70
80
150
50

1001 DREAM CARS
YOU MUST DRIVE BEFORE YOU DIE

1001 DREAM CARS

YOU MUST DRIVE BEFORE YOU DIE

GENERAL EDITOR **SIMON HEPTINSTALL**

PREFACE BY **NICK MASON**

UNIVERSE

A Quintessence Book

First published in the United States of America in 2012 by
UNIVERSE PUBLISHING
A Division of Rizzoli International Publications, Inc.
300 Park Avenue South
New York, NY 10010
www.rizzoliusa.com

Second printing, 2012
2012 2013 2014 2015 / 10 9 8 7 6 5 4 3 2

ISBN: 978-0-7893-2437-5

Library of Congress Control Number: 2012934937

QSS.KCAR

This book was designed and produced by
Quintessence Editions Ltd.
230 City Road
London EC1V 2TT
www.1001beforeyoudie.com

Project Editor Elspeth Beidas
Editors Frank Ritter, Fiona Plowman
Designers Tea Aganovic, Tom Howey, Alison Hau
Picture Researchers Giles Chapman, Sara Di Girolamo
Production Manager Anna Pauletti

Editorial Director Jane Laing
Publisher Mark Fletcher

Color separation by KHL Chromagraphics, Singapore
Printed in China by Midas Printing Ltd.

Contents

Preface | Nick Mason

The American cowboy, actor, and commentator Will Rogers famously said, "I never met a man I didn't like." Well, I feel rather the same about cars.

It's been like that since I was a young boy. Even if you assembled the 1,001 worst cars of all time I could probably find something of interest in any one of them to justify inspecting, driving, and, very sadly, occasionally buying the offending vehicle.

Even after many years of driving, racing, and restoring cars this enthusiasm remains unabated, and the thought of a list of 1,001 of the very best of the best seems like a cracking idea.

Like most best-of lists, the pleasure of this one lies in the affirmation of one's own immaculate judgement, tempered with the occasional outburst at some missed favorite. It's worth remembering that, a little like music, there is no final arbiter of good taste. While you may be able to collect that full set of postage stamps (and increase the value), no car collector can assemble the cars that will perfectly suit someone else.

For the enthusiast, cars are perpetually interesting. They often forge international bonds, as brand loyalists form clubs and organize events to celebrate their particular (and sometimes misguided—oh, there I go with my own prejudices!) dream machines.

I've been lucky enough to own some wonderful cars, and I've driven a lot more fantastic vehicles. Yet as soon as I contemplate an assembly of cars like this, I can't help but start thinking about what they might be like to actually experience on the road. Whether it's an ancient racing car or an ultraexclusive futuristic new supercar, this desire doesn't seem to fade with age. In fact, the more you experience the driving, the greater the interest in making those comparisons, and there's nothing like having those facts and figures on hand to assist in daydreaming!

As an outsider, it seems that this book is the result of an amazing global publishing project. A unique and enormous collection of cars from more than thirty different countries has been put together, with contributions from writers across the world and a huge selection of photographs sourced from libraries, private collections, and archives. All that work has created something very special and long lasting for enthusiasts everywhere.

I think all of my favorite cars are in here—and, as I've said, a few I might argue over. I suspect most readers will undergo a similar experience: smiling at their favorites, becoming apoplectic at a loved one rejected, or being enraged by a pet horror included.

For me, the greatest cars are the ones that transcend regular vehicle engineering, and often bear the mark of a specific designer or engineer's vision; Bugatti springs to mind as an early exponent. I still have a Type 35B that I started restoring in the mid-1970s and have been racing ever since. Cars like this involve innovative engineering, but also beautiful mechanical design. The fact that it runs on methanol rather than gasoline and does about four miles to the gallon seems only a minor setback . . .

And then there's the Ferrari 250GTO. Nowadays more famous for its value rather than its sporting ability, it personifies the timelessness of some of these great automobiles, and it is clear to see why it influenced Gordon Murray when he designed the McLaren F1. I still feel some pride in having loaned the Ferrari to Gordon when he was first assembling his ideas on what exactly the F1 should be.

But enough of supercars. There's also plenty of room for the cars that changed the sociology of the world we live in. I still have great affection for the Austin 7 chummy that was my first car, and taught me as much about do-it-yourself maintenance as driving, as well as my Model T Ford whose previous owner, Coco the clown, ensured that the car's doors fall off and its radiator shoots out steam on a regular basis.

Whether your motoring tastes are varied or specific, I don't think you will find it hard to discover some fascinating cars in this book. In fact, I think there's a fair chance you'll find 1,001 of those delights as you open the pages . . .

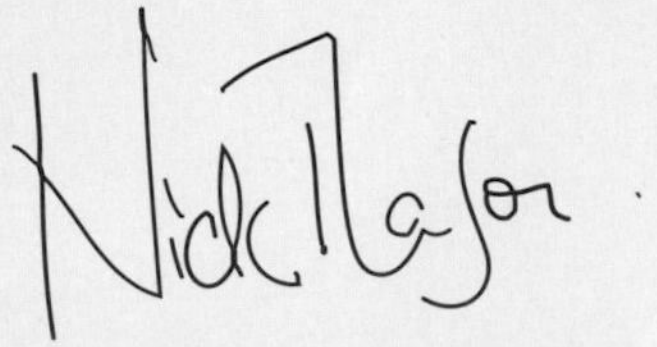

London, UK

Introduction | Simon Heptinstall

It all started on the morning that Bertha Benz sneaked into her husband Karl's workshop while he was asleep. This shed was where he kept his strange new motorized contraption.

Karl and his technicians had carefully tested the horseless carriage on a few short experimental runs around their house, but he was not very confident about taking it much further. Maybe this odd device would never come to anything. It was an extraordinary machine, after all.

Bertha, however, decided to take the Motorwagen and drive it for 66 miles (106 km) to visit her mother—without telling Karl. This was the first proper journey ever taken by motorized road transport.

Bertha took her two teenage sons along for the ride and together they had to negotiate the precar world of rough, unmarked tracks. It took all day, as they took turns driving and sometimes had to get out and push, too. There were no filling stations in 1888, so when they ran out of fuel Bertha showed great ingenuity by managing to buy a chemical that worked the engine at a pharmacy. Along the way she also cleared a blocked fuel pipe with her hairpin, insulated a loose wire with a garter, and persuaded a village shoemaker to construct new leather pads for the brakes. As they chugged along the 66-mile route, some people were frightened, some were shocked, but most were amazed. That evening, Bertha sent a telegram to her husband to say they'd arrived.

Her short car journey would be a mundane occurence today, but in 1888 it caused an international sensation. Newspapers carried headline stories about this marvelous event. Suddenly, everyone wanted one of Karl Benz's machines. More than 120 years later, people living along Bertha's route still celebrate her achievement. Her humble route has become a major tourist attraction.

Fast forward to the present. Around the world there are now more than 800 million cars on our roads doing trips just like Bertha's. Today, our cities, economies, and our very lives are organized around cars, the roads they drive on, and the fuel they use. Many of us love our cars more than our homes, more than some members of our families. We drool over and crave cars that are out of our budget.

In fact, Karl Benz's humble Motorwagen has evolved to become a major part of the heated debate about the future of the planet. To some, cars have become symbols of human greed and environmental indifference. They're dangerous, destructive, and polluting . . . yet somehow, the vast majority of us still love them. Anyone lucky enough to have a huge lottery win will most likely rush out and buy not a life-long train season ticket or a private bus service, but an exotic supercar.

And we don't just love driving cars—we even love dreaming about driving them, too. That's where this book comes in: it is designed to be a treat for armchair drivers everywhere.

Armchair? Well, although it would be a nice way to spend a few years, no one in the world has actually driven *all* of these cars. No one ever will. However rich or well-connected you are, you couldn't trace all 1,001 of them just to take a quick turn behind the wheel. It's true that many of these cars are still on the roads or for sale in showrooms, but plenty more of them only live in museums or exclusive collections. Some have sadly disappeared altogether.

So the massive and wonderful collection of vehicles in this book has been designed to inform, educate, and entertain anyone with an interest in cars. Think of it as an automotive wish list.

The 1,001 collection spans more than 125 years and includes cars built on six different continents. You'll find vehicles from thirty-one different countries, ranging from Austria to Australia and the United States to Ukraine. There are gasoline/petrol cars, diesels, cars powered by steam, electricity, hydrogen, and even jet motors.

There are multimillion sellers in here, alongside obscure one-offs. You'll find household names next to rarities that few have heard of. But they all have one thing in common: they are very special machines. Of course, "special" can mean many things to many people . . .

Special can mean particularly innovative. There are lots of those in this book. The technological pioneers range from the Cadillac Model 30 of 1910 that introduced the simple idea of having an enclosed body to sit inside, to the Mercedes SLS AMG E-Cell that's being developed as this book is being produced. It uses an electric motor on each wheel to reach an emission-free top speed of 155 mph (250 kph).

But special can also mean cars that changed the course of motoring history. Cars like the original Mini of 1959, which introduced a sideways engine driving the front wheels and became one of the most influential mechanical layouts of the modern era, or the Willy's Jeep that not only helped win World War II, but also inadvertently introduced the concept of SUVs to the world.

Cars can be special record-breakers, like the Thrust SSC that is currently the world's fastest car, or they can be special technological showcases, like the Mitsubishi GTO or Mercedes CL600. They can be a special part of social culture like the Trabant in Eastern Europe or the Holden pickup trucks in Australia. They can even be artistically special—seen as beautiful automotive sculptures—like most of the early Bugattis and many modern supercars.

This book also includes special celebrity cars like James Bond's Aston Martin or Bob Hope's Skylark. Or cars that played big roles in popular culture, like Chitty Chitty Bang Bang or the Batmobile. Then there are cars chosen for their special significance in particular countries, like China's Great Wall Haval that surely signals the start of what will become a major car-producing nation. Or the Popemobile, surely the most iconic vehicle in the Catholic world.

So in this book you'll find 1,001 vehicles that are special for lots of different reasons. But one thing unites them all: if you get the chance to drive them, at any time in your life before you die, you owe it to the rest of us car lovers to take it.

Of course, any selection from all the cars in history is subjective. We think this is the best possible collection of 1,001 cars, but one of your favorites may be missing. We've certainly omitted plenty of multimillion sellers and gorgeous vehicles, but I hope you'll see that we chose a similar alternative that we thought was perhaps a little more special and we can agree to disagree. One of the joys of browsing through this enormous collection is choosing your own favorites. If you did scoop that massive lottery win, which five would you fill your garage with? And why limit yourself to five?

Work on this book began many years ago, and included whittling down a list of possibles from all the vehicles ever produced to a final 1,001 cars, recruiting a specialist team of twelve writers from across the globe, and tracking down more than 800 photographs and technical details for all 1,001 cars. Around a third of a million words have been written and edited carefully so they are understood by readers on different continents. That means considering the use of regional automotive words such as ute, saloon, and estate. Apologies in advance if there are unfamiliar words within the text; it's impossible to please everyone all the time.

Even more demanding were the technical specifications. We opted to give all speeds in both miles per hour (mph) and kilometers per hour (kph), and engine power in brake horsepower (bhp) and kilowatts (kW). Similarly, fuel consumption, where mentioned, is given in miles-per-gallon (mpg) and in liters-per-100 km.

Unfortunately the situation with measuring acceleration is not so straightforward. Some cars are measured on a 0–60 mph (97 kph) sprint, others on a 0–62 mph (100 kph) run. If only one set of figures is available then that is all we are able to give. The danger is in comparing the acceleration of different cars using the two different systems. Don't assume they are virtually the same measurements. The timing of a gear change could make the 0–62 mph much slower than 0–60 mph.

The date given for each car is another potential minefield for diligent car students. The cars are arranged in chronological order, to create an overall picture of the development of the automobile over time. It should surely be simple to give the date each car was launched?

Yet it rarely is. Cars are usually presented to the public or unveiled at one of the major motor shows. Production usually follows some months afterward, but sometimes many years afterward. The production date isn't always the same as the on-sale date.

And cars are often given a date as part of their identity, known as the "model year." This may or may not relate to the year it goes on sale. So, like a car's 0–60 mph acceleration time, the date is another rather gray area.

We've tried to date each car entry accurately to keep the book in chronological order, but this sometimes means we have featured a car several years into its production life. In the modern era cars are generally changed every year. Sometimes we have chosen a version that was significantly improved from the launch model. The date given is of the version we feature in the words and photograph. We hope you'll find that the text beneath the picture explains what we have done.

In comparison, top speed is much easier. Usually this is taken from figures given by the manufacturers. These can sometimes be either very conservative or very optimistic depending on the carmaker's marketing strategy. In some instances we've tried to use the most reliable independent test results. Note that many high performance cars now have limited top speeds. If the speed limiter is removed, then obviously the speed would be much higher and, if this is reliably known, it is mentioned in the text.

When figures aren't available we haven't made them up or taken an informed guess, we've written "unknown."

The country given as an international badge under each car photograph is simply the nation that is most closely associated with the car. In years gone by that was a straightforward matter of where it was conceived and built. Today's motor industry is global. A company based in one country may use a research team based in another and a factory based in a third, then sell the car in another part of the world altogether. We've tried to explain this in the text if the car's origins are unclear.

We have specified engine sizes using the modern universal measurement of liters and centiliters. This, of course, is a measurement of the engine displacement, or the total volume swept by the pistons within the cylinders. For those still fond of the old cubic inch system, the simple sum you need to do is multiply each liter (or 1,000 cc) by sixty-one. We've also explained what the engine configuration is—how many cylinders it has and how they are arranged. Straight engines are indicated with an "S" and flat engines with an "F"; the number of cylinders follows the letter (eg: S4).

The initials given in bold at the end of each piece refer to the writer. You can find a brief biography of each of the contributors at the end of the book.

Finally, there is a downside to motoring that must be mentioned. Cars, as we all know, cost money. Lots of it. The fabulous cars collected in this volume would have a combined value of many millions today. We've given any prices in both British pounds and U.S. dollars. Unless you are very, very rich, try not to dwell on them—instead, just sit back and enjoy.

Index of Cars by Manufacturer

Key to Licence Plate Country Codes

A Austria
AUS Australia
B Belgium
BR Brazil
CDN Canada
CH Switzerland
CN China
CS Czechoslovakia
CZ Czech Republic
D Germany
DK Denmark
E Spain
F France
FL Liechtenstein
GB United Kingdom
I Italy
IL Israel
IND India
J Japan
MA Morocco
MAL Malaysia
MEX Mexico
N Norway
NL The Netherlands
NZ New Zealand
PL Poland
ROK Republic of Korea
RUS Russia
S Sweden
SU USSR
UA Ukraine
USA United States
ZA South Africa

ROLLS
ROYCE

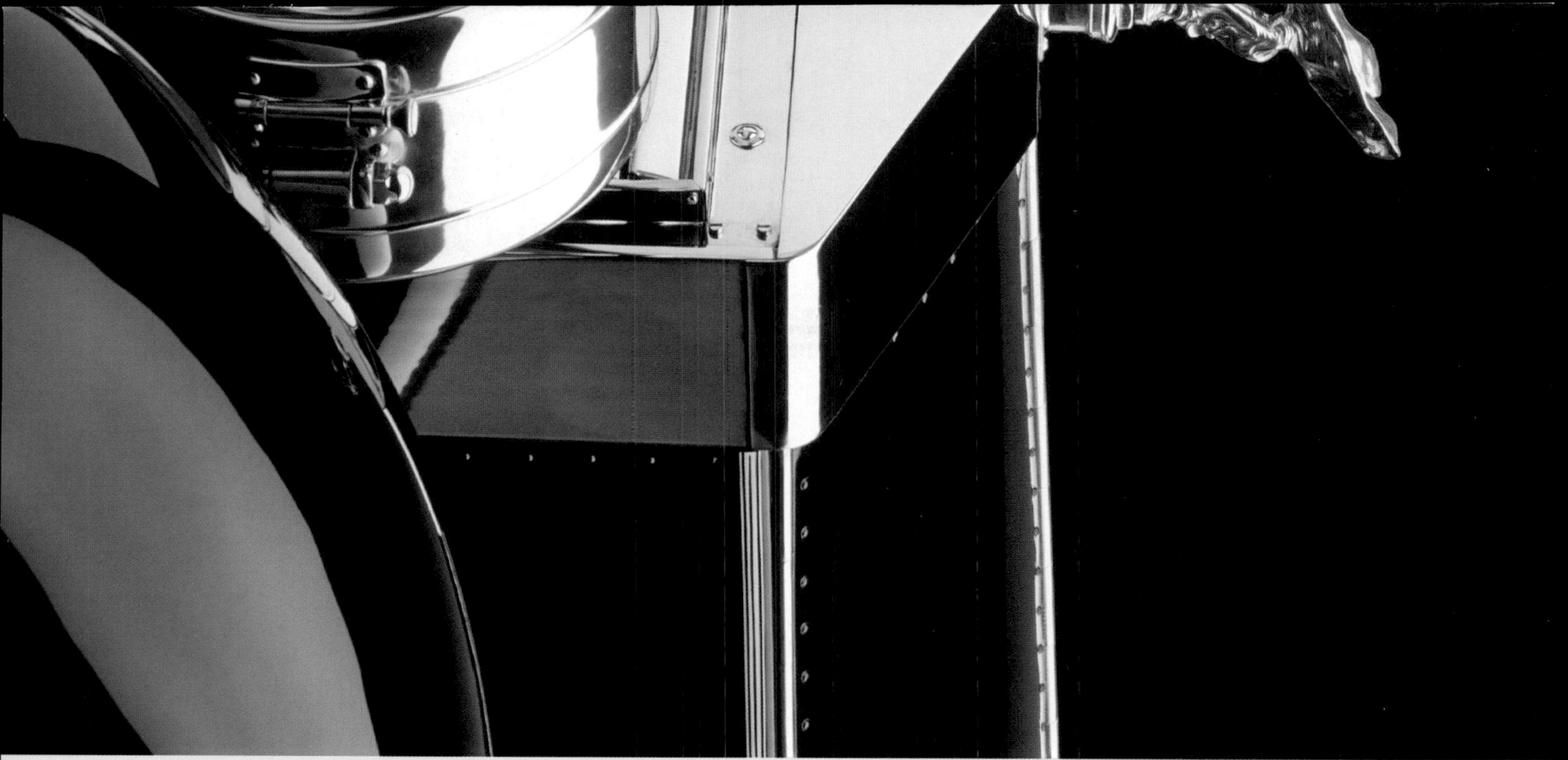

Close up of a 1925 black Rolls-Royce ornament, a badge that would become symbolic of luxury.

1886–1944

Motorized Carriage | Daimler

(D)

1886 • 93 cu in/1,526 cc, single-cylinder • 1 bhp/0.7 kW • unknown • 10 mph/16 kph

The internal combustion engine arrived gradually. In 1824 it was realized that there should be a system using compression, and the first petrol-vapor engine appeared in 1826. In-cylinder compression followed in 1838, and a working 5-bhp (4-kW) engine was designed by Italian Pietro Benini in 1856, although he never thought to put it in a carriage.

In 1860 the Belgian engineer Jean Lenoir built a gas-fired 1.5-bhp (1-kW) engine with pistons, connecting rods, and cylinders. Installing it in a wooden wagon he called the "hippomobile," he drove 11 miles (18 km) from Paris to Joinville-le-Pont. In 1876 Nicolaus Otto invented a four-stroke, piston-cycle, gas motor engine and built the world's first motorcycle.

Gottlieb Daimler and William Maybach attached their own engines to bicycles and even to a boat before they created the design for a new grandfather clock-shaped, lightweight, gasoline-injected 1-bhp (0.7-kW) engine with a single vertical cylinder and a float-feed carburetor that allowed problem-free combustion of gasoline. In early 1886 Daimler purchased a dark blue carriage with black leather seating and bright red trim from Wilhelm Wimpff & Sohn stagecoaches of Stuttgart, mounted his engine just forward of the carriage's rear bench seat, and on March 8, 1886—after suitable modifications to the frame—the Daimler motorized carriage was born.

A water-cooled variant followed in 1887, and not long after that came another development, the driver's license. Of his own volition, Daimler applied for a permit on July 17, 1888, to drive his very own "light four-seater chaise with a small engine." **BS**

Victoria | Benz

(D)

1893 • 104 cu in/1,720 cc, single-cylinder • 3 bhp/2.2 kW • unknown • 11 mph/18 kph

Late on New Year's Eve in 1878, the German designer and engineer Karl Benz was putting the finishing touches to his newest invention: a two-stroke, water-cooled, internal combustion engine. Powered by gasoline, it was lighter and more compact than the cumbersome steam engines of the past.

In 1885 Benz combined this with several other recent inventions—the carburetor, car battery, coil ignition, spark plug, and differential drive—in a three-wheeled motorized tricycle that he named the "Motorwagon." However, its single front wheel made for a bumpy ride over Europe's wagon-rutted roads and an unconvinced public stayed away.

Finally, in 1893, in the face of pleas from within his own company to produce a four-wheeled vehicle, Benz reluctantly followed the approach of his rival Gottlieb Daimler and added an extra wheel to the Motorwagon. The Benz Victoria, as it was named, became Benz's favorite car. Designed to carry two passengers, it featured a revolutionary pivoting front axle that the driver could steer using a tiller connected to the axle by a chain and a patented knuckle joint.

In the summer of 1894 Benz's inventiveness was put to the test when the Austrian-born industrialist Theodor von Liebig drove Production Number 76 on a largely incident-free 538-mile (939-km) journey from Reichenberg in Bohemia to the Moselle River and back, visiting Benz himself in Mannheim and making several other impromptu, whimsical detours along the way. Regarded as the world's first long-distance motor trip, on that occasion the Victoria averaged 8.4 mph (13.6 kph) along roads that were cobbled at best. **BS**

10HP Dogcart | Arrol-Johnston

GB

1897 • 197 cu in/3,230 cc, F2 • 10 bhp/7.5 kW • unknown • 25 mph/40 kph

Forth Road Bridge engineer Sir William Arrol and locomotive engineer George Johnston combined their talents to create the first British production car. Like many early cars, the Scottish-built "Dogcart" was like a horse-drawn carriage without the horse, but compared to many rivals the Arrol-Johnston was a neat and practical design. The engine, which lay under the floor and was started by pulling on a rope, drove the rear wheels by chain.

Like a carriage, the Dogcart had a light wooden body, large wooden wheels with solid tires, and a hand-operated brake shoe that was pressed onto the back of the rear tire. The vehicle was almost useless in wet weather. The suspension, however, was fairly effective, thanks to full elliptic leaf springs all around. Horse-drawn passengers would be familiar with the layout of the six seats, too; the driver and two passengers faced forward, and the three passengers in the rear faced backward. The Dogcart proved a strong and popular vehicle and was produced, with only minor changes, until 1907, when it was replaced by a conventional front-engined model.

"A-J," as the Arrol-Johnston company was widely known, operated in Glasgow from 1896 to 1931. It developed the world's first off-roader for the Egyptian government. It also designed a car to travel on snow for Ernest Shackleton's expedition to the South Pole, but this turned out to be useless when it arrived in Antarctica.

The first postwar Arrol-Johnston was 1919's Victory, which was sold to the Prince of Wales but broke down on a royal tour of the West of England with much attendant bad publicity. One of A-J's final highlights was building the body of Malcolm Campbell's Bluebird land-speed record-breaker in 1929. **SH**

Curved Dash | Oldsmobile

(USA)

1899 • 95 cu in/1,563 cc, single-cylinder • 4.5 bhp/3.4 kW • unknown • 20 mph/32 kph

By rights, Ransom E. Olds, the man who founded the Oldsmobile company, ought to be as well known as his contemporary, Henry Ford: the two were born just a year apart, in 1863 and 1864 respectively. As Olds battled Ford to be the first to manufacture a successful car for the mass American market, the Oldsmobile Curved Dash became the first American car to be built on an assembly line.

The Curved Dash took its name from its curved footboard, styled after the horse-drawn carriages of the period. The model might never have seen the light of day had there not been a fire at the first Oldsmobile factory in East Jefferson, Michigan. Before the fire, Olds and his engineers had built eleven prototype cars, in different sizes and to different designs, including a couple of electric vehicles. The Curved Dash was popular with the workers, but they saw it more as a plaything than a contender for their first commercial offering. However, the factory fire, in March 1901, destroyed all the prototypes except for the Curved Dash. Olds redesigned it and put all his energies into it.

The factory fire made news, though, and Olds was receiving orders for the Curved Dash even before it was offered for sale. In the event, 425 were produced in 1901 at a price of $650 (£419). Most were delivered to their new owners by train, often with an Oldsmobile sales representative on board to hand over the two-seater car personally. In total, 19,000 were built before production ceased in 1907, by which time Oldsmobile had gotten into financial trouble and was bought by General Motors. Even so, Ransom E. Olds had beaten Ford to the mass market. **MG**

‹ English-born American actress Julia Marlowe and her dog try out the Columbia Electric Coach, circa 1910.

Electric Coach | Columbia (USA)

1899 • 44-cell battery • 2 bhp/1.49 kW • unknown • 15 mph/24 kph

By 1899, the statistics of the Columbia Automobile Company of Hartford, Connecticut, were bold enough even before they began mass-producing one of the first American electric cars. The factory was spread under an enormous 17-acre (68,800 sq m) roof, and the company employed in excess of 10,000 people. In 1898 it produced America's first chainless bicycle, and in 1899 it was producing hundreds of cars a year at a time when most carmakers in the United States were making only dozens.

The Columbia Electric Coach was powered by four sets of batteries—totaling forty-four cells—that produced almost 2 bhp (1.49 kW) and offered a range of about 30 miles (48 km). But for those who could afford it, the novelty of not having to walk or take a buggy proved irresistible. The coachwork was not unlike that of a traditional horse-drawn stagecoach, with similar joints and methods of reinforcement, a heavily lacquered oak frame, and goatskin upholstery. The vehicle's most exceptional feature, however, was its rubber pneumatic tires, capable of running for 3,500 miles (5,633 km) on every change, and even more "if the roads are good and free from mud."

Columbia Electric Coaches were sold to the New York City Transit Authority for transporting dignitaries from Grand Central Station to offices throughout Manhattan. Company brochures promised customers a vehicle as close to perfection as the times would allow: "No consideration of the cost of production," it read, "has been permitted to interfere with making perfect every part and piece of every model." In 2011 one of the few surviving "perfect" Columbia Electrics sold at auction in the United States for $550,000 (£354,300). **BS**

Runabout | Stanley (USA)

1901 • two-cylinder, steam-powered • 3.5 bhp/ 2.57 kW • unknown • 27 mph/44 kph

Twin brothers Francis E. and Freelan O. Stanley of Kingfield, Maine, were in their forties and the owners of a successful photographic plate company when they attended a "horseless carriage" display in Massachusetts in 1896. The event persuaded them to spend the remainder of their lives designing and building automobiles. Within weeks they had sold their business to Kodak, and just twelve months later had produced their very first working car, a steam-powered vehicle they named the Stanley Runabout.

The 3.5-bhp (2.57-kW) twin-cylinder double-action engine had fewer than twenty-five moving parts and powered the rear wheels via a single chain drive courtesy of a 14-inch (35-cm) diameter, 90-pound (41-kg) vertical boiler. Mounted beneath the seat, this was able to withstand 2,000 lb (907 kg) of pressure thanks to steel wires wound around its exterior. Any combustible material could be used for fuel, including wood, kerosene, even whale oil, but there were drawbacks. It took up to forty minutes for the engine to generate sufficient steam to drive the chain, and one tank of water would last only about 20 miles (32 km). Nevertheless, the Stanleys sold in excess of 200 cars in 1898.

Freelan and his wife Flora became the first to drive a car to the summit of Mt. Washington, at 6,288 feet (1,916 m) the highest point in the northeast United States. They made the trip, involving a winding carriage road with a demanding 12 percent gradient, in just over two hours. In 1898 two customers, John Walker and Amzi Barber, were so enamoured with their steamers that they bought the company. **BS**

999 | Ford

USA

1902 • 1,147 cu in/18,800 cc, S4 • 70 bhp/51 kW • unknown • 91 mph/147 kph

Ford 999 was a number plate, not a model number, and only two cars were ever built. They were a world away from the mass-produced Ford Model A that was making Henry Ford's name at about the same time.

The Ford 999 was designed by Ford and arose from his fondness for motor racing. The car was an amazing-looking beast, with no bodywork at all, just a driver's seat perched behind a massive 1,146-cubic-inch (18,800-cc) engine that sat on a wooden chassis. Often a mechanic was perched somewhere alongside the driver, both to help with breakdowns and to make adjustments while the car was actually being driven. As it had no suspension, it must have been quite a ride.

The original 999 was painted red, while an identical car built at the same time was yellow and called the Arrow. However, the cars and their number plates became interchangeable, and both were later known as the Ford 999. The number actually came from a steam train, the Empire State Express No. 999, which was the first man-made vehicle to exceed 100 mph (160 kph) under its own propulsion when it reached a speed of 112.5 mph (181.1 kph) on May 10, 1893.

The Ford 999 never matched its namesake, its record speed being 91.37 mph (147.05 kph), achieved on the ice of Lake St. Clair (lying between Ontario and Michigan) on January 12, 1904. This was in the Arrow model, now renamed the 999, and driven by Henry Ford himself. The land speed record lasted only for a month, but the publicity it generated was a real boost to the one-year-old Ford Motor Company. The original 999 is now on display at the Henry Ford Museum in Dearborn, Michigan. **MG**

Simplex | Mercedes

D

1902 • 408 cu in/6,700 cc, S4 • 40 bhp/29.8 kW • unknown • 70 mph/119 kph

On March 29, 1901, German driver Wilhelm Werner entered a 35-bhp (26-kW) Mercedes in the Nice–La Turbie Hill Climb on the Côte d'Azur; he finished forty-three seconds ahead of his nearest rival after averaging an unheard-of 32 mph (51 kph). Word of Werner's victory spread like brushfire through motoring circles. By the time a 40-bhp (29.8-kW) road version of his 1901 stripped-down racer was released the following year, the car was already on its way to becoming a legend. That was before a single unit of the road version had been sold.

Designer William Maybach wanted his 1902 creation to provide "comfort by means of simplicity." An extended wheelbase gave the car a lower center of gravity. The addition of a shift lever made automatic declutching possible. A second foot brake was added to keep in check the modified 6.7-liter engine, and a new cooling system made use of vanes to direct air more efficiently through the honeycombed radiator. Trendsetting coachwork and accoutrements such as oversized oxyacetylene brass headlights and a charming brass bulb-horn gave it the Mercedes flourish.

The ancestor of generations of Mercedes to come, the Simplex is recognized today as the world's first authentic automobile, built upon timeless principles such as a four-speed gear shift, rear-wheel (albeit chain) drive, and a four-passenger seating configuration.

In 1902 William K. Vanderbilt Jr. set a world speed record of 69.5 mph (111.8 kph) in a Simplex. Everywhere it went, the car seduced all who laid eyes on it, from commoners to royalty. Remarked Emperor Wilhelm II to Maybach at the 1903 Berlin Motor Show: "A truly beautiful engine you have here, sir." **BS**

Model A | Cadillac

(USA)

1903 • 98 cu in/1,609 cc, single-cylinder • 8 bhp/6 kW • unknown • 30 mph/48 kph

The oldest known surviving Cadillac is one of the first three Model As that were sold at the New York Auto Show in January 1903. A $10 (£6) deposit at the show secured the $750 (£485) two-seater runabout, one of which was bought by a Mr. Homas, who owned the Thomas Winery in Cucamonga, California. The car stayed in the Homas family until 1973, and was sold at auction in 2007 for $300,000 (£193,350).

The Cadillac Automobile Company had been established in 1902 in Detroit, and named after the city's founder, the impressively titled French explorer, Antoine Laumet de La Mothe, Sieur de Cadillac (Cadillac is a town in southwestern France). The company's founder, and the builder of the first American Cadillacs, was Henry Martyn Leland, an inventor and motoring pioneer from Vermont, who later also founded the Lincoln company, which was subsequently sold to Henry Ford.

The Model A was only referred to as such when a Model B came out in the following year, during which 1903 models also continued to be sold. The two original 1903 Cadillacs were actually the two-seater Cadillac Runabout, while for an extra $100 (£65) buyers could have two additional seats strapped on; this car was called the Cadillac Tonneau. The single-cylinder engines were rated at just under 8 bhp (6 kW) but in practice achieved 10 bhp (7.5 kW) for a top speed that matched its contemporary, the Ford Model A.

An original Model A from 1903 was sold in 2011 for $99,000 (£63,800). Only 2,497 were ever built, and by 1908 the Cadillac had progressed as far as the Model T. In 1909 Cadillac was bought by General Motors. **MG**

Model A | Ford

(USA)

1903 • 101 cu in/1,668 cc, V2 • 8 bhp/5.9 kW • unknown • 30 mph/48 kph

When Henry Ford sold his first Model A to Dr. Ernst Pfenning of Chicago on July 20, 1903, the newly formed Ford Motor Company of Detroit had just $223.65 (£144) remaining in the bank. The company had been incorporated one month earlier with $28,000 (£18,502) in capital, and fortunately for Ford the $750 (£484) two-seater Model A proved to be a success. He sold 1,750 of them in 1903 and 1904, making a profit of almost $39,000 (£25,150) in the first three months alone. In 1904 the vehicle was superseded by the Ford Model C (the Model B had been a larger four-cylinder touring model that cost $2,000 [£1,289]).

The Model A was more successful than its nearest rival, the Oldsmobile Curved Dash, despite being $100 (£64) more expensive. (For an additional $100 (£64) customers could have the four-seater version, and for a further $30 (£19) a rubber top. Another $20 (£13) could buy a leather top.) Ford advertised the car as being so simple that a fifteen-year-old boy could operate it—an important sales ploy as other cars on the road had a reputation for being hard to drive and maintain.

Two more buyers were just behind Dr. Pfenning in the line to buy a Ford Model A in July 1903, and one of those cars still survives. It was bought by Herbert L. McNary, a butter maker from Britt, Iowa, and bore the chassis number thirty. The cars had not been numbered in logical sequence, and Dr. Pfenning, the first buyer of a Ford car, only got number eleven. Mr. McNary kept his car for fifty years and it has had only four subsequent owners. It came up for auction in California in 2010, but the highest bid of $325,000 (£210,000) did not reach the reserve price. **MG**

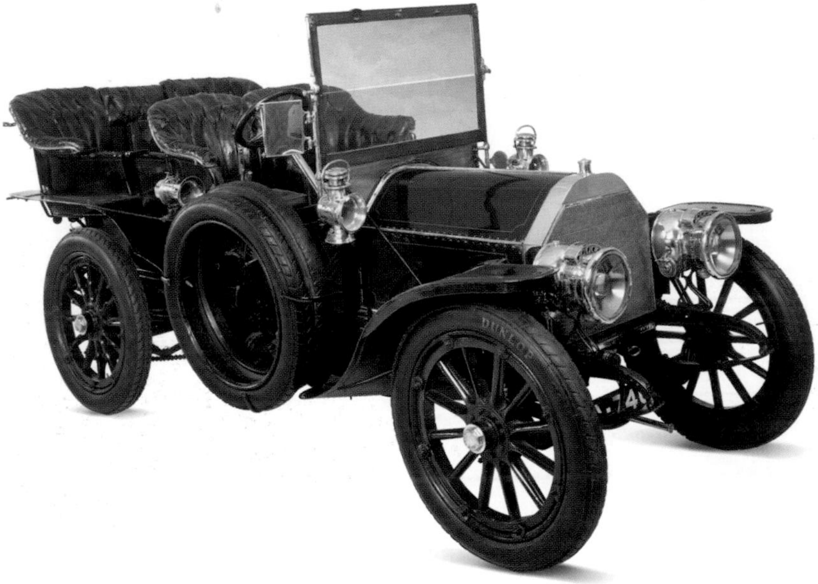

60HP | Mercedes

D

1903 • 567 cu in/9,293 cc, S4 • 60 bhp/44 kW • unknown • 65 mph/104 kph

Wilhelm Maybach was a German engineer who worked with Gottlieb Daimler of the Daimler company. After Daimler died in 1900, Maybach went on to work with Gottlieb's son, Paul, and in 1901 they produced the first car to bear the Mercedes name: the Mercedes 35HP. The Mercedes part of its name came from the daughter of one of the Daimler board members, Emil Jellinek. Jellinek was prepared to pay a huge sum of money for Daimler to develop a new racing car, on the condition that it was named after his daughter, Mercedes.

The Mercedes 35HP begat the Simplex 28HP Tourer, a less powerful commercial version of the racer, and also the first road-going car in the world to carry the name of Mercedes. This was followed by the 60HP model, distinguished by its huge 567-cubic-inch (9,293-cc) engine. Its official top speed of 65 mph (104 kph) was impressive for the time, but it was said that drivers could coax a full 75 mph (120 kph) out of the car at a time when the speed limit on British roads was all of 12 mph (19 kph).

In 1906 the "Rest and Be Thankful Hill Climb" took place in Scotland for the first time, although a long period elapsed before it was officially revived in 1949. The winner of the inaugural race was a Mercedes 60HP, which managed the stretch of scenic road, roughly 1 mile (1.6 km) long, in two minutes and nineteen seconds.

Only 200 60HPs were built, in either a two-seater or four-seater version. Five of those original cars are known to survive today. When one of the two-seater 60HP Mercedes came up at auction in 1991, it sold for £1.6 million ($2.49 million). In 1996 that car participated in the Centenary London to Brighton Veteran Car Run. **MG**

60HP | Spyker

NL

1903 • 538 cu in/8,821 cc, S6 • 60 bhp/44 kW • unknown • 80 mph/129 kph

Jacobus and Hendrik-Jan Spijker were coach builders in Hilversum, northern Holland, and in 1880 they founded the Spijker company, in a plan to move into the car-making business. In 1898 they relocated to Amsterdam, where they had been commissioned to build a golden carriage for the coronation of Queen Wilhelmina on September 6. Because the queen had decided that she would not receive any gifts on the day of her crowning, and the carriage was going to be a gift from the citizens of Amsterdam, she received it the following day. The carriage was not used officially until her marriage in 1901, and it remains in use today.

The coach commission was a pivotal point in the Dutch brothers' lives, and in 1899, after a great deal of positive publicity, they decided to devote themselves to the manufacture of cars. After producing a few early and conventional models, in 1903 two major things happened. The brothers changed their name and the name of their company from Spijker to the more internationally friendly Spyker, and they built one of the first cars to bear that name, the Spyker 60HP. It was a remarkable car in many ways, not least in that it was the first in the world to have four-wheel drive, and the first in the world to have a six-cylinder engine. Having brakes on all four wheels was also a first.

The brothers were noted as innovative designers, and in 1903 they also patented their idea for a "dust-shield chassis." This was a device that fit under cars and prevented them from creating dust on unpaved roads. Spyker cars also had distinctive circular radiators, and the brothers later became known in Britain as the Rolls and Royce of Continental Europe. **MG**

GENEVIEVE
27
HXR

⊲ A scene from the 1953 movie *Genevieve*, in which a Darracq 12HP played a starring role.

12HP | Darracq (F)

1904 • 113 cu in/1,886 cc, S2 • 12 bhp/9 kW • unknown • 45 mph/72 kph

Alexandre Darracq was born in Bordeaux in 1855 and trained as a draftsman at Tarbes in the Haute-Pyrenees. In 1891 he established the Gladiator Cycle Company before selling it in 1896 for a substantial profit and turning his attention to the manufacture of cars. Darracq was in many ways the Henry Ford of his day, one of the first automakers in Europe to seriously consider and plan for the mass production of automobiles.

In 1902 he signed an agreement with German carmaker Adam Opel to build cars at their factory in Russelsheim, Germany, and by 1904 the new company, Opel Darracq, was the largest carmaker in the world, with an annual output of 1,600 vehicles, responsible for one of every ten vehicles being driven on French roads.

In 1904 Darracq designed a four-stroke, 12-bhp (9-kW), twin-cylinder two-seat roadster with a pressed steel chassis, one of which would, forty years later, have a profound impact upon the British motoring public and their attitude toward older cars. In 1953 Darracq's roadster became the star of *Genevieve*, a movie about the London to Brighton Veteran Car Run, first organized in 1896 to celebrate the lifting of the national speed limit to 14 mph (23 kph). The film inspired "Genevieve rallies" and fueled interest in period automobiles.

"Genevieve" was the product of two discarded Darracq 12s, one a rusted chassis, the other a stripped-down body found abandoned in a junkyard in 1945. Restored over four years, it competed in its first rally in 1949. Reborn with gleaming brasswork and flared front wings, Darracq's roadster achieved stardom and became, in the words of Britain's National Motor Museum, "the mascot of the old car movement." **BS**

200HP | Darracq (F)

1904 • 1,550 cu in/25,400 cc, V8 • 200 bhp/147 kW • unknown • 122 mph/196 kph

In 1889 a French draftsman named Alexander Darracq designed a sewing machine that won a gold medal at that year's Paris Exhibition. In the 1890s he turned his attention to building motor tricycles, before flirting with electric cars and radial engines.

He produced a vertical twin-cylinder engine in 1900, and in 1902 began to make four-cylinder, 20-bhp (15-kW) cars with pressed-steel chassis. It had been an inexorable progression, each time to a larger, more complex machine—but Darracq wasn't done yet.

In 1905 he designed an engine the like of which had never been seen before: a 1,550-cubic-inch (25,400-cc), water-cooled V8 engine that took up fully two-thirds of the chassis. There was no bodywork, because bodywork meant weight, just two seats, a steering wheel, pedals, and a lightweight radiator. This wasn't a racing car, it was a monster—and quite an achievement for a man who didn't enjoy driving.

Darracq only ever built one, and he built it to break records. Debuting in France on December 28, 1905, untried and untested, it took just two days to break the existing world land speed record when it clocked 109.65 mph (176.5 kph) near Salon-de-Provence. On Ormond Beach, Florida, in 1906 it became the first gasoline car to cover 2 miles (3.2 km)in a minute, at a new record speed of 122.449 mph (197 kph).

The Darracq 200HP ended its competitive career in 1909 and lay neglected and in pieces in an English garage until purchased by a Darracq enthusiast in 1954. The car underwent a mammoth fifty-year restoration, finally roaring back to life before an enthralled public in Worcestershire on July 4, 2006. **BS**

8HP | Rover

GB

1904 • 80 cu in/1,327 cc, single-cylinder • 8 bhp/ 5.9 kW • unknown • 24 mph/38.6 kph

The Rover 8HP, designed by Edmund Lewis, chief engineer of the Daimler Motor Company, represented a key moment in the development of the automobile. With the majority of designs still favoring a chassis that bore an uncanny resemblance to the horse-drawn carriage, Lewis opted instead for a world first: a steel backbone frame comprising the crankcase, gearbox housing, prop shaft, and integrated rear axle. The engine was, by contrast, more conventional, a vertically mounted single-cylinder 80-cubic-inch (1,327-cc) version with three forward gears easily changed via a lever on the car's steering column.

A foot pedal allowed the engine's natural compression to assist the car in braking, while the use of aluminum gave the car the very low weight of 10.5 cwt (533 kg). The first prototype was completed on July 1, 1904. Two- and three-seat configurations went on sale to the public on December 1, 1904, for the relatively modest price of £200 ($314), or £220 ($345) for the three-seat version. It proved an instant success.

Sure, the car may have lacked the beauty and sophistication of the Mercedes Simplex, but this was always designed to be a common person's vehicle, without unnecessary (and expensive) adornments. Lewis had clearly hit upon the right formula—the Rover 8HP became Britain's top-selling car. **BS**

16-24HP | Fiat

I

1904 • 255 cu in/4,181 cc, S4 • 24 bhp/18 kW • unknown • 43 mph/70 kph

In 1899 the Fabbrica Italiana Automobili Torino (Italian Automobile Factory of Turin) was established, and would become the biggest car manufacturer in Italy. Its first vehicle in 1899 was the 3½ CV, with a 42-cubic-inch (697-cc) engine, and only eight of those were made. The 1904 16-24HP, with its 255-cubic-inch (4,181-cc) engine, was a much more powerful car.

Fiat's 1903 model was called the 16-20HP, for its 20-bhp (15-kW) engine, and this time 100 were built. They made 130 of the larger 16-24HP model, which came out in 1904, then reverted to producing 171 of a modified 16-20 in 1905. The 16-20 and 16-24HP models were significant in several ways. One glance at the Fiat 20HP that was being built in 1903 shows it to look very much like a motorized version of a horse and cart. It was open to the elements, and the driver and passenger sat in two separate seats, side by side. The 1904 model was recognizably a car, with a removable roof, an elevated body, and two single-bench seats for four people.

The 1904 development also had innovative features, such as a water-cooling system powered by a pump and a four-speed manual gearbox that drove the rear. It was also exported to the United States where it sold for $6,700 (£4,300). This was at a time when the early Cadillac Model A was being sold for $750 (£485). **MG**

28HP Landaulette | Lanchester (GB)

1906 • 231 cu in/3,800 cc, S6 • 28 bhp/20.9 kW • unknown • 44 mph/71 kph

The Lanchester Engine Company was started in 1899 by the three Lanchester brothers: Frank, George, and Frederick. Success was immediate with the production of a single-cylinder 79-cubic-inch (1,306-cc) vehicle in 1896. Their first two-cylinder, 246-cubic-inch (4,033-cc) production cars appeared in 1900, and by 1905 the Lanchesters were producing 350 cars a year.

Frederick was a gifted engineer and the driving force behind the company's innovation, credited with inventing the wick carburetor, the accelerator pedal, oil-fed bearings, and piston rings. In 1905 he designed a machine to produce the gears for a new worm-drive transmission, and another machine to make the roller bearings for a new rear axle. To lessen tortional vibration on the company's new 231-cubic-inch (3,800 cc) engine, he designed a unique harmonic balancer as well as a dampener that he attached to the crankshaft.

The 1906 Lanchester Landaulette's individualized, aluminum-paneled coachwork was cut on a jig and shaped in their Birmingham factory. The engine, mounted between the front seats, allowed the hood (bonnet) to be replaced by an elegant leather-clad dashboard apron. The car's aesthetic appeal combined with its technical innovation to make the Landaulette a uniquely engineered motor car ahead of its time. **BS**

Silver Ghost | Rolls-Royce (GB)

1906 • 429 cu in/7,036 cc, S6 • 48 bhp/35 kW • unknown • 78 mph/126 kph

The Rolls-Royce model known as the Silver Ghost was originally named the "40/50HP," with the Silver Ghost being a name applied to just one car that rolled out of the Rolls-Royce factory. Soon, however, everyone was referring to the 40/50HP as the Silver Ghost.

With a massive 429-cubic-inch (7,036 cc) engine producing what seems today a tiny output, and two spark plugs firing into each of the six cylinders, the car stood at the cutting edge of automotive technology. By modern standards, though, the car is terrifying: the brakes only worked on the rear wheels (by hand), and electric lights only became an option in 1914, just in time for World War I, when production was put on hold to allow the company to begin making armored cars.

But it was the Silver Ghost's reliability that made it really stand out from the crowd. The car was put through trial after trial, with motoring journalists doing everything they could to find its weak spot. It sailed through every time, breaking records for performance and endurance along the way. In 1907 it won a 15,000-mile (24,000-km) trial set by the Royal Automobile Club.

Even at launch this was no car for the masses. A new model in 1906 would cost several times the average professional wage. A vintage one now could fetch around $60 million (£40 million) at auction. **JI**

Alpha | Lancia

I

1908 • 155 cu in/2,543 cc, S4 • 56 bhp/41 kW • unknown • 56 mph/90 kph

The Lancia 12HP was the first production car made by the company's founder, Vincenzo Lancia. In 1908 the car was unveiled at the Turin Motor Show.

Lancia was born in 1881 and began working at his first job as an accountant in a bicycle factory in Turin. When Fiat bought the bicycle company in 1899, Lancia was named chief inspector. He worked with Fiat for eight years, during which he started test-driving the company's cars, as well as driving Fiat's racing models, winning in many events. When, in 1906, he created the Lancia company he was not concerned with comfort or practicality; he was thinking only of racing.

Lancia began with a 12-bhp (9-kW) engine that was available on a straight chassis. A variety of different body styles were dropped on later, including everything from closed landaulets to a sporting two-seater. The Lancia Corsa was one example of that first car and was raced at Savannah, Georgia, in 1908. These early Lancia pre-production cars were known for being lightweight and were acknowledged as well-engineered vehicles.

Also in 1908, Lancia started work on production of his first automobile. Lancia's first car, called the Alpha, had a 155-cubic-inch (2,543-cc) four-cylinder engine with a side-valve.

Lancia developed into a company unafraid of engineering innovations. It manufactured the first standard production V6, the first electrical system in a car, and the first five-speed standard transmission.

Perhaps Vincenzo Lancia's most enduring legacy is found in the world of motorsports. Lancia can claim ten world rally championship titles, a record that exceeds that of any other car manufacturer. **BK**

Cadillac | Cadillac

(USA)

1908 • single-cylinder • 10 bhp (7.45 kW) • unknown • unknown

In its six years of independence, from the day of its founding by Henry Leland in 1902 to when it was swallowed up by General Motors in 1908, the Cadillac Automobile Company had a lot to be proud of. Cadillac engineers invented the first synchronized transmission, the self-starter, and independent front suspension. And its single-cylinder engines—dubbed "Little Hercules"—produced 10 bhp (7.5 kW), far more than the single-cylinder engines of its competitors.

In 1908 Cadillac offered customers a choice of five carryover models from the previous year: the four-cylinder models H and G, made for the luxury market, and the smaller, single-cylinder models S, T, and M. Cadillac claimed that the parts of any one model could be interchanged with another car of the same model. Interchangeability had become a byword for precision engineering. Britain's Royal Automobile Club had thrown a gauntlet down at the feet of the world's carmakers to prove interchangeability of parts, and only Cadillac dared pick it up.

In 1908 three 1907 Model Ks were driven to Brooklands racetrack at Weybridge, England, and disassembled, piece by piece, into 721 individual components. The pieces were then mixed together and two mechanics unfamiliar with Cadillacs were asked to reassemble them into three working vehicles. When they did, Cadillac became the first American car company to win the Royal Automobile Club's coveted Dewar Trophy for automotive advancement. Cadillac gave their marque a new slogan—the "Standard of the World"—and reinvigorated Henry Leland's motto, "Craftsmanship a creed, accuracy a law." **BS**

Coachwork is lowered onto a waiting Model T, while workers prepare to swing the next unit over the following car, 1914.

S61 Corsa | Fiat (I)

1908 • 615 cu in/10,087 cc, S4 • 130 bhp/96 kW • unknown • 93 mph/150 kph

At the turn of the twentieth century, the newly formed Fabbrica Italiana Automobili Torino, FIAT for short, believed that building engines with enormous cubic capacities and winning auto races was the best way to prove the reliability and strength of its emerging brand.

Fiat did not go racing for the fun of it; racing was essential to the company's development. Its engines, such as the enormous four-cylinder S74 of 1904 with a 854-cubic-inch (14,000-cc) displacement, were capable of speeds in excess of 100 mph (161 kph) and were "sauce for the goose" in an era when racing restrictions only applied to the overall weight of a vehicle and not to any aspect of the engines they carried.

Originally built to race in the 1909 Grand Prix de l'Automobile Club de France (ACF), the S61 was considered a baby when compared in capacity to the S74, despite being one of the day's most powerful racing cars, courtesy of a straight four-cylinder, 615-cubic-inch (10,087-cc) engine that produced 130 bhp (97 kW) at 1,900 rpm. Mounted on a modified 1908 racing frame, the S61 had four valves per cylinder—the first time an engine was fitted with mechanically operated multivalves—pressurized lubrication, dual ignition, and a chain-driven, bevel-geared engine. The car may have been heavy and lacking in agility, but in an era of open-banked racetracks, such as Brooklands and Montlhéry, it was speed, not handling, that was key to winning races.

In 1909 a S61 lapped Brooklands at an average speed of 112 mph (180 kph), and in 1911 three S61s were sent overseas to the United States, where one finished third in that year's Indianapolis 500. An S61 can be seen today in the Indianapolis Motor Speedway Hall of Fame. **BS**

Model T | Ford (USA)

1908 • 176 cu in/2,900 cc, S4 • 20 bhp/15 kW • unknown • 45 mph/72 kph

"Most of the babies of the period were conceived in Model T Fords and not a few were born in them," wrote John Steinbeck in his 1945 novel *Cannery Row*, giving one unexpected and yet persuasive reason why Henry Ford's Model T has been described as the most important car of the twentieth century.

This was the model about which its maker famously said, "Any customer can have a car painted any color that he wants so long as it is black." In fact, a black model was not available for the first few years of the Model T's existence; the options were gray, green, blue, and red. It was not until 1914 that black became the only color, said to be due to the fact that black paint dried the quickest, which speeded up production. By 1918 half the cars in the United States were Model T Fords. The model was so successful that between the years of 1917 and 1923 Ford saw no need to pay for advertising.

The first Model Ts sold for $850 (£550), but the car was such a huge hit that by the time Ford called a halt in 1927 after 16.5 million had been made the vast scale of production had enabled the unit price to be reduced to $300 (£193).

By 1927 the car was also being manufactured at several factories in Europe. Only the Volkswagen Beetle has had such a long production run. The Model T therefore achieved and exceeded Ford's dream of creating a mass-produced car that the average man could afford. It was also the first car to have a radio fitted, and the first car to drive to the top of Ben Nevis, Britain's highest mountain—although no babies were conceived or born on that journey. **MG**

Model 30 | Cadillac

(USA)

1910 • 255 cu in/4,185 cc, S4 • 33 bhp/24.3 kW • unknown • 60 mph/97 kph

The term "unique selling point" was unknown back in 1910, but Cadillac's Model 30 from that year certainly had a USP. It was the first automobile with an enclosed body that offered protection against the elements. An open version had been introduced in December 1909, but it was the 1910 model that really took off when it was introduced in April 1910. The enclosed "Thirty" sold for $1,600 (£1,030), over twice the cost of the average car and $200 (£130) more than its predecessor. The only surprise is that it took so long for manufacturers to come up with an enclosed body. Most were being built in Michigan, which has a record cold temperature of –51°F (–46°C), recorded on February 9, 1934.

The Model 30 was only produced until 1911, when it was superseded by designs that were numbered after the year, such as the Cadillac Model 1912 (the first car to use an electric starter), although they were essentially the same vehicle. The electric starter and ignition system was invented for Cadillac by engineer Charles Kettering, and remains the basis of what is used today. Kettering also invented leaded gasoline.

The Model 30 was an imposing car, standing 7 feet 5 inches (226 cm) tall and weighing in at about 3,500 pounds (1,588 kg). This Cadillac has been described as the precursor of the modern car.

The cars were not cheap—Cadillacs never had been—and the price increased to $1,800 (£1,160) in 1912, and $1,980 (£1,275) in 1913. Despite the price hike, sales increased from just over 8,000 in 1910 to 14,000 in 1912 and more than 15,000 in 1913. Perhaps it was something to do with those bitter Midwest winters. Today they sell at auction for up to $100,000 (£64,400). **MG**

Type 126 12/15HP Touring | Peugeot

(F)

1910 • 134 cu in/2,212 cc, S4 • 12 bhp/9 kW • unknown • 34 mph/55 kph

In France, the Peugeot name did not get off to a good start because its first steam-powered cars got a reputation for, well, falling to pieces. When Peugeot had one driven from Paris to Lyon to show what the new horseless carriages could do, it left components scattered in its wake and attracted ridicule rather than enthusiasm. Although the company's vehicle-manufacturing arm was established in 1882, by 1891 Peugeot had managed to build and sell only five cars.

Nearly twenty years later, things had improved dramatically, with the company managing to build 350 of their new Type 126 model in 1910. The car could achieve a giddy top speed of 34 mph (55 kph), although if this was too much for some customers they could purchase a less powerful version with a 47-cubic-inch (785-cc), one-cylinder engine. The Type 126 had a lot of competition, though, because by this time other manufacturers were offering cars that could go twice as fast. Peugeot's plan to build inexpensive cars resulted in vehicles like the Type 126, which were simply not powerful enough, and too cumbersome to drive easily.

In other ways, 1910 was a big year for Peugeot. The parent company had been a family firm founded in 1810 to make coffee mills, to which bicycles had been added in 1830. In 1896 an argument had resulted in Armand Peugeot leaving the family firm and setting up a rival company that also used the Peugeot name. In 1910 the warring parties decided to get back together and merge the companies. The company is, of course, still going strong, and in recent years has won several European Car of the Year Awards. Generally, bits dropping off their cars has become a thing of the past. **MG**

Tipo 55 Corsa | Lancia

(I)

1910 • 210 cu in/3,456 cc, S4 • 68 bhp/110kW • unknown • 68 mph/110 kph

Lancia was founded in 1906 in Turin, also the home of Fiat, and in 1907 had started its journey through the Greek alphabet by launching the Lancia Alfa-12HP. The Lancia Dialfa-18HP (dialfa is a nonexistent letter) followed in 1908, and the Lancia Beta-15/20HP in 1909. In 1910 it was to be the turn of the Lancia Gamma-20HP, although the car is equally well known by its original name, Lancia Tipo 55 Corsa. (In fact, all Lancia's cars had alternate names, the Alfa being the Tipo 51, the Beta the Tipo 54, and so on.)

The rate at which Lancia built up its markets and its production runs was quite slow, just as it was at Fiat. Only twenty-three Dialfas were built, and 150 of the Beta model. The Tipo 55, or Gamma-20HP, was a step up from the previous model, with a bigger engine and, at 258 units, a longer production run. It was a handsome car, and by now Lancia was making a name for itself by modeling its cars on the Fiats then being produced, but giving them a classier look and appealing to a more upscale market.

The Tipo 55 had the Torpedo body style that had been introduced in 1908 to give cars a more streamlined look. For competition racing, the car was also available with a 286-cubic-inch (4,700-cc) engine, which helped it win races in both Italy and in the United States. One very unusual feature was that the frame could also be configured in different ways to suit the customer, which is why photographs of the surviving models show them to be quite varied in appearance. The angle of the steps up into the body and the angle of the long steering wheel were just two of the ways in which the Tipo 55 could be customized. **MG**

S76 | Fiat

(I)

1911 • 1,726 cu in/28,300 cc, S4 • 300 bhp/224 kW • unknown • 180 mph/228 kph

One look at the specifications of the Fiat S76 and it is apparent that this was no ordinary car. Its engine was so big that it took up almost the entire 9 feet (2.7 m) of the wheelbase, with the driver and his mechanic perched at the back. The S76 looked not unlike a rocket made out of a gigantic tin can and plunked down on its side. In its performance, too, it was exactly like a rocket placed on its side and fired horizontally along the ground rather than vertically.

The body of this beast—and for once that word is not out of place—was so huge that drivers had trouble seeing over the hood (bonnet) and were obliged to lean out and look around the side instead. Two big exhaust pipes came out of the side and merged, like something usually seen only in a huge industrial factory. The engine was twice as big as that of the car's predecessor, the Fiat S74. One was later used to power an airship, while another is rumored to be still functioning and operating a pump on an oil field in Mexico.

It seems that only two S76s were ever built, and these were used purely for racing and for breaking speed records. They were driven by some of the top racing drivers of the era, including Felice Nazzaro, Antonio Fagnano, and Pietro Bordino, who between them won several European Grand Prix and other races.

In those days there were no official land speed records; instead, manufacturers competed to claim the accolade of the fastest mile and fastest kilometer. One estimate of the S76's top speed can be reached using the fact that, in tests on Long Island, New York, it traveled a mile (1.6 km) in 20.2 seconds, equivalent to just under 180 mph (288 kph). **MG**

EI 641

◁ The Vauxhall Prince Henry was famous for its speed, and caught the eye of royalty across Europe.

Prince Henry | Vauxhall (GB)

1911 • 183 cu in/3,000 cc, S4 • 19.9 bhp/15 kW • unknown • 65 mph/104 kph

Widely held up as the first English sports car, Vauxhall's Prince Henry was certainly one of the fastest in its day. It was often known to hit 70 mph (113 kph) or more, much quicker than its official top speed.

With its distinctive pointed nose, the Prince Henry won countless trophies in speed trials between 1911 and 1914, and took center stage in one of the most enduring photographs of the era. At the Shelsley Walsh hill climb course near Worcester in the United Kingdom, Vauxhall director A. J. Hancock is seen at the wheel of a Prince Henry with his mechanic hanging out of the opposite side as a weight counterbalance.

The car was officially named the C10 Type but rechristened for Prince Henry of Prussia, who sponsored early vehicle reliability trials. After it competed in a St. Petersburg-to-Sebastopol race in the year it was launched, Tsar Nicholas was so impressed he bought two. Based on the Vauxhall 20HP model, the car was marketed to well-heeled Edwardian gentlemen who regarded the new sport of motoring as an entertaining way to pass the time. London's *Daily Telegraph* newspaper reviewed the car on October 6, 1910, and labeled it "the most remarkable Twenty in the motor car world." A Prince Henry cost £485 ($752) at the time, but that only bought a rolling chassis—the four-seater coachwork was extra. Fewer than ten worldwide are thought to have survived.

A later version was renamed the 30/98, but production was halted during World War I. When it restarted in 1919, the car was badged the E-Type—a moniker today more commonly associated with the Jaguar of the same name launched in 1961. **RY**

40 | Amherst (CDN)

1912 • unknown • 40 bhp/29 kW • unknown unknown

This quirky early Amherst was one of Canada's first ever cars. Although built from imported parts in Ontario, it was designed just across the border in Detroit. Little is known of the specifications of the 40, but it was clearly a uniquely practical concept. It served as a seven-passenger touring car, or the rear seat could be removed to enable it to be used as a pickup truck.

The Amherst was named for the small town in Ontario where it was built, Amherstburg. The car was made by a group of Detroit entrepreneurs along with a few enthusiastic Canadians. They called themselves the Two-in-One Auto Company. It is believed that only nine Amherst 40s were built in the one year that the company operated. It was the only model they made.

The idea of a vehicle that could be so easily switched from a passenger car to a light truck clearly appealed to the citizens of Amherstburg. The town itself took a major financial share in the Two-in-One Auto Company. A finished Amherst 40 proudly stood on display in the town.

In August 1912 a prototype Amherst 40 was used to pull a broken-down vehicle 20 miles (32 km) along rough roads back into the town. A 40 was also displayed in Toronto at that year's Canadian National Exhibition. However, in September 1912 the Detroit backers were fired. It seems they had refused to pay their promised contribution.

Only a few more Amherst 40 cars were completed before the company was forced into bankruptcy and disappeared forever. Fortunately, one of their vehicles lives on and is on display at the Canadian Transportation Museum in Kingsville, Ontario. **SH**

Bearcat | Stutz

USA

1912 • 389 cu in/6,388 cc, S4 • 60 bhp/44 kW • unknown • 80 mph/128 kph

From Mr. Magoo to the Sultan of Brunei, the Stutz Bearcat has been driven by a wide range of owners. A 1936 model owned by the character Mr. Burns has appeared in *The Simpsons*, and in 1971 two full-scale Bearcat replicas were used for the short-lived American television series, *Bearcats!*, in which two private investigators drove a Bearcat in adventures set just before World War I.

The Bearcat was the first American sports car. It initially came to the world's notice in 1911, when an early version of the four-cylinder car finished eleventh in the very first Indianapolis 500 motor race. That might not seem a great achievement, but it was a brand-new and untried car, racing in its home city in front of 80,000 people, and it covered the 500 miles (805 km) in an impressive 442 minutes. As a result, an advertising slogan was born: "The car that made good in a day."

When an almost identical commercial version of that prototype Bearcat went on sale in 1912, the public

snapped it up. The car was still being raced, and in 1912 it won twenty-five of the thirty races in which it competed. By 1915 the Stutz Bearcat had been named as the United States' champion racer. With such fame, the car was now generating its own publicity.

The Bearcat—which is a nickname for the mountain lion—was the first car to bear the Stutz name. Harry C. Stutz was an automotive pioneer who grew up on a farm in Ohio; he built his first car when he was twenty-one years old. He went on to design and build his own gasoline engine, and founded the Ideal Motor Company in 1911; this was renamed the Stutz Motor Company in the following year. Stutz also invented the low-slung chassis, which was designed to lower the center of gravity of his cars and make them both safer and more maneuverable. Such was their legendary stability that even humorously clumsy cartoon character Mr. Magoo was able to drive one. **MG**

Model 51 | Cadillac (USA)

1914 • 314 cu in/5,150 cc, V8 • 70 bhp/52.1 kW • unknown • 62 mph/100 kph

In 1914 Cadillac founder Henry Leland needed a replacement for the company's dependable, though dated, four-cylinder Model 30. Sales had plummeted in 1913–14 from 17,000 to 7,000 units. Cadillac's competitors had shifted to producing smoother, more powerful six-cylinder engines, and they were taking Cadillac's customers with them. Seeing that Europe was years ahead of American carmakers in the development of high-performance engines, Leland entrusted Scottish-born D. McCall White, formerly of Daimler, with the job of bringing his customers back.

Leland's brief was simple: design and build America's first mass-produced V8 engine, and do it away from prying eyes. Development took place inside a small concrete building in the Detroit suburb of Mt. Clemens, with only those employees vital to the project permitted access. What emerged was a 314-cubic-inch (5,150-cc) V8 engine that gave out an impressive 70 bhp (52 kW). That was almost 10 percent more punch than the comparable Packard Model 38, which cost consumers twice as much. White had excelled himself; although the engine wasn't perfect—the crankshaft design led to an out-of-balance wobble in the 40–50 mph (64–80 kph) speed range—sales rebounded with 13,002 units selling in 1915. **BS**

Touring Car | Cunningham (USA)

1916 • 439 cu/7,200 cc, V8 • 90 bhp /67 kW • unknown • 80 mph/129 kph

The conservative-minded Cunningham family began handmaking horse carriages in 1842 and by the turn of the century were known for their elaborately carved sleighs and exquisite funeral wagons. In 1907 the company produced an electric car, followed in 1908 by their first gasoline-driven automobiles powered with borrowed engines, and in 1911 made their first touring car—the Model J—powered by their very own 40-bhp (29-kW) four-cylinder engine.

It was not until the unveiling in 1916 of their 439-cubic-inch (7,200-cc), 45-bhp (33-kW) side-valve V8, with its state-of-the-art Brown Lipe dry multidisk clutch, however, that the Cunningham family finally let its hair down. Boasting more bhp than its closest rival, the Cadillac V8, this new, European-looking touring car, with its cellular core air tube radiator clad in German silver, set a new benchmark in style, sophistication, and "oomph."

The car included innovations such as built-in air pumps, water-heated intake manifolds, and a tire hose that extended from beneath the front seat. Twelve configurations were available, including a two-passenger roadster and five- and seven-seat versions, all priced at \$3,750 (£2,400), though extensive customizing of the chassis and interior meant that a Cunningham tourer rarely sold at its advertised price. **BS**

Dual Power | Woods (USA)

1917 • 95 cu in/1,560 cc, S4 • 12 bhp/9 kW • unknown • 35 mph/56 kph

Hybrid cars might seem a modern idea, but the first to go into production was the Woods Dual Power, back in 1917. Electric cars were quite common in the early days of motoring but, like today, there were problems with their range and their power. Gasoline engines were popular but gave a less smooth ride. The Dual Power was created to try to give the best of both worlds.

Clinton Edgar Woods, a great enthusiast for electric vehicles, had founded the Woods Motor Vehicle Company in Chicago in 1899. Some of his early cars used twin electric motors for a top speed of 18 mph (29 kph), considerably less than gasoline engines were able to achieve. In 1915 the company patented a car that would use both electric and internal combustion engines. By 1917 it was on the road.

The electric engine could get the speed up to 20 mph (32 kph), at which point the gas engine would take over to save the battery and take the car up to 35 mph (56 kph). Alternatively, both engines could be used simultaneously, though only the electric engine could operate in reverse. At a price of $2,650 (£1,700) the car was considerably more expensive than equivalent conventional vehicles, and was much harder to service. This early hybrid may have been on the road in 1917, but it was off the road by 1918. **MG**

38HP Model 51 | Pierce-Arrow (USA)

1919 • 524 cu in/8,587 cc, S6 • 38 bhp/28.3 kW • unknown • 70 mph/113 kph

In 1909 two Pierce-Arrow Model 38s were ordered as part of a new presidential motorcade. Ten years later, President Woodrow Wilson was presented with one for his own personal use. Wilson became so enamored with the car that upon leaving office in 1921, he purchased it.

Model 51s were sold overseas to ambassadors, prime ministers, even emperors. This wasn't just another luxury car, it was a symbol of status. The 524 cubic inches (8,587 cc) of the dual-valve six-cylinder engine produced more horsepower than older single-valve motors. The engine was built as a replacement for the previous Model 66's massive 823-cubic-inch (13,502-cc) motor, which was the largest production engine ever made.

Engines aside, the car had perfectly cast aluminum body panels, supplied by the Aluminum Company of America. The result of years of experimentation, the panels—some as thin as an eighth of an inch (3 mm)—made the Model 51 both strong and light, reducing vibration but also adding to the car's rather hefty price.

There were many other wonderful Pierce-Arrow touches, too, such as its patented headlights; instead of being mounted on either side of a radiator, these were set within exquisite molds extending forward from its front fenders (bumpers). Such flourishes were not surprising for a carmaker that had its very own art department. **BS**

CITROËN
2416-E3
PARIS
JACOTIN
1, Faubg. de Marne
CHÂLONS-S/-MARNE

(<) The Citroën Type A was the epitome of bourgeois motoring in its time, as exemplified by this 1923 poster.

Type A | Citroën (F)

1919 • 80 cu in/1,327 cc, S4 • 18 bhp/13 kW • unknown • 41 mph/65 kph

The father of high-volume car manufacturing is Henry Ford, who in 1908 pioneered the production-line approach with the Model T in Detroit. Eleven years later, the concept crossed the Atlantic, with the result that the Citroën Type A became Europe's first car to be assembled using Ford's groundbreaking principles. What is perhaps most impressive is that the French company had never before built a car.

During World War I, company boss André Citroën's factory had worked on munitions. But even as the guns were blazing, he had been considering the idea of a medium-sized car. When hostilities ceased, he finalized the design. Also known as the 10HP, the Type A went on sale in July 1919, and was an immediate success. Within a year, up to a hundred Type As a day were rolling out of the factory gates. By the time the model was phased out twenty-three months later, ten different versions had been created and sales had reached just short of 25,000.

With the Type A's success, car manufacture changed. Instead of supplying a rolling chassis to a coachbuilder for a bespoke body to be fitted, cars began to be made exclusively on one site.

Citroën became the first mass-production carmaker outside North America, but its achievement went further. The company took the industry into uncharted waters by creating a customer-focused sales and service network—a legacy that remains in place today. In less than a decade, Citroën became Europe's largest carmaker, and the fourth largest worldwide. It was also a pioneer of employee rights, providing staff with medical facilities, a gym, and a daycare center. **RY**

A | Essex (USA)

1919 • 178 cu in/2,930 cc, S4 • 55 bhp/40 kW • unknown • 60 mph/97 kph

Henry Ford may have been responsible for producing the first affordable open-sided automobile in the Model T, but it was the Essex Motor Company, established by the Hudson Motor Company in 1917, that first gave the average American inexpensive, comfortable, enclosed motoring with the introduction of the Essex Model A sedan (saloon) in 1919. Designed to compete with the Model T, the A's affordability soon made it one of the most common cars on American roads. In six years it helped lift Hudson/Essex from the seventh-largest U.S. carmaker into third, snapping confidently at the heels of Chevrolet and Ford.

The Essex A was a two-door sedan produced on two parallel assembly lines capable of turning out 150 cars a day, a woefully low figure considering the volume of orders the company was receiving. Timber was used to brace and frame the car's squarish steel panels (the A was one of the first American cars to use pressed-steel coachwork). This simplistic approach to design kept costs down, but also made the A's cab overwhelmingly boxlike. However, almost 22,000 units were sold in the A's first year alone, and sales increased in 1920 after an Essex roadster set a New York-to-San-Francisco speed record of four days, nineteen hours and seventeen minutes. The A's 55 bhp (40 kW) was almost three times that of the Model T.

By 1920 the model range had expanded to include a four-to-five-seat tourer, a two-seat roadster, and a two-seat cabriolet. But it was the sedan that had changed the buying habits of Americans, who wanted more power and greater protection from the elements than Ford's open-sided Model Ts could provide. **BS**

H6 | Hispano-Suiza

F

1919 • 402 cu in/6,597 cc, S6 • 135 bhp/101 kW • unknown • 80 mph/130 kph

The Hispano-Suiza H6 oozes luxury. Its makers referred to it in their catalog as "an undoubted masterpiece," and for once the hyperbole could be forgiven—the car looks as classy as anything ever built. The car's merits did not lie only in its appearance, however, as it also had power and some groundbreaking features. The engine was designed by the Swiss engineer Marc Birkigt, who had previously worked on designing aircraft engines. One thing he knew was how to give an engine some "oomph."

The braking system on the car, which was first shown at the Paris Motor Show in 1919, was also new and unique. Each wheel had its own power-assisted brake, so that when the driver hit the brake pedal, the very act of decelerating provided additional power to the brakes. This resulted in greater control, with no locking, and a very short braking distance. Tests showed that the car could come to a stop in only 115 feet (35 m) when traveling at 62 mph (100 kph). The brakes were so good that the system was licensed to Rolls-Royce, which paid a royalty for every one of its cars that used it.

The cars stayed in production until 1933, with two later versions (the H6B and H6C) being yet again more powerful. Five special racing versions of the H6B went on to break several international speed records. About 2,600 cars were built in all, mostly in France, although some were built under a sublicense to, of all companies, Skoda in Czechoslovakia. There, they built one for the Czech president and founder of the country, President Masaryk. Other illustrious owners included King Alfonso XIII of Spain, the American movie director D. W. Griffith, and the future Earl Mountbatten of Burma in Britain. **MG**

Six Convertible | Australian

(AUS)

1919 • unknown, S6 • 25 bhp/20 kW • unknown • 40 mph/64 kph

It wasn't until the late 1940s that the Australian government finally committed itself to help develop a national automotive industry. The government agreed to subsidise General Motors company Holden in the manufacture of their Holden sedan (saloon). The first of their cars came off the production line on 29 October, 1948, and the demand was such that there was a waiting list that stretched well into 1950.

The era of truly "Australian" motoring had at last arrived. Buyers no longer had to ingloriously import vehicles from overseas manufacturers. In some ways, however, this had come thirty years too late. In 1919, if the government had paid more attention—and given more assistance—to Sydney engineer, inventor, and automotive pioneer Frederick Hugh Gordon, it could have happened a generation earlier.

In 1918 Gordon traveled to the United States, and He met with Louis Chevrolet, who agreed to sell Gordon several components of the Light Six he was producing at American Motors. Gordon sourced other parts from around the globe: Rutenber six-cylinder engines from Illinois, Muncie gearboxes, Salisbury differentials, and Rolls-Royce-like Grecian-shaped radiators.

Production of his Australian sedan began at his factory in Sydney in 1919. The car debuted on June 28 with six homegrown Australian models to choose from, all with luxurious, pleated, full-hide leather seats. A hundred or so units were made a year until a series of financial reversals, a bankruptcy, a subsequent bailout, and then a fire combined to see the end of Gordon's vision. Around 500 Australian Sixes were built during that time, but sadly today only sixteen of them remain. **BS**

Hélica | Leyat

(F)

1919 • 73 cu in/1,203 cc, two-cylinder, propeller-driven • 8 bhp/6 kW • unknown • 43 mph/70 kph

Deriving from a French word for "propeller," Hélica was the name given to French inventor Marcel Leyat's propeller-driven light car, a vehicle requiring no clutch, transmission, or differential. Leyat was concerned more with weight and aerodynamics than complex mechanics. There were, however, several design modifications along the way.

One early model had the driver and passenger in an open cabin, with nothing resembling a guard for the twin-bladed wooden propeller spinning mere inches in front of the driver's worried face. A windshield for the passenger was later added, then taken away, as was a horizontal stabilizer.

The later models for which Leyat is best known included a monocoque—the body and chassis form a single unit—plywood-framed and aluminum-clad cockpit that weighed just 625 pounds (284 kg). The occupants were now enclosed, still with room for only two people, one sitting behind the other. Steering was via wires connected to the rear wheels. The 54-inch (137-cm) propeller remained attached to the front of the Hélica, bolted directly on to the crankshaft of its air-cooled, twin-cylinder Scorpion engine; at least it was now encased by a protective wooden shroud.

Between 1919 and 1925, Leyat sold between twenty-five and thirty units. At the 1921 Paris Auto Show he received orders for 600 of a four-bladed version that was quieter and reduced vibration—despite its top speed being a modest 43 mph (69 kph).

In World War II the Germans commandeered a Hélica, but the driver was confused by its "backward" method of steering and drove it into a tree. **BS**

3-Litre | Bentley

GB

1921 • 182 cu in/2,996 cc, S4 • 80 bhp/59 kW • unknown • 80 mph/129 kph

If ever a company's first car set the tone for what came later, the Bentley 3-litre did. As well as establishing the elegant Edwardian styling that all Bentleys of the era would share, it spearheaded the brand's outstanding success at the legendary 24 Hours of Le Mans race in France. In lightweight "open" trim, versions of the 3-litre secured victories in 1924, 1927, 1928, 1929 (when it took the first four places), and 1930. There was further success in the Isle of Man Tourist Trophy (TT) races and the Indianapolis 500. The team of brave drivers, known as the "Bentley Boys," became front-page news.

Prior to World War I, motorcycle-racing enthusiast Walter Bentley was a successful importer of DFP sports cars from France. He was also the designer of lightweight aluminum pistons for aircraft engines, such as that of the Sopwith Camel fighter.

When peace came, Bentley set about creating a fast car of his own. It was unveiled in 1919 at London's Olympia Motor Show and went on sale two years later. Manufactured in the capital's northern suburb of Cricklewood, the price was £1,100 ($1,750) for a chassis. Customers had the choice of three coachwork options: touring, sports, or sedan (saloon). By the time production ceased in 1928, when it was replaced by the 4½-litre, more than 1,600 had been built.

Despite public acclaim and racing triumphs, Bentley Motors was beset by financial difficulties and came close to bankruptcy several times during the 1920s. Ironically, taking up racing was supposed to provide publicity to stabilize the balance sheet, but that wasn't to be. Bentley finally went into receivership in June 1931, to be rescued by Rolls-Royce. **RY**

A diminuitive 1922 Austin Seven passes spectators during the 1926 Lord Mayor's Show in the City of London. ▷

C4 Torpedo | Spyker

NL

1921 • 347 cu in/5,700 cc, S6 • 40 bhp/30 kW • unknown • 87 mph/140 kph

In 1898 the Spyker brothers, Jacobus and Hendrik-Jan, built the famous "Golden Carriage" for the coronation of Wilhelmina as Queen of the Netherlands. The recognition and patronage that flowed from that commission was a turning point, enabling them to turn their attention to their true passion: the making of luxury automobiles.

In 1907 a privately owned Spyker 14/18HP tourer took second place in the grueling Peking-to-Paris race. This was something of an irony, as the Spykers believed their cars to have no need to prove themselves in competitions. The brothers turned from cars to building aircraft in World War I, returning to automaking in 1919. In 1921 their greatest creation was unveiled: the Spyker C4.

With an engine designed by German engineer Wilhelm Maybach, with two spark plugs for each cylinder, it set a new record in the 1921 Nijmegen–Sittard–Nijmegen endurance race, driving 18,642 miles (30,000 km) in thirty days and averaging 21.7 mph (35 kph), beating the previous record held by Rolls- Royce without having to make a single repair. In 1922 record-breaker Selwyn Edge chose a C4 for his attempt to break his own double twelve-hour average speed record of 60 mph (96.5 kph), set at Brooklands in 1907. The C4 achieved 74.5 mph (120 kph); Edge called it "faultless."

The Autocar magazine thought its power and acceleration "extraordinary," and driving it akin to "the nature of a glide." Spykers were guaranteed for life, and the company enjoyed the constant patronage of Queen Wilhelmina. But praise, precision, and patronage would not be enough. The C4 was expensive and Spyker—selling just 150 units in five years—closed its doors for good in 1926. **BS**

Seven | Austin

GB

1922 • 42 cu in/696 cc, S4 • 10 bhp/7 kW • unknown • 48 mph/77 kph

The Austin Seven, which was in production from 1922 until 1939, has been described as the United Kingdom's Model T Ford. Nicknamed the "Baby Austin," it brought motoring to the masses at an affordable price, and was hugely popular around the world. Around 290,000 were built in those seventeen years, including many built under license and sold under different names in various countries. The very first BMW car was actually an Austin Seven built under license. In France they were called "Rosengarts" and the cars were even exported to the United States and sold as the "American Austin." Some countries imported parts from England; others simply copied the design and built their own "bootleg" versions of the car.

Sir Herbert Austin had founded the Austin Motor Company in 1905, and in 1909 it had put out a 7-bhp (5.2-kW) car, also called the Austin Seven. The company's main production had always been of larger and more expensive vehicles, though, and when Sir Herbert later wanted to try another smaller vehicle, the company's board of directors refused. It was only when he threatened to take his design to their great rivals, Wolseley, that Sir Herbert got his way; the new Austin Seven went into production in 1922. Sir Herbert collected a royalty payment of just over £2 ($3.10) for each one sold, although he had put a lot of his own money into seeing the car through.

In 1927 a two-tone tourer, the Austin Seven Swallow, was equally popular, and in 1928 the Austin Seven Swallow saloon (sedan) arrived. An estimated 10,000 Austin Sevens still survive around the world, a testimony to their sturdy construction. **MG**

FIRST FLOOR
50
17

5CV Type C | Citroën

F

1922 • 51 cu in/850 cc, S4 • 13 bhp/9.7 kW • unknown • 37 mph/60 kph

The Citroën 5CV Type C was called the "little lemon" because its initial production color was the brightest of yellows. It also came with an electric starter as standard because the company believed this would help endear it to women drivers. The 5CV had an open body, a fish-tailed rear end that doubled as a storage compartment, a spare wheel attached to the outside of the driver's door, and a simple, wooden-framed, no-nonsense roof. It was unashamedly quaint, cute, and feminine. Or so it seemed.

The 5CV was designed to be France's answer to Henry Ford's Model T—cheap, no frills, and plentiful. The 51-cubic-inch (850-cc) engine made it smaller than almost all of the Citroëns that had recently preceded it, and placed it only a rung or two above the lightweight cycle cars that were popular in France at the time. Having brakes only to the rear wheels would normally raise an eyebrow, but when a vehicle's top speed is just 37 mph (60 kph), why invest in unnecessary mechanics?

In 1925, along came Neville Westwood, a twenty-two-year-old Seventh Day Adventist from Perth in Western Australia, of all places, who would turn Europe's opinions of the 5CV on its collective head. Westwood became the first person to drive his car, a quaint-looking Citroën 5CV, around Australia—a distance of 5,600 miles (9,012 km). Carried across the Fitzroy River by local Aborigines, its punctured tires stuffed with grass and cowhide, it made a remarkable journey, the envy of all the organizers of those so-called "endurance races" back in tiny Europe. The legacy of the 5CV's ability to keep going, going, and going can be seen today in Westwood's fully restored little battler, which is now on permanent display at the National Museum in Canberra. **BS**

40CV Type JP | Renault

(F)

1922 • 556 cu in/9,123 cc, S6 • unknown • unknown • 90 mph/145 kph

Although Renault's name will be forever linked in many people's minds with its diminutive 2CV—a people's car with some physical resemblance to the Morris Minor—the company has also produced some rather more powerful machines. The 40CV was one of them, built like a horse-drawn coach and looking big enough to carry a sizable party in the back. The first 40CV came out in 1911; when it was shown at a motor show in St. Petersburg in 1913, the Tsar of Russia immediately ordered two of them.

Different models followed, named as types with different two-letter combinations, including 1922's 40CV Type JP. This has the distinction of having been voted among the most dangerous cars of all time, because the driver's visibility was very poor. When the top was up, it blocked out much of the area behind the vehicle, and the comparatively small rearview mirror did not help much. Mirrors were only becoming commonplace in the 1920s, and although the JP had one, the driver still needed help from his passengers before he could pull out to overtake anything. But one innovative feature the JP did have was a hydraulic servo-brake system, a development of the basic hydraulic brake that had only been invented in 1918.

The 40CV was still a success, and in 1925 one of them won the Monte Carlo Rally. Although the first rally was held in 1911, the 1925 race was only the fourth in its history due to the interruption of the war years. Winning the race was seen as a real test of a car's ability, so the 1925 result was a coup for Renault. Production of the 40CV ceased in 1928 when Renault replaced it with the Reinastella. **MG**

Practical Motorist

⊂ Although Delage enjoyed great success on the racetrack, the marque is better known for its stylish luxury automobiles.

DH-V12 "La Torpille" | Delage (F)

1923 • 645 cu in/10,570 cc, V12 • 95 bhp/70.8 kW • unknown • 149 mph/240 kph

Louis Delage was a racer at heart. He established the Delage Automobile Company in 1905 and began making his own engines in 1909. By the time war broke out in 1914, his cars were proving so effective at winning races that the French government enlisted him to help improve their inventory of military vehicles.

That pause in carmaking ended in the early 1920s with a plea to Delage from racing-car driver René Thomas to design a special, one-off racer the like of which had never been seen before. Delage agreed to do it, then gave designer Charles Planchon just three months to design the car so it could debut at the French Grand Prix in Tours. When the car was finished, Delage called it "a work of art" and named it, appropriately, "La Torpille"—the Torpedo.

The car's chassis was streamlined and tapered at the back—a torpedo indeed, but in reverse. What mattered with the Delage V12 was not what you could see, however, but what you couldn't. The engine was so heavy that it had to be bolted onto a steel ladder-shaped frame with dampeners on each corner to maximize stability. It was thought capable of producing 120 bhp (88 kW), though 95 bhp (70 kW) was probably closer to the mark, and it was fitted with front wheel brakes, a rarity at the time, even for racing cars.

The Delage V12 that debuted at the 1923 Gaillon Hillclimb was a supercar. With René Thomas at the wheel it smashed the land speed record at Arpajon, clocking 143.3 mph (230 kph) on July 6, 1924 (the record stood for a week until beaten by Ernest Eldridge in the Fiat Mefistofele). The DH-V12 continued as a successful sprint racer until it was retired in 1935. **BS**

Type 35 | Bugatti (F)

1924 • 138 cu in/2,262 cc, S8 • 130 bhp/97 kW • 0–60mph/96 kph in 6 seconds • 125 mph/201 kph

Some experts claim that the Bugatti Type 35 was the world's first proper sports car. Between 1924 and 1931, Type 35s won almost 2,000 races, including the first Grand Prix World Championship in 1926. The distinctive Bugatti-blue cars with the arch-shaped radiator won the Targa Florio race for five consecutive years. At its peak, the Type 35 averaged fourteen race wins per week, yet it was the only car of the time that could be driven both on the racetrack and on the road.

The Type 35's performance would be thought fast even today, and the handling was considered exemplary. The French racing driver René Dreyfus commented, "You could place the car wherever you wanted, the roadholding was fantastic. The precision of the steering was something fantastic." Little wonder that more than 300 of the two-seaters were built at Bugatti's factory in Molsheim, Alsace.

Although the simple but charming looks of the Type 35 remained unchanged over the years, the model evolved through a variety of engine sizes. Supercharging was introduced in the Type 35B, which won the 1929 French Grand Prix.

Innovative features of the Type 35 included alloy wheels, when other manufacturers were still using wire wheels, and a weight-saving hollow front axle, at a time when rivals were still clinging to the belief that making cars heavier improved their roadholding.

The story was not all state of the art, though. When rivals began to use hydraulic brakes, Bugatti stuck with brake cables. When one of his customers complained about this, Ettore Bugatti was said to have replied, "I make my cars to go, not to stop." **SH**

CGS | Amilcar (F)

1924 • 63 cu in/1,047 cc, S4 • 35 bhp/26.1 kW • unknown • 75 mph/120 kph (estimated)

The French-made, doorless, pointy-tailed Amilcar CGS was known lightheartedly among the interwar racing fraternity as the "poor man's Bugatti." It was the latest in a line of lightweight sports cars that had begun with the 550-cubic-inch (903-cc) CC in 1920. Amilcar had lost no time building an enviable reputation in the 67-cubic-inch (1,100-cc) -class auto races that proliferated throughout France in the early 1920s.

The CGS began production in 1924. Here was the MG of its era: inexpensive and fun and with a surprisingly piercing, throaty exhaust. The CGS introduced a new generation of racing enthusiasts to the sport and was deceptively quick for a side-valved engine. It had a classic sports car design, with a high-geared engine and direct steering. It also had a revolutionary four-wheel braking system that allowed the brakes to be constantly applied to the wheels when cornering.

The CGS was handmade at a rate of one or two a day. In total, 984 were made in its two-year production run, of which between eighty and a hundred survive today. Commentators saw it as a miniature Bugatti, with its long-blade fenders (bumpers), racing radiator, and wire wheels. The French auto magazine *Moto-Revue* also fell under its spell, writing in 1924, "The Amilcar is the dream machine of anyone who loves fast, responsive cars." **BS**

Phantom I | Rolls-Royce (GB)

1925 • 467 cu in/7,668 cc, S6 • 108 bhp/80.5 kW • unknown • 90 mph/145 kph

Expectations were high when the Phantom I was finally revealed to the world in May 1925. It was the successor to the famed Silver Ghost, Rolls-Royce's emblem for the previous eighteen years. The engine was a push-rod OHV straight-six, cast in three groups of two cylinders with never-before-seen detachable heads. The chassis was entirely handmade and the interior had a wind-up chauffeur's window and an intercar telephone. Its headlights were nickel and silver-plated Paris opera lamps, and there were silk blinds on the windows.

The Phantom I was designed and built amid almost unheard-of secrecy. It was code-named the EAC (Easter Armored Car), and armor plating was placed in plain view to throw other carmakers off the scent. It received overwhelmingly favorable reviews, of course, but nothing could hide the fact that it was built over the Silver Ghost's old chassis, a decision that affected its performance and forced Rolls-Royce to reexamine the relationship between aerodynamics and performance.

A 1925 model Phantom I Barker Boattail was purchased by the Maharajah of Jodhpur and used as a hunting vehicle until he sold it to the Maharajah of Bikaner in 1927. The car sold at auction in 2008 for $1.21 million (£750,000). Even if slightly flawed, no marque holds its value quite like a Rolls. **BS**

3-Litre | Sunbeam (GB)

1925 • 178 cu in/2,920 cc, S6 • 21 bhp/16 kW • unknown • 151 mph/242 kph

Sunbeam had been making 3-liter cars for some time, and in 1912 they came first, second, and third in the Coupe de l'Auto run in Dieppe. Sunbeams were stormingly successful on the Grand Prix circuit, and finished first, second, and fourth in the 1923 French Grand Prix, and won the 1924 Spanish Grand Prix, too. However, when a new 3-liter Bentley won the 1924 Le Mans race, the company decided it had to act.

A brand-new Sunbeam 3-litre was unveiled at the London Motor Show in October 1924; it was the first production car in Britain to have a twin overhead camshaft, and the first in the world to use the dry sump lubrication system. Two Sunbeams were entered in the 1925 Le Mans race, and although one was forced to retire, the other came in second, beating the Bentleys. The success was ephemeral, however, as Bentley went on to dominate Le Mans in subsequent years.

Only 250 of the Sunbeam 3-litre Super Sport, to give it its full name, were made before production ceased in 1930, and the company sadly went into receivership in 1935. It had originally been founded in Wolverhampton in 1888, it made the first British car to win a Grand Prix victory, and it set several land speed records. In 1925 Malcolm Campbell drove a Sunbeam to become the first driver to break the 150-mph (242-kph) barrier. **MG**

4.5-Litre | Bentley (GB)

1927 • 274 cu in/4,400 cc, S4 • 110 bhp/82 kW • unknown • 98 mph/158 kph

The Bentley 4.5-litre of 1927 superseded the underpowered Bentley 3-litre, the car Ettore Bugatti once disparaged as "the fastest lorry in the world." It had all the aerodynamics of a barn door yet still managed to exude sophistication and precision. The hand-built open bodies were sheathed in Vanden Plas leather, and there were 19-inch (48-cm) seventy-spoke wire wheels, fold-down windshields, and silver-winged "B" badges and hood (bonnet) ornaments. Four massive 17-inch (43-cm) cable-operated brakes helped slow down the 3,580-lb (1,625-kg) behemoth. The naturally aspirated engine had four valves per cylinder at a time when most other performance models had two.

At the urging of racing-car driver Henry Birkin, who was desperate to have a win at Le Mans, a supercharged 175-bhp (130-kW) version—known as the "Blower Bentley"—would follow, but this would prove unreliable in competition (two Blowers entered at Le Mans in 1930 failed to finish). The Blower is now considered something of a motor-racing diversion, one that founder Walter Owen Bentley felt played a large part—together with the Wall Street stockmarket crash in 1929—in the eventual decline of the company in 1931. "To supercharge a Bentley engine," he said, "was to pervert its design and corrupt its performance." **BS**

Type 43 | Bugatti

(F)

1927 • 138 cu in/2,262 cc, S8 • 120 bhp/89 kW • 0–60 mph/96 kph in 12 seconds • 106mph/170kph

When it was introduced in 1927, the Bugatti Type 43 was touted as the world's first 100-mph (160-kph) production car; this was at a time when 70 mph (112 kph) was a more typical top speed for a road vehicle. The Bugatti was actually capable of even more than that, with early tests achieving 112 mph (179 kph). The car could also accelerate to 60 mph (96 kph) in about twelve seconds, when many cars struggled to get there at all. It was the arrival of the Type 43 that helped confirm Bugatti as one of Europe's top car manufacturers, as well as its reputation for combining automotive beauty and beast.

That this beautiful car had such beastly power was hardly surprising. It had the same engine that went into the Bugatti Type 35B racing car, which would go on to win the French Grand Prix in 1929. The basic Type 35 engine had been a phenomenal success worldwide, powering wins in more than 1,000 races. In the Type 43,

the engine was loaded onto a Bugatti Type 38 chassis, although Bugatti did make a few concessions to the fact that this was going to be used on the road rather than the racetrack by providing the model with bigger brakes and a larger radiator.

Only 160 of the Type 43, which was essentially a "supercar" hybrid, were ever built, from its launch in 1927 until it was retired in 1931 in favor of the Type 43A roadster, which itself was introduced in 1931 and continued in production during 1932. Not surprisingly, the Bugatti Type 43 rarely appears at auction, although when one was put up for sale by Bonhams and Butterfields in 2011 at an estimated price of $1.3–1.5 million (£840,000–960,000) it failed to meet its reserve price and remained unsold.

With its aerodynamic styling and V-shapes, the Type 43 has been described as being the epitome of the art deco automobile. **MG**

The 1927 Model A was the second Ford car to carry that name, but it proved just as popular as the original 1903 model. ▷

Type S 36/220 | Mercedes-Benz (D)

1927 • 414 cu in/6,789 cc, S6 • 180 bhp/132 kW • unknown • 110 mph/177 kph

The Mercedes Type S secured its place in the automotive history books for three reasons. First, it was the first vehicle to appear following the formal joining of the Daimler and Benz companies in 1926. Second, the man credited with creating the car is one Professor Ferdinand Porsche, the company's technical director who left in 1928 and three years later formed a new business that bore his name. Third, the great German racing driver Rudolf Caracciola was at the wheel of an early Type S when he won his class at the inaugural event at the now-legendary Nürburgring circuit in June 1927. The car was the first of a generation of iconic Mercedes, including the SS, SSK, and SSKL.

Taking advantage of its aero-engine expertise, Mercedes led the way in supercharging cars during the early 1920s. In common with all its models of the era, the Type S's "on demand" system only activated when the throttle pedal was fully depressed. Raising the power output from 140 to 180 bhp (100 to 132 kW), it was also noted for assaulting the ears of race spectators. British car magazine *Motor* called it "a threatening, high-pitched whine," while another writer of the time suggested that Mercedes had somehow harnessed a "howling goddess of vengeance" under the hood (bonnet).

The Type S was a reworking of the Mercedes-Benz Type K, which claimed to be the first road car to achieve 100 mph (177 kph). The newcomer's handling was said to be much improved over its predecessor as a result of simple physics—it had a much lower center of gravity. The Type S was also known as the 36/220, with the first figure representing Germany's fiscal horsepower for taxation, and the second, the peak power rating when the supercharger was engaged. **RY**

Model A | Ford (USA)

1927 • 201 cu in/3,300 cc, S4 • 40 bhp/29 kW • unknown • 65 mph/104 kph

Henry Ford introduced his first Model A in 1903, and by 1908 his cars had already progressed alphabetically to the Model T, a car that was so successful that it lasted until 1927. But Ford saw his next car as such a huge leap forward that he went back to the Model A name. The new car proved to be just as much of a hit; in the first eighteen months Ford sold two million of them, and they were soon being manufactured everywhere from Argentina to Australia. By 1932 Ford Model As were even being built in the Soviet Union. Worldwide, they were selling at a rate of almost 4,000 cars a day.

In its later years, the Model T had famously been available in any color as long as it was black. When it was introduced, the new Model A could be bought in four colors, but not black, which helped to set it apart from its predecessor. However, there were soon nine different styles available—with black now as an option—ranging in price from $385 to $1,400 (£250 to £900). There was even a taxicab version—taxicab and police-car versions of the Model A can be identified in the 2005 remake of *King Kong*.

By modern standards the engines were still large, but their fuel consumption, at 25–30 mpg (8–12 km/l) was impressively low. The Model A was also the first car to use safety glass in its windshield. Henry Ford handed over responsibility for the body design of the car to his son, Edsel, who had in fact been president of the company since 1919. It was Edsel who persuaded his father to incorporate a more modern look and some technological innovations, and the father–son partnership ensured that the Model A was just as successful as the Model T had been. **MG**

LONE PINE DR

AF | Minerva

B

1927 • 360 cu in/5,900 cc, S6 • 34 bhp/25 kW • unknown • 80 mph/129 kph

Minerva was a long-standing Belgian marque that started by making bicycles in 1897. Motorized bikes followed, and eventually Minerva started making cars, too. They were beautifully built, upmarket machines—Rolls-Royce founder Charles Rolls was a Minerva dealer in England. Minerva cars were bought by the kings of Sweden, Norway, and Belgium; even Henry Ford bought one. By the 1920s, Minerva cars were on a par with Rolls-Royce for quality, and they were slightly cheaper.

Minerva cars all used an unusual type of "Silent Knight" engine with a double-sleeve valve design from the United States. A metal sleeve between the piston and the cylinder wall slid at appropriate stages of the internal combustion cycle to reveal the openings to the inlet and outlet ports. While much quieter than rival poppet-valve engines, it was much more expensive to produce. In 1927 Minerva's AK series was launched with the ultimate version of the Silent Knight engine, a sumptuous 360-cubic-inch (5,900-cc), straight six-cylinder unit.

The cars—known as the AD, AF, AG, AK, and so on—were distinguished by their coachwork. Most designs included wire wheels, an upright windshield, and long running boards that swooped up over the front wheels. The radiator cap featured a distinctive bust of the Greek goddess Minerva with her name embossed below. She was featured on the company's red-and-white badge, too. A Landaulette version was particularly sought-after; this type of car had a solid roof with a folding top that exposed the rear seat only. Many Minerva models were shipped across the Atlantic for wealthy American film stars and industrialists, despite being among the most expensive cars in the world at the time. **SH**

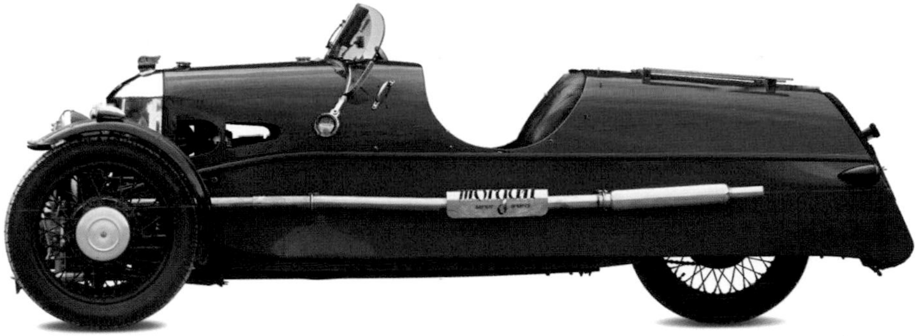

Super Sports Aero | Morgan

GB

1927 • 66 cu in/1,096 cc, V2 • 40 bhp/29.8 kW • unknown • 115 mph/185 kph

When it came to building three-wheeled vehicles, few carmakers could match the passion of the Morgan Motor Company. Henry Frederick Morgan's three-wheelers were simple, durable, and, most of all, popular, thanks to a tax break that allowed three-wheeled cars to be registered as motorcycles. Beginning with a standard model three-wheeler at the 1911 Olympia Motor Show, there followed a deluxe model, a sports model, a family model, and a Grand Prix model, from which would evolve Morgan's record-breaking Aero and Super Sports Aero models.

The Super Sports Aero was built for speed. Its bodywork was streamlined, and it had a low chassis to maximize its center of gravity—so low that the driver's seat lay a mere 8 inches (20 cm) off the ground; this left just 6 inches (15 cm) of clearance between chassis and road. Drivers were wise to note a warning from Morgan: "We do not recommend its use on roads which are not at least reasonably good."

The Matchless MX4 40-bhp (29.8-kW) engine was totally exposed between its two front wheels, a feature that went on to become a Morgan trademark. Other features included Ghost silencers on its exhaust pipes and a tapered tail. It is no wonder that Sterling Moss once claimed, "My Morgan was a great babe magnet."

At Brooklands in the late 1920s, a Super Sports Aero was deemed so fast it was required to start a lap behind its four-wheeled competitors. It gained dozens of speed records, but the days of the three-wheeler were numbered. Uncomfortably cramped cockpits and a harsh ride saw sales gradually decrease, forcing Morgan to switch to four-wheelers with its 4/4 in 1936. **BS**

Speed Six | Bentley

GB

1928 • 396 cu in/6,500 cc, S6 • 180 bhp/134.2 kW • 0–60 mph/97 kph in 10 seconds • 95 mph/192.9 kph

One of the most famous models of the Bentley marque, the Speed Six debuted in 1928 and extended the company's growing stranglehold on Le Mans. It finished first in 1929 and again in 1930 (gaining Bentley five wins in seven years). With Bentley chairman Joel Woolf Barnato, rescuer of the financially ailing company in 1926, behind the wheel, the success of the Speed Six in race meets came to be so total that other teams began to decline invitations to race against it.

Identified by its parallel-sided radiator and green enameled badge, the Speed Six came in sedan (saloon), coupe, and open sports models, all with bodies by Gurney Nutting, one of the United Kingdom's leading design firms. High-geared and with a lovely rumbling exhaust, the Speed Six—the "car that most worried Rolls-Royce"—cruised comfortably at 80 mph (129 kph), had twin SU carburetors, and had the distinction of being the first car ever to have four valves per cylinder.

In a famous wager, Barnato bet £100 ($160) that he and his sedan-model Speed Six could beat the famous Blue Train in a race from the French Riviera to London. It was a feat Rover had already managed with its Light Six, which Barnato derided as being of "no special merit." He claimed that he would be seated in his favorite London club before *Le train bleu* even reached Calais.

The race took place on March 13, 1930. Barnato battled fog, thunderstorms, a hard-to-find refueling stop outside Auxerre in Burgundy, a burst tire, and France's rutted *routes nationales* before crossing the Channel in a packet steamer and pulling up outside the Conservative Club in London four minutes before the Blue Train steamed its way into Calais Station. **BS**

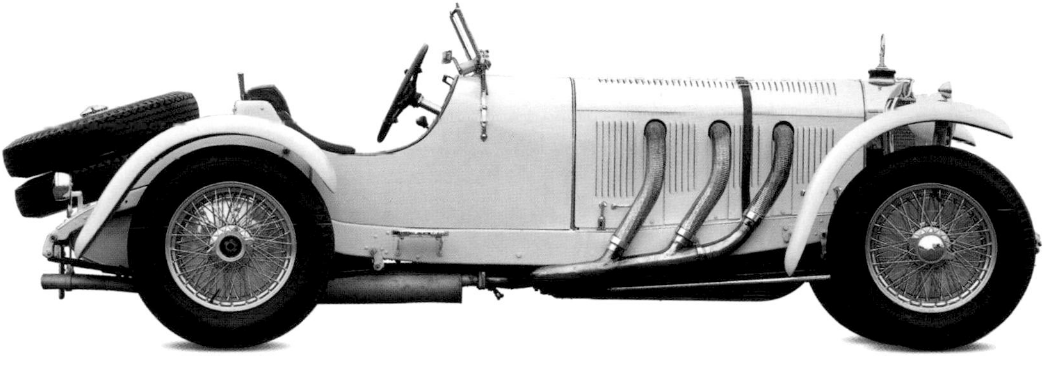

SSK | Mercedes-Benz

D

1928 • 427 cu in/7,000 cc, S6 • 225 bhp/68 kW • 0–60 mph/97 kph in 14 seconds • 120 mph/193.1 kph

The Mercedes SSK, the "Fastest Sports Car in the World" according to its maker, was the last car a disillusioned Ferdinand Porsche designed for Mercedes-Benz. Porsche left after the merger of Daimler and Benz in December 1928 to establish a company of his own.

Designed to be a sporty road car, the SS (Super Sport) series' Model K had unparalleled straight-line pace with a top speed of 108 mph (173.8 kph), making it the fastest production model of its type anywhere in the world. To improve weight distribution, Porsche shortened the previous SS chassis by 19 inches (48 cm). The radiator and supercharged engine were lowered and placed closer to the driver to lower the center of gravity. The hood (bonnet) and chassis were also lowered, giving the car a leaner body. The car was the epitome of "long hood, short deck" elegance.

The list of SSK track victories reads like a gourmet race guide: the German Grand Prix, the Irish Grand Prix, the 500 Miles [805 km] of Argentina, and the British Tourist Trophy Race. Yet today, very few SSKs remain; only forty were built, most of which were crashed while racing and cannibalized for parts.

The final version in the SS series was the SSKL (L for "light"). Only six SSKLs were ever built. The car weighed just 2,976 pounds (1,350 kg) thanks to a drilled ladder frame. In April 1931, Rudolf Carraciola became the first foreigner to win Italy's famous Mille Miglia road race, driving his SSKL 1,015 miles (1,635 km) at an average speed of 63 mph (101.4 kph). But given that the frame was the foundation for a weighty 300-bhp (224-kW) engine, drilling risked structural integrity and the SSKL suffered several embarrassing failures. **SH**

443 Custom Eight | Packard (USA)

1928 • 382 cu in/6,306 cc, S8 • 106 bhp/79 kW • unknown • 85 mph/137 kph

In the late 1920s and early '30s, Packard expanded its association with coachbuilders such as Rollston, Le Baron, and Fleetwood to become the undisputed king of American prestige motoring.

The Custom Eight was available in nine standard body styles. The "custom" part of the name is a bit of a misnomer, although customized versions were available. The lengthy 143-inch (363-cm) wheel-based chassis was specifically designed to be the foundation for heavy, customized bodies. Customized or not, it was a weighty vehicle at 5,045 pounds (2,293 kg). To reduce the weight, Custom Eights, and variants such as the Phaeton, employed superthin aluminum castings, named "Sylentlyte," developed by the Paris-based coachbuilders Carrosserie Hibbard et Darrin.

The car had an advanced lubrication system that delivered oil effortlessly to thirty-eight points. Customized 443 bodies, such as the Phaeton four-door convertible, featured patented hydraulic two-way action shock absorbers. Though state of the art, these made turning the car at slow speeds a real chore. Huge, barrel-like chrome headlights were among the Phaeton's most recognizable features. Convertible coupe bodies came courtesy of designer Raymond Dietrich, complete with wooden steering wheel and dashboard. **BS**

Type 41 Royale | Bugatti (F)

1929 • 778 cu in/12,763 cc, S8 • 300 bhp/220 kW • 0–60 mph in 18 seconds • 100 mph/161 kph

After being told that his cars had been outclassed by Rolls-Royce, Ettore Bugatti decided to build an extraordinary luxury vehicle, 21 feet (6.4 m) long and powered by a huge 778-cubic-inch (12,763-cc) engine designed for the French Air Force. Called the Bugatti Type 41, it is better known as the Royale because Bugatti pompously planned to sell it only to royalty. At $30,000 (£18,750) for just the chassis (bodywork was extra), the Royale cost twice as much as a Rolls-Royce. In the event, only commoners ended up buying the Royale.

The Royale's engine alone is almost 5 feet (1.6 m) long, but the car was surprisingly sporty to drive, with precise steering and firm ride. Luxury features included whalebone switchgear, a walnut steering wheel, and a sculpted elephant on the radiator. The three-speed, centrally mounted gearbox was topped by an ivory knob.

All six cars still exist, but now with different bodies. Three were bricked up at Bugatti's home in Ermenonville during World War II to avoid Nazi commandeers; another was hidden in a Paris sewer. One, fitted with a 897-cubic-inch (14,700-cc) engine, was Ettore's own. Two were later sold to gentleman racer Briggs Cunningham for $3,000 plus two fridges, then unavailable in France.

In 1999, VW, new owner of the Bugatti brand, bought one for around $20 million (£12.5 million). **BS**

S4 | Salmson

(F)

1929 • 79 cu in/1,300 cc, S4 • 30 bhp/22 kW • unknown • 62 mph/100 kph

Between 1921 and 1928, Emile Salmson's company, Salmson of Billancourt, won 550 races and set ten world records. Yet, despite its success on the racetrack, it was Salmson's touring cars that added the most to the balance sheets. In 1929 the company closed its racing division and concentrated on touring cars, specifically the groundbreaking S4 series.

The S4 succeeded the Salmson D-type and was available in a sedan (saloon), cabriolet, and coupe, and was targeted at the middle class. Among its nice external flourishes were a radiator and badge work designed by the noted Art Deco stylist Andre Kow.

But what set the Salmson S4 apart from its competition was substance, not style. It was powered by a double overhead camshaft engine, an advance that most other carmakers shied away from in the 1920s due to its complexity and high cost. The advantages, however, were clear: the double overhead camshaft was a higher-revving, more responsive engine, and was a generation ahead of single camshaft motors. Emile Salmson had founded his company as a manufacturer of radial aircraft engines in 1912, so it should come as no surprise that he should do this. A pioneer of French aviation, it seemed perfectly proper to him that he should be a pioneer of cars, too. **BS**

Minor | Morris

(GB)

1929 • 51 cu in/847 cc, S4 • 20 bhp/15 kW • unknown • 55 mph/88 kph

Founded in 1910 by bicycle manufacturer William Morris, by 1924 the Morris Motor Company was the United Kingdom's biggest car manufacturer. In 1928 Morris entered Ford's market of affordable cars by producing the first version of the car that would be forever associated with its name: the Morris Minor.

The original came in different styles over the next few years, from a two-seater sports version to a four-seater tourer, plus a van. The touring version sold for £125 ($194) when it first went on display at the 1928 London Motor Show. The 51-cubic-inch (847-cc) engine was 100 cc more powerful than that of its main rival, the Austin Seven, the United Kingdom's best-selling car.

The 1929 Morris Minor had an overhead camshaft engine, a sales feature as this type of engine was normally used on racing cars and large touring cars. However, the engine proved susceptible to excess oil getting into the dynamo, and it was also expensive to make. In 1932 it was replaced by a side-valve unit, which not only overcame the oil problem, but was cheaper to manufacture, enabling the company to sell the cars at a lead-in price of £100 ($155).

In 1934, after sales of more than 86,000, the Morris Minor was replaced by the Morris Eight, although the well-established name was revived in 1948. **MG**

AM 80 Veth Coupe | Hotchkiss

(F)

1929 • 183 cu in/3,015 cc, S6 • 70 bhp/52 kW • unknown • 93 mph/150 kph

The Hotchkiss AM 80 Veth Coupe was the automotive equivalent of the League of Nations: a French car with a Dutch body and an English name. In terms of bodywork it was a standard touring car of the day, but the Veth Coupe is remembered for having a rubberized, impact-absorbing front fender (bumper) designed by the Dutch firm Overman. The fender, protruding 16 inches (400 cm) from beneath the radiator, would flex backward when impacted, courtesy of two V-shaped, spring-loaded arms; this would leave the car undamaged in collisions at up to 29 mph (40 kph). Though still rare in the late 1920s, fenders were becoming an increasingly desirable option as they attracted a discounted insurance premium.

The majority of the AM 80s had factory cabins, though some were given coupe bodies designed by Veth & Sons of Arnhem. All had the powerful six-cylinder, 183-cubic-inch (3,000-cc) engine that premiered at the 1928 Paris Salon and which replaced the 134-cubic-inch (2,200-cc) that had been the company's standard engine since 1923. The 183-cubic-inch cemented the company's reputation for precision engineering, and in September 1929 an AM 80 with a new torque tube transmission was driven 25,000 miles (40,233 km) on the Montlhéry racetrack over sixteen days at an average speed of 65.85 mph (106 kph).

The Hotchkiss emblem of two crossed cannons and a cannonball harked back to the company's beginnings as a weapons manufacturer. The AM 80 had a long run, and continued to be produced in various guises until Hotchkiss ended its involvement in passenger cars in 1955. **BS**

6C 1750 | Alfa Romeo

(I)

1929 • 106 cu in/1,752 cc, S6 • 46 bhp/35 kW • unknown • 68 mph/109 kph

The Alfa Romeo 6C had been around since 1925, but when the 6C 1750 was launched in Rome in 1929, people were seeing the arrival of a million-dollar car. Quite literally so, as it turned out; when a 1930 Alfa Romeo 6C 1750 Gran Sport Spyder came up for sale in 2011 at Bonhams and Butterfields, the asking price was €950,000 to €1.25 million ($1.2 to $1.6 million). A 1929 model of the car was on offer in the same sale for slightly less. These are clearly very sought-after cars.

The original 1925 cars had only a 90-cubic-inch (1,487-cc) engine. The 1929 models remained much the same, but they did benefit from several major improvements, the most important being under the hood (bonnet): a new and more powerful 106-cubic-inch (1,752-cc) engine. That improved engine made all the difference. During the brief four-year lifespan of the 6C 1750 it was established as one of the best Alfa Romeos ever. It began as a superior road car, but transformed itself into one of the best racing machines.

A 1928 version of the car had been good enough to win that year's Mille Miglia, but the 1929 6C 1750 topped that. It won not only the Mille Miglia but every race in which it was entered, including Grand Prix victories in Monza, Belgium, and Spain. It won the Mille Miglia in 1930, too.

In all, six versions of the 6C 1750 were produced, each one outdoing its predecessor. They ranged from the basic 1750 Turismo, capable of about 68 mph (109 kph), through to the Super Sport–Gran Sport–TF model, which could reach 110 mph (176 kph). Just under 2,500 of the various 6C 1750s were built in total. If you want one, you had better start saving now. **MG**

Midget M Type | MG (GB)

1929 • 51 cu in/1,752 cc, S6 • 46 bhp/35 kW • unknown • 68 mph/109 kph

When *Autocar* magazine first saw the Midget M Type, it said that it would "make sports car history." It was cheap, fast, had exceptional handling due to its low weight (1,120 pounds/508 kg), and soon was racing everywhere.

The prototype was designed in 1928 by MG's cofounder, Cecil Kimber, who adapted a Morris Minor chassis to have a lowered suspension, a repositioned steering column, a V-shaped windshield, and a mesh-grilled radiator. Unashamedly built to a price, the first models shown at the 1928 Motor Show had bodies of fabric-covered plywood over ash frames (though metal panels would follow in production). A simple folding roof stowed in the car's boattail, and there were bolt-on wire wheels. Notably cheaper than almost any other sports car, it promised to wrest sports motoring and hill-climb events out of the grip of the idle rich, and open them up to the middle class. Interest was so high that Kimber ordered almost 500 bodies to be made.

Within a year of the Midget's release, its camshaft was modified to provide 30 percent more horsepower and the braking system was redesigned. With a standard three-speed gearbox, or optional four-speed, and a choice of a closed coupe body or open two-seater, it was on its way to becoming Britain's best-selling sports car. Even Henry Ford's son, Edsel, bought one. **BS**

Model U | Plymouth (USA)

1929 • 175 cu in/2,874 cc, S4 • 45 bhp/34 kW • unknown • 65 mph/105 kph

Chrysler's Plymouth line got its name from Plymouth Binder Twine, a household string popular among farmers. It was a neat reference to the everyday needs of ordinary working families, and the name probably didn't receive a lot of analysis at Chrysler prior to the stock market crash of October 1929. In the end, however, it was because of the affordable practicality of the Plymouth Model U that the company survived while others were failing.

Made from January 1929 to April 1930, the Model U was more than just Chrysler's first foray into the lower-end market; it was also a car that was years ahead of its rivals. Its engine had aluminum-alloy pistons and full-pressure lubrication, internal expanding hydraulic brakes on both front and rear wheels, and an independent hand brake—features that Ford and Chevrolet would not offer for another decade. Chrysler also offered as standard cars with all-steel construction, in an era largely of wooden-framed bodies. It was due to the Model U that Chrysler, almost alone in the automotive world, was able to boast higher sales in 1930–31 compared to 1929–30.

"Every goddamn farmer in America has heard of Plymouth Binder Twine," Chrysler's sales manager Joseph Frazer told Walter Chrysler in his argument to adopt the Plymouth name. By the end of the Depression, everyone had heard of the Model U, too. **BS**

L-29 | Cord (USA)

1929 • 298 cu in/4,893 cc, S8 • 120 bhp/88 kW • 0–60 mph/97 kph in 32 seconds • 78 mph/125 kph

The Cord L-29 debuted shortly before the October 1929 stock market crash. It was appalling timing. The L-29 was beautiful and innovative, the first car on the American market with front-wheel drive. It had de Dion suspension, and inboard brakes borrowed from Indianapolis 500 race cars. It also had a fully gauged dashboard, rare for the time, showing gas, oil, and water temperature, an ammeter, and speedometer. However, just 5,010 were made during 1929–31, with a mere 4,400 sales.

The L-29 was created by Errett Loban Cord, who also made the Auburn Speedster and the Model J Duesenberg. The car's hood housed a 298-cubic-inch (4,893-cc) Lycoming straight-eight engine, fronted by a Duesenberg-styled grille and radiator designed by engineer Al Leamy. Despite its size, the engine produced just 120 bhp (88 kW), sufficient only to propel the 4,700-pound (2,100-kg) car at a top speed of 78 mph (125 kph).

But the L-29 had those "little things" that count: a body trimmed with the finest broadcloth, leather seats, silver-plated internal fittings, and an adjustable steering column with fingertip gearshift. Success in a string of European Concours d'Elegance events also saw it pave the way for the great Cords to come—the 810 and the 812—although those would have to wait another seven frugal years, until people could afford them again. **BS**

8-Litre | Bentley (GB)

1930 • 488 cu in/8,000 cc, S6 • 220 bhp/162 kW • 0–60 mph/97 kph in 13.5 seconds • 100 mph/160 kph

The 8-litre was the last of the "W O-era" Bentleys, and would overtake the Rolls-Royce Phantom II as the most luxurious British car. Rolls-Royce must have been worried: when Bentley faced bankruptcy in 1931, it bought out the company and refocused it on only "entry-level" luxury.

The 8-litre was composed of truly special stuff. Its crankcase was made of elektron, a rare alloy that increased tensile strength and helped resist corrosion. Its cylinder heads had four valves for every cylinder, and twin-spark ignition enabled the car to accelerate from walking pace to top speed even when in fourth gear. The 156-inch (396-cm) wheelbase version was the largest car ever made in Britain, weighing more than two tons and supported by a double-dropped frame strengthened by seven tubular cross braces. The six-cylinder engine could push the heavy car along at 100 mph (161 kph) even when fully laden, 10 mph (16 kph) faster than the Phantom II, and every bit as silently.

All of the great English coachbuilders made bodies for the 8-litre, and the various models all had their options. Short-chassis, four-seat tourers had French pillar-mounted swivel spotlights, Vanden Plas tourers had fold-down windshields, and sportsman's coupes had sliding sunroofs. But sales were hit hard by the Depression. Of the 100 8-litres that were built, seventy-eight survive. **BS**

The Riley Brooklands was so low-slung that its occupants could touch the ground from the cockpit. ⊡

Valve Special | Miller Boyle (USA)

1930 • 269 cu in/4,424 cc, S4 • unknown • unknown • 117 mph/188 kph

The Miller Boyle Valve Special is a motoring legend from a period in American motor sport that made heroes out of racing cars and men alike—an era when the press called the cars "rockets" and drivers "pilots." The "Miller Boyle" will always be remembered for its association with the Indianapolis 500, where it raced on four occasions, three times with a four-cylinder engine and once with an eight-cylinder. "Wild Bill" Cummings drove one to victory in record time in 1934.

The Miller Boyle began as an eight-cylinder racer in 1930, when it was owned by the Chicago-based underworld enforcer Mike "Umbrella" Boyle. It was then purchased by Lou Meyer, who gave it a transverse sprung rear axle and removed the eight-cylinder engine, replacing it with a four-cylinder, 269-cubic-inch (4,424-cc) Miller engine to conform with new Indy regulations. These called for cars to be less complicated and less expensive in the hope that Indy engineers would develop practical mechanics that would trickle down to benefit everyday Americans.

In all, nine derivatives of the Miller Boyle de Dion rear-axle, rear-drive racers are believed to have been constructed, but these were more variants than additional examples, reflecting a time when racing cars were often improvised and recycled with bits and pieces from other vehicles. Whether a derivative of the original Miller Boyle Valve Special can be identical enough even to be called an additional example is debatable, but in any case none has survived to this day, and those seen at rallies now are replicas only. One example may have reappeared as the so-called "rocket car" of pioneering stockcar racer Sig Haugdahl in the early 1930s. **BS**

Brooklands | Riley (GB)

1930 • 66 cu in/1,087 cc, S4 • 50 bhp/37.2 kW • unknown • 80 mph/129 kph

It is easy to be swayed by the idea that, in order for any performance car to be a success, it has to be propelled by a monstrous engine. The Riley Brooklands turns that myth on its head. This 1930s racing machine was powered by an engine of less than 67 cubic inches (1,100 cc) but still won races and motoring challenges the world over.

Small it may have been, but the Riley Nine engine (the brainchild of Percy Riley himself) was ahead of its time. It was a small-capacity, high-revving motor whose blueprint would seem equally at home in a fast motorcycle or modern Japanese "hot hatch." The engine had hemispherical combustion chambers with inclined valves and twin camshafts set high in the block. As such, it is widely regarded as the most influential engine design to have come out of the 1920s.

Unsurprisingly, the Riley Nine attracted the attention of engine tuners and racing engineers. Among them was J. G. Parry-Thomas, who ran a workshop next to the famous banked circuit at Brooklands racetrack in Surrey, England. It was in Parry-Thomas's workshop that the Riley Brooklands was born, with a lowered body and a distinctive tapered rear end. Sadly, Parry-Thomas was killed during a speed record attempt in 1927, but his friend Reid Railton took over the project and saw it through to fruition.

One of the outstanding features of the Riley Brooklands was just how low it was. The seats were only 6 inches (15 cm) off the ground, with only 36 inches (91 cm) between the ground and the top of the radiator cap. This low profile gave the car a winning edge on the track; from Le Mans to the Ulster TT, and, of course, at Brooklands itself, it took the checkered flag with ease. **JI**

238
G 8541

V16 Two-seater Roadster | Cadillac

(USA)

1930 • 451 cu in/7,400 cc, V16 • 165 bhp/123 kW • unknown • 80–100 mph/130–160 kph, depending on model

The timing of the launch of the costliest Cadillac ever built left something to be desired. The V16 was first shown at the New York Auto Show in January 1930, less than three months after the stock market crash. Nevertheless, despite the financial crisis, the V16 continued to sell for the next ten years, and it was only the advent of World War II that brought production to a halt. The Cadillac had the first sixteen-cylinder engine in a V configuration to be mass produced in the United States, and each car was hand-built. Only 4,076 were ever made, but half of those were built in the first twelve months of the production run, before the Depression of the 1930s really took hold.

While the V16 engine was more expensive than the V12 or the V8, it was no more powerful; its selling point was its smoothness, and it was only ever used in high-end cars like the Cadillac V16. Among the more famous owners of the V16 were Marlene Dietrich,

Cecil B. DeMille, and the infamous gangster Al Capone. Purchased for $30,000 (£19,000), Capone's 1930 model was built to his specification with possible attempts on his life in mind. As much a battle wagon as a luxury limousine, it included such features as bulletproof glass, armor plating, tires that would run when flat, a device for adding oil to the exhaust to produce a smokescreen, a police siren, and a tube through the floorboards down which he could drop tire-puncturing nails.

Production of the "1940" models stopped in December 1939, although not before Capone bought one of those, too. By this time, Cadillac was only making about one a month—and was losing money on each one. The singer Eddie Cantor was one of the last people to buy a V16. It remains, however, one of the best-built cars made in the first half of the twentieth century, and a model in good condition can fetch more than $500,000 (£320,000). **MG**

A Rolls-Royce Phantom II with coachwork by U.S. firm Brewster & Co., the epitome of motoring elegance. ▷

Grosser 770K | Mercedes-Benz (D)

1930 • 467 cu in/7,655cc, S8 • 200 bhp/150 kW • unknown • 93 mph/150 kph (estimated)

Given the chance to be famous for something, few would select an association with Adolf Hitler. But, as archive movie footage reveals, the Mercedes 770K, otherwise known as the Grosser (meaning "bigger"), was the limousine of choice for the Führer. Time and time again his often standing figure can be seen in this enormous armor-plated monster as it cruises past the massed ranks of the Nazi war machine. Almost all of the 200 or so Grossers that were built between 1930 and 1943 were used as German state vehicles, transporting either high-ranking military officers or Nazi party officials. Herman Goering had one, and so did Rommel.

The standard car was built around a box chassis with leaf-spring suspension all round, although in 1938 a revised version had an all-new tubular chassis and coil-spring suspension. It had a wheelbase more than 12 feet (3.75 m) long, and fully loaded weighed 7,716 pounds (3,500 kg). Hitler's car, however, or cars—he possibly had several—was armor-plated, and thus may well have weighed more than five tons.

To shift this vast mass took an eight-cylinder engine with a capacity of nearly 488 cubic inches (8,000 cc). But even the optional supercharger could only make it produce 200 bhp (150 kW). This took the vehicle to a fairly conservative 90 mph (150 kph) down the new autobahn.

At the end of the war, Hitler's Grosser passed through several owners, including a Las Vegas casino proprietor. It eventually made its way back to Germany, but was recently sold to an unknown Russian buyer. The exact price he paid was not disclosed, but it is thought to be around €210 million ($13 million/£8.4 million). And it has gone to Moscow, which is more than Hitler did. **JI**

Phantom II | Rolls-Royce (GB)

1930 • 469 cu in/7,668 cc, S6 • 120 bhp/88 kW • unknown • 92 mph/149 kph

Prompted by increasing competition from the likes of Buick and Sunbeam, Rolls-Royce replaced the Phantom I with the Phantom II after four years of improvements that went far beyond mere tinkering. The car sat on an entirely new chassis and had semielliptic rather than cantilevered rear springs, a sleeker, more racy low-slung frame, and a radiator set well back, which helped designers move away from the more boxlike look of its predecessor. It also had an extensively modified engine and transmission. Manifolds were improved, combustion chambers redesigned, and a new cross-flow cylinder head fitted. And just to make sure it all went smoothly, the last of the company's great six-cylinder vehicles was supervised at every stage of its production—from first draft to completion—by F. Henry Royce himself, proving that Rolls-Royce was never a company to rest on its laurels.

Upon receipt of a commission, the car, meaning just the chassis and associated running gear, was taken from the Rolls-Royce factory in Derby to the client's designated coachbuilder, where its interior and fittings were installed as per the owner's requests. The Phantom II's options were legendary, all the way from an exquisite sloping Veed windshield—years before the "streamlining" era made them fashionable—down to toolboxes recessed into its running boards.

The Phantom II was Henry Royce's ultimate masterpiece and represented the zenith of the coachbuilt era. It was designed for the chauffeur-driven passenger, who could tell the driver what to do by operating a series of lights in the chauffeur's compartment—"turn left," "turn right," "speed up," "slow down," "go home." In a Phantom II, no one need ever take a wrong turn. **BS**

20/25 | Rolls-Royce

GB

1930 • 223 cu in/3,669 cc, S6 • 65 bhp/48 kW • 0–50 mph/80 kph in 28 seconds • 75 mph/121 kph

The 20/25 was Rolls-Royce's so-called "small car," a replacement for the six-cylinder 20HP, which had been in production since 1922. In keeping with the company's traditional two-model policy, it was built alongside the larger Phantom II. Like its sibling, it was supplied on a rolling chassis so that owners could select the coachbuilder of their choice.

The 20/25 was unfairly considered slow for its time, for owners tended to add considerable weight to the chassis with bodies designed more for comfort and appearance than performance.

The chassis was identical to that of the 20HP, except for a slight variance allowing it to accommodate the larger 223-cubic-inch (3,669-cc) engine needed to compensate for the heavier coachwork. Changes, however, did come. The carburetors, brakes, clutch, and ignition were all modified. Within a year the chassis had been lengthened, flexible wheel mountings added, and the exhaust improved, while an increase in the engine's compression ratio in late 1930 added more power. Of all the models Rolls-Royce built between the wars, none sold more than the 20/25—almost 4,000 chassis—due in part to a decision to absorb some costs and sell it for the same price as the 20HP before it.

All the usual coachbuilders—Brewster, Vanden Plas, Park Ward—added their requisite luxury to Rolls-Royce's precision engineering, and racing-car drivers and adventurers such as Tommy Sopwith, Prince Bira of Siam, and Sir Malcolm Campbell all owned one. What wasn't to like? As automotive magazine *The Motor* wrote in a 1929 review: "It is a car from which the most critical would derive considerable pleasure." **BS**

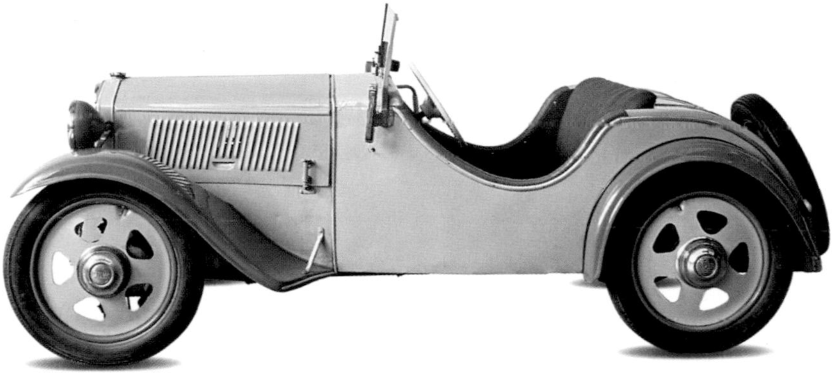

FA | DKW

(D)

1931 • 35 cu in/584 cc, S2 • 15 bhp/11 kW • unknown • 47 mph/75 kph

The DKW FA was the first mass-produced front-wheel-drive car. It was also Germany's cheapest car during the Depression and helped DKW become the country's second-biggest carmaker at the time.

Danish designer Jørgen Rasmussen had started the company by building a steam-driven car, or *Dampf-Kraft-Wagen* in German—hence DKW. Later he produced cars and motorcycles. But when the Depression hit in 1930, DKW needed to boost sales urgently. The times inspired quickly built, cost-cutting innovations and DKW came up with the new car in a few weeks. One idea was front-wheel drive, which it implemented ahead of Citroën in France. Later it became clear that several manufacturers were thinking along the same lines.

DKW's factory in Saxony started churning out F Series cars that in retrospect offered a very modern layout: a transverse engine, sited in the front, drove the front wheels. There was all-around independent suspension and a gear selector in the center of the simple dashboard.

The FA was available as a two-seater cabriolet and a four-seater sedan (saloon). Both were rather handsome, with a long, tapering hood (bonnet), imperious grille, and spacious cabin. The two-stroke engine was small, however. Driving the front wheels through a three-speed gearbox, it could only reach 47 mph (75 kph), despite the car's ultralow weight of just 992 pounds (450 kg).

Slightly bigger engines and inventive engineering trials followed until World War II. The engine was linked to the gearbox by a chain; a 41-cubic-inch (684-cc) engine was introduced; various suspension arrangements were made; and the generator was replaced by a "Dynastart" combined alternator and starter motor. **SH**

8C | Alfa Romeo

(I)

1931 • 142 cu in/2,336cc, S8 • 180 bhp/132 kW • unknown • 115 mph/185 kph

Alfa Romeo had enjoyed phenomenal success with its 6C 1750 series, introduced in 1929 (and continued until 1933), but even that was overshadowed by the various eight-cylinder models the firm introduced in 1931. One of these, specifically aimed at the grueling Le Mans 24 Hours race, certainly hit its target. Called the 8C 2300 Le Mans, it won the race for Alfa Romeo from 1931 to 1934, without a break. In the 1931 victory, the 8C completed the 1,875-mile (3,000-km) course with an average speed of more than 78 mph (125 kph).

Even the standard cars continued to win races for Alfa Romeo. The first model to appear, the 8C 2300, was designed as a racing car, but also sold as a road car. It won the 1931 Italian Grand Prix at Monza, among other races, and Alfa Romeo continued its tradition of adding the name of such victories to the name of the car—thus the model became the Alfa Romeo 8C 2300 Monza. One of these, built in 1933, was sold at auction in 2010 and fetched an impressive $6,710,000 (£4,300,000). A Drophead Coupe version of the 1933 8C 2300 also came up for sale in 2009 and was bought for $4,180,000 (£2,700,000).

Alfa Romeo carried on ringing in the changes on its 8C 2300 models, although not always with comparable success. In 1935 it produced a single-seat racing version, the Monoposto 8C 35 Type C, but that car did not perform well. The year 1935 also saw the arrival of the Bimotore model, which was given two 3.2-liter engines, one at the front and one at the back, but the gain in speed was offset by tire damage and extra time in the pits. Oh well, it didn't win all the races, but Alfa Romeo certainly tried. **MG**

Type 50 | Bugatti

(F)

1931 • 305 cu in/4,972 cc, S8 • 200 bhp/164 kW • 0–60 mph/97 kph in 8 seconds • 106 mph/170 kph

The Bugatti Type 50 may have been designed for the road and not the racetrack, but that didn't stop Ettore Bugatti's son Jean from wanting to use it to wrest Le Mans from the clutches of Bentley in 1931. Jean persuaded his father to give him three Type 50s for the great race, then painted them black in protest against the French government, which refused to sponsor them. He well may have won, too, but a tire failure caused his car to veer off the track and kill a spectator, which prompted Bugatti to abandon the race.

Jean could not be faulted for wanting to try, considering what he had at his disposal: three supercharged 5-liter, eight-cylinder, double overhead camshaft engines capable of generating 200 bhp (164 kW), matched only by the Duesenberg SJ. The engines, developed under his own supervision, were so powerful they made their chassis flex. It was the first double overhead camshaft engine Bugatti ever made, and the company's most powerful production engine.

The Type 50's design was in many ways a miniature version of the company's massive, 73-cubic-inch (13,000-cc) Type 46 Royale tourer, which had been in production since 1929. With a choice of a "sports" wheelbase or a longer "touring" version (known as the 50T), customers could order a standard Bugatti body or a custom-designed one, such as the Coupe Profilée, with its raked windshield and eye-catching elliptical paintwork.

Only sixty-five Type 50s, including the Le Mans racers, were built. They were outsold by other Bugatti models—notably Types 46 and 57—yet the Type 50 is now considered by many enthusiasts to have been the finest achievement of Automobiles E. Bugatti. **BS**

Roy D. Chapin, one of Hudson's founders, shows the new Hudson Terraplane to aviator Orville Wright, 1934.

Pioneer | Goliath (D)

1931 • 12 cu in/198 cc, single-cylinder • 5.5 bhp/4 kW • unknown • 37 mph/60 kph

Times were hard in the 1930s. So hard, in fact, that having four wheels on your car was a luxury some just couldn't quite afford: three would just have to do.

The Pioneer was made for three years in Germany during the Great Depression. It was built in various shapes and varieties by Goliath, a small part of the Borgward company, based in Bremen. Its back-to-basics design involved a tiny, single-cylinder, two-stroke engine sited in the rear of the car. This drove the two back wheels through a three-speed manual gearbox; the single front wheel was for steering.

There were just two seats inside, but steel bodywork was beyond the budget. Pioneer owners made do with a wooden frame covered by body panels of a fabric described rather flatteringly at the time as "imitation leather." The whole vehicle was called a "tricycle sedan." A rather cheekily beguiling convertible model with a folding fabric roof was also produced.

At the time, the Pioneer was considered a more sophisticated version of engineer and designer Carl Borgward's earlier Blitzkarren three-wheel utility pickup cart. An amazing 4,000 Pioneers were sold, and at its peak there were 300 employees working on building the cars. However, during World War II the Goliath factory was bombed and production terminated.

After the war, Goliath went on to build three-wheeler trucks. From 1958 these Goliath models were sold under the brand name Hansa—the Borgward group wanted to distance itself as far as possible from its prewar history of two-stroke three-wheelers. But the heyday of such vehicles had passed; three years later, in 1961, the Borgward group went bankrupt. **SH**

Terraplane | Hudson (USA)

1932 • 244 cu in/4,000 cc, S8 • 88 hp/65 kW • 0–60 mph/97 kph in 14.4 seconds • 85 mph/137 kph

World-famous solo aviator Amelia Earhart was employed to launch the new Terraplane at a huge party in Detroit in the United States. More than 2,000 car dealers from across North America were invited and the event was reported in newspapers across the country.

The new Hudson was deliberately named to cash in on the contemporary public fervor for anything to do with flying. Earhart had completed her famed solo transatlantic flight only two months before. The Terraplane also caught the eye of pioneer aviator Orville Wright, who promptly bought one for himself.

The car's unique mechanical feature was nothing to do with flying, however. It had "duo-automatic" brakes, or two separate brake systems—a hydraulic one, as on a modern car, and a mechanical one using a cable as a stand-by, in case the other failed.

The next year Hudson offered an eight-cylinder model that was claimed to have the highest horsepower-to-weight ratio of any car in the world (figures above). This made it a magnet for those who wanted speed—particularly the big gangsters of the day. Gang leader John Dillinger, bank robber John Paul Chase, and Baby Face Nelson (named Public Enemy Number One by the FBI) all drove Terraplanes. In 1933 one of the eight-cylinder models raced up to the top of Mount Washington in a record time that wasn't beaten for another twenty years.

The car was cheap, durable, and fast—and sold well despite the Depression-era economy. Its sales slogan was: "On the sea that's aquaplaning, in the air that's aeroplaning, but on the land, in the traffic, on the hills, hot diggity dog, that's Terraplaning." **SH**

SJ | Duesenberg

USA

1932 • 421 cu in/6,900 cc, S8 • 320 bhp/239 kW • 0–60 mph/97 kph in 8 seconds • 127 mph/204 kph

The Duesenberg Automobile and Motor Company was founded by Frederick and August Duesenberg in Des Moines, Iowa, in 1913. Self-taught engineers, the brothers had a passion for designing hand-built sports cars. They finished tenth in the 1914 Indianapolis 500, then won it in 1924, 1925, and 1927.

The brothers were great engineers but poor businessmen. In 1926 their company was saved from bankruptcy by being purchased by the owner of the Auburn Automobile Company, Errett Cord. An admirer of what the Duesenbergs had achieved, Cord did not wait long before meeting Fred Duesenberg to give him a challenge. "I want you, Fred," Cord said, "to build me the greatest car in the world." And in fact Duesenberg came close to giving Cord what he had asked for with the debut of the Model J at the 1928 New York Car Show. It was the Model J that inspired an expression for greatness that is still used today: "It's a Duesy."

The Model J was a great car, but it would be made even better. In May 1932 a supercharger was fitted so close to the Lycoming Straight-8 engine that the eight exhaust pipes had to be creased and bent so that they could exit through the side panels of the hood (bonnet), inadvertently giving the Duesenberg SJ its timeless signature look. With the supercharger, power increased from 265 to 320 bhp, enabling the car to hit 104 mph (167 kph) in second gear, and eclipse in performance all other production cars of the period.

Errett Cord's brief had been realized exquisitely. Fred's brother "Augie" observed, "The only car that could pass a Duesenberg was another Duesenberg—and that with the first owner's consent." **BS**

Type 55 | Bugatti

(F)

1932 • 138 cu in/2,262 cc, S8 • 130 bhp/97 kW • 0–60 mph/97 kph in 13 seconds • 112 mph/180 kph

When the Bugatti Type 55 went on sale in 1932, one of its early buyers was Baron Philippe de Rothschild. A member of the wealthy Rothschild banking family, Philippe for a period had been a Grand Prix racing driver. Driving a Bugatti Type 35C, one of three that he owned, he had managed a respectable fourth-place finish in the 1929 Monaco Grand Prix. When the more powerful Type 55 made its appearance, he was waiting with his checkbook, although by this time he had given up competitive racing to devote more time to the family's prestigious vineyards.

The Type 55, which was the road-going version of the Bugatti Type 54 Grand Prix racing car, suited the baron perfectly. It had the same body as the original, but with a detuned engine that was less than half as powerful as the racing version. Only thirty-eight Type 55s were made, of which fifteen had exclusive coachwork designed by Jean Bugatti himself. Little wonder that one of these attracted the fashion designer Ralph Lauren, who owned one for a time. Bugatti actually designed two types, a roadster and a coupe, and his roadster has been described as the most exclusive sports car of all time. The Type 55 has been called a car that was as much a pleasure to look at as it was to drive, with its gracefully sculpted design.

When a rare example of a Type 55 came up at auction in 2008, it sold for $1,760,000 (£1,100,000). For collectors, this particular example carried extra kudos because it was the car's prototype—the engine is even numbered "1." The car had been previously sold in 1960, when it was no longer running, for just $1,200 (£770). After that, the car had received a superb re-creation of Jean Bugatti's roadster coachwork. **MG**

SS1 | Swallow Coachbuilding Company

GB

1932 • 125 cu in/2,054 cc, S6 • 48 bhp/36 kW • unknown • 75 mph/121 kph

It's incredible to think that Jaguar, the marque now known for "grace, pace, and space," began as a tiny company making motorcycle sidecars (boxy things bolted alongside a motorcycle that offered one person an uncomfortable ride). Admittedly, those made by the Swallow Sidecar Company—formed by William Lyons and William Walmsley in 1922—were stylish sidecars for the likes of the Norton and Brough Superior motorcycles. Their first proper car, five years later, was the Austin Seven–based Swallow, and at that point the company became the Swallow Coachbuilding Company. As the 1930s approached, Lyons decided he wanted to build a beautiful, sporty—yet affordable—coupe.

One of his major skills was choosing the right people to work with. He commissioned a chassis from Rubery Owen and chose the reliable Standard 16 engine, which was offered in 2-liter or 2.5-liter form. He employed Cyril Holland to create the coachwork, which had a long hood (bonnet) and superlow roofline. Its performance was modest, but its looks blew away crowds at the 1931 London Motor Show. U.K. magazine *The Motor* wrote, "The SS1 is a new type of automobile in the sense that it is a car built for the connoisseur, but is relatively low priced."

Lyons was in the hospital when the plans were finalized, and it's probably just as well. His preferred roofline was so low that drivers of average height wouldn't have been able to get inside, so Walmsley had it raised. Lyons hated it and made serious revisions for 1933.

The tag "SS" meant either Standard Swallow or Swallow Special (Lyons himself said this was never resolved), but after World War II the initials had a more negative association, so "Jaguar" was chosen instead. **LT**

Model B | Ford

USA

1932 • 124 cu in/2,033 cc, S4 • 65 hp/48 kW • unknown • 65 mph/104 kph

In 1927 something extraordinary happened in the cutthroat world of the American auto industry. For the first time ever, Chevrolet outsold Ford—and not by a little bit, but by more than 250,000 registrations. The next year, they did it again. The Model T had become obsolete, and the Model A that followed was underpowered and already dated. Ford's grip on America's roads was slipping, so he decided he'd design and build, in typical Ford fashion, a mass-produced solution: the Model B.

The B came with what was essentially an upgraded A engine (sometimes called a C by enthusiasts, although this designation never formally existed), and was available as a two- or four-door sedan (saloon), a roadster, and a three- or five-windowed coupe. It had hydraulic suspension, an upright rectangular grille, and, according to press reviews upon its release on March 31, 1932, was, from fender to fender (bumper to bumper) all dipped in striking black enamel, "the best looking" Ford yet. It was lower than the A and sleeker too, with a lower center of gravity, lower running boards, and nice touches like rust-proof steel headlights. When Ford decided the gas tank should be at the rear of the car and no longer protrude from its cowl, his son Edsel and designer Eugene Gregorie rejoiced at the extra styling options this gave them. (Though they wouldn't take full advantage of this until 1933 with the introduction of a new raked grille.)

Despite its improved looks, the launch of the Ford V8 with its 85 bhp (63 kW) flathead engine spelled the end not only of the Model B, but of Henry Ford's four-cylindered revolution. **BS**

Twin Six | Packard

USA

1932 • 445 cu in/7,292 cc, V12 • 160 bhp/119 kW • unknown • 100 mph/161 kph

In 1912 Packard became the first automobile company in the world to build a V12 engine, and their 1915 Twin Six was the first production car to get it. Manufacture was halted in 1920, however, and twelve V12-less years followed. Then, in 1932, to meet competition from Buick, Duesenberg, and the 165 bhp (121 kW) of Cadillac's new V16, Packard premiered their new V12 at the Roosevelt Hotel in New York City. This was during a depression that was seeing demand for luxury cars shrink faster than the nation's economy. Yet despite the economic gloom, its arrival created such a stir among the well-to-do that news of its unveiling was broadcast on the ticker tape across the trading floor of the ailing New York Stock Exchange.

The heart of the car was its 445-cubic-inch (7,292 cc), side-valve V12 engine. This was augmented by state-of-the-art Stromberg carburetors and a specially modified combustion chamber that allowed the engine to produce a whopping 160 bhp (119 kW). That was enough torque to power all the models in the range comfortably at 100 mph (161 kph). Zero spacing between valve-train components also meant it could go 50,000 miles before the valves needed adjusting—one less thing for its owners to worry about in troubled times.

The interior had sumptuous leather-clad seats, an aircraft-style instrument display, and a fold-up windshield for the comfort of its rear passengers, who could also rest their feet on its full-width, cloth-trimmed footrest. But the real beauty of the Packard Twin Six lay in its accessories: elongated cat's-eye headlights designed by Ray Dietrich, a rear trunk (boot) rack, sidebars, and a tiny door just behind the driver's door to store your Great Depression–mocking bag of golf clubs. **BS**

V8 | Ford

(USA)

1932 • 220 cu in/3,621 cc, flat V8 • 65 bhp/48 kW • 0–60 mph/97 kph in 21.5 seconds • 75 mph/121 kph

The Ford V8 was conceived by the great Henry Ford and given impetus by the success of arch rival Chrysler. Also known as the Model 18, the car came in fourteen body styles that grew out of two basic configurations—the three-window deluxe coupe and the five-window coupe. All were powered by Henry Ford's last great contribution to the evolution of the American motorcar: the compact, revolutionary flathead V8.

It was the engine the masses had been waiting for, born in Ford's own mind and dictated in detail to his engineers. Cast in a one-piece block and enhanced with a new down-draft carburetor, it out-performed all its competitors and was decades ahead of its time. Its development was achieved with typical Ford frugality and would sell, he said, for under $700 (£450). Everyone at Ford told him it couldn't be done, that a V8 couldn't be made in a single cast. "We're going from a four to an eight because Chrysler is going to a six," he insisted. "And anything that can be drawn up, can be cast."

V8s were complicated and expensive to build, and most carmakers preferred straight eights and sixes. Ford, who treated his engineers like draftsmen, was undaunted. His V8 proved a watershed in engine development, and was continually tweaked in postproduction to "up" its performance. An improved ignition system took horsepower from 65 bhp (48 kW) to 75 bhp (56 kW). In 1934 its grille was given straight hood (bonnet) louvers to improve airflow, raising it further still to 85 bhp (63 kW). The bank robber John Dillinger was so enamored with Ford's V8 that he used them for his getaways. At the time, there wasn't a better recommendation than that. **BS**

THX 138

🅒 A canary-yellow Deuce Coupe played a starring role in the 1973 movie *American Graffiti*.

Deuce Coupe | Ford (USA)

1932 • 220 cu in/3,621 cc, flat V8 • 65 bhp/48 kW • 0–60 mph/97 kph in 21.5 seconds • 75 mph/121 kph

By the early 1940s over four million Model Bs were being driven on America's roads. They were plentiful, and they were cheap. Their performance figures are given above.

One day, someone took a closer look at a B and began to imagine the fun they could have by stripping down all those inconveniently weighty elements not essential to performance and maybe making a few minor modifications to its already powerful V8. They could make it go as fast as their budget and ingenuity would allow. Those are the figures not given above . . .

Young people all over America started to realize that they could "soup up" an inexpensive car so it could outperform other, more expensive, cars. The era of the hot rod had arrived. It was the birth of DIY customization.

This fashion gave new life to the 1932 Model B—and the Ford V8 that followed it—and would, in time, turn them both into the most replicated automobiles in American automotive history. Hot-rodders called their new machines "Deuce Coupes," and they have since become the classic image of what a hot rod should be. Anything not considered vital was discarded in the transformation from family car to street machine: fenders (bumpers), hoods (bonnets), and windshields, with engines either refined or replaced by larger ones.

In 1963 the Beach Boys immortalized the Deuce in their hit song "Little Deuce Coupe." A bright-yellow, five-window highboy Deuce achieved fame as John Milner's street machine in the 1973 movie *American Graffiti*. Endlessly re-created, revised, modified, and sometimes even deified, the Deuce Coupe has remained the quintessential American hot rod for seventy years. **SH**

Model Y | Ford (USA)

1932 • 56 cu in/933 cc, S4 • 8 bhp/6 kW • 0–50 mph/80 kph in 24 seconds • 59 mph/98 kph

When people think of Henry Ford they think of America. But the fact is that Ford's U.S. expansion closely paralleled his ventures in Europe. The first Ford factory opened in the United Kingdom in 1911, and in 1917 a tractor plant began production in Ireland. Automobile assembly plants quickly followed in Copenhagen, Bordeaux, Cadiz, Trieste, Berlin, and even Moscow. Yet despite Ford's growing European empire, sales of the continental Model T and unpopular Model A had plummeted with the onset of the Great Depression—and Henry Ford was in need of a savior.

Designed in under five months specifically for the U.K. market, the Model Y was the car that Depression-era families in Britain were waiting for. Built at the Dagenham factory in Essex—the largest automotive factory in England—the Model Y did much to recoup the company's investment there. It sold over 157,000 units during its five-year production run. At its peak it captured 41 percent of its target market, much to the chagrin of Hillman, Morris, Singer, and Austin.

Materials and options in the Model Y were basic: a steel body over a pressed steel chassis, and choice of a fixed or sliding "sun" roof. Available in two- and four-door versions, the two door became the first closed-body car to sell in Great Britain for £100 ($160). The price naturally made the Model Y an instant hit with the masses, who were happy to forgive it its flaws: it was slow, had an uninspiring three-speed gearbox with no synchromesh, a worrying tendency to drift from side to side at speed, and, according to the British motoring magazine *Autocar*, had "an almost unbelievable lack of brakes." Still, what do you expect for that price? **BS**

AM80S | Hotchkiss

(F)

1933 • 212 cu in/3,485 cc, S6 • 100 bhp/75 kW • unknown • 90 mph/145 kph

Benjamin Hotchkiss was born in Connecticut in 1826, and worked as an armaments maker in Hartford before moving to St. Denis, just north of Paris, in 1867. His company produced the Hotchkiss machine gun and also—during idle periods of peace—dabbled in the manufacture of motor parts. The company made its first car in 1903, and after World War I specialized in the construction of superluxury cars such as the 6.6-liter Type AK. In 1928 Hotchkiss engineers designed a new series of six-cylinder tourers that would form the basis of all their future cars: the AM80. The French government were so impressed by it that they bought the cars to patrol French colonial outposts in the Syrian Desert. In 1929 an AM80 broke forty-six international records at the Autodrome de Montlhéry track when it covered 25,000 miles (40,233 km) in sixteen days.

The French motoring journalist Charles Faroux described the AM80S, the sporting version of the AM80, as having a simplicity of line and purity of design that combined to guarantee "an assurance of perfection." It was an AM80S prototype that was driven to victory by Maurice Vasselle in the Rallye Automobile Monte Carlo of 1932, a race that would become something of a Hotchkiss "benefit" in subsequent years with victories in 1933, 1934, and again in 1939. The AM80S was born for hill climbs, with its specially lowered chassis and rear springs facing outward from the chassis to help eliminate sideways roll. While its mechanics were essentially those of the AM80, it did come with an enlarged 100 bhp engine. The AM80S was available in a four- and seven-seat sedan (saloon), a coupe, roadster, cabriolet, and limousine. **BS**

Trumpf Junior | Adler

D

1934 • 60 cu in/995 cc, S4 • 28 bhp/21 kW • unknown • 56 mph/90 kph

The Trumpf Junior marked the transition from cars of the past to vehicles of the new modern era. Heinrich Kleyer's company had manufactured everything from bicycles to typewriters, and cars seemed just one part of his plans. Yet before World War I, his sons had raced his cars successfully and an Adler was bought by Kaiser Wilhelm. The company was always keen to try new ideas and in the interwar period, Adlers featured Europe's first hydraulic brake system. Also at this time, German racer Clärenore Stinnes used an Adler in her attempt to be the first person to drive around the world. She succeeded, doing 29,000 miles (47,000 km) in her Adler Standard.

In the 1930s Adler focused on building the new style of front-wheel-drive cars introduced by fellow German manufacturer DKW. The Trumpf was launched in 1932, and the smaller Trumpf Junior in 1934. The range had a wide choice of side-valve engines from 60 cubic inches (995 cc) to 100 cubic inches (1,645 cc). Buyers could choose between two- and four-door sedans (saloons), cabriolet, semicabriolet, tourer, and two-seater sports car. The cars were well received and were also manufactured by Rosengart in France and Imperia in Belgium. Sporting success soon followed, with a Trumpf winning the Le Mans 24 Hour race.

Some Trumpf features were from the old world, such as the mechanical brakes and four-speed manual "crash" nonsyncromesh gearboxes. But others heralded the start of a more modern type of car—like all-round independent suspension and pioneering rack-and-pinion steering. Sales were good and despite the Depression, Trumpf Junior production exceeded 100,000 cars before it ended with World War II. **SH**

Type 57 | Bugatti

(F)

1934 • 198 cu in/3,257 cc, S8 • 135 bhp/101 kW • 0–60 mph/97 kph in 10 seconds • 95 mph/153 kph

A supercharged 57SC Atlantic (one of only two surviving) became one of the most expensive used cars ever when it sold for $30 million (£18.9 million) at auction in America. Fashion designer Ralph Lauren owns the other one. Even a humble "standard" 57 version sold recently in the U.K. for £3 million ($4.6 million). The buyer wasn't deterred by the fact that it had been found covered in dust in a garage and hadn't started for fifty years.

This obscure French prewar sportscar is extremely sought-after because of its striking looks, and because it was rare and exclusive even back in the 1930s. Fewer than 700 of the Type 57 were made in six years, and yet owners included many of the rich and famous faces of the 1930s—such as prominent French circus director Jérôme Médrano, British motor-racing MP Earl Howe, and world land speed record chasers Malcolm and Donald Campbell.

The 57 used the engine from Bugatti's Grand Prix car, sometimes tuned or supercharged to reach 120 mph (193 kph). Some were convertibles, others coupes. The specially made "S" models were named after the French word *surbaissé*, or "lowered." These cars had a revised chassis to make them ride closer to the road—giving more handling and performance potential. The Atlantic fastback version is often judged the most beautiful prewar car.

Nevertheless, even on such acclaimed cars some details didn't date well. The interior originally came with mock crocodile-skin leather, there were "spats," or covers, enclosing the rear wheels, and some models will never be seen with the roof up. That's because its awkward assembly was likened to a tall greenhouse. Today that's not really a problem, because, of course, anyone owning a Type 57 knows it is far too valuable to take out in the rain. **SH**

Ulster | Aston Martin (GB)

1934 • 91 cu in/1,500 cc, S4 • 80 bhp/60 kW • 0–60 mph/97 kph in 25 seconds • 102 mph/164.2 kph

Of all the vintage automobiles ever made, none can match the Ulster for survivability. All twenty-one that were built are still with us today—an impressive statistic for a purpose-built racing car only slightly bigger than a go-cart. And it is even more impressive when seen in the light of a 1935 review in *Motor Sport* magazine: "The car inspired confidence, had an inherent sense of rightness . . . and moved like a rocket."

Developed by Italian designer and race-car driver Augustus Cesari Bertelli, the "Father of Aston Martin," the Ulster was the culmination of over ten years of racing experience. Its time on the racetracks of Europe, though brief, was spectacular. Fitted with external manifolds, stiff suspension, an advanced overhead camshaft, dry sump engine, and made entirely from aluminum, the 2,068-pound (940-kg) "rocket" took first, second, and third place at the 1934 British Tourist Trophy at Goodwood, and came in third at Le Mans in 1935, winning its 1,101–1,500 cc category. It was the closest thing to a pure racing car Aston Martin ever produced.

The last unrestored Ulster was sold—in bits and with just a "few" pieces missing—at Christies, in 1996. Most are still registered and roadworthy, and—as Aston Martin themselves promised seventy-eight years ago—they are still "ready to race without further preparation." **BS**

401 Eclipse | Peugeot (F)

1934 • 103 cu in/1,700 cc, S4 • 44 bhp/33 kW • unknown • 62 mph/100 kph

Introduced at the 1934 Paris Motor Show, the 401's classic, sculpted lines and art deco appearance made it an instant design classic. But there was more to this new Peugeot than its looks: the 401 came with the world's first electrically powered, fully retractable metal roof.

The result of one of the most unusual collaborations in automotive history, the 401 was built by a curious mix of dedicated enthusiasts. The revolutionary roof was the brainchild of Georges Paulin, dental technician and prolific inventor; the French coachbuilding firm Carrosserie Pourtout provided the body; and a Parisian Peugeot car-dealer-turned-designer, Emile Darl'mat, designed the car's signature art deco lines. But it was the roof that had everyone talking: a curved, single-piece detachable roof that stowed away beneath the car's similarly curved trunk (boot) thanks to a special power mechanism that Paulin immediately patented and then incorporated in the 402 the following year.

The 401 was robust and economical, and well received by the French motoring public. It was adopted by the Paris taxi company G7, which outfitted them with a heating system and wireless radios. However, only seventy-nine were built before they were phased out by the 402 in 1935. Paulin's roof would never go out of style, though, and is still offered on Peugeots today. **BS**

500K | Mercedes-Benz (D)

1934 • 306 cu in/5,019 cc, S8 • 160 bhp/118 kW • 0–60 mph/97 kph in 16 seconds • 99 mph/160 kph

First shown in 1934, the 500K would come to be viewed by many as the ultimate Mercedes-Benz. It succeeded the 380, which had only been introduced in 1933, and soon was the company's number one product. This was hardly surprising. It had the same 5-liter engine that went into the 500 model sedan (saloon), but the addition of a K to its name indicated the *kompressor*, or supercharger, which turned it into a sports car.

The 500K appealed unashamedly to the luxury market, with a more powerful engine, more expensive bodywork, and a brand-new independent suspension system. It gave one of the smoothest drives around. Other cutting-edge features included safety glass, hydraulic brakes, and electric door locks. It came in three different chassis and eight different body types, including two-seater and four-seater versions. An even faster and lighter version, the 540K, was released in 1935, which pushed the top speed up to 110 mph (176 kph).

Only 342 Mercedes 500Ks were made, one of which ended up owned by Formula One's Bernie Eccleston. When his collection was sold in 2007, his 500K Special Roadster sold for just under £700,000 ($1,100,000). That was small fry, however, compared to the 540K model put up for sale in 2011—it fetched $9,680,000 (£6,200,000), having cost £7,700 ($12,000) when new. **MG**

Type 77 | Tatra (CS)

1934 • 181 cu in/2,969 cc, V8 • 59 bhp/44 kW • 0–60 mph/97 kph in 38 seconds • 90 mph/145 kph

It may not look it at first glance, but the Tatra 77 was the first car to be aerodynamically designed. One of its engineers was Paul Jaray, who had worked on the design of Zeppelin airships, and the Tatra 77 certainly has a Zeppelin feel about it. Another of its creators was an Austrian engineer, Hans Ledwinka, who had helped design railroad cars. In theory, the resulting car should have been a clunky, sturdy Middle European piece of automobile stodge. This was very far from the case.

The Tatra Company was founded in 1850 and produced its first motor vehicle in 1897. It went on to make a steady series of reliable luxury cars, with the Tatra name being first used in 1919. In the 1930s Hans Ledwinka, his son Erich, and a German engineer Erich Übelacker, began working as a team with Paul Jaray, having bought licenses from Jaray for his designs. The result was the Tatra 77, or T77 as it's also known.

The Tatra 77 was not only the first car to have been designed on aerodynamic principles, using a rear-mounted, air-cooled V8 engine, it was also to have a long-lasting impact on car design thanks to Adolf Hitler, a big Tatra fan. In 1934 when Hitler instructed Ferdinand Porsche to produce a "people's car" for the German nation, his design for the Volkswagen was heavily influenced by the Tatra 77. **MG**

7CV Traction Avant | Citroën

F

1934 • 79 cu in/1,303 cc, S4 • 32 bhp/24 kW • unknown • unknown

We take the concept of front-wheel-drive for granted these days, but somebody had to do it first. That wasn't Citroën with the Traction Avant, despite the car's name being a direct translation. Alvis in the United Kingdom, Cord in the United States, and DKW in Germany had already pioneered the concept, but the Traction Avant was the first model with a steel monocoque body to use it, and the first to take it to the masses. Citroën countered criticism of this new production technique by driving a car off a cliff to show how strong it was.

At its debut in May 1934, the car—also known as the Citroën 7CV—won praise for being packed with innovations. Aside from the welded unibody, which made it notably lighter than other cars of that era, it featured hydraulic brakes on all four wheels, and independent torsion bar suspension.

But Citroën paid the price for its ambition. Development costs and factory refurbishment pushed the company into bankruptcy later that year. It was rescued by Michelin, who owned it until 1976.

There were many versions of the Traction Avant—the 7A, 7B, 7C, 11, and 15—each with different engines. The numbers referred to the European system of "taxable horsepower," known as CV, based not on how powerful the car was but on its cylinder dimensions. This is why the Traction Avant is often called the 7CV, even though the model in question might not be.

Production ended in July 1957 after twenty-three years, four months, and fifteen days—a world record for a single car at the time. More than 750,000 had been built. What's believed to be the oldest surviving 7A is currently on display at the Citroën Museum in Paris. **RY**

150H Sport Roadster | Mercedes-Benz

D

1934 • 91 cu in/1,498 cc, S4 • 55 bhp/41 kW • unknown • 78 mph/126 kph

There aren't too many Mercedes that bring to mind the styling and principles of a Volkswagen. But with its rear-mounted engine placed just behind the driver and forward of the rear wheels, and its decidedly Volkswagen-like nose, the Mercedes 150H Sport Roadster invites the comparison.

The world's first mid-engine sports car, the 150H was designed by Hans Nibel and Mercedes chassis engineer Max Wagner, who merged aerodynamic principles, art deco, and aspects of the less appealing mid-engine 130H roadster sedan (saloon), to create a new mid-engine car. It must have seemed revolutionary in a world of front-engine roadsters. After all, an engine under the front hood (bonnet) was the way cars had always been, and the 150H might well have been dismissed as an oddity—had it been designed by anyone else but Mercedes.

The design could also have been considered good timing. Germans in the mid-1930s were developing a liking for mid- and rear-engine autos. The 150H (the "H" standing for *heck*, the German word for "rear") was built on a backbone chassis that united its front and rear axles, with its centrally located engine cooled by a centrifugal fan that drew air into the engine compartment via a system of louvers, similar again to the cooling system in the Volkswagen Type 1.

Innovation, however, does not always mean something is practical. A third headlight embedded into the bottom of the hood looked gawky, and the gas tank, which was over the engine in the 130H, was moved into the front compartment, thus reducing the car's carrying capacity. Whatever the reason, the 150H sold poorly and was discontinued in 1936. **BS**

K6 | Hispano-Suiza

(F)

1934 • 505 cu in/5,000 cc, S6 • 125 bhp/93 kW • unknown • 90 mph/145 kph

The Hispano-Suiza K6 premiered at the Paris Auto Salon in 1934 and immediately carried on from where the company's previous automotive masterpiece, the H6, had left off. Following a classic is never easy, but the K6 reflected founder Marc Birkirgt's ability to sense and respond to what his customers were seeking, despite its high price tag and the ravages of the Great Depression.

The K6 was offered on a rolling Hispano-designed chassis so customers could select the coachwork of their choice. This saw the car adorned with some exquisite bodies that were often indistinguishable from—or better than—those of the company's flagship, the J12. Master French coachbuilders loved the K6 because of its sophistication and attention to detail, and Birkirgt knew his clientele preferred luxury and sumptuous surroundings over speed and performance. Thus freed to sacrifice power for comfort, the 305-cubic-inch (5,000-cc), straight-six engine of designer Rodolphe Herrmann did away with chain and gear driven camshafts, instead using older-style push-rod driven valves, along with a precision steering box, to deliver what his clients were looking for: responsiveness and silence.

The K6 ceased production in 1938 as Europe lurched ever closer to war and Hispano-Suiza was forced to focus increasingly on the other string to its bow—the production of aircraft engines. As many as thirty-six custom-built, handmade K6s survive today, a reminder that motoring isn't always about speed. The survivors ensure that Hispano-Suiza's reputation for being the preferred marque for those who sought comfort, grandeur, precision engineering, and the smoothest of rides is not forgotten. **BS**

NA 8/90 | Buick

USA

1934 • 344 cu in/5,644 cc, S8 • 116 bhp/86 kW • unknown • 100 mph/161 kph

The Series 90 Buicks boasted an impressive list of innovations: safety glass, vacuum-powered brake boosters, a starter switch connected to the accelerator, and a cowl-mounted fresh air ventilator. They had a new type of front suspension called "knee-action" suspension, so named because of the way the wheels were connected to the axle. Together with a rear ride stabilizer, the new suspension impressed Rolls-Royce so much that it adopted the design under license and added it to its new Phantom III V-12.

Series 90s were available in a sports coupe, convertible coupe, seven-passenger sedan (saloon), and convertible phaeton, all of which were fitted out with plush mohair velvet upholstery; the tourer also had a fold-out armrest between its rear seats. The sedan had silk shades over its rear doors and rear quarter windows, and a glass partition separated the driver from the rear passengers, who had the luxury of reading lights and door pouches for storage. The sports coupe had a rumble seat, allowing it to seat four, while the phaeton had side-mounted spare tires and a luggage rack as standard, as well as "suicide"-style forward-opening front doors. The 8/90 was powered by Buick's own straight-eight engine, one of the most advanced engines of its day. It was developed in 1931 at the height of the Depression and remained a mainstay of Buick automobiles until 1953.

The Depression was difficult period for Buick—as it was for almost all American car manufacturers—and although the introduction of the Series 40 helped the company to ride out the downturn, the Series 90 continued to reign as Buick's top-of-the-line "flagship of innovation." **BS**

The 1934 Chrysler CU Airflow Eight was a pioneering design in the development of aerodynamic vehicles.

CU Airflow Eight | Chrysler (USA)

1934 • 323 cu in/5,302 cc, S8 • 130 bhp/97 kW • 0–60 mph/97 kph in 19.5 seconds • 95 mph/153 kph

In 1933 the great Chrysler engineer and one of the company's legendary "three musketeers," Carl Breer, was either watching an airship moving overhead or following a V-shaped flight of geese—there are several versions of the story—when he began to consider how an object's shape might govern how economically it moves through the air. Whatever the prompt, it wasn't long before he and his other musketeers, Owen Skelton and Fred Zeder, began wind tunnel tests at Chrysler's Highland Park headquarters in Michigan to see what might be the most aerodynamically efficient shape for a four-door sedan (saloon).

The elimination of drag was the main principle that guided their design. Headlights, windshields, fenders (bumpers), even radiator grills—anything that trapped air and increased drag—was either redesigned or jettisoned. Weight distribution also came under the microscope—sedans when loaded with passengers often had three-quarters of their weight over the rear wheels, making the vehicles unstable. Finally, after months of experimentation, a new car was designed that met all the aerodynamic requirements they threw at it: the Chrysler Airflow.

But Americans didn't like it. The *Harper's Bazaar* fashion writer, Carolyn Edmundson, summed up the confusion by calling it "breathlessly different-looking." Nobody seemed to care about its drag-free body or its steel space frame construction or its 50/50 front-to-rear weight distribution—it just looked awkward. Chrysler responded by redesigning the grill, but to no avail. Sales were poor over its four-year run, and in 1937 the Airflow floated away into automotive oblivion. **BS**

402BL | Peugeot (F)

1935 • 131 cu in/2,148 cc, S4 • 68 bhp/50 kW • unknown • 75 mph/120 kph

Like the Lincoln Zephyr and the Chrysler Airflow before it, the Peugeot 402 was an example of the growing fascination of mid-1930s automakers with "streamlining." Peugeot's bevy of talented designers had been closely following the development of Amercian airflow designs, and set about designing a landmark new automobile.

The result was the 402BL Eclipse Decapotable, which came with a 131-cubic-inch (2,148-cc) engine, a 9-cubic-inch (151-cc) increase over a standard 402. The body was replete with lovely accents—all cast in aluminum—such as faux running boards, taillight and indicator surrounds, Peugeot's lion-headed hood (bonnet) release handle, and fender (bumper) skirts. Despite this, it was—as with the 401 and 402—Georges Paulin's mechanical retractable metal roof (which Paulin sold to Peugeot in 1935) that had everyone talking, although this time the roof was stowed manually rather than electrically.

But the 402BL wasn't all innovation. Hidden beneath its distracting exterior were some disappointingly dated concepts such as a conventional rear-drive chassis and cable-actuated, rather than hydraulic, brakes. But what couldn't be seen failed to deter the French motoring public who were enthralled by the car's all-too-obvious elegance. There was the rounded nose and reverse-teardrop waterfall-styled grille; a striking V-shaped windshield; a gearstick lever and handbrake that extended from behind the art deco–styled dashboard with its brown Bakelite switches; and, soaring above it all, the cutting-edge genius of Georges Paulin's disappearing roof. **BS**

Roadster | Squire

GB

1935 • 91 cu in/1,500 cc, S4 • 110 bhp/81 kW • 0–60 mph/97kph in 12 seconds • 100 mph/161 kph

The story of the Squire Roadster is the story of Adrian Squire. By the time he was twenty-one, Squire, an Englishman, had already worked for Bentley and MG. He decided to build his own car, forming the Squire Motors company to do so. He wanted to build a car that could be driven on the roads, but was also capable of winning a Grand Prix. Friends aided him in his pet project, providing him both with labor and with financial backing. Squire also invested some money that he had inherited in his company.

Squire commissioned the Vanden Plas company to design the bodywork of his vehicle, and acquired a stock of powerful engines from the Anzani engine manufacturers. He built two versions, a two-seater and a four-seater, and the result was a car that was fast and also had exceptional braking capacity.

Unfortunately, Squire was only able to produce a handful of cars—one estimate is that he built just three two-seaters and four four-seaters. Exact figures aren't known for sure, and there may have been as many as ten cars built in all.

But Squire simply could not produce his cars at a price that could compete with what else was on the market. His first vehicles sold for £1,220 ($1,900), for which price people at the time could buy a Bugatti. Squire then changed to cheaper bodywork and managed to bring the price down to £995 ($1,550), but it wasn't enough. He was forced to stop building the cars in 1936 due to lack of funds. Squire went to work for the Bristol Aeroplane Company, where he was tragically killed in an air raid in 1940. He was only thirty years old. **MG**

Speedster | Auburn

(USA)

1935 • 280 cu in/4,596 cc, S8 • 150 bhp/112 kW • 0–60 mph/97kph in 15 seconds • 100 mph/160 kph

The Auburn Automobile Company was founded in 1900 by the Eckhart brothers in Auburn, Indiana. Their father built horse-drawn carriages, but the two sons preferred the emerging world of horseless carriages. They had a checkered but mainly unsuccessful career, and had to sell the company to a group of Chicago businessmen in 1919.

The businessmen fared little better, and though various cars were produced, none of them took off. They sold the company to the hugely successful automobile salesman E. L. Cord in 1925, and Cord immediately sold off the existing stock of cars by painting them two-tone and selling them cheap. In 1926 Cord went into partnership with the Duesenberg Company, and together they produced several Speedster models, the first in 1928. In 1932 a Speedster first recorded a speed of 100 mph (160 kph) on the Bonneville Salt Flats in Utah.

The classic 851 and 852 Auburn Speedsters came along in 1935 and it was these jaunty, redesigned 1935 models, with their powerful engine and even faster speed, that really caught the public's eye. Unfortunately the company was still in a very poor financial state, worsened by the Depression, and despite the acclaim for the latest Speedsters the Auburn Automobile Company went out of business in 1937, taking the rest of E. L. Cord's vast business empire with it. The company headquarters survived, though, and is now home to the Auburn Cord Duesenberg Automobile Museum—which includes, naturally, several Speedster models.

Today the Speedster is one of the most sought-after classic cars, and original 1935–37 models sell for £300,000 ($465,000) and upward—rather too late for the Eckhart Brothers, E. L. Cord, and those Chicago businessmen. **MG**

A 1930s poster celebrating the multiple world-record-breaking achievement of Citroen's 8CV "Petite Rosalie." ▷

11CV Normale | Citroën (F)

1935 • 116 cu in/1,911 cc, S4 • 46 bhp/34 kW • unknown • 68 mph/109 kph

Andre Citroën wanted his new 11-series line to include a striking new two-door roadster to show off at the upcoming Salon de l'Automobile, to be held at the Grand Palais in Paris in October. He gave instructions to his two best designers—Flaminio Bertoni and Jean Daninos—to make him one.

They came up with the 11CV Normale Roadster, a wide-bodied version of Citroën's 1934 7A saloon (the "11" referred to the taxable horsepower of the car; taxation rates for autos were based upon their engine's cylinder dimensions). Although its fenders (bumpers), hood (bonnet), and many of its body parts came from the previous year's 7-series sedans (saloons), Bertoni and Daninos designed an elegant sweeping body on a longer wheelbase that resulted in a roadster with plenty of room for driver and passenger and was a thrill to drive.

The new roadster came with a list of standards that saw Citroën at the forefront of automotive innovation: independent front-wheel torsion bar and wishbone suspension, front-wheel drive, and a new "monocoque" construction approach that welded the body and chassis together to form a single unit. A faux cabriolet version (a two-door fixed-head coupe with roadster-type lines) was also available.

The U.K. right-hand drive version of the 11CV was known as the "Light 15," and its interior came with leather upholstery, a wood-grained dashboard, and, it has to be said, a rather optimistic 80 mph (129 kph) speedometer. The 11CV Normale Roadster further enhanced Citroën's reputation for excellence in design and engineering, and made real the company's motto: "Citroën: Creative Technologie." **BS**

Rosalie | Citroën (F)

1935 • 88 cu in/1,452 cc, S4 • 32 bhp/24kW unknown • 70 mph/113 kph

The Three Rosalies might sound like a female country band, but they were in fact three car models produced by Citroën in the 1930s: the 8CV, the 10CV, and the 15CV. The performances of the bigger cars were, of course, more impressive than the 8CV statistics given above—the 15CV, for instance, had a 161-cubic-inch (2,650-cc) engine and a top speed of 75 mph (120 kph).

However, even the humble 8CV created a stir in 1933 when it appeared at the Montlhéry racing circuit to the south of Paris. It was driven for 134 days and nights, covering a distance of 187,500 miles (300,000 km) at an average speed of 58.125 mph (93 kph), beating 106 world records. It was an astonishing achievement.

It was also a revolutionary event in the history of Citroën. Throughout the 1920s it had established a name for itself for selling cars that were small, inexpensive, and not very exciting. In the 1930s it began improving the design and increasing the power of its cars, and the commercial launch of the Rosalie in 1935 was a landmark for the company. Not only did its achievement at Montlhéry give it immediate impact in the market, but it had a much more contemporary look that was more in line with other European and American car designs of the time. More importantly from Citroën's point of view, the lessons that the company had learned from studying Ford's assembly-line techniques in the United States meant that it could be produced efficiently and at an affordable price. And if you had plans to drive for 134 days and nights, then Rosalie was your girl. **MG**

6689 RG 1
4
YACCO
UNE 8 CV
CITROËN
DE SERIE "PETITE ROSALIE"
A PARCOURU
30000 KMS
EN 134 JOURS A 93 DE MOYENNE
AVEC UTILISATION CONSTANTE D'HUILE YACCO DU COMMERCE
CHASSIS DE PETITE ROSALIE EST STRICTEMENT IDENTIQUE

Zephyr | Lincoln (USA)

1935 • 268 cu in/4,400 cc, V12 • 110 bhp/82 kW • 0–60 mph/97 kph in 16 seconds • 87 mph/140 kph

In the early 1930s manufacturers began to experiment with "streamlining," a concept designed to reduce air resistance. The first American car to use this in its design was the poorly received Chrysler Airflow, which the press derided as "an anonymous lump." Undaunted by this response, Lincoln's new head of design, Eugene Gregorie, went to work. Using stress-analysis formulas that tested the structural integrity of airplanes, he designed pontoon fenders (bumpers) with inlaid circular headlights, a flat-topped "iron board" hood (bonnet) hinged at the rear, and a vertical V-shaped grille inlaid with delicate horizontal bars—and gave America the Lincoln Zephyr.

But it wasn't just its aerodynamic design that made the Zephyr unique. The engine was a cleverly designed, compact V12 with a tiny 2.75-inch (6.8-cm) bore—the smallest of any American-made car—which meant it needed less space than the big V8s of other carmakers, yet was comparable in power. It was also competitively priced, with 17,700 units sold in its first year (80 percent of Lincoln's total sales). Available in a four-door fastback and a two-door coupe, its interior was almost cavernous, helped by a shallow, heavily chromed dashboard layout that allowed front-seat passengers to sit close to the windshield, thus providing ample room for six people—all sitting in streamlined, aerodynamic comfort. **BS**

4/4 | Morgan (GB)

1935 • 68 cu in/1,122 cc, S4 • 34 bhp/25 kW • 0–60 mph/97 kph in 28.4 seconds • 75 mph/120.7 kph

From 1910 to 1935, Henry Morgan was known for his three-wheeled, tax-free cyclecars. By 1935, however, cheap four-wheelers from Morris and Austin were bringing the three-wheeler era to an end, so Morgan reluctantly decided he, too, had to enter the four-wheeled world. He did so in the most remarkable and profound way, with a car that can still be purchased today, looking much as it did back in 1935.

4/4 meant "four cylinders, four wheels," but from the windshield forward you could easily mistake it as an F4 three-wheeler. From the windshield back, however, and under the hood (bonnet), there had been some remarkable transformations. The car was heavier, with the F4's 60-cubic-inch (993-cc) engine replaced by a 34-bhp (25-kW) 68-cubic-inch (1,122-cc) Coventry Climax. Chassis rails and the suspension were strengthened, and rubber engine mounts were fitted. No sooner had the paint dried on the first 4/4 than Morgan decided to generate publicity by entering it in the London to Exeter trial, where its racing pedigree began humbly with a Premier Award.

The 4/4 had its official launch at the London Motor Show in March 1936 and has been with us ever since—making it the longest running model nameplate in the history of automobiles. **BS**

C28 Aerosport | Voisin (F)

1935 • 182 cu in/2,994 cc, S6 • 102 bhp/75 kW • unknown • 93 mph/150 kph

Voisin cars were designed by the company founder, Gabriel B. Voisin, and it is little wonder that the vehicles looked so good, as Voisin was a student at the École des Beaux-Arts in Lyons as well as being a talented engineer. He produced some striking cars, notable for their lightness and their low-slung chassis, and it's no surprise that what was probably his masterpiece, the C28 Aerosport, later proved popular with filmmakers. C28s can be seen in the 2005 movie *Sahara* and 2008's *Indiana Jones and the Kingdom of the Crystal Skull*.

Sadly for Voisin, fame only came retrospectively—while at the peak of his design powers, in the mid-1930s, his company faced severe financial problems. In 1934 he unveiled the C24 Aerodyne at the Paris Salon, which combined his interest in aerodynamic cars with a love for art deco design. Among the car's more unusual features was a sliding roof, which had a row of portholes along it, so that when it slid down behind the driver he could still see behind him.

The C28 Aerosport evolved from this and became Voisin's supreme design, selling for 92,000 French francs (about $88,500/£56,500 today)—vastly more than even a Bugatti at the time. Hardly anyone could afford them and only three or four were even made, just one of which is known to survive. **MG**

50 | Steyr (A)

1936 • 60 cu in/984 cc, S4 • 22 bhp/16 kW • unknown • 56 mph/90 kph

The Steyr 50 may look like a cartoon car, but it was very fondly regarded. It was built for the Austrian mass public, to cope with driving in the Alps, and was fondly nicknamed the "Steyr Baby." Thirteen-thousand were sold before it was replaced by the Steyr 55 in 1940. As the Austrian population at the time was only about 6.7 million, this was a respectable number, and it helped confirm the Steyr 50's place as the "Austrian People's Car."

It may have looked like a car whose top speed could only be attained by going downhill on one of the steeper Alps, but it was, in fact, designed using the latest aerodynamic principles of the time. Its hood (bonnet) curved gently, its windshield leaned back, and the air flow continued down the rounded rear, which looked not unlike the Volkswagen, or "German People's Car." The Steyr 50's features included a sliding roof, to take advantage of Alpine summer days, and it also offered more luggage space than the Volkswagen.

On the grille of the Steyr 50 is a company logo in the shape of a target. Steyr had made rifles since the mid-1800s, but at the end of World War I it was banned from producing anything other than bicycles. They had already been planning to go into the automobile industry, however, so their car production began. The Steyr 50 would be their best-selling vehicle. **MG**

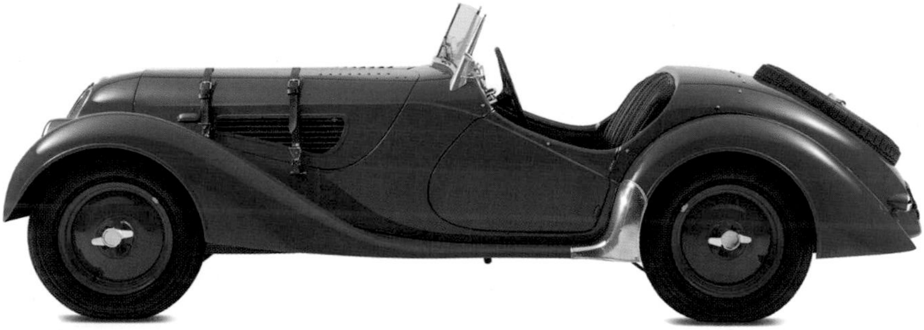

328 | BMW

D

1936 • 120 cu in/1,971 cc, S6 • 55 bhp/41 kW • 0–60 mph/97 kph in 10 seconds • 93 mph/150 kph

It was not particularly surprising that in 1999 the BMW 328 made the short list of cars nominated by an international panel of motoring writers for their choice of Car of the Century. (The eventual winner was the Model T Ford.) It was the only BMW to make the short list, and is widely regarded as the best car that the company ever built. The design may have looked a little bulky, but the Bavarian Motor Company had used the latest aerodynamic techniques to style the bodywork, and it proved to be both easy to drive and fast. Its lightweight alloy body helped it zip along at an impressive speed.

As well as being a fine roadster, the BMW 328 was a remarkable success on the racing circuit. It can lay claim to an astonishing list of achievements that were amassed during its brief lifespan from 1936 to 1940, during which time 464 models were built. Three of those were entered in the 2-liter class for the 1939 Le Mans race, and finished in the first three positions. The car also won the 1939 RAC Rally, and, adding yet more silverware to the BMW trophy cabinet, the Mille Miglia version won the 1940 Mille Miglia race.

Production of the BMW 328 was interrupted because of the outbreak of World War II, although it was always intended to resume manufacture again once hostilities ceased. However, the plant was located in Eisenach in Germany, which became part of East Germany following the conclusion of the war, and only state-sanctioned vehicles could be produced there. The car's pedigree and rarity mean that today it fetches very high prices at auctions. One was sold in 2010 for $667,000 (£428,000). **MG**

853 Phaeton | Horch

D

1936 • 301 cu in/4,944 cc, S8 • 120 bhp/89 kW • unknown • 81 mph/130 kph

German blacksmith-turned-engineer August Horch built his first car in 1901. In 1909, when he left the company he had founded, he wasn't allowed to take his own name with him because it was ruled to now be a registered trademark, so he called his new company by the Latin version of his name: Audi. The Horch company remained in business after his departure, though it was now a kind of "Horchless carriage," until 1932 when it eventually merged with Audi and three other car manufacturers to form the Auto Union group.

The Horch name continued as a distinct brand within the group, however, and in 1936 produced what would be the finest car to carry that marque, the Horch 853 Phaeton. It was a handsome and imposing car, a luxury model, but as it was less expensive than its Mercedes rivals, it was soon achieving healthy sales figures. Its design still seems to fit perfectly into the rather grandiose German image of the mid- to late 1930s, although it looks to be the perfect vehicle for Chicago gangsters just as much as SS Generals. Its huge body weighed 5,798 pounds (2,630 kg), and inside it housed a nearly 5-liter engine. It was built like a tank, which proved to be a useful skill for the manufacturers as the Auto Union group was soon making tanks and other vehicles for the German army with the outbreak of World War II.

When war ceased in 1945, the world had changed. The Audi factory where the 853s had been built was in Zwickau, which now found itself under Soviet control in East Germany. The factories where this magnificent car had been built were dismantled. **MG**

135M | Delahaye

(F)

1936 • 217 cu in/3,557 cc, S6 • 90 hp/67 kW • unknown • 99 mph/160 kph

Delahaye introduced its imposing but graceful 135 model in 1935, and quickly followed it with the more dynamic racing version, the 135M, the following year. A souped-up version of the 135 had become known as the Coupe des Alpes after it won the Alpine rally in its first year of production. It was an impressive win, and confirmed for Delahaye that it was making the right decision in trying to give its cars a sportier look and performance. The last few models had been rather staid, and the company wanted to return to the flair and fun that had been more associated with its image in the 1920s and earlier.

Delahaye decided to build an even more powerful version of the 135, which became the 135M, to continue the company's return to its old form. The 135 was notable for its low chassis, among other features, and the chassis of the new car would be even lower still. It was shorter, too, and with a more powerful engine, the 135M was even better received than its predecessor. It offered a choice of one-, two- or three-carb engines.

More variations on the basic successful model followed, including a 135MS that was produced in both touring and high-performance racing versions. Race victories continued, including scoring the first two places at Le Mans in 1938, and production continued too, with versions of the 135 being sold by Delahaye right through until 1954. In that year the company was bought by another French car manufacturer, Hotchkiss, who stopped Delahaye's car production completely, and retired the illustrious Delahaye name. Many of the 2,000 or so 135s that were built live on, though. One sold in 2007 for $1,320,000 (£850,000). **MG**

810 | Cord

USA

1936 • 288 cu in/4,730 cc, V8 • 125 bhp/92.3 kW • 0–60 mph/97 kph in 20.1 seconds • 90 mph/145 kph

Looking at the Cord 810 it should come as no surprise that its designer, Gordon Buehrig, was a finalist in the Car Designer of the Century award given by the Global Automotive Elections Foundation in 1999. Buehrig began his working life at Packard and in 1929, at the age of twenty-five, became the chief body designer at Duesenberg. In 1934 he joined the Auburn Automobile Company, and the following year gave the world the Auburn Boattail Speedster. His greatest achievement, however, would come in 1936 when he designed the car that New York City's Metropolitan Museum of Art has described as "the outstanding American contribution to automobile design"—the Cord 810.

The Cord's most striking feature (and also that of the 812 that followed) was its louvered, wraparound Venetian blind grille. It was this that led to its nickname "the coffin-nose." The car was so low to the ground it didn't require running boards. The interior, too, was striking, with an instrument panel bristling with chromed appliqué, fingertip levers, easy-to-read dials, and even a dashboard-mounted radio. The hand brake had a pistol grip and the car's headlights—concealed within its sweeping, streamlined fenders (bumpers)—could be raised and lowered via two chromed internal hand cranks. Crowds pressing around the Cord at car shows were so dense that people stood on other vehicles just to get a look. And, at long last, instead of sounding your horn only after painstakingly searching out a little button on the dashboard, you could signal your displeasure with the guy in front by banging repeatedly on the Cord's conveniently placed, hard-to-miss chrome ring right there on the steering wheel. **BS**

540K | Mercedes-Benz

(D)

1936 • 329 cu in/5,401 cc, S8 • 115 bhp/86 kW • 0–60 mph/97 kph in 16.4 seconds • 110 mph/170 kph

The Mercedes 540K is the most expensive roadster you'll find anywhere. If you can find one, that is, and also find the few million dollars that you'll need in order to buy it. Fortunately for the Formula One supremo Bernie Ecclestone, he did have a spare $8.25 million (£5.3 million) lying around when one came up for sale in 2007 and he was able to add it to his car collection. Others have sold for about $1–3 million (£640,000–£1,920,000) in recent years, depending on their condition, and the cars do come up surprisingly often given that only 419 were ever made, between 1936 and 1940. One of the reasons for this is that when World War II broke out in 1939, which effectively brought production to a halt, many people hid and even buried their 540Ks alongside their cash, works of art, and other valuables.

The 540K was first shown at the Paris Salon in 1936, and it followed on from the 500K model that had been launched in 1934. The name drew attention to the increase from a 5-liter (305-cubic-inch/5,000-cc) engine to a 5.4-liter (329-cubic-inch/5,400-cc) one, which boosted the car's top speed from 100 mph (160 kph) to 110 mph (170 kph).

The car wasn't merely big, it was one of the largest that had ever been made at that time and weighed 5,952 pounds (2,700 kg). Buyers were offered several options, including a seven-seater limousine with armored sides and glass, but the cars were so high end that Mercedes-Benz would customize them—at a price. One of the most sought-after models was the Tourenwagen, a two-door tourer that was roomy enough to seat four people in complete comfort. **MG**

SS100 | Jaguar

GB

1936 • 162 cu in/2,663 cc, S6 • 125 bhp/93 kW • 0–60 mph/97 kph in 10.4 seconds • 101 mph/162 kph

Only 314 Jaguar SS100s were ever manufactured over the period from 1936 to 1940 when the model was in production, making it one of the most sought-after, as well as stylish, British sports cars. It was the vehicle that, quite literally, made the Jaguar name. They were built not by Jaguar but by SS Cars of Coventry, which had previously been the Swallow Sidecar Company. SS Cars had already begun using the name Jaguar for some of their models, but after World War II, when the initials SS had strong associations with Nazi Germany, the company changed its name completely to Jaguar Cars in 1945.

The SS100 was a jaunty two-seater sports car, which began life with a 2.7-liter engine, although from 1938 onward the capacity was increased to 3.5 liters (213 cubic inches/3,500 cc). It evolved from the SS90 model and, while they were very similar, it was the subtle differences that turned the SS100 into a star car. It had better suspension, got more power from the same engine, its acceleration left other sports cars trailing in its wake, and its slightly redesigned front and rear gave it a sleeker and more sporty look. Reports on its top speed vary, but it was certainly one of the first cars that could happily cruise along at 75 mph (120 kph) without feeling the strain. It also sold for a relatively low price of £395 ($600).

If you can find a good-quality model on sale today, you can expect to pay about £200,000 ($310,000) for it. A cheaper option is to buy one of the replicas still being made by the Suffolk Jaguar company, which has made about 200 of them so far—almost as many as were originally built. **MG**

A new batch of Topolinos roll off the production line at the Fiat plant in Turin, Italy, 1947. ▷

101 | ZIS (SU)

1936 • 351 cu in/5,766 cc, S8 • 90 bhp/67 kW • unknown • 71 mph/115 kph

The ZIS 101 was born when Communist Party officials in the prewar Soviet Union decided they needed a car that fitted their lofty status. It was designed using inspiration (and unlicensed imported parts) from old American cars such as Cadillac, Buick, and Stalin's favorite, Packard. The head of the ZIS factory bought a prototype to the Kremlin for the leader himself to inspect. Stalin decided he didn't like the flamboyant hood (bonnet) mascot. This was hurriedly replaced.

The big old Buick engine was mated to a three-speed automatic gearbox and mounted in a long, heavy body using Buick panels. Some were cabriolets, some sedans (saloons), but almost all were painted black. The car's engine only did 11 miles per gallon (26.5 liters per 100 km) and barely topped 70 mph (115 kph). A few models were made into bulletproof armored cars with iron cladding; their engines had to be upgraded to 180 bhp (134 kW) to cope with the extra weight. A few 101s became ambulances.

Meanwhile, three young ZIS engineers developed their own version of the new vehicle: the 101A Sport, probably the most beautiful Russian car of all time. This two-door convertible had a long swooping body with a 141 bhp (105 kW) engine. Top speed was 100 mph (162 kph), although in a front-page article *Pravda* boasted it was 112 mph (180 kph). Only one was built in 1939 and sadly it hasn't survived.

At the beginning of World War II, most ZIS cars were put into storage as they couldn't cope with Russia's wartime roads. After the war, the car was slightly altered to become the 110, which, although very dated, continued in production until 1958. **SH**

500 Topolino | Fiat (I)

1936 • 34 cu in/569 cc, S4 • 13 bhp/10 kW • unknown • 53 mph/85 kph

Mickey Mouse, in most languages, is Mickey Mouse, but in Italy he's *Topolino*, meaning "Little Mouse." When Fiat launched its cute 500, it, too, became affectionately known as *il Topolino*.

This was Italy's Model T, 2CV or VW Bug. Fiat's managing director Giovanni Agnelli first got the idea for his "people's car" after visiting Ford's factory in 1922. He envisioned a car costing 5,000 lire (about £5,300 or $8,100 in modern money), capable of carrying two people in comfort with 110 pounds (50 kg) of luggage. In 1934, he gave the task to talented young designer Dante Giacosa, who looked after the engine, transmission, and chassis, while Rudolfo Schaffer, Fiat's resident coachwork designer, created the body.

At launch, the result was the world's smallest car, measuring only 10 feet 6 inches (3.2 m) long and weighing only 1,190 pounds (540 kg). It came with a fixed roof or a strip of fabric that rolled right back to the rear deck to let the sunshine in. The Topolino was never as cheap as Agnelli hoped, selling at 8,900 lire (£5,800 or $8,900 now). Its 569-cc engine gave it a pace just faster than a professional racing cyclist, but the payoff was 46.8 miles per gallon (6 liters per 100 km) economy. Classic-car enthusiasts prefer the restyled version with the overhead valve engine introduced in 1948, which increased the top speed to a heady 59 mph (95 kph).

The car ceased production in 1955, after 511,000 were made. It then began a second career on U.S. drag strips. Its light weight made it a popular choice for the Fuel Altered class, after Jim "Jazzy" Nelson made his name in an un-mouse-like "Topo" with a nitro-injected flathead Mercury V8. **LT**

57 Atlantic | Bugatti

(F)

1936 • 198 cu in/3,257 cc, S8 • 200 bhp/149 kW • 0–60 mph/97 kph in 10 seconds • 124 mph/200 kph

Got a spare $40 million lying around and fancy something a bit different? Then how about one of the most beautiful cars of all time, the Bugatti 57 Atlantic? One tiny problem: only four were ever produced, and only two of those still exist.

This striking, art deco coupe was designed personally by Jean Bugatti, son of the company founder Ettore. The car has a distinctive seam running up the body, which is actually a throwback to the original prototype: this was made of the alloy Elektron, which is highly flammable and had to be riveted together rather than welded. This created a ridge in the bodywork that was then replicated in the production cars, made of boring old aluminum.

Powering this work of art was an eight-cylinder engine that produced 175 bhp (130 kW) in standard form, but which reached 200 bhp (149 kW) with the addition of a supercharger. This took the rear-wheel-drive Atlantic up to 124 mph (200 kph).

Not everything about the car was as futuristic as its looks, though. It had a solid rear axle and leaf spring suspension, something more at home on an American muscle car than a European sportster.

But that can't eclipse the Atlantic's beauty or its legendary status. No one knows what happened to the prototype and only two of the aluminum cars have survived. One is owned by the American fashion designer Ralph Lauren. The other was owned by Peter Williamson, an American doctor and car collector. The car went up for auction in 2010 after he died. The exact sale price and the buyer remain a mystery but it's believed it changed hands for around $40 million. **SH**

W25K | Wanderer

(D)

1936 • 119 cu in/1,963 cc, S6 • 85 bhp/63 kW • unknown • 90 mph/145 kph

The familiar Audi symbol of four rings in a row came about when the company joined forces with three others to form the Auto Union in 1932. It was an attempt to band together to try to help each other ride out the country's economic problems. One of those four rings was for the Wanderer company, which first came into existence in 1896 and had been using the Wanderer name for its cars since 1911. One thing Wanderer brought to the Auto Union was its popular and powerful lightweight six-cylinder engine, with interchangeable cylinders, which had been designed by the renowned Dr. Ferdinand Porsche.

That engine was used in the company's 1936 W25K. It was an attractive, racy-looking two-seater car, much lighter in design than many of the mid-1930s German heavyweights. The cars were handmade, but still managed to be priced to appeal to a middle class audience. They, therefore, did not compete with the other members of the Auto Union, who made either upmarket or cheap cars. Apart from the four-rings trademark, the Wanderers were distinguished by a radiator grille shaped like a heraldic shield, which strangely enough gave the front of the car almost a smiling look.

The W25K had an exclusivity about it, with only 149 built in 1936, and a mere 250 manufactured in total when the car ceased production in 1939 with the prospect of war on the horizon. The war brought a complete end to the Wanderer's existence as the factories were destroyed by bombing and never rebuilt. In 2006 an original 1936 W25—the non-*kompressor* (supercharged) version of the car—came up for auction and was sold for $103,400 (£66,000). **MG**

Thanks to its successful racing past, the Alfa Romeo 8C 2900B is today one of the world's most expensive cars.

12/4 Continental | Riley (GB)

1937 • 91 cu in/1,496 cc, S4 • 51 bhp/38 kW • 0–50 mph/80 kph in 23.1 seconds • 73 mph/117 kph

The Riley 12/4 Continental didn't remain a Continental for long. Bentley had a monopoly on the term, and in the face of a Bentley legal challenge it was renamed the "Close-Couple Touring Saloon." The timing of the name change came late in production, after all the advertising was in place and catalogs had been printed praising the new "Riley Continental." Customers were confused and sales poor. The production run of the car lasted barely a year, with just twenty being made. Even though its body went on to survive in various guises on Riley's new 1938 chassis, customers remained unmoved, despite the body sitting prettier on the larger frame. To be fair, its departure may have been unfairly hastened by financial storm clouds that gathered throughout 1937, and which resulted in Riley going into receivership in February 1938.

The Continental was powered by one of Riley's most popular interwar engines, the 12/4, first launched in 1935. A complete departure from the Riley engines of the past, the 1.5-liter 12/4 replaced the 12/6, though it wouldn't be long until it, too, was replaced by Riley's new 2.5-liter, four-cylinder "Big 4."

Riley loved making automobiles, but they may have loved it too much. When the Continental was released in 1937 it joined an impressive list of twenty-two models in the Riley garage, all of which had a variety of body types available. It was easy for an individual Riley to be overlooked, even if it was a potentially good seller like the 12/4. "We make far too many models, of course," a Riley executive admitted in September 1936. "But then we have a pretty fertile design department, and we like making nice, interesting cars." **BS**

8C 2900B | Alfa Romeo (I)

1937 • 177 cu in/2,905 cc, S8 • 180 bhp/132 kW • 0–60 mph/97 kph in 9 seconds • 140 mph/225 kph

The 2900B was yet another successful development from the original Alfa Romeo 8C. The Mille Miglia Roadster (also known as the Spyder) is one of the most desirable cars in the world, helped by the fact that it had the ability not just to get up to 140 mph (224 kph) but to beat the competition over a thousand miles. That's some car.

In 1938 the 2900B took the first two places in the Mille Miglia, and one of those vehicles ended up in the car collection of fashion designer Ralph Lauren (who has over seventy rare cars in his possession). This was a special lightweight competition version of the car, but even the road-going version was the fastest roadster in the world when it appeared.

There was also a 2900B Le Mans Speciale version, although this proved less successful than the Mille Miglia. One was entered in the 1938 Le Mans and quickly built up a commanding lead of 100 miles (160 km), but technical problems forced it to withdraw. It did still manage to notch up the fastest lap speed, though, at 96.74 mph (154.78 kph). As late as 1951, the 2900B was still winning races.

When one of the Mille Miglia models—and not even one of the winning cars—came up for auction in 1999 it sold for over $4 million (£2.5 million), making it one of the world's most expensive cars. One of the Touring Berlinetta versions, of which only thirty-three were ever produced, is owned by the former president of Microsoft, Jon Shirley, and won a Best of Show at the Pebble Beach Concours d'Élégance in 2008. It was a benchmark model, the one from which all modern Alfa Romeos have subsequently emerged. **MG**

Alfa Romeo

Aprilia | Lancia

(I)

1937 • 82 cu in/1,352 cc, V4 • 47 bhp/55 kW • 0–60 mph/97 kph in 26 seconds • 80mph/128 kph

Vincenzo Lancia was born in a small village near Turin, Italy, in 1881, and had worked variously as a pilot, an engineer, and a Fiat racing driver before founding the Lancia car company in 1906. His first car, the Lancia Alfa, went on sale in 1908, but it was his revolutionary Lancia Aprilia for which he will be best remembered. It came out in February 1937—the month in which Lancia died from a heart attack. The Aprilia was the last car that he designed.

The Aprilia was also one of the first cars to be designed using a wind tunnel. Wind tunnels had been around for some time—the Wright brothers used one in 1901—but no one had ever applied one to a car's aerodynamic design before. The car doesn't look especially aerodynamic for its time, but the sleekly shaped rear end helped it achieve a record low drag coefficient of 0.47, even though its top speed remained comparatively modest. The main benefit to motorists was in its low fuel consumption.

An unusual feature was that its four doors had no pillars supporting them. The front doors opened forward and the rear doors opened backward, the doors meeting in the middle when closed.

The first series of the Aprilia sold 10,000 models, and a second series began production in 1939, with a beefed-up 1,486-cc engine. This remained in production until the Aprilia was retired in 1949. Around 18,000 were sold, which is one reason it remains a coveted car. Other models of the time were being produced in the hundreds of thousands. The actor Peter Ustinov drove a Lancia Aprilia, as did the cartoon character Tintin in his *Land of Black Gold* adventure. **MG**

T150C SS Goute d'Eau (Teardrop) | Talbot

F

1937 • 243 cu in/3,994 cc, S6 • 140 bhp/104 kW • 0–60 mph/97 kph in 13 seconds • 109 mph/175 kph

The Talbot T150C SS is one of the few cars that fitted the description "rolling sculpture," the ultimate expression of late 1930s streamlining when form was, for one brief, flamboyant moment, every bit as important as function. It was a racing car for drivers who weren't just interested in racing; they wanted to enter their curvaceously lined autos in concours d'elegance events when the race was over. There were two versions: five notchback coupes called "Jeancart," and eleven "Model New York" fastbacks. Each was unique, detailed according to the whims of its owner.

The Teardrop is remembered for its stunning futuristic body, the product of the collaboration between designer Giuseppe Figoni and businessman Ovidio Falaschi, who combined in 1935 to create the Parisian coachbuilding firm of Figoni et Falaschi. A protest against the squared-off designs of the 1920s, there was barely a straight line to be seen, prompting Figoni to claim he had achieved "speed without moving." It wasn't, however, just about looks. It also had a lightweight body, independent front suspension, and was powered by an Antonio Lago and Walter Brecchia–designed six-cylinder 140-bhp (104-kW) engine good enough to gain a podium finish at Le Mans in 1938.

The Teardrop was the most expensive car in the world, and it remains today one of the most expensive to purchase secondhand. Few cars can claim to be the most sought-after car in history, but the Teardrop—exclusive, expensive, fast, and designed to seduce from any angle—can make as good a case as any for that title. It was the high-water mark of car design, the automobile as art. **BS**

V12 | Lagonda (D)

1937 • 273 cu in/4,480 cc, V12 • 177 bhp/130 kW • unknown • 105 mph/169 kph

Wilbur Gunn began by building motorcycles, and in 1906 established the Lagonda company. He produced his first car in 1907, and when it won a trial drive between Moscow and St. Petersburg in 1910, success followed.

Sadly, Gunn died in 1920 before the company's first sports cars were built, but he would have been proud of the landmark V12. It was designed by W. O. Bentley, founder of Bentley Motors, which had been bought by Rolls-Royce in 1931. When relations between Bentley and Rolls-Royce soured, Bentley was lured to Lagonda by the offer to design a car that would better the V12 model that Rolls-Royce was working on, the Phantom III.

This Bentley did—eventually. Many early models had technical problems and had to be shipped back by their owners. It wasn't until the 1939 versions that perfection was reached, and when these were displayed at the 1939 New York Motor Show they were the highest-priced cars on display at $8,900 (£5,700).

Six months before the 1939 Le Mans race, Bentley was challenged by Lagonda's owner, Alan P. Good, to produce a V12 that could compete. Two Lagondas were ultimately entered for the twenty-four-hour race and, astonishingly, finished third and fourth. Only 190 Lagonda V12s were ever built, with production coming to a halt with the advent of World War II. **MG**

Y-Job | Buick (USA)

1938 • 320 cu in/5,247 cc, V8 • 141 bhp/105 kW • unknown • unknown

It is amazing what carmakers can conjure up when they don't need to actually sell something, when a car is created not to be driven but to provoke and inspire designers. This is the lot of the "concept car"—the one-offs destined for lives in museums or corporate headquarters. Well, it's better that way. Why mass produce even a few hundred of something like the Y-Job? It would only create envy. Better to make just one then squirrel it away somewhere so that the rest of us don't have to look at it. Life is hard enough already.

The Y-Job was invented by the great GM designer Harley Earl, who used it as his own personal car, but it was stylist, George Snyder, who penned the drawings. The car's dimensions are audacious—20 feet (6 m) long and just 5 feet (1.8 m) high. It sat on a production Buick chassis and previewed a host of design themes that Buick would use in years to come: power-operated concealed headlights, flush door handles, electric doors and windows, even an electric, foldaway roof.

But it was the look of the Y-Job that was so thrilling—fenders disappeared into doors, bumpers into bodywork. Earl named the car with a Y and not the usual X because he felt it went one step beyond other prototypes. The only Y-Job in existence can be found today at the GM Design Center in Michigan. And thank God for that. **BS**

Sixty Special | Cadillac (USA)

1938 • 346 cu in/5,670 cc, V8 • 130 bhp/97 kW • unknown • 90 mph/145 kph

The Sixty Special has been called the most important Cadillac ever made. That the name was only retired in 1993, after fifty-five years of production, says a lot. There was only a short gap in its lifespan, from 1976 to 1984, when Sixty Specials weren't being built in America.

The car was designed by Bill Mitchell, who spent all his life with General Motors and went on to design the 1963 Buick Riviera and the 1963 Corvette Stingray. For the Sixty Special, he did away with running boards, made the vehicle longer and lower, used Cadillac's standard powerful V8 engine, and put out a car that sold for a relatively modest sum of $2,080 (£1,340). It was a raging success from day one, and accounted for 39 percent of the total Cadillacs that were sold in 1938.

The 1939 model added a few more innovations, including an early sunroof design and retractable glass panels between the front and rear seats. The 1941 model was the last one to be taken from Mitchell's original design, but the new look did not detract from the car's popularity. In fact, a 1955 Sixty Special became one of the most famous cars in the world: Elvis Presley bought it for his mother, though she never drove it, and it became one of the King's favorite cars, which he painted pink. You can see it today at the Elvis Presley Car Museum near Graceland, in Memphis. **MG**

Dolomite Roadster | Triumph (GB)

1938 • 121 cu in/1,991 cc, S6 • 60 bhp/44 kW • 0–50 mph/80 kph in 15 seconds • 80 mph/129 kph

The Roadster grew out of the successful Triumph Dolomite series, but it was to have a rather short lifespan. The car was announced in April 1938, then in July 1939, Triumph went into receivership. It was bought out and production of the car continued, but the plant where they were made was destroyed in a German air raid in 1940. And that was the end of the Dolomite Roadster, of which only 200 were ever made.

This was a shame as it was an attractive-looking sports car, which could seat five people. On the down side, it was both less powerful and more expensive than the similar-looking Jaguar SS100. The Roadsters did incorporate some of the motoring world's latest features, however, such as windows that wound down, a leather-covered steering wheel, and spot lamps.

One of the brains behind the Triumph Dolomite series was Donald Healey, a racing driver and automotive engineer who won the 1931 Monte Carlo Rally. In 1935 he entered the Rally driving the very first Dolomite, the Straight 8, but he had to withdraw after colliding with a train in Denmark.

In 1944 Triumph was bought by Standard Motors. The Roadster name lived on with the introduction of new models, but they bore little resemblance to the originals. **MD**

Two Volkswagen Beetle prototypes are tested out on the new *autobahn* between Potsdam and Berlin, Germany, 1938. ⊡

328 Mille Miglia | BMW (D)

1939 • 120 cu in/1,971 cc, S6 • 135 bhp/99 kW • unknown • 120 mph/193 kph

When the BMW 328 came out in 1936, the standard model was impressive enough. But the ultimate car in the 328 series was the Mille Miglia model. Never was a car more worthy of the Mille Miglia name. In 1939 the 328 had already taken the first three places at Le Mans. The Mille Miglia race wasn't held in Italy that year after a fatal accident in 1938 caused the Italian leader Benito Mussolini to suspend it. Instead it was held in North Africa, on a stretch of road in Libya between Tobruk and Tripoli, and was a one-off event known as the African Mille Miglia. BMW entered three of their Mille Miglia specials in the race and took the top three places at the finishing line.

In 1940 Mussolini saw the wisdom of bringing the race back to Italy, and there were even some French entries despite the fact that the two countries had been at war for seven months. BMW entered again and this time didn't manage one-two-three, but instead finished first, third, fifth, and sixth; the winning car averaging 103.6 mph (166.7 kph). It's said that the BMW that finished third had been ordered to slow down so that an Italian Alfa Romeo could take second place to please Germany's Italian ally. The race wasn't quite a thousand miles, but was instead only 939 miles (1,502 km), as the cars drove nine laps of a closed 104.4-mile (167-km) triangular circuit between Brescia, Cremona, and Mantua.

As if the car's Mille Miglia performances at the time weren't enough, in 2004, in the Mille Miglia Storica race for classic cars, a 1939 BMW 328 became the first car to win both the original and the classic versions of the race. **MG**

Beetle | Volkswagen (D)

1939 • 60 cu in/995 cc, F4 • 29 bhp/19 kW • unknown • 56 mph/90 kph

German leader Adolf Hitler couldn't drive, but was a great car enthusiast. He recognized the impact cars from Ford, Citroen, and Austin were having across the world and in 1933 asked German carmaker Dr. Ferdinand Porsche to develop a *volkswagen*, or "people's car." National Socialists were fond of using *volks* to describe anything they did as a benefit for the mass of the population.

Hitler had some strict requirements for the design. It had to be built to carry two adults and three children at a speed of 100 kph (62 mph). It was also to have a very low price—just under 990 Reichsmarks, or about thirty weeks pay for an average worker, just above the cost of a motorcycle.

Porsche was the right choice. He had already been planning "a car for everybody" with a rear-mounted flat-four engine. By 1935 he had prototype Beetles testing on Germany's new autobahns. Production at a grand new purpose-built factory finally started in 1939—just months before World War II started. So it wasn't until 1946 that Beetles were rolling off the production line at speed. The car that finally emerged was one of motoring's biggest ever success stories. More than 21 million were built during the longest production run of any single car design. It was still being built in 2003.

The ingredients were simple: an air-cooled engine was sited in the back of a curved body and powered the rear wheels. There were only two doors, but seats for five. For the era, it was well built, reliable, sturdy, economical, and simple to fix. And—most importantly of all—the *volks'* car had a likable character that endeared it to millions. **BK**

Champion | Studebaker

USA

1939 • 163 cu in/2,687 cc, S6 • 78 bhp/57 kW • unknown • 80 mph/128 kph

The Studebaker company had been founded back in 1852 to make, among other things, farm wagons. They eventually went into automobile production, but suffered more than most during the Depression. By 1933 they were $6 million (£3.9 million) in debt and company president Russel Erskine committed suicide. Through restructuring and refinancing with the aid of others such as Lehman Brothers, Studebaker continued trading and put all their energies into what would be a new low-price, lightweight automobile. This became the Studebaker Champion, an apt name as it turned out because the car transformed the company's fortunes.

People have described the Champion as the world's first green car, as its fuel consumption was low for the time at an average of 27.25 miles per gallon (11.6 km per liter). It was also one of the lightest cars on the market, and cost a modest $660 (£425). Studebaker sold 30,000 of them in the first year, which doubled the company's sales figures and ensured the survival of the company's name (although it eventually disappeared in 1979).

While the outbreak of World War II caused many U.S. car manufacturers to suffer, Studebaker's Champion thrived thanks to its low fuel consumption in the years when gasoline was rationed by the U.S. government. Studebaker had also always been a supplier of military vehicles during times of conflict, right back to the Civil War, and this, too, helped the company's fortunes.

By 1947, after a successful relaunch, the Champion was responsible for 65 percent of all Studebaker sales. It remained the company's main car right up to 1958, when production ceased and it was replaced by the rather less impressively named Studebaker Lark. **MG**

Continental | Lincoln

USA

1939 • 292 cu in/4,789 cc, V12 • 120 bhp/89 kW • unknown • 78 mph/125 kph

The Lincoln Continental ought to have a good pedigree, as the first model was built as a one-off production model intended for the personal use of Edsel Ford, Henry Ford's son. He wanted it built in time for his March 1939 holiday in Florida, the kind of thing you can request when you own a motor company. At this point Lincoln was a subdivision of the Ford Motor Company. The car had to be shipped out to Ford in Palm Springs, but the reaction of his friends and neighbors to his new car was so positive that he decided to put it out commercially. It went into production in December 1939, almost identical in design to the private prototype, and it remained virtually unchanged until 1942.

Production of the Continental was interrupted after the Japanese attack on Pearl Harbor in December 1941, brought the United States into World War II. The 1942 Continentals were the last to be made for a few years, although the design had changed a lot by that point and the cars were longer and wider than their predecessors, with a bigger front end.

Production resumed in 1946, but only lasted for a couple of years. The 1948 models of the Lincoln Continental were the last in the United States to feature a V12 engine, although some cars in Europe and in Japan have subsequently used V12s. In 1956 Ford introduced the Lincoln Continental Mark II, and gave it some "oomph." At a price of $10,000 (£6,400), the same as a Rolls-Royce, it was one of the most expensive cars in the world. The Continental stayed in production until 2002, giving it one of the longest overall production runs of any vehicle. **MG**

Jeep | Willys

USA

1941 • 134 cu in/2,199 cc, S4 • 60 bhp/45 kW • unknown • 60 mph/96 kph

The Jeep was the first mass-produced off-roader and is the forerunner of all modern SUVs. Today this lightweight four-wheel-drive utility vehicle could be classed as the world's most recognizable car and its famous name has become a generic term.

Where exactly this name came from remains a mystery, though. Some say it derives from the military abbreviation "GP" (short for "General Purpose"), others say it was named after the Eugene the Jeep character in 1930s Popeye cartoons.

The Jeep's main claim to fame is, of course, as the utility vehicle for the Allied forces in World War II. At the request of the American government it had been roughly designed in forty-nine days and was produced in huge numbers very quickly. The vehicle could climb a 40-degree slope, tilt sideways at 50 degrees without tipping, and had a tiny 30-feet (9-m) turning circle. With special adaptors on the wheels it could run on railroad tracks and could pull 25 tons at 20 mph. Its flat hood (bonnet) could serve as a map table, church altar, or card table. The Jeep itself could serve as an ambulance, gun-carriage, or reconnaissance vehicle.

The spartan build was so simple that military engineers are still trained to swap their drivetrains and bodies within minutes. And according to legend, the original rudimentary engine would run on either gasoline or diesel.

Willys was the creator of this ultimate symbol of American industrial power that helped win the war, but many other vehicle manufacturers were licensed to build the Jeep for the Allied forces during the war, including Ford, Kaiser, and Bantam. **JB**

Town & Country | Chrysler

(USA)

1941 • 241 cu in/3, 957 cc, S6 • 115 bhp/84.6 kW • unknown • unknown

It's been described as "a lumberyard on wheels," and although the Chrysler Town & Country that was introduced in 1941 wasn't the first station wagon to have wooden sides, it was the first model to combine them with a sturdy steel roof. It was also the first model to be referred to as a "woody wagon," a style of vehicle that became incredibly popular with the Californian surfing community in the 1950s and 1960s. The steel roof gave it extra strength, to carry all those surfboards, while inside there was room for either six or nine passengers (at least officially), as the cars contained either two or three three-person bench seats. Only 797 of the nine-passenger Town & Country models were built in 1941, of which just a handful survive today—thereby making them eminently collectible.

One reason they are so rare is, of course, the fact that the wood can easily deteriorate. The first models used a mix of ash and mahogany, and it was recommended that the wood be revarnished every year. Many owners either forgot or couldn't be bothered.

The unusual name came about because Chrysler wanted it to be a car that could be used in both the town and the country, though some people said the front was designed for the town and the back for the country, rather than having an integrated design. One of the first models to come off the production line was bought by Warner Bros. Studios, which used it in films by Our Gang and Charlie Chaplin, among others. You can also see the Town & Country in the 1978 version of *Superman*, in *Starsky and Hutch* (1970s), and in the Woody Allen movie, *Play it Again, Sam* (1972). **MG**

50 60 70 80

The interior of a 1953 Cadillac Eldorado; the model underwent a major redesign in 1959.

1945–1959

TC Midget | MG

GB

1945 • 76 cu in/1,250 cc, S4 • 54.5 bhp/40.6 kW • 0–60 mph/97 kph in 22.7 seconds • 79 mph/126 kph

The MG Car Company was founded in 1924, and made a permanent name for itself from the 1930s onward through its open-top, two-seater MG Midget sports cars—though it did produce other cars, too. The first model, the TA, appeared in 1936, and the TB in 1939 (a rare vehicle as only 379 were ever made).

After the interruption of the war years, the TC Midget appeared in 1945 and was a great success. MG produced 10,000 of them in its four-year existence, many of which were exported to the United States, even though the company only ever built a British right-hand-drive version. It was the start of a productive relationship for MG, and later, in the 1960s and 1970s, over 70 percent of its MGB models were sold in the U.S.

Quite why the TC Midget was such a hit is open to debate. It wasn't a particularly powerful car, and could barely reach 80 mph (128 kph) for brief periods when flat out. The plus side of this was that it was much more maneuverable than other cars, especially American models, and was very low on fuel consumption. Its appeal also had something to do with a feeling of British optimism, following the horrors of war. But whatever the reason, the TC Midget became the archetypal British sports car of its day—even in the United States. One of the more peculiar aspects of its design was that the speedometer was in front of the passenger's seat, not the driver's, but this certainly didn't harm sales.

Sadly, the man who founded MG Motors, Cecil Kimber, died in a train accident at King's Cross Station in London in February 1945, and never saw the postwar success that MG enjoyed. **MG**

Silver Wraith | Rolls-Royce

GB

1946 • 259 cu in/4,257 cc, S6 • unknown • 0–60 mph/97 kph in 16.2 seconds • 88 mph/141 kph

The Silver Wraith was the first postwar car made by Rolls-Royce, and it demonstrates just why the company's name was synonymous with exclusivity. Although the Silver Wraith remained in production for thirteen years, until 1959, only 1,883 of them were ever built. Interestingly, for the first two years of its life, the car was only available for export—it didn't go on sale in Britain until 1948.

In 1951 the engine capacity was increased to 278 cubic inches (4,566 cc), and again to 298 cubic inches (4,887 cc) three years later. The power that the Rolls-Royce engines generated is unknown, as Rolls-Royce never gave out the figures. What is known, however, is that what was regarded at the time as the best car in the world was unwieldy to drive and very expensive to run. If you were to buy one today you would also find the spare parts hard to find, and a Silver Wraith in excellent condition costs about £30,000 ($46,500), which is relatively modest for a classic car.

The first Silver Wraiths continued the Rolls-Royce tradition of only delivering a chassis to the car owner, who then had to find someone to build the car's body for them—that's why so many of the early model Wraiths look so different. Nevertheless, the car remained photogenic and has appeared in numerous movies from the 1960s through the 1990s, including *Batman*, *Victim*, *Withnail and I*, *Get Carter*, *Annie Hall*, *The Talented Mr. Ripley*, *From Russia with Love*, *The Return of the Pink Panther*, and *The Love Bug*. The Silver Wraith was the last car to be sold on the basis of the body being built separately, as the number of companies who were able to do this work was dwindling. **MG**

1955-D

The rear-engine design of the Renault 4CV meant that the trunk (boot) was located at the front of the car.

4CV | Renault (F)

1946 • 46 cu in/760 cc, S4 • 21 bhp/16 kW • 0–56 mph/90 kph in 38 seconds • 62 mph/100 kph

With cheeky good looks and frugal running costs, it's no surprise that the Renault 4CV sold so well in its fourteen-year production run. It was the first French model to sell over a million cars.

The 4CV had been developed secretly during World War II. Renault factories in France had been taken over by Nazi occupiers, so engineers kept their development ideas hidden. Their plan was to make a car that would be cheap and simple, to cope with anticipated postwar austerity.

So when the war ended Renault had the designs ready. A former French Resistance hero was put in charge of the newly nationalized company and a year later the first 4CV car was shown at the Paris Motor Show, to great acclaim. The next year, the new car started rolling off the production line.

The prediction about the state of France after the war was accurate. There was little money available. The 4CV matched the national mood. It was offered in only blue, with just one engine available. The curvaceous little car had a durable build with four doors, four seats, and an engine at the rear driving the wheels at the back.

That rear engine allowed space for a roomy cabin and the light weight (just 1,234 lbs/560 kg) made it fun and economical to drive, although it broke no speed records. Later there was an attractive convertible and a sporty version with a much larger 1,063-cc engine.

This sporting 4CV notched several notable victories, including the Monte Carlo Rally and Le Mans 24 Hour Race. It was easily modifiable and attracted the attention of Jean Redele, whose Alpine race tuning company would later become closely linked to Renault. **SH**

115 | ZIS (SU)

1946 • 366 cu in/6,005 cc, S8 • 160 bhp/118 kW • unknown • 87 mph/140 kph

Plenty of people have had cars named after them, but how about an entire car company? Soviet leader Joseph Stalin had no problem with the idea, adding his own name to the Russian car firm ZIS—Zavod Imeni Stalina, or "factory dedicated to Stalin."

Uncle Joe liked his cars, particularly the American luxury brand Packard (the Communist leader had been given one by President Roosevelt as a gift during World War II). In fact, he liked them so much he made ZIS build their own version, possibly with dies taken from the Packard factory.

The ZIS 115 was his own personal transport—if you can call a chauffeur driven, six-tonne beast personal. The reason it weighed so much was partly down to its overall size—it was nearly 20 feet (6 m) long. But it was also weighed down by Stalin's own paranoia. The passenger compartment inside the 115 was actually an armored chamber, virtually a car within a car, kept separate from the driver. It had windows that were raised and lowered by hydraulics. The glass was 3 inches (7.5 cm) thick, strong enough to fend off not just capitalist bullets but imperialist grenades, too.

To handle all this weight the tires had to be of a special industrial design (which sadly meant Stalin couldn't use the same white-walled tires as the Packard) and the solid rear axle was taken from a ZIS truck. Its 366-cubic-inch (6,005-cc), eight-cylinder engine strained to move it, reaching only 87 mph (140kph).

Around forty 115s were produced in total, which is just as well because it's said that Stalin, terrified of assassination attempts, refused to use the same car for two days running. **JI**

A T26 Grand Sport with bodywork designed by Jacques Saoutchik, displayed at an auto show in Paris, France, 1948. ⊡

Tama Electric | Prince (J)

1947 • electric motor • 4.5 bhp/3.3 kW • unknown • 22 mph/35 kph

Prince had switched from making Zero fighters for the Japanese air force during the war to trying to build cars in an old borrowed factory in postwar Tokyo. Japan was suffering an extreme shortage of fuel. There seemed little point building a gasoline-powered car with strict rationing in place.

So the unemployed aircraft engineers created a pioneering electric car with surprisingly cute looks. The body was steel, but it was mounted on a wooden frame. There was a truck version and a passenger car, with simple robust interiors featuring bench seats and metal dashboards. It had flick-out orange indicators, a vertical trunk (boot) lid below the back window, and a flip-up hood (bonnet) accessed by a lever hidden under the badge. In here was a cable to connect the car to a domestic electricity supply for charging.

This two-door, four-seater Tama was slow, but had a useful range of more than 60 miles (96 km) per charge. The lead-acid batteries were stored under the cockpit floor. You simply opened flaps under the door to access them. They were large and heavy, but had built-in rollers so they could be easily extracted and replaced with charged substitute units. By 1949 the larger Tama Senior was capable of 124 miles (200 km) on a charge. Tama Electrics were widely used as taxis in Japan until 1950.

Prince went on to become part of Nissan, which still owns the first Tama Electric that rolled off the production line. It was recently used to entertain motoring journalist passengers at the launch of the Leaf electric car. More than sixty years after it was built, the Tama astonished the writers by accelerating briskly and almost silently from a standstill to round a special test track. **SH**

T26 Grand Sport | Talbot-Lago (F)

1947 • 273 cu in/4,482 cc, S6 • 170 bhp/126.8 kW • 0–60 mph/97 kph in 10 seconds • 124 mph/200 kph

The Talbot-Lago company emerged from the ashes of the collapse of Sunbeam-Talbot-Darracq in 1935, when the Austrian engineer Anthony Lago stepped in and founded what would become a potent name in automotive history. Lago's aim was to produce both exceptional racing cars and luxurious roadsters, and it would be the cars designed for him by the Italian duo of Figoni and Falaschi that would prove to be the company's landmark machines.

Falaschi was the business brain of the team, but Figoni was an artist who sculpted in metal. Thankfully for car lovers he chose automobile design as a way of expressing himself. It is said that he hated the wind, and his striking car shapes were his way of trying to get the better of it. Figoni and Falaschi also designed the Delahaye 135M, among other Delahaye models, as well as working for Bugatti and Alfa Romeo, but it is the several fine vehicles they designed for Talbot-Lago for which they are best known.

The greatest of these was the T26 Grand Sport, although they didn't make all of them. It was common then for the car company to produce the chassis and for the bodywork to be farmed out to different companies, or for the customer to arrange their own. Figoni and Falaschi vehicles were the most sought-after, though, and still are. They were prized for their looks but also their performance, beating the competition—and the wind—to win the 1950 Le Mans 24-Hour Race. A 1947 T26 was bought by the movie director George Sidney, known for films such as *Pal Joey* (1957), *Viva Las Vegas* (1964), and *Kiss Me, Kate* (1953). The car was as much a hit in Hollywood as it was at Le Mans. **MG**

LE L'AUTOMOBILE
CATALOGUE
Carrosserie
SAOUTCHIK

PV444 | Volvo

(S)

1947 • 86 cu in/1,414 cc, S4 • 44 bhp/33 kW unknown • 76 mph/122 kph

The PV444 was the car that established Volvo. It was a tough, go-anywhere vehicle, capable of delivering Swedes to their destination despite freezing winters and loose-surfaced roads. It was also gutsy and fun to drive.

Most carmakers were busy making planes and munitions during World War II. In neutral Sweden, Volvo decided that a new, smaller car, with good fuel economy, would assure the company's future come peacetime.The PV444 was presented in September 1944, but it didn't hit the road until 1947. The price was attractive at 4,800 Swedish krona ($695 or £451), the same as for Volvo's first car in 1927. Its looks were influenced by prewar Yank-tanks, with chunky fenders (bumpers) and a rounded fastback with a divided rear window. Modern features included a unitary body and a laminated windshield. Interest was huge and production soared to almost 200,000 before the PV444 became the PV544 in 1958.

In 1956, it gained a 70 bhp (52 kW) 96-cubic-inch (1,583-cc) engine with one Zenith carburetor, then in 1957 it was given twin SU carburetors and 85 bhp (63.5 kW), and reached 95 mph (153 kph). The PV gathered more plaudits at international rallies; Gunnar Andersson became European Rally Champion driving one in 1958. The Volvo badge now meant solid, resilient, and safe—a reputation that stuck. **LT**

202SC | Cisitalia

(I)

1947 • 66 cu in/1,088 cc, S4 • 55 bhp/40 kW • 0–60 mph/97 kph in 13 seconds • 100 mph/161 kph

Car writers can sometimes get carried away in describing certain models as works of art or masterpieces. In the case of the Cisitalia 202SC the description is justified as the car was chosen for an art exhibition called "Eight Automobiles" that went on show at New York's prestigious Museum of Modern Art (MoMA) in 1951.

Cisitalia made its debut in 1946 with the D46, a small car that met with success on the racing circuit. The company was already looking to build on this, and had commissioned Ferdinand Porsche to design them a more powerful single-seater car that could compete on the Grand Prix circuit. This would have been the Cisitalia 360 if it hadn't been too expensive to proceed with.

In the meantime, along came the 202 series. The design chosen for the 202SC was by Battista Farina, who excelled himself. The body was conceived as a single shell, a first at the time, and the result was a beautiful car with smooth, flowing lines that give the impression of speed and air sweeping over it even when standing still.

Not only was the car chosen by MoMA for its exhibition, it also appeared in the hugely successful 2011 video game L.A. Noire. It is far from being just an object of beauty, though. In the 1947 Mille Miglia, Cisitalia took three of the first four places. **MG**

8C Monterosa | Isotta Fraschini (I)

1947 • 207 cu in/3,400 cc, V8 • 125 bhp/92 kW • unknown • over 100 mph/161 kph

Before the war, John Wayne, Claudette Colbert, the Pope, the Aga Khan, and Mussolini had all driven Isotta Fraschini cars. Surely, all this luxury carmaker needed was a sleek new model to recapture its past glories?

The problem was that the 8C was launched into a destitute postwar Europe needing small, economical "people's cars." What Isotta Fraschini released was the huge 8C Monterosa. At around $10,000 (£6,300), it cost more than twice as much as the biggest, most luxurious chauffeur-driven Cadillac or Packard. It was doomed.

The eccentric 8C had a rear-mounted V8 and an aluminum body. Zagato designed the huge, sweeping four-door sedan (saloon) body that was first shown at the motor show in Paris. There was also a two-door model and a boat-tailed cabriolet—all by different designers.

The mechanics were a mix of quirky and advanced: the engine drove the rear wheels through an advanced all-syncromesh five-speed gearbox with overdrive. There were hydraulic brakes and rubber suspension. Features included spring-opening doors, plastic rear window, camelskin seats, and powered-opening wheel fenders.

Only a handful were made and it was the company's last ever car. The name lived on briefly, though, when actor James Dean drove an Isotta Fraschini 8A from the 1930s in his last film, *Giant* (1956). **SH**

A90 Atlantic | Austin (GB)

1948 • 162 cu in/2,660 cc, S4 • 88 bhp/66 kW • 0–60 mph/97 kph in 15.8 seconds • 91 mph/146 kph

One look at the Austin A90 Atlantic and you can tell it was designed with both the U.K. and U.S. markets in mind. It is halfway between a sprightly two-seater British sports car and a more solid-looking American sedan (saloon) of the time. It provided fairly good performance, but was heavy on fuel usage and rather clumsy to drive.

The Atlantic first went on sale in 1948, and Austin put a lot of money and effort into launching it in the United States. One reason behind this was that at that time in Britain, the government restricted the supply of steel to those manufacturers who needed it to create exports. To try to increase appeal to the American market, Austin made the car available in a range of what, to British tastes, were quite garish colors.

The result of all this was that the car fell between two stools. Only about 350 models were ever sold in the States, even after the price was dropped by $1,000 (£650). To the American car buyer the Atlantic wasn't as powerful as equivalent U.S. models, nor was it as nimble and appealing as the TC Midget, which was already being successfully exported to the United States by MG.

Less than 8,000 Atlantics were ever built, and few survive today because it was prone to rust. Production ceased in 1952, but the car can still claim its place in history as a bold but flawed experiment. **MG**

401 | Bristol

GB

1948 • 122 cu in/2,000 cc, S6 • 85 bhp/62 kW • 0–60 mph (97 kph) in 17.4 seconds • 97 mph/156 kph

The car division of the Bristol Aeroplane Company was born after World War II, and the Bristol 401 was its second production model. With room for five passengers, the 401 was luxurious and fast and soon won the acclaim of journalists and enthusiasts. It was obvious that the world-famous Bristol Aeroplane Company had successfully applied its know-how and experience to build a high-quality, first-class automobile.

The body of the earlier Bristol 400 had taken design cues from the prewar BMW 326, 327, and 328, partly because Bristol had acquired the plans for those cars as war reparations. Four prototypes were built by 1946, all featuring desirable parts of the prewar BMWs.

After a short production run of the Bristol 400, the Bristol 401 sedan (saloon) was launched in 1948. The new 401 was fast, and its finish compared well with the more expensive and prestigious cars of its day. But it was also very expensive, selling for £2,000 ($3,000).

The 401's 122-cubic-inch (2-liter), six-cylinder engine produced an 85-bhp (62-kW) output, which was impressive for the time. The Bristol could cruise at almost 100 mph (156 kph), and, again, this was impressive in the late 1940s. More, the Bristol did it in a relaxed, refined manner, and the roomy interior was very quiet at speed.

The Bristol 401 was one of very few cars of the day that had been developed in a wind tunnel, and that was due to the company's aeronautical background. Its body was built with complete rigidity, too, and was well braced for maximum stiffness. The body panels were made of aircraft-quality light alloy, and panel gaps were tight and well crafted. The 401 was very much the car for the dashing postwar British gentleman. **BK**

2CV | Citroën

(F)

1948 • 22 cu in/375 cc, S2 • 9 bhp/6.6 kW • unknown • 40 mph/64 kph

While the Volkswagen Beetle is championed as the original people's car, the Citroën 2CV would have got there first had it not been for the outbreak of World War II.

The concept of the 2CV (pronounced *deux chevaux* by the French) dates back to research done in the 1920s by the Michelin tire company. The idea was to progress the masses from the horse and cart by creating a cheap and rugged "umbrella on four wheels" capable of carrying four people and 110 pounds (50 kg) of farm goods at 30 mph (50 kph). Work on turning the vision into reality began in 1936, but the launch date of October 1939 was postponed because of the war. The car was finally unveiled at the 1948 Paris Motor Show. Going on sale twelve months later, it lasted for forty-two years.

Key to its appeal was its user-friendly practicality. The simple engine was easily maintained, the long-travel suspension created a soft ride, and high sills gave excellent clearance over rough ground.

The car was an instant hit. Within months of its launch there was a three-year waiting list, and that eventually increased to five years. A secondhand 2CV commanded a higher price than a new one simply because buyers were impatient to become owners.

Close to 9 million of the original 2CV were eventually built, including mechanically identical versions such as the Ami, Dyane, and Mehari. There was even a delivery van version. Manufacture of the 2CV took place everywhere, including the United Kingdom, Uruguay, Portugal, Spain, Slovenia, and Chile. Numerous special editions were launched to maintain the public's interest, including the Cocorico, in support of the French football team competing in the 1986 FIFA World Cup. **RY**

A 1954 advertisement for the Porsche 356: hopeful buyers have been circling its image in pen ever since it launched.

T600 Tatraplan | Tatra (CS)

1948 • 119 cu in/1,952 cc, S4 • 52 bhp/39 kW • 0–50 mph/80 km in 22 seconds • 80 mph/130 kph

The Tatra T600 Tatraplan was built in postwar Czechoslovakia, and it is tempting to say that it was too beautiful a car for the only customers permitted to purchase it: Czech government departments and state security services. After all, the Eastern Bloc was a world full of Zaporozhets, Volgas, and Trabants, whose rear windows were heated—as the joke went—so that their owners' hands could be warmed when pushing them. For a car like the T600 to emerge from such a design desert was nothing short of miraculous.

The car's Austrian-born designer, Hans Ledwinka, burst onto the world stage in 1933 with the streamlined T77, which caused a sensation at that year's Berlin Autosalon. The T77 was good, but with the T600, Ledwinka had outdone himself. The T600 was a "fastback," meaning its roof sloped continuously all the way to its rear fender (bumper), a classic teardrop shape that fully enclosed the chassis and the wheels to produce a drag coefficient of just 0.32. Ledwinka had reduced the weight of the T600's predecessor, the T97, and distributed it evenly across the chassis. He had improved its economy, given it a futuristic, pressed-steel body, and vastly increased its interior space and comfort. And it was fast—T600s took the first four places at the 1949 Rally of Austria.

Tatra was unusual for its time in faithfully pursuing aerodynamic principles in car design, and it paid off. The T600 was a timeless milestone in the continuing evolution of the motorcar. In 2010 British enthusiasts voted the T600 the classic car of the 1940s, when, for one brief moment, it was entirely proper to say, "Move over Porsche, Ferrari, and Fiat—the Czechs are coming." **BS**

356 | Porsche (D)

1948 • 67 cu in/1,100 cc, S4 • 40 bhp/29.8 kW • 0–60 mph/97 kph in 17 seconds • 87 mph/139 kph

Quite simply, this is the car on which the entire Porsche reputation is built. It was compact and simple, and remains as classically beautiful today as it did at launch.

After leaving Mercedes, Ferdinand Porsche set up his own design consultancy in 1931. However, it would be another seventeen years before a production car appeared that bore his name—actually created by his son, Ferdinand "Ferry" Porsche. The company hadn't been resting on its laurels, though; the name related to the 356th project Porsche had undertaken.

Available as a two-door coupe or cabrio with a rear-mounted engine and rear-wheel drive, the car was famed for its low weight and nimble handling. It was closely related to the Volkswagen Beetle—another Porsche design—and used much of the mechanical hardware of that car. But the 356 was updated regularly, with a focus on performance that quickly moved it away from its roots. It achieved regular success on the racetrack and rally circuits, notably at the 24 Hours of Le Mans in France and the Mille Miglia in Italy.

Assured of its place in automotive history, the Porsche 356 is much loved. Experts believe that around half of the 76,000 built—before the car was replaced by the 911—have survived. One of the most desirable is the Speedster from 1954. The American importer Max Hoffman told Porsche that a stripped-out, cut-price convertible would go down well stateside, so the company got to work on it. Californians loved its removable windshield and bucket seats. Iconic American actor James Dean owned and raced a Speedster, and the Porsche 550 Spyder in which he crashed and died was based on the 356. **RY**

PORSCHE
Drive it and be envied
Typ 356
Cabriolet

48-215 | Holden

(AUS)

1948 • 131 cu in/2,160 cc, S6 • 60 bhp/44 kW • 0–60 mph/97 kph in 28 seconds • 80 mph/130 kph

The Holden name goes back to the Australian gold rush of the 1850s, when the company began to make saddles and other outback essentials. It later began to build and repair horse-drawn carriages, before starting in the auto business in 1908. The company later flourished as a subsidiary of General Motors, and the two companies merged in 1931 to establish the name of General Motors-Holden's Limited.

Early cars in Australia either came from overseas or were only partly built at home. It was only in 1948, with the arrival of the Holden 48-215 (also known as the FX), that Australians were able to buy the first all-Australian mass-produced car. It was not 100 percent Aussie, however. Chevrolet had designed it for production in 1938, but it was ultimately rejected as being too small a vehicle for American buyers. Holden stepped in, and had three prototypes built in Detroit before deciding to produce the car in Australia for the home market. It was an important step for Australia, and the car was launched by the country's prime minister, Ben Chifley.

The Holden was a great success, as naturally Australians liked the thought of buying an Australian car rather than an American or European model. The 48-215 had a respectable top speed, and could cruise comfortably for hours at a steady 65 mph (104 kph). It had a dustproof body, which was popular with buyers, as was the fact that it had enough brute force to climb even steep hills without moving out of top gear. It was definitely an Australian car, and Holden went on to monopolize the car market there. Only one of those three original 48-215 prototypes has survived, and it resides today at the National Museum of Australia. **MG**

Dyna 110 | Panhard

(F)

1948 • 37 cu in/610 cc, S2 • 24 bhp/18 kW • unknown • 60 mph/110 kph

When movie and TV producers need a vehicle to set the scene for postwar rural France, they often choose a Panhard Dyna 110 van. Bakers and postmen are seen chugging around in these vans, which definitely have a lovable look to them as well as a period charm.

The Dyna 110, also known as the Dyna X, was a complete change in direction for the Panhard company, which had been selling cars since 1890 and had built up a reputation for producing plush and luxurious cars for the upper echelons of French society.

Seeing postwar austerity ahead, however, the company made the wise move toward building a cheap little vehicle that would have a simple engine and wouldn't use much gas. The move saw the company chug along just like the Dyna 110 did, without ostentation but most importantly without going out of business, as happened to some prewar rivals who remained too focused on pricier cars.

As well as its useful little van, Panhard offered the Dyna in two-door, three-door, and four-door versions. The Dyna 110, Dyna 120, and Dyna 130 were named after the maximum speeds in kilometers per hour that their engine sizes could produce. None of the engines had a radiator; instead, all were air-cooled, requiring only a tiny grille low down on the front.

The car stayed in production until 1954, by which time about 47,000 had been sold, a respectable number for a modest car, especially in the context of rival models from the much larger Renault and Citroën. The Dyna family certainly made enough money to usher Panhard through the postwar years and to help it stay in business until 1967. **MG**

Boxer Sugar Ray Robinson leans on his pink Series 61 Cadillac in front of part of his New York business empire in 1950. ▷

DeLuxe | Ford

USA

1948 • 225 cu in/3,700 cc, V8 • 95 bhp/71 kW • 0–60 mph/97 kph in 21.2 seconds • 81 mph/130 kph

In 1938 Ford introduced its Deluxe line of cars, and movie history was made. It is on the trunk (boot) of a 1948 Deluxe that John Travolta bounces his butt in the film version of *Grease* (1978) in the well-known "Greased Lightning" scene, and it is a 1946 Super Deluxe that bad guy Biff Tannen drives in the first two *Back to the Future* films. It is this car that gets filled with manure in the films, although when it came up for sale recently, the sellers wanted to point out that it was cork rather than real manure that was used. The car was on offer, incidentally, for $29,998 (£19,200).

The movie roll call doesn't end there. The Deluxe features in dozens of other films, including *American Graffiti* (1973), *The Wild One* (1953), *The Last Picture Show* (1971), *Bad Day at Black Rock* (1955), *Lolita* (1962), *North by Northwest* (1959), and in car chases in *The Twilight Zone* (1983) and *It's a Wonderful Life* (1946). Perhaps one of the reasons for the car's popularity with moviemakers was its heart-shaped grille, which was one of the few features that differentiated it from other Ford models when it was first introduced. In later years, the heart shape was altered to make it less emphatic.

In 1941 Ford introduced another level of car, installing its Super Deluxe models alongside those merely termed Deluxe. The Super Deluxe was available in several styles, including a convertible with an impressive new feature: an electrically operated top.

By 1947 the Fords were showing their age, as indeed was Henry Ford, who died that year. The year 1948 saw the end of the main Deluxe production run. As it happened, the last car Henry drove was a dark-blue 1942 Ford Super Deluxe sedan (saloon). **MG**

Series 61 | Cadillac

USA

1948 • 346 cu in/5,670 cc, S6 • 150 bhp/112 kW • unknown • 95 mph/152 kph

The Cadillac Series 61 had a checkered and slightly confusing history. It was introduced in 1939 to replace the Series 60 (although the luxurious Sixty Special remained in production). The Series 61 was then retired in 1940 in favor of the Series 62, only to be brought back into production again in 1941. It was then retired from 1943 to 1945, and reintroduced in 1946. It was the 1948 redesign, though, that made it stand out from the crowd—at least for a short while. It was finally retired in 1951 as a result of falling sales.

The most distinctive change made for the 1948 model was the addition of tail fins for a slightly more space-age look, although the interior of the car remained fairly plain. The new Series 61 was reasonably light and fast, too, and initially it attracted buyers.

In 1949 the model received a boost—as did most Cadillacs—when the company introduced its revolutionary V8 engine. This boosted the 61's power from 150 bhp (112 kW) to 160 bhp (119 kW). All the later Series 61 models benefited from the V8.

The 1951 model was redesigned yet again. It kept the tail fins, had a shorter wheelbase and a longer hood (bonnet), and it sat lower to the ground. But the changes were not enough to save it from the scrap heap. By 1951 sales had taken a turn for the worse, despite the improvements, and production ceased.

Images of the Series 61 still live on, though, most recently in the award-winning video game, L.A. Noire, where both the hardtop and convertible versions of the 1947 model appear. The 1948 model, recognizable by its tail fins, often could be seen being driven in the background of period Hollywood movies. **MG**

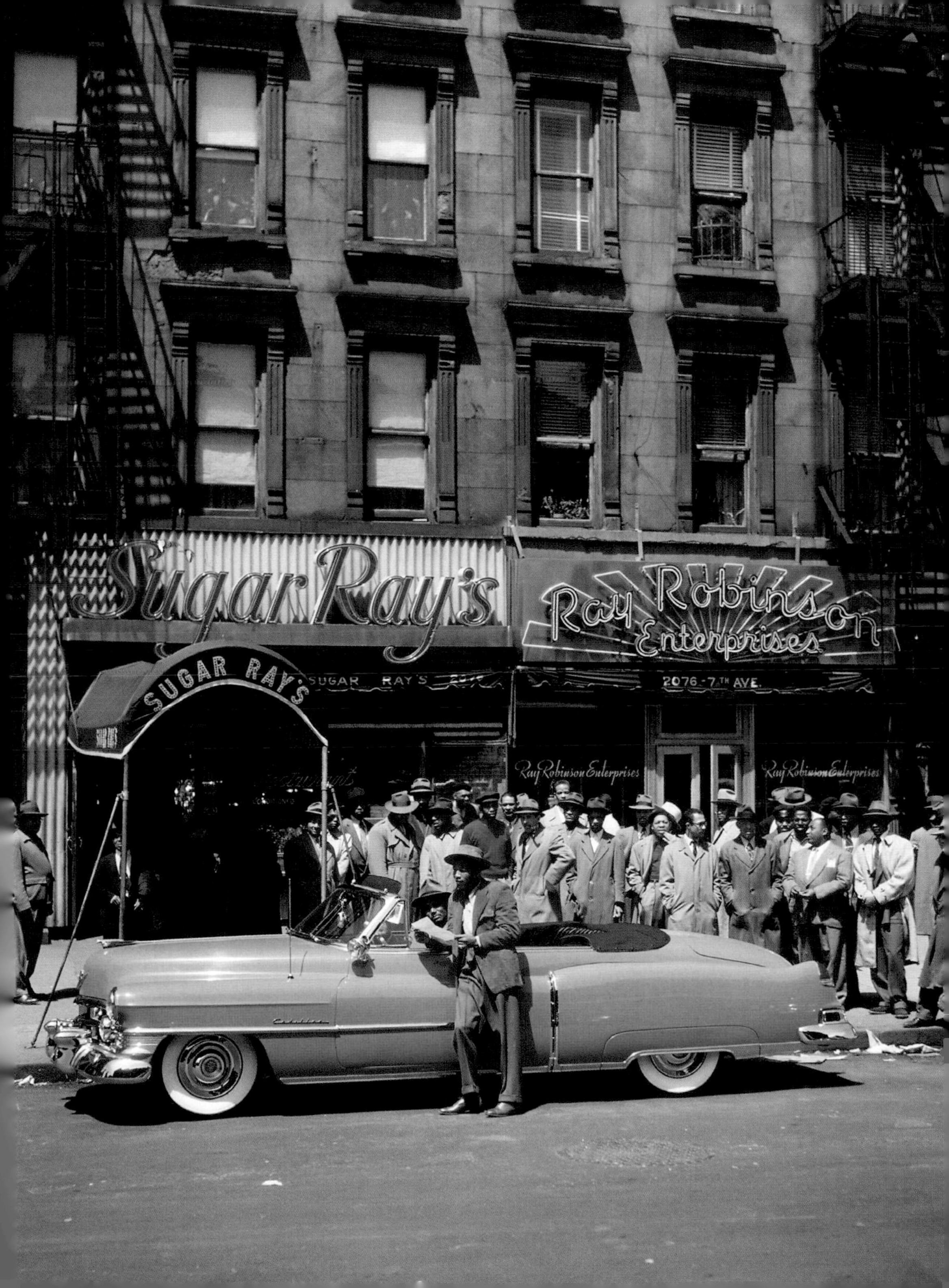

Sugar Ray's
Ray Robinson Enterprises
SUGAR RAY'S
2076-7TH AVE.
Ray Robinson Enterprises
Ray Robinson Enterprises

'48 Sedan | Tucker

USA

1948 • 333 cu in/5,470 cc, F6 • 166 bhp/124 kW • 0–60 mph/97 kph in 10 seconds • 120 mph/192 kph

On June 15, 1948, the American businessman and automobile designer Preston Tucker sent an open letter to the automobile industry that was published in many U.S. newspapers. The long and rambling epistle tried to settle a few scores, but its main purpose was to publicize the imminent arrival of the rear-end Tucker, nicknamed the "Tucker Torpedo." Tucker claimed that "hundreds of thousands have written us that they are ready and waiting to buy it." Never was it truer that pride comes before a fall. Tucker's company would only ever produce fifty finished models (and one unfinished one) of the Torpedo, which became the Tucker '48 Sedan, and nine months after he wrote the letter, Tucker's company went out of business.

There was nothing wrong with the actual cars, once the design had been refined from Tucker's plans, many of which proved to be overly ambitious. He had initially wanted a massive 588-cubic-inch (9,650-cc) engine, but that proved impractical. The replacement, an aircraft engine, did not fit into the space available at the rear of the car. Other innovative ideas did make it into the '48 Sedan, including the world's first car seat belts, a strengthened frame, padded dashboard, and a design that brought all the instruments within easy sight and reach of the driver. But the car received a lot of negative publicity, some of it attributed to U.S car manufacturers trying to snuff out Tucker's challenge.

In 1988 Tucker's controversial life was turned into a movie, *Tucker*, directed by Francis Ford Coppola and starring Jeff Bridges as Preston Tucker. Today, forty-seven of his Sedans survive, and some have fetched more than $1 million (£640,000) at auction. **MG**

XK120 | Jaguar

GB

1948 • 210 cu in/3,442 cc, S6 • 160 bhp/119 kW • 0–60 mph/97 kph in 9.9 seconds • 121 mph/185 kph

The Jaguar XK120 is one of the most beautiful, stylish, and sexy cars ever made. When Clark Gable bought one of the first to be imported to the United States in 1949, his Hollywood neighbors Humphrey Bogart and Lauren Bacall loved it and bought one, too.

This mobile sculpture, created by Jaguar's founder Sir William Lyons, was far more than a pretty face. The six-cylinder XK engine introduced to mass production a layout that remains modern: twin overhead camshafts in an aluminum cylinder head. Many racing drivers had their first taste of success in the XK120, including Sir Stirling Moss and the first U.S. F1 World Champion, Phil Hill. Ian Appleyard—Jaguar dealer and Lyons's son-in-law—and his wife Pat won many grueling international rallies in their car, NUB 120. The special-bodied XK120C (or C-type), won the Le Mans endurance race in 1951 and 1953.

When the car was launched in 1948 at the Earl's Court Motor Show in London, everyone who saw it was smitten, and astonished that it was offered at around half the price of a Ferrari. So soon after World War II, though, building such a car was a risk. Britain was broke, its citizens suffering austerity and food rationing. Only car companies that exported a large proportion of their production got the precious raw materials they needed. Lyons thought this sports car would only sell a few hundred, but almost 12,000 were made, most being left-hand drive for export to the United States.

These days, the driving experience feels vintage and the footwell is painfully cramped, but good examples sell for $300,000 (£200,000). They are still popular with celebrities—such as pop guru Simon Cowell and actor Patrick Dempsey (Dr. Shepherd in *Grey's Anatomy*). **LT**

(<) Queen Elizabeth II and the Duke of Edinburgh travel in a Land Rover Series 1 converted for travel while standing.

Series 1 | Land Rover (GB)

1948 • 97 cu in/1,595 cc, S4 • 51 bhp/38 kW • unknown • 60 mph/96 kph

The original Land Rover—the Series 1 of 1948—was a motorized workhorse far removed from today's Land Rover. While celebrities frequently turn up to city restaurants in a "Landie" today, the first version was an extremely rough-and-ready vehicle.

Brothers Maurice and Spencer Wilks, respectively chief designer and general manager of Rover, came up with the idea in the aftermath of World War II. Maurice had been using a Willys Jeep on his estate on the Isle of Anglesey in Wales. Despite the postwar shortage of raw materials, the duo decided to try to build a better car themselves. They started work on a prototype using parts from the Rover P3 luxury sedan (saloon) and from wartime aircraft. The eccentric result was shown in April 1948, at the Amsterdam Motor Show.

The Land Rover was a utility vehicle in every respect, halfway between a tractor and a truck. For the first forty-eight preproduction cars a pale green paint originally intended for the interiors of Spitfire fighter planes was used—it was the only color available.

The vehicle had a steel box-section chassis and a 97-cubic-inch (1.6-liter) gasoline engine. The four-speed gearbox came from the Rover P3 with an additional two-speed transfer box for high and low ratio conditions. The body was aluminum as this, too, was available from the British aircraft industry after the war. Even today, Land Rover's Defender model has aluminum body panels. A roof was an optional extra.

Buyers loved the Land Rover's go-anywhere abilities, but the vehicle was too spartan for most. Within a year a seven-seater station wagon (estate) was built. It even included the luxury of a heater. **JB**

Minor | Morris (GB)

1948 • 56 cu in/918 cc, S4 • 27 bhp/20 kW • 0–60 mph/97 kph in 36.5 seconds • 62 mph/99 kph

Although an earlier Morris Minor went into production from 1928 to 1933, it was the car relaunched under the same name in 1948 that became one of Britain's best-loved cars. With a top speed of 62 mph (99 kph), this was not the speed freak's first choice, but it was a cozy family car that provided economic fuel consumption—40 miles per British gallon (33 miles per U.S. gallon, or 7.1 liters per 100 km). In postwar Britain, where rationing of gas remained in place until 1950, this mattered. So too did the modest price of £359 ($560).

The Morris Minor became the first British car to sell over a million, with the eventual production run totaling about 1.3 million vehicles. It only ceased production in Britain in 1971, although some were still being made in New Zealand as late as 1974. Despite the fact that the car has not been built for almost forty years, it remains as popular as ever, with owners' clubs around the world and many cars still in service in the United Kingdom.

The Minor has been described as a British design classic. Its creator was the Anglo-Greek automobile designer Sir Alexander Arnold Constantine Issigonis, the man who was also responsible for the BMC Mini. The original model had only two doors, with the headlamps mounted in the grille. A four-door sedan (saloon) version came out in 1950, with the headlights mounted on the wings, followed in 1952 by a station wagon (estate) version with a visible wooden frame; this, the Morris Minor Traveler, was just as enthusiastically received.

The Morris Minor has been a major movie star, too, appearing in films ranging from *Gandhi* (1982) and *Shadowlands* (1993) to *Austin Powers* (1997), *Thunderball* (1965), and even (briefly) in *American Graffiti* (1973). **SH**

6/80 | Wolseley

GB

1948 • 135 cu in/2,215 cc, S6 • 72 bhp/54 kW • 0–60 mph/97 kph in 21 seconds • 85 mph/137 kph

The Wolseley 6/80 may have appeared in the late 1950s British TV series *The Invisible Man*, but it was certainly a very visible car in TV cop shows and movies throughout the 1950s. That is because it was a popular police car in reality, which is a testimony to both its speed and its sturdiness; it could cope with real car chases, not just the movie kind. But it was also selected to play roles in comedies, such as the Norman Wisdom film *A Stitch in Time* (1963), and it is seen pulling over Dirk Bogarde in *Doctor at Large* (1957), as well as in *The Ladykillers* (1955), *The Saint* (1997), and *Blue Murder at St Trinian's* (1957).

After the war, Wolseley wanted to demonstrate that it was business as usual for Britain's car industry. The 6/80 came out in 1948 alongside the firm's slightly less powerful 4/50 model, with the 4/50 using a four-cylinder engine and the 6/80 a six-cylinder. These were the company's first two postwar cars. As well as being more powerful, the 6/80 was a longer car, and over the next few years would sell twice as many as its little brother. This is despite the fact that some of its engines were known to have problems with the exhaust valve burning out. To prevent this from happening, the police had the valves of their 6/80s "Stellited," or specially coated with a virtually indestructible cobalt-chromium material.

The cost of a 6/80 on its first introduction was £767 ($1,200). That was expensive for the time, but the price included leather seats, a heater, and a one-speed electric windshield wiper; it was also, as they say in real estate, fully carpeted throughout. The 6/80 remained on sale until 1954, by which time 25,000 had been built and Wolseley's postwar blues were well behind them—thanks, in part, to the boys in blue. **MG**

Silverstone | Healey

GB

1949 • 149 cu in/2,443 cc, S4 • 104 bhp/78 kW • 0–60 mph/97 kph in 12.2 seconds • 113 mph/182 kph

In World War I, Donald Healey was invalided out of the Royal Flying Corps after being shot down by home antiaircraft fire. While recuperating he took a correspondence course in automobile engineering. A skilled driver, he won the 1931 Monte Carlo Rally.

In World War II Healey first conceived the idea of building his own sports cars. The Donald Healey Motor Company was eventually founded in 1945, producing elegant sports cars on his own rigid steel chassis and front suspension setups; bodywork was outsourced and the necessary running gear was bought in.

The 1948 Healey Elliott sedan (saloon) was said to be the world's fastest closed-cockpit car of its time, thanks largely to Healey's pioneering use of wind tunnels to improve aerodynamics. But these early cars were expensive and out of the reach of most British motoring enthusiasts. The 1949 Healey Silverstone was the answer to the club racer's prayers: a spartan, roofless two-seater, on a shortened and stiffened chassis, could be bought for less than £1,000 ($1,500). Clever design features included twin headlights recessed behind the radiator grille, a retracting windshield for racing, and a partly exposed spare wheel that doubled as the rear fender (bumper). With lightweight aluminum bodywork, excellent roadholding, and a reliable Riley 2.4-liter twin-cam engine, the Silverstone went on to several class wins in the Alpine and the Liège–Rome–Liège rallies.

In the 1950s, bigger Nash engines took the Healey on to further Le Mans and Mille Miglia successes. Only 104 Silverstones were built, and a high attrition rate has meant that genuine cars are now extremely rare. **DS**

P·264 39

⟨ A Saab 92 and its driver attract waterborne interest in a publicity photo staged by a chilly Swedish lake.

92 | Saab (S)

1949 • 46 cu in/764 cc, S2 • 25 bhp/19kW • unknown • 65 mph/105 kph

Saab was always the Swedish make that wasn't Volvo: the cars were more subtle and executive. The company was proud that its products were tough enough to protect occupants in its frequent collisions with Swedish moose, and the marketing department never failed to mention that Saab originally made aircraft.

After World War II, Svenska Aeroplan AB—SAAB—branched out into making cars with the Model 92. The car's teardrop styling was sleek, futuristic, and highly aerodynamic for the time, with a drag coefficient of only 0.30. It also had an integral safety cage to protect occupants in an accident, which made this one of the first cars designed with safety in mind.

The 92 was not fast. The two-cylinder, two-stroke, 46-cubic-inch (764-cc) engine put out a maximum 25 bhp (19 kW), and three gears were selected using a lever mounted on the steering column. A radical touch for the time, though, was that power went to the front wheels.

The 92's toughness and reliability were proven by Eric Carlsson, whose driving style on international rallies is summed up by his nickname "Carlsson on the roof." To beat more powerful machines, Carlsson kept his foot flat on the accelerator at all times and braked with his left foot to keep the car (mostly) on the road. Left-foot braking was always the best way to go downhill because if the driver lifted off the gas, the two-stroke engine got nothing but oil. Another option was a "freewheel" button that disconnected the drive.

Dutch boutique supercar company Spyker bought Saab from General Motors in 2010. Its ambition was to build a 92-inspired retro model following in the treads of the new Beetle, Mini, and Fiat 500. **LT**

1500 | Hansa (D)

1949 • 91 cu in/1,498 cc, S4 • 48 bhp/35 kW • 0–60 mph/97 kph in 30.6 seconds • 75 mph/120 kph

Motorists tend to forget how easily they take for granted simple inventions that were revolutionary when they first appeared. The Hansa 1500 from Germany had several innovations of note. It was the first car to incorporate flashing turning signals alongside its rear brake lights, all together in one unit—electric signals had been around since 1907, but this arrangement was a first. In another original piece of design, the trunk (boot) was given a hinged lid so that it could be accessed from outside the vehicle instead of inside. One other new feature was the design of the hood (bonnet), which enabled it to be opened from either the left or right side of the car.

The design team at the Bremen-based Borgward car factory, which produced the Hansa brand, was determined to pull out all the stops because the Hansa 1500 was to be the first completely new German car to be designed and built after the end of World War II. Another of the team's simple but effective features, not yet very common, was the steering-wheel design. This had a very slim outer rim linked to the hub by three sets of ultrathin spokes, which made the whole of the dashboard behind the wheel clearly visible to the driver. It was a design borrowed from Porsche racing cars (and one that some modern manufacturers would do well to copy).

Even the seating created a stir when the Hansa 1500 was first shown in March 1949 at the Geneva Motor Show. Bench seats, already much favored in the United States, ran the full width of the car, creating a vehicle that could easily seat three people in both the front and back. All these features attracted buyers and the 1500 remained in production until 1954. **MG**

Series 62 | Cadillac

USA

1949 • 330 cu in/5,424 cc, V8 • 160 bhp/118 kW • unknown • 100 mph/160 kph

Cadillac sales were sluggish in 1948, even those of their popular Series 62. That year the designers had added tail fins, a feature that caught everyone's attention and was soon being copied by every other American manufacturer, and yet sales of the car still fell.

The following year was another story, however. The design was tweaked a little more, but what really impressed was the introduction of a new, lightweight V8 engine. This boosted the car's top speed to the coveted figure of 100 mph (160 kph), and the public came back in droves; sales increased by more than 50 percent. Cadillac was relieved, and the engine was so good that it was still in use eighteen years later.

Another news-making stroke in 1949 was that Cadillac added a hardtop convertible model, the Coupe de Ville, to the Series 62. The hardtop cost $3,497 (£2,230), only $55 (£35) more than the soft-top convertible, and although the soft-top easily outsold the hardtop in the first year, Cadillac had hit on a success; sales of the hardtop would soar over the next few years. Models in good condition can fetch well in excess of $100,000 (£64,000) when they come on the market today.

Strictly speaking, the car wasn't actually a Coupe de Ville. The original French term, *coupé de ville*, indicated a town (*ville*) car that had been cut (*coupe*) in two with an interior division to separate the driver from the passengers in the rear seat. This 1949 Americanized version did not include the division, but it did feature a telephone in the glove compartment. Mobile phone services had been in existence since 1946, when the first call from a car was made using Bell's revolutionary new Mobile Telephone Service (MTS). **MG**

P1 | Allard

GB

1949 • 219 cu in/3,600 cc, V8 • 85 bhp/63 kW • 0–60 mph/97 kph in 15 seconds • 85 mph/137 kph

Sydney Allard was a rare creature in the motoring world, one of the few men who was successful both as a racing driver and as a car manufacturer. His reputation was built by winning races while driving cars built by his own company. The Allard P1 was a notable example, and Sydney Allard drove it to victory in the Monte Carlo Rally in 1952. In second place, narrowly, was a young driver named Stirling Moss, competing in his first rally.

Allard founded the Allard Motor Company in England in 1936, when he was twenty-six years old. The following year he tried to drive an Allard to the top of Ben Nevis, Britain's highest mountain, but it wasn't one of his finest moments as the car crashed and rolled over. Luckily, Allard was unharmed.

The P1 was one of Allard's most successful vehicles, and 155 were sold over the model's three-year lifespan. Many of them were exported to the United States; in postwar Britain a healthy export business was essential for obtaining access to scarce supplies of materials such as steel and aluminum. Allard sourced his engines from Ford, which meant that the cars were easy to service in the United States, and his ability to pack a huge engine into a fairly small space also appealed to the American market.

For the Allard Motor Company it was always a case of quality rather than quantity. The manufacturer stayed in business until 1966, the year its founder died, and in the thirty years of its existence it built fewer than than 2,000 cars—only a little more than one a week. Yet thirty years is an impressive length of time for a small company in the automobile industry, where many minnows have faltered and failed. **MG**

166 Inter | Ferrari

I

1949 • 121 cu in/1,995 cc, V12 • 109 bhp/81 kW • 0–60 mph/97 kph in 11 seconds • 111 mph/178 kph

Enzo Ferrari's motor company, Scudo Ferrari (literally "the Ferrari stable"), had been making winning racing cars since the company was founded in 1929, so when the firm announced its first road vehicle in its twentieth anniversary year, it is hardly surprising that there was tremendous interest. Developed out of the 166 S race car, the Ferrari 166 Inter was essentially a racing car redesigned for road use, and its speed and handling were phenomenally good.

Ferrari introduced several 166 models, one of the most popular being the 166 MM "Barchetta," a simple, low-slung car that got its name when the Italian motoring writer Giovanni Canestrini saw it for the first time and likened it to a little boat, a *barchetta*. The car actually looked and drove more like a little bullet. The MM in its name stood for the Mille Miglia, the "Thousand Miles" road endurance race in Italy that Ferrari had won in 1948 with its 166 S model, driving at

an average speed of 76 mph (121 kph). Fittingly, in 1949 it was the Ferrari 166 MM that took first place, at an even faster average of 82 mph (131 kph) over the 1,000-mile (1,600-km) course. It turned out to be but a stage of a winning streak, because Ferrari went on to win the event in 1950, 1951, and 1952. The five consecutive wins earned Ferrari priceless publicity that reached far beyond the world of motor racing and did sales of their first road vehicle no harm at all.

The cars designated the Ferrari 166 Inter all look very different, because Ferrari adopted the common practice of the day in only selling the chassis to the customer, who would then take it to a favored coachbuilder to have a body put on it. When a 166 comes up for auction today, there is at least as much interest as when the cars were first introduced. The highest price so far paid for one was $801,350 (£511,000) in 2008. **MG**

1949 | Ford (USA)

1949 • 224 cu in/3,687 cc, V6 • 90 bhp/67 kW • unknown • 81 mph/130 kph

Known as the car that saved Ford, the 1949 was the company's first postwar model. Almost everything bar the engine was overhauled, and even the engine was souped up a little and moved to provide more space inside. It came in both V6 and V8 versions, indicated by V6 or V8 appearing after the Ford name on the grille.

Unusually, company president Henry Ford II had invited designs from outsiders as well as from Ford's in-house team, and it was a freelance group that won the contract. Ford knew that this car had to be a success to keep his company afloat, and he was willing to do whatever he could to make sure of that. The 1949 Ford was shorter, lighter, and set 3 inches (8 cm) lower than previous Fords, and it introduced a few innovations such as independent front suspension.

There were initially four basic models, a coupe, a sedan (saloon), and two- and four-door, eight-seater "woodie" station wagons (estates), but with the two engine sizes they provided a new range of eight different models. Prices ranged from $1,333 (£850) to $2,119 (£1,350). The 1949 would help Ford sell over a million cars that year, which did, indeed, turn around the company's finances. New variations were introduced in 1950 and 1951, and by the time the 1949 was phased out in favor of the 1952 Ford, the company's future was secured. **MG**

J2 | Allard (GB)

1949 • 239 cu in/3,920 cc, V8 • 140 bhp/105 kW • 0–60 mph/97 kph in 9.3 seconds • 110 mph/177 kph

Following quickly on from the Allard P1, the J2 had only a slightly bigger engine, but was capable of a much better performance. It was primarily built for the U.S. market, which company founder Sydney Allard had noticed was still lacking a nippy little sports car. Allard, who was a Ford dealer in the United Kingdom in addition to being a manufacturer in his own right, continued to use the Ford V8 engine that made his cars easy to service across the Atlantic.

The J2 was also a successor of the earlier Allard J (also known as the J1), which was built in 1946. The Allard J had been designed both for racing and for road use, and the J2 was also seen as a racing car that could be driven on the road. To improve this latest model Allard gave the J2 independent rear suspension. The car did moderately well, given the company's limited production, and it was followed by variations like 1951's J2X and 1953's J2R.

About 200 J2s were made in all, and while it was not a huge success on the racing circuit, it did manage a creditable third place in the 1950 Le Mans 24 Hour Race, driven by Sydney Allard himself with Tom Cole. That J2 was equipped with a larger, 329-cubic-inch (5.4-liter) Cadillac engine.

The highest price a J2 has fetched was $308,000 (£196,000), the result of an auction in 2008. **MG**

205 | Abarth (I)

1950 • 66 cu in/1,090 cc, S4 • 75 bhp/55 kW • unknown • 106 mph/170 kph

Carlo Abarth was an Austrian-born motorcycle champion and a fine motoring engineer who was known as a tuning expert. He worked for Cisitalia in the 1940s, but when the Cisitalia finances became shaky in 1949, Abarth left the company by mutual agreement, although he continued to race its cars.

In 1950 Abarth began creating a car of his own, the Abarth 205, but only three of these were built in that year. He entered his first car in the 1950 Mille Miglia, where it was driven by Guido Scagliarini, Carlo's partner in his new company. The race was from Brescia to Rome and back, but the Abarth had to withdraw before reaching Rome.

Another of Abarth's three cars won the 1,100-cc class at Monza in 1950, but it did not perform as well in the 1951 Mille Miglia. Abarth continued to produce cars, and also to build exhaust systems, which were another passion of his. In 1971, he sold his company to Fiat.

In 2009 the very first Abarth 205 was entered in the Mille Miglia again by its now-owner, Mark Gessler. History repeated itself when it had to drop out in Florence. Undeterred, Gessler entered it for the 2011 Mille Miglia and this time it completed the race, finishing 234th out of 376 classic cars, all of which had been in Mille Miglia races previously. That may not have been a victory, but it wasn't bad for a sixty-one-year-old. **MG**

1900 | Alfa Romeo (I)

1950 • 114 cu in/1,884 cc, S4 • 80 bhp/59 kW • 0–60 mph/97 kph in 15 seconds • 93 mph/150 kph

The Alfa Romeo 1900 was an important car for the company. From a practical aspect, it was the first car it would build on a production line, so quality control had to be rigorous. Alfa Romeo did not want its reputation to be damaged by any production problems.

The car was also important because it represented an attempt by Alfa Romeo to change direction, but without losing its upmarket image. At the end of World War II it was clear that Europe had changed, and Italians in particular would not have much money to spare. Alfa Romeo, therefore, needed a car that would maintain its luxury image but which would be affordable and drivable by not-so-wealthy customers. The 1900 was it.

Switching to a production line meant that the car had to be conceived as a whole, rather than built as a chassis that then had a body bolted to it. Parts of the car that previously would have been integrated into the chassis construction could be incorporated into the body design, and the result was a sleekly elegant car.

By 1954 the 1900 had become Alfa Romeo's best-selling car and 21,000 had been built by the time production ended in 1959. More importantly, Alfa Romeo was still in business; other companies that had focused only on luxury cars after the war realized too late that the market had disappeared and were forced to close. **MG**

Jet 1 | Rover (GB)

1950 • gas turbine • 100 bhp/74 kW • 0–60 mph/97 kph in 14 seconds • 90 mph/145 kph

World War II proved the jet engine would revolutionize air travel. Perhaps, thought Rover, it would do the same for road transport, too? The idea was not as unrealistic as it might seem now. The Jet 1 was not rocket-powered with a flame coming out the back; the jet powered a turbine that turned the wheels in the normal way. The small, light engine could run on a wide variety of fuels and created few emissions. With fewer complex components, it was easier to install, run, and maintain.

On the outside, the prototype looked like an open-topped roadster—but underneath it was the world's first jet-turbine car. But Rover soon discovered there were problems. Jet 1 ran beautifully at high speed, but it was very sluggish to start and run at the low speeds that most cars usually drive at. Its exhaust blew at 100 mph (160 km) with scalding temperatures. Worst of all was fuel consumption: 6 mpg (39 liters per 100 km) at best. Yet Rover persisted with turbine research. Together with race team BRM, it produced a 142-mph (229-kph) turbine-powered sports cars that raced at Le Mans in the 1960s, driven by Jackie Stewart and Graham Hill.

British musician and TV host Jools Holland owns an authentic-looking Rover Jet 1 replica built from a Rover 80 powered by a 150-mph (241-kph) Jaguar engine. The original is in London's Science Museum. **SH**

DB2 | Aston Martin (GB)

1950 • 157 cu in/2,580 cc, S6 • 105 bhp/93.2 kW • 0–60 mph/97 kph in 11.2 seconds • 116 mph/187 kph

The Aston Martin DB2 has seeds of virtually every Aston that came after it—it embodies Aston Martin DNA in the curves of its bodywork, the shape of its posterior, and that famous Aston front end. The gaping radiator grille and wide headlights were a first in 1950, but have now became a trademark of this iconic British firm.

The DB2 was the second car that Aston Martin made after the company was taken over by entrepreneur and engineer David Brown—DB—in 1947. The previous model, officially called the Two Litre Sports, had been successful in racing and the DB2 borrowed its tube-frame chassis. A 2.6-liter, six-cylinder Lagonda engine provided the power, and the bodywork was made of aluminum.

The DB2 was unveiled to the public at the 1950 New York Motor Show. Buyers would have to wait a while though, because the first few cars made were destined for Le Mans, where they were first and second in class that year. It was not simply outright speed that made the DB2 so good. The handling was superb, with coil-spring suspension on each corner. This was at a time when rivals were still using leaf springs, something better suited to a truck than a race-bred sports car. One reviewer said the coupe DB2 handled better than any passenger car and as well as any sports car he knew. **JI**

1400 | Fiat (I)

1950 • 85 cu in/1,400 cc, S4 • 44 bhp/33 kW • 0–60 mph/97 kph in 35.7 seconds • 75 mph/120 kph

According to advertisements for the Fiat 1400, it was the "car of progress." Its attractive, rounded body signaled a new direction for Fiat, and it was the company's first car without a sturdy, old-fashioned chassis. The 1400 was significant in many ways: it was Fiat's first monocoque construction, it introduced Fiat's first diesel engine, and in 1953 it became the first car to be produced by Seat in Spain.

Advanced features included the five-speed gearbox and hydraulic clutch. Buyers found armrests built into the doors, a hand brake sited under the dashboard, a "radio receiver," and a cigar lighter. Advertisements featured a uniformed chauffeur loading seemingly impossible amounts of luggage into the generous trunk (boot) while a smartly dressed family looked on.

The 1400 was available as either a four-door sedan (saloon), two-door cabriolet, or two-door coupe. All had sleek, modern lines with simple curves, distinctive chrome trim, and an aggressive front grille.

The convertible was the pick of the bunch, though, offering a new type of sexy glamour to the mass market. This was typified by sunny publicity shots showing five models in the car, two men and three women. The driver and two passengers were squeezed into the front seat, while the remaining two spread out in the back. **SH**

Champion | Studebaker (USA)

1950 • 2,786 cc, S6 • 85 bhp/63 kW • 0–60 mph/97 kph in 17.6 seconds • 82 mph/132 kph

American car design often looked to the skies in the 1950s, but only one car wore a propeller on its nose: the 1950 Studebaker Champion.

Flamboyant Frenchman Raymond Loewy had been a consultant designer for Studebaker since 1938. His design for the radical 1950 model was almost sunk by his Chief Designer, Virgil Exner. "Ex," who would go on to create the Forward Look for Chrysler, presented Studebaker chiefs with a shock rival design. Loewy won the spat, however, and the simple ultra-modern lines of the Champion were penned by Robert E. Bourke.

Sadly, the Champion doesn't fly—with a 170-cubic-inch (2,786 cc) straight-six delivering just 85 bhp (63 kW) at 4,000 rpm, the 1950 toddles. It gets round corners neatly, however, thanks to relatively firm double A-arm and coil spring front suspension with an anti-roll bar. It also offered Automatic Drive, developed with Borg Warner. This excellent system featured a non-slip direct-drive torque converter preventing "creep" or auto-destruction if reverse was selected on the move.

Some 343,164 of the 1950 models sold at around $1,500 (£960), but, as jets took over from propellers, Studebaker couldn't compete with Detroit's low prices. Today's classic car buyers should be able to get into the cockpit for around $6,000 (£3,800). **LT**

We also make a funny-looking car.

We make a car that looks like a beetle.

And a station wagon that looks like a bus. (Or so we're told.)

But we think of them a little differently; both Volkswagens look just like what they are.

The VW Sedan is for carrying 4 people. The station wagon is for carrying 8, bag and baggage. (With almost as much headroom and legroom as you get in a real bus.)

The wagon also handles a staggering amount of just stuff. (It has 170 cubic feet of space, compared to about 105 in conventional wagons.)

Both Volkswagens have air-cooled rear engines. No water or anti-freeze needed; terrific traction on ice and snow.

Both park in practically the same space. (The wagon is only 9 inches longer.)

Both defy obsolescence. Nobody knows what year VW you drive. Except you.

Our sedan is a pretty familiar sight; not many people laugh at it any more. But our station wagon is still good for a few chuckles.

« This 1960s advertisement for the Volkswagen Type 2 shows off the campervan's spacious interior.

Type 2 | Volkswagen (D)

1950 • 72 cu in/1,192 cc, F4 • 30 bhp/22.3 kW • 0–60 mph/97 kph in 31 seconds • 54 mph/86 kph

The wheels that powered a revolution, the Volkswagen Type 2 campervan will forever be associated with the West Coast hippie movement of the 1960s.

A practical and versatile forerunner to the modern people carrier, the Type 2 earned its name because it was the next production vehicle after the Type 1, the Beetle. But it had a multitude of other badges: "Transporter" if it was the commercial vehicle, or "Kombi" (short for "Kombinationskraftwagen") if it was the home-from-home camper. As with the Beetle, devoted enthusiasts around the world came up with their own, including "Campervan" in the United Kingdom, "Microbus" or simply "Bus" in the United States, and "Bulli" in its native Germany.

Each of the different models also got its own unique nickname, so the launch version, the T1, was the "Splittie"—after its vertically split windshield—while the T2 was the "Breadloaf" because of its exterior shape. The most recent version, sadly lacking any nickname, is the T5 and was launched in 2003. The camper version is known as the "California" in some markets, a tribute to its counterculture roots.

The story goes that the Type 2's concept came from a Dutch businessman called Ben Pon. A local importer of Volkswagen vehicles, he sketched the idea in the spring of 1947. It was approved for production two years later and went on sale in 1950. Later modifications have led to various formats of commercial vehicles: a pickup truck, flatbed truck, a camper with and without a popup roof. It has even been an Alpine tourist coach with a removable canvas roof for improved skyward visibility. **RY**

50-2106 | Holden (AUS)

1951 • 132 cu in/2,171 cc, S6 • 60 bhp/45 kW • 0–60 mph/97 kph in 27.7 seconds • 65 mph/105 kph

The Australian car firm Holden (part of the U.S. giant General Motors) might easily be thought to have invented the "Ute," or Utility Vehicle, the kind of car that has a conventional front half but a flat load bed at rear. Aussies are fiercely loyal to the Ute, which represents a combination of hard work (the back bit) and a laid-back way of life (the front).

In fact, it was Ford that built the first Ute, in 1932; a farmer's wife had written to the company, asking for a car that could take her "to church on Sunday and pigs to market on Monday." But who cares about the history books—it is the iconic Holden 50-2106 that matters. It was based on Holden's 1948 six-cylinder sedan (saloon), the 48-215, which was originally designed in the United States, but considered too small for American buyers.

The Australians loved it, though, and the "Coupe Utility" version followed in 1951. This offered great versatility, performance, and strength, being able to carry heavy loads across farmland as well as passengers in comfort. The Holden also undercut its rivals on price, and it is no surprise that demand went through the roof. By the end of the 50-2106's first year on sale, there was a waiting list in Australia of 70,000.

The original sedan's all-steel welded body was carried over to the Ute, as was its overhead-valve six-cylinder engine. Although the load bay had an official weight limit, most buyers found they could happily ignore it and load the Ute to the gunnels without mishap.

When the 50-2106 was launched, the advertisers claimed, "Holden is designed for Australia and built in Australia . . . the result is a vehicle you will be proud to own." For once, the ad men were right. **JI**

235 | Delahaye

F

1951 • 217 cu in/3,558 cc, S6 • 152 bhp/112 kW • 0–60 mph/97 kph in 12 seconds • 105 mph/169 kph

While some carmakers, such as Panhard and even Alfa Romeo, adjusted their products to take account of the new postwar austerity, Delahaye and others plowed on doing what they knew they did best: building luxury cars. Delahaye must have been wondering whether plowing on was the right thing to do, though, because in 1951 its previous models, the 135 and the 175, sold a grand total of seventy-seven between them. The future rested on its latest hope, 1951's Delahaye 235.

The 235 certainly looked good and was well received when first shown at the 1951 Paris Auto Show. It was quite clearly a successor of the 135, but its potent six-cylinder engine could push it to about 105 mph (169 kph). It was quite clearly a modern car for the modern world, and it became Delahaye's only model, which enabled them to put everything behind it.

Unfortunately, the Delahaye company simply could not sell the car cheaply enough, in part due to its small-scale production. It was twice the price of Jaguar's XK120, which had come out in 1949 and offered similar features. By 1954 only eighty-four of the 235s had been built, which compared badly even with sales of the previous models. The company continued to be sustained by the building of military vehicles, but it desperately needed a viable car as well. And good as it was technically, the 235 was not what was required.

Delahaye was taken over by Hotchkiss, which shut down the firm's car production and, soon afterward, dropped the distinguished Delahaye name altogether. Today, the cars are more sought-after than they were in the 1950s, and in 2009 a 1952 Delahaye 235 sold in Monaco for €117,600 (£99,000/$156,000). **MG**

Land Cruiser | Toyota

(J)

1951 • 207 cu in/3,400 cc, S6 • 84 bhp/62 kW • unknown • unknown

Loved by foreign-aid charities and nongovernment organizations the world over, the Toyota Land Cruiser has been in continuous development since 1951. Its ancestral line can be traced back to the Toyota BJ, a truck-based mud-plugger developed for the military—a sort of Japanese Jeep. The story goes that a Toyota driver piloted the prototype higher up Mount Fuji—the slopes of which proved excellent as a local test track—than anyone had ever driven before.

The following year it became the first Toyota passenger car to be exported, and in 1959 the first to be manufactured outside the home market of Japan, when a factory opened in Brazil. The BJ name gave way to the more descriptive Land Cruiser in 1955, and ever since, this 4x4 has built a reputation for durability, reliability, and outstanding off-road performance.

To date, more than 5 million have been sold in more than 180 different countries and territories. Ironically, it was the success of the European and U.S. carmakers during those early decades that helped make the Land Cruiser the global phenomenon that it is today. That is because when Toyota began to explore the export opportunities, it found that many of the established markets were already well penetrated by the likes of Jeep and Land Rover. That encouraged Toyota's top brass to focus on the emerging markets in the Middle East, East Asia, and South America, where the Land Cruiser is still massively popular to this day.

The vehicle is also a big seller in Australia, where Toyota carries out new model development work in the outback. Local magazine *4WD Monthly* voted it "4x4 of the Year" four times in a row, from 1998 to 2001. **RY**

A 1953 French magazine advertisement for the Frégate celebrates its ability to endure the passing of the seasons. ›

Comète | Ford

(F)

1951 • 131 cu in/2,158 cc, V8 • 73 bhp/55 kW • 0–60 mph/97 kph in 24 seconds • 81 mph/130 kph

The genesis of the Ford Comète was extraordinary. It was a pet project of Ford president François Lehideux, who said that the company's new luxury car should be developed outside the Ford organization, without anyone's knowledge. Lehideux collaborated with the French coachbuilding firm of Facel-Metallon to produce the Comète, which was designed in Italy in cloak-and-dagger conditions. Like a magician pulling a rabbit out of a hat, Lehideux unveiled the car with a flourish in Biarritz in the summer of 1951.

The appearance of the handsome four-seater sports car gave more than a nod toward the futuristic styles of larger cars that were appearing in the United States at the time. But for all the buzz created by the secrecy, the engine in the Comète was unfortunately not nearly powerful enough to carry the larger body. While the car was admired for its looks, its performance was less impressive, and the engine was also prone to breakdown due to the strain being put on it.

When a new model was launched at the Paris Motor Show in 1952, it had a slightly larger engine, which certainly helped, but its image was dented again when the Ford Comète Monte Carlo model was brought out in 1953. This had a 239-cubic-inch (3,923-cc) V8 engine that was normally used only on Ford trucks, and while there was a boost in performance, people did not like the thought of driving a car powered by a truck engine. Consequently, the Ford Comète plummeted with less than cometlike grace, and died in 1954. It even lost its name in its afterlife, becoming known as the Simca Comète—a result of the French Ford subsidiary being taken over by Simca, also in 1954. **MG**

Frégate | Renault

(F)

1951 • 121 cu in/1,997 cc, S4 • 56 bhp/42 kW • 0–60 mph/97 kph in 29 seconds • 77 mph/124 kph

In 1949 Renault was developing a car that would be modern and fairly luxurious, an upmarket model designed to show that in France the years of postwar austerity were over. Renault had been nationalized by the French state in 1945, with Pierre Lefaucheux being put in charge. Lefaucheux had no particular interest in cars, and indeed rode to work on a bike, but he had been a hero of the French Resistance, imprisoned at Buchenwald, and at the start of World War II had been the director of a boiler manufacturing company.

This unlikely hero was charged with producing the car that would change Renault's image and fortunes, and from several options being considered, his team chose the Frégate. This was going to be a typical Renault with its engine at the rear, but rather late in the day the engine was moved to the front. It was launched at the 1950 Paris Motor Show, but the first ones would not be on sale until November 1951.

The Frégate was a solid and stately looking vehicle, and in 1953 Renault sold about 25,000 of them, a decent amount but not exceptional. Performance was boosted on some later models, but Citroën, Renault's big rival, continued to dominate the French market for executive sedans (saloons).

By the time production was halted in 1960, 163,383 Frégates had been made. In February 1955, Pierre Lefaucheux set out in one of these to give a presentation in Strasbourg. The car hit a patch of black ice in the Alps and rolled over. Although the car's solid body protected him, Lefaucheux was killed when his briefcase, which had been loose on the rear seat, struck him on the back of the neck. **MG**

us en rêviez à l'automne
us y avez songé tout l'hiver
us allez l'essayer au printemps
us en serez heureux cet été
t pendant de longues années encore.

Frégate
RENAULT
RÉGIE NATIONALE

Z-102 | Pegaso

E

1951 • 170 cu in/2,800 cc, V8 • 360 bhp/265 kW • 0–60 mph/97 kph in 10.5 seconds • 155 mph/250 kph

Spanish manufacturer Pegaso was best known for making trucks, tractors, coaches, and military vehicles. However, it also built the remarkable Pegasus Z-102 series of cars in the 1950s. Not only was this a groundbreaking car for the Spanish motor industry, but in 1953 a supercharged version of the Z-102 became the world's fastest production car (figures above). It was a brutal machine with little handling subtlety, just a series of big aluminum overhead-cam V8 engines powering a small light car rapidly, preferably in a straight line.

The car was designed by Wifredo Ricart, who had been forced to flee Spain during the Spanish Civil War. He'd joined Alfa Romeo for eight years, designing the Alfa 512 and working alongside Enzo Ferrari. The two men reputedly didn't get on well. In 1945 he was about to leave for the United States to work for Studebaker, when he was persuaded instead to lead a team to produce a Ferrari-beater—the Z-102—in the old Hispano Suiza factory in Spain. The car was aimed right at the new prancing horse Ferraris and was even named after the winged horse Pegasus from Greek mythology.

When it was introduced at the 1951 Paris Motor Show it received an enormous amount of acclaim. It was Spain's first postwar car, and every part was produced in Barcelona. It was a matter of great national pride and a large amount of both cash and ingenuity had been thrown into its production, which was one reason it took six years from conception to birth.

Unfortunately, it was simply too expensive to produce economically. The cars continued to be built right through till 1958, although only 88 were ever produced. **MG**

Hornet | Hudson

USA

1951 • 305 cu in/5,000 cc, S6 • 145 bhp/106 kW • 0–60 mph/97 kph in 12.1 seconds • 107 mph/172 kph

The 2006 Pixar animation film *Cars* featured a retired racing champion voiced by actor Paul Newman; Doc Hudson had dominated the racetracks of the 1950s and taught the star Lighting McQueen how to drive properly. This was probably the most accurate part of the successful children's film, if only because the Hudson Hornet of 1951 was indeed a classic that, for a few years, left all its rivals in its wake.

The all-new Hornet was launched with a "step-down" design that was first used in the 1948 Hudson Commodore. Having the floor pan set low between the axles and frame of the car meant a smooth ride, a fashionable low-slung appearance, and a low center of gravity for extra handling prowess. Further, the new Hornet had the most powerful six-cylinder engine available in an American car at the time. The 5-liter engine was also said to be the largest six-cylinder engine in the world. In the "big is best" culture of 1950s America, this made the Hornet very desirable. It was considered fast, cool, and fun, and was available as a two-door coupe, a four-door sedan (saloon), a convertible, and a hardtop coupe. Not surprisingly, the Hornet had a great racing career, taking NASCAR and AAA stock car championships. Hornets won everywhere there was a racetrack.

Yet by 1953 the big Hudson saw its sales slipping away. Fashions were changing fast, and anything old had to be quickly refreshed to survive. But to revamp the step-down design was too costly, and the big V8 engines of Hudson's competitors were beginning to take over. So as quickly as it had arrived, the Hornet was gone; production ended in 1954. **BK**

Stirling Moss in the Jaguar works C-Type wins the Sports Car Race at Goodwood, England, on September 29, 1951. ›

Traveler | Kaiser (USA)

1951 • 226 cu in/3,707 cc, S6 • 100 bhp/75 kW • 0–60 mph/97 kph in 16 seconds • 90 mph/145 kph

The most commonly accepted version of the birth of the Kaiser Traveler goes like this: one day in July 1948, Henry Kaiser, the father of Kaiser–Frazer Corporation's general manager Edgar Kaiser, telephoned his son at the carmaker's headquarters in Willow Run, Michigan, and implored: "You've got to get out here [to Oakland, California], I've got an idea."

Edgar flew to California and listened to his father list the faults of a station wagon (estate) he had just driven back from a Tahoe fishing trip. The car rattled and squeaked, he said, and handled like a tank. Its rear seat had to be unbolted and removed to provide space for his camping gear. Something had to be done. So he took his son over to one of his Kaisers and drew what he wanted in the dust of its side panels. Edgar was convinced, and the largest independent U.S. carmaker—fourth in size behind the "Big Three" of Ford, GM, and Chrysler—got to work on what became known in closed circles as "Henry's fishing car."

What made the Traveler unique was its dividable rear door, with the rear window embedded in its upper half and its bottom half folding down flat, like the tailgate of a pickup truck. The passenger seat folded down, too, for extra space—for fishing rods, maybe? Advertised as a luxurious family sedan (saloon) that could convert in ten seconds into a rugged cargo carrier—"One car for your money, and two for your use!" was the slogan—it was the first true hatchback. Its designer, the great Howard Darrin, had determined to produce a winner. And why wouldn't he? Henry had, after all, agreed to pay him a 75-cent royalty on every Darrin-designed "fishing sedan" they sold. **BS**

C-Type | Jaguar (GB)

1951 • 210 cu in/3,442 cc, S6 • 200 bhp/149 kW • 0–60 mph/97 kph in 6.5 seconds • 144 mph/231 kph

The basic story behind Jaguar's C-Type is a simple and pleasing one. It was designed and built with the express purpose of winning the Le Mans 24 Hour Race, which it did—twice. It grew out of Jaguar's XK120C model, which did well in competition at Le Mans, but did not win. Jaguar—or more specifically, the company founder, Sir William Lyons—wanted a win, so Lyons commissioned a car that would do that. His engineers crammed an engine that was full of power into a lightweight aluminum body that had been aerodynamically designed. Everything that was deemed superfluous to a winning car was ditched from the design; more than 1,000 pounds (454 kg) were shed. The result of all this effort was the C-Type, with the "C" standing for "Competition." The car won at Le Mans in 1951, and again in 1953.

In the 1951 race, a twenty-two-year-old and fairly inexperienced driver named Stirling Moss was also driving a C-Type, but mechanical problems forced his withdrawal while the Jaguar team of Peter Walker and Peter Whitehead drove to victory. But by the time the 1953 race came around, the C-Type had been improved, being even faster and lighter, and it won again. It even managed to better Jaguar's delight in its first victory. In 1953 the car was the first to win the race at an average speed of over 100 mph (160 kph), with an impressive 105.85 mph (169.36 kph) over the twenty-four hours.

The C-Type was only built from 1951 to 1953, with an estimated fifty-four machines being made. Despite their record and rarity, they can be bought quite cheaply at auction, although when a fine model came up for sale in 2006 it fetched a whopping $1,512,500 (£961,000). **MG**

8V | Fiat

(I)

1952 • 121 cu in/1,996 cc, V8 • 106 bhp/78 kW • unknown • 118 mph/190 kph (estimated)

Back in the early 1950s, when Fiat's designers were working toward creating a new sports coupe, they mistakenly believed that Ford had trademarked the term "V8" for that engine configuration. So, to avoid a costly lawsuit, they simply switched the characters around and called their new baby "8V," or Otto Vu.

Whatever they had chosen to call it, the car was undeniably stunning. It was built around a tubular steel chassis with a double-skinned body. The outer one gave it its shape while the inner one was welded to the chassis.

The alloy V8 (or 8V) engine at its heart was originally meant to go into a Fiat sedan (saloon). But that project was shelved and the engine was redirected to a limited run of sports cars. Developed with the aim of boosting Fiat's image in the sporting arena, that engine remains to this day the only V8 Fiat has ever built.

With plenty of power on tap and fully independent suspension, the 8V excelled in competition. Even in 1959, five years after production of the car was stopped, the Otto Vu won the Italian 2-liter championship.

There are actually several different-looking 8Vs. After the car initially launched in 1952 with factory-produced coachwork, Fiat outsourced the body building to a number of different design houses. One of the most important of these was Carozzeria Zagato, which produced one of the most beautiful Fiats ever, a model that seems like a quintessential 1960s sports car—except that it was made a full decade before.

The Ghia design house also came up with something that was way ahead of its time—the Fiat 8V Supersonic. An unrestored one of these was sold in the United States in 2011 for $1.55 million (£985,000). **JI**

C-3 | Cunningham

(USA)

1952 • 331 cu in/5,425 cc, V8 • 223 bhp/164 kW • 0–60 mph/97 kph in 10 seconds • 130 mph/208 kph

The C-3 was the brainchild of the appropriately named American racing driver and car builder Briggs Swift Cunningham II. During his illustrious career, he also won the 1958 America's Cup, invented the Cunningham—a winch used on racing yachts—and appeared on the cover of *Time* magazine in 1956.

Since the 1940s, Cunningham had been building cars for himself, for both racing and road use, as well as cars for other drivers to race. In 1952 he decided to build a car and make it commercially available, although only to a select few—only twenty-seven Cunningham Continental C-3s were ever built. (It was thought there were only twenty-five of them until a definitive register was published by the Briggs Cunningham company in 2011.) The reason for the low number is that Cunningham wanted to enter the car at Le Mans, and the rules stated that in order to do so, there had to be at least twenty-five examples built, or planned to be built. Cunningham decided to make the completed cars available for purchase.

Cunningham began work on the cars at his factory in Florida. They were then shipped to Italy where the very European-looking steel bodies were added, before being shipped back to Florida to be finished. Little wonder that each one carried a price tag of almost $12,000 (£7,700), the equivalent of three Cadillacs, and that Nelson Rockefeller was among the buyers.

In its day, the Cunningham C-3 had the cachet of a Ferrari. Of the original twenty-seven cars, twenty-four are known to have survived, and eleven of these turned up at a Cunningham Gathering outside his old factory in West Palm Beach in January 2011. **MG**

R-Type Continental | Bentley (GB)

1952 • 278 cu in/4,564 cc, S6 • 150 bhp/110 kW • 0–60 mph/97 kph in 9.4 seconds • 117 mph/188 kph

Only 2,323 of the Bentley R-Type would be built from its launch in 1952 to its replacement in 1955 by the Bentley S1. Of these, only 165 were the Continental model, which despite its name was aimed mainly at the U.K. domestic market, with three times as many right-hand drives being built compared to left-hand export models. The main difference between the Continental and the basic R-Type was a fine tuning of the engine, although Continental models from 1954 onward would have a larger, 4.9-liter engine.

The R-Type's attractions were speed and the smoothness of the ride. The cars were hand-built at the Rolls-Royce factory in Crewe. Although customers could arrange to have the coachwork done elsewhere, most opted for the simpler option of having Bentley finish the job with their standard body. And what a body! Its closest rival was the Rolls-Royce Silver Dawn, and the R-Type's front shared the Dawn's stately grandeur, but where the Roller was only stately, the R-Type had a tapering and less boxy body that made it look like a giant sports car.

No expense was spared on its plush leather interior, with its carpeted floor and wooden dash. It sold for £7,608 ($12,000) when new, and with its built-to-last qualities is still in demand today, with an average auction price of just over £33,700 ($53,000). **MG**

Capri | Lincoln (USA)

1952 • 317 cu in/5,203 cc, V8 • 205 bhp/151 kW • 0–60 mph/97 kph in 14.1 seconds • 99 mph/159 kph

Cars rarely win road races, win awards for their safety features, and are commercially successful all at the same time, but the Lincoln Capri series, made from 1952 to 1959, did just that. It was seen as a replacement for the Lincoln Cosmopolitan, but right from the start it was a remarkable success in its own right.

Part of this was due to its amazing achievements in the famous Mexican Road Races that ran from 1950 to 1954. The cars raced for about 2,000 miles (3,200 km) across Mexico, including some very tough terrain, and in the first year it entered, in 1952, the Capri took the first five places in the International Standard Class. It beat the 1951 winner, a Ferrari, by more than an hour. In 1953 it claimed the first four places, and in 1954 the Capri finished first and second in its class.

Regarding safety, the Capri was able to offer this reassurance when *Life* magazine named it the safest car of 1955. By then the car was already selling in healthy quantities for a luxury model: 29,552 in 1954, and another 23,673 the following year. But sales went into decline when Ford repositioned the car for the mass market, rather than its original luxury market, and it ceased production in 1959. The early models are still sought after at auction, though, for those prize-winning Mexican Road Race qualities. **MG**

Mark VI | Lotus

GB

1952 • 71 cu in/1,172 cc, S4 • 50 bhp/37 kW • 0–60 mph/97 kph in 15 seconds • 93 mph/150 kph

The Lotus Mark VI was the first production sports car made by founder Colin Chapman's team. Up until then they had produced cars for trials and competition. The Mark VI was sold as a kit with a Lotus chassis, and then customers could specify which parts they wanted.

The chassis was of a space-frame design and weighed only 55 pounds (24 kg). Wrapped around this was an aluminum body that was minimalist, to say the least. The mechanics were largely based around the Ford Prefect, which may not have been very exciting, but were at least cheap and easy to come by.

The base engine was Ford's side-valve 71-cubic-inch (1,172-cc) unit, which may have only produced 50 bhp (37 kW) but could fire the little car along at more than 90 mph (145 kph). Given the low ride height and lack of weather protection, it was an exhilarating experience. The chassis also had mounting points for several other engines, including Ford's own 91-cubic-inch (1,500-cc) motor from the Consul.

Additional appeal lay in how Lotus offered a wide range of special parts to boost performance and handling; they would even take in the owner's existing components and modify them for the new car. The little Mark VI laid the foundation of Lotus's reputation for building light, fast, brilliantly handling machines. **JI**

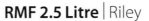

RMF 2.5 Litre | Riley

GB

1952 • 149 cu in/2,443 cc, S4 • 100 bhp/75kW • 0–60 mph/97 kph in 16.4 seconds • 95 mph/153kph

The Riley RM series copied the successful front independent suspension and steering system of the 1930s' Citroën Traction Avant. Its classic, flowing long-bonnet design was in the finest prewar tradition.

The RMC was a three-seater roadster that unsuccessfully attempted to break into the U.S. market, while the RMD was an elegant two-door convertible. The 91-cubic-inch (1.5-liter) RME was a sedan (saloon), which continued in production into the mid-1950s.

By the time the RMF came along, the car had modern features such as headlight fairings and hydraulic brakes all around, although the split screen and wooden roof (covered with vinyl) remained. Inside, it was wood and leather everywhere. The "Big Four" engine originated in the 1930s, but it was a sophisticated unit with twin camshafts and hemispherical combustion chambers. With twin SU carburetors it could reach 100 mph (160 kph) on a downward slope and return around 20 miles to the gallon (14 liters per 100 km).

More than 1,000 RMFs were built in twenty months at the MG works in Abingdon. But after Riley became part of BMC, the RMF was replaced by the Riley Pathfinder. With the same engine but a more modern body, the Pathfinder was produced until 1957. **SH**

RAE 345

◄ A Bristol 404 is posed with a Bristol Aeroplane Company Britannia, introduced one year earlier than the car, in 1952.

404 | Bristol (GB)

1953 • 120 cu in/1,971 cc, S6 • 105 bhp/78 kW • 0–60 mph/97 kph in 12.3 seconds • 115 mph/185 kph

The look of the exclusive Bristol 404 sports coupe borrowed details from aircraft design of the time. The 404 was made by the car division of the Bristol Aeroplane Company. Its radiator grille looked much like a jet's air intake, and observers likened the overall shape to parts of the company's rather unsuccessful Brabazon airliner. The fastback body had an aircraft-style mixture of steel and light-alloy panels over a wooden frame.

Engineers tweaked the BMW-derived straight-six engine to produce 105 bhp (78 kW). There was a 125-bhp (93-kW) option for competition use. Bristol 404s took first, second, and third places in their class at Le Mans in 1955.

The compact two-seater had upmarket aspirations. Inside, the ambience was that of a classic British sports car—with leather seats and door panels, and a wooden dashboard dotted with Smith's instruments. Stylistic quirks abound—both front wings feature gull-wing cupboards that open to reveal the spare wheel, jack, and battery, carefully positioned on shelves. The front end features a single central spotlight. Brakes were sophisticated alloy drums.

Without a dealer network, sales were low. Cars were sold through a factory showroom in London, and an old-fashioned sales claim that it had "the dignity of a town carriage" didn't help. Only fifty-two were made in three years. Jaguar's XK coupes were faster and cost half as much. A longer, four-door model called the 405 was launched in 1955. Available as a convertible or sedan (saloon), it was more popular, selling 308 cars until 1958.

A pristine maroon 405 is featured prominently throughout the 2009 British film *An Education*, which was nominated for three Academy Awards. **SH**

F-100 | Ford (USA)

1953 • 291 cu in/4,785 cc, V8 • 100 bhp/70 kW • 0–60 mph/97 kph in 18.5 seconds • 70 mph/113 kph

In 1948 the Ford Motor Company abandoned its car-based trucks and delivered its first purpose-built pickup, the F-1. Then, in 1953, as part of the company's fiftieth anniversary celebrations, came the F-100. This was the first of Ford's second generation of F-series pickups. Far more than just the F-1 with a facelift, the F-100 had a cab that had become, in Henry Ford's own words, "driverized," meaning everything was either higher, wider, or more accessible.

The cab was higher and 7 inches (17.5 cm) wider than the F-1's. More headroom meant longer, more comfortable seats. Better springs and an adjustable backrest gave the seats "hammock-like" comfort. A new curved windscreen was 55 percent larger than the F-1's. Buyers had the choice of a six-cylinder or flathead-V8 engine and, providing they could overcome their skepticism about its place in a working vehicle, could request the Ford-O-Matic automatic transmission, the first time such a thing was available in a Ford truck.

It also had a stylishly reinvented front grille, an enlarged 45-cubic-foot (1.27-cubic-meter) tray area, dashboard switches that were easier to reach, and a centralized instrument panel. Its almost sedanlike interior reflected Ford's belief that pickups were increasingly being seen as alternatives to the family car. Ford loved its "million-dollar cab" so much it invited prospective buyers to walk into their nearest Ford dealership and take the "15-second sit-down test."

The F-100 was beautiful, with two-tone color schemes in dramatic hues such as Glacier Blue, Raven Black, and Vermilion. It was one of Ford's best ideas and has been in production for over six decades. **SH**

Skylark | Buick

USA

1953 • 321 cu in/5,276 cc, V8 • 188 bhp/140 kW • 0–60 mph/97 kph in 12 seconds • 105 mph/169 kph

General Motors called the Skylark, their new two-door convertible, "the answer to the European sports car." Right from the start, it was intended to be glamorous, with a low-slung body and wheel-wells fully open to show off its 15-inch (38-cm) chromed wire wheels and whitewall tires. Its designer was the legendarily tall, fedora-wearing Harley Earl, whose first Skylark model was perhaps the best-looking Buick of all time, and also the first with a V8 engine installed.

The top-of-the-line car was built to celebrate Buick's fiftieth anniversary and was well equipped with all-leather interior, powered fabric roof, power steering, 12-volt electrics, and a radio boasting a power aerial operated by the driver's foot. The Skylark drove well for the period, too, thanks to coil springs in each corner and lever-arm shock absorbers that ensured good handling and ride qualities. The transmission was automatic and the drum brakes power-assisted, but the steering would seem very sloppy to modern drivers—the turning circle was a huge 42 feet (13 m).

The Skylark was very expensive. Buyers included TV comedian Milton Berle, actor Jackie Gleason, and movie star and comedian Bob Hope, whose cream, custom-built Skylark had his name embedded in silver in the center of the steering wheel. That car is now displayed in an auto museum in Gatlinburg, Tennessee.

Production of the Skylark lasted only a year. Its misjudged price of $5,000 (£3,200) forced General Motors to cut its losses after only 1,690 were made. The low total has helped to make the Skylark one of the world's most collectible classic cars, and pristine models now fetch at least $500,000 (£320,000). **SH**

Corvette C1 | Chevrolet

USA

1953 • 235 cu in/3,859 cc, S6 • 150 bhp/110kW • 0–60 mph/97 kph in 11 seconds • 100 mph/160 kph

The Corvette was the first American production sports car, and the first production car to be built using a lightweight fiberglass body. Only 300 were built in 1953, its first year, and they were as desirable then as they are today. In 1954 Chevrolet built 3,640 Corvettes with a more powerful engine, and the 1955 model was faster and lighter still. By 1956 the top speed had increased from the initial modest 100 mph (160 kph) to a more impressive 129 mph (206 kph) and the acceleration to 60 mph (97 kph) had been reduced to under nine seconds. By the time the final 1962 model came around, that acceleration was under six seconds and Chevrolet sold 14,531 of them.

The all-American Corvette name, synonymous with fast sports cars, was originally the name of a type of seventeenth-century frigate. The boats were small and maneuverable, both qualities Chevrolet sought to emulate, and so the name of its hand-built car was changed to Corvette; otherwise, the cars would have been known as Chevy Opels.

The first American in space, Alan Shepard, was a big Corvette fan and owned an original 1953 model, as well as Corvettes from 1957 and 1962. Rock star Jon Bon Jovi has a 1958 Corvette, and Tico Torres, the drummer with Jon Bon Jovi, has one from 1960, as does Burt Reynolds. Bruce Springsteen and George Clooney both own 1959 roadster-model Corvettes.

The Corvette was a huge success, and the first model was only retired in order to launch the second-generation Corvette C2, the Sting Ray. The car, still going strong as one of the most desirable sports cars in the world, has reached its sixth generation, the C6. **MG**

Popular | Ford

GB

1953 • 71 cu in/1,172 cc, S4 • 30 bhp/22 kW • 0–60 mph/97 kph in 80 seconds • 62 mph/100 kph

The Ford company's claim for the Popular when it launched in 1953 was that it was Britain's cheapest car. It cost £390 ($610), and that money certainly did not buy Britain's speediest car, as its top speed and acceleration figures show. One motoring magazine of its time estimated that it could get up to 50 mph (80 kph) in about twenty-four seconds, but it took the car almost another minute to get up to its maximum speed.

The car was, nevertheless, aptly named, and throughout the 1950s and 1960s it was to become one of the most popular and most recognizable cars on the British roads. Although production ceased in 1962, the sturdy little car plodded on toward a new kind of popularity, this time with moviemakers looking for an easy way to get period detail into a film or TV series, such as *Heartbeat* (1992–2010) and *The Sweeney* (1975–78). The car even took the starring role in a sketch on *Monty Python's Flying Circus* (1969–74) entitled "Mr. and Mrs. Brian Norris's Ford Popular."

Ford had to make several sacrifices in the Popular's design to keep the price down to an affordable level. The price of the Popular represented forty weeks' wages for the average worker, at a time when the typical car cost the equivalent of two years' worth of pay packets. One thing that went was a heater, without even the option of having one as an added extra. There was only one windshield wiper, for the driver, so the car was not exactly perfectly suited for driving in British winters.

The original Ford Popular 103E lasted until 1959, when it was replaced by the 100E. This had a better engine and a faster top speed, and, at last, a heater and an extra windshield wiper became optional. **MG**

Minor Traveller | Morris

GB

1953 • 49 cu in/803 cc, S4 • 30 bhp/22 kW • 0–60 mph/97 kph in 52 seconds • 62 mph/100 kph

Ah, the crack of leather on willow, old ladies cycling to church, high tea on the lawn—the Morris Minor Traveller fits into a period picture of English life. Those cheeky looks and that distinctive ashwood framing the rear end earned this car a place in many people's hearts.

The Traveller was actually born a few years into the Morris Minor's twenty-three-year lifespan and was its station wagon (estate) version. With its trademark varnished woodwork and rear side-hinged doors, it may seem something of a quirky antique, but the design of the car was full of innovations—less of a surprise when it is realized that it was penned by Sir Alec Issigonis, the man who went on to create the original Mini.

The Minor Traveller had a monocoque construction (where the body shell and chassis are one and the same), and independent front suspension.

The engine was far from tailor-made for the car. A stock item from the BMC (British Motor Corporation), it originally produced just 27 bhp (20 kW). However, by the time the Traveller was launched, this had been boosted to a heady 30 bhp (22 kW), which could power the car to 62 mph (100 kph). The car's rate of acceleration is best ascertained using a sundial, but raw performance matters little to fans of this car. They remember the Traveller providing simple, dependable family transport in the postwar era. For many, this is the ultimate Morris Minor.

Forty years since the last one rolled off the production line at the Cowley factory in Oxford (where the relaunched BMW Mini is made), the Traveller is still very much in demand. Specialist British dealers sell immaculate versions, both restored and original, for as much as £20,000 ($31,000). **JI**

An advertisement for a late-model Panhard Dyna Z stresses its roominess, economical gas consumption, and speed. ⊡

FJ | Holden (AUS)

1953 • 131 cu in/2,160 cc, S6 • 60 bhp/45 kW • 0–60 mph/97 kph in 19 seconds • 72 mph/116 kph

In October 1953, five years after Australia's pioneering FX Holden became the country's first locally produced car, along came the evolutionary FJ. The FJ was similar in shape to the FX, but rather than a staid, vertical grille, it had an open grille with an oversized horizontal chrome fender (bumper). Chrome was everywhere: on the hubcaps, fenders, the rear guard fins, and the surround of its centrally mounted rear stoplight.

Looking decidedly more American than European, the four-person family sedan (saloon) was roomy enough to seat six comfortably. It had excellent ground clearance for out-of-city driving on the nation's rough country roads, and its door seals kept out the Aussie dust. A panel van and a utility model were also available, and by the early 1960s, the three incarnations of the FJ had captured an unprecedented 50 percent of the nation's automotive market.

When Australians produce something that is unprecedented, the first thing they do is shorten its name. Sir Donald Bradman has always been "the Don"; Rod Laver is "the Rocket." The process makes people we cannot know or things we cannot own familiar to us. Legends become somehow accessible. The FJ Holden has always been, simply, the "FJ." There is no need to mention Holden because every Australian knows who made it. A movie, *The FJ Holden* (1977), has lauded it, and it has become as much a symbol of what it means to be Australian as the national anthem and meat pies at the footy. The automobile has come a long way in the last fifty years, but in 2012, if you want to impress your neighbor, there is still no better way to do it than to say, "I bought an FJ yesterday." **BS**

Dyna Z | Panhard (F)

1953 • 51 cu in/851 cc, F2 • 42 bhp/31 kW • unknown • 78 mph/126 kph

The Panhard Dyna Z debuted before the French press at Les Ambassadeurs restaurant in Paris on June 17, 1953. It was the latest in an impressive line of light, economical Panhard designs, made so in part through extensive use of aluminum panels over steel subframes. The Z replaced the Dyna X and had a considerably roomier interior, along with an unusually dipping front fender (bumper) and headlights embedded into its hood (bonnet), which gave the Dyna Z an exceptionally low drag coefficient and an animated—or, dare it be said, goofy—facelike appearance. It also had a heavily padded and surprisingly instrument-free dashboard—a concession to safety that was years ahead of its time.

The motor car company Panhard et Levassor was established by pioneering engineers René Panhard and Émile Levassor in 1887. Their first car was built in 1890 under a Daimler license. In 1895 they created the first modern transmission, and by the early 1900s they were regularly winning races such as the Paris–Bordeaux–Paris event. In 1925 it was a Panhard/Levassor that set a world hour speed record of 115 mph (185 kph).

In France after World War II, the Panhard company was highly prestigious. This was a period when its designers and engineers were buoyed by the success of their early Dyna sedan (saloon) in 1946, which had revived the company's flagging fortunes. They considered themselves the equal of Citroën when it came to mechanical innovation and setting trends in automotive design. So if cars had feelings, a 1950s Packard Dyna would have felt justifiably cocky when parked alongside the great motor cars of Europe. **BS**

PROBLÈME SIMPLE
6 personnes
+ 6 litres d'essence
+ 130 km.-heure
DYNA PANHARD
19, AVENUE D'IVRY - PARIS XIIIE - GOB. & POR. 65-60

At a gas station, James Dean prepares to climb into the Porsche 550 Spyder in which he died hours later, 1955. ⊡

Starlight | Studebaker (USA)

1953 • 168 cu in/2,779 cc, S6 • 120 bhp/90 kW • 0–60 mph/97 kph in 17 seconds • 93 mph/149 kph

The Studebaker Starlight coupe had been around since 1947, but it was the radical redesign of 1953 that gained notice when it emerged from the Studebaker plant at South Bend, Indiana. Some commentators named it one of the classic designs of 1950s America; others went further and described it as one of the best U.S. car designs of all time. The Museum of Modern Art in New York City even called it a work of art.

The Starlight had a more European look to it than other U.S. cars of its era. It sat lower, and had a more deeply sloping front and rear. People joked that they could not tell whether the car was coming or going.

The style was mainly the work of designer Robert E. Bourke, who started his career with Sears Roebuck & Co., but joined Studebaker in 1944. His design for the 1950 Studebaker was acclaimed but did not sell well; neither did his bold redesign of 1953 help prevent Studebaker's financial decline in the early 1950s. Again, the car was praised to the skies, but failed to sell, and by 1956 the company was almost bankrupt.

It did not help that Studebaker confused the public in the naming of their cars, which could and should have been commercial as well as critical successes. In 1953 Studebaker produced both Starlights and Starliners, and both were available as either Champion or Commander models, giving the public four options of what was basically the same car. Further confusion reigned in the following year. In 1956 all the cars became Studebaker Hawks, before the Starlight name was revived in 1958 and then dropped after a year. Studebaker's plant in South Bend finally closed just before Christmas of 1963. **MG**

550 Spyder | Porsche (D)

1953 • 91 cu in/1,498 cc, F4 • 110 bhp/82 kW • 0–60 mph/97 kph in 8.2 seconds • 137 mph/220 kph

The Porsche 550 Spyder was so low-slung that German racer Hans Herrman famously drove his under the closed barriers of a railway crossing during the 1954 Mille Miglia—and was narrowly missed by an oncoming train. The Spyder won at Nürburgring in its first race, went on to win its class at Le Mans, and established Porsche as a major force in motor sport.

The air-cooled engine was a comparatively small 91-cubic-inch (1,498-cc) flat-four unit, but it produced 110 bhp (82 kW) at a screaming 7,800 rpm, thanks to a complex and temperamental design that involved twin-carburetors, dual distributors, and four camshafts. The Spyder was a lightweight, mid-engined racer with few compromises for road use. The ladder-frame tubular steel chassis supported a hand-built aluminum body with a tiny windshield. The idea was for customers to race on weekends and use it on the road during the week.

The Spyder became famous as the car driven by actor James Dean, whose infamous words "Live fast, die young," came tragically true at the wheel on September 30, 1955. The young Hollywood star had imported a silver Spyder 550 from Germany at huge cost, met by earnings from his first two films. Dean named the car "Little Bastard," which he had painted on the rear panel. He had the Spyder for only nine days before he crashed it at top speed and was killed instantly. The wreck was supposedly cursed; people who got involved with it invariably met some misfortune.

Only 135 Spyders were built in the factory, but a large number of replicas have been made since. The scarcity of surviving originals means that their auction value would be at least $1 million (£500,000) today. **SH**

MOTEL
130
PORSCHE

1900 | Alfa Romeo (I)

1954 • 114 cu in/1,884 cc, S4 • 115 bhp/86 kW •
0–60 mph/97 kph in 11 seconds • 112 mph/180 kph

The Alfa Romeo 1900 series, commencing in 1950, was the company's first foray into mass production after a history of making exotic race cars. Curiously, it was the first left-hand-drive Alfa and came with a twin-cam, four-cylinder engine that was to become one of Alfa's most distinctive features. The 1900 is credited with starting the category of sports sedans (saloons).

The simple, spacious, and swift range evolved very quickly. Within a couple of years there were coupes, convertibles, and a short-wheelbase version. Various competing Italian coachbuilders created their own bodies on the Alfa 1900 chassis. By 1954 the car had a faster engine, five-speed gearbox (instead of four), and even more striking good looks.

Alfa began to make inroads into the U.S. market. A special one-off 1900 coupe developed by Ghia was displayed at the Los Angeles Auto Show of 1954 and was voted the most beautiful car in the show. It was bought by the owner of San Francisco's Fairmont Hotel who added a customized backseat for his dog.

Milan-based family-run styling company Zagato made the best version of all: the 1900 Super Sprint. The performance figures given above are for the Zagato model, now much sought after by collectors, which had an even more beguiling body and an uprated engine. **SH**

Century | Buick (USA)

1954 • 322 cu in/5,277 cc, V8 • 195 bhp/144 kW •
0–60 mph/97 kph in 13.3 seconds • 93 mph/149 kph

The Buick Century has come and gone, and come back again. The original car was launched in 1936, but phased out in 1942 after a poor sales performance. When the California Highway Patrol ordered a fleet of custom-built cars for their own use in 1954, the name was brought back again. The model gained priceless publicity when the TV series *Highway Patrol* launched in 1955, starring Broderick Crawford as a gruff patrolman. The show was an immediate hit and ran until 1959, being syndicated all over the world. The location of the fictional Highway Patrol was never specified, but as it was shot in California they used the same cars as the real Highway Patrol: Buick Centuries.

Buick's design for the new Century put a large engine in a small body, and this blend of power and nimble performance appealed to the public as much as to the police. Engine power was soon increased, too, in 1955 and again in 1956, to take the top speed over that magic 100-mph (160-kph) mark. By the time this series of the Century ceased production in 1958, the car had a full 366-cubic-inch (6-liter) engine. In fact the vehicle itself remained substantially the same when it came out in 1959 with a differently designed body, but now called the Invicta. The Century then came out in a third-generation incarnation in 1973. **MG**

Isabella TS | Borgward (D)

1954 • 91 cu in/1,493 cc, S4 • 59 bhp/44 kW • 0–60 mph/97 kph in 18 seconds • 81 mph/130 kph

Isabella, the Spanish version of Isabel, is a name that sits oddly with the Germanic-sounding Borgward company. The Bremen-based business had been making a small range of cars since the 1930s, and its founder, Carl Borgward, was noted for coming up with quirky vehicles that were always distinctive.

The Isabella was, at first, going to be another version of the Borgward Hansa 1500, which had arrived in 1949 to acclaim for its strikingly modern looks. But it changed in the production process and became a more spacious and gracious car. The name Isabella was coined to hint at what was considered to be its rather Mediterranean look and character. In truth, no other German car of the time could compete with the Isabella's combination of spaciousness, looks, handling, and price, and it became Borgward's best-selling car.

The best in the line was the Isabella TS, a two-door cabriolet. This had an upgraded 75 bhp (56 kW) engine, which also powered the sleek TS Coupe, launched in 1957. Borgward's wife liked the coupe he gave her so much that she drove it for the next twenty-five years.

By the time production ended in 1962, over 200,000 Isabellas had been made. But it still was not successful enough to stave off financial problems and the company went into liquidation. **MG**

2300S | Salmson (F)

1954 • 141 cu in/2,320 cc, S4 • 105 bhp/78 kW • 0–60 mph/97 kph in 13 seconds • 105 mph/169 kph

After World War II, sales of Salmson cars were sluggish. The French socialist government disapproved of luxury, high-end performance cars and imposed a tax on large engines that kept demand low and eroded profits. A new direction was needed, toward smaller cars with smaller engines—and a smaller price tag.

The Italian-styled 2300S two-seat coupe (and the convertible that followed in 1955) arrived too late to reverse the company's declining fortunes. Designed by Eugène Martin with a body supplied by the respected Parisian coachbuilders Chapron, the 2300S was intended to appeal to Salmson's small but dedicated rallying clientele. What the cars lacked in chassis design and low-speed torque they made up for with superb handling that saw both versions entered in various national and international rallies. Yet, despite having a four-speed gearbox, rack and pinion steering, a reputation for reliability and robustness, and a powerful 105-bhp (78-kW) engine that saw it compete at Le Mans from 1955 through to 1957, the 2300S never truly impressed.

Together, the coupe and convertible 2300S would be Salmson's swan song, the last two cars produced before the company went into receivership and was purchased by Renault in 1957. Of the 236 coupes produced, fewer than eighty examples have survived to this day. **BS**

Guiletta Sprint | Alfa Romeo

(I)

1954 • 78 cu in/1,290 cc, S4 • 80 bhp/60 kW • unknown • 88 mph/142 kph

Arriving in late 1954, the Sprint coupe was the first car to appear in Alfa Romeo's original Guiletta model range. Various other versions, including a stunning Spider soft-top, would follow later.

Less than a decade after the end of World War II, the Italian carmaker was determined to produce something that would revive its prewar reputation for building small, nippy cars that handled very well. The result of its efforts was the front-engine, rear-wheel-drive Guiletta Sprint. It was powered by a relatively small motor that was technologically advanced for its time, with twin overhead cams and a lightweight alloy block and head. By modern standards its power output of 80 bhp (60 kW) may seem modest, but it was enough to take the Guiletta Sprint up to nearly 90 mph (145 kph). The Bertone-designed bodywork may have been understated, but there was no mistaking the iconic Alfa grille at the front end.

Higher-powered versions were developed, and one of these was the Zagato. Legend has it that after a Sprint crashed during a race and damaged its bodywork, it went to the Zagato coachbuilder for repair. It received an all-new, all-aluminium body.

After making a small number of similar cars for racing, Zagato was eventually supplied with Guiletta Sprint rolling chassis by Alfa Romeo itself. The result was the Guiletta Sprint Zagato, or SZ. This model had 116 bhp (87 kW) and could reach 120 mph (193 kph)—not bad for a car with a 79-cubic-inch (1.3-liter) engine.

The Guiletta Sprint is still very much in demand. An original example sold in Eastern Europe in 2011 fetched in excess of $40,000 (£26,000). **JI**

220 | Mercedes

D

1954 • 133 cu in/2,195 cc, S6 • 83 bhp/62 kW • 0–60 mph/97 kph in 18.1 seconds • 90 mph/145 kph

The Mercedes 220 series was first unveiled at the 1951 Frankfurt Motor Show. It was the company's first all-new postwar design, with a pontoon-type body welded to the floor frame. The 220 was similar in appearance to the 170S and had an almost identical chassis to the 180, although lengthened by 6.75 inches (17 cm) to provide 2.75 inches (7 cm) more legroom for rear-seat passengers and 4 inches (10 cm) over the front end to accommodate the new six-cylinder engine. The headlights, no longer freestanding, were integrated into the front fenders (bumpers), and turn indicators set further forward in smart chrome housings gave the series a brand-new face. Fog lights were standard. All four wheels had ribbed brake drums with turbo cooling, ventilation slits were cut into the wheel rims to increase airflow, and the engine was given an octane compensator so it could take a variety of different fuels. The cars were nicknamed "pontons," from the German word for pontoon, referring to pontoon fenders that encased the wheels.

The 220 was available as a sedan (saloon); a two-door, two-seat Cabriolet A with rear jump seat; a four-door, four-seat Cabriolet B; and a coupe, probably the most exclusive 220 version, with just eighty-five being produced and available with an optional sunroof. Both the coupe and Cabriolet A had new, improved 85-bhp (63-kW) engines. All had magnificent solid-ash dashboards full of colored lights: blue for high beam, red for the generator, white for choke, and green for the turn signals. The sedan was discontinued in May 1954, but the coupe and Cabriolet A (figures given above), of which just 1,278 were made, continued through to August1955. **BS**

A Jaguar D-Type competition roadster is posed in front of San Francisco's spectacular Golden Gate Bridge. ▷

Vega FVS | Facel

F

1954 • 276 cu in/4,524 cc, V8 • 180 bhp/134 kW • 0–60 mph/97 kph in 10.7 seconds • 112 mph/181 kph

Facel may no longer be a well-known name in the automobile industry, but some famous people have wanted to own one of the company's cars over the years, including Albert Camus, Tony Curtis, Pablo Picasso, Dean Martin, Fred Astaire, and Ringo Starr.

The Facel company was founded in 1939 by French engineer Jean Daninos and had supplied body parts for cars, including the Ford Comète and the Panhard Dyna. It had always been Daninos's dream to build a car of his own one day, and with the Facel Vega in 1954, his dream came true. The car was named after a star, Vega, the fifth-brightest star in the night sky.

The Vega FVS was one of the first European cars to use an American V8 engine, which, with Daninos's proven skill in producing stylish bodywork, made the car rather special. The Vega FVS was hand-built, and fewer than 3,000 were produced over the next eight years. They were expensive and exclusive, and were designed by Daninos himself, with more than a nod to the striking styles coming out of the United States.

Daninos made various models, but the FVS was one of the more unusual. It had a wraparound windshield, unlike any other car on the road, and although the factory quoted a top speed of about 112 mph (181 kph), some tests found speeds of up to 130 mph (208 kph). Little wonder that racing drivers, including Stirling Moss and Maurice Trintignant, wanted one for themselves.

The Facel company went out of business in 1964 after a failed attempt at producing a racing car, the Facellia, which cost a fortune to develop, but had mechanical problems and sold badly. Having risen to a great height, Daninos's star had finally fallen. **MG**

D-Type | Jaguar

GB

1954 • 210 cu in/3,442 cc, S6 • 250 bhp/187 kW • 0–60 mph/97 kph in 5.7 seconds • 160 mph/257 kph

After the outstanding success of the Jaguar C-Type, what could the company do next? The C-Type had been built specifically to win at Le Mans, and it had done so twice. Jaguar faced either repeating the success ad nauseam or, eventually, failing to do so. So it set out to build a better car: the D-Type.

In fact, the company built six of them in 1954, improving the car by cramming even more power into the engine, shortening the engine area, and adding a tail fin behind the driver to make the car more stable at top speed. The result was a spectacularly beautiful car that was simple in its lines and yet managed to display all the pent-up power of a wild animal when quivering and about to pounce on its prey.

Unfortunately the car failed to pounce effectively at Le Mans, and although Jaguar entered four of the six D-Types it had built, the checkered flag went to Ferrari. Undeterred, the Jaguar engineers and designers carried on working on the D-Type, trying to squeeze every ounce of power from it. They returned to Le Mans in 1955 and this time their determination paid off. One of the D-Types took first place, although it was a victory overshadowed by an appalling accident. A Mercedes-Benz clipped the back of an Austin-Healey, crashed into a barrier, then burst into flames and exploded, killing the driver and eighty spectators. Mercedes withdrew from the race, which included stopping the lead car, which was two laps ahead of the Jaguar. The D-Type went on to a victory that inevitably seemed hollow.

Mercedes withdrew from racing, and soon after Jaguar did too, with the remaining stock of D-Types being sold instead as road cars. **MG**

Metropolitan | Nash

USA

1954 • 90 cu in/1,489 cc, S4 • 52 bhp/39 kW • 0–60 mph/97 kph in 22.4 seconds • 76 mph/122 kph

Development of "the world's smartest smaller car" began in 1946 when George W. Mason, visionary boss of Nash-Kelvinator, decided to target female, urban, and thrifty buyers. Its designer, William Flajole, worked independently with the Nash design department, but inspiration leaked from Italian design house Pininfarina, which also had been working for Nash.

The company had no small-car experience, so Austin in the United Kingdom was contracted for the build, and most of the running gear was sourced there. All this might have caused an identity crisis, and to make it worse Nash merged with Hudson to become American Motors Corporation (AMC) just as the Metropolitan was launched in 1954. This meant the car was sold by Nash and Hudson in the United States. From 1957 there was a right-hand-drive Austin version.

In the end, however, Metropolitan became a brand in its own right. The car itself came into its own in 1956 when it gained a perky 1500 B-series engine (used by the MGA) and its distinctive zig-zag two-tone color scheme. Inside, a simple Bakelite dash contained an integral radio. A "three on the tree" gear lever added space and suited American tastes. Behind the two-person front bench in chic houndstooth fabric, a flap gave access to the trunk (boot).

AMC used savvy ad campaigns to push sales of the hardtop at $1,527 (£973) and convertible at $1,551 (£988). U.S. sales were healthy until the early 1960s, but buyers preferred the larger Rambler. In Britain, the Met proved too brash and wallowy, and AMC pulled the plug in 1962. U.S. enthusiasts now pay up to $12,000 (£7,500) for a convertible; U.K. buyers will pay more. **LT**

Monterey | Mercury

(USA)

1954 • 255 cu in/4,195 cc, V8 • 162 bhp/119 kW • 0–60 mph/97 kph in 14 seconds • 100 mph/161 kph

The first Mercury Monterey came out in 1950, Mercury being a subdivision of Ford, and the Monterey was created to be the most luxurious and most expensive model in the Mercury range. The Monterey name lasted until 1974, but it was the models made from 1952 to 1954 that stood out, in particular the '54 Monterey. This was fitted with a new Ford V8 engine that boosted the horsepower from 125 bhp (93 kW) to a much more impressive 162 bhp (119 kW). This gave a big leap in performance, even though the car looked similar on the outside. New wraparound taillights and a restyled grille were the most noticeable changes.

In 1954 Ford built its 40-millionth vehicle, and it was a Mercury Monterey Convertible in siren red that got the honor. The Monterey was produced in four different body styles including a hardtop coupe, which was Ford's best-selling model of 1954 with almost 80,000 units. Ford also sold almost 66,000 of the four-door sedans (saloons). There was a four-door station wagon (estate), too, the famous "woodie wagon" so beloved of surfers, of which some wonderful examples have survived and occasionally turn up at auction. A regular 1954 Mercury Monterey today, in good condition, is likely to fetch about $45,000 (£29,000).

A one-off preproduction Monterey was built in Detroit in 1953, and although it was much touted and shown at the 1954 Detroit Auto Show, the design was killed off and the Monterey that appeared was nothing like the prototype. The prototype had no functioning engine so had to be hauled into position. It was later sold off, then found again in the legendary barn where old cars are always found, only to end up on eBay. **MG**

Thunderbird | Ford

USA

1954 • 312 cu in/5,114 cc, V8 • 225 bhp/165 kW • 0–50 mph/80 kph in 7.5 seconds • 116 mph/187 kph

The Thunderbird is a mythological American Indian creature of great power and strength, and the Ford Thunderbird certainly justified its name. It lasted for fifty years through eleven generations, and 4.4 million cars were sold. Strangely enough, Thunderbird was not one of the thousands of names considered for the new car (including Apache, Eagle, and Thunderbolt); it was adopted at the last minute in the race to get a car out to compete with Chevrolet's 1953 Corvette.

Ford's first Thunderbird was put on show at the Detroit Motor Show in January 1954 and was on sale by October. Its V8 engine was capable of 116 mph (187 kph), and it was marketed as a two-seater personal touring car rather than a sports car. The Thunderbird soon achieved celebrity status with Frank Sinatra buying a 1955 model, and Marilyn Monroe and Arthur Miller driving around in two 1956 Thunderbirds—one in New York and one in California. Other Thunderbird fans over the years have included Elvis Presley, Bing Crosby, Oprah Winfrey, and John Travolta.

Despite selling over 53,000 Thunderbirds in the first three years, Ford felt there was a bigger family market still to be tapped. The four-seater second-generation model was introduced for 1958. Sales doubled, and doubled again in 1959 when Ford targeted the female market. Ford then relaunched a new-generation Thunderbird every three years.

A 1966 Thunderbird convertible featured in the classic road movie *Thelma and Louise* (1991), and a 2003 model was driven by Halle Berry in the James Bond film *Die Another Day* (2002). But sales finally began to fall and production ceased in 2005. It was the end of an era. **MG**

300SL | Mercedes

D

1954 • 182 cu in/2,995 cc, S6 • 212 bhp/156 kW • 0–60 mph/97 kph in 10 seconds • 160 mph/257 kph

Beyond the Mercedes 300SL's most obvious feature—its gull-wing doors—lies some technology that made this possibly the world's first supercar. It has a tubular "space frame" chassis, a kind of metal skeleton upon which the bodywork hangs. This makes the 300SL incredibly strong and stiff, without weighing it down. Then there is the engine, which was the first in the world to have gasoline direct injection, where fuel is squirted straight into each cylinder. Although the basic straight six-cylinder engine design was carried over from the earlier four-door Mercedes 300, direct injection almost doubled the power output. At its launch at the New York Motor Show in 1954, the 300SL was the world's fastest production car.

But what about those gull-wing doors? They came about out of an engineering necessity rather than a design fancy. The car's advanced space frame dictated that a key chassis member should run right through the space where the lower part of any normal door would be. The answer? Hinge the doors at the top and make them lift upward.

When Mercedes designed the 300SL, they were encouraged to do so by an Austrian-born American named Max Hoffman. He was the chief importer of several European car brands into the United States at the time, and he often advised manufacturers about what sort of models would sell there. With the 300SL he was absolutely right: more than three-quarters of the total made was sold in that market, and the car helped to cement the Mercedes brand in the United States.

In 2009 two 300SLs were offered for sale in the United States for more than $1.3 million (£840,000). **JI**

Darrin | Kaiser

USA

1954 • 159 cu in/2,621 cc, S6 • 125 bhp/93 kW • unknown • 96 mph/154 kph

Some cars sum up the time and place of their birth. For the Kaiser Darrin that would be the United States in the early 1950s. After the sacrifices of the war years, this was a country determined to enjoy itself. It was a time of bold designs, and few come any bolder than this.

The car was the brainchild of Howard A. "Dutch" Darrin, a designer who had had something of a love-hate relationship with the Kaiser car company, repeatedly joining then leaving the firm. He was so determined to design a sports car, against the management's wishes, that he did it all in his own time. He even got as far as building a prototype in 1952.

The two-seater convertible had a fiberglass body on a steel chassis, and sliding doors based on a design that Darrin had patented in 1946. It also had a small, shell-shaped front grille that was described as "looking like it wants to give you a kiss." When the work was presented to the company boss, Henry J. Kaiser, his response was less than positive. "We're not in the business of selling sports cars!" he raged. But things changed when his wife gave her opinion: "It's the most beautiful thing I've ever seen."

Won over, Henry gave it his approval and the Kaiser Darrin went into production, although the car did not go on sale until 1954. Sadly, it never really took off, with the market resisting its combination of an exotic design and a relatively high price.

Only 435 were made before the Kaiser company ceased production. Darrin himself sold a hundred more, each fitted with a Cadillac V8. Shortlived though it was, the Kaiser Darrin remains one of the most beautiful and bold examples of American car design. **JI**

Magnette ZA | MG

GB

1954 • 90 cu in/1,489 cc, S4 • 60 bhp/45 kW • 0–60 mph/97 kph in 22.6 seconds • 82 mph/132 kph

In 1952 the British Motor Corporation (BMC) accounted for almost 40 percent of all British cars made, having in its stable such brands as Austin, Wolseley, Morris, and MG. Austin, the dominant partner in the group, merged with Nuffield in 1952 at a time when one of Nuffield's chief designers, Gerald Palmer, was at work designing a replacement for MG's popular Y-Type series. Drawing inspiration from Italian stylists, Palmer came up with a car that would be, until the advent of the MGA, the best-selling MG of all time: the Magnette ZA.

The ZA received only a lukewarm reception when it premiered at the 1953 London Motor Show, but this would soon change. MG devotees began to be won over by its new look and superior handling, achieved with a new coil-and-wishbone suspension and rack-and-pinion steering hidden beneath the ZA's sleek, curvaceous skin. The ZA was also the first MG with a monocoque pressed-steel body, which allowed the car to be made lighter while still retaining structural strength. Inside were leather-trimmed front seats, a fully carpeted floor, a polished wood dashboard, and a pull-down armrest in the rear seat.

The ZA sold almost 4,000 units in its first year, despite a delayed debut to allow the fitting of BMC's new B-series 60-bhp (45-kW) engine, which former MG designer H. N. Charles described as "horrible . . . but free from bugs." Such an engine would, of course, always struggle to provide adequate power to a car weighing 2,500 pounds (1,136 kg), which raises the question of whether *Autocar*'s review in 1954 that "wet roads or dry make little difference to its performance" was meant as a critique or a compliment. **BS**

XK140 | Jaguar

GB

1954 • 210 cu in/3,442 cc, S6 • 190 bhp/142 kW • 0–60 mph/97 kph in 8.4 seconds • 120 mph/193 kph

Britain was in its sports car heyday when the Jaguar XK140 appeared as the replacement for the highly regarded XK120. In production for just three years from its launch in 1954, the XK140 was the definitively glamorous, eye-catching British two-seater of its age. It was the car any upwardly mobile motorist wanted to be seen in, until the 1957 arrival of its even more powerful successor, the XK150.

The 1950s were a time of growing prosperity and optimism. The XK140 arrived on the scene just one year on from Queen Elizabeth II's coronation. With the new young monarch adding glamour to Britain's image at home and abroad, the twin-seat Jaguar was perfectly placed to capitalize on the mood of the moment.

The car encapsulated all the elements of Jaguar founder Sir William Lyons's famous slogan, "Grace, space, and pace," as well as fulfilling his strict value-for-money mantra. Powered by Jaguar's own twin-cam straight-six-cylinder engine with twin carburetors, the Coventry-built XK140 was the core of the company's success throughout the 1950s. To improve on its illustrious predecessor, the car was given more interior space and a power boost of 10 bhp (7.5 kW), as well as better brakes and more supple suspension that improved the ride and handling. Buyers were offered a choice of two body styles: steel-roof coupe or soft-top roadster.

The car was built on Jaguar's motorsport success early in the decade, and wore a trunk- (boot-) lid emblem that proclaimed "Winner Le Mans 1951-3." In 1956 the XK140 became the first Jaguar sports car to be offered with an automatic gearbox, an option that increased its appeal as an import in the United States. **SB**

Aurelia B20 GT | Lancia

(I)

1955 • 149 cu in/2,451 cc, V6 • 110 bhp/82 kW • 0–60 mph/97 kph in 12.3 seconds • 112 mph/180 kph

When Lancia's founder, Vincenzo Lancia, died suddenly of a heart attack in February 1937 at the age of fifty-six, his son Gianni and widow Adele vowed to continue in his visionary footsteps. One of their many decisions was to lure the talented engineer Vittorio Jano away from Ferrari to work on Lancia's impressive line of heavy trucks. World War II intervened and Lancia production suffered under the occupation, but Jano continued to work on designs from a secret location in Padova.

The Aurelia line of Jano-designed sedans (saloons) and coupes began in 1951 with the B10 and continued through six series to 1958, all possessing a classic form and benefiting from trim and performance enhancements through each series (the B20 GT alone went through six series upgrades). All had the distinction of having the world's first production V6 engine, as well as being one of the first cars to be fitted with radial tires as standard. Of all the variants produced, however, only the two-door, 149-cubic-inch (2,451-cc) B20 GT Coupe would go on to earn the title of the world's first Gran Turismo (GT). The B-20 GT was also known as "the connoisseur's car," due in part to the involvement of the legendary Sergio "Pinin" Farina, who provided the car with its beautiful bodywork and gave the public a glimpse of a stylish automotive future.

Although it can be said the B20 GT's interior was rather austere and sported a very unsporting column change (a Lancia sedan leftover that could in any case be replaced by a floor-mounted conversion), that did not stop the great Juan Manuel Fangio—the man whose job it was to race Ferraris and Maseratis—from describing the B20 GT as "invigorating." **BS**

403 Convertible | Peugeot

F

1955 • 89 cu in/1,468 cc, S4 • 64 bhp/48 kW • 0–60 mph/97 kph in 20.8 seconds • 84 mph/135 kph

The Peugeot 403 is an unlikely looking movie star, but then so is Peter Falk, who portrayed the rumpled but unforgettable Lieutenant Columbo in the 1970s U.S. TV series *Columbo*. The 403 was Columbo's car, but it also appeared in countless other TV series and movies, especially in its native country, France, including *À Bout de Souffle* (1960), *Bonjour Tristesse* (1958), *Les Quatres Cents Coups* (1959), various Maigret movies and TV episodes, and in the TV cartoon series *Les Aventures de Tintin* (1991–92). One even appears in *Bullitt* (1968), though only in the background behind Steve McQueen, as this was not a car built with car chases in San Francisco in mind. In fact, just negotiating the slopes of some of the streets might have been a major challenge.

The standard 403 model, a chunky sedan (saloon), came in various configurations. There was the basic four-door sedan, a five-door station wagon (estate), and a two-door pickup. Columbo's car, however, was probably a 1959 403 convertible, which was the least successful of the models produced, perhaps because it looked about as elegant and racy as Columbo's famous raincoat. He would also have driven a 1960 version of the car, which was used as a backup, but it is almost impossible to tell the two years apart.

When Columbo describes his car as "very rare," he is putting a positive spin on the fact that only 504 examples of his convertible were made in 1959. This is out of the grand total of 1.2 million Peugeot 403s that were sold in all. Peugeot used the famous Columbo connection in advertising campaigns, even though its 403 ceased production in 1966, two years before the TV series first aired in the United States. **MG**

507 | BMW

(D)

1955 • 193 cu in/3,168 cc, V8 • 150 bhp/112 kW • 0–60 mph/97 kph in 8.8 seconds • 124 mph/200 kph

Max Hoffman was an Austrian-born businessman who lived in the United States, intimately knew the U.S. car market and the whims of its motoring public, and made a good living as sole importer of what were then referred to as "foreign" cars. He saw the United States as a lifeline for European carmakers still struggling with depressed postwar economies, and his intuition regarding what would appeal to U.S. car buyers was renowned. The Mercedes 300SL and the Porsche 356 Speedster were Hoffman suggestions, and in 1954 he convinced BMW that it ought to consider producing a midpriced roadster to compete with the 300SL. Hoffman wanted the great engineer and designer Albrecht von Goertz to create it.

Unveiled in New York in 1955, the von Goertz-designed BMW 507 set a new benchmark in car design with its classic lines and sweeping hood (bonnet). The 507 was an important car for the German automaker as it struggled out of a ruined postwar economy to reestablish its place as one of Europe's great brands.

Though the 507 was mounted on a 503 frame, that was where similarities to anything produced in the past ended. The engine was a new lightweight V8 capable of producing 150 bhp (112 kW), and no two 507s were the same, each one being almost entirely hand-shaped from aluminum, with bodies so individual that their fabric hardtops had to be customized to fit. Unfortunately, the absence of an assembly line made the 507 expensive (it was twice the price of a Jaguar XK140) and BMW reportedly lost money on every one of the 252 units it made. Nevertheless, for many it remains the all-time icon of the BMW brand. **BS**

502 | BMW (D)

1955 • 157 cu in/2,580 cc, V8 • 100 bhp/75 kW • 0–60 mph/97 kph in 14.5 seconds • 99 mph/160 kph

When BMW unveiled its new 501 sedan (saloon) at the inaugural Frankfurt Motor Show in 1951, the company's first postwar luxury car made such an impression on a public starved of beauty, that the car was nicknamed the "Baroque Angel." But there was a problem: the six-cylinder engine was not big enough to power a car weighing 3,175 pounds (1,440 kg) adequately. With a real prospect of losing its precious market share, BMW set about making a derivative of the 501: the 502.

The 502 was available as a two-door and four-door sedan, and a cabriolet. Its engine, designed by longtime BMW engineer Fritz Fiedler, was the world's first light alloy V8 to go into standard production, and the first V8 engine built in Germany since 1945. A number of so-called Super V8s with increased compression and twin carburetors were also made, capable of producing 160 bhp (119 kW).

The BMW 502 also received some luxurious appointments that were denied the 501, such as individualized front seats, fog lights, and additional chrome trimming. The "new, improved" 502 "Baroque Angel" was undeniably beautiful, but it was also expensive—some of its voluptuous panels required three pressings to get right—and only 3,840 units were sold, barely one-sixth of the total BMW executives had hoped for. **BS**

1955 | Chevrolet (USA)

1955 • 265 cu in/4,343 cc, V8 • 162 bhp/121 kW • 0–60 mph/97 kph in 9.9 seconds • 110 mph/176 kph

By the 1950s, U.S. car manufacturers were seeking a particular Holy Grail: a vehicle that combined the new fashion for eye-catching design with both power and price. Chevrolet achieved that with its 1955 Chevy, a car that is now regarded as one of the classic American designs. The 1955 came in three versions: the 150, 210, and the Bel Air. Between them, the three models came in nine different configurations, ranging from a two-door sedan (saloon) to a six-passenger station wagon (estate), although they all used the same powerful V8 engine.

The '55 Chevy was born in 1952 when designer Edward Nicholas Cole was challenged to design a new car from scratch. The end result not only changed the image of Chevrolet cars but the company's fortunes, too. Despite being shorter and narrower than previous Chevrolets, its design made it look longer and wider.

The '55 Chevy had its fair share of film roles. Three specially built examples feature in the road movie *Two-Lane Backtop* (1971), one of which was strengthened so that it could support the cameras filming the action while the actors were driving. Two of them were later painted black and used in *American Graffiti* (1973), one appearing in the crash scene at the end of the movie, although the car seen burning was simply a wreck salvaged from a scrapyard. **MG**

Super 88 | Oldsmobile (USA)

1955 • 323 cu in/5,309 cc, V8 • 240 bhp/177 kW • 0–60 mph/97 kph in 8 seconds • 110 mph/176 kph

The Oldsmobile 88 name had existed since 1949, but it is the 1955 model that is among the best remembered, going on sale in what was to be a momentous year for the U.S. car industry. The 1955 Chevrolet, Chrysler C-300, Chrysler Imperial, and Studebaker Speedster—every one a classic—would all emerge in that same year.

The 1949 Oldsmobile 88 had introduced a new V8 engine, known as "the Rocket." The cars inspired what many people consider to be the first rock 'n' roll song, "Rocket 88." The year 1951 saw the launch of the first Oldsmobile Super 88, a more powerful and more expensive version of the plain old Oldsmobile 88.

By 1955 the Rocket engine was even bigger, and the Super 88 of that year now matched the style and power of rival models, but at a cheaper price. The 1955 Super 88 offered a new grille design, a one-piece windshield, turn signals, stainless-steel trim moldings, rocket badges, a dimmer rearview mirror, dual trumpet horns, a cigar lighter, floor mats front and rear, and optional air-conditioning. In this same year the Oldsmobile company sold its five-millionth vehicle since its founding in 1896.

A 1955 Super 88 can be bought today for around $20,000 (£13,000). As well as inspiring a song, Oldsmobile 88s have appeared in movies such as *Goldfinger* (1964), *Walk the Line* (2005), and *Pulp Fiction* (1994). **MG**

C-300 | Chrysler (USA)

1955 • 331 cu in/5,426 cc, V8 • 225 bhp/166 kW • unknown • 128 mph/206 kph

The naming of the Chrysler 300 series has a confusing history. The first to appear was the C-300. This was followed by, obviously, the 300B and then the 300C, and that pattern continued through to 1965's 300L. There was no 300I, however, and the 300M did not appear until thirty-four years after the 300L.

The C-300 itself was a bit of a mongrel, too, having been cobbled together from the front end of a Chrysler Imperial, the middle of a Chrysler New Yorker, and the rear end of a Chrysler Windsor. Astonishingly, the amalgam worked. It was modern in style, thanks to designer Bob Rodger, and it was powerful under the hood (bonnet). It had a bigger engine and a better performance than its biggest rival, the 1955 Chevy.

The C-300 was a star on the racetrack rather than the road, helping Chrysler win the NASCAR Grand National title, and the AAA Championship. It was a breakthrough car whose speedometer went up to the new magical figure of 150 mph (240 kph). People lined up to see the car in showrooms, but did not line up to buy it. The C-300 was very heavy on gasoline, and with a price of $4,110 (£2,670) was clearly aimed at the high-end market—it cost more than twice as much as the Chevy '55. Only 1,725 C-300s were built in its first year, and scarcity makes it a desirable and equally expensive car today. **MG**

« Few could resist the charm of an Isetta. Here Cary Grant poses in a 1955 model during a visit to Munich, Germany.

Isetta 250 | BMW

D

1955 • 15 cu in/247 cc, one-cylinder • 13 bhp/9.6 kW • 0–30 mph/48 kph in 30 seconds • 53 mph/85 kph

Most of the world had never seen a car like this before: bubble windows, a canvas roof for ventilation, and a single front door that opened outward, taking the steering wheel with it. While BMW transformed the two-seater Isetta into a success when it launched it in April 1955, the idea was not its own—the car had been on sale in Italy for two years previously. It was the brainchild of Italian firm Iso SpA, best known for its scooters and three-wheeled trucks, and in postwar Italy it provided cheap and cheerful urban transport for the masses. The name Isetta, translating as "Little Iso," alluded to the Iso company.

The German giant bought a license to build the car and all the tooling, and modified the design around its own 15-cubic-inch (247-cc) single-cylinder motorcycle engine. The car—badged the Isetta 250—could be driven on a bike license. In just eight months 10,000 were produced for a hungry German market. When time was called in May 1962, more than 160,000 had been sold.

In the fall of 1956, a larger-engined version called the Isetta 300 was launched, followed a year later by a four-seater called the 600; bizarrely, the latter retained the front-opening door. The 600 did not sell well because customers preferred the Volkswagen Beetle.

The Isetta was an international hit and was built at factories in Spain, France, Brazil, and the United Kingdom, where cars were built for the National Health Service and offered free to wheelchair users to improve their mobility.

The Isetta's unique appeal has kept it popular with enthusiastic collectors. BMW's simple and cost-conscious approach to its construction, both in terms of price and fuel economy, has led many carmakers today to consider making modern-day equivalents. **RY**

Karmann Ghia | Volkswagen

D

1955 • 72 cu in/1,192 cc, F4 • 30 bhp/22.3 kW • 0–60 mph/97 kph in 25 seconds • 72 mph/115 kph

Three elements went into the Volkswagen Karmann Ghia: the mechanical talent of Volkswagen, the coachbuilding skill of Karmann, and a design penned by Italian styling house Ghia. The result is a classic of automotive art, often appearing in lists of the best-looking cars of all time. It is a pity that it lacked the performance to go with the looks.

In the early 1950s, Volkswagen's iconic Beetle was selling well, but senior executives wanted a different version to act as a halo (flagship) for the base model. They hired Karmann, who brought in Ghia, and the result was the Type 14, which debuted as a concept vehicle on the Ghia stand at the 1953 Paris Motor Show. It was the work of Luigi Segre, who a year later helped develop the Renault Dauphine.

The idea of a 2+2 (two seats in both front and rear) in both coupe and convertible body types went down well with Volkswagen and in August 1955, the first production coupe—now renamed in honor of the three companies involved—rolled out of the factory gates. The public loved its sleek styling and 10,000 were sold in the first year. Buyers, willing to overlook that it was basically a Beetle underneath, loved it for its timeless design rather than its handling.

The cabriolet followed in 1957, and a decade later it achieved fame in the United States when it appeared in the credits of the popular spy comedy *Get Smart*.

More than 445,000 Karmann Ghias were manufactured in Germany before the axe fell in 1974, when it was succeeded by the Scirocco. From 1962 to 1975, Karmann's South American operation in Brazil built 41,000 more for the local market. **RY**

3100 Series | Chevrolet

USA

1955 • 265 cu in/4,343 cc, V8 • 123 bhp/91 kW • unknown • 120 mph/192 kph

Once seen, never forgotten: the Chevy 3100 pickup is a classic American car design.

When Chevrolet unveiled a new line of pickup trucks in 1947, it used the phrase "Advance Design" to describe the vehicle's striking new looks. The cabs were built wider and taller, and for the first time the pickup could seat three people across the bench seat. There was a heater and a defroster, which in those days were luxury features for cars, let alone trucks. But Americans have always loved their trucks, and there is a huge market for them. With its 1947 Advance Design models, Chevrolet established itself as the leading truck manufacturer in the United States.

Then in 1955 came the Chevrolet 3100 Task Force series, which featured various first-time features for Chevy trucks such as powered steering and brakes. The wraparound windshield was the first seen on any truck, but most important was the powerful new V8 engine. A star was born. As well as being a tough truck for the all-American guy, these monsters could drive at speeds that would leave many cars standing. There was a boom in sales as drivers bought them to do double duty as a truck and as a family's main passenger vehicle.

The new 3100s had looks that were stylish and fun. Appealing features included the egg-crate grille, and headlights that for the first time were modeled after car headlights. Selling for $1,619 (£1,000), they were not only affordable but a bargain, especially to rural families who previously had been used to running both a pickup and a family car. They were durable, too, and there is now an active market in lovingly restored examples of Chevy 3100 Task Force pickups. **MG**

Bel Air Nomad | Chevrolet

(USA)

1955 • 235 cu in/3,859 cc, S6 • 140 bhp/103 kW • 0–60 mph/97 kph in 16.8 seconds • 86 mph/138 kph

Chevrolet had created a stir when the company introduced its Bel Air model back in 1950. The Bel Air was both a hardtop and a "convertible" (the roof was of solid construction, so while it could be swung back, it could not be detached from the car). Sold at a competitive price, it was advertised as offering the best of both summer and winter driving: the top could be shifted in summer, but in the freezing winter occupants had the benefit of a solid roof. The Bel Air did moderately well, certainly well enough to keep the models rolling off the production line for the next few years.

The big change came in 1955 when the car was given a sleek new styling that definitely angled it toward the convertible market and turned it into a hot rod. In addition, a new model was introduced, one that was also quite revolutionary and represented another attempt by Chevrolet to blend two types of car into one. The Bel Air Nomad was a combination of hardtop and station wagon (estate). No one had seen anything quite like it before, and for Chevrolet it was a bold gamble.

The station wagon sold at a modest $2,571 (£1,700) and gave the American driver what looked more or less like a conventional car but with a lot of additional space to pack kids, luggage, groceries, and bulkier items in the back. The disadvantage was that it proved to be a hot and stuffy car to drive, with its large windows turning it into a soporific greenhouse on sunny days.

Only 8,386 were sold in the first year and sales dropped year after year, but the Bel Air Nomad stuck around until 1965. By then the Nomad name was established and well loved, and Chevrolet brought it back in the 1990s for its Nomad van line. **MG**

Fireflite | DeSoto

USA

1955 • 291 cu in/4,769 cc, V8 • 200 bhp/147 kW • 0–60 mph/97 kph in 11 seconds • 110 mph/175 kph

Introduced in 1955, the Fireflite was the first of two new vehicles that put the DeSoto name firmly on the motoring map. The other was the Adventurer, which came out in 1956. DeSoto was a brand founded by Walter Chrysler in 1928, and both cars were part of a special "Forward Look" plan introduced by Chrysler designer Virgil Exner throughout the company's range. Until the arrival of the Fireflite, DeSoto had been a fairly conservative part of the Chrysler empire.

Among other things, Exner emphasized the tail fins on the new Fireflite, which made the car stand out, even at a time when everyone else was trying to outdo one another in their tail-fin design. Exner also gave the Fireflites a two-tone look, with some eye-catching combinations, and the cars often featured a white, black, or red stripe down the side to stress their speed.

In the case of the Fireflite, the visual trick of "go-faster" stripes was amply supported by the car's capacity for

speed. This was the year DeSoto added "oomph" to its range by switching from six-cylinder to eight-cylinder engines. The cars gained added pubicity, too, because since 1950 Chrysler had been sponsoring the immensely popular Groucho Marx radio series, *You Bet Your Life*. When the show later appeared on TV, the sponsorship deal involved the host peering through a DeSoto logo and telling the audience, "Friends . . . go in to see your DeSoto-Plymouth dealer tomorrow. And when you do, tell 'em Groucho sent you." That probably was not the wittiest line the master of comedy had ever uttered, but it helped DeSoto's sales figures. The Fireflite sold more than 37,000 examples in 1955, and another 31,000 in 1956, when its engine was given even more power. Also in 1956, a striking gold and white Fireflite convertible served as the official pace car for the Indianapolis 500. Sadly, the model was phased out in 1957, superseded by an updated DeSoto Adventurer. **MG**

Crown Victoria | Ford

USA

1955 • 222 cu in/3,654 cc, S6 • 120 bhp/89 kW • unknown • unknown

When Ford launched its 1955 range of cars, it boasted of how the bodywork made it look like it was moving, even when it wasn't. The flowing lines and jutting headlights gave an impression of speed, apparently.

That contention speaks more for the competition between 1950s U.S. carmakers than it does for the Ford Crown Victoria. Ford was keen to fight back against thriving rivals, and needed to pull out all the stops. This was the year of two-tone paint schemes, wraparound windshields, and flying-saucer hubcaps.

The Crown Victoria was lower than a standard Ford Victoria, less than 5 feet (152 cm) from the floor to the top of the roof, and its panoramic windshield was lifted from a convertible. The standard engine was a 222-cubic-inch (3.6-liter) straight-six, but other options were available, even including a muscular 292-cubic-inch (4.8-liter) V8 shared with the legendary Thunderbird. But what made the Crown Victoria stand out was its over-the-roof "tiara." This was a chrome molding—also called a "basket handle"—that ran up and over the roof from one side of the car to the other. The aim of the design was to separate visually the driver's compartment from the rear passengers.

Another visual effect of the Crown Victoria's squashed roof height was that the car appeared longer than it actually was. In fact, every Ford model on the market in 1955 was of the same length.

One version of the Crown Victoria—the Skyline—was produced with a clear acrylic roof section. This did not sell very well, particularly in the hotter U.S. southern states, but quite a few found their way to Sweden, where intense sunshine was less of an issue. **JI**

410 Superamerica | Ferrari

I

1955 • 302 cu in/4,963 cc, V12 • 400 bhp/298 kW • 0–60 mph/97 kph in 6.6 seconds • 165 mph/265 kph

What would sell more exotic Italian sports cars across the Atlantic? Make them bigger and more luxurious, and call them "America," of course. That was Ferrari's plan, anyway, with a series of V12-powered touring sports cars in the 1950s and 1960s. The name was American, but the styling and build quality from the Modena factory was more European, with high-quality details, such as thickly bolstered hide seats and leather-trimmed glove boxes, to seduce wealthy buyers.

Movie star Ingrid Bergman drove one, as did Texas oil heiress Sandra West, whose will stipulated that she be buried inside hers wearing a lace nightgown. Her family complied, covering the car with concrete to deter thieves.

The epitome of the series was the 410 Superamerica, which had even more power than the already very rapid Americas. It was correspondingly superexpensive, too. At $16,800 (£10,800), the 410 was almost double the price of a Mercedes 300SL, and three times the cost of a Corvette. The 410's list of buyers reflected this price tag: the Shah of Iran, Aga Khan, Gianni Agnelli, Enzo Ferrari, Nelson Rockefeller, Emperor Bao Dai of Vietnam, and U.S. casino baron Bill Harrah all owned one.

Disregarding slight variations in the 410's technical details and different customized bodies, all buyers got a car that would still be considered very fast today. With triple Weber carburetors, the track-bred V12 5-liter engine produced up to 400 bhp (298 kW) and it could do 0–60 mph (97 kph) in 6.6 seconds.

The car's top speed was 165 mph (265 kph), a mind-boggling performance in the late 1950s. One owner said, "When you put your foot down, you hope the road goes where the car is going." **SH**

Silver Cloud | Rolls-Royce (GB)

1955 • 299 cu in/4,900 cc, S6 • 155 bhp/116 kW • 0–60 mph/97 kph in 13.5 seconds • 103 mph/165 kph

The Rolls-Royce Silver Cloud was a majestic car that had an eleven-year reign as the top model produced at the company's factory in Crewe. Some 7,372 were made between April 1955 and March 1966.

The much-admired curvaceous body, designed by J. P. Blatchley, represented a major change from its predecessor—the Silver Dawn—and all previous Rolls-Royce models. The Silver Cloud was the last Rolls-Royce made in the traditional way with a steel box-section chassis, welded together into a very rigid construction, and a steel and aluminum coachwork body on top. All subsequent Rolls-Royces have had the more modern unibody construction. The Silver Cloud appeared first with a 4.9-liter straight-six-cylinder engine, but from the arrival of the Mark II in 1959 this was changed to a 378-cubic-inch (6.2-liter) V8.

Traditionally Rolls-Royces had been the preserve of royalty, aristocrats, and rich industrialists. After World War II, ownership expanded to include a wider range of customers. Perhaps the most famous owner of a Silver Cloud was Elvis Presley. Oddly, for such a wealthy pop star, he had a penchant for buying used cars. The Silver Cloud that became a familiar sight at his Gracelands mansion in Memphis had had three previous owners, an actor and two country musicians. **SB**

MGA | MG (GB)

1955 • 91 cu in/1,498 cc, S4 • 68 bhp/50 kW • 0–60 mph/97 kph in 16 seconds • 98 mph/157 kph

The MGA was one of the classic English sports cars. It arrived in 1955 as a fresh-faced roadster that was seen as a complete break from MGs of the past. The new sleek lines were an instant hit, especially abroad. There weren't even any exterior door handles to disturb the streamlined sides. The two-door car also came as a coupe, but with the optional wire wheels and folding fabric roof, the MGA soft-top set the tone for a generation of British roadsters.

Beneath this stylish skin was an engine from the MG Magnette sedan (saloon), which drove the back wheels through a four-speed manual gearbox. The floor was slung low between the chassis members, creating a lower center of gravity for better handling. By 1958 there was a twin-cam engine producing a more muscular 108 bhp (81 kW) and disc brakes replaced the previous drums. The acceleration time was almost halved. The MGA was built until 1962 when it was succeeded by the MGB, which built steadily on the dynasty's success

How cool was the MGA at the time? Certainly many Americans took to the little roadster—it was exported across the Atlantic in one of the highest proportions of any British car ever. In 1962 Elvis Presley sang a number in the film *Blue Hawaii* from the back of a red MGA. He liked it so much he bought one. It is still on display at his former home, Graceland. **BK**

TR3 | Triumph (GB)

1955 • 121 cu in/1,991 cc, S4 • 95 bhp/71 kW •
0–60 mph/97 kph in 10.8 seconds • 105 mph/169 kph

In the early 1950s, the Standard-Triumph company, based in Coventry, produced sedans (saloons) under the Standard brand, and sports cars with the Triumph badge. The Triumph TR3 was designed to do battle with a rival product from MG, the MGA 1500. An updated version, produced from 1957, became known as the TR3A, although it was never badged as such.

The basic TR3 was a two-seater soft-top, but an occasional rear seat and a bolt-on steel hardtop were available as optional extras. A distinctive feature of the TR3 was its "egg-box" mesh "small mouth" grille. This was later extended to improve airflow into the engine, and as a result the TR3A is easily recognized by its "wide mouth" grille. At the same time, the updated car was fitted with front disc brakes, becoming the first series-built British car to have them as standard equipment. It was also given exterior door-handles and a lockable trunk (boot), both of which the 1955 TR3 lacked.

Sold in an era when Britain was the acclaimed leader in designing and building sports cars, the TR3 became popular around the world. It was regarded as a relatively simple, reliable, and affordable model with a breezy insouciance, and it was not only produced in Coventry but also assembled in Belgium, South Africa, and Australia. It sold particularly well in the United States. **SB**

Speedster | Studebaker (USA)

1955 • 258 cu in/4,244 cc, V8 • 185 bhp/136 kW •
0–60 mph/97 kph in 10 seconds • 110 mph/176 kph

Only 2,215 Studebaker Speedsters were built in 1955, so it hardly set the world alight, but it is a car whose name has lived on. Its full name was actually the Studebaker President Speedster, as it was part of the firm's President series. President cars had been, as the name suggests, solid and dependable upmarket vehicles. (Studebaker finally dropped its President name in 1958.) Studebaker wanted to keep the upmarket feeling while giving the new Speedster a much sportier look, in particular by adding the bigger grilles and fenders (bumpers) that other manufacturers were introducing at the same time.

The Studebaker Speedster cost $3,252 (£2,100), much more than the standard President model because it incorporated many features that were optional extras with the basic car. The extras included such luxuries of the day as a radio, a cigarette lighter, chrome-plated ashtrays, a clock, two-speed windshield wipers, and leather upholstery.

The cars came in either two-tone or three-tone colors. The combination of lemon and lime caused some derision at the time, and gray/white and pale blue/dark blue are also startling. But the combinations, while not always totally successful, help to give the cars a desirably retro look today. **MG**

Potential customers examine serried ranks of Fiat 600s parked by Fiat in a Turin square during the car's launch in 1955. ⊡

DS Safari | Citroën (F)

1955 • 132 cu in/2,175 cc, S4 • 99 bhp/74 kW • unknown • 101 mph/163 kph

The Citroën DS (from the French *déesse*, meaning "goddess"), is regarded as one of the most beautiful cars the French company ever made. Have a guess at which decade it first rolled onto the streets. The groovy 1960s? The futuristic 1970s? Neither. This landmark car was launched in 1955 when the term "aerodynamic" was far from most car designers' vocabularies.

If the design would turn heads today, it was considered revolutionary just a decade after the end of World War II. The philosopher Roland Barthes said, "It is obvious the new Citroën has fallen from the sky."

Under the skin, the DS was just as futuristic and laid the foundations for much car design to come. It had hydraulic self-leveling suspension (a future Citroën trademark), a semiautomatic gearbox with shift paddles around the steering wheel, and powered disc brakes.

The DS Safari was the station wagon (estate) version and a truly massive beast at nearly 16½ feet (5 m) long. Despite its immense proportions, it handled smoothly, thanks to its clever suspension system, which kept the Safari on an even keel, even with a family on board. The enormous trunk (boot) had a trick up its sleeve in the form of two folding, rear-facing seats that were raised from the floor to make the car an occasional seven-seater. With blinds in the rear windows, owners could easily turn the back of the car into a spacious bedroom, and some Safaris were even converted into ambulances.

The Citroën DS appeared in numerous movies and TV shows during the 1960s and 1970s. Even today, in the U.S. TV series *The Mentalist*, the central character, a quirky former show-business psychic turned sleuth, uses a later DS model as his everyday transport. **JI**

600 | Fiat (I)

1955 • 38 cu in/633 cc, S4 • 21 bhp/15. 5kW • unknown • 59 mph/95 kph

The Fiat 600 was devised in the early 1950s as Italy's "people's car." Eyeing the success of the Volkswagen Beetle and the Citroën 2CV, which were doing well for neighboring Germany and France, Fiat wanted its own budget model to put ordinary Italians in the driving seat. The idea behind the Seicento, as it was known in its native Italy, was to produce a car that the men who built it would be able to buy.

So the 600 became the model that put Italy on the road. It was designed by famed engineer Dante Giacosa, who spent four years developing the small, lightweight four-seater runabout that would also be Fiat's first rear-engined car. It was launched at the 1955 Geneva Motor Show, causing an immediate stir, while back at home Fiat staged a mass introduction by filling the streets of every Italian city with hundreds of cars.

Italy, at the time still recovering from World War II, was entering a new era of social and political history. The Fiat 600 symbolized hope for the future, and quickly became the status symbol of Italian society. Its desirability was reinforced by a famous poster of the time. Created by Felice Casorati, it featured the car set against an iconic view of nighttime Turin, Fiat's home city.

Small and light, the Fiat 600 was so called because of its 0.6-liter engine size. In length the car was only 10½ feet (3.2 m), and it weighed just 1,240 pounds (585 kg). The engine was water-cooled, and there was a four-speed gearbox. A slightly more powerful 46-cubicinch (767-cc) version was also produced. Although it is now outshone by the Fiat 500, which came later, the 600 was a big sales success for the Fiat company, which produced a million cars within only six years. **SB**

DS | Citroën

F

1955 • 116 cu in/1,911 cc, S4 • 75 bhp/55.9 kW • 0–60 mph/97 kph in 23.3 seconds • 87 mph/139 kph

Any car that keeps a president safe during an assassination attempt is assured of greatness, and the Citroën DS did just that. On August 22, 1962, General Charles de Gaulle of France was being chauffeured through the town of Clamart when terrorists opened fire with submachine guns. Despite its bodywork and tires being riddled by bullets, the big Citroën escaped the scene at high speed and no one was seriously hurt.

Unveiled at the Paris Motor Show in 1955 as a successor to the Traction Avant, the DS was a sensation. Almost 750 orders were taken in the first forty-five minutes, and 12,000 by the end of the day.

Today we view its smooth flanks and swept-back lines and call it a design classic, but at the time such futuristic styling was a risk. Citroën's creative team even labeled the first prototype "the hippopotamus." Yet the car went on to unprecedented showroom success. When production ended after twenty years and the DS was replaced by the CX, almost 1.5 million cars had been built. It sold in the United States from 1956 to 1972, but was not a hit because it lacked features that buyers expected, such as an automatic transmission.

In the 1950s it pushed automotive innovation and comfort to new levels, the star performer being its high-pressure hydraulic power unit. This controlled several of the car's main functions, including the hydropneumatic suspension. Able to keep the car at a constant height above the ground whatever the load, this was a revelation. The system made life easier for the driver by offering power steering, and it also improved safety with powered front disc brakes—another first for a mass-produced car. **RY**

190SL | Mercedes-Benz

(D)

1955 • 115 cu in/1,897 cc, S4 • 103 bhp/77 kW • 0–60 mph/97 kph in 12.4 seconds • 112 mph/180 kph

If it were not for Max Hoffman, the Mercedes 190SL—and several other classy cars—might never have existed. Born in Austria, Hoffman had moved to the United States where he became a major importer of European cars. He knew his market well, thanks to American car dealers who let him know what their customers were looking for.

When Mercedes announced the 300SL, Hoffman agreed to sell it, but asked the company if they could also come up with a cheaper car with a smaller engine than the 300SL's 183-cubic-inch (3-liter) one. Mercedes produced the 190SL for Hoffman's U.S. market. The 190 in its name came from the 1.9-liter engine, while the SL of both models stood for Sports Lightweight.

A prototype of the vehicle had debuted at the 1954 New York Auto Show, and its positive reception encouraged Mercedes to put it into production. The production model was ready for the Geneva Auto Show in 1955. That it continued selling until 1963, and sold almost 26,000 during its eight-year production run, shows why manufacturers such as Mercedes-Benz listened to Max Hoffman. The 300SL also stayed in production until 1963, and Mercedes sold 3,258 of them in the same period, but allegedly lost money on each one.

The 300SL may have been faster (in fact it was the fastest production car on the road at that time), but not by much. The 190SL was hardly sluggish, with good acceleration, and otherwise the cars looked very similar. The 190SL got better mileage, too. The major factor was that the 300SL cost $7,460 (£4,760) stateside, compared to the smaller model's price of only $3,998 (£2,550). Hoffman was right on the money. **MG**

Imperial | Chrysler

(USA)

1955 • 331 cu in/5,426 cc, V8 • 225 bhp/165 kW • 0–60 mph/97 kph in 12 seconds • 128 mph/205 kph

Chrysler Imperials had been made since 1926, but in 1955 the company decided to reposition the car under its own name and market it as simply the Imperial. It achieved one target in that sales doubled from the 1954 model, but even that hardly made a dent in the sales leads enjoyed by Chrysler's rivals, Lincoln and Cadillac.

The Imperial was still a powerful car, though, and a tough one, too: it was banned from competing in many of the demolition derbies popular at the time due to its being almost indestructible. The 1957 model also had the distinction of being the widest American car ever produced, at 81¾ inches (207.5cm).

Whether due to their sheer size or their presence, Imperials appeared in many movies, and in particular those of Elvis Presley, including *Jailhouse Rock* (1957), *It Happened at the World's Fair* (1963), and *King Creole* (1958). Imperials can also be seen in *Blade Runner* (1982), *The Godfather Part II* (1974), *Breakfast at Tiffany's* (1961) and *Indiana Jones and the Kingdom of the Crystal Skull* (2008).

The 1958 Imperial was the first car to feature cruise control, then called Auto-Pilot and invented by the blind mechanical engineer Ralph Teetor. By 1959 the Imperial was at last outselling the Lincoln, which it did again the following year. However, an outlandish 1960 redesign proved unpopular and sales then fell behind those of the Lincoln, remaining steady but unspectacular.

Two 1972 Imperial limousines were bought by the United States Secret Service and used at the inaugurations of Presidents Ford, Nixon, Carter, and Reagan. The car remained in production until 1982, but people never considered it quite as desirable or high-status as other cars of the period. **MG**

Adventurer | DeSoto

(USA)

1956 • 341 cu in/5,595 cc, V8 • 320 bhp/235 kW • 0–60 mph/97 kph in 8.7 seconds • 144 mph/230 kph

The DeSoto Adventurer was a new and powerful vehicle that came from virtually nowhere in 1956. Not only could it do 0–60 mph (97 kph) in under nine seconds, DeSoto boasted that its new heater achieved 0–100°F (38°C) in fifteen seconds. It also featured, as an optional extra, a record player mounted under the dashboard—yes, one that played old-fashioned vinyl discs. Bumps in the road caused this to be discontinued, although the 1960 Adventurer would have a record player that played the new (and slightly less vulnerable when driving) 45-rpm discs.

DeSoto was a Chrysler company that had been around since 1929, but the name was never very fashionable, nor were its cars especially worthy of note. That changed in 1955 and 1956 with both its Fireflite and Adventurer models. The Adventurer initially only came as a limited-edition two-door hardtop; all of the 996 units built in its first year were sold. For the $3,678 (£2,400) price tag the car included gold plating on its grille and wheels, and an engine packed with power. It was recorded at 137 mph (219 kph) while racing at Daytona Beach, and at 144 mph (230 kph) at one of the proving grounds that Chrysler operated around the United States for the testing of their vehicles.

The power was not only under the hood (bonnet); the car also offered power steering, power seats, power windows, and power brakes. In 1957 the design was tweaked and fins were added at the rear, to emulate other cars of that period. It sold 1,950 in this second year, but then recession and increased competition hit DeSoto and sales dwindled again. DeSoto decided to end the Adventurer adventure in 1960. **MG**

A 1957 *Autocar* magazine cover shows off the American styling of the Ford Zodiac Mark II convertible to best advantage. ⊡

M-72 Pobeda | GAZ (SU)

1956 • 129 cu in/2,120 cc, S4 • 51 bhp/38 kW • unknown • 56 mph/90 kph

The GAZ M-20 Pobeda (Russian for "Victory") was a Soviet four-door fastback sedan (saloon) that first appeared in 1946 and remained in production until 1958. It was the first Soviet car to have turn indicators, an electric heater, wiper blades, and a cigarette lighter, and was a symbol of the Soviet Union's economic resurgence from the ashes of World War II. According to GAZ, its new M-20s were "as secure as a bank, as strong as a safe, and as simple as a bicycle."

In the mid 1950s a limited number of M-20s had their monocoque bodies removed, reconstructed, and then grafted onto the GAZ M-69 4WD, an off-road truck designed for use by the Soviet army. The result, called the M-72, was a typical 1950s piece of Soviet ingenuity, a triumph of sorts, combining an M-20 body with the 4WD capability of the GAZ M-69. Soviet engineers took just three days to work out how to strengthen the body for its new role, but they were unable to alter its ungainly appearance. The M-72 had oversized wheel rims, which gave it exceptional ground clearance but caused its two-door, sedanlike body to sit so high above the ground that a stepladder was almost needed to climb into it. However, the closed, unitized body did provide for a reasonably comfortable ride, with exceptional visibility forward and to the sides, although the narrow rear window was so high it gave the driver a better view of aircraft than it did automobiles.

Not only did the new hybrid vehicle prove popular, it also grabbed for itself a slice of motoring history. If Soviet Cold War hyperbole can be believed, with the M-72 they had just invented the world's first proper all-terrain sports utility vehicle, or SUV. **BS**

Zodiac Mark II | Ford (GB)

1956 • 154 cu in/2,553 cc, S6 • 86 bhp/64 kW • 0–60 mph/97 kph in 17.1 seconds • 88 mph/142 kph

There was a time, in the late 1950s and 1960s, when many of Ford's British and European cars looked very much like smaller versions of their American cousins. The Ford Zodiac is one such car. With its angled front and rear wings, wraparound rear windshield, slab-sided body, and two-color paintwork, it's like a slice of Americana in miniature.

The Zodiac began life as the upmarket version of Ford's Zephyr, which originally launched at London's Earl's Court Motor Show in 1953. The Zodiac stood out from its British- and European-made peers by having two-tone paintwork, lots of decorative chrome, and spotlights, but it was not until the 1956 Mark II version that it really began to have a transatlantic look.

The Zodiac Mark II was powered by a 2.5-liter straight six-cylinder engine, a fairly large unit by British standards at the time, that gave the car a top speed of 88 mph (142 kph). By now the body had become more angular, with more elaborate rear-end styling, gold badging, and chrome hubcaps. The chrome fog lights of the original were dropped, but it kept the two-tone paintwork.

For the first time, there would now also be a convertible version of the Zodiac. This was even flashier than its sedan (saloon) brothers, with a three-position powered folding roof. Its luxury extras included leather upholstery, whitewall tires, and even a radio.

Cutting the roof off a sedan to make a convertible version often causes structural problems, which is one reason that so few Zodiac soft-tops survive. But a slightly battered example that used to belong to one of the comic artists behind the "Dan Dare" stories was sold at auction in 2010 for around £7,000 ($10,000). **JI**

The Autocar
31 MAY 1957

BRITISH CARS AND ACCESSORIES

1/-

The Autocar

FOUNDED 1895

LARGEST CIRCULATION

TC 108G | Alvis

USA

1956 • 182 cu in/2,993 cc, S6 • 105 bhp/78 kW • unknown • 108 mph/161 kph

The Alvis marque was nothing if not innovative. As early as 1926, it was building front-wheel-drive grand prix racing cars; it was the first company to bring a front-wheel sports car to market; and in the late 1920s it perfected all-around independent suspension—thirty years before its late-1950s "debut" with the Mini.

In 1956, when Alvis lost its two coachbuilders, it decided to reinvent itself and ditch its reputation for stodgy, outdated bodies. Custom coachwork was becoming a disappearing art in postwar Europe, but several outstanding designers still remained. One of the most prominent was Carrosserie Graber of Switzerland, designer of the Bentley Mark VI. Graber gave Alvis a two-door coupe with beautiful, modern lines. The bodies, which were placed on the Alvis TC 21 sports tourer chassis, were crafted at Willowbrooks in Loughborough.

The TC 108G gave a very smooth, quiet ride thanks to the use of resin-bonded plywood as a dampener in the floor, and sponge-rubber sheets overlaying the fluted Connolly leather seats. But only sixteen hand-built examples were ever made, despite its being a sporty two-door car with a speed of 108 mph (161 kph). If only buyers had heeded Alvis's enthusiasm for its new creation; according to the car's own brochure, it was no less than "one of the world's most beautiful cars." **BS**

503 | BMW

D

1956 • 193 cu in/3,168 cc, V8 • 138 bhp/103 kW • 0–60 mph/97 kph in 10.4 seconds • 118 mph/190 kph

At the top end of BMW's production range in the 1950s was the BMW 503, which could be afforded by only a few. It launched in 1956 and was in production for almost three years, during which time few more than 400 were built—273 coupes and 129 convertibles.

The 503 was designed by German-born Albrecht Goertz, who began his car-design career after emigrating to the United States. While there, Goertz got to know Austria-born Max Hoffman, a pivotal figure in encouraging European brands to export across the Atlantic. Hoffman put him in touch with BMW, for whom he designed both the 503 and the 507 in 1955.

The BMW 503 was built to compete with the Mercedes 300SL, although in a straight race the much faster 300SL would easily leave the 503 in its wake. The 503 could not compete on price, either, and it was also somewhat overshadowed by its big brother, the 507.

The 503's sleek design was much admired, and featured a top that could be removed electronically—an industry first. It outsold the 507, but undoubtedly the very existence of that car prevented the 503 from claiming its true place in automotive history. However, the fact that so few were produced gives it a rarity value for today's collector, and models in good condition sell for about $165,000 (£105,000) at auction. **MG**

D-500 | Dual-Ghia (USA)

1956 • 314 cu in/5,155 cc, V8 • 240 bhp/179 kW • 0–60 mph/97 kph in 9.2 seconds • 114 mph/184 kph

Only 117 Dual-Ghias were ever built, between 1956 and 1958, and all of them lost the company money. Dual Motors had been set up in Detroit by Eugene Casaroll, with the express purpose of building an exclusive car at an affordable price. The company succeeded on both counts, and there was soon a waiting list of people desperate to get their hands on the new car. The car was very reasonably priced for a high-power vehicle—although the reasonable price benefited the public more than the Dual Motors balance sheet.

Casaroll's plan was to buy the design of a car that Chrysler had built prototypes for, but never put into production: the Dodge Firearrow. The Firearrow had been designed by Chrysler's talented Virgil Exner, who used a Dodge chassis and had the Turin-based Ghia company build the body. The result was costly because the vehicles had to be transported to Italy and back, and only four were ever built.

The Dual-Ghia D-500 did not lack for publicity. Frank Sinatra and his Rat Pack buddies all owned one, and Dean Martin drove his car in the 1964 Billy Wilder film, *Kiss Me, Stupid*. The cars were actually more successful in retrospect, and no fewer than three U.S. presidents drove a Dual-Ghia at some point: Richard Nixon, Ronald Reagan, and Lyndon B. Johnson. **MG**

Ace | AC (GB)

1956 • 121 cu in/1,991 cc, S6 • 90 bhp/66 kW • 0–60 mph/97 kph in 10.5 seconds • 103 mph/165 kph

AC was one of the oldest independent carmakers in Britain, having produced its first car in 1903. It made a steady series of good cars over the next few decades, but never established itself as one of the big names.

That changed in 1953 when the AC Ace arrived. It was the work of the innovative engineer and designer John Tojeiro, and was partly inspired by the wonderfully sleek Ferraris that were being produced in those days, especially the Barchetta. Tojeiro built a low-slung open-top sports car out of lightweight alloy, and managed to coax a healthy top speed out of a fairly modest 122-cubic-inch (2-liter) engine. The Ace debuted at the 1953 London Motor Show and production began the following year, although only sixty were built.

The initial Ace was followed by the Aceca version, but in 1956 AC really hit its stride with a new Ace, capable of even better performance, and the Ace Bristol. The latter used a 122-cubic-inch (2-liter) Bristol engine that boosted the car's top speed to 116 mph (186 kph) and provided an even nippier performance. Tojeiro had always been good at balancing the weight of his cars, placing front-mounted engines as close to the center as possible, and the result was a design that would inspire one of the greatest of sports cars, the Carroll Shelby–inspired AC Cobra. **MG**

Romance sold the Renault Dauphine to buyers, as per this 1961 advertisement, but the car's handling wasn't so charming. ⊡

Troll | Troll Plastik & Bilindustri (N)

1956 • 42 cu in/700 cc, S2 • 30 bhp/22 kW • unknown • 81 mph/130 kph

Troll Plastik & Bilindustri was a Norwegian carmaker from the Telemark district of southern Norway. Despite being small, the company had a big ambition, to be the nucleus of a new, dynamic Norwegian automotive sector—with its Troll vehicle in the vanguard. The Troll was developed by Hans Trippel, a former race car driver who was the inspiration for the Mercedes 300SL's gull-wing doors. He had also invented the Amphicar, the first amphibious vehicle ever to be offered to the public, which went on to became one of the most popular hybrids of its type ever made.

Developed from a series of German molds brought to Norway by Norwegian engineer Per Kohl-Larsen, Trippel's Troll was the first car ever made in Norway. Its body was made from fiberglass, the most expensive material available for car bodies at the time. It made the Troll almost 286 pounds (130 kg) lighter than a metal-bodied equivalent, and not prone to rust, either. The body sat on a chassis developed by German carmaker Gutbrod and was powered by an economical fuel-injected 42-cubic-inch (700-cc) two-stroke engine that achieved 47 miles per gallon (97 km per 5 liters) of gasoline.

Norway's flirtation with the idea of a Volvo-like automotive sector was never destined to get very far, however, due to a complex bartering agreement Norway had with the Soviet Union, which required Norway to buy cars from the Soviets in return for an assured market for its fish products. The Norwegian government permitted the production of just fifteen Trolls before the company closed in 1958. To this day, Norwegians are entitled to feel a sense of pride and achievement whenever a Troll passes by—which is not, obviously, all that often. **BS**

Dauphine | Renault (F)

1956 • 51 cu in/845 cc, S4 • 32 bhp/24 kW • 0–60 mph/97 kph in 32 seconds • 50 mph/80 kph

When, in March 1956, the Renault Dauphine was unveiled at the Palais de Chaillot in Paris, more than 20,000 people came to see it. So enamored by its looks were they that nobody seemed to care what might be underneath. The Dauphine was a product of "Ponton" styling, a postwar trend in car design that did away with running boards and heavily articulated fenders (bumpers) in favor of the bulbous, all-enveloping bodywork that presaged modern automatic styling.

Its engineering and internal design presented problems, however. Over 60 percent of its weight—including its rear-mounted engine and gearbox—lay over its rear axle. That degree of lopsided weight distribution, combined with a mostly empty front trunk (boot) area, resulted in a tail-heavy swing and poor handling that made it not a car for the fainthearted. An inadequate spring axle in the rear, combined with a light front end, offered no relief from impending doom—occupants surviving the corners and sideways drift still faced poor handling at speed on the straight, which was potential lethal if they hit something.

Los Angeles Times automotive critic Dan Neil included the Dauphine in his list of Fifty Worst Cars of All Time. This "most ineffective piece of French engineering since the Maginot Line," he said despairingly, had a rate of acceleration so slow it could be "measured with a calendar." But the car did have an undeniable elegance, a heater, an automatic choke, and it was cheap: "A penny-farthing a mile and you travel in style," said Renault. A four-door sedan (saloon) that could make anyone look like a sophisticated Manhattan urbanite, it could just about cope with even the worst of New York traffic jams. **BS**

make
a
DATE
with
the
DAUPHINE
t your
ENAULT
ealer
OW!

Continental | Lincoln

(USA)

1956 • 366 cu in/6,000 cc, V8 • 285 bhp/213 kW • 0–60 mph/97 kph in 10 seconds • 110 mph/186 kph

The Lincoln Continental has its origins back in the 1930s, when a car built as a one-off personal vehicle for Edsel Ford in 1938 became a production model that was made until 1949. The best-known Lincoln Continental, however, was launched in 1956, when the name was revived for a model to rival a Rolls-Royce.

The Detroit-built Lincoln Continental of the mid-1950s was a two-door hardtop model with a distinctive hump in the trunk (boot) lid where the covered spare wheel was located. It was one of the most expensive cars in the world in its day, costing five times the price of a mainstream Ford model of its time.

With such an astronomical price tag, the Continental sold in relatively modest numbers. Only 2,996 were made during the two years it was in production. It was not a profitable venture for Ford, and the company was said to have made a loss on every car sold. As a result, some regard it as one of the most expensive flops in automobile history. But the car was intended as a halo model to burnish Ford's image. It was pitched at the world's wealthiest people, those with international fame and status. There were stories of dealers turning away potential buyers of the Continental because they were not deemed to be "the right kind of people" to own one.

Some famous owners gave the car a special cachet and earned it an elevated status in automotive history that now makes it almost legendary. They included Frank Sinatra, Elvis Presley, and the Shah of Iran. In 1957 the car featured in a Hollywood film *Sweet Smell of Success*, driven by Burt Lancaster as J. J. Hunsecker, an unscrupulous Broadway columnist. **SB**

Holiday 88 Coupe | Oldsmobile

(USA)

1956 • 324 cu in/5,310 cc, V8 • 240 bhp/179 kW • unknown • 112 mph/179 kph

Oldsmobile had been making their 88 models since 1949, but sometimes a year comes along where a particular model stands out. That happened in 1955 with the Super 88, and in 1956 Oldsmobile built on that success with the Holiday 88 coupe, which has been called one of the handsomest cars that General Motors ever built. Many of the changes were subtle, such as splitting the grille, changing the design for the tail lights, and using an oval rather than a round speedometer, but the overall effect, coupled with an increase in the 88's power, was to produce a car that is now considered a piece of classic Americana.

The Holiday 88 came in several configurations, including two-door and four-door sedans (saloons), and two-door and four-door hardtops, and they all sold well. It was the two-door hardtop coupe version that sold the best of all, though, accounting for almost 75,000 of the vehicles made. That represented over 15 percent of Oldsmobile's sales for the year.

Some of the Holiday 88 coupes came in a really impressive two-tone look, including the tires. The two-tone look extended inside the car, too, determining the color scheme of the interior door panels, the dashboard, and the seats. Some of the cars were made in a particularly eye-catching combination of turquoise and white that really expresses the feel of the mid-1950s, when car design was a part of a whole series of dramatic changes taking place in American society.

Thanks in no small way to the success of the 1956 Holiday 88 Coupe, Oldsmobile moved up from fifth place at the start of 1956 to fourth place at the end of 1957 in the league table of U.S. car manufacturers. **MG**

A poster for the 1983 movie *Christine* depicts the murderous Plymouth Fury at the center of Stephen King's horror story. ⊡

Multipla | Fiat

(I)

1956 • 38 cu in/633 cc, S4 • 21 bhp/15.6 kW • 0–30 mph/48 kph in 43 seconds • 57 mph/92 kph

Car enthusiasts have to take their hats off to Fiat when it comes to the 1956 Multipla. Not only is the company great at making cute small cars (both the original and reborn Fiat 500 are testament to that), but it has never been scared to push things a little bit further

Forget the Renault Espace or Mitsubishi Space Wagon—it is the Multipla that can claim to be the first people carrier or MPV. And unlike its year-2000 namesake (a striking machine in its own right), the original Multipla was based on a micro car. Fiat really did take its 1955 rear-engined 600 and turn it into a six-seater car. With no motor up front, the front seats could be shifted forward, directly between the wheels. This gave the Multipla a square, vanlike nose, but made the most of the small floorpan: the whole car was only 20 inches (50 cm) longer than the original BMC Mini.

Behind the front seats customers could choose to have a flat load bay, or either one or two bench seats. Passengers were able to travel in relative comfort as the water-cooled engine (an improvement on the air-cooled engine of the trendier Fiat 500) provided a proper heating system for the boxlike cabin. The pocket-sized people carrier also had the benefit of a clever front suspension. Unlike the standard Fiat 600's leaf-spring setup, the Multipla had a smart (and compact) wishbone arrangement.

Several different versions were made, including a taxi variant fitted with a spacious luggage rack next to the driver. There was also a Pininfarina-designed open-sided Multipla called the Marine that had wicker seats and a wraparound bench—similar to those installed in some motorboats—for passengers in the back. **JI**

Fury | Plymouth

(USA)

1956 • 302 cu in/4,965 cc, V8 • 240 bhp/179 kW • 0–60 mph/97 kph in 9.5 seconds • 144 mph/230 kph

The Fury was a good and powerful 1950s name for a good and very powerful 1950s classic car. Plymouth intended it to be a showcase vehicle for its brand—the kind of car that people would read about and lust over, even if they could only afford a less illustrious Plymouth model. The tactic worked, and the car stayed in production from 1956 until 1978, with the company also bringing out a Gran Fury model from 1980 to 1989.

Establishing the top speed that the Fury was capable of led to various claims. It was clocked at 124 mph (198 kph) in the Flying Mile at Daytona on the very same day that the car was being launched at the Chicago Auto Show in February 1956. Good timing, indeed. A few weeks later it recorded almost 144 mph (230 kph) at Daytona Speed Weeks. The Daytona car was a special preproduction performance model, though, and the top speeds of street versions made available that year to the Average Joe were said to be more like 114–120 mph (182–192 kph), which was still an amazing achievement for a road car of the day.

The Fury looked pretty amazing, too. At first it was available in any color as long as it was white and gold. The main body color was an eggshell white—a color used exclusively for the model—and it had a stripe of gold aluminum down each side, shaped to look something like a lightning bolt. The car cost $2,866 (£1,850) to buy and was the most expensive car that Plymouth produced. While it was only ever intended for an exclusive market, the Fury still sold an impressive 4,485 units. A 1958 Plymouth Fury was the car that was supernaturally possessed in Stephen King's 1983 horror novel *Christine*, and one featured in the movie version, too. **MG**

A bright red Volvo Amazon—or 122S as it was known in America—cruises through the streets of New York, 1958. ⊡

603 | Tatra (CS)

1956 • 155 cu in/2,545 cc, V8 • 95 bhp/70kW • 0–60 mph/97 kph in 16 seconds • 105 mph/169 kph

At what point after the release of the beautiful streamlined Tatra 600 of 1948 did Tatra's management tell its designers that their services were no longer required? In the eight years intervening between that launch and the arrival of the Tatra 603, the company obliterated all that was once beautiful in the 600: its tear-shaped, elliptical body, its low drag coefficient and aerodynamic principles, and its enclosed chassis.

Yet the Tatra 603 six-seater sedan (saloon) remained in continuous production through three versions—the T603-1, T603-2, and T603-3—until 1975. Promoted as "rear-engined luxury," its most distinguishing feature was a row of three headlights mounted inside a chromed, oval surround. It also had rear-mounted air catchers to cool its engine in the absence of a radiator, but these too, although designed to be integrated into the body, could not help but look awkward. Two-thirds of all the 603s produced were exported to China, Cuba, and various Soviet bloc countries. To this day, former Cuban president Fidel Castro still has his air-conditioned 603, although this is more likely to be a result of the strictly enforced U.S. embargo than an enduring automotive love affair.

The 603 did, however, have some attractive touches, including a dome-shaped cowl, white levers and steering wheel, and distinctly U.S.-looking oversized chrome fenders (bumpers). The model offered a smooth ride and was almost entirely hand-built, but in the end it fell victim to the increasingly militarized Soviet economy and the government's preference for manufacturing trucks and light military vehicles rather than automobiles. **BS**

Amazon | Volvo (S)

1956 • 96 cu in/1,583 cc, S4 • 60 bhp/40 kW • 0–60 mph/97 kph in 17 seconds • 90 mph/143 kph

Volvo has long been associated with automotive safety, and the car that did most to establish this reputation was the Volvo Amazon. Launched in 1956, it was the first car in the world to be fitted with standard lap-strap front seat belts, a feature added in 1959. It also became the first car to feature three-point seat belts when Volvo later upgraded its safety provision. The Amazon was notable for other safety features that were innovative at the time, including a padded upper dashboard and a laminated windshield.

The Amazon was named after the fierce female warriors of Greek mythology, but initially it was badged as the Amason because a motorcycle manufacturer had already registered the spelling Volvo wanted. Production started in Gothenburg but later moved to Torlanda, an island just to the northwest of Volvo's home city. The car had a long lifespan, remaining in production until 1970. It was also assembled in Belgium, South Africa, Canada, and Chile. In export markets it was latterly known as the 121 or the 122S.

The styling of the Amazon took its cues from U.S. cars of the early 1950s. Designer Jan Wilsgaard said he had been inspired by a Kaiser automobile he saw one day at Gothenburg harbor. His design included strong "shoulders" and faintly visible tail fins, reminiscent of some Detroit models of the time. The car had quite a tall posture, a long hood (bonnet), and a chunky tail overhang. The best-known version is the two-door model, but there was also a four-door sedan (saloon). An Amazon station wagon (estate) was introduced in 1962. A total of 667,791 of the three versions were produced during the car's lifetime. **SB**

TAXI
VOLVO
N.J.
FTW-219
GARDEN STATE

A 1961 Lancia promotional shot shows actress Brigitte Bardot seated on the hood (bonnet) of a Flaminia Berlina. ⊡

Sports SE492 | Berkeley (GB)

1957 • 26 cu in/429 cc, S3 • 30 bhp/22 kW • 0–60 mph/97 kph in 21.8 seconds • 81 mph/130 kph

Coachworks factory owner Charles Panter made his fortune by becoming the United Kingdom's leading caravan manufacturer. In 1956, along with newfound partner Laurie Bond, Panter began building small-engined motorcars under the Berkeley brand, utilizing his workforce's experience with glass-reinforced plastic. Panter wanted to build "something good enough to win world 750-cc races," but also attractive to ordinary motorists by being cheap, pretty, and easily repairable.

Built almost entirely of fiberglass, Berkeley's first car was chain-driven through the front wheels and powered by a small-capacity motorcycle engine. In the absence of a traditional steel chassis it weighed in at a mere 725 pounds (329 kg). Berkeleys campaigned successfully during the 1950s in the smaller engine classes at races, rallies, and auto tests. In one famous race at the Goodwood circuit in June 1957, the BBC caught the amazing spectacle of a tiny 328-cc twin-cylinder Berkeley Sports snapping at the heels of a 3,442-cc Jaguar Mark VII to set a lap record in its class.

In 1957 the 10-foot-long (3-m) Berkeley Sports received a new 30-cubic-inch (492-cc) three-cylinder engine. Designated the SE492, the car was nicknamed the "mini-Ferrari." In 1958 Italian Formula 1 driver Lorenzo Bandini took a race-prepared SE492 to victory in the 750-cc GT class at the Monza 12 Hour Race, the car's limpetlike handling more than compensating for its limited horsepower. About 2,100 Berkeley Sports were eventually built, 900 of which were exported to the United States. Sales of the SE492 began to slump only when the better engineered and similarly priced Austin-Healey Sprite was launched in 1958. **DS**

Flaminia Berlina | Lancia (I)

1957 • 149 cu in/2,458 cc, V6 • 98 bhp/72 kW • 0–60 mph/97 kph in 14.5 seconds • 99 mph/159 kph

When the motoring press first laid eyes on the Flaminia (named after the ancient road connecting Rome with Rimini), it was love at first sight. *Autocar* said it represented the "highest level in current Italian workmanship." Walt Woron of *Motor Trend* enthused, "If you have the money to buy a Cadillac Eldorado, take a long hard look at the Flaminia." *Road & Track* wrote, "If every owner of an expensive U.S. sedan could drive a Flaminia for a day, there would be changes made."

Enzo Ferrari himself declared it to be one of the best-handling cars he had ever driven. Sophia Loren, Audrey Hepburn, and Juan Manuel Fangio all owned one. With styling from Pininfarina and Zagato, suspension courtesy of De Dion, a brand-new 119-bhp (89-kW) V6 engine, and the enviable Lancia pedigree, the Flaminia Berlina was a car for the ages.

Although a prototype was released in 1956, the production version was first revealed at the Geneva Motor Show in 1957. Based on the 1956 Florida, the four-door Flaminia Berlina sedan (saloon) represented a radical break from tradition for Lancia. Designed from scratch, it had a more angular shape than its predecessor, an all-new universal wishbone suspension, and Dunlop inboard rear brakes for increased agility when cornering. Its four doors came with no central pillars, though each window had its own frame so the sides would not be completely open when the windows were down. Later limousine, cabriolet, and coupe versions were coachbuilt with individualized custom features that kept production to a minimum. Although sales were low, the last Flaminia would not roll off the production line until 1970. **BS**

MIRAMONTI

Bel Air | Chevrolet

USA

1957 • 283 cu in/4,640 cc, V8 • 283 bhp/211 kW • 0–60 mph/97 kph in 8.9 seconds • 120 mph/193 kph

"Tramps like us, baby, we were born to run," sang Bruce Springsteen, and the car they ran in was the Bel Air. The inspiration for Springsteen's first hit was what he bought after signing his first record contract: a '57 Chevy Bel Air. That car captured the spirit of mid-1950s America as surely as Elvis, Tom & Jerry, and drive-in movies.

The Bel Air was the open-top version of the Chevy '57 sedan (saloon), with a powered roof that "makes snug protection automatically yours at the touch of a button." With copious decorative fins and chrome being typical at the time, the Bel Air was considered rather understated.

The '57 Bel Air was actually no more than a face-lifted version of the '55 model in the last year of its production run before being replaced by a new model. Yet it looked longer, lower, and wider, thanks to wheels reduced from 15 to 14 inches (38 to 36 cm) and restyled tail fins. Somehow this Chevy just struck the right stylistic chord at the right time. Out of sight, the gearbox, called the "Powerglide," was a three-speed manual or two-speed automatic. A more sophisticated "Turboglide" transmission—a continuously variable gear ratio that provided imperceptible gear shifts—was an option.

The hottest Bel Air was the Super Turbo Fire V8, whose bored-out engine produced a tire-squealing 283 bhp (211 kW) and a 120-mph (193-kph) top speed thanks to mechanical "Ramjet" fuel injection.

The Bel Air sold well and most examples were kept running long after contemporary rivals reached the junkyards. It is still popular today, especially among restorers and customizers. Springsteen sold his inspirational Bel Air in 1976, and it has since been bought by a collector for $400,000 (£258,000). **SH**

Galaxie Skyliner | Ford

USA

1957 • 291 cu in/4,785 cc, V8 • 206 bhp/ 153 kW • 0–60 mph/97 kph in 11.6 seconds • 101 mph/163 kph

The Ford Galaxie Skyliner was not the first car with a powered retractable hardtop; that honor goes to the 1934 Peugeot 402 Éclipse Décapotable. But it was probably the largest car ever to lift its lid that way.

During the 1950s consumer boom in the United States, companies loaded their wares with every electrical gadget they could think of. Because a simple electric roof was boring, this long, low flagship for Ford's full-sized range was given a new trick: it could stow its roof in the trunk (boot), or uncurl it again like the tail of a lobster, in sixty seconds flat.

Operation of the roof relied on hydraulic rams and worm gears plus 600 feet (18 m) of wiring, ten power relays, eight circuit breakers, ten limit switches, three drive motors, and a safety interlock that ensured the roof would only operate when the car was in neutral. The system was actually relatively simple because each motor performed just one task before tripping a switch to activate the next. A hand-cranked manual override was provided should the rams fail. All this made the car heavy, though, and when the roof was stowed, it left a tub-shaped hole just 3 feet (0.9 m) square for luggage. The 1960 Sunliner reverted to an ordinary electric roof.

The basic factory price for a Galaxie Skyliner was around $3,346 (£2,130), but most were laden with options, including two more powerful engines: 225 bhp (168 kW) or 300 bhp (224 kW). One of those cars would cost close to $40,000 or £25,500 today.

A total of 20,000 were made in 1957; 14,713 in 1958; and 12,915 in 1959; and in that final year the Galaxie Skyliner won the gold medal for exceptional styling at the Brussels World's Fair. **LT**

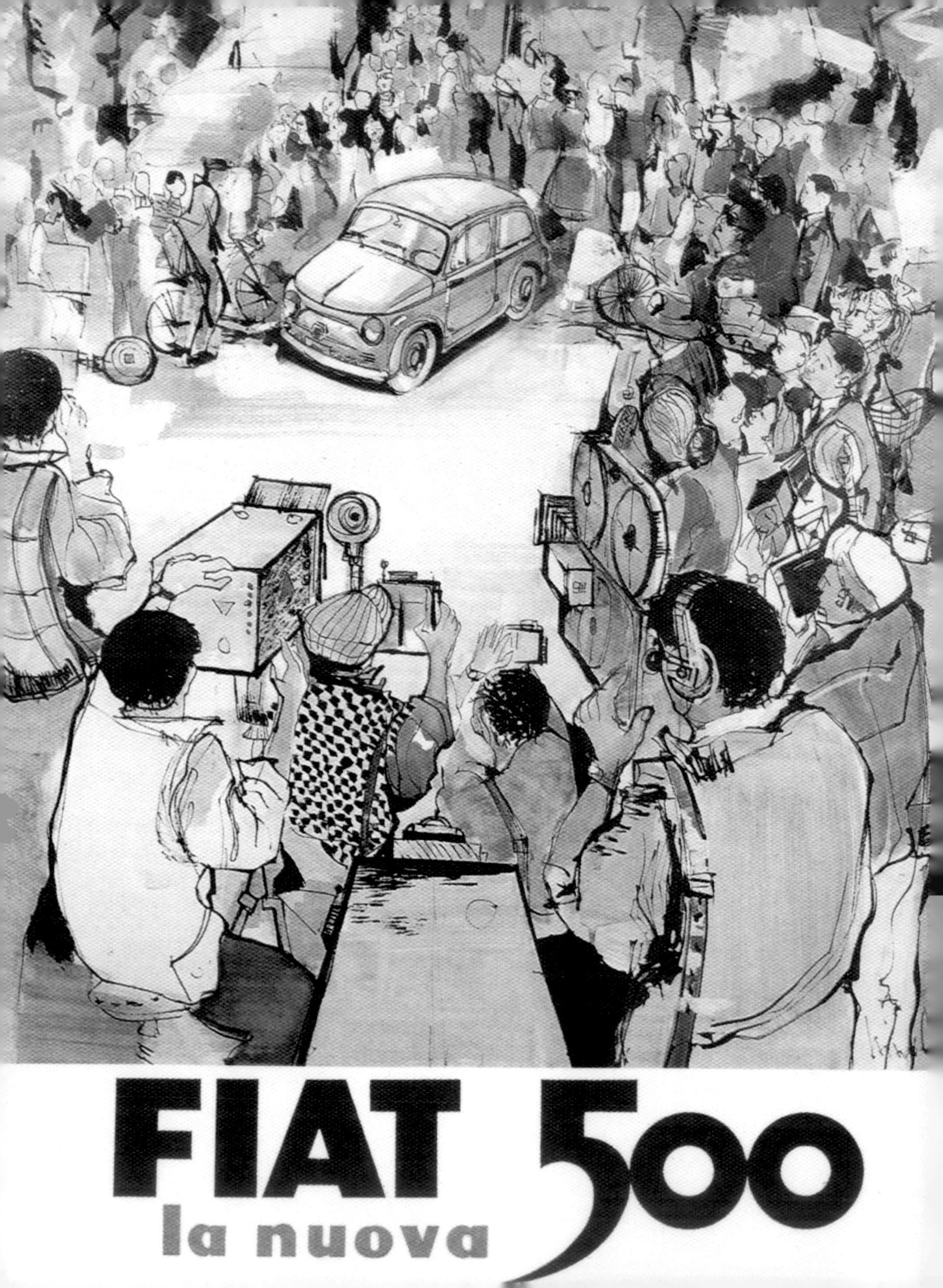
FIAT
la nuova
500

◁ A 1957 advertisement celebrates the launch of the Fiat 500, Italy's answer to the German Volkswagen Beetle.

500 | Fiat

(I)

1957 • 29 cu in/479 cc, S2 • 13 bhp/9.7 kW • unknown • 51 mph/82 kph

The Fiat 500 was Italy's second attempt to emulate the success of Germany's Volkswagen after the 600 of 1955. Offering economical transport for the Italian masses, the 500 pioneered what today is called the city car—a compact and highly maneuverable model that is cheap to run, simple to maintain, and easy to park.

This was not the first time that Fiat had used the "500" name (which is known as "Cinquecento" in its home market); its 500 Topolino—meaning "little mouse"—was on sale from 1936 to 1955 and was actually slightly bigger than the first of the new 500s.

Dreamed up by designer Dante Giacosa, the 500 of 1957 was created along similar lines as the Volkswagen Beetle with a rear-mounted engine. Measuring 9.8 feet (3 m) between its fenders (bumpers), the earliest versions had a canvas roof similar to that of the Citroën 2CV and doors with hinges to the rear.

The 500 spawned a huge number of variants. The longest running of these was the Giardiniera—also known as the K—which was launched in 1960 and sold until 1977, two years after all other 500s had been replaced by the boxier 126. Essentially a 500 station wagon (estate), the K featured the same front end, but ditched the coupelike roofline for a squared-off, vertical, side-hinged rear door.

More than 4 million 500s were built during its twenty-year run. In 2007, exactly fifty years after the 500's launch in 1957, Fiat unveiled a modern-day reworking that has proved massively successful around the world. There is huge affection for the original, though, and a 1959 version called Luigi is immortalized by Pixar in the 2006 animated movie *Cars*. **RY**

3500GT | Maserati

(I)

1957 • 212 cu in/3,485 cc, S6 • 220 bhp/164 kW • 0–60 mph/97 kph in 7.6 seconds • 137 mph/220 kph

In late 1957, after a series of disastrous crashes that saw many of Maserati's works cars scrapped, the company decided to abandon racing and focus its attention on passenger cars. The change of direction coincided nicely with Europe building increasingly sophisticated autobahns and autostradas, which made it possible for anyone to drive fast, high-performance automobiles. These were called Grand Tourers: comfortable, production road cars that were practical on city roads but could also go very fast.

Maserati had tinkered with road cars in the past, but these were little more than thinly disguised racing cars. What Maserati's owner, Adolfo Orsi, and chief engineer, Giulio Alfieri, wanted was a machine that would mark a true transition from the racing cars of the past to an era of powerful, passenger-friendly production vehicles. For the first time in the company's history the responsibility for this new car would be handed entirely over to Maserati's engineers. What they came up with was the stunning Maserati 3500GT.

The 3500GT was powered by a detuned V6 Maserati racing engine capable of producing in excess of 220 bhp (164 kW). Its interior was full of chrome, leather, indicator lights, levers, and switches. It shook the world of sports-car makers to its core, not a bad achievement considering it was Maserati's first outright challenge to the dominance of its old rival, Ferrari. But the confident air that Maserati showed in unveiling its new offering—delivered with little fanfare and an almost cocky self-assurance—was enough to make people think, although Ferrari would doubtless disagree, that really there was no rivalry at all. **BS**

XKSS | Jaguar

GB

1957 • 210 cu in/3,442 cc, S6 • 250 bhp/184 kW • 0–60 mph/97 kph in 7.3 seconds • 150 mph/241 kph

Consider these specifications: a lightweight, race-bred sports car achieving 250 bhp (184 kW) from a straight-six, twin overhead cam engine. Plus an acceleration of 0–60 mph (97 kph) in seven seconds and a top speed of over 150 mph (241 kph). The specs could easily refer to a hot modern hatchback, maybe something from Japan or Germany. But they do not. They refer to a British sports car that was launched in front of a thrilled public at the New York Motor Show in 1957.

When Jaguar decided to close its racing program in the late 1950s, the company still had twenty-five D-Type racing cars on its books without buyers. As sometimes happened in that era, they decided to turn them into roadsters. First of all, Jaguar removed the D-Type's trademark rear fin, which had added stability on the racetrack. Then it added a front passenger seat with its own door. A canvas roof was added (the racers had been open-topped), together with a rudimentary windshield and some fenders (bumpers).

Despite the alterations, this was still a racing car for the road. It had disc brakes all around (quite uncommon in 1957), which enabled it to balance its phenomenal speed with real stopping power. The flowing bodywork formed part of the monocoque chassis that was bolted to a rigid subframe. Because the motor had to be tilted slightly to get it into the engine bay, there was a noticeable off-center hump in the hood (bonnet).

Sixteen private buyers bought the XKSS and most went to the United States. Probably the most famous owner was movie star and car enthusiast Steve McQueen. He owned one from 1959 to 1969, then rebought the same car in 1977 and kept it until he died in 1980. **JI**

300SL Roadster | Mercedes-Benz

(D)

1957 • 182 cu in/2,996 cc, S6 • 212 bhp/158 kW • 0–60 mph/97 kph in 8.1 seconds • 155 mph/249 kph

One of the most desirable automobiles ever built, the Mercedes 300SL roadster owes its existence to the influential U.S.-based car importer Max Hoffman, who traveled to Stuttgart in Germany to convince Mercedes executives they needed to take their 1954 300SL gull-wing coupe and use it as a template to develop a new roadster for the U.S. market. Hoffman's argument was presented persuasively, to say the least, and the 300SL roadster took the motoring world by storm when it was introduced at the 1957 Geneva Motor Show.

The roadster retained essentially the same engine as the 300SL, which was tilted to the left to fit it under the low-slung hood (bonnet), but externally and structurally the car required extensive redesigning to transform it from coupe to convertible. Additional tubing was fitted to the chassis' lower half to maintain its rigidity and allow for the installation of conventional doors in place of the iconic gull-wings, which had proved impractical in parking lots and narrow garages. The changes meant that, even without its roof, the new soft-top roadster was 77 pounds (35 kg) heavier than its predecessor. The weight was overcome by a modified engine that produced an extra 20 bhp (15 kW), while a rear low-pivot axle improved the handling. Cosmetically, there were changes, too. The fenders (bumpers) were enlarged, and so were the headlights. The front grille became smaller and the windshield was given more of a curve.

The 300SL gull-wing and roadster were the most advanced cars of their day and the first to have direct port fuel injection. More than any other Mercedes before or since, they invoke the mythology of the brand. No two "Mercs" ever wore the three-pointed star so proudly. **BS**

Workers attend to hardtop Trabants at the VEB Sachsenring factory in 1956. On the right is a line of EMW convertibles.

Aronde Plein Ceil | Simca (F)

1957 • 78 cu in/1,290 cc, S4 • 57 bhp/42 kW • unknown • 82 mph/132 kph

The French car company Simca was founded by an Italian, Henri Pigozzi, who was born in Turin in 1898. In 1924, after setting up a business as a distributor of U.S. and British motorcycles, he began to import scrap metal from France, which he sold on to Fiat. In 1926 Fiat's founder, Giovanni Agnelli, appointed Pigozzi as Fiat's representative in France. Later that year, Pigozzi established a Fiat distribution and manufacturing company near Paris and, by 1934, had sold in excess of 30,000 vehicles. But Pigozzi was no longer content with merely selling cars—he wanted to make them. On November 2, 1934, he purchased a factory in Nanterre, northwest of Paris, and created the Société Industrielle de Mécanique et de Carrosserie Automobile—SIMCA for short. Henri Pigozzi was a carmaker at last.

Thanks mostly to the intervention of World War II, not much happened at Simca until the arrival in 1951 of its first in-house-designed automobile, the 9 Aronde, named after the French word for a swallow, the company's emblem. The Aronde brand was continued until 1964. Its second series, the 90A Aronde of 1955 to 1958, had two variants, both of which appeared in October 1957: the two-door convertible Oceane and the hardtop coupe, the Plein Ciel.

Plein Ciel is French for "full sky," a reference to the car's oversized windshield. Its shape had echoes of the Ford Thunderbird, but essentially it was a typical Simca. Rather than being innovative, it represented just another careful step forward, a consolidation of past tried-and-tested formulas for a company that began with nothing to become, by the late 1950s, France's second-largest maker of family cars. **BS**

Trabant | VEB Sachsenring (DDR)

1957 • 36 cu in/600 cc, S2 • 26 bhp/9 kW • 0–60 mph/97 kph in 21 seconds • 70 mph/113 kph

Many people outside the Soviet bloc had never heard of the humble "Trabbi" until the Berlin Wall came down in 1989. But as thousands of East Germans flooded into West Germany, the cars were impossible to miss.

Made in the German Democratic Republic by VEB Sachsenring Automobilwerke in the city of Zwickau, the Trabant became a symbol of life in the former Soviet bloc. The Trabant had been intended as a basic four-seater transport for the masses during the Cold War. More than 3 million left the VEB Sachsenring factory between 1957 and 1991, when production ended.

The name, which comes from astronomy and translates as "satellite," celebrated Russia's Sputnik, which had recently become the first man-made object to orbit Earth. Strictly speaking, there were four versions of the car, but while each had a different engine, little else changed. The car was built from a steel body frame with plastic resin panels bolted on. During the Trabant's time in the spotlight it was widely reported the panels were made of cardboard, but that was an urban myth.

The two-cylinder, two-stroke engine offered easy maintenance, and the average car ran for twenty-eight years. But environmental concerns were not high on the political agenda; two-stroke oil had to be added after every stop at a filling station. The car had no fuel gauge, and the only way to know whether fuel was running low was to check a dipstick that went into the tank.

The car was celebrated by Irish rockers U2 on the cover of the *Achtung Baby* (1981) album two years after the Berlin Wall fell, and formed part of the stage set on their subsequent tour. Two are now on show in the Rock and Roll Hall of Fame in Cleveland, Ohio. **RY**

F

TS-250 | Goggomobil

D

1957 • 15 cu in/247 cc, S2 • 13 bhp/10 kW • unknown • 52 mph/84 kph

It is tempting to look at Goggomobil minicars, with their modest 13–20 bhp (10–15 kW) engines and screwed-on fenders (bumpers), and dismiss them and their designer Hans Glas as little more than automotive oddities. But Glas managed to achieve what most entrepreneurs could only dream of; he built a car that proved enormously popular, then went on to manufacture it in large quantities over many years.

Working from a small factory in the Bavarian town of Dingolfing, Glas introduced his first "Goggo" at the 1954 IFMA International Bicycle and Motorcycle Show. The car's quirky features included a single windshield wiper (present in pre-1957 models only) and sliding windows. In time, Glas began to expand his range to include a convertible version (the Dart) and a coupe, and later on even a van and a pickup truck.

The TS-250 came along in 1957 with a 15-cubic-inch (247-cc), 13-bhp (10-kW) rear-mounted engine—there was also an 18-cubic-inch (300-cc), 15-bhp (11-kW) option)—ventilated via two small intake scoops on the rear fenders. The interior was predictably spartan with individual, squared-off front seats and a speedometer—the dashboard's only gauge. Clean and uncluttered, the cabin was not without flourishes, including a white steering wheel and white highlighted levers commonly found in more expensive sedans (saloons).

Quickly acquiring a reputation for reliability, Glas's Goggomobil in its several variations soon became Germany's largest-selling microcar. Each had hydraulic brakes and electric preselective transmission. In no way could they be seen as toys—these were serious, dependable, economical "cars in miniature." **BS**

Elite | Lotus

GB

1957 • 74 cu in/1,216 cc, S4 • 75 bhp/55 kW • 0–60 mph/97 kph in 9.7 seconds • 116 mph/187 kph

Can a car with only 75 bhp (55 kW) on tap really achieve 116 mph (187 kph)? Yes, it can. The Lotus Elite was a highly successful track car and roadster thanks to its clever design and low weight: 1,110 pounds (505 kg).

The Elite was fitted with a groundbreaking fiberglass monocoque chassis. Other cars had fiberglass as parts of their bodywork, but in the little Lotus it was used for the key structure of the car, with the body acting as the chassis. There were steel elements also, chiefly holding the engine in place, but the use of GRP (glass-reinforced plastic) made the Elite a proper lightweight. As such, it gained a sports-car performance from a four-cylinder engine that was not only small, but actually originated as the water-pump in fire trucks. It was not the first time Lotus has used Coventry Climax FWE motors—they had also been an option for the early Lotus Six.

The Elite had independent suspension all around, with a system called the "Chapman Strut" at the rear, named after Lotus founder Colin Chapman. The car was also aerodynamic, with some of the bodywork final design being done by Mike Costin, chief aerodynamic engineer at the de Havilland Aircraft Company.

With disk brakes all around (unusual for 1957), the Lotus was a car that went like a rocket, handled as though it was on rails, and could stop on a dime. Quick, light, and maneuverable, the Elite excelled on the racetrack, winning its class at Le Mans six times and racking up countless other victories.

Of the 1,000 Elites made, around 700 still survive. Given that the Elite was one of the world's first cars to use fiberglass so extensively, it has proven to a resilient and enduring little beast and a testament to the material. **JI**

VESPA 400
MOTORE: 2 cilindri
393 cmc.
CAMBIO: 3 velocità
SOSPENSIONI
FRENI
CARROZZERIA
VELOCITÀ: 90
CONSUMO

◁ The compactness of the ACMA Vespa 400 is demonstrated at the 1958 Turin Motor Show.

Vespa 400 | ACMA (F)

1957 • 24 cu in/400 cc, S2 • 18 bhp/13 kW • 0–40 mph/64 kph in 23 seconds • 55 mph/90 kph

Similar in size and design to the German Goggomobil, the Vespa was a rear-engined minicar manufactured by French company ACMA (Ateliers de construction de motocycles et d'automobiles), which also made the Vespa scooter. It was officially a two-seater, but two very small children could conceivably be shoehorned into the back, providing that the optional cushion had been purchased. Space for luggage was minimal, just a small luggage tray over the rear trunk (boot).

With space at a premium, the doors of the Vespa had plastic internal panels to provide extra elbow room. And as if that were not restrictive enough, early models had fixed side windows. Would-be purchasers who happened to suffer from claustrophobia or car sickness were better advised to consider buying a larger car, or at least think about the cabriolet version. This came with a fabric roof that rolled back from the windshield rail all the way to the trunk (boot), enough to allow ACMA to market the car as a convertible. A front slide-out panel in the hood (bonnet) housed the Vespa's 12-volt battery. There were hydraulic drum brakes front and rear and a forward-mounted roll bar.

The dashboard was basic, arrayed with the barest of warning lights, a speedometer, and an open glove box. The starter and choke were mounted in between the two front seats, which were comfortable enough, being made from tubular steel with cloth stretched over mattresslike springs. Prior to the Vespa's Monaco release on September 26, 1957, race driver Juan Manuel Fangio drove one over the French Alps and later claimed, "It was so comfortable that I felt I was driving a much bigger car." **BS**

Cresta PA | Vauxhall (GB)

1957 • 138 cu in/2,262 cc, S6 • 83 bhp/62 kW • 0–60 mph/97 kph in 18 seconds • 87 mph/139 kph

Auto manufacturers are always looking for a celebrity customer to give their cars a seal of approval. In the United Kingdom, having Queen Elizabeth II drive one as her personal transport comes pretty high on the list. For Vauxhall, that is what happened, and it helped to make the PA the best known of its Cresta family.

The Cresta PA four-door sedan (saloon), which shared its body style with the less well equipped Vauxhall Velox, was Vauxhall's answer to the Ford Zodiac. Totally different in design to the Cresta E of 1954, it was a truly elegant car with more than a nod in its design to the 1950s fashion for all things American. It had fins topping the rear wings and wraparound glass front and rear. But while the optional whitewall tires emphasized the transatlantic influences, it remained more understated and "British" than many of the American models of the era.

Queen Elizabeth's car was the PA Estate (station wagon), an official Vauxhall model but actually a postsale conversion carried out by a British company. The car managed to keep its fins by having its restyled and extended rear end built inside and between them.

The PA was one of the first vehicles to be adopted as part of a cultural phenomenon. Its U.S. image, albeit diluted, made it a hit with the "teddy boy" and rock'n'roll fashion movements in the United Kingdom.

The original 138-cubic-inch (2,262-cc) engine was replaced in 1961 by a 158-cubic-inch (2,600-cc) unit that increased power from 83 bhp (62 kW) to 95 bhp (71 kW). More than 80,000 PAs were built before it was replaced in 1962 by the PB. This had more conservative styling, and before long the 2.6-liter engine was swapped for a more powerful 201-cubic-inch (3,300-cc) unit. **RY**

M-21 Volga | GAZ

SU

1957 • 146 cu in/2,400 cc, S4 • 70 bhp/52 kW • unknown • 81 mph/130 kph

When President George W. Bush visited Vladimir Putin's home in 2005, the Russian president could not wait to show off his prized classic car. Putin and Bush surprised waiting photographers as they jumped in the beautifully restored white GAZ M-21 Volga—or GAZ-21—sharing the front bench seat as Bush took the wheel for a drive.

For Russians the GAZ-21 is as much an icon of the 1950s as a Chevy Bel Air is for Americans. The earliest models were used in much-publicized promotional drives across the vast expanse of the Soviet Union, during which they notched up 18,000 miles (29,000 km). Only a few private civilians were able to afford one. The GAZ-21 served as police cars and taxis, and station wagon (estate) versions were used as ambulances. A high-performance version, the GAZ-23, was produced for Soviet Special Services, deliberately made to look exactly the same as the standard GAZ-21. The GAZ-23 had a 195-bhp (145-kW) V8 engine and reached 106 mph (170 kph).

The Volga's chrome and curves were obviously heavily influenced by American designs, but the Volga had higher ground clearance, unbreakable suspension, 0.04 inch- (1mm-) thick steel, and effective rustproofing to cope with the Soviet Union's demanding climate and conditions. The engine was a strong and forgiving overhead-valve unit. Drivers used a three-speed manual gearshift on the steering column. Luxury features included a reclining front seat, cigarette lighter, heater, windshield washer, and three-wave radio.

The GAZ-21 has appeared in dozens of movies, ranging from *Casino Royale* (2006) to *Segment '76* (2003). Around 30,000 were built and today they remain highly desirable for car collectors, including Mr. Putin. **SH**

Caravelle | Renault

(F)

1958 • 51 cu in/845 cc, S4 • 40 bhp/30 kW • 0–60 mph/97 kph in 18 seconds • 89 mph/143 kph

Unveiled at the 1958 Paris Motor Show, the Caravelle was Renault's attempt at the North American market, where it was introduced at the New York Auto Show in December 1959. It was only in the United States and Canada that it was called the Caravelle; in Europe it was launched as the Renault Floride. The name was changed in North America in case it was too closely linked with the state of Florida, which might have put off buyers from all the other states.

It turned out that American buyers did want one, at least initially. The problem was that they couldn't get them. Renault took orders for 13,000 Caravelles at the 1959 New York Auto Show, but the purchasers would not see their cars for several months. When they did, the performance was less than impressive. The cars certainly looked good, with an attractive design that was along the latest American lines, but in the trunk (boot) the rear-mounted engine was tiny by U.S. standards.

In the United States, the mere fact that the engine was rear-mounted counted against the car. Rear-mounted engines were common in many European countries but American drivers were not used to them and encountered handling problems. They were not too pleased by the floor-mounted gear lever, either.

Three versions were produced: a two-door coupe, a two-door cabriolet, and a two-door convertible (a cabriolet in which the retractable hardtop could be removed completely). In 1962 the engine was upgraded to 956 cc, the Floride name was dropped, and every car worldwide was named the Caravelle. It continued to sell, steadily if not spectacularly: 117,000 were built between its 1958 arrival and its 1968 departure. **MG**

Dozens of identical "Amby" taxis line up outside a railway station in Kolkata, home of Hindustan Motors, in 2009. ▷

Grantura | TVR (GB)

1958 • 74 cu in/1,216 cc, S4 • 83 bhp/61 kW • 0–60 mph/97 kph in 10.8 seconds • 101 mph/163 kph

The Grantura was the first real production car made by British sports car company TVR at its factory in Blackpool, which sadly is now closed.

The company was founded by engineer Trevor Wilkinson; "TVR" derives from his first name. Wilkinson built his first car in 1949 using a tubular chassis, mechanical parts borrowed from various other cars, and a handmade steel body. But he soon realized that he could make a lightweight body more cheaply if he used fiberglass instead of metal. So the design of future TVRs was born: front-engine, rear-wheel drive, steel chassis, with a glass-reinforced plastic (GRP) body on top. It was a recipe for speed and thrills.

To get around a tax imposed on finished cars, the Grantura was available in kit form. Mechanically it was generally a mix of VW Beetle or Triumph suspension, Austin-Healey brakes, and BMC rear axles. Engines also came from a number of sources. They initially included Coventry Climax four-cylinder motors that were usually put to work driving the water pumps on fire engines. Other favorites included Ford engines and the MGA B series. Customers could choose the exact final specification of each car that left the factory.

The GRP body was made on-site at TVR's Blackpool plant. It had a hood (bonnet) that hinged at the front, and no trunk (boot) lid. Getting into the rear storage area meant clambering around in the back of the car; the spare wheel had to be heaved out over the front seats.

The Grantura was continually modified and stayed in production until replaced by the TVR Mark IV in 1965. This had a longer, stiffer chassis and was available with a more powerful 109-cubic-inch (1,800-cc) MG engine. **JI**

Ambassador | Hindustan (IND)

1958 • 90 cu in/1,489 cc, S4 • 55 bhp/41 kW • 0–60 mph/97 kph in 30.5 seconds • 74 mph/118 kph

Old British cars never die. The tooling is just shipped off to far-flung corners of the former empire, to be built there until the end of the world. The Ambassador has been in production in India since 1958. Little has changed since it was the Morris Oxford Series III, sold in the United Kingdom from 1956 to 1959 and assembled at the Cowley plant, where the Mini is now made.

The "Amby," as it is known across India, is built by Hindustan Motors at its facility near Kolkata (Calcutta) in West Bengal. Hindustan's first car was the Landmaster of 1942, based on another British classic, the Morris Ten, and popular with the Indian middle class.

Soon after the Amby went on sale, the Indian government changed the regulations on imported cars, making them prohibitively expensive for most people. Those rules, which remain in place today, resulted in the Amby being unchallenged as the transport of choice for decades; for twenty-three years after its launch it was Hindustan Motors' only vehicle.

Today an Amby can be bought with a 71-bhp (52.9-kW) 109-cubic-inch (1,800-cc) gasoline engine or a 35-bhp (26.1-kW) 91-cubic-inch (1,500-cc) diesel. Various minor upgrades have taken place over the years, but the car's heritage is still instantly recognizable.

An amusing footnote to the Oxford/Amby's global adventure is its reappearance in the United Kingdom. In the 1990s it was briefly rebadged as the Fullbore Mark 10, and during the early 2000s a company in Wales imported some under Single Vehicle Approval laws that bypassed full homologation. That became impossible in 2008 when the U.K. government upgraded mandatory vehicle safety standards. **RY**

TAXI
WB 19
WB 04
B 0238

Series 62 Convertible Coupe | Cadillac

USA

1958 • 364 cu in/5,972 cc, V8 • 310 bhp/228 kW • 0–60 mph/97 kph in 10.9 seconds • 113 mph/182 kph

In the United States during the 1950s, owning a family car had become a national obsession. Americans were spending more and more time in their automobiles, which were evolving as never before to keep pace with the nation's expanding infrastructure. Americans were accustomed to long drives, but the U.S. interstate highway system, inaugurated in 1956, meant people were no longer content with driving from town to town—they were driving from coast to coast.

Even in these circumstances, U.S. carmakers found 1958 to be a bad year for releasing a new model of anything. The country was in recession, and Cadillac's latest offering—the Series 62 convertible coupe—sold poorly. Nevertheless, the 1950s were still the "anything is possible" decade, and manufacturers were not ready to make concessions to tough times just yet. Car sales were lower than at any time since 1954, but that did not stop the 1958 Series 62 premiering several new

features, including a signal-seeking radio and powered door locks. Also present were chrome fins on the front fenders (bumpers), an innovative and wider jewelled grille incorporating quad dual-mounted headlights, and, of course, there were still those ubiquitous, space-race-inspired tail fins—though a little less pronounced than on previous models. The only hint at frugality was under the hood (bonnet); the high-compression V8 engine was detuned in an ineffective nod to fuel efficiency.

The Series 62 still had its drawbacks, of course: drum brakes that quickly wore out trying to slow down its V8-powered 4,400 pounds (2,000 kg); a turning radius of 24 feet (7.3 m) that required the driver to perform a minor circumnavigation whenever a U-turn was required; and air domes in its new air-suspension system that constantly leaked. But none of that mattered, really. If Elvis Presley's car was a 1955 pink Cadillac Series 60, then most people would take any Cadillac on offer. **BS**

TG500 | Messerschmitt

D

1958 • 30 cu in/492 cc, S2 • 19.5 bhp/15 kW • 0–60 mph/97 kph in 27.8 seconds • 78 mph/126 kph

Park a Messerschmitt TG500 next to one of its predecessors and a key difference becomes apparent. The earlier "bubble cars" produced by the Messerschmitt company were three-wheelers, but the TG500 was given a 33 percent increase. Putting a wheel at each corner made the little vehicle a lot more stable. The car continued to be powered by a small two-stroke engine that sat above the rear end, with the power being taken to what were now two rear wheels by a chain drive.

The extra wheel also made the car more conventional, although that is relative, of course. The passenger still sat behind the driver, rather than at his or her side. Both driver and passenger got into the TG500 through the hinged bubble canopy, as they would into a Messerschmitt fighter aircraft, although there was a Sportster version with no top whatsoever.

The two-cylinder motor may have put out less than 20 bhp (15 kW), but it managed to push the lightweight TG500 up to nearly 80 mph (126 kph). That was better than full-sized cars of the era such as the Morris Minor.

The four-wheeler also had great handling, thanks to its low ride height and wheel-at-each-corner design. The fully adjustable rear suspension played its part, too.

Ultimately fewer than 500 TG500s were built. Sales were hampered by its relatively high cost. In the United Kingdom a TG500 was almost as expensive as a Mini, which had the benefit of an extra pair of seats and a metal roof. More and more people were now able to afford a "real" car, which left vehicles like the TG500 out in the cold.

But, like the Mini, these are cult machines. Park one next to a Ferrari or a Porsche and it is the tiny German bubble car that draws the crowd. **JI**

Sprite | Austin-Healey

GB

1958 • 57 cu in/948 cc, S4 • 43 bhp/32 kW • 0–60 mph/97 kph in 20.5 seconds • 83 mph/136 kph

One of the most distinctive features of this small British sports car came into being as an attempt to cut costs. When Donald Healey first designed the Sprite on behalf of the British Motor Corporation (BMC), he intended the headlights to retract when not in use, so that they would point upward and lie flush with the body. However, BMC decided that the retracting mechanism was too expensive. The lights were left stranded in their upright position, which gave the "face" of the Mark 1 version a slightly startled expression. The car was quickly dubbed the "Frog-eyed" or "Bug-eyed" Sprite.

Today, the comically prominent headlights simply add to the charm of this car, which was launched by BMC just before the 1958 Monte Carlo Rally. It was an affordable sports car, one that "a chap could keep in the bike shed," and it made up for its lack of performance by having more than its fair share of character. Opening the doors required reaching inside to grab a lever, and the only way to access the trunk (boot) was to tilt the seats forward and rummage around behind them.

The sporty-looking model also had the same modest engine as the Morris Minor, but with different carburetors for extra power. That still only added up to 43 bhp (32 kW) of pulling power, though.

The Austin-Healey Sprite was the definitive small British sports car, with low power but great handling. BMC began entering Sprites in motorsport and in 1958 one won the Alpine Rally. In the same year, a team of three Sprites was sent to the United States to compete in a twelve-hour endurance race at the Sebring circuit in Florida. They took the first three places in their class and won the Sprite a devoted American following. **JI**

PV544 | Volvo

(S)

1958 • 96 cu in/1,584 cc, S4 • 66 bhp/49 kW • 0–60 mph/97 kph in 14.3 seconds • 96 mph/155 kph

Volvo has a name for sturdy reliability; witness its rather unexcitingly named PV444 model, which first came out in 1943 and was still in production fifteen years later. When, in 1958, the company introduced the PV444's successor, the PV544, the differences were small and certainly not earth-shattering. Not that Volvo was worried; if the 544 sold as well and as steadily as the 444 had done, it would be, if not exactly laughing, at least smiling contentedly all the way to the bank.

The PV544 would not manage quite as long a production run as its predecessor, although it would keep rolling off the production line for eight years. What was important, however, was that it was the first Volvo to make any significant impact on the U.S. market. The differences between the 544 and the 444 all helped: its curved one-piece windscreen, a much larger rear window for better visibility, a four-speed rather than a three-speed manual gearbox, a larger rear seat that could accommodate three people in comfort, a dashboard with a padded upper half, and a ribbon-style speedometer.

As far as the U.S. market was concerned, at least some of the greater appeal of the new model lay in how its slight redesign made it look like a scaled-down version of the classic 1946 Ford, which had been hugely popular. The Americans cared less about the economic fuel consumption of the standard model, so Volvo mainly exported its better-performing but fuel-hungry "S" tune model. Despite Volvo's image of staid respectability, and the PV544's solid, dependable look, this import was quite a nippy performer and even had some competition successes stateside. **MG**

360 | Subaru

J

1958 • 21 cu in/356 cc, S2 • 16 bhp/12 kW • 0–50 mph/80 kph in 37 seconds • 60 mph/96 kph

The 360 of 1958 was the first car that Subaru ever built. The name refers to the tiny engine size, a twin-cylinder, 356-cc (21-cubic-inch) two-stroke that would be more at home in a motorbike of that era; indeed, it puts out less power that many modern ride-on lawnmowers.

For Subaru, choosing such an engine meant that the 360 fell within the "kei-car" or "light automobile" class, which made it exempt from certain tax and insurance regulations. Owners did not even have to prove that they had a parking space. Making such cheap, light automobiles was a way of encouraging the Japanese masses to take up motoring after the war.

The 360, or "Ladybug" to its Japanese devotees, was the first kei-car to have four wheels and to carry four passengers. The rear-mounted engine may have been small but, being a two-stroke, was deceptively powerful. However, owners were required to premix two-stroke oil and fuel and add the mixture to the engine at regular intervals.

The design was fairly advanced for its day, using a monocoque chassis, in which the bodyshell also serves as the car's loadbearing frame.

The Subaru 360 was made from 1958 to 1971, but sadly was never exported to Europe—a continent famous for its passion for small cars. Oddly enough, it was sold in small numbers in the United States, where unfavorable crash reports did not help its case. In one test collision, the fender (bumper) of an American car ended up inside the 360's passenger compartment.

The kei-car class has been continued in Japan to this day, but it is doubtful that any models will prove as groundbreaking as Subaru's firstborn. **JI**

A 1960 advertisement trumpets the arrival of the new Ford Anglia range, including the 105E. ▷

A40 | Austin (GB)

1958 • 57 cu in/948 cc, S4 • 34 bhp/24 kW • 0–60 mph/97 kph in 35.6 seconds • 73 mph/123 kph

BMC, the British Motor Corporation, was created from a merger in 1952 between the Austin Motor Company and Nuffield Corporation, owners of Morris, MG, Riley, and Wolseley. In 1956 BMC introduced the Austin A40, a new model with the same A-Series engine and gearbox as its predecessor, the Austin A35, but with radical new styling that was more square-shaped than most cars of the time. The Farina suffix that is often applied to the name of the A40 denotes that its styling was by Pininfarina, the famous Italian auto designer.

The A40 first appeared at the 1958 London Motor Show at Earls Court as a sedan (saloon). At the back, a panel opened downward as a trunk (boot) lid, while the rear windshield above it was fixed in position. In late 1959 the Countryman version appeared. The rear window of this version could be opened, and had its own support, while the lower panel was redesigned with longer and stronger hinges that allowed it to open level with the trunk floor, which was helpful when loading the car.

This change at the rear led to the A40 being widely credited as the first hatchback car. Its upward-opening hinged rear door was an innovative feature that has subsequently become a key part of one of the most popular car body styles.

In January 1959, within months of the car's launch, an A40 was driven with great success by Pat Moss and Ann Wisdom in the Monte Carlo Rally, then the most famous motorsport event in the world. It won several prestigious awards, including the Coupe des Dames, was runner-up in the class for standard production cars of up to 1,000 cc, and was tenth overall. This gave the A40 huge publicity that put it on the motoring map.. **SB**

Anglia 105E | Ford (GB)

1959 • 60 cu in/997 cc, S4 • 39 bhp/29.1 kW • 0–60 mph/97 kph in 26.9 seconds • 76 mph/112 kph

Not one car, but four named Anglia were sold in the United Kingdom between 1939 and 1967. The last of the these, the 105E, has become the best known thanks to its high-flying appearances in the best-selling book and movie *Harry Potter and the Chamber of Secrets*. Prior to that, the Anglia's biggest claim to fame was a bit part in British TV police drama *Z-Cars* during the 1960s and 1970s. Around the same time, former British prime minister Margaret Thatcher also drove one.

The first Ford Anglia, the E04A, was launched just after the outbreak of World War II and was a facelifted version of the Ford 7Y. Hostilities hindered production, which resumed at full speed when they ended in 1945. The Mark II was another facelift and sold from 1949 to 1953, when it was rebadged as the ultrabasic Ford Popular and continued to be made for another six years.

The first all-new Anglia, the 100E, arrived shortly after and featured a totally different design based on the styling cues of the larger Consul. It was easily the best-selling Anglia to date, with almost 350,000 finding homes over the next six years. Two station wagon (estate) versions of the 100E appeared in 1955, one of which marked the debut of the Escort name on a Ford.

With more American styling—its inwardly sloping rear window was a Lincoln trait—the fourth and final Anglia hit showrooms in 1959. It thankfully did away with one of the range's less endearing features, the vacuum-powered front wipers, which were famous for slowing down when the Anglia went uphill. The 105E was the most successful version of the Anglia and in eight years more than a million were built. The Anglia name was killed off in 1968 with the arrival of the Escort. **RY**

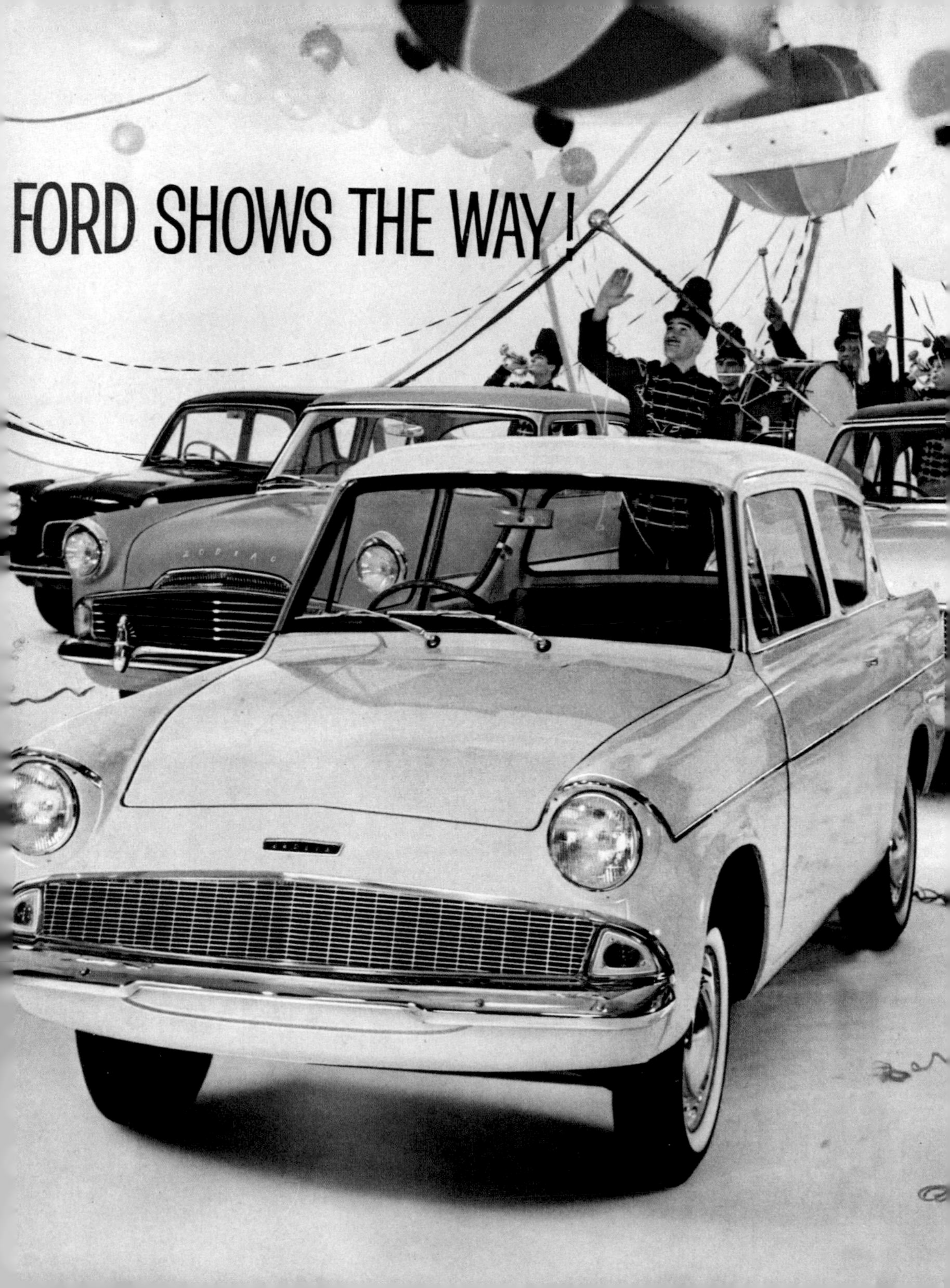
FORD SHOWS THE WAY!

GT | Gilbern

GB

1959 • 109 cu in/1,799 cc, S4 • 96 bhp/71 kW • 0–60 mph/97 kph in 9.7 seconds • 103 mph/163 kph

The Gilbern Sports Cars company was set up in the Welsh village of Llantwit Fardre after a chance meeting between local butcher Giles Smith and German former prisoner of war Bernhard Friese. Earlier in the 1950s Friese had worked on fiberglass cars and Smith had asked his opinion on the various models available with a view to building a component car of his own. Eventually the two men custom-built their own car in an outbuilding behind the butcher's shop.

The GT was a pretty 2+2 fastback sports coupe, resembling a mini Aston Martin. Featuring a fiberglass body and Austin A35 mechanicals, the very first GT was tested by *Autosport* magazine, which was very complimentary about its handling, performance, and build quality. Seeing a potential market for the new car, the pair set about producing part-assembled Gilbern GTs in kit form, retailing at £748 ($1,176). All that was left to do was fit an engine, gearbox, rear axle, and wheels—a weekend's work for most customers. In that way British buyers avoided paying a hefty purchase tax that was applied to completed factory-built cars; even Lotus supplied the majority of its cars in kit form until the 1970s.

As demand grew, Gilbern increased its staff to five. In the early 1960s, cars were offered with MGA running gear, and were produced at the rate of one a month. By 1965 the 109-cubic-inch (1,799-cc) MGB engine was used, and a staff of twenty was making one Gilbern GT 1800 a week.

In all, 277 Gilbern GTs were built; today, they are highly sought after, particularly in their native Welsh homeland. Many are still competing in historic sports car racing events thanks to their lightweight construction and robust mechanicals. **GT**

Sport Prinz | NSU

D

1959 • 35 cu in/583 cc, S2 • 30 bhp/22 kW • 0–60 mph/97 kph in 27.8 seconds • 78 mph/126 kph

NSU (formally NSU Motorenwerke AG) of Germany had its fingers in a lot of pies: first sewing machines, then pedal cycles, scooters, and motorcycles. NSU was the largest producer of motorcycles in the world by the mid-1950s and set several land-speed records.

From 1905 to 1932, when it sold its auto division to FIAT, the company also manufactured motorcars. Turning again to cars in the 1950s, executives contacted Franco Scaglioni of Bertone and told him they wanted a sporty car to add to their rather staid but growing stable. Scaglioni, who was busy designing cars for Alfa Romeo and was the man behind the Aston Martin DB2 and the Maserati 3500 GT, accepted the offer. In 1959 NSU released Scaglioni's Sport Prinz.

The hit of the 1958 Frankfurt Motor Show, the Sport Prinz was a racy little coupe, a sort of jazzed-up version of Hans Glas's Goggomobil, some thought, with lines that echoed the popular, though larger, Chevrolet Corvair. The first 250 examples were built at Bertone's Turin factory, but later models were manufactured in Germany at NSU's own factory at Neckarsulm. More than 20,000 were built between 1959 and 1967.

The Sport Prinz was smart, with lovely, tapered lines, hooded taillights, chrome trim, and typical "microcar" features including two-spoke wheels. A spartan interior had the driver's legs straddling a rather inconvenient steering column that disappeared into the floor between the accelerator and the brake.

However, the German light car industry would not last. The Deutschmark was gathering strength, and people began abandoning little cars as they embraced another form of cc: conspicuous consumption. **BS**

3000 | Austin-Healey

GB

1959 • 177 cu in/2,912 cc, S6 • 124 bhp/92.4 kW • 0–60 mph/97 kph in 11.4 seconds • 114 mph/182 kph

Essentially an Austin-Healey 100-6 with a new and larger 177-cubic-inch (2,912-cc) engine, the 3000 is an iconic British sports car of the 1950s. It was the last and best known of what later became known as the "big Healeys," a name dreamed up to differentiate the 100, 100-6, and 3000 from the smaller Austin-Healey Sprite.

The 3000 is most fondly remembered for its competition successes and it remains a favorite of many enthusiasts. It raced at circuits all over the world, including Sebring and Le Mans, but also triumphed in rally stages. Legend has it that the British Motor Corporation, which assembled the 3000 at its factory in Abingdon, only stopped developing it as a works racer after the success of the Mini Cooper S.

Launched in 1959 with a convertible canvas roof and bodywork designed by Jensen Motors, the Austin-Healey 3000 was available as a two- or four-seater. The latter was by far the more popular model, accounting for more than 10,000 of the 13,000 sold. The Mark I, which only became known as that when the Mark II made its debut, was phased out in March 1961. Although a 2+2 Mark II option was added to the range, the seat in the back was tiny and rarely used by passengers. A Mark III was launched in 1963 and remained in showrooms for five years.

Production of the 3000 ended because new safety legislation in North America, which constituted the 3000's largest customer base, made reengineering it uneconomic. By that time, more than 40,000 had been sold. Imitation is the sincerest form of flattery, and the 3000 lived again during the 1980s and 1990s when various replicas were made available. **RY**

356B | Porsche

D

1959 • 119 cu in/1,966 cc, F4 • 130 bhp/97 kW • 0–60 mph/97 kph in 9.7 seconds • 125 mph/201 kph

When Porsche's first full production year began in 1950, the 356 was little more than modified Volkswagen Beetle mechanics beneath a handcrafted sports car body. However, over the next fifteen years Porsche continually refined its car, replacing Volkswagen components with its own improved designs to make the car perform and handle better. As the car became more "Porsche," it also became more expensive.

Until 1959 Porsche had sold a stripped-down open-top version of the 356 called the Speedster. This was built to compete with cheaper British sports cars, and also to appeal to amateur club racers. By the late 1950s, however, the lucrative U.S. market was looking for greater levels of comfort and refinement. In response, the new Porsche 356B was launched at the 1959 Frankfurt Auto Show, featuring a facelifted front end with improved steering and braking, and a few more creature comforts for its occupants. The Speedster was dropped from the lineup in favor of a better trimmed, coachbuilt cabriolet.

The new entry-level 60-bhp (45-kW) "Damen" might have looked the part, but Porsche's desire to prove itself on the racetrack inspired some much hotter versions of the 356B. The most impressive of these was the fabulous Carrera 2 (so named because of its 2-liter engine), which was to become the fastest 356 ever built. The Carrera 2 was described in Porsche sales brochures as "a racehorse tamed by a master's hand"; capable of 125 mph (201 kph), and with only drum brakes to stop it, this was a car for serious drivers only. British motorsport legend John Surtees, the only person to have won world championships on both two and four wheels, chose to drive his ivory 1963 Carrera 2 for nearly twenty years. **DS**

The ncredible AUSTIN SEVEN &
MORRIS MINI-MINOR

⊂ A 1959 display of the new Mini suggests the number of passengers and the amount of luggage it could carry.

Mini | Austin (GB)

1959 • 51 cu in/848 cc, S4 • 34 bhp/25 kW • 0–60 mph/97 kph in 25 seconds • 72 mph/116 kph

History has decreed that the little car with its engine turned sideways and its wheels pushed out to the corners of a 10-foot-long (3-m) body will forever be known simply as the Mini. When it started life back in 1959, though, it was a badge-engineered pair of cars, called the Austin Seven and the Morris Mini Minor, later to become the Austin Mini and then the Mini.

The Mini incorporated a brilliant notion of designer Alec Issigonis. The engine was located sideways along the front axle, instead of placed in the conventional fore-aft position in the engine bay, and was made to drive the front wheels instead of the back ones. By this means, Issigonis shortened the hood (bonnet) and did away with the usual driveshaft needed for power delivery from front engine to back axle.

Enough space was saved to shorten the car's overall length considerably. Now 80 percent of the car floor area could be used for passengers and luggage, with minimal space allocated to accommodating the engine and long body overhangs. At a stroke, the boxy little car made its contemporaries look cumbersome and old-fashioned. Its very direct, "go-kart" handling also transformed the way a small, modestly powered car could be expected to drive.

The Mini erupted onto the British scene just a few months before the arrival of what became the "Swinging '60s" heyday of The Beatles, with the glamour of London's Carnaby Street and the excitement of space exploration. It is often forgotten, though, that the Mini was not an instant success. Sales started slowly, until chic trendsetters such as Princess Margaret and Lord Snowden began to be seen around London in a Mini. Then the little car took off in a big way. **SB**

M-13 | Chaika (SU)

1959 • 337 cu in/5,526 cc, V8 • 195 bhp/143 kW • 0–60 mph/97 kph in 15 seconds • 99 mph/160 kph

In the Soviet Union's planned economy of the 1950s, the concept of producing enough cars for its citizens, to say nothing of being able to buy one "off the street" (in the unlikely event that anyone had the money), was unheard of. Anyone wanting a car placed their name on a waiting list and then waited, often for up to ten years. That is, unless they were a low-ranking party member, scientist, trade delegate, or other VIP; then the car they would most likely get was a Chaika.

The Chaika 337-cubic-inch (5,526-cc) V8 M-13 weighed more than 5,511 pounds (2,500 kg) and needed all of its 195 bhp (143 kW) just to pull it along. It was available only to politburo members and high-echelon bureaucrats. A few more than 3,000 Chaikas were built during its twenty-year production run—long by Western standards but common in a planned economy where there was no need for stylistic changes, and no need to stay ahead of the pack.

Officially the Chaika was designed in-house in Russia, although it looked suspiciously like a Packard with its typically 1950s oversized chrome fenders (bumpers) and trim, and faint echoes of a Cadillac Series 62. A 1955 Packard Patrician had been imported from the United States to give the Chaika's design team some Western inspiration to draw from, so the similarities are, therefore, unsurprising.

The Soviet premier, Nikita Khrushchev, preferred a Chaika to the more sophisticated ZiL, and kept one in the garage of his summer dacha. Most were sedans (saloons), but a small number of four-door convertibles were made. Like Ford's Model T, they were available in a variety of colors as long as it was black. **BS**

SP250 | Daimler

GB

1959 • 155 cu in/2,548 cc, V8 • 142 bhp/106 kW • 0–60 mph/97 kph in 8.9 seconds • 124 mph/200 kph

Daimler of England, a subsidiary of Germany's Daimler-Benz, never built many sports cars, and when they did they were not terribly successful. Its 1953 Conquest roadster had been an attempt at a more affordable Daimler, but production ceased after just two years of poor sales. The late 1950s, however, saw a change in management and direction.

Daimler's new chairman, Jack Sangster, decided in a board meeting on May 22, 1958, that it was time to look anew at developing a sports car for the lucrative U.S. market. The demand for British sports cars in the United States had grown by 82 percent in 1957, fueled by new models from MG, Jaguar, Triumph, and Austin-Healey. Daimler wanted a piece of the action. Engineer Edward Turner's brief was a simple one: design a sports car that would be reliable, easy to service, and most of all a joy to drive. The result, the Daimler SP250, was almost everything that Jack Sangster was looking for.

The problem was the shape. Tooling costs for pressed steel were prohibitive, but the odd-looking fiberglass body appeared to have been designed in haste, with headlights awkwardly pushing forward from the fender (bumper) and exaggerated tail fins.

Questionable looks aside, the rigid chassis and oversized shock absorbers gave superb comfort and handling, and an exuberant new V8 engine with patented valve gears provided up to 6,000 rpm. The car had disc brakes all around (still a rarity), and rear seats that comfortably accommodated two children.

In 1960 Daimler was bought out by Jaguar. The SP250 was improved upon with the Model B, but it still lacked popularity and was discontinued in 1964. **BS**

Eldorado | Cadillac

(USA)

1959 • 390 cu in/6,391 cc, V8 • 345 bhp/254 kW • 0–60 mph/97 kph in 9.6 seconds • 124 mph/199 kph

Cadillac introduced a model named the Eldorado back in 1953, but the redesign that appeared at the end of the 1950s now clearly represents the ultimate in that decade's extravagant auto styling.

The new Eldorado was particularly notable for taking tail-fin design just about as far as it could go. At the back, the fins were the tallest that had ever been made, measuring 45 inches (114 cm) from top to bottom. They were angled in at the rear in a V-shape, and at the point of each V were a pair of red taillights. The great fins gave the 1959 Eldorado the appearance more of a rocket ship than a car.

Tail fins had been introduced on the Eldorado back in 1956, and had grown bigger in 1957, and bigger yet again in 1958. But 1959 brought the biggest and brashest yet. Some critics, notably the Cadillac historian Walter McCall, called them "ludicrous" and "of questionable taste," but the public seemed to go for the space-age look. In 1959, sales of not only the Eldorado but all Cadillacs went up as a consequence.

The car really was quite special, and at a price of $7,401 (£4,790) buyers expected something out of the ordinary. Under the hood (bonnet) was a massive 390-cubic-inch (6,391-cc) engine, and more horsepower than had been packed into previous Cadillacs. Again, that went about as far as it could go, making the 1959 Eldorado the most powerful 1950s Cadillac. A six-way power seat was offered as an optional extra, along with electric door locks; the sides were elaborately decorated in chrome trim. Anyone wanting one today can expect to pay well in excess of $200,000 (£129,400) for a model in good condition. **MG**

Impala | Chevrolet

(USA)

1959 • 235 cu in/3,859 cc, S6 • 135 bhp/99kW • unknown • 90 mph/145 kph

Drivers certainly knew when they were driving behind a Chevrolet Impala in 1959. Although the model had been introduced the year before, the 1959 model had been redesigned to produce a style classic. One of the changes involved the introduction of a large teardrop-shaped taillight on each side, which sat beneath curving, eyebrowlike tail fins. The combination gave the impression of some kind of monster, or maybe even a superhero, staring beady-eyed at the car behind, and it ensured that the Impala got noticed.

When it first appeared in 1958, the Impala (named after a leaping African antelope) had three small taillights in a row on each side instead of one big one. The look was dramatic, but not as dramatic as the following year's change. Curiously, Chevrolet then reverted to a more conservative taillight style for 1960. Their decision cannot be faulted, though, because by 1965 the Impala had become the best-selling car in the United States.

The 1959 Impala was designed by Harley Earl, who produced a number of great U.S. cars, and this was to be the last car he designed for the company before he retired. He definitely went out with a bang, producing a car that was called "the wild one" by admirers, and any number of names by those who did not like it.

Chevrolet's intention with the Impala was, according to Ed Cole, the company's chief engineer, to build a "prestige car within the reach of the average American citizen." As such, the looks were more important than power. The basic model had a fairly modest top speed, but Earl designed the car so that customers could order more powerful engines if they wanted to. The Impala name is still going strong today. **MG**

5000 GT | Maserati

(I)

1959 • 301 cu in/4,940 cc, V8 • 340 bhp/254 kW • 0–60 mph/97 kph in 6.5 seconds • 170 mph/274 kph

The Maserati 5000 GT has secured its place among the world's greatest luxury grand tourers. It has racing pedigree, immense power, superb handling, and a level of exclusivity that few cars have matched.

In 1958 the Shah of Persia (now Iran) visited Maserati, looking for something special to add to his expanding stable of supercars. Shah Reza Pahlavi was impressed by Maserati's new 3500 GT, but he desired something more exclusive, and considerably more powerful. After lengthy discussions with the chief engineers, the shah commissioned Maserati to build a unique grand tourer, the 5000 GT. Styled by Italian coachbuilder Touring, and powered by a lusty V8 derived from the ill-fated 450S race car, the 5000 GT was an unrivaled masterpiece.

When details of the shah's 5000 GT leaked out, Maserati received a stream of enquiries from the world's wealthiest car fanatics. Over the next six years, another thirty-two were built; bodied by eight different Italian coachbuilders, including Ghia, Bertone, and Michelotti, each was unique. These later cars, now sporting a 305-cubic-inch (5,000-cc) V8, became known as the "superstars' supercars"; customers ranged from actor Stewart Grainger and sportsman Briggs Cunningham to world leaders, including King Saud of Saudi Arabia and Mexico's President Adolfo Lopez Mateos.

In August 1962, Karim Aga Khan took delivery of a purple Maserati 5000 GT at his home in Paris, France. Specially ordered with disc brakes all around and bespoke bodywork from Frua, it also featured a 45-rpm record player in the front dashboard. In 2007 this car sold at Gooding & Co. car auctions in Pebble Beach, California, for $1.1 million (£696,000). **DS**

Bill Murray drives "Ecto-1," a Cadillac Miller-Meteor ambulance converted to battle the paranormal, in *Ghostbusters* (1984).

Dart | Goggomobil (AUS)

1959 • 18 cu in/300 cc or 24 cu in/400 cc, S2 • 15 bhp/11 kW • unknown • 62 mph/100 kph

It is a very Australian thing to do: take a stock-standard automobile, remove the factory-fitted engine, and put in a bigger one. This is what Buckle Motors of Punchbowl, Sydney, did with 700 Darts, the Australian-made sports version of the popular German Goggomobil TS, which Buckle made from 1959 to 1961.

To Bill Buckle, the TS's 215-cubic-inch (50-cc) engine seemed way too small, so when the chassis and running gear were purchased from Goggomobil's inventor, Hans Glas of Dingolfing, Germany, and production began, the new-generation Dart received a typical Aussie upgrade with a choice of either 18 cubic-inch (300-cc) or 24-cubic-inch (400-cc) engines.

The German Goggomobile had steel panels, but Buckle reduced its weight to just 838 pounds (380 kg) by fitting a fiberglass body. Bill Buckle already had had some success racing fiberglass six-cylinder sports cars in Australia, and he approached a Sydney-based engineer, Stan Brown, to design a convertible.

Aussies were used to eclectic-looking vehicles, and the Dart certainly was that. Sure, it had no roof, no doors, and an engine the size of a go-cart, but what it lacked in the usual necessities it more than made up for in sheer likability. It wasn't fast, but a flattering power-to-weight ratio meant it wasn't slow, either.

This "stubby-nosed E-Type" with its wheelbarrow-sized tires was as cute as could be, though large drivers would soon tire of climbing in and out of its cramped, doorless cockpit. But it had a lovely curved windshield (based on the Renault Dauphine), and its simple flowing lines and enclosed headlights turned heads wherever it went—and for all the right reasons. **BS**

Miller-Meteor | Cadillac (USA)

1959 • 389 cu in/6,390 cc, V8 • 325 bhp/242 kW • 0–60 mph/97 kph in 11.5 seconds • 120 mph/193 kph

In 1957 the two most respected names in the U.S. funeral car and ambulance market were acquired by the industrial giant Wayne Works of Indiana and merged into a single, powerful entity: Miller-Meteor. The A. J. Miller Company had first began crafting buggies, hearses, and surreys in 1853, while the Meteor Motor Car Company, first established in Ohio in 1913, had become the largest manufacturer of funeral cars and ambulances in the world. The Miller plant in Bellafontaine, Ohio, was sold and operations consolidated at Meteor's factory at Piqua, Ohio.

Miller-Meteor's first coaches were built on Cadillac chassis. Cadillac had been the undisputed leader in ambulances and hearses since the late 1940s thanks to its extralong, 163-inch (414-cm) Series 75 commercial chassis. By 1962 Cadillac had managed to snare an impressive 50 percent of its market thanks to the demise in 1954 of their fiercest competitor, the Henney-bodied Packards, after several years of falling sales.

The most popular Miller-Meteor model ever made was the 1959 Cadillac Futura. Coachbuilt by Miller-Meteor, the Futura's exaggerated 42-inch (107-cm) rocketlike tail fins place it among the most collectible ambulances and hearses of all time. Sure, it might seem that such outrageously ornamented cars were inappropriate for carrying out such solemn duties, but for those making that final journey, Cadillac and the Miller-Meteor firm made sure that they went in style.

A 1959 Cadillac Miller-Meteor became famous in 1984 with the release of the movie *Ghostbusters*. It played "Ecto-1," the car used by actor Bill Murray and his team to sniff out various spooky ectoplasmic disturbances. **BS**

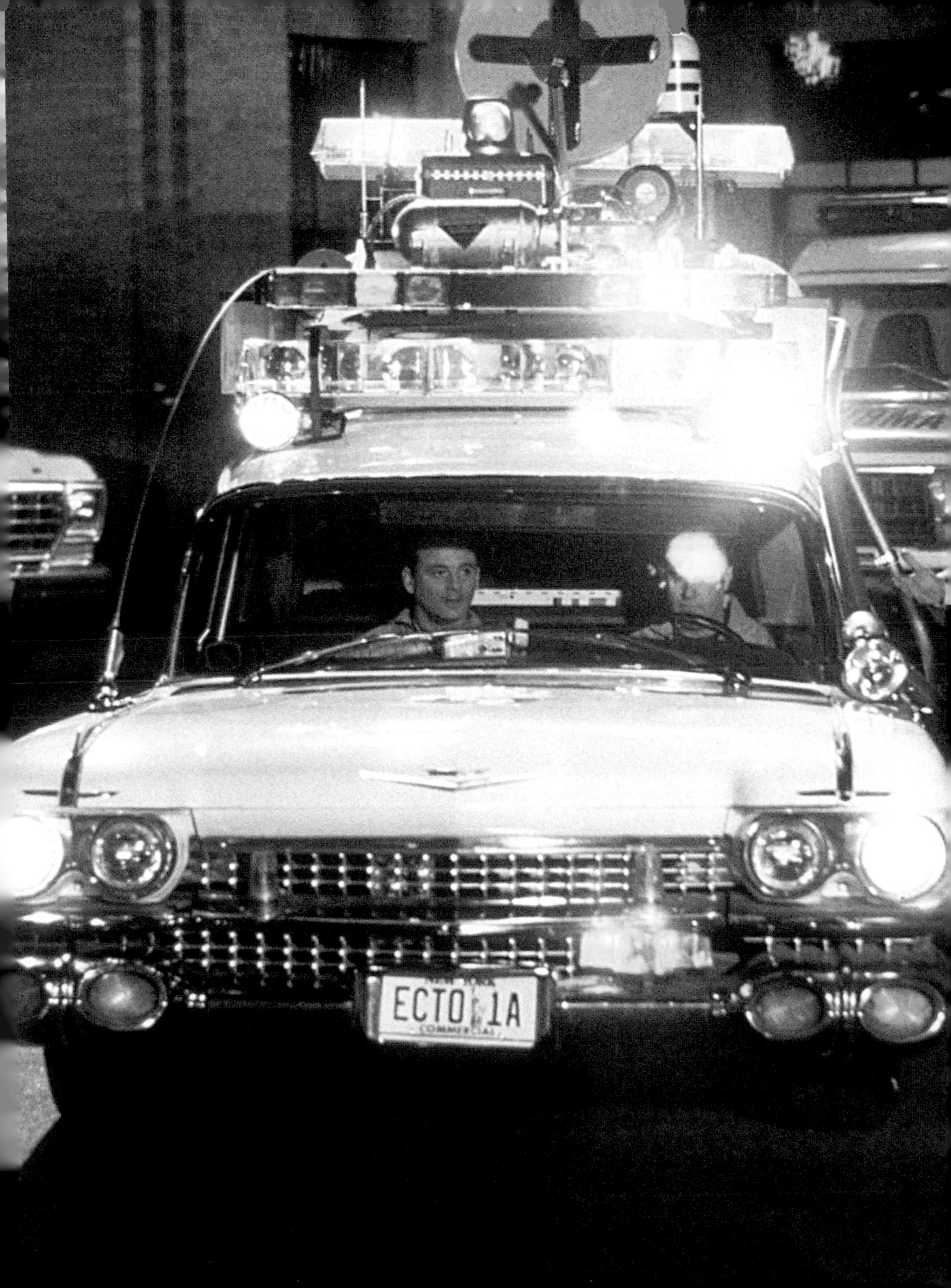
ECTO 1A
COMMERCIAL

400 GT Superamerica | Ferrari

I

1959 • 242 cu in/3,967 cc, V12 • 340 bhp/250kW • unknown • 165 mph/265 kph

Launched as the successor of the 410 Superamerica models, the limited-edition 400 GT Superamerica two-seater was sold from 1959 to 1964. The majority were standard "aerodynamica" coupes, but one "berlinetta" coupe and nine convertibles also rolled out of the factory gates. All but two were designed by Pininfarina, all but one were left-hand drive, and each featured a mighty 242-cubic-inch (3,967-cc) V12 engine.

The car's name made history because it was the first time a production Ferrari did not follow the convention of having a three-digit number representing the swept volume of a single cylinder. So, instead of being the 330, it is the 400, the total cubic capacity of 4 liters. And Superamerica? To meet the demands of the U.S. market, while the "super" prefix remains a common Ferrari way of announcing an improved version.

Aimed at the überrich, the cars were designed and built along the same lines as the Ferrari 250 GT series, also in production at the time. Customers were able to select the body style they wanted, and then have it personalized as they chose. No two cars were the same.

The first example went to Fiat boss Gianni Agnelli in 1959 and was presented to him at that year's Turin Motor Show. Suitably impressed, he eventually secured a controlling stake in Ferrari a decade later.

Only forty-six 400 GTs were ever built and they do not come up for sale very often. One example, a 1962 cabriolet, went under the hammer in May 2010 in Monaco for €2.8 million ($3.8 million/£2.3 million). It was a world record price for a 400 Superamerica and, needless to say, the new owner did not roar off down the French Riviera to celebrate. **RY**

250 GT SWB | Ferrari

(I)

1959 • 180 cu in/2,953 cc, V12 • 280 bhp/209 kW • 0–60 mph/97 kph in 6.2 seconds • 152 mph/245 kph

The Ferrari 250 family of sports cars began with the Europa model of 1953. Over the next eleven years Ferrari's annual output rose from thirty-five to 670 units per year, such was the popularity of this V12 supercar.

With its light, 180-cubic-inch (2,953-cc) Columbo engine, and a finely balanced chassis, the Ferrari 250 was always a race car at heart. The 250 GT SWB (short wheel base) was the world's fastest, and quickest accelerating, sports car of its day. On track it was virtually unbeatable; in 1960, Ferrari claimed the top four places at the 24 Hours of Le Mans in the GT class. The following year, motorsport legends Stirling Moss and Graham Hill beat the lap record. Moss has been quoted as saying that the 250 GT SWB was "the best GT car ever."

Ferrari needed to sell road cars to fund their racing ambitions. Capitalizing on the 250's recent successes on track, Ferrari launched the Lusso (meaning "luxury") and the beautiful, open-topped California—a replica of which famously appears in the 1986 hit movie *Ferris Bueller's Day Off*.

In 1961 Hollywood actor James Coburn bought a black 250 GT California, which he owned for the next twenty-four years. While filming *The Great Escape* (1963) he convinced his costar, and fellow gearhead, Steve McQueen to try one. In 1963 McQueen bought his first Ferrari—a chestnut brown 250 GT Lusso; years later, this was sold for $2,310,000 (£1,472,600) at the 2007 Monterey Sports Car Auctions. However, the following year, British radio presenter Chris Evans bid an astonishing £5,089,280 ($7,983,600) for Coburn's California, setting a world record for the highest price ever paid for a car at auction. **DS**

MPH

The sumptuous red interior of a customized 1961 Ford Thunderbird.

1960–1969

A staged publicity photograph of the Citroën DS Décapotable hints at the lifestyle that typical owners might enjoy. ⊡

Sabra | Autocars (IL)

1960 • 103 cu in/1,703 cc, S4 • 74 bhp/55 kW • 0–60 mph/97 kph in 15 seconds • 93 mph/150 kph

Brought into being only in 1948, the state of Israel had no historic opportunity to establish itself as a major center of motor manufacturing. In the 1950s, Yitzhak Shubinski saw no reason why that should not change. He established a brand-new firm, Autocars, in Haifa, 25 miles (40 km) west of Nazareth.

Shubinski teamed up with Reliant in the United Kingdom, which provided him with the necessary knowledge and helped him to build several models. All were straightforward cars with boxy shapes, and by 1960 Shubinski knew that he needed a more challenging car.

Paying a visit to the 1960 Racing Car Show in central London, Shubinski noticed a fiberglass body that a company named Ashley Laminates had to offer. Ashley was selling the bodies to enthusiasts handy enough to turn a rusty old Ford Popular or Austin Ten into something much more sporty. These were kit car bodies.

With additional technical help from Reliant plus a Bellamy chassis and a tuned Ford Consul engine, Shubinski imported Ashley bodies and used them to manufacture the Autocars Sabra. The model designation referred to "cactus" in Hebrew, which also appeared in the Autocars logo. The Sabra was unveiled at the New York Motor Show of 1961. Back in Haifa, the plant was not yet ready for production, so the first cars were built at Reliant's plant in Tamworth.

Even when production in Israel started, demand for the Israeli sports car was limited. The fact that Reliant continued to build them (now as the Reliant Sabre) did not help. Eventually some 380 Sabras were built before Autocars signed a contract with Standard Triumph and began to produce cars under their license. **SH**

DS Décapotable | Citroën (F)

1960 • 116 cu in/1,911 cc, S4 • 83 bhp/62 kW • 0–60 mph/97 kph in 18.3 seconds • 99 mph/159 kph

The Citroën DS Décapotable (convertible) always had an air of inevitability about it because its predecessor, the DS sedan (saloon) was, quite simply, one of the most popular and influential automobiles of all time. The sedan featured self-leveling hydropneumatic suspension and power steering, and was the first production car to have powered front disc brakes. It was considered uncommonly beautiful by some—*Classic & Sports Car* magazine named it as the most beautiful car ever made, and it was only a matter of time before the loud chorus of "Take off its roof!" would force the great French car maker to do so.

The Décapotable was designed and built by the gifted coachbuilder Henri Chapron, a traditional *carrossier* who continued to craft and remodel bodies long after the monocoque age had consigned most of his contemporaries to the history books. His design owed nothing to any motor vehicle that had come before it. A gently tapering body, all-new panels aft of the front fender (bumper), and a new single-piece rear wing with cutaway wheel arches produced a look that was both futuristic and timeless. Now a strict 2+2, it had some lovely innovations, including headlights that turned in sync with the steering. A central division between the front and rear seats offered rear passengers their own heating and ventilation controls. The DS Décapotable was a true limousine.

Of the more than 1.5 million DS sedans built, only 1,365 were the sought-after Chapron-designed classics that reminded drivers with long memories of the grandes routières of days gone by—and gave the rest of us a glimpse of what might come. **BS**

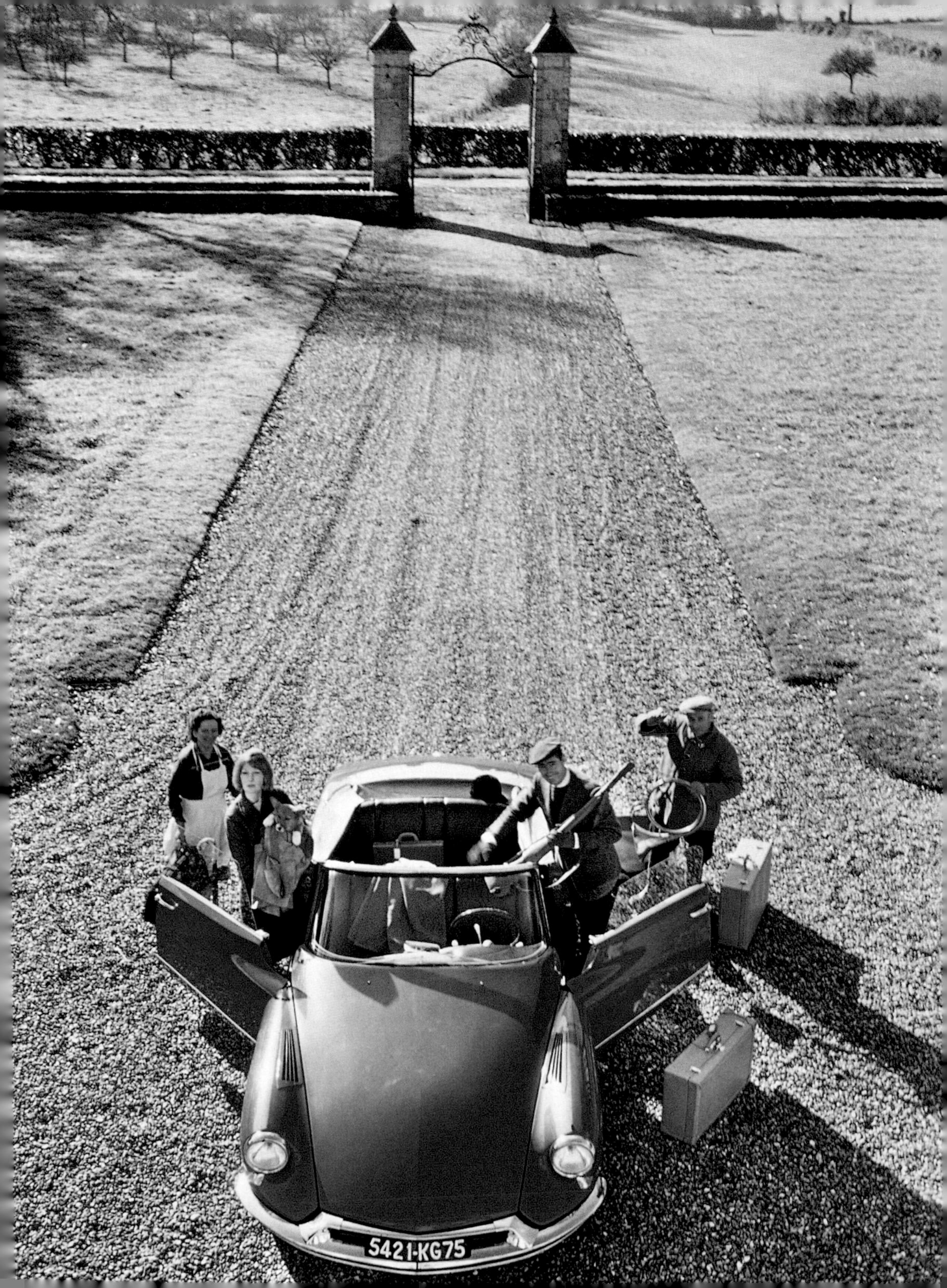
5421-KG75

411 JX 75

⊂ The Peugeot 404, pictured here in 1960, proved as much a success with French families as it did in African rallies.

404 | Peugeot (F)

1960 • 98 cu in/1,618 cc, S4 • 71 bhp/5 kW • 0–60 mph/97 kph in 22 seconds • 84 mph/135 kph

Italian design studio Pininfarina has penned some classically beautiful cars, but it is doubtful that any has been as well used worldwide as the Peugeot 404.

Built as a replacement for the 403, although the pair did sell alongside one another for a while, the 404 was a four-door family car. More than 1.8 million were assembled in France from 1960 to 1975. It was popular as a sedan (saloon) or station wagon (estate) and many were used in the taxi trade. A convertible and coupe were added in 1962 and 1963 respectively, and the pickup version proved a hit with France's agricultural communities—so much so that when production of the 404 car ended, strong sales of the truck kept it in showrooms for another thirteen years.

Yet the Peugeot 404 will be remembered as much for its conquest of Africa as anything else. In a continent where smooth bitumen was almost nonexistent, its rugged durability made it hugely desirable with the locals. Demand was so great that Peugeot agreed to it being built under license there and various factories were opened. The last of these, in Kenya, closed in 1988.

Much of the 404's reputation in Africa was built on its successes in the Safari Rally, a grueling desert endurance race that eventually became part of the World Rally Championship (WRC). One 404, driven by Kenyans Nick Nowicki and Paddy Cliff, became Peugeot's first winner of the event in 1963. The model then secured an additional hattrick of titles with straight victories in 1966, 1967, and 1968.

The car was also popular in South America, where it was built under license for the Argentinian market by local manufacturer Sevel. **RY**

New Yorker | Chrysler (USA)

1960 • 413 cu in/6,771 cc, V8 • 350 bhp/261 kW • 0–60 mph/97 kph in 7 seconds • 124 mph/199 kph

The 1960 New Yorker was available as a two-door hardtop and convertible, a four-door sedan (saloon) and hardtop, and a four-door hardtop station wagon (estate). Only 556 of the convertible were built, all in that first year. All of the models moved to full-unit construction, meaning that their panels were attached with welds rather than nuts and bolts. This resulted in a safer and far more rigid body, but also an increased tendency to rust. Styling changes centered on a large, inverted trapezoid grille, while for the first time the station wagons sported elongated tail fins that ran half the length of the car. One of the more popular optional extras consisted of front seats that swiveled to the outside when the front doors were opened.

The Chrysler New Yorker had been first unveiled in 1938 as the New Yorker Special; that name was later simplified to just "New Yorker." New Yorkers continued in production uninterrupted until 1996, and for many of those years they were Chrysler's flagship models. The U.S. motorist saw Chrysler, and the New Yorker in particular, as not as fancy as a Cadillac, but superior to a Ford or Chevrolet. And it wasn't all about dignity; "When you go for a drive, 'You'll feel like a kid at the circus,'" went the advertising. This was no less than "The car of your life for the time of your life."

The New Yorker was the car that told Americans where the company stood. When it was finally laid to rest, looking too much like a weary version of Chrysler's new high-end, solid-performing LH sedan, it was more than just the demise of another motorcar. It was the end of an institution, the longest continually used nameplate in U.S. automotive history. **BS**

300F | Chrysler

USA

1960 • 413 cu in/6,768 cc, V8 • 375 bhp/279 kW • 0–60 mph/97 kph in 7.1 seconds • 127 mph/205 kph

The first of the Chrysler 300 series, the C-300 of 1955 had been a success from the start, and the cars continued to roll off the production line, year by year. After moving up a notch to the 300B in 1956, the series names descended letter by letter until the Chrysler 300E of 1959, by which time sales were down to a sluggish 647 cars. Something had to be done to revitalize the brand, and what was done was the 300F of 1960. And there was nothing sluggish about this beast—in fact, it became one of the first examples from Chrysler of what became known as "muscle cars."

The 300F had the same engine as the previous model, but with more power, and it was also given a lighter body, which enabled more speed and a more impressive acceleration figure. The rear was redesigned, with Chrysler producing its own stylized version of the all-important tail fin. Tail fins had been one of the key elements of U.S. car design through the latter half of the 1950s, and by 1960 they had gone just about as far as they could go and were beginning to turn into parodies of themselves. The 300F's fins sloped both upward and outward, and each had a huge, V-shaped taillight in it, like the open mouth of a snake. A spare tire rested in a recess in the top of the trunk (boot), but this became known as the "toilet seat" and was done away with for the following year.

Air-conditioning was an optional extra, and the basic price of the car when it came out was $5,411 (£3,500). There were only two versions, a two-door coupe and a two-door convertible. The redesign and extra power paid off for Chrysler as they were able to almost double production to 1,217 vehicles. **MG**

Ghia L6.4 | Chrysler

USA

1960 • 383 cu in/6,279 cc, V8 • 335 bhp/250 kW • unknown • 140 mph/224 kph

When it comes to rare and collectible automobiles, few cars anywhere are as prized as the Chrysler Ghia L6.4. It had all the necessary ingredients: it was hand-built, designed in Italy, had the most frugal of production runs (just twenty-six made), and its celebrity connections were the coolest of cool. Six handpicked examples of the Ghia L6.4 were set apart from the rest, given extraspecial headlights designed by the Barris Kustom Company of Hollywood, then delivered to their new owners: Frank Sinatra, Dean Martin, Sammy Davis Jr., and the other members of the Hollywood Rat Pack. In the early 1960s, the Rat Pack was very best PR crew that an automobile company could hope for.

The Italian-American hybrid (based in part on a Dodge concept car, the Firearrow) was almost entirely manufactured in Italy, but had a classic Chrysler V8 engine at its core. This involved an around trip from Detroit to Torino—the "longest production line on earth," as the joke went. The model's rarity and high cost (fully twice that of its predecessor, the Dual Ghia) meant that it would only ever be a car for the wealthy, lucky few. The fact the Italian bodies were prone to rust, together with the project's massive cost overruns, deterred noone; if anything, the rising costs just added to the frenzy of interest. In the end, however, it was the high ongoing costs of production that doomed it to obscurity.

But everybody, it seemed, wanted one, and no other Chrysler has ever been so unashamedly coveted. "The Rolls-Royce," said one Hollywood columnist, "has become a status symbol for those who can't get a Dual-Ghia." Rarely had anything on wheels ever looked so ring-a-ding-ding, as the Rat Packers would have said. **BS**

The hardy Citroën 2CV Sahara housed two engines, which enabled it to tackle all manner of terrain.

2CV Sahara | Citroën (F)

1960 • 29 cu in/478 cc, S4 • 12 bhp/9 kW • unknown • 65 mph/105 kph (both engines)

The first standard Citroën 2CV adapted for use as a four-wheel drive was devised in 1954 by a private citizen. A Mr. Bonnafous from Landes in southern France placed a second 22-cubic-inch (375-cc) engine in the car's rear compartment and transformed the bitumen-bred sedan (saloon) into a twin-engined, all-terrain vehicle. On undemanding roads the factory-fitted front engine was used, with the second engine engaged only when the terrain demanded more traction. A prototype, completed with the assistance of Panhard in 1958, had driven more than 60,000 miles (96,500 km) before it came to the attention of a curious Citroën executive.

Demand for a vehicle like the 2CV Sahara had been growing from expatriate French citizens in North Africa. Also, since the end of World War II oil companies had been expanding their operations in Algeria and were in need of all-terrain vehicles that could negotiate the remote, trackless, often sandy regions of the country's interior. The adapted 2CV proved ideal. In addition to its four-wheel-drive capability, its front and rear coil-spring suspension was considerably strengthened to cope with the conditions that lay ahead. Specially designed carburetors were installed that would feed the engines at whatever angle the car might be traveling. There were separate ignition switches, and the twin gas tanks under the driver and front passenger seats could be accessed through cutouts in the front doors.

As impressed as critics were by its design, the Sahara was also expensive: twice the cost of a standard 2CV, which had always been "the car that peasants can afford." In the end it was a financial flop. Only 694 were built, and production ended in 1971. **BS**

112 Sports | ZiL (USSR)

1960 • 364 cu in/5,980 cc, V8 • 230 bhp/172 kW • 0–60 mph/97 kph in 9 seconds • 162 mph/260 kph

As the first-ever Russian sports car, the ZiL 112S (Sports) was a surprisingly good first effort. The two-seater had real power and sports-car handling. A huge step forward for the Soviet motor industry, it marked the nation's first use of all-around disc brakes, limited slip differentials, and radial tyres. It certainly matched its contemporary, the Ferrari Superamerica, for performance, if not for luxury, glamour, and refinement.

The car was ingeniously assembled from Russian parts available at the time: a big, powerful V8 and gearbox from the ZiL-111 limousine, plus steering and front suspension from the GAZ-21 Volga. The rear suspension was all original, and aluminum components were used to reduce the car's weight.

From the front and back, the two-seater, rear-wheel-drive ZiL, with its big air scoop on the hood (bonnet) and modern front grille, looked like a Western-styled sports car of the time. From the side, the car had a more utilitarian, stripped-down look, with the front wheel arches swooping back to the doors without covering the backs of the front wheels at all.

Not surprisingly, the ZiL 112S soon broke the nation's own land-speed record, and also won the Soviet Racing Championship. But only two cars were built because ZiL decided that such sports machines were a waste of precious resources. For years the two cars were stored in an unused part of ZiL's Moscow factory. Somehow they found their way to a car museum in Riga, Latvia, where they still stand. Because they have been repainted red and white, classic car enthusiasts sometimes refer to them as the "Testa Russas"—Russian equivalents of the Ferrari Testarossa. **SH**

96 | Saab

S

1960 • 51 cu in/841 cc, S3 • 40 bhp/30 kW • 0–60 mph/97 kph in 25.6 seconds • 75 mph/121 kph

Saab was a little-known Swedish carmaker until its 96 model arrived on the scene in 1960. This was the model that first earned the Trollhattan-based brand international recognition. It was the first Saab to be exported to the United Kingdom and other markets.

The car's styling, by designer Sixten Sasen, was iconic. The shape was bulbous, but made the vehicle look as if it was going fast even when standing still. The design originally had a 45-cubic-inch (750-cc) two-stroke engine, but this was soon upgraded to the 51-cubic-inch (841-cc) engine by which the car became best known. The car was notable for its distinctive two-stroke sound and for having its gear lever mounted on the steering column, a feature it retained throughout its twenty years of production.

Controlling the gearbox from the steering column had been common in older cars of the 1950s and earlier, but by the 1960s floor-mounted gear levers were becoming dominant across the whole of the motor industry. Saab favored the steering column lever, though, because it allowed faster gear changes, and this helped make the car popular with rally drivers.

The most famous of these was Erik Carlsson, who drove a Saab 96 to victory in three RAC Rallies and two Monte Carlo Rallies between 1960 and 1963. He also competed in the East African Safari. In Carlsson's hands, driven to its limit and beyond, the Saab 96 became as almost as famous upside-down as it was the right way up—hence his nickname of "On-the-roof Carlsson."

Carlsson's British wife, Pat Moss Carlsson, Stirling Moss's sister, was another famous rally driver associated with the Saab 96. Others included Per Eklund, Simo Lampinen, and Stig Blomqvist. **SB**

DB4 GT Zagato | Aston Martin

GB

1961 • 229 cu in/3,760 cc, S6 • 314 bhp/234 kW • 0–60 mph/97 kph in 6.1 seconds • 154 mph/247 kph

Collaborations between car designers in different countries have often produced spectacular results, and the Aston Martin DB4 GT Zagato is a prime example.

Aston sent its DB4 GT coupe chassis over to the Zagato design house in Milan, where the chief stylist was the legendary Ercole Spada. He came up with a body that was lighter, smaller (it lost the rear seats), and more aerodynamic than that of the original car. Using a technique called Superleggera (meaning "superlight"), he stretched a skin of aluminum over a steel frame. By using Perspex instead of glass he saved yet more weight.

The DB4 GT Zagato is rated as one of the most beautiful cars of its era, being a blend of Aston's sleek "Britishness" and Spada's Italian flair. Comparisons are made to Ferrari's 250 GT Berlinetta, which was always considered the Zagato's main rival and inspiration.

The engine was equally impressive: a six-cylinder, 229-cubic-inch (3,760-cc) aluminum block with two spark plugs per cylinder. This put out 314 bhp (234 kW), quite a bit more than the original DB4 GT's 302 bhp (225 kW). There were no fenders (bumpers), although a number of owners have added them to protect that stunning body. The interior was fairly minimalist in style.

Being an Aston Martin, the car had racing in its genes. Of only nineteen Zagatos built, four were made to racing specifications. They competed in numerous events, including the 24 Hours of Le Mans.

In 1991, thirty years after the car's launch, Aston Martin upgraded four DB4 chassis to GT specification. These were shipped to Zagato and given new bodywork, using the same techniques as the original coachbuilders. Each one was sold for more than $1 million (£635,000). **JI**

E-Type Series 1 | Jaguar

GB

1961 • 230 cu in/3,781 cc, S6 • 265 bhp/198 kW • 0–60 mph/97 kph in 6.7 seconds • 153 mph/275 kph

Few cars stir the emotions like the Jaguar E-Type, with its long, almost phallic hood (bonnet). When the design first appeared in 1954, Enzo Ferrari complimented it as "the most beautiful car ever made." Designer Malcolm Sayer drew heavily on the shape of Jaguar's D-Type Le Mans race car, reinterpreting it for the road. Undoubtedly one of the most iconic cars in automotive history, the E-Type was ranked number one on a list of the one hundred most beautiful cars of all time drawn up by the *Daily Telegraph* newspaper in 2008.

The Jaguar E-Type made its debut in March 1961, but bizarrely it was initially intended for export only. It did not go on sale in its British homeland until the summer, four months later. Early E-Types were powered by a 3.8-liter, triple-carburetor engine carried over from a predecessor model, the XK150S (within Jaguar, the E-Type was originally designated as the XK-E). The car's success was immediate. The E-Type arrived on the scene just as Britain was entering the colorful and buoyant 1960s, and the mood was right for a dramatic-looking British sports car that seemed to herald what later would be dubbed the Swinging Sixties.

Gorgeous though it looked, the E-Type was far from perfect. It had a cramped cabin, was short of legroom, and had limited trunk (boot) space and a clunky gear change. But during the car's fourteen-year lifespan it improved as new versions were developed, including a 2+2 with a lengthened wheelbase. Series 1 models are generally regarded as the best-looking, Series 2 cars drove better, and the Series 3 included the most powerful roadgoing E-Type, the 323-cubic-inch (5,300-cc) V12. Production of the E-Type ended in 1975. **SB**

Imperial | Chrysler

(USA)

1961 • 412 cu in/6,767 cc, V8 • 340 bhp/254 kW • unknown • unknown

Chrysler, launching the Imperial in 1961, called it "the finest car America has yet produced." That might be a point of debate, but there is no getting away from the fact that it was an exceedingly large automobile. The 1961 model was 19 feet (5.77 m) long, making it the biggest car, aside from limousines, in the United States.

The design is best described as extravagant. Apart from its sheer bulk, there were enormous tail fins stretching up and outward at the back. Some variants even had headlights freestanding on stalks in front of the grille, looking more at home on a car from the prewar era than cutting-edge. And in some ways this Imperial was the first retro car, built in the 1960s but harking back to the more elaborate U.S. car designs of previous decades. Either that or Chrysler was simply clinging on to a style that was already out of fashion.

Mechanically, the car was up to date. It had push-button transmission, air-conditioning, swiveling seats, and a 412-cubic inch (6,767-cc) V8 engine. There were two upright banks of gauges on either side of the main dash that made it look vaguely space age. The steering wheel was squarer than it was round.

The Imperial was designed by the legendary Virgil Exner, who had worked for Pontiac and Studebaker before joining Chrysler. He has been described as a "great American artist," but sadly this was the last car he designed for Chrysler before retiring for health reasons. Subsequent Imperials were much less flamboyant, and those rampant tail fins were never seen again.

The current value of a pristine Imperial hovers around the $20,000 (£12,500) mark. Collectors get an awful lot of car for that money. **JI**

This 1962 publicity shot for the Innocenti 950 Spider perfectly captures the charm of the luxurious Italian sportster. ⊡

967 | LuAZ

USSR

1961 • 54 cu in/887 cc, V4 • 30 bhp/22 kW • unknown • 47 mph/75 kph on land; 1.9 mph/3 kph on water

A small and lightweight Soviet amphibious jeep, the LuAZ 967 was mass-produced nonstop for fourteen years behind the Iron Curtain. The military version was deployed all across the Warsaw Pact countries, and now civilian versions are still seen everywhere in Eastern Europe, being used by farmers, rescue services, and people just having fun around water.

This half-boat, half-car was originally designed by Russia's Moskvitch carmaker for military use, mainly for evacuating frontline casualties. It ended up being built at the LuAZ car plant in northern Ukraine. No production numbers are available for the 967, but it was made until 1975. In the 1980s the LuAZ-969, a nonamphibious version powered by a Ford Fiesta 67-cubic-inch (1,100-cc engine), was exported to Italy.

The body/hull contains a bilge pump as well as the small, air-cooled gasoline engine. But with no propeller system, the driver has to rely on the spinning of the wheels to gain movement through water. The steering is even less effective; as there is no rudder, navigation is achieved by turning the front wheels. On dry land, the four-wheel-drive system is permanent and has a high and low ratio. Each wheel has independent suspension for negotiating difficult terrain. With its light but torquey engine, the LuAZ 967 is a capable off-roader.

The 967 has an open top, but a canopy can be fitted over detachable roof bars. There is a flat load bay behind the passengers, with a drop-down tailgate, removable side body panels, and a powerful winch. The driver sits in the center with two passengers to either side, below and to the rear. This is because the 967 was originally designed to carry stretchers. **SH**

950 Spider | Innocenti

I

1961 • 57 cu in/948 cc, S4 • 50 bhp/37 kW • 0–60 mph/97 kph in 17 seconds • 87 mph/140 kph

The Italian car company Innocenti began life as the maker of Lambretta scooters. In the early 1960s it began to build cars under license from BMC, beginning with the Austin A40 and the original Mini.

The Innocenti Spider was essentially an Austin-Healey Sprite, rebodied by the Ghia design house and built at its factory in Turin. The car was based on the Mark II Sprite, which had lost its trademark "bug-eyed" headlights in favor of lights on the end of each wing.

The Spider was an upmarket car, sporting such luxuries as wind-up windows—it would be years before its British cousins, the Sprite and MG, adopted such a flamboyant feature. The Spider also had a glove box, a heater, interior lighting, wider doors, and a lockable trunk (boot).

The Italian car had a monocoque chassis, in which the body of the car and chassis are one and the same, and a four-speed gearbox. The engine was not especially powerful, and the first models had only a 948-cc BMC A-Series motor under the hood (bonnet). The car also weighed more than the Sprite, and that hampered performance even further.

But what mattered more was charm—and the Spider had that in bucketloads. It also handled well, as befitted a front-engined, rear-wheel-drive European sportster. In the mid-1960s the model would inherit a larger engine from BMC and have a number of chassis upgrades. It stayed in production until 1970.

Innocenti was eventually snapped up by British Leyland in 1972. When Leyland was nationalized in 1975, the company fell back into Italian ownership as de Tomaso, but it ceased trading altogether in 1996. **JI**

2300S Coupe | Fiat

I

1961 • 139 cu in/2,279 cc, S6 • 136 bhp/254 kW • 0–60 mph/97 kph in 10.5 seconds • 120 mph/193 kph

Fiat should be saluted for trying. In the late 1950s it built a station wagon (estate), the Fiat 2100, that was designed to appeal to the U.S. market. Sadly, the car appealed neither to American drivers nor to their European counterparts. All was not lost, though. The Italian coachbuilders Ghia took a 2100 and used it as the platform for a stylish coupe with straight sides and a wraparound rear windshield. The coupe was duly unveiled at the 1960 Turin Motor Show.

Fiat (which had itself wanted to build a performance car) was impressed and agreed to supply Ghia with floorpans, upon which the stylish body could be installed. The car, called the Fiat 2300S coupe, was built at the Ghia-owned OSI factory in Turin.

Mechanically the coupe was relatively simple, with torsion-bar suspension at the front and a solid beam and leaf spring at the back. The six-cylinder Fiat engine had originally been designed by a former Ferrari engine guru, Aurelio Lampredi. For the 2300S it was breathed on a little more (as many Fiat engines are); the tuner Abarth added an extra carburetor and a different cam to take peak power to 136 bhp (254 kW). A four-speed gearbox was installed, together with disc brakes all around—a step forward in 1961.

The interior was made as pleasing on the eye as the body. Although the seats are vinyl rather than leather, there was plenty of chrome trim and the wooden dashboard was lined with classic Veglia dials.

The great strength of the Fiat 2300S coupe lay not in its outright performance but in its ability to carry on comfortably all day at 100 mph (160 kph). That was the sign of a true grand tourer. **JI**

Continental | Lincoln

USA

1961 • 429 cu in/7,045 cc, V8 • 345 bhp/257 kW • 0–60 mph/97 kph in 12.4 seconds • 130 mph/210 kph

Lincoln joined the Ford empire in 1922. It used the Continental model designation for the first time in 1939, but the name became most famous in its fourth incarnation, made between 1961 and 1969.

In 1961, Ford's top brand competed with Cadillac to build the best U.S. car. Lincoln's fourth-generation Continental was dubbed "America's answer to the Rolls-Royce," especially with its Rolls-styled front grille. Yet its design was shared with the 1961 Ford Thunderbird, and was essentially the same car with a different badge. Both were produced on the same line in Michigan.

After the chrome-laden and high-finned cars of the 1950s, the Continental's understated square styling was considered very elegant and the car soon became a hit. One of its trademark features was back doors hinged at the rear, giving an extremely wide entry. The Continental Mark IV also featured an antilock braking system, a vinyl roof, and a distinctive, optional small "opera window" in the rear three-quarter pillar. Its tried-and-tested Ford V8, which had appeared in the Mark III, was mated to a three-speed automatic transmission. Soon after the 1961 launch, a convertible version appeared with an electrically operated roof.

An open-top Continental was purchased by the U.S. Secret Service and drove John F. Kennedy through Dallas on the day he was assassinated in 1963. The car was subsequently fitted with bulletproof armor and a fixed roof and continued to serve U.S. presidents. It is now in the Ford Museum in Dearborn, Michigan.

Where most U.S. cars of the era had a rather short life cycle, this fourth-generation Lincoln Continental lasted until 1969, by which time 267,266 were sold. **JB**

Consul Capri | Ford

GB

1958 • 81 cu in/5,972 cc, V8 • 310 bhp/228 kW • 0–60 mph/97 kph in 10.9 seconds • 113 mph/182 kph

The Ford Consul Capri did not have a long run, only lasting for three years, from 1961 to 1964. It may be slightly overshadowed by its later namesake (without the Consul), but that does not stop this neat two-door coupe from being something a little special.

The Consul Capri was based on the U.K.-made Ford Classic sedan (saloon), with a restyled body but the same four round headlights and wrapover hood (bonnet). The design, a combination of slab sides and undulating curves, was influenced by Ford's Thunderbird and Galaxie Sunliner, but it was all done with a very European twist.

Although the Consul Capri was built at the Ford factory at Dagenham in Essex, it was initially produced for export only. Drivers in the U.K. eventually got their hands on the car in 1962, when they were treated to a range of deluxe features: disc brakes, variable-speed wipers, and even a cigar lighter.

Technically, the Consul Capri was pretty impressive: a monocoque chassis/body, independent front suspension, and a four-speed gearbox. The front-mounted motor ran through the rear wheels. The first cars were thought to be underpowered and the engine capacity was increased to 91 cubic inches (1,498 cc). Then, in 1963, Ford went one step further by introducing a GT version, driven by a Cosworth engine that raised power to 78 bhp (58 kW).

Sadly, the Consul Capri's pretty body was complex to manufacture and expensive to produce. The model ended up competing not just with its rivals but with other cars in the Ford range, including a new boy in 1963, the now-legendary Cortina.

For these reasons, the Consul Capri unfortunately came to a premature end, but nowadays it is regarded as a true Ford classic . Surviving examples are much sought after. **JI**

Spacious, affordable, and reliable, the 1961 Renault Four was designed to meet all the varied demands of family life.

Starfire | Oldsmobile (USA)

1961 • 394 cu in/6,457 cc, V8 • 330 bhp/243 kW • 0–60 mph/97 kph in 9 seconds • 120 mph/192 kph

In the 1950s Oldsmobile had used the Starfire name in association with its "98" series of cars, but 1961 saw the Oldsmobile Starfire appear in its own right. The name had been borrowed from a Lockheed jet fighter aircraft, and the 1961 version of the car, with its big engine and impressive top speed and acceleration, certainly deserved the comparison.

Initially the Starfire was built only as a convertible, and it had a cleaner and leaner style than some of the brash designs that were popular with many automobile manufacturers of the time. It had a smoothly tapering rear end, in contrast with the rocket-style tail fins that had grown increasingly tall as the 1950s wore on, and when it came out it was greeted with great acclaim as a classy and powerful car.

The Starfire was available in colors that were relatively tasteful for the time, along with whitewall tires. Only 7,600 were built in its first year, but in 1962 it was made available as both the original convertible and as a two-door hardtop. The convertible sold fewer than the previous year, just 7,149 examples, but the hardtop was a big success and Oldsmobile went on to build 34,839 of them.

Despite its initial popularity and good reception, 1962 proved to be its peak year and production slowly tailed off over the next few years. For 1966 only the hardtop was put on sale, and 13,019 of them were built. No longer Oldsmobile's most powerful car, it did not reappear in 1967.

The original 1961 Starfire sold for a basic price of $3,564 (£2,300), but buyers of a good model today are prepared to pay about ten times that amount. **MG**

Four | Renault (F)

1961 • 45 cu in/747 cc, S4 • 24 bhp/17.9 kW • unknown • 68 mph/110 kph

Marketing men often talk about the concept of a car that is designed to fit in with "how the buyer lives." Brochures for any modern multipurpose vehicle show happy children smiling from the back seat and maybe even a dog in its own space in the rear. But the idea could well have started back in 1961 with the Renault Four, the *voiture à vivre*, or "livable car."

Renault wanted to build a car capable of dealing with the rough and tumble of family life, a car to take parents to work in the week, and then out with the kids on the weekend.

The Renault Four was designed to appeal as much to women drivers as men. It had a spacious, square body with a simple, uncluttered interior. There were five doors that opened wide—yes, five doors, as even the rear opened like a hatch, something new and exciting in 1961. The rear bench seat could be folded flat to turn the car into a load carrier, and there was even a flap in the roof to make it easy to carry long objects.

The car was also rugged and easy to maintain. The small engine was married to a three-speed gearbox, even though the older Renault 2CV had a four-speed. The coolant system was sealed, meaning that it would never need topping up in the entire lifetime of the car.

The Renault Four and its variants were an immediate success, and after its launch only four-and-a-half years passed before the company had built one million of them. With its popularity spreading well beyond French shores, it was eventually manufactured in around twenty countries worldwide.

Many cars are called "iconic" or "legendary," but few deserve the title more than this original lifestyle car. **JI**

REMARKABLE
REMARKABLE
REMARKABLE
REMARKABLE
REMARKABLE
719 NMY

P1800 | Volvo

(S)

1961 • 108 cu in/1,778 cc, S4 • 97 bhp/72 kW • 0–60 mph/97 kph in 13.8 seconds • 105 mph/169 kph

At the 1961 Geneva Motor Show, the hottest two new cars were the Jaguar E-Type and the Volvo P1800. Jaguar was offered the chance to feature the E-Type in a new TV drama series due to start the following year; it declined, and the chance went to Volvo instead.

That was how the Volvo P1800 became a star in the popular 1960s TV program *The Saint*. Driven by actor Roger Moore in his role as detective Simon Templar, a white P1800 was featured throughout the series. Moore was so enamored with the car he drove on screen that he bought one for his personal use.

The P1800 started life in 1957, when Volvo tasked its engineering consultant, Helmer Pettersen, with adding a sports car to its range. His son, Pelle, did the design work, shaping the body that would clothe Pettersen Sr.'s technical kit. At first the design was credited to Italian designer Pietro Frua, for whom Pelle Pettersen worked, but it was later acknowledged as his.

The P1800 was initially assembled in the United Kingdom by the British company Jensen, based in West Bromwich, using a body shell made at Linwood in Scotland. After two years, production moved to Sweden. Between 1961 and 1973, almost 40,000 P1800s were produced, as well as another 8,000 of a three-door station wagon (estate) version. **SB**

Felicia Super | Skoda

(CS)

1961 • 74 cu in/1,221 cc, S4 • 55 bhp/41 kW • unknown • 81 mph/130 kph

Skoda's transformation from the butt of cruel jokes to a respected manufacturer of award-winning cars was completed in the early 2000s with the launch of the Fabia, Superb, and Yeti. But the Felicia proves that Skoda has always known a thing or two about car design.

Originally known as the 450, this two-door convertible was reworked and rebadged as the Felicia in 1959. The name is derived from the Latin for "happiness." The convertible came in two formats: the standard Felicia, which had a 66-cubic-inch (1,089-cc) engine, and a more powerful 74-cubic-inch (1,221-cc) version that was launched in 1961 as the Felicia Super.

Under a folding canvas and plastic roof stretched over a tubular steel frame, the Felicia Super seated five, with three on the bench-style front seat and two passengers behind. The exterior styling was similar to that of the slightly larger Octavia, which debuted in 1959.

When production ended in 1964, almost 15,000 Felicias had been built at the factory in the Czech city of Mlada Boleslav. Sadly, there was no replacement for the Felicia at the time, nor at any point since. The brand has never produced another cabriolet. In 1994 a small family hatchback Felicia was born, and a station wagon (estate) the following year, but these had none of the original's charm. **RY**

Tempest LeMans | Pontiac (USA)

1962 • 214 cu in/3,523cc, V8 • 190 bhp/142 kW • 0–60 mph/97 kph in 9.9 seconds • 115 mph/184 kph

The Pontiac Tempest, designed by John DeLorean, was launched in 1960. It packed such power in its small but stylish frame that it was named the "Car of the Year" by *Motor Trend* magazine. It was very light and had a new, eye-catching design, with a split grille at the front. Independent suspension provided a smooth ride, and the car also managed to consume fuel economically.

In 1962, Pontiac brought out the LeMans variant, which became the company's top-of-the-line car. It was a wise move because in its various versions it would stay on the market for almost twenty years. The LeMans was even smaller and sportier than the standard Tempest, and had an attractively redesigned interior.

But Pontiac also wanted a model that could compete at the top level of stock car racing, especially at the all-important NASCAR events, where it was losing ground to its main rivals. The firm, therefore, also built a Super Duty Tempest LeMans, a more rugged version of the car.

Whether or not it would have succeeded is unknown because, soon after this, parent company General Motors made the decision to withdraw from all racing activities. That did not detract from the success of the LeMans name, though, as it continued to provide half the sales of the whole Tempest range and was only finally retired in 1982, when it was replaced by the Bonneville. **MG**

Cedric | Nissan (J)

1962 • 90 cu in/1,488 cc, S4 • 87 bhp/65 kW • unknown • unknown

How did a Japanese executive car get named Cedric? Apparently Nissan's CEO, Katsuji Kawamata, loved the children's book *Little Lord Fauntleroy* by Francis Hodgson Burnett, about a boy called Cedric.

Nissan had just finished producing A40s and A50s under license from Austin, and had decided to create its own luxury sedan (saloon). The Cedric was an odd mix of old Austins and contemporary U.S. car designs. There was some Japanese influence; the front lights were inspired by a local commuter train, and the U.S.-style wraparound windshield was something not yet tackled by Austin.

The car had a 90-cubic-inch (1,488-cc) or 115-cubic-inch (1,900-cc) engine, and a stretched long-wheel-base version was Japan's largest vehicle. Station wagon (estate) and van versions were soon added (with an electrically operated rear window). Top-end models had net curtains in the back windows. The radio had its own batteries and could be taken from the car and used portably.

The Cedric continued until 2004 and was constantly updated, including a new grille design every year. By 1964 it had a wood veneer dash and an automatic option.

The Cedric was promoted with charming naivety abroad. One advertisement in Australia showed a Japanese model in sunglasses bizarrely lying in the open trunk (boot) alongside the spare wheel. **SH**

250 GTO | Ferrari

(I)

1962 • 180 cu in/2,953 cc, V12 • 302 bhp/225 kW • 0–60 mph/97 kph in 4.9 seconds • 176 mph/283 kph

The Ferrari 250 GTO (Gran Turismo Omologata) picked up where the 250 GT SWB left off. However, this time it would be a dedicated track weapon, with a stiffer, lightweight chassis and Plexiglass windows.

Due to a change in Fédération Internationale de l'Automobile (FIA) regulations, each manufacturer was now required to build at least one hundred examples of its race cars if they were to be allowed in the International Championship for GT Manufacturers. However, just thirty-nine GTOs were ever built; Ferrari fooled FIA officials by skipping numbers when stamping each car's chassis.

Yet again, Ferrari dominated the GT championship, winning the world title in 1962, 1963, and 1964. Its 250 GTO was also entered in long-distance endurance races. It debuted at the 12 Hours of Sebring in 1962, where spectators were amazed to see it battle to second place overall with U.S. Formula 1 world champion Phil Hill at the wheel, beating purebred race cars from the class above.

Performance statistics were mind blowing, but it was the car's aerodynamics that gave it the edge. The GTO's integrated spoiler—the first to appear on a road car—made this 250 both quicker and more stable at speed.

When it was launched, the car cost $18,000 (£6,430); however, all buyers had to be personally approved by Enzo Ferrari himself before they were given the keys. Today, the very rare GTO is the most highly prized of all classic Ferraris. In February 2012, an immaculate example, with genuine racing pedigree, sold for $31.7 million (£20.2 million); it was the most expensive car ever to be sold in the United Kingdom.

Famous GTO owners include Pink Floyd drummer, Nick Mason, and fashion designer Ralph Lauren. **DS**

Vega II | Facel

(F)

1962 • 383 cu in/6,277 cc, V8 • 355 bhp/265 kW • 0–60 mph/97 kph in 6.7 seconds • 149 mph/240 kph

Despite the lavish praise heaped upon its automobiles, and the fact that they were bought enthusiastically by the people who could afford them, the Facel company was facing bankruptcy in 1962. It was not the best of times to be launching a new luxury car. In particular, it was not the best time to be launching one like the Facel Vega II, which was going to be bigger, faster, and more expensive than anything the company had built before. All was in the balance; the fate of Facel depended on the success or failure of this venture.

The car certainly looked good. It was the most stylish the company had made, which is high praise indeed, and its simple, graceful, angular style still looks good today. The most fuss was at the front, where a five-part grille was framed by high headlights, with the effect that the new model looked bigger than its predecessor, the Facel Vega HK500, even though it was actually slightly smaller. It was also almost 20 mph (32 kph) faster than the previous model. On paper, at least, it had everything going for it.

Unfortunately Facel's cars were still incredibly expensive to produce, and there were still only a finite number of people who could afford to buy them. The names of those who owned Facel Vegas over the years were legendary, the crème de la crème of the rich and famous—people like the Shah of Persia, Princess Grace of Monaco, Christian Dior, Frank Sinatra, and King Hassan II of Morocco. There are only so many shahs and kings, so many princesses and pop stars in the world, and only 182 of the cars were built and sold.

The Vega II ceased production in 1964, and Facel went out of business in the same year. **MG**

407 | Bristol (GB)

1962 • 313 cu in/5,130 cc, V8 • 250 bhp/186 kW • 0–60 mph/97 kph in 8.3 seconds • 125 mph/200 kph

The 407 was the first model to be made after Bristol Cars became a separate entity from the Bristol Aeroplane Company, maker of all the previous models.

The most remarkable thing about the Bristol 407 was its engine. Bristol ditched the 123-cubic-inch (2,216-cc) six-cylinder engine that had been in the Bristol 406, believing that it was not powerful enough to compete with rival luxury sports cars. Bristol had always made its own engines, but now the company wanted to buy one. It settled on Chrysler's V8, but the U.S. carmaker was no longer making them, although Chrysler in Canada still was. The Canadian engines also could be tailored to Bristol's specific requirements.

Apart from the imported engine, there were hidden improvements in the front suspension and steering mechanism. The exterior of the 407 looked very much like that of the 406, although there was now a second exhaust pipe at the back and a slightly redesigned radiator grille—neither of which alteration would have had the average buyer showing much excitement. That engine, however, did make a huge difference, and it put Bristol's name back in the forefront of British sports-car makers. The 407 was only shortlived, being replaced by the 408 in 1963. Only eighty-eight 407s were built, yet the car was a vital step forward for the Bristol name. **MG**

Vitesse | Triumph (GB)

1962 • 97 cu in/1,596 cc, S6 • 70 bhp/52 kW • 0–60 mph/97 kph in 17 seconds • 90 mph (145 kph)

The Triumph Vitesse was one of the most highly regarded sports sedans (saloons) of the 1960s. It was launched as a six-cylinder performance model to join the company's mainstay, the four-cylinder Triumph Herald. The Italian auto designer Giovanni Michelotti was responsible for the look of both cars.

With almost all the same body panels as the Herald, the Vitesse had a much bolder and more eye-catching front end. The model was available in two body types, sedan and convertible. The twin headlights and racier styling of both instantly differentiated them from their more mundane sibling.

The Vitesse had a similar snug cabin to the Herald but with extra flourishes that elevated the interior ambience and made it feel more plush. There were wood veneer door cappings to match the polished wood dashboard, better seats, and an optional sunroof.

An update in 1966 increased the engine size to 122 cubic inches (2,000 cc), and raised the top speed to 96 mph (154 kph). When the Mark II arrived in 1968, the engine was given a power boost and the Vitesse became a "ton-up" model, now capable of 106 mph (171 kph); it also had a new front grille and revised rear suspension.

More than 51,000 Vitesses were made over nine years before production was discontinued in 1971. **SB**

Avanti | Studebaker (D)

1962 • 288 cu in/4,734 cc, V8 • 240 bhp/177 kW • 0–60 mph/97 kph in 9.5 seconds • 139 mph/224 kph

Sherwood Egbert became president of the troubled Studebaker Corporation in February 1961. It is said that, while on a flight, he made a few rough sketches for the kind of sports car he wanted to see built. Egbert gave the sketches to Studebaker's design team, under the talented Raymond Loewy, and the team turned the sketches into a finished car design in forty days.

In April 1962 the car was unveiled at the New York International Automobile Show. It was certainly striking visually. The Avanti had a boxlike design, with a light, fiberglass body. A more powerful race version was built, and this achieved an astonishing 170 mph (272 kph) at the Bonneville salt flats, making it the fastest production car in the world. Studebaker presented an Avanti to the winner of the 1962 Indianapolis 500, Rodger Ward, who therefore became the first person to own one of these remarkable new cars.

Studebaker was hoping to sell 20,000 Avantis in the first year, but in the event it was only able to build 1,200 of them, due to supply and other problems. Orders were cancelled. The company's financial woes continued, and by December 1963 it had to close down the South Bend factory where the Avanti was being made. It was a sad end to a car that could have been a world-beater, dreamed up by a man on an airplane. **MG**

S3 Continental | Bentley (GB)

1962 • 379 cu in/6,227 cc, V8 • 205 bhp/151 kW • unknown • 115 mph/185 kph

Wanting to continue the success of its S1 and S2 models, Bentley showed off their successor, the S3, at the Paris Motor Show in October 1962. It was another solid success, but what was really eye-catching was the S3 Continental version, which Bentley also produced.

The standard S3 was an imposing and rather grand-looking car, one that seemed designed with the British aristocracy in mind. It had a new twin-headlight arrangement, with beams that were significantly more powerful than before, while a padded dashboard offered extra safety. The rear seat was pushed back a little to give the passengers extra legroom, and the hood (bonnet) was a little lower, giving the car a sleeker appearance. The S3 also had a bigger engine than the S2.

The Continental, however, was an even racier vehicle, particularly the convertible coupe version. It had all of Bentley's elegance and stateliness, but with the top down it also had a European sportiness about it. The top speed of 115 mph (185 kph) seemed much faster in the Continental than it did in the standard, stately S3.

Drivers had to pay for that feeling, though, as the Continental was about half as much again as the standard S3 model. It has held that premium price well, and these coachbuilt Bentleys are still in demand, with one selling in 2011 for more than $130,000 (£82,000). **MG**

S-XC 768

(<) Pictured in its native Germany, the Mercedes 300SEC was as large and gasoline-thirsty as many U.S. luxury models.

300SEC | Mercedes-Benz (D)

1962 • 183 cu in/3,000 cc, S6 • 160 bhp/118 kW • 0–60 mph/97 kph in 13 seconds • 112 mph/180 kph

Mercedes' new flagship line for the early 1960s was a mix of company heritage and state-of-the-art features. The design was long and chrome-laden with long overhangs beyond the front and rear axles, while the radiator, headlights, and windshield were big and upright. But the unadventurous design has aged well, and today the big Mercedes, particularly in coupe guise, looks imposing and desirable.

Mechanically, the 300 Series was given everything to differentiate it from the lesser 200 Series. Mercedes had to justify a price tag almost double that of the 200, even though the cars, unusually for the brand, shared a chassis. So pneumatic suspension, power steering, four-wheel disc brakes and automatic transmission were standard. There were bigger wheels with whitewall tires. Most important, there was a big straight-six overhead-valve engine under the long hood (bonnet).

The two-door coupe and cabriolet versions arrived in 1962, a year after the sedan (saloon). Looking back today, the 300SEC (coupe) was a wonderfully sleek design, with pillarless side windows and delicate tail fins. The interior was garnished with leather and burr walnut, with a big steering wheel, column-shift gearshift, and dashboard with a radio and clock. There were four enormous padded seats with bulky fold-down armrests between them. A courtesy delay light that stayed on briefly after the doors were closed was considered a luxurious touch.

The 300SEC was all about making refined comfortable progress rather than screeching around corners. In fact, the car, weighing 3,505 pounds (1,590 kg), returned fuel consumption that would seem appalling today—just 12 mpg (17 liters per 100 km) on average. **SH**

Djet | Matra (F)

1962 • 67 cu in/1,108 cc, S4 • 68 bhp/51 kW • unknown • 103 mph/165 kph

Yes, the name of this car should have been "Jet," but its designer and first builder, René Bonnet, imagined that the French would not be able to pronounce the name properly without a little phonetic help.

These days the car is more often referred to as the Matra, which is the name of the larger French company that took control of René Bonnet's operation when it got into financial difficulty. Over the five-year lifespan of the Djet, the naming of subsequent models became quite confused, with the René Bonnet Djet being followed by the Matra Bonnet Djet, the Matra Sports Djet, the Djet 5, the Djet 5S, and the Matra Sports Jet.

Whatever it was called, the car was always a little bit special. It did not have a huge engine, but Bonnet coaxed an impressive performance out of it, and its light, fiberglass body meant that it was very nippy to drive. The car had anti-roll bars at front and rear for safety, independent suspension, and disc brakes, and the design of the body had a lovely flowing line. The streamlined look of the hood (bonnet) concealed the fact that the engine was actually mounted very centrally, for better balance and control.

The 1962 Djet was a very advanced car for its time, and can claim to be the world's first mass-produced, mid-engined, roadgoing sports car, traveling that route before Porsche and Lamborghini got started. In total, only about 1,500 Djet cars were built, which makes them very collectible today.

In 1967 the Djet was retired and replaced by the first car that was totally Matra's own. This was the M530, which was named after one of the missiles that Matra also built. The Djet could not compete with that. **MG**

Elan Sprint | Lotus

GB

1962 • 95 cu in/1,559 cc, S4 • 126 bhp/94 kW • 0–60 mph/97 kph in 5.9 seconds • 130 mph/209 kph

By the early 1960s Lotus was in financial trouble and needed to replace the Elite with something far simpler and cheaper to produce. The answer was the Lotus Elan, with a steel backbone chassis, perky twin-cam engines, and fully independent suspension. Weighing a mere 1,500 pounds (680 kg), thanks to its lightweight fiberglass body, the Elan embodied the Lotus mantra of adding "lightness" to improve performance.

Initially launched as a roadster, the Elan was later sold as a coupe and a 2+2. Almost 90 percent of Elans produced for the U.K. market were sold as kits, enabling British buyers to avoid taxes imposed on new production cars. At its U.K. launch, a factory-built car cost £1,499 ($2,300), versus £1,095 ($1,700) in kit form.

The spirited little two-seater soon became an icon of the Swinging Sixties. When producers of the cult 1960s TV series *The Avengers* cast Diana Rigg as the stylish, aristocratic superspy Emma Peel, an Elan seemed the natural choice as her mode of transport.

It is well known that the Elan was the spiritual forefather of the best-selling Mazda MX-5; rumor has it that two Elans were dissected by Mazda engineers in the course of its development.

Guinness heir Tara Browne was killed after crashing his Elan at over 100 mph (161 kph). Browne, who was a friend of John Lennon's, became the inspiration for the 1967 Beatles' song *A Day in the Life*.

F1-car design guru Gordon Murray has often said that his favorite car of all time was the Lotus Elan. On his recommendation, Jay Leno, the car-mad U.S. talk show host, bought two for his collection. Specifications for the Series-4 Elan Sprint are given above. **DS**

MGB | MG

GB

1962 • 109 cu in/1,798 cc, S4 • 94 bhp/70 kW • 0–60 mph/97 kph in 12.5 seconds • 106 mph/170 kph

The MGB is the best known of the sports cars produced by the Abingdon-based MG car company. In production from 1962 to 1980, it started life under an independent MG, but the company later came under the ownership of the British Motor Corporation (BMC).

The MGB first appeared in May 1962 as the replacement for the MGA. It represented a major change from the MGA's body-on-frame construction, and was the first MG with an all-in-one monocoque design. This combined body-chassis structure, relatively lightweight but strong, helped keep down manufacturing costs.

Considered to be quite a lively performer for its day, the MGB was one of the first cars to feature crash-protective "crumple zones." The original model was a soft-top roadster, with steel fenders (bumpers). Later models with fat rubber fenders are considered less attractive and are not as sought after as the early cars.

Total production of the MGB roadster during its eighteen-year lifespan was over 386,000 cars, of which nine out of ten were exported, mostly to the United States. A further 125,000-plus of the station wagon (estate) MGB GT were made, boosting the total of MGB production to over half a million cars. In the United Kingdom, the GT was an even bigger sales success than the roadster, possibly due to the fickle climate.

In the mid-1960s the MGB was notable for outright victories in major events at the Nürburgring and Brands Hatch, as well as class wins at Sebring, Spa, and on the Targa Florio. Famous owners in the 1960s included American singer Roy Orbison, who owned a green roadster, and Prince Charles, who drove an MGB GT. **SB**

89

◁ This 1964 Shelby Cobra, 289 CSX2473, has been nominated the "Winningest Cobra" in recognition of its track successes.

Cobra | Shelby (USA)

1962 • 260 cu in/4,261 cc, V8 • 264 bhp/197 kW • 0–60 mph/97 kph in 5.5 seconds • 143 mph/230 kph

The Shelby Cobra (its U.K. name is the AC Cobra) was the result of an extreme makeover on a quintessential British roadster—the AC Ace—by a former Texan chicken farmer who had won at Le Mans. Carroll Shelby managed to transform the restrained and understated Ace into one of the iconic muscle cars of a generation.

The Ace's engine was replaced by a 260-cubic-inch (4,261-cc) Ford V8. Shelby also stiffened the chassis and fitted disc brakes all around. Some seventy-five of these models were built, but a 286-cubic-inch (4,700-cc) version was soon made available; with 300 bhp (224 kW), it produced a top speed of 155 mph (250 kph).

Many Cobras found their way to the racetrack, where they soon began to bother even Enzo Ferrari. In 1964 the car appeared in its ultimate shape at the 24 Hour of Le Mans race as the Cobra 427, armed with with a 427-cubic-inch (7,000-cc) V8 "big block" engine.

Road versions of that car were available from 1965. They were built upon a new chassis and had coil-spring rather then leaf-spring suspension. Several coupe versions were built for racing, of which the seven Shelby Daytona Coupes are the most famous.

Cobra production then languished, and it was not until 1982 that Scottish company Autokraft took over the rights and began to offer replicas. Some years later, Carroll Shelby, too, started up production of new Cobras marketed as "continuation cars."

Today there are as many Cobra copies ("Fake Snakes," as they are known) as original cars. Original 427s are now among the most sought-after cars in the United States. Shelby's personal Cobra was auctioned in 2007 for $5 million (£3,250,000). **JB**

Flamingo | GSM (ZA)

1962 • 107 cu in/1,758 cc, S4 • 80 bhp/60 kW • 0–60 mph/97 kph in 11 seconds • 112 mph/80 kph

Two students from Stellenbosch, Bob van Niekirk and Willie Meissner, set up GSM (the Glass Sport Motor Company) in Cape Town in 1958. South Africa had never been known for motor industry, but Van Niekirk and Meisner wanted to change that. On a visit to the United Kingdom they had been inspired by specialist sports car companies mushrooming at the time.

The pair teamed up with former Rootes stylist Verster de Wit to design a body from fiberglass. This was the wonder material of the era, and the source of the company name. The trio created the initial plasticine quarter-scale models in a rented one-bedroom flat in London's Earls Court. Heading back to Africa, they carried with them the design for a two-seat sports car with a ladder frame and Ford Anglia engine. Daimler had claimed their preferred Dart name, so the new car's name was changed to Delta. Production took place in both South Africa and the United Kingdom until British production stopped in 1961.

The 1962 GSM Flamingo, made exclusively in South Africa, was a 2+2 coupe version, again with a fiberglass body. The styling was outstanding, with a sharp-sloping rear split in two by a central fin. The engine was now a 107-cubic-inch (1,758-cc) German-made Ford Taunus, which drove the rear wheels. A 91-cubic-inch (1,500-cc) Cortina GT engine also became available as an option. The Flamingo was heavier than the GSM roadster, but its suspension was more sophisticated; instead of the Delta's transverse leafs the Flamingo had coil springs.

GSM built 144 Flamingos between 1962 and 1965. Gordon Murray, Formula One race designer and creator of the McLaren F1, owns an original Flamingo. **JB**

SX1000 | Ogle (GB)

1962 • 60 cu in/997 cc, S4 • 68 bhp/51 kW • 0–60 mph/97 kph in 13.5 seconds • 99 mph/159 kph

David Ogle entered the motor industry in 1960 to design attractive versions of existing BMC models. The first car that his company made was the Ogle 1.5 coupe, based on the Riley 1.5-liter. With just eight cars built, it was not a great success, but that changed with his next car.

The SX1000 was based on the Mini and caused a stir when launched in 1961. Much of the Mini—floorpan, inner wings, and part of the bulkhead, engine, and gearbox plus subframes, steering, and suspension—was retained, but now with a fiberglass coupe body on top.

The car went on sale in 1962 and, thanks to its good design, excellent finish, and £550 ($848) price tag, was not short of customers. That it cost far more to build each car was later revealed by Ogle's then-chairman John Ogier, who said, "It would have been cheaper to give any customer £300 ($463) and told him to go away."

BMC initially refused to supply new parts, but later agreed to do so as long as the word "mini" was never used in promotional material. From then on, Ogle supplied brand-new cars with Cooper 60-cubic-inch (997-cc) engines at £1,190 ($1,836).

One race model was made, and that was the car that David Ogle was driving in May 1962 when he was killed in a road accident. Production of the SX1000 stopped after his death, and only sixty-nine cars were built. **JB**

Wagoneer | Jeep (USA)

1963 • 230 cu in/3,780 cc, S6 • 140 bhp/104.4 kW • 0–60 mph/97 kph in 15.5 seconds • 92 mph/147 kph

Pioneering what is now called the Sport Utility Vehicle (SUV), the Wagoneer was the world's first luxury 4x4. It was marketed from 1963 as a station wagon (estate).

The Wagoneer was designed by Brooks Stevens, the man who coined the phrase "planned obsolescence"—the notion that consumer goods should deliberately be made not to last forever. That is ironic, given Jeep's reputation for bulletproof reliability and longevity.

With features including an automatic transmission and power steering, the Wagoneer was like no other 4x4. Initially available as a two-wheel-drive vehicle and with a two-door body shell, both were axed in 1967, although the two-door returned as the first Jeep Cherokee.

The Wagoneer was popular due to its powerful engines and towing capacity. Sales continued with only minor modifications under AMC ownership (1970–87), and later when Jeep was part of the Chrysler Group. When the last one was built in June 1991, the same basic chassis had been used for almost three decades. The model was superseded by the Grand Cherokee, but the name lived on in a Grand Wagoneer edition launched in 1993; this did not sell well and lasted only a year.

However, at the 2011 Detroit Motor Show, Chrysler boss Sergio Marchionne said that the Wagoneer would live again as a seven-seater SUV, due in 2013. **RY**

Mistral Spyder | Maserati (I)

1963 • 152 cu in/2,500 cc, S6 • 255 bhp/190 kW • 0–60 mph/97 kph in 6.8 seconds • 147 mph/236 kph

Originally to be called the Due Posti, or Two Seater, the Maserati Mistral Spyder was first shown in November 1963 in Turin, Italy. The name Mistral, suggested by a Maserati dealer in France, referred to a cold northerly wind of southern France, while Spyder spelled with a "y" meant convertible. A rare and delicate machine, the car carries significant historical relevance today.

The car was the last production Maserati to use its famous straight six-cylinder, twin-spark, double overhead cam engine. This engine had powered one of the world's most iconic Formula 1 cars, Maserati's 250F, which won eight races and the F1 championship for Juan Manuel Fangio in 1957. There were three variants of the engine: the 213-cubic-inch (3,500-cc), 225-cubic-inch (3,700-cc), and 244-cubic-inch (4,000-cc).

With a graceful steel body, the hood (bonnet), trunk (boot) lid, and doors were made from alloy. The delicate wire wheels of early models came from Borrani. The interior was stylish but decidedly fragile. For example, the indicator stalks snapped off easily in the driver's hand.

In 1968 a Mistral Spyder became the most modern car ever to win the Best in Show award at the Pebble Beach Concours d'Elegance. Only 125 were built, with an original price of $13,600 (£8,670). At auction today, one would cost around twenty times that figure. **RD**

Corvette C2 | Chevrolet (USA)

1963 • 327 cu in/5,360 cc, V8 • 360 bhp/268.4 kW • 0–60 mph/97 kph in 6.2 seconds • 147 mph/235 kph

In the 1960s, in the pioneering days of space travel, Chevrolet's parent company GM decided to use astronauts to promote its new all-American sports car. In return for the exposure, the former fighter pilots were offered two cars each; most chose something sensible for the wife while reserving a Corvette for themselves.

Production of the Corvette C1 had ended in 1962. Its replacement, the C2, is often included on lists of the best-looking cars of all time. The first 'Vette to come as a coupe, it was known as the Sting Ray. The car is said to be styled after a mako shark that head designer Bill Mitchell caught when out deep-sea fishing. For a short time only, the design included sharklike hood (bonnet) vents, which were purely decorative, and a split rear window.

Power was boosted to 375 bhp (280 kW) in 1964. The following year a "big block" 396-cubic-inch (6,4900-cc) V8 engine option was launched, to be uprated to 427 cubic inches (7,000 cc) in 1966. Customers in 1967 saw the first use of a layout featuring four red taillights that is now considered an iconic Corvette styling cue.

The C2 was replaced in 1968 by the C3, loosely based on the Mako Shark II concept car. The C3, which premiered the use of T-top cutaway roof panels, was loved by the public. It sold until 1982, when it was replaced, quite predictably, by the Corvette C4. **RY**

In 1964, the mix of Sean Connery as James Bond and the Aston Martin DB5 was as powerful as one of Bond's dry Martinis.

Imp | Hillman (GB)

1963 • 55 cu in/874 cc, S4 • 39 bhp/29 kW • 0–60 mph/97 kph in 25.4 seconds • 80 mph/129 kph

The famous Mini was not the only small car built by Britain in the 1960s. An equally small, sporty, and innovative rival was produced by Hillman—the Imp. But while the Mini was trendy, the Imp wasn't, despite the fact that it was easily as much fun to drive.

The Imp was a rear-engined, two-door, four-seater with surprisingly sophisticated all-independent suspension. The engine was a pioneering all-aluminum overhead cam unit that was readily tuned to produce sportier outputs. This meant that the Imp was destined for a successful career in track and rally events. An Imp won the British Saloon [Sedan] Car Championship for three consecutive years.

The Imp was built in a special factory near Glasgow, Scotland, and by 1976 more than 440,000 rolled off the computerized production line. It was seen as a Scottish car and was more popular north of the border. Apart from the standard sedan, there was a coupe, sometimes called the Californian, a station wagon (estate), called the Husky, and even a van. The range soon included the more luxurious Singer Chamois version and a twin-carburetor Sunbeam Sport.

At just 1,598 pounds (725 kg), the Imp was very light for a mass production car. It was just 11.75 feet (358 cm) in length. The rear window gave access to the small luggage area behind the fold-down rear seats, which made the Imp a rare early form of hatchback.

Arriving later than the little Austin, the Imp always seemed to be in the Mini's shadow. Sales were not as high as was hoped, and that fact helped to force Hillman's parent company, Rootes, into the arms of Chrysler, from where it went into oblivion. **SH**

DB5 | Aston Martin (GB)

1963 • 244 cu in/4,000 cc, S4 • 282 bhp/210 kW • 0–60 mph/97 kph in 7.1 seconds • 142 mph/229 kph

The DB5's traditional leather-and-wood interior, hand-finished coachwork, and race-bred power added up to a very expensive, cultured, and desirable machine.

Its cult status was assured when it was chosen to reflect the stylish brutality of James Bond in the early films. Sean Connery drove a DB5 in *Goldfinger* (1964), and the car also appeared with 007 in *Thunderball* (1965), *Tomorrow Never Dies* (1997), *Casino Royale* (2006), and *GoldenEye* (1995). At £4,175 ($11,690), it cost twice as much as an E-Type but only did 15 mpg (19 liters per 100 km), yet sales soared after *Goldfinger* made Aston Martin a worldwide symbol of 1960s Britain.

The car featured a new 244-cubic-inch (4,000-cc) engine—big by European standards—and state-of-the-art technology such as disc brakes and a five-speed gearbox. Features included electric windows, reclining seats, and a fire extinguisher. Unusually for a European car, air-conditioning was available as an option.

Aston Martin's "DB" series was named for wealthy tractor maker David Brown, who bought the company in 1947. Only 886 DB5s were produced as sedans (saloons), and 123 as the Convertible. Even rarer were DB5 Shooting Brake estates; only twelve were made.

DB5 modifications for the Bond movies included a passenger ejector seat (through a removable roof panel), oil-slick and smokescreen facilities, front machine guns and battering rams, wheel-mounted tire slashers, radar scanner, and a bulletproof shield.

The DB5/Bond link was strongly advertised. For *Goldfinger*, Sean Connery once drove a silver DB5 along the Champs-Élysées in Paris accompanied by sixty women whose bodies were painted gold. **SH**

BNT 216A

P6 2000 | Rover

(GB)

1963 • 120 cu in/1,978 cc, S4 • 90 bhp/67 kW • 0–60 mph/97 kph in 14.6 seconds • 104 mph/167 kph

This underestimated executive sedan (saloon) is sadly infamous as the car Princess Stephanie of Monaco drove off the road in 1982, fatally injuring her mother, Princess Grace, who was in the passenger seat.

Rover called its car the "P6" to differentiate it from the previous-generation P5, but its official launch name was the Rover 2000, a reference to its 1,978-cc (120-cubic-inch) engine. The car's design was crisp and modern compared with the old-fashioned gentleman's club styling of the P5, and its technology was cutting-edge.

Advanced features included all-synchro gears, four-wheel disc brakes, and a unitary body. A unique front suspension system and sophisticated features at the rear gave a superbly comfortable ride.

From 1968, a modified version of Buick's alloy V8 engine transformed the model into the mighty, 3,528-cc (215-cubic-inch) Rover 3500. Its power was much appreciated by the U.K. police, with the sight of its grille frightening villains as it roared up behind them. The 3500 can be seen in action, sirens blaring, in the cult TV cop drama *The Sweeney* (1975–78).

In the 1960s and early 1970s, the Rover badge still meant "posh." A P6 called "the Rover" almost became a character in its own right in the iconic British TV soap *Coronation Street* (1960–present), used by barman Fred Gee to ferry around pub landlady Annie Walker.

Prices for Rover classics have never been high. Rust sent plenty to breakers' yards, and the 3500 can overheat. The 2200 TC, with twin SU carburetors, handles better and is less fuel-thirsty. Few people are in the know about this modern classic, so prices have remained reasonable at around £2,500 ($3,900). **LT**

Quattroporte | Maserati

(I)

1963 • 252 cu in/4,136 cc, V8 • 256 bhp/191 kW • 0–60 mph/97 kph in 8.3 seconds • 130 mph/209 kph

The Quattroporte (Four Door) from Maserati is pretty much head boy in a class of one, being an Italian supercar that also has the benefit of four doors and a full complement of seats. It was the quintessential grand tourer, seemingly able to traverse a space such as continental Europe just in time for lunch.

The first Quattroporte was unveiled in 1963. It was designed by Turin-based Pietro Frua, one of the leading Italian car designers at the time. It was based on an early design he had done as a one-off for the Aga Khan.

The Quattroporte was V8-powered and ran with either a five-speed manual or three-speed automatic gearbox. The motor was based on Maserati's racing unit, but detuned and civilized for the road. The combination of sheer muscle and gearing meant that it could cruise comfortable at high speed all day.

The chassis was a blend of tubular steel and box sections; crucially, there were disc brakes all around. The first models had a complicated rear suspension system known as De Dion, which uses a solid axle but joints at each wheel. This was later switched to a simpler live axle design with leaf springs. At the same time the engine was boosted to 286 cubic inches (4,700 cc).

The Quattroporte's trademark was, of course, not simply its power but its ability to carry a full quota of five passengers and all their luggage in comfort. Air-conditioning was standard on later models; the seats were leather and the windows electric.

If you were "someone," chances were you wanted a Quattroporte. Communist leaders, Hollywood stars, and European royalty would all discover that high-speed motoring had never been quite so civilized. **JI**

Lotus Cortina Mark 1 | Ford

GB

1963 • 95 cu in/1,558cc, S4 • 105 bhp/78 kW • 0–60 mph/97 kph in 9.2 seconds • 108 mph/174 kph

Behind the Lotus Cortina, the car that quickened pulses when it arrived on the motoring scene in 1963, were three key men. The first was Lotus boss Colin Chapman, who wanted his company to build its own engines instead of very expensively buying them.

The second was his close friend, the multitalented Harry Mundy, who was both an engineering wizard and a magazine technical editor. Chapman tasked Mundy to design a new engine, and the resulting 95-cubic-inch (1,558-cc) twin-cam was excellent.

The third person, acknowledged as the brain behind the car, was Ford Motor Company executive Walter Hayes. Then head of public affairs at Ford's Warley headquarters in Essex, he was a very astute operator, and he saw the potential for a high-performance version of the regular Ford Cortina.

Hayes asked Chapman if he would supply 1,000 of Mundy's new Lotus engine to power a short production run of cars. This would enable the car to be homologated, or built in sufficient numbers to comply with motorsport regulations stipulating that a car should be produced as a road version before it being eligible for certain categories of motor racing.

The first version of the new Lotus engine was fitted into a Lotus 23 race car that Jim Clark drove at the Nürburgring in 1962. It was also used to power Lotus Elan road cars. The notion of using the same racing engine in a Cortina was inspired, and the result was a car that has become legendary. The Lotus Cortina, produced from 1963 to 1966, was quickly recognized as a connoisseur's car. It now enjoys a place in motoring history as the original fast Ford. **SB**

SL "Pagoda" | Mercedes-Benz

(D)

1963 • 140 cu in/2,300 cc, S6 • 150 bhp/110 kW • 0–60 mph/97 kph in 11 seconds • 150 mph/110 kph

Whether cruising along a Paris boulevard or along the San Francisco waterfront, the "pagoda"-roofed SL was one of the most distinctive car designs of the 1960s.

The two-door roadster's designer, Paul Bracq, also styled several French presidential cars, a popemobile, and the TGV high-speed train. However, the removable hardtop that makes this influential Mercedes sports car so special was the work of colorful Austrian engineer Bela Barenyi, who conceived the subtle pagoda shape to give the lightweight roof extra strength.

Barenyi was also responsible for more than 2,500 patented inventions in his life, including Merecedes-pioneered car safety features such as crumple zones and collapsible steering columns. Some say he was the real designer of the original VW Beetle, years before Ferdinand Porsche even thought of the shape.

With its short, wide chassis and independent suspension, the SL handled well for its time. It even had some rally successes. The straight six-cylinder, fuel-injected engine delivered a smooth, refined performance, although this was not in same sports car league as its contemporary rival, the Jaguar E-Type. Instead, this was a car designed for people wishing to travel swiftly in style, luxury, and comfort.

The list of celebrity owners tells its own story. Despite the hardtop design, this was a car for getting rid of the roof, cruising slowly in the sunshine, and being seen, as SL owners Charlton Heston, Tony Curtis, Peter Ustinov, Sophia Loren, Stirling Moss, and John Lennon would all testify. In later years the car still attracts buyers, including John Travolta, race driver David Coulthard, and supermodel Kate Moss. **SH**

31

A Porsche 904 at Le Mans, 1964; despite only spending a brief time on the race circuit, the 904 racked up many wins.

904 | Porsche

D

1963 • 119 cu in/1,966 cc, F4 • 198 bhp/148 kW • 0–60 mph/97 kph in 5.3 seconds • 160 mph/260 kph

The 904 was the last of Porsche's dual-purpose street-legal race cars, and was designed to get Porsche back into competition after leaving Formula 1 in 1962. Preliminary sketches made by "Butzi" Porsche were virtually unaltered throughout the project. The 904's 119-cubic-inch (1,966-cc) air-cooled flat-four engine was mid-mounted for the first time to improve weight distribution and handling. The construction of a lightweight fiberglass shell was outsourced to Heinkel.

Homologation regulations set out by the FIA required at least one hundred roadgoing examples of the 904 to be made available for sale to the general public. The street-legal variant was renamed the Carrera GTS; despite its high price tag, all 106 cars were quickly snapped up by Porsche fanatics across the world.

The purebred 904 began a very successful, albeit short, race career in 1964. The extremely flexible machine soon racked up dozens of class wins at circuits like Le Mans and Sebring, as well as several grueling endurance events such as the Tulip and Alpine rallies. Despite having a highly complex four-cam powerplant, the 904 proved to be extremely robust and reliable.

Drivers loved the sheer thrill of piloting the 904, but the road car was cramped, noisy, and poorly ventilated. In one infamous episode, the half-frozen Eugen Böhringer and Rudolf Wütherich were forced to thaw themselves with shots of brandy while navigating the snow-covered Alpine hairpins of the 1965 Monte Carlo Rally, because the cockpit's heater was practically useless. Despite this, they battled to second place overall in a treacherous rally that saw only twenty-two teams finish from a field of 237 starters. **DS**

Bellett GT-R | Isuzu

J

1963 • 96 cu in/1,584 cc, S4 • 120 bhp/89 kW • 0–60 mph/97 kph in 12.8 seconds • 118 mph/190 kph

The Isuzu Bellett GT-R was, in many ways, ahead of its time. It was one of the first Japanese cars to bear the badge GT-R ("R" stood for "racing"), which is now a trademark of drift racers and highly tuned Japanese street cars.

Striking for its black hood (bonnet), the GT-R was an evolution of Isuzu's two-door Bellett GT coupe, which was itself developed from the Japanese firm's standard Bellett sedan (saloon). The Bellett was Isuzu's first in-house design, as previously it had been building rebadged Hillman Minxes under license from the British manufacturer. But now Isuzu had learned its craft and wanted to build its own cars.

The GT-R was the line-topping race version, with a distinctive paint scheme and spotlights that made it look like a European rally car. The 1600 twin-carburetor engine was inherited from Isuzu's 117 coupe and produced 120 bhp (89 kW). Given that the car weighed only 1,474 pounds (670 kg), that power made for a sprightly straight-line performance.

Owners enjoyed the very pleasing, throaty rasp the GT-R made as it went along. Benefiting from rear-wheel drive and a four-speed gearbox, the small Japanese car behaved more like a European sportster. Indeed, the GT-R was very European in style, with a dashboard and clocks that would have looked at home in anything from Britain or mainland Europe at that time. At its launch in 1963 it also had fully independent suspension and front disc brakes, which were not always found on its Western rivals. It now has something of a cult following, and in Japan it has been rated as one of the best-ever Japanese cars. **JI**

600 | Mercedes-Benz

D

1963 • 386 cu in/6,329 cc, V8 • 300 bhp/221 kW • 0–60 mph/97 kph in 9.7 seconds • 125 mph/200 kph

When Elvis Presley met The Beatles at his Graceland home in the summer of 1965, they might well have talked about cars. Both Elvis and John Lennon were numbered among the celebrity owners of the Mercedes-Benz 600, a car built as the ultimate in comfort and luxury for the wealthy. Other members of the "600 club" included the kind of people who could have afforded any car in the world, such as Hugh Hefner, Elizabeth Taylor, and Aristotle Onassis.

There were two basic types of the 600 when it was launched in September 1963 (the same month that The Beatles' single "She Loves You" had its U.S. release after going straight to number one in the British charts). The 600 SWB (short wheel base) version was designed for those who were not quite wealthy enough to afford a chauffeur, while the LWB (long wheel base) was available with a central divider that had a power-operated window, allowing passengers in the back

to issue instructions to their driver. Luxury features inside included anatomically-shaped seats, leather upholstery, and push-button controls.

There was a six-door limousine version that offered even more space for its passengers—a kind of precursor of the stretch limo—and Mercedes also built several special landaulet versions. These had a fold-down top and were designed for VIPs who were expected to be visible on official visits. Users of the landaulet model included Queen Elizabeth II of the United Kingdom and the Pope.

For celebrities such as The Beatles and Elvis, the 600 was not simply a self-indulgence. The bodies were sturdy enough to withstand the barrage of fans, and the huge engine had the acceleration needed to get the stars out of hazardous situations. The 600 did its job well and stayed in production until 1981, by which time Mercedes had made 2,677 of them. **MG**

The Mini Cooper S has been a style icon ever since its launch in 1963, as well as achieving success as a rally car. ▷

Turbine | Chrysler (D)

1963 • turbine engine • 130 bhp/97 kW •
0–60 mph/97 kph in 12 seconds • 108 mph/174 kph

When the President of Mexico got hold of one of the first Chrysler Turbine cars he tested the claim that it could run on any fuel by filling the tank with tequila. It worked. In fact, the gas-turbine-powered two-door hardtop coupe could also run on petrol, diesel, kerosene, jet fuel, vegetable oil—even Chanel No. 5.

The engine was inspired by the Rover Jet 1, an experimental British prototype that evolved from Sir Frank Whittle's pioneering jet aircraft design. Like Rover, Chrysler found the turbine was powerful and smooth but had technical difficulties. Rover struggled with the turbine's tremendous thirst for fuel. Chrysler found their engine revved to an incredible 48,000 rpm, but sadly sounded like a giant vacuum cleaner.

The car was designed by the Italian styling house Ghia and was only available in "Turbine bronze" with a black vinyl roof. The design was distinctive, with heavy chrome-laden light clusters at the rear and striking light units at the front, both featuring a bladed turbine motif. The leather-clad bronze interior had four bucket seats, automatic gearshift, and a strange cylindrically-shaped turbine-themed centre console.

Only fifty-five were built. Over three months they were given to 200 random members of the American public for ordinary day-to-day testing. One car was taken on a world tour of twenty-one countries (including Mexico). None were sold, although one has ended up in the collection of comedian and chat show host Jay Leno.

Chrysler were encouraged by the potential of the turbine engine and continued to develop it. In 1977 they produced turbine-powered Le Baron. The next year they started producing M1 turbine tanks for the army. **SH**

Mini Cooper S | BMC (GB)

1963 • 65 cu in/1,071cc, S4 • 70 bhp/52 kW •
0–60 mph/97 kph in 13.5 seconds • 90 mph/145 kph

The Mini Cooper S burst on to the motoring scene in 1963 to immediate acclaim. This "pocket rocket" of a car was quickly recognized as something special. The Mini was already riding the crest of a wave of popularity, and the Cooper S had instant cachet as the most charismatic and desirable new model in the Mini line. It wore the family name of John Cooper, a gifted engineer who was also a close friend of the Mini's brilliant designer, Alec Issigonis.

For the Cooper S, BMC's standard A-Series engine was increased in size to 65 cubic inches (1,071 cc) and tuned to optimal performance. Small, light, nimble, and quick, it was an exciting car to drive. It had classless appeal and was the trendiest model of the moment in an era of miniskirts, Twiggy, and Mary Quant.

In January 1964, a cheeky Irishman took the world by storm when he snatched victory on the Monte Carlo Rally at the wheel of a Cooper S. Forever after, the fame of the Mini Cooper S has been interlinked with the name of Patrick "Paddy" Hopkirk. In his bright red works Cooper S, codriven by Henry Liddon, Hopkirk stole rally glory from under the noses of far more powerful competitors. After this stunning victory, the reputation of the little car was flying high.

In the following year another Mini Cooper S won the Monte, driven by Hopkirk's teammate Rauno Aaltonen. Then, in 1966, the works team tried for a hat trick, fielding four cars and setting a blistering pace. Three of them finished first, second, and third. But in a highly questionable decision, the rally stewards disqualified the three Cooper S Minis on the grounds of a supposed obscure lighting infringement. **SB**

COUPE
ALPES
24PK

A model at the Peel P50's 1963 launch in London shows that it is impossible to drive the tiny vehicle without laughing.

911 | Porsche (D)

1963 • 121 cu in/1,991 cc, F6 • 128 bhp/96 kW • 0–60 mph/97 kph in 8.5 seconds • 131 mph/211 kph

Porsche's classic 911 is one of the world's most recognizable sports car designs. Like its predecessor, the 356, it employed a rear-mounted powerplant, but here was a completely new design that distanced Porsche cars from their humble origins in the Volkswagen Type 1 "Beetle."

The original design concept had been penned in 1959 by Ferdinand "Butzi" Porsche, grandson of the company's founder, as a rival to the sporty four- seaters offered by Mercedes and Alfa Romeo. The all-new air-cooled flat-six engine hung behind the rear axle, which allowed cabin space for two small rear seats.

Launching it at the 1963 Frankfurt Motor Show as the 901, Porsche hastily changed the moniker to 911 after a wrangle with Peugeot, which had claimed the rights to the central zero numbering series. Surprisingly, Porsche aficionados were slow to take to the new car, bemoaning that this heavier, more luxurious model was not the true driver's car that the little 356 had been. It was also nearly twice the price. However, opinion soon changed: in early 1965 *Car & Driver* magazine trumpeted that the "new 911 model is unquestionably the finest Porsche ever built. More than that, it's one of the best Gran Turismo cars in the world."

Despite its "tail happy" character, the handling was highly praised thanks to its all-independent suspension. This, combined with brisk performance and robust mechanicals, meant that the 911 was soon campaigning on the international rallying circuit. By the late 1960s the 911 completely dominated the famous Monte Carlo rally, taking both first and second places for three consecutive years. **JI**

P50 | Peel (GB)

1963 • 3 cu in/49 cc, one-cylinder • 4.5 bhp/3.3 kW • unknown • 38 mph/61 kph

Guinness World Records awards the Peel P50 the title of smallest-ever production car; it is just 54 inches (137 cm) long and 41 inches (104 cm) wide.

Launched in 1963 by Peel Engineering on the Isle of Man in the United Kingdom, it had a singular theme. It carried one adult (and one shopping bag, according to advertising of the time), it had one rear-hinged door on the left-hand side, a single headlights, one wiper blade, and a single-cylinder two-stroke moped engine supplied by DKW. It did, at least, have three wheels.

The P50 was one of many "bubble cars" then made in Europe to motorbike specifications in order to avoid road tax. One criterion was that the vehicle must have no reverse gear, so the Peel driver simply got out and used a handle on the back to pull the car around.

In 2008 the TV program *Top Gear* in the United Kingdom showed the six-foot five-inch (196-cm) presenter Jeremy Clarkson driving a P50 around inside BBC Television Centre in London. Having driven forward into the elevator, he needed passing news anchorwoman Fiona Bruce to push him out again.

In 2010 entrepreneurs Gary Hillman and Faizal Khan bought the Peel name and rights. They won an investment of £80,000 ($129,464) from James Caan on the hit TV show *Dragon's Den* (2005–present) and began to remanufacture the P50 and its Sputnik-style sister the Trident.

Just forty-seven P50s were sold between 1963 and 1964 for £198 ($310). Originals are worth Mercedes S-class money. The reinvented Peel Engineering began to sell cars to Ripley's Believe it or Not! museums, and was taking orders from the public in 2012. **LT**

PEEL 50

24CT | Panhard

(F)

1963 • 51 cu in/848 cc, F2 • 50 bhp/37 kW • 0–60 mph/97 kph in 22.3 seconds • 89 mph/143 kph

It was in 1890 that the name Panhard was first seen on a car, although the original company was called Panhard et Levassor. In the 1890s its cars won events such the Paris–Bordeaux race, and the Paris–Marseille–Paris race, and it was among the first mass-producers of cars in the world—mass-produced by the standards of the day, that is. The company went on to produce a steady stream of cars in the twentieth century, including the popular Dyna series after World War II.

In 1962 the company had a moderate success with its PL17 model (giving cars snappy names was never a company forte), and in 1963 it announced its successors, the 24 series. The best-selling model by far was the 24CT two-door coupe, which in the course of the next four years would sell more than 14,000, about half the 24's entire production run.

The Panhard 24CT was a very handsome car with a low-slung, modern look and big windows all around for excellent visibility. Sadly, what it did not possess was a very powerful engine. The Panhard company designers had included a more forceful four-cylinder engine in their plans, but implementation of this was blocked on grounds of cost by the parent company, Citroën, and a two-cylinder engine was used instead.

Citroën had taken a 25 percent stake in Panhard in 1955, going on to take full control in 1965. It did not want any Panhard cars encroaching upon what it saw as Citroën's territory of high-speed automobiles. The problem was not to exist for much longer because Panhard's carmaking arm was closed down with the 24 series in 1967, when the Panhard name appeared on a car for the final time. **MG**

Corvair Monza | Chevrolet (USA)

1963 • 163 cu in/2,687 cc, F6 • 95 bhp/70 kW • 0–60 mph/97 kph in 14.7 seconds • 92 mph/148 kph

Unfortunately for Chevrolet, its 1963 Monza is best remembered for being included in the consumer campaigner Ralph Nader's 1965 book, *Unsafe at Any Speed*. This was the book that made Ralph Nader's name, and in it he criticized the Monza's design flaws. By the time the book was published, those design flaws had already been fixed, but mud sticks and the Corvair never lived the complaints down; it was named by *Time* magazine as one of the Fifty Worst Cars of All Time.

Bad press—and the Monza had more of that than almost any other modern car—was not what Chevrolet needed. The Monza was its attempt to produce a more compact car to combat the inroads that were being made into the U.S. market by European manufacturers such as Volkswagen. The Volkswagen Beetle was doing surprisingly well in a country dominated by huge and flashy cars. In retrospect, some U.S. carmakers had lost sight of the fact that there existed a sizable section of the American public that wanted smaller and more energy-efficient cars. Hard though it was to believe, plenty of drivers preferred a Beetle to a Bel Air.

The Corvair's design borrowed heavily from successful European compacts, particularly the Beetle. The trunk (boot) was put at the front of the car, and the engine was rear-mounted and air-cooled, both of which were unusual in the United States. Chevrolet also used swing-axle rear suspension, similar to the Volkswagen's. The German manufacturer had been producing this for years, but it was a new style for Chevrolet. It was to cause the handling problems that made Ralph Nader come down so hard on the car. Chevrolet ceased its production in 1969. **MG**

Actor Peter Sellers poses in his ice-blue Ferrari 275 GTB. He was making 1965's *What's New Pussycat?* at the time.

Mini Moke | BMC (GB)

1964 • 51 cu in/850 cc, S4 • 33 bhp/25 kW • 0–60 mph/97 kph in 22 seconds • 65 mph/105 kph

"Moke" is an archaic name for a donkey, and the Mini Moke—a kind of diminutive beach buggy—was the rugged workhorse of the Mini line. It was originally designed as a lightweight military vehicle, a miniature Jeep, but its small wheels and the lack of ground clearance were unsuitable. Only the Royal Navy showed interest in the "Buckboard" prototype as a vehicle for use on the decks of aircraft carriers.

The British Motor Corporation (BMC), maker of the Mini, abandoned the idea of a military Moke and instead developed a civilian version, launched in 1964. It was intended as a low-cost and easily maintained utility vehicle, and was targeted at farmers and light commercial users. As a commercial vehicle it would have been exempt from purchase tax, but British Customs and Excise ruled that it was a passenger car. This made it expensive and limited its potential.

The Moke was built in the United Kingdom from 1964 to 1968, first in Oxford at the Morris factory, and then in Birmingham at the BMC Longbridge plant. From 1966 to 1981 it was produced in Australia, and from 1980 in Portugal. Production ended in 1993.

A little more than 50,000 Mini Mokes were made: 14,500 in Britain, 26,000 in Australia, and 10,000 in Portugal. The car was marketed under various names, including Morris Mini Moke, Austin Mini Moke, and Leyland Moke. In the 1960s Mini Mokes would be seen in British seaside towns, but the little Mini-based buggy enjoyed its main popularity overseas, becoming something of a cult vehicle in some of the world's warm-weather leisure centers, including Barbados, the Seychelles, California, and Queensland, Australia. **SB**

275 GTB | Ferrari (I)

1964 • 200 cu in/3,286 cc, V12 • 300 bhp/224 kW • 0–60 mph/97 kph in 6.2 seconds • 165 mph/266 kph

While the Ferrari 250 spawned some of the most successful race cars in motorsport history, the roadgoing versions were mechanically outdated in comparison to cars produced by Lamborghini and Maserati. The arrival of the Ferrari 275 in 1964 signaled a technological leap forward; the new car now featured fully independent suspension, disc brakes all around, and a five-speed rear-mounted transaxle.

Customers could opt for the GTB Berlinetta coupe, or the open-topped GTS Spyder. Although these shared the same chassis and V12 powerplant, their styling was quite different. The more streamlined Berlinetta had clearly evolved from the 250 GTO, while the Spyder was more of a U.S.-targeted grand tourer.

In 1966 the 275 GTB/4 was launched. Powered by a heavily revised four-cam V12, with six Weber carburetors, it was a direct response to Lamborghini's newly launched supercar, the Miura.

Only sixteen lightweight Competizione versions of the 275 GTB were built; in 1966 a GTB/C entered the 24 Hours of Le Mans, coming first in the GT class. However, the rarest and most valuable performance variants were the ten 275 GTS NART (North American Race Team) cars; custom-built for a U.S. dealer at a cost of $8,000 (£3,330) each, a NART car came in second in the 1968 12 Hours of Sebring endurance race.

The Ferrari 275's most famous movie appearance was in 1968's *The Thomas Crown Affair*, in which a Ferrari dismissed by Faye Dunaway as "one of those red Italian things" is actually the same car that raced at Sebring. But her costar, Steve McQueen, was so impressed that he bought a 275 GTS NART for himself. **DS**

Wankel Spider | NSU

D

1964 • 30 cu in/498 cc, rotary • 50 bhp/37 kW • 0–60 mph/97 kph in 14.5 seconds • 92 mph/148 kph

In 1964 the NSU car company, which was absorbed into the mighty Audi/Volkswagen empire in the 1970s, decided to make a spider (open-top) version of its Prinz sedan (saloon), which was powered by an air-cooled, 36-cubic-inch (600-cc) twin-cylinder engine. For the Spider, however, NSU opted instead for a Wankel rotary engine. This dispenses with pistons and instead uses a spinning rotor, which does not waste energy by shifting heavy pistons up and down.

At the time rotaries were seen as a great leap forward, but time has shown that it will take a lot more than that to knock the piston engine off its throne. The NSU engineers were not to know this, though, and they shoehorned a Wankel motor into the rear of their new Spider. Being liquid-cooled, it needed a radiator, which could only be placed up front in the luggage area.

The rotary engine was actually sweet and free-revving. On paper it produced 50 bhp (37 kW), but revving it past its 7,000 rpm redline yielded a some more horsepower. NSU eventually upped its official figure to 55 bhp (41 kW).

The car itself was a neat little roadster, styled by Bertone. The rear-mounted engine (it was perched directly above the rear wheels) gave it nimble handling.

Unfortunately, rotary engines put a lot of strain on their components, and the Spider gained a reputation for unreliability. The Spider's Wankel motor needed regular rebuilds, something that no manufacturer wants to contemplate. Consequently, the rotary Spider remains something of a one-off, with respect to Mazda's RX. The dream of replacing the piston with the rotor was not to become a reality for NSU. **JI**

GT40 | Ford

(USA)

1964 • 426 cu in/6,997 cc, V8 • 485 bhp/362 kW • 0–60 mph/97 kph in 4.2 seconds • 213 mph/343 kph (Le Mans car)

The Ford GT40 is inextricably linked with the 24 Hours of Le Mans motor race in western France, the most famous motorsport event in the world. Expressly developed to pursue victory at Le Mans, this ground-hugging, missile-shaped, high-performance sports race car won the iconic endurance motor race four times in a row, from 1966 to 1969.

The clear plan behind the GT40 was to win long-distance sports car races as a serious rival for the dominant Ferrari, which won Le Mans six times in a row from 1960 to 1965. Henry Ford II had harbored an ambition to see a Ford car win at Le Mans since the beginning of the Ferrari landslide of victories in the early 1960s. Looking at the results the GT40 achieved during the car's distinguished motorsport career, it is obvious that it amply achieved that aim.

The GT40 was a collaboration between Ford and race car company Lola, steered by Lola's owner and chief designer Eric Broadley. Former Aston Martin team manager John Wyer was hired to work on the project, joined by respected Ford engineers Roy Lunn and Harley Copp. The significance of the car's name was simple. GT stood for Grand Touring, and 40 represented the overall height of 40 inches (102 cm) as measured at the top of the windshield; the height was dictated by the rules governing the GT40's racing category.

The GT40's four victories at Le Mans put both the car and its drivers in the record books. The winning drivers were Chris Amon and Bruce McLaren in 1966, Dan Gurney and A. J. Foyt in 1967, Pedro Rodrigues and Lucien Bianchi in 1968, and Jacky Icky and Jackie Oliver in 1969. **SB**

SUNBEAM
Tiger

⊲ Steve Carrell, playing spy Maxwell Smart, takes a flying leap in a Tiger Sunbeam in the 2008 movie *Get Smart*.

Tiger | Sunbeam (GB)

1964 • 259 cu in/4,260 cc, V8 • 164 bhp/121 kW • 0–60 mph/97 kph in 9 seconds • 120 mph/193 kph

With the Sunbeam Tiger, auto designer Carroll Shelby and his team were at it again. Having hot-rodded the AC Ace with a 259-cubic-inch (4,260-cc) V8 to create the Cobra, they shoehorned the same engine into the pretty Sunbeam Alpine for the United Kingdom's Rootes Group. Much of the reengineering work was done by chief engineer Ken Miles, best known for his success racing GT40s. A Mark II appeared in 1967 with a 288-cubic-inch (4,727-cc) V8, but Chrysler's takeover of Rootes ended the deal with Ford.

The Alpine chassis needed plenty of stiffening, and a rack-and-pinion steering system was sourced from MG. The Tiger would remain a wolf in the Alpine's clothing, though, with just the twin exhausts, badges, and chrome side strips to give away its identity. That is, until the car fired up and its deep gurgling set off every car alarm within range.

From 1964 to 1967, works Tigers drove head-to-head against Austin-Healey 3000s in European rallies. The car also became an on-screen star with agent Maxwell Smart at the wheel in the 1960s TV series and 2008 movie *Get Smart*, featuring almost as many gadgets as James Bond's Aston Martin.

The Tiger is fun to drive, but its brakes are not the best, and the steering and pedals give the driver a good workout. Also, the V8 has no space in the compact bay and can boil over if the car is stuck in traffic.

The Tiger originally cost $3,499 in the United States and £1,445 in the United Kingdom. Prices remained average for a long time, but began to climb in 2010. Now a good Mark I can cost up to $40,000 (£24,571), but that is still a lot cheaper than an AC Cobra. **LT**

Malibu SS | Chevrolet (USA)

1964 • 326 cu in/5,354 cc, V8 • 300 bhp/220 kW • 0–60 mph/97 kph in 8 seconds • 126 mph/203 kph

In 1964 in America, there wasn't a much cooler car than a Chevrolet Malibu. With the roof down and the Beach Boys "I Get Around" playing on the radio, drivers could feel like they were in the movies.

The SS (Super Sports) version added an all-vinyl interior, sexy bucket seats, and a centre console—a luxury extra for the time. Buyers could choose between the four-speed manual gearbox or the two-speed Powerglide automatic. More lavish extra features included engine gauges on the dashboard, deep-twist carpeting, and special distinctive SS wheel covers. The most muscular power option was the 326-cubic-inch (5,354-cc) V8 with 300 bhp (320 kW). The figures for the automatic version are given above.

Buyers were attracted by the fact that the Malibu wasn't as enormous as its 1950s predecessors. The fuel consumption of 12 mpg (5 km per liter) wasn't considered a problem. The Malibu marked a change from fantastical chrome-laden styling to more understated decoration. The SS unusually had less body decoration than more basic models. But its clean lines and comfortable proportions won lots of fans. Adverts proclaimed that it was "a good foot shorter and a few inches narrower than the BIG cars." The SS cost around $2,600 (£1,600) and almost 77,000 were sold before an all-new model took over in 1967.

The Malibu had begun as merely a top-level trim on the Chevelle range, but proved so popular that it soon became a model in its own right. In fact it was the start of a dynasty of Chevy Malibus that continues today. The eighth generation Malibu—a global four-door sedan (saloon)—was launched in 2012. **SH**

Grifo | Iso

(I)

1964 • 327 cu in/5,359 cc, V8 • 405 bhp/302 kW • 0–60 mph/97 kph in 7 seconds • 190 mph/304 kph

The asking price for an Iso Grifo when it was a new model was roughly $9,500 (£6,000), but an example in good condition costs ten times that today. The Grifo was considered a rich playboy's car; with a roaring acceleration from its huge engine, it achieved a top speed that was about twice the legal speed limit in most countries where it was driven. In fact, it was able to break most speed limits without even leaving first gear, which could get up to 68 mph (109 kph).

The car was engineered by Giotto Bizzarrini, who had worked for Alfa Romeo and then made his name as the chief engineer at Ferrari for many years. He left the company in 1961 and eventually set up his own business, Bizzarrini, with the aim of producing the most advanced and desirable road and racing cars possible. He worked with companies such as Lamborghini and Iso Rivolta, which was famous for its 1950s "bubble car." But anything less like a bubble car than the powerful Iso Grifo is hard to imagine.

Although Bizzarrini worked on the engineering, the beautiful bodywork design was the work of Giorgetto Giugiaro, who was one of the best, if not *the* best, car designers in the world. Named as Car Designer of the Century by an international panel in 1999, Giugiaro worked for names including Ferrari and Maserati, but the Iso Grifo is definitely one of his career highlights.

Despite its playboy image, the Grifo was no lightweight built only for show and speed. It competed at Le Mans, and although its best result was a fourth place, it did win a "first in class," evidence that it could cope with the demands of the grueling 24 Hours of Le Mans Race. **MG**

Gordon-Keeble | Gordon-Keeble

GB

1964 • 329 cu in/5,395 cc, V8 • 300 bhp/224 kW • 0–60 mph/97 kph in 7.7 seconds • 135 mph/217 kph

With Italian styling, American muscle, and British engineering know-how, the Gordon-Keeble was pitched at wealthy motorists as an interesting and alluring alternative to the luxury grand tourers made by Alvis, Aston Martin, and Jaguar.

The company was formed when John Gordon, formerly of Peerless Cars, teamed up with race car engineer Jim Keeble. At the suggestion of a USAF pilot based in the United Kingdom, they first experimented with a 213-cubic-inch (3,500-cc) Buick engine in the space-frame chassis of a Peerless GT. This was shipped to Italy where auto designer Giorgetto Giugiaro styled the car's elegant bodywork in lightweight aluminum.

The finished prototype was completed just in time for the 1960 Geneva Motor Show, before being rushed to Detroit to help persuade Chevrolet bosses to supply the firm with the Corvette's 329-cubic-inch (5,395-cc) engine. Chevy was so impressed that it agreed to supply a thousand.

Built in Southampton, England, the production cars had lightweight fiberglass bodywork. The cockpit was well trimmed and its thunderous V8 gave incredible performance for a 2+2 executive sedan (saloon). As a private joke, the Gordon-Keeble company had selected as its emblem a tortoise, inspired by a family pet that had ambled into an early factory photo shoot.

Gordon-Keeble should have flourished, but at £2,798 ($4,410) it had underpriced an excellent product. When a supply of vital components was delayed, sixteen cars stood unfinished; subsequent cash-flow problems forced the company into liquidation after only ninety-nine cars were built. **DS**

Tony Curtis, pictured here with his Excalibur in 1965, was just one of the car's many celebrity owners. ▷

SH760 | Shanghai (CN)

1964 • 134 cu in/2,200 cc, S6 • 90 bhp/67 kW • 0–60 mph/97 kph in 21 seconds • 81 mph/130 kph

The solid, sensible, and inoffensive lines of the Shanghai hint to what it really was: the car of medium status for middle-ranking officials of a Communist regime. Yet in terms of China's infant motor industry, this dull-looking four-door car was a big step forward.

The company Shanghai Automobile, based in Shanghai, first built a vehicle, a truck, in 1956. Its first car was the Hongqui limosine, a two-and-a-half-ton Soviet ZiL clone built in tiny numbers from 1958 exclusively for party leaders, including Chairman Mao.

From around 1958, Shanghai began to make its first totally locally-made mass-produced car. Initially intended for lesser party officials, it occupied the next rung down the ladder from the Hongqui. The car appeared in very small numbers at first, gradually building to a peak of about 6,000 cars a year in 1984.

The earliest model, called the Fenghuang (Phoenix), had big fins to the rear and a U.S.-influenced front. But there was certainly nothing innovative about this boxy four-door sedan (saloon). The design was an unimaginative and dated mix of old Mercedes, Soviet, and U.S. shapes. The engine was rumored to be a copy of the Mercedes straight-six unit. It had rear-wheel drive and a four-speed manual gearbox.

The Shanghai Fenghuang was renamed the SH760 in 1964, and, incredibly, the car stayed in production with only minor cosmetic changes until 1991, when it was finally dumped when Shanghai Automobile started making Volkswagens under license. By that time a total of 80,000 SH760s had been made. A few of these were made into crew-cab pickups and rare convertibles; many others ended up as taxis. **SH**

Excalibur | Excalibur (USA)

1964 • 326 cu in/5,354 cc, V8 • 300 bhp/224 kW • 0–60 mph/97 kph in 5.2 seconds • 121 mph/194 kph

The Excalibur was a true one-off example of car design, an attempt to put modern muscle into a classic car body. The car was conceived in 1964 by Brooks Stevens, an American designer who worked on furniture and home appliances as well as cars and motorcycles. Stevens was acting as consultant to Studebaker, who asked him to come up with a show-stopping new model to rejuvenate the company at the 1964 New York Auto Show. The designer is said to have sketched his vision for the Excalibur on a restaurant place mat.

Stevens looked at the body of the 1928 Mercedes-Benz SSK and decided to pack it with the power of Studebaker's Avanti engine. The latter had made a huge impact on the car trade and on the public until, in late 1963, Studebaker closed down the factory where it was made to cut costs. Stevens's great idea was to take the Avanti's muscle and wrap it in a classy body inspired by the stunning looks of the SSK.

A prototype was ready three days before the New York show, at which point Stevens was told that Studebaker was pulling the plug on the project. Stevens decided to show the car anyway, and it was admired so much that he looked into building it himself. Encouraged by early orders, he proceeded, and since 1964 his company has sold over 3,500 cars, some to celebrities such as Steve McQueen, Bill Cosby, Frank Sinatra, Tony Curtis, Sonny Bono and Cher, and Dean Martin. The comedienne Phyllis Diller has owned four of them. Stevens went on to design Harley-Davidson motorcycles, and his bike designs are still being used today. Studebaker, meanwhile, was bought by Wagner Electric in 1967, only to disappear in 1979. **MG**

442 | Oldsmobile

USA

1964 • 329 cu in/5,400 cc, V8 • 310 bhp/228 kW • 0–60 mph/97 kph in 7.5 seconds • 116 mph/186 kph

The Oldsmobile 88 series, introduced in 1949, led the early postwar muscle car field by such a distance that the maker, General Motors (GM), rather lost interest in the sector. However, it was awoken from its complacent reverie in 1964 when the rival Pontiac had great success with its new GTO.

GM's response, the Oldsmobile 442, was produced quickly, but showed no signs of having been made in a panic. The series number referred to the four-barrel carburetor, the four-speed gearbox, and the twin exhausts. It was a car to savor, with a top-of-the-line 329-cubic-inch (5,400-cc) engine. The same power unit was installed in the maker's highway patrol cars, and the so-called "police package" 442 proved a major attraction.

Although the 442 was originally launched as only two models—a two-door coupe and a two-door convertible—the identical format was also made available on all midsize Oldsmobiles, including every four-door except the station wagon (estate). Confused potential buyers struggled to tell whether the 442 was a wolf in sheep's clothing or vice versa. When road tests revealed that it was not the fastest around the block—from a standing start it took almost a second longer than the GTO to hit 60 mph (97 kph)—its fate was sealed. It became a niche car for those already hooked on Olds rather than the market leader GM had hoped it would be. Sales turned out to be disappointing; one fewer than 3,000 in the first year of production.

For all its shortcomings, the 442 reasserted Oldsmobile's marker in the sports sector at a time when commentators were beginning to wonder if it had thrown in its hand. **GL**

Barracuda V8 | Plymouth

USA

1964 • 273 cu in/4,474 cc, V8 • 180 bhp/130 kW • 0–60 mph/97 kph in 12.9 seconds • 106 mph/171 kph

Despite the fact that the Plymouth Barracuda debuted a full two weeks before Ford's Mustang, the car took a real beating from the originator of the pony car class. In 1964 alone, the Mustang outsold the Barracuda eight to one. That was more about the Mustang's runaway success than any failure of the Barracuda, which, over time, has won its own place in automotive history.

Plymouth built the Barracuda as a small—by U.S. standards—compact car with a sporty twist, as was the fashion in the mid-1960s. The company borrowed many parts from its Valiant sedan (saloon), including body panels and mechanicals, which saved a lot of time and money in the new car's development cycle.

At the heart of any pony car was its engine, and the Barracuda was available with any of the motors in the Valiant range, starting with the 225-cubic-inch (3,700-cc) straight-six. The most powerful on offer was Chrysler's all-new 274-cubic-inch (4,500-cc) V8, which had only just arrived on the market. At 180 bhp (130 kW), this gave the Barracuda the real muscle and acceleration it needed to match its rivals.

Most cars were bought with an automatic gearbox, available on the 1964 model with a push-button selector. Most notably, the Barracuda had a vast rear window, stretching virtually all the way back to the rear fender (bumper). A specialist company was brought in to help design this one-off piece of glass.

The Barracuda went through many updates and redesigns during its lifetime, but never quite attained the status of the Mustang. Its fate could have been worse though—Chrysler bosses had originally wanted to call it the Panda. **JI**

The 1964 Pontiac GTO epitomized the U.S. muscle car and is viewed by some people to be the first genuine one. ⊡

8 Gordini | Renault (F)

1964 • 67 cu in/1,108 cc, S4 • 89 bhp/66 kW • 0–60 mph/97 kph in 12.3 seconds • 107 mph/171 kph

Most car manufacturers have a tuning arm, or at least a brand name that they apply to the hotter versions of their standard machinery. With Renault this is Gordini, named after Amédée Gordini, an Italian-born engineering wizard nicknamed "the sorcerer."

Gordini began his relationship with Renault in 1956, working first on the Dauphine, its small economy car. He was so successful in wringing extra performance out of the standard car with little extra cost that he was assigned to do the same to its successor, the Renault 8. This small family car was so boxy in profile that it resembled a child's drawing. Yet it had one or two interesting design quirks, such as the rear-mounted engine and disc brakes all around (a first for a car of this size).

Gordini took the 67-cubic-inch (1,108-cc) liquid-cooled engine and raised its peak power from 49 bhp (37 kW) to a more exciting 89 bhp (66 kW). This was done by adding twin Weber carburetors, reworking the cylinder head, altering the exhaust ducts, and redesigning the intake and exhaust manifolds. Further, the car had a close-ratio, five-speed gearbox fitted, and its suspension was also lowered and stiffened.

The Renault 8 Gordini could only be bought in one color, vivid blue, with two white stripes up the length of the car. The fact that it now looked like a racing car was no mere coincidence; the Gordini was hugely successful on the track and in rallying.

The little blue Renault established the method of taking a small European car and giving it more power and better handling. The fact that many makers now do so shows how great the Renault 8 Gordini was. **JI**

GTO | Pontiac (USA)

1964 • 389 cu in/6,375cc, V8 • 325 bhp/242 kW • 0–60 mph/97 kph in 7.5 seconds • 125 mph/201 kph

The Pontiac GTO, which debuted in 1964, grew out of a decision by parent company General Motors to ban its various divisions from being involved in competitive racing. This was a major blow to Pontiac, in particular, which was closely tied into the auto-racing world as part of its image and promotional strategies. Several senior Pontiac people, including John DeLorean, decided they would, therefore, produce mighty Pontiac "muscle cars" but focus on the performances their cars could achieve on the streets.

The 1964 GTO was the first result, and it has gone down in history as one of the finest muscle cars ever made. Some people even regard it as the first genuine muscle car, even though the term had been around for some time. DeLorean came up with the name GTO, which stood for the Italian phrase "Gran Turismo Omologato," meaning a Grand Tourer car that was officially certified for racing. Of course, that was not true of the Pontiac—but hey, they were only initials.

General Motors had also forbidden its companies from using any engine greater than 329-cubic-inches (5,400-cc) on a medium-sized car frame. Pontiac bent the rules by making the vastly bigger engine an optional extra, rather than part of the standard fitting, but as it was offered at only $300 (£196) it was an option that everyone wanted.

The GTO was a raging success. Although the price was kept down to an affordable $4,500 (£2,940), it was still considered an exclusive car. Pontiac expected to sell about 5,000 of them, but they had to ramp up production. In the end they sold more than 32,000, a result that General Motors could hardly argue with. **MG**

RANDY'S
DONUTS
Chocolate Chip Cookies
24hr.
Randy's

350GT | Lamborghini

(I)

1964 • 211 cu in/3,464 cc, V12 • 280 bhp/209 kW • 0–60 mph/97 kph in 6.7 seconds • 155 mph/250 kph

Ferruccio Lamborghini was a skilled engineer who had made his fortune in postwar Italy converting surplus military vehicles into agricultural machinery. The wealthy entrepreneur had an interest in sports cars and owned three Ferrari 250s during the early 1960s. However, the engineer eventually grew weary of his Ferrari's uncompromising race-car dynamics, not to mention repeated problems with the 250's clutch.

One fateful day, upon deciding to take his complaints to Enzo Ferrari in person, he was dismissed by the Ferrari boss as a mere "tractor salesman," with the problem more likely being due to his driving than the 250's engineering. Legend has it that a furious Lamborghini vowed then and there to beat Ferrari at his own game, and so began the money-is-no-object development program of the Lamborghini 350GT.

The new luxury grand tourer had a 211-cubic-inch (3,464-cc) quad-cam V12. Deep bucket seats faced a well-trimmed leather and aluminum dashboard beset with Jaeger clocks and steel toggle switches. Several early cars also featured an unusual 2+1 arrangement courtesy of a small rear seat. The rakish fastback had supercar presence, but was never quite as pretty as the Ferrari alternatives. Yet it was technically superior, with a five-speed gearbox, lightweight aluminum bodywork, independent suspension, and disc brakes all around.

While most accepted that Lamborghini had indeed built a better grand tourer than Ferrari, wealthy customers were slow to switch allegiance. Only 120 cars were built in the three-year production run, far short of the original target of 500 per annum, but the tractor salesman had shown he meant business. **DS**

Imperial | Humber

GB

1964 • 180 cu in/2,965 cc, S6 • 135 bhp/101 kW • 0–60 mph/97 kph in 13.7 seconds • 101 mph/163 kph

The Humber Imperial was a luxury sedan (saloon) sold for just three years during the mid-1960s. The Imperial name had originally been used by the British manufacturer in the 1930s and 1940s. The car's emphasis was on comfort and quality, with lots of interior wood and generous plush carpet.

The Imperial was an upmarket version of another of Humber's cars, the Super Snipe. This had originated before World War II (during which many were used as military staff cars), but by the late 1950s it had been updated with a design that echoed American styles. This was hardly surprising, given that Humber was under the control of the Chrysler Corporation.

The power for both the Imperial and Super Snipe came from a 180-cubic-inch (2,965-cc), six-cylinder engine fed by twin carburetors. The Imperial had an automatic gearbox as standard (although manual was an option), with power steering and a heater for the rear passengers. It also had rear "Selectaride" shock absorbers that could be adjusted electrically. The roof was covered in black leather as another sign of the car's prestige. There were some luxury touches inside, like fold-down wooden picnic tables for the rear passengers and individual reading lights. There were even rugs on the floor. The Imperial was available in an even more upmarket version, as a limousine with a sliding glass partition between the passengers and chauffeur.

While some manufacturers in the 1960s were aiming to build an "everyman" car, Humber was unashamedly class-conscious, marketing the Imperial as the car people drove, or were driven in, when they had arrived at society's very top. **JI**

◀ The 1964 Ford Mustang Mark I was an instant hit, and today is a cult classic after being immortalized in film and song.

Mustang Mark I | Ford (USA)

1964 • 301 cu in/4,942 cc, V8 • 240 bhp/179 kW • 0–60 mph/97 kph in 7.5 seconds • 116 mph/187 kph

The Ford Mustang was the originator of the pony car class of U.S. muscle cars, sports car–like coupes with long hoods (bonnets) and short trunks (boots). Where the Mustang led, others followed, and the hunky Ford spawned a generation of "me-too" models, such as General Motors' Chevrolet Camaro, Chrysler's Plymouth Barracuda, and the AMC Javelin. But the Mustang was the best, enjoying cult status and even immortalized in a popular song; "Mustang Sally" was first recorded by Mack Rice in 1965 and became a rhythm 'n' blues hit for Wilson Pickett the following year.

The Ford Mustang was manufactured in Dearborn, Michigan, starting in March 1964. The public first saw it on April 17 of that year at the New York World's Fair. Credit for the name went to Ford's executive stylist, John Najjar, who loved the World War II P-51 Mustang fighter aircraft. The car's chief designer was Joe Oros.

The Mustang drew heavily on existing Ford technology, and its chassis, suspension, and drivetrain were mostly derived from Ford's Falcon and Fairlane models. But it was the muscular-looking styling that made the Mustang a standout; 22,000 Mustangs were sold on the first day. Originally forecast to sell 100,000 in the first year, that number was achieved within three months; the Mustang actually sold 418,000 in its first year, and a million within two years of going on sale.

The Mustang Mark I proved to be the first of a very long line of cars to bear the name, and the original car's descendants are still in production today. The Mustang has been immortalized in film, most famously driven by Steve McQueen in *Bullitt* (1968), in what is widely regarded as the best-ever movie car chase. **SB**

1800 | Marcos (GB)

1964 • 108 cu in/1,786 cc, S4 • 114 bhp/85 kW • 0–60 mph/97 kph in 9.1 seconds • 115 mph/185 kph

The Marcos car company was founded by Jem Marsh and Frank Costin; the first parts of their surnames make up the name. Costin had worked on the De Havilland Mosquito fighter-bomber during World War II and it was his idea to use plywood to build sports cars.

The 1800 was not the first Marcos car; that was the odd-looking GT, which had gull-wing doors and a four-piece windshield. But the 1800 was the car that helped put the company on the map of auto manufacturers.

The chassis had a steel subframe and made extensive use of wood. On top of that there was a gloriously curvaceous fiberglass body. The rear suspension was sophisticated, using the De Dion system, which mixes a solid axle with floating joints at each wheel hub. This gives a supple ride, even over poor surfaces, but is complicated to build.

At launch the engine was a Volvo 108-cubic-inch (1,786-cc), four-cylinder unit—an unusual choice for a sports-car company—to which Marcos added an overdrive gearbox. In 1966 this was swapped for a Ford engine, and the rear suspension was switched to a simpler and more conventional live-axle design.

In 1969 the 1800's wooden chassis was abandoned in favor of steel. This gave Marcos the opportunity to use more powerful engines such as Ford's Essex V6; with 140 bhp (104 kW) on tap, this could push the lightweight Marcos up to 120 mph (190 kph).

Marcos wanted to sell the car in the United States, but delays in getting it through emissions tests were the company's undoing. Mounting costs forced the company to close its doors; it was to be just the first occasion on which Marcos ran into difficulties. **JI**

DB6 | Aston Martin

GB

1965 • 243 cu in/3,995 cc, S6 • 282 bhp/210 kW • 0–60 mph/97 kph in 8.4 seconds • 150 mph/241 kph

Carmakers love to see the profile of their cars raised when someone famous drives one while lots of people are watching. In the United Kingdom, after the formal part of Prince William's marriage to Catherine Middleton in April 2011, the newlyweds broke with tradition and drove themselves from Buckingham Palace to the nearby reception in a convertible sports car. It was an Aston Martin DB6 Volante, owned by Prince Charles and given to him fresh from the factory by his mother, Queen Elizabeth II, on his twenty-first birthday in 1969. Billions of people saw William behind the wheel and interest in the DB6 spiked.

On sale from 1965, the coupe debuted at that year's London Motor Show. The Volante—Aston's regular name for a convertible—appeared exactly a year later. The DB6 was a grand tourer and successor to the DB5, which famously had been driven by fictional British spy James Bond on the silver screen.

The DB6 had about 2 inches (5 cm) of headroom more than its predecessor, which improved comfort for rear passengers. Legroom in the back was also better, making the car a genuinely practical four-seater. There were also aerodynamic changes, and even though the car was heavier, its extra stability at high speeds was considered to be worth any tiny loss in top-end performance. Optional extras included power steering and air-conditioning.

Almost 2,000 examples were built, including a handful of "shooting brake-style" station wagons (estates), before the axe fell in January 1971. The model was ultimately replaced by the DBS, although the pair were on sale at the same time from 1967. **RY**

MGB GT | MG

GB

1965 • 109 cu in/1,798 cc, S4 • 95 bhp/71 kW • 0–60 mph/97 kph in 13.5 seconds • 105 mph/169 kph

Many have argued that the MGB GT, designed by Italian styling house Pininfarina, was a better-looking sports car than its open-topped sibling. It was certainly a more practical proposition for drivers in wetter climes. The GT's cockpit was also considerably quieter, and its 2+2 layout could accommodate children on the rear bench seat. The large, sloping tailgate allowed easy access to a generous luggage space and began the trend for sporting hatchbacks.

Although the GT was 160 pounds (73 kg) heavier than the roadster, handling remained good by the standards of its day; the roof helped to reduce body flexing and marginally improved aerodynamics.

In 1966 two newly appointed female traffic officers from the Sussex Police Force were assigned a mildly tuned MGB GT patrol car. Although the placement of two attractive policewomen in a marked police sports car was largely seen as a PR stunt, the car performed remarkably well and proved to be one of the most reliable vehicles within the force's car pool.

While the standard 109-cubic-inch (1,798-cc) engine was a trusty unit, MG heeded the demands of its ever power-hungry customers. In 1967 the Austin-Healey 183-cubic-inch (3,000-cc) straight-six was fitted and the car rebranded as the MGC. Soon after its launch, a young Prince Charles purchased a cobalt-blue GT, which became his daily transport while at university.

However, it was not until 1973 that the GT got the powerplant it deserved: the fabulous 213-cubic-inch (3,500-cc) Rover V8, with a top speed of 125 mph (201 kph). Celebrity owners include Peter Tork, guitarist with the Monkees, who wrote a song entitled "MGB GT." **DS**

Calais | Cadillac

USA

1965 • 428 cu in/7,025 cc, V8 • 308 bhp/230 kW • 0–60 mph/97 kph in 8.8 seconds • 117 mph/189 kph

In 1965 Cadillac replaced its 62 series of cars with the 682 series, giving it the classy name of Cadillac Calais. The name may have referred incidentally to the well-known town and ferry port in northern France, but it was mainly for Calais, one of the gods of Greek mythology, who was able to travel as fast as the wind. The Cadillac Calais certainly had an engine size to justify that claim, a massive 428 cubic inches (7,025 cc).

The Calais was available in three different styles in that first year: a two-door hardtop coupe, a four-door sedan (saloon), and a four-door hardtop sedan. All of them sold very respectably for a brand-new luxury car, and about 35,000 units in total were made.

One reason for the Calais's popularity was that buyers could feel that they were custom-building their car, thanks to the huge number of optional extras. These included air-conditioning for $495 (£325), cruise control for $97 (£65), and a radio with a rear speaker and remote control for $246 (£160). For the safety conscious, rear seat belts were available for $18 (£12). One of the people for whom safety might especially have been a factor was an early Cadillac Calais buyer, June Carter, the wife of singer Johnny Cash, who had written off their 1964 Cadillac in a crash.

Actor Morgan Freeman fared better as the chauffeur in the movie *Driving Miss Daisy* (1989). One of Daisy's cars over the years was a 1965 Cadillac Calais, and it was still being driven when she later also bought a 1970 model. The Calais can also be glimpsed in movies including *Dirty Harry* (1971) and *Almost Famous* (2000), and on 1970s TV cop shows such as *Columbo* and *Kojak*. It stayed in production until 1976. **MG**

TR4A | Triumph

GB

1965 • 130 cu in/2,138 cc, S4 • 104 bhp/78 kW • 0–60 mph/97 kph in 11.4 seconds • 109 mph/175 kph

There are certain things that technically minded car owners now take for granted. They assume that a gas-powered car will have no fewer than four valves per cylinder, and that carburetors belong in the past. But when Triumph updated its highly regarded sportster, the TR4, in 1965, it added something exciting and new: independent rear suspension.

Rather than have a solid rear axle, perhaps moving on leaf springs, the TR4A had coil springs and semitrailing links. This removed the previous car's bugbear of an uncomfortable, jiggly ride. It also removed the first TR4's tendency to be bounced off line on a poorly surfaced road.

Triumph was so proud of the suspension that it emblazoned the back of the car with a badge that read "IRS," in the same way that more recent cars might carry "16V" or "turbocharged" decals. Actually, the new independent suspension began as an optional extra, and a number of buyers still specifically requested the previous type of axle. But nothing can halt progress, and soon the innovation became a standard feature.

The bodywork was quite masculine and square, compared with the cheekier "bug-eyed" look of early Triumphs and some other contemporaries. One noteworthy option was a lift-off hardtop that had a canvas section in it. This was a forerunner of the Targa top, which officially saw the light of day a year later on the Porsche 911.

Less exciting, perhaps, were some of the other "firsts" carried by the TR4A. It had roll-up windows at the front and the first dashboard air vents found on a British car. No badge was affixed to the car for those. **JI**

A contemporary advertisement for the 1965 Holden HD shows off the luxury interior of the Premier model. ⊃

GT | Broadspeed (GB)

1965 • 77 cu in/1,275 cc, S4 • 100 bhp/74.6 kWr
0–60 mph/97 kph in 9 seconds • 120 mph/193 kph

The Broadspeed GT was a British-built 1960s fastback that was quick and nimble on the road and a winner on the track, outpacing even mighty AC Cobras on some circuits. All the more amazing, then, that it was based on a 1965 BMC (British Motor Corporation) Mini Cooper.

Broadspeed Engineering of Birmingham took BMC's baby and chopped the body off at the base of the screen pillars, removing the entire back end. A new roof and rear body section was then molded from a single piece of fiberglass and married to the car. Even the seams in the front bodywork were taken off to give the Broadspeed GT a smooth exterior. The GT was also lower than the standard car, both in roofline and ground clearance, and the handling was pin-sharp.

Broadspeed was a race-tuning company that even beat the BMC works team in its own car in Mini races. It offered various engine options for the GT. The top-of-the-line road model was based on the Mini Cooper S1275 engine, which was taken up to 100 bhp (74.6 kW) through extensive modifications to the engine and exhaust. There were luxury touches, too, including a new wraparound windshield, 150-mph (240-kph) speedometer, 10,000-rpm rev counter, plush carpeting, and extra soundproofing material in the cabin. There were also more storage options than were offered for a standard Mini.

What impressed most, though, was the car's race-bred performance. There was even a racer version—the GTS—that had a 83-cubic-inch (1,366-cc) engine and unofficially recorded a top speed of 145 mph (233 kph).

Only twenty-one Broadspeed GTs were ever built. Sadly, only a few of those have survived. **JI**

HD | Holden (AUS)

1965 • 178 cu in/2,933 cc, S6 • 140 bhp/104 kW
0–60 mph/97 kph in 15.8 seconds • 88 mph/141 kph

When the Holden HD sedan (saloon) was released in 1965, its maker told Australians that its new motoring milestone was about to change their world. The HD would be available in three engine sizes: 100 bhp (75 kW); 115 bhp (86 kW); and the top-of-the-line X2, with 140 bhp (104 kW), courtesy of twin carburetors and a modified camshaft. Here, at last, was "power to go as never before, power for effortless highway passing." But when all the hype and rhetoric finally settled down, nobody liked it.

Holden had been number one in automobile production for almost twenty years, with Ford its only competition in Australia. But with the introduction of the HD, the unthinkable happened. The press had a field day, reinterpreting the HD name as the "Horrendous Disaster" or the "Horrible Design."

After the extraordinarily popular EH model, made between 1963 and 1965, nobody saw the criticism coming. The HD had a new and much-improved two-speed Powerglide automatic transmission, improved suspension, and wraparound taillights. It was longer and wider than previous Holdens, and an expanded list of options (including, for the first time, all-around disc brakes) gave buyers unprecedented choice. The X2 even came with an improved dashboard in which factors such as oil pressure and water temperature were at last given proper gauges instead of just colored lights. But the public was unmoved.

The HD was a harsh reminder for its designers—all of whom resided in Detroit, Michigan—that creating a new car for another country from the ground up is a job that is probably best left to the locals. **BS**

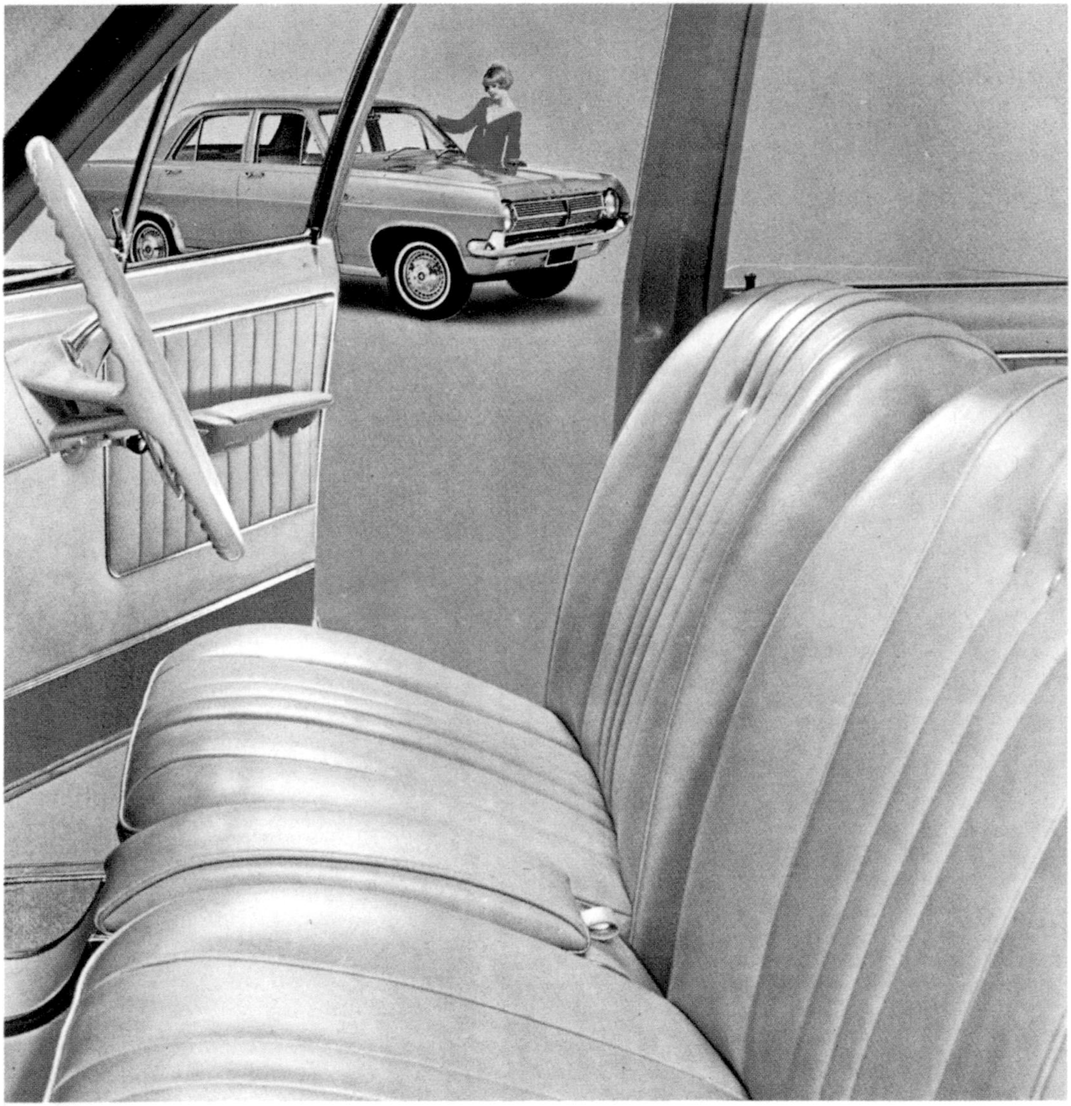

Luxury and elegance wherever you turn

Sitting in the new luxury Holden Premier reminds you of cars costing at least £2,000.

The extra spaciousness, for example, that goes with Premier's new curved doors and windows. Or Premier's sumptuous new front bucket seats, with spongy bolster edges for extra comfort.

And much more besides . . . a centre console with driver's glove-box and heater-demister . . . deep pile carpet, and more. Wherever you turn, there's luxury and elegance.

Savour this, and the performance you get from your choice of engines up to the fiery 140-hp X2, and you'll appreciate that this car at its price is unmatched for sheer driving pleasure.

HOLDEN PREMIER

AUSTRALIA'S TOP VALUE LUXURY CAR — FROM £1,100 PLUS TAX

GENERAL MOTORS-HOLDEN'S

Silver Shadow | Rolls-Royce (GB)

1965 • 379 cu in/6,227 cc, V8 • 200 bhp/147 kW • 0–60 mph/97 kph in 10.9 seconds • 115 mph/184 kph

The Rolls-Royce Silver Shadow was described when it was introduced in 1965 as a "car for the masses." Well, up to a point; a Silver Shadow cost £6,557 ($10,400) when it first went on sale, which was far from cheap.

Nevertheless, the Silver Shadow did represent a shift in the aims and the image of the venerable British carmaker. It was the first Rolls to be marketed as being for people who actually wanted to drive a Rolls-Royce, rather than just sit in the back. The carmaker's plan worked very effectively. For all of the prestige that Rolls-Royce had long enjoyed, it is said that the Silver Shadow was the first car that actually turned a profit since the discontinuation of the Silver Ghost in 1925.

A subtle change in design also helped its success. Without losing the classic appeal of the traditional Roller, the design team grafted a modern, stylish look onto the car. Famous owners of the Silver Shadow included Freddie Mercury of the rock band Queen.

Rolls-Royce built 20,604 of the Silver Shadow in its various forms over the model's fifteen-year lifespan, more than it made of any other car. The car that succeeded it was called the Silver Spirit, although the watershed basic design and outline of the Silver Shadow would stay evident in the appearance of future Rollers for several more years. **MG**

Fairlady SP311 | Datsun (J)

1965 • 97 cu in/1,595 cc, S4 • 95 bhp/71 kW • unknown • 105 mph/169 kph

If the Fairlady SP311 looks like a British sports car or an Italian design, it is no coincidence. Datsun wanted to break the European grip on small sports cars, particularly in the lucrative U.S. market. This they managed, and without falling prey to the European cars' weaknesses, such as poor reliability and a tendency to rust.

While sales of earlier Fairlady variants were slow, the SP311 was more successful. It had Datsun's new R-series engine, plus larger wheels than previous versions. Beneath the fabric roof was a sporty interior with many of the most up-to-date developments: vinyl seats, carpeting, and a proper transistor radio.

Other parts of the car were less modern, with a ladder-type chassis separate from the body shell. But the SP311 did have one first for a Japanese car: a four-speed manual gearbox with synchromesh of all four gears to allow smoother gearchanges.

The style of the car really was very European-looking, with smooth lines and a chrome strip running down each flank. The stylistic similarities continued inside, with banks of dials and toggle switches that looked familiar to anyone who had ever driven an MG or Triumph.

All this and Japanese build quality. It is no wonder that the Fairlady SP311 helped to forge Datsun/Nissan's future reputation as a performance car builder. **JI**

President | Nissan (J)

1965 • 243 cu in/3,988 cc, V8 • 197 bhp/145 kW • unknown • 115 mph/185 kph

The Nissan President was a luxury car produced from 1965 until 2010. It was aimed at businessmen and politicians in the Japanese home market. Japanese Prime Minister Eisaku Satō was one prominent user.

Until Nissan's President arrived, most luxury cars in Japan had been imports. At much the same time, several Japanese manufacturers decided to fill this gap in the home market themselves; Toyota, for example, built the Crown Eight in 1964. But at more than 16.5 feet (5 m) long, the Nissan President was the biggest and most powerful car ever produced in Japan.

Externally, the design was unashamedly American, with a slab-sided body and angular front grille. The engine could be either an all-new 243-cubic-inch (3,988-cc) V8 or Nissan's older and less powerful 183-cubic-inch (3,000-cc) straight-six. The car had a three-speed automatic gearbox and rear-wheel drive. The car was fitted with an antilock braking system (ABS) in 1971, making it the first Japanese car to get one.

The final-generation President was launched in 2001, powered by a 274-cubic-inch (4,500-cc) V8. But with ever stricter safety regulations looming, Nissan did the math and realized that the model was no longer commercially viable; in 2010 the car was discontinued. Since 1965 around 56,000 Presidents had been sold. **JI**

Fulvia Coupe | Lancia (I)

1965 • 74 cu in/1,216 cc, V4 • 80 bhp/60 kW
0–60 mph/97 kph in 15.8 seconds • 104 mph/167 kph

The 1963 Fulvia, a boxy sedan (saloon), had been a very smooth package, unusual for its revvy 67-cubic-inch (1,098-cc) V4 engine, four-wheel disc brakes, and transverse-leaf-spring front suspension. Two years later, the elegant Fulvia coupe was launched. This car stayed in production until 1976 and became a rallying icon. Its wheelbase was 5.9 inches (15 cm) shorter than the sedan's, and its 74-cubic-inch (1,216-cc) engine was tuned to deliver 80 bhp (60 kW) at 6,000 rpm. A top-of-the-line performance model, the HF, benefited from aluminum bodywork and plexiglass windows.

From 1967, the coupe's engine was reengineered and a longer stroke gave it 75 cubic inches (1,231 cc), delivering 87 bhp (65 kW), or 101 bhp (75 kW) for the HF. Buyers could also opt for the more muscular Zagato-bodied Sport. All Fulvia variations shared the same precision on a twisty road. The ride was exceptional, the steering tactile, and the handling pin-sharp.

Lancia had always been a name to beat in motorsport, and the Fulvia Coupe Rally HF, with its 96-cubic-inch (1,584-cc), 115-bhp (86-kW) engine, was a serious competitor on the rally circuits. The Lancia works team won the International Championship for Manufacturers in 1972, forcing Fiat into second place and Porsche into third. **LT**

Miura | Lamborghini

(I)

1966 • 239 cu in/3,929 cc, V12 • 370 bhp/276 kW • 0–60 mph/97 kph in 6.7 seconds • 170 mph/273 kph

The opening sequence of the 1969 cult heist movie *The Italian Job* is considered the finest in movie history by many auto enthusiasts. A Lamborghini Miura sweeps through the curves of the Grand St. Bernard Pass while Matt Munroe croons "On Days Like These." It all ends badly, but fortunately the wreck dumped over the mountainside was not a complete car.

On any list of the Most Beautiful Cars, the Miura is near the top. It was Marcello Gandini's first project for Italian styling house Bertone, before he sealed his reputation by creating the Lamborghini Countach, Lancia Stratos, and the first-generation BMW 5 series. The lithe, sinuous body, which still looks modern, made all the other cars at the 1966 Geneva Motor Show look like a row of potatoes. Even under the skin it looked good. The deep-throated V12 engine was transversely mounted ahead of the rear axle, and two triple-choke Weber carburetors nestled between each set of cam covers. The cylinder block, gearbox, and final drive casing were all one magnificent light-alloy casting.

Early cars suffered from terrifying oversteer and front-end lift, so most customers favored the 1971 SV, which benefited from greatly uprated suspension.

The driving position was always awkward, requiring bent-up knees and outstretched arms. The clutch was heavy and the gearshift was stiff enough to build biceps. The flightdeck-inspired dash layout also created a reflection problem. But drivers tolerated those things to hear that wonderful burble, gurgle, and roar behind their heads and feel the car's force while looking down its curvaceous nose. On a winding road, the Lamborghini Miura was driving heaven. **LT**

400GT | Lamborghini

(I)

1966 • 239 cu in/3,929 cc, V12 • 320 bhp/239 kW • 0–60 mph/97 kph in 7.5 seconds • 156 mph/251 kph

While Ferruccio Lamborghini's first production car, the 350GT, had not been a huge sales success, it had been a technological triumph. History did not stop there. In early 1966 the 350GT was being fitted with a 239-cubic-inch (3,929-cc) version of its quad-cam V12; veteran test driver Valentino Balboni later said that this was Lamborghini's best-sounding engine of all time. Known as the 400GT Interim, the car had the same elegant body shape as the 350GT, but it remained compromised as a practical GT car by its lack of rear seats.

At the 1966 Geneva Auto Show, Lamborghini unveiled the 400GT 2+2, which now featured an enlarged steel body and a lengthened wheelbase to accommodate comfortable rear seats. At first glance it was hard to tell it apart from its predecessor; the main clue was the double-oval headlights used to comply with new U.S. safety legislation. Mechanically, an improvement had been made to the 400GT's transmission by adding Porsche-style synchromesh to the new Lamborghini-built five-speed gearbox.

British motoring journalists from *Autocar* magazine were very impressed, exclaiming that the 400GT was "better than all the equivalent exotic and home-bred machinery in this glamorous corner of the fast-car market." During testing in the United States, *Road & Track* magazine hit 150 mph (241 kph), the fastest speed any member of its team had then ever clocked.

Eventually, 247 400GT 2+2s were built. Famous owners include Sir Paul McCartney, who imported his orange Lamborghini in 1967, while The Beatles were at the height of their fame. In 2011 this car sold at auction for $197,000 (£122,500). **DS**

The new "Coke-bottle look" of the 1966 Pontiac GTO helped sales of the GTO to more than triple.

Sonett II | Saab

(S)

1966 • 91 cu in/1,500 cc, V4 • 65 bhp/48 kW • 0–60 mph/97 kph in 12.5 seconds • 100 mph/160 kph

In the 1950s, Saab ideas man Rolf Mellde was given a tiny budget and told to create a two-seater sports car in secret. Saab hoped to lift the image of the whole brand by creating an exciting race-winning car.

In his remote barn, Mellde came up with the fiberglass prototype and the name, which resulted from him exclaiming in Swedish, "That's so neat!" The first Sonett (or Saab 94) had a small, two-stroke, three-cylinder engine. The little front-wheel drive roadster could reach 100 mph (160 kph), but after it ran into problems with race regulations only six were made.

It was ten years before the pretty Sonett II appeared in 1966. The front-drive coupe's little two-stroke engine had been upgraded to a 91-cubic-inch (1,500-cc) Ford V4 with a corresponding bulge in the hood (bonnet) to accommodate the bigger unit. The car now had advanced safety features, such as a roll bar, high-backed bucket seats, and three-point seat belts. The entire front section of bodywork hinged forward to allow access to the engine, suspension, and gearbox.

The Sonett II was acclaimed for its front-wheel-drive handling and its track performance. But only 1,868 of this generation were made, almost all of them exported to the United States. Buyers were deterred by the quality of the four-speed column gearshift and a strange freewheeling system that disengaged the clutch when drivers took their foot off the accelerator.

In the 1970s a more conventional and Italian-inspired Sonett III took over. The engine was enlarged to 103 cubic inches (1,700 cc), but the car was slower and less appealing than before, and production ended in 1974. **SH**

GTO | Pontiac

(USA)

1966 • 389 cu in/6,375 cc, V8 • 335 bhp /247 kW • 0–60 mph/97 kph in 7.9 seconds • 120 mph/193 kph

When it launched in 1964, the GTO had surprised even Pontiac with the level of its sales, with more than 32,000 units leaving the showroom. The company was not content to rest on its laurels, however, and in 1966 the GTO had a big makeover that increased sales to 96,946 cars. This was not only the GTO's highest annual sales figure, it was the most any muscle car had ever sold in one year. From 1966 the GTO would be available as a model in its own right, without Pontaic having to sell it as an optional upgrade to get around rules set by General Motors on engine sizes.

Part of the design change involved giving the revamped model what has become known as the "Coke-bottle look," a style that involved the car having (or giving the visual impression of) a body with a narrow center along with emphasized tail fins that suggested a flashy, more youthful style.

Youth in the United States had already had some fun with the GTO, whose initials came from the Italian phrase "Gran Turismo Omologato." The kids, however, had started calling it the "Goat," a nickname that, although quite affectionate, did not go down well with the besuited businessmen of General Motors. They preferred to focus on the new-look 1966 GTO, which was slightly longer and wider than its predecessor, had new bucket seats with adjustable headrests, a stylish and graceful new roofline, real wood fitted in the interior, unique fluted taillights, and a grille with a plastic mesh insert, which had never been seen before. Further changes would come in for the 1967 GTO, whose famous owners have included Vin Diesel and Snoop Dogg. **MG**

GTO
CALIFORNIA
MHS 619
BALESTRA
XP 2000

Toronado | Oldsmobile

(USA)

1966 • 425 cu in/6,965 cc, V8 • 385 bhp/287 kW • 0–60 mph • (97 kph) in 7.5 seconds • 135 mph/216 kph

Evoking images of powerful natural forces, the name "Toronado" was meaningless and originally created for a 1963 show car. The two-door production model was a mechanical sibling of the Buick Riviera and Cadillac Eldorado for most of its life. Going head to head with the Ford Thunderbird in dealerships, the luxuriously appointed Toro was also historically significant for being front-wheel drive. It sounds bizarre now, but such technology was a genuine rarity at the time. The last volume model to opt for such a setup was a Cord, launched a full three decades earlier.

Oldsmobile engineers famously spent more than seven years developing the Toronado, driving hundreds of thousands of test miles to reassure the public of front-wheel drive's durability. Their efforts were not in vain; the Toro handled surprisingly well and was critically well received. It was voted Car of the Year in 1966 by influential consumer magazine *Motor Trend*.

The Mark II version of this luxury coupe, available from 1971 to 1978, was notable for its pioneering use of safety technology. It debuted high-level rear brake lights and, from 1974, the front airbag, based around a custom-made steering wheel. Parent company General Motors named the airbag the Air Cushion Restraint System and installed it on the passenger side, too.

After selling for more than twenty-five years over four generations, the last Toronado rolled off the assembly line on May 28, 1992. In subsequent years, differentiating between General Motors' brands became increasingly difficult. Finally, in 2004, the parent company made the cost-cutting decision to sacrifice the Oldsmobile brand completely. **RY**

Charger | Dodge

(USA)

1966 • 317 cu in/5,210 cc, V8 • 230 bhp /171.5 kW • 0–60 mph/97 kph in 9 seconds • 117 mph/187 kph

The first generation Dodge Charger was a mid-sized muscle coupe that made its public debut during a commercial break in coverage of the Rose Bowl college football game on January 1 1966. It was billed as the "new leader of the Dodge rebellion."

Later that year, Dodge went NASCAR racing with the Charger. During testing it had acted like an airplane wing with the back end going light, so a trunk (boot) spoiler was fitted to add downforce. NASCAR rules stated that the production version must have it, too, so the Charger became the first U.S. road car to feature one. NASCAR driver David Pearson took the Grand National Championship in 1966 with fourteen wins.

The road-going version introduced other features, too. It had one of the first fastback rooflines and a new grille style that looked like an electric razor to bemused customers in the mid 1960s. Soon it seemed normal though, and was widely copied.

Part of this innovative front-end design was that the headlamps rotated sideways through 180 degrees. When they were hidden away they were replaced by a section of grille that made it seem as if there were no headlamps at all. There were soon sportier versions—including a 427-cubic-inch (7,000-cc) V8 hemi-powered monster.

The most famous Charger is a 1969 model—the General Lee that featured in almost every episode of 1980s U.S. TV drama *The Dukes of Hazzard*. But the car had another other brush with stardom. In the 1968 Steve McQueen classic *Bullitt*, a first generation Dodge Charger took part in one of the most celebrated and influential chase sequences in movie history. **RY**

◀ Weighing nearly 3 tons, the 1966 Batmobile probably required all the power of its turbine engine just to get moving.

Batmobile | George Barris (USA)

1966 • 389 cu in/6,390 cc, V8 • 500 bhp/373 kW • unknown • unknown

Whack! Crack! Kappow! For anyone growing up in the 1960s or 1970s, the TV series of *Batman*, starring Adam West, was their first introduction to the caped crusader. In more recent movies, the Batmobile became more akin to a fearsome military vehicle, but the version that rolled onto TV screens every Saturday morning was more like some crazy 1950s concept car—which is exactly how it started out.

Back in 1955, the design team at Lincoln—part of Ford—came up with a space-age design called the Futura. The concept car was built by hand at the Ghia workshops in Turin and cost the equivalent of $2 million (£1.3 million). Its distinctive fins and angular body shape were inspired by the mako shark and manta ray. But the car never went into production and the prototype was eventually sold to custom-car designer George Barris for just one dollar.

Barris supplied cars to Hollywood, and in 1965 he was asked to build a Batmobile at short notice—less than three weeks. He decided to use the Futura. Amazingly, the finished Batmobile actually contained many of the features seen on TV, including the gas turbine at the back, although this could only run for fifteen seconds at a time. The options list also included two parachutes for making emergency 180-degree turns, a cable cutter, smoke screen, and a bat phone.

Under all that steel and fiberglass was a 389-cubic-inch (6,390-cc) V8 that put out around 500 bhp (373 kW). The engine was unreliable (the Futura was ten years old by the time filming started) and was replaced by a Ford V8 and gearbox. The car was never speed-tested, but it needed all that grunt to catch the Joker. **JI**

124 | Fiat (I)

1966 • 96 cu in/1,592 cc, S4 • 94 bhp/70 kW • 0–60 mph/97 kph in 10.3 seconds • 104 mph/168 kph

The Fiat 124 was the successor to the 1300 and 1500 sedans (saloons). Since the Italian carmaker had never produced a model called the 123, sales brochures quipped that "Fiat is one jump ahead with the new Fiat 124." Indeed, the car was revealed in a most theatrical fashion at the back of an airborne cargo plane, before parachuting down to an incredulous press.

While the styling was rather staid, the car's mechanical underpinnings were quite impressive; disc brakes all around, rear coil suspension, and a front anti-roll bar made the lightweight sedan a fun car to drive. In 1967 it became the first Italian car to win the prestigious European Car of the Year Award.

Base models had a perky 73-cubic-inch (1,200-cc) engine capable of 90 mph (145 kph); the Fiat 124 Special T was the most entertaining of all, and had a high-revving twin-cam 97-cubic-inch (1,592-cc) engine (performance figures are given above).

However, it was not without its faults. The small fuel tank and thirsty engine meant range was limited; many people also disliked the car's spartan interior and boxy body shape. But its biggest downfall was rust; poor-quality Russian steel, given in part-payment for Fiat's help in setting up Lada, meant that Fiats of this era gained a terrible reputation for "metal moth."

While production of the Fiat 124 stopped in 1974, the car lived on as the blueprint for the Russian-built Lada. Clones have also been assembled in Turkey, Spain, India, Bulgaria, Korea, and Egypt; total sales are believed to be in excess of 16 million, and qualify the Fiat 124 as the second best-selling model of all time, bested only by Volkswagen's Beetle. **DS**

Interceptor | Jensen

GB

1966 • 382 cu in/6,276 cc, V8 • 284 bhp (212 kW) • 0–60 mph/97 kph in 7.3 seconds • 137 mph/220 kph

The Jensen company was founded by brothers Alan and Richard Jensen in their workshop in Britain's West Midlands. They had previously created an acclaimed one-off car for Amercian actor Clark Gable in 1934.

The Interceptor was a stylish, high-performance sports car that was technically way ahead of its time. It came with four-wheel drive well before Audi created its Quattro. It also featured a retractable steering column, traction control, lift-up glass tailgate, and even deformation zones. One version, the Jensen FF, was equipped with antilock brakes years before Mercedes-Benz claimed to have invented them. But it was also complicated, expensive, and extremely thirsty.

The Interceptor's lines, with the huge, panoramic rear screen, came from Italian designer Vignale, while the hefty 382-cubic-inch (6,276-cc) V8 was sourced from Chrysler. There was also a 439-cubic-inch (7,200-cc) version with 330 bhp (246 kW).

The FF initials of that version stood for "Formula Ferguson," after the farm tractor manufacturer that had designed its four-wheel-drive system. With a wheelbase that was slightly longer than usual, the FF was recognizable by an air intake on the hood (bonnet) and double air outtakes behind the front wheels.

A convertible was later launched in the hope of making a hit in the United States. However, the first oil crisis of 1974 stifled demand and few were sold.

Jensen went bankrupt in 1976 after a total of 7,408 Interceptors were built. Attempts have been made to revamp the model several times. At the time of writing, a Coventry-based company is hoping to launch an all-new Interceptor based on an aluminum chassis. **JB**

Camaro | Chevrolet

(USA)

1966 • 327 cu in/5,359 cc, V8 • 210 bhp/155 kW • unknown • 120 mph/192 kph

The Camaro was Chevrolet's entry in the power-car market, competing with the likes of the Ford Mustang, which launched successfully in 1964. It was that competition with the Mustang, in particular, that led to debate about what the word "Camaro" actually meant. Chevrolet said at the time that it sounded like a friend, which a car should be to its owner. Yet the Camaro was originally to be named the Panther, and there were rumors that some Chevrolet staff were joking that their car was an animal that ate Mustangs. In fact, Chevrolet was looking for a name that started with a "C" and not a "P," and Camaro was a slang word—indeed meaning "friend" or "comrade"—that General Motors researchers found in an old French dictionary.

The car was launched with some pizzazz in 1966, with a press conference held simultaneously in fourteen different cities, all hooked up together by telephone. It was the first time that such an audio conferencing event had ever been attempted. With all the publicity and power under the hood (bonnet), Chevrolet was able to sell the Camaro for the reasonable price of $2,466 (£1,600). One of those original Camaros today would be likely to sell at auction for around $150,000 (£98,000).

The first-generation Camaro went on sale in 1966 (which was the 1967 model year) and lasted through to 1969. There were several configurations available, including the eye-catching SS model with two contrasting thick stripes running over the hood. In 1967 the various Camaros sold over 221,000 between them, a respectable enough figure but still only half the sales of the rival Ford Mustang. **MG**

Susan Sarandon and Geena Davis pose in character with the famous Ford Thunderbird from *Thelma and Louise* (1991). ▷

Spider | Alfa Romeo (I)

1966 • 95 cu in/1,570 cc, S4 • 108 bhp/80 kW • 0–60 mph/97 kph in 9.9 seconds • 114 mph/183 kph

Starring Dustin Hoffman, the seminal 1967 movie *The Graduate* launched the young actor's career into the stratosphere. It also made a star of the little red sports car his character, Ben, drove in it: the Alfa Romeo Spider.

The car was made in Italy by Pininfarina, the design house and coachbuilder. After its first exposure as a prototype at the 1961 Turin Motor Show there was a long wait before production of the car began in late 1965; it went on sale early the following year.

Following a competition inviting Alfa fans to come up with a suitable suggestion, the sports car was originally named Duetto, Italian for "duet," in celebration of its being a two-seater. But when a slightly revamped version was named Spider, a term commonly used for open-top cars, it had a more international ring about it and the original name was eclipsed. In its native Italy the car also had a popular nickname, di Seppia, or "cuttlefish," which referred to the Spider's unusually long-tailed design, resembling the fish's internal shell, commonly found on beaches.

The car was designed with a monocoque construction and incorporated the then relatively new feature of crash-protection crumple zones at the front and rear. The engine was a 95-cubic-inch (1,570-cc) twin-cam, and technical features included disc brakes and independent suspension. The cabin was quite roomy but rather sparse, with bucket seats. The styling of the Spider was the work of Franco Martinengo, then design director at Pininfarina, and he did a remarkable job in creating a car with such an unmistakable silhouette, instantly recognizable among all the other two-seater sports cars across the decades. **SB**

Thunderbird | Ford (USA)

1966 • 427 cu in/7,013 cc, V8 • 345 bhp/257 kW • 0–60 mph/97 kph in 8.4 seconds • 115 mph/185 kph

Lots of cars have a particular claim to fame, but few have been driven off a cliff by a pair of fugitives. At the end of the 1991 movie *Thelma and Louise*, the two central characters choose to end it all rather than face capture, and they do it in just that dramatic fashion—in a 1966 Ford Thunderbird.

This was neither the first Thunderbird (the car was first launched in 1995) nor the last (it briefly resurfaced in retro form in 2001). But 1966 saw the last convertible T'Bird and was the last year in which it was built as a unibody, with the chassis and body shell as one whole.

The fourth-generation Thunderbird bowed out in style: a new front end with a more distinctive grille, better trim, more standard equipment (including rear seat belts), and more power. The base model V8 was boosted to 315 bhp (235 kW), while the all-new 425 V8 produced 345 bhp (257 kW).

The most popular version in 1966 was not actually the convertible, always the favorite previously. Instead it would be the Thunderbird Town Landau, a hardtop with a slightly ungainly extension to the rear roofline. More than 35,000 of these were made in 1966 alone. Purchasers could choose from four different shades of vinyl for the roof covering.

The fifth-generation 1967 model saw a change in direction for the Thunderbird toward a harder-edged design that included muscle-car elements. In fact, from 1967 onward, each new version would move away from the T'Bird's initial concept as a "personal car." So, for many, the 1966 Ford Thunderbird represented an ending that was every bit as tragic as the ending of Hollywood's *Thelma and Louise*. **JI**

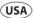

Thunderbird

S800 | Honda

J

1966 • 48 cu in/791 cc, S4 • 70 bhp/52 kW • 0–60 mph/97 kph in 13.4 seconds • 100 mph/160 kph

Every auto manufacturer wants a car to grab people's attention. With Honda it was the S800 roadster, a car that showed the world that the acclaimed motorcycle producer could also make decent four-wheelers.

The S800 was not Honda's first car; the Japanese company had previously produced numerous Kei cars: ultracompact, small-engined cars designed to take advantage of low taxation rules. Its immediate predecessor was the S600, a 306-cubic-inch (606-cc) roadster and coupe. But the S800 raised the bar much higher and helped Honda to become a global brand.

For a start, it was powered by a bigger, 48-cubic-inch (791-cc) aluminum engine fed by four carburetors. It produced 70 bhp (52 kW) at a high-revving 8,000 rpm, running through a four-speed full-synchromesh gearbox. It was Honda's first true 100-mph (160-kph) car and showed how years of extracting every ounce of power from small motorbike engines had paid off for the company.

At launch, the S800 was equipped with chain drive to the rear wheels and independent suspension at the back. The latter was carried over from the earlier S600 and gave good performance and excellent handling, But it was complicated and more expensive to produce than a more conventional driveshaft and live-axle setup. On later models, particularly those built for export, the system was ditched.

In 1967 the S800 became Honda's first car to be sold in the United Kingdom, competing against the likes of the Triumph Spitfire and Mini Cooper at a cheaper price. With the high-revving S800, Honda showed the world what it was capable of. **JI**

GT6 | Triumph

GB

1966 • 121 u in/1,998 cc, S6 • 95 bhp/71 kW • 0–60 mph/97 kph in 10.4 seconds • 106 mph/171 kph

With a stylish fastback body by Giovanni Michelotti, designer of the chic BMW 2002, a silky smooth straight-six engine, and a well-appointed wood and leather cabin, the Triumph GT6 was dubbed the "poor man's E-Type." In fact, its combination of looks and performance was unbeatable in the 1960s, and the price undercut even that of the slower MGB GT.

The GT6 was more luxuriously equipped than its open-topped sister, the Spitfire. It came with an all-synchro gearbox, comfortable bucket seats, and a padded center armrest. The leather-trimmed alloy-spoked steering wheel and two-speed heater were optional at first, but standard later.

On pressing the accelerator, the straight-six engine made a wonderful growl, its wide spread of torque making the car feel faster than it was. It did not seem to care which gear it was in, it just kept on pulling. The handling was lots of fun, too. The tail could be brought out by a stab on the throttle or a tweak of the wheel.

No wonder so many enthusiastic owners chose the GT6 for historic track events on both sides of the pond. The GT6 itself was not a works hero, though. Spitfires were raced with fiberglass fastback bodies instead, taking some silver awards at Le Mans.

At launch, the separate chassis seemed crude and old-fashioned, but today it makes life easier for restorers. No surprise for a British car, rust is a major problem, and both the chassis and body need to be inspected with a magnifying glass and a magnet. At least parts are plentiful. And owners of a GT6 can hope to get as many admiring glances as they would driving a Jaguar E-Type costing twice as much. **LT**

Dino Spider | Fiat

I

1966 • 121 cu in/1,987 cc, V6 • 160 bhp/119 kW • 0–60 mph/97 kph in 8.1 seconds • 127 mph/204 kph

The Fiat Dino Spider marks an interesting chapter in the history of Italian car manufacturing; it was the car that finally formalized the partnership between Enzo Ferrari and the larger, Turin-based carmaker.

Ferrari always knew that if he wished to continue in motorsport at the highest level he would need to increase sales of his roadgoing cars to fund it. He also needed to nurture new talent for Scuderia Ferrari by encouraging young drivers to race in Formula 2. Supported by his son Alfredo (nicknamed "Dino"), Ferrari's engineers had begun developing a 91-cubic-inch (1,500-cc) quad-cam V6 for use in the 1956 F2 season. Unfortunately, Dino died of muscular dystrophy in June 1956, and never saw the project come to fruition.

New regulations for the 1966 F2 season required a minimum of 500 engines to be built; at the time, this was twice Ferrari's yearly output. The cunning solution was to team up with Fiat and produce 500 pretty 2+2 convertibles powered by a reworked version of Dino's racing V6. Fiat was happy to be linked with such a prestigious partner, so much so that, in 1969, it bought a 50 percent stake in the Ferrari company.

The beautiful, flowing lines of the Dino Spider are the work of Pininfarina; hunched arches and frowning quad-headlights give the car a purposeful look. Early cars received the Fiat-built 122-cubic-inch (1,987-cc) quad-cam V6, which later found its way into Ferrari's first midengined sports car, the Dino 206. While a good Dino Spider today costs around $25,000 (£16,000), it would be a mistake to think of it as the "poor man's Ferrari." New, it cost about the same as a Mercedes 280SL, and at the time it had running costs similar to Ferrari's Dino. **DS**

Midget Mark III | MG

GB

1966 • 77 cu in/1,275 cc, S4 • 65 bhp/47 kW • 0–60 mph/97 kph in 14.6 seconds • 96 mph/154 kph

The quirky little Austin-Healey "Frog-eye" Sprite, launched in 1958, had proven the perfect formula to bring fun, affordable motoring to the masses—and it sold well in the lucrative American markets. In 1961 the diminutive convertible was restyled and badged as both the Austin-Healey Sprite and the MG Midget. In Britain the newly nicknamed "Spridgets" sold for just £680 ($1,070), including taxes; they were marketed as the sports car a "chap could maintain in his bike shed."

Over the next few years, the design was gradually tweaked: engine capacity grew to 77 cubic inches (1,275 cc) in 1966 when Spridgets received a detuned A-series powerplant from the lauded Mini Cooper S. However, aftermarket tuning parts were readily available by this time, and the little two-seaters became a popular sight in grassroots motorsport thanks to their lightweight construction and nimble handling. It is the 1966 Mark III Midget/Mark IV Sprite that is most highly prized.

Being narrower than the Mini, and measuring only 12.5 feet (3.5 m) in length, the MG Midget Mark III looks miniscule in modern-day traffic and remains a sports car that raises a smile for its looks rather its performance. But by 1975 the car's design was getting a little long in the tooth. With no company alternative on offer, the Midget struggled on with a modified ride height, and ugly plastic bumpers, installed to meet strict new U.S. crash-test legislation. To add insult to injury, the venerable old A-series engine was replaced with a less reliable 91-cubic-inch (1,500-cc) lump lifted from its archrival, the Triumph Spitfire. Still, when production ceased in 1979, it was estimated that more than 350,000 Spridgets had been sold. **SH**

Volvo created this stack of 144s for a 1971 campaign to demonstrate the strength of each hardtop. ⊡

Prince Royal | Nissan (J)

1966 • 390 cu in/6,400 cc, V8 • 256 bhp/191 kW • unknown • unknown

The Emperor of Japan in the 1960s was lucky enough to have a enormous luxury limousine specially built by his own countrymen for him. The Nissan Prince Royal was a huge, 20-foot (6.1-m) sedan (saloon) weighing 7,054 pounds (3,800 kg). It needed all of its massive 390-cubic-inch (6,400-cc) engine just to pull it around. The engine was machined from a solid block of steel. Even the tires had to be custom-made.

The transmission had to come from the United States. Japanese engineers did not yet have a gear system capable of handling the Prince Royal's huge torque, so they used a three-speed, column-mounted GM Turbo-Hydramatic unit often used in Cadillacs.

The stately Nissan had four large doors and three rows of seats with room for eight passengers. The security staff who often traveled with the emperor had leather seats; the emperor's was distinguished by a pure woolen fabric covering. The rear windows had curtains and double glazing, and the emperor had his own telephone to communicate to the driver.

The Prince Royal was the first Japanese-built official emperor's car. It had a long life in service, from 1967 to 2008, when a specially prepared bulletproof Toyota Century Royal replaced it. Before the Japanese motor industry was established, the emperor was obliged to travel in a succession of Rolls-Royce, Cadillac, and Mercedes-Benz limousines.

The Prince Royal demonstrated that the Japanese motor industry could now compete with the world's finest carmakers. And the technology used in its construction was not wasted; it was used to help develop the Nissan President luxury car series. **SH**

144 | Volvo (S)

1966 • 108 cu in/1,778 cc, S4 • 115 bhp/86 kW • 0–60 mph/97 kph in 14.1 seconds • 92 mph/148 kph

The mid-1960s saw the launch of Volvo's biggest business venture to date. Bravely, it replaced the curvy quasi-Americana of the Volvo Amazon with something completely different: a sluggish, wallowing, boxy-looking car whose main claim to fame was safety. Other manufacturers must have tittered behind their hands, yet Volvo had the last laugh because the pioneering 140 Series transformed the car market.

The Volvo 144 was an elegant four-door sedan (saloon) with a big luggage compartment. A two-door and the cavernous 145 station wagon (estate) were soon to follow. Spacious, sensible, and simple, the big Volvo's shape did not date like that of most contemporary rivals. In fact, more than a million 140 Series cars were sold around the world in an eight-year production run, and the basic design was retained throughout the 240 Series until the mid-1990s.

Buyers cared little that performance and handling were average for the time. All the 140 Series cars bristled with new safety ideas: energy-absorbing zones at the front and rear, a safety cage for the occupants, pioneering dual-circuit brakes, and three-point safety belts for driver and passenger. For the first time, the car's interior was designed with safety padding, and without the dangerous edges and protrusions that characterized many cars. There were disc brakes all around with a primitive new antilocking system. The center of the collapsible steering wheel was deeply recessed and drivers found they had good visibility in all directions. After this, manufacturers all over the world began to realize that safety and practicality could sell cars just as quickly as high performance. **SH**

Corolla | Toyota (J)

1966 • 65 cu in/1,068 cc, S4 • 59 bhp/44 kW • unknown • unknown

Toyota's Corolla is the world's top-selling model, beating the Model T Ford and the Volkswagen Beetle. In 2008 *Time* magazine described it as one of the most influential cars of all time, also saying that it was "as boring as hell."

The Corolla proves that a car does not have to have be superpowerful and superexciting to be popular. What millions of drivers the world over really want is a way to move themselves and their family in comfort.

The Corolla was launched in 1966 through Toyota's direct sales network, a system of dealers dedicated to selling particular models. Rather than stay under 61 cubic inches (1,000 cc) and benefit from tax exemptions, Toyota installed a new, larger motor. It also put in a four-speed gearbox at a time when many people thought this was a sign of an underpowered engine. The front suspension copied British and European designs in having McPherson struts and a leaf spring across the width of the car, under the engine. More conventional solid axle and leaf springs were used at the back.

Such decisions paid off and the Corolla was established as a competent family car. Across eight generations it has been sold (and built) around the globe. The success of the automobile in general in giving people freedom through personal transport is mirrored by the global success of the Corolla. **JI**

Cortina Mark II | Ford (GB)

1966 • 79 cu in/1,298 cc, S4 • 62 bhp/46 kW • 0–60 mph/97 kph in 18 seconds • 82 mph/132 kph

Four years after the original Ford Cortina debuted, it was succeeeded by the plumper and more voluptuous Mark II, styled by Roy Haynes. It was intended to have more interior space and improved ride comfort, and it did.

The slogan that accompanied the launch of the Mark II was "New Cortina More Cortina," so it was ironic that the car was actually slightly shorter in length, at precisely 14 feet long (4.27 m). The track between the wheels was wider, and so was the body. Curved side panels allowed an extra 2.5 inches (6 cm) in the cabin.

Important improvements included a smaller turning circle, softer suspension, and self-adjusting brakes and clutch. A new 79-cubic-inch (1,300-cc) engine was added to the range. This certainly helped to boost sales, for in the year following its launch the Cortina Mark II became the best-selling car in Britain.

Between 1966 and 1970, when its successor arrived, the Mark II racked up more than a million sales. Engines ranged from a 73-cubic-inch (1,200-cc) "Kent" to a 183-cubic-inch (3,000-cc) V6 "Essex," and body styles were two- and four-door sedans (saloons) and a five-door station wagon (estate), with four trim levels: base, Deluxe, Super, and GT. From 1967 a 1600E version, with tuned engine, lowered suspension, and walnut interior, joined the line. **SB**

Europa | Lotus (GB)

1966 • 95 cu in/1,558 cc, S4 • 126 bhp/94 kW • 0–60 mph/97 kph in 6.6 seconds • 127 mph/204 kph

In 1958, Ron Hickman was tasked by Lotus to design a Ford-powered GT car capable of beating Ferrari at Le Mans; he also sketched out plans for a lightweight midengined racer. Lotus didn't win the contract, but Lotus boss Colin Chapman liked Hickman's designs and decided that Lotus itself should build a scaled-down roadgoing version; this became the Europa.

The Europa was Britain's first midengined sports car. It was also the last Lotus model to be offered in kit form. The high buttresses surrounding the rear engine compartment had the car called "the bread van," but they helped reduce the car's drag coefficient to just 0.29, an incredible figure for its day. The fixed seats, poor visibility, and nonopening windows were also criticized.

The first Europas were powered by a mildly tuned 95-cubic-inch (1,558-cc) four-cylinder lifted from the Renault 16. With only 78 bhp (58 kW) on tap, straight-line performance was rather modest. However, the well- balanced chassis and low center of gravity more than made up for this along twisty sections of road.

It was not until the bigger Lotus-Ford twin-cam engine was shoehorned into the Europa Special that the car got the horsepower it deserved. These limited-edition Specials commemorated Team Lotus's wins in the 1972 and 1973 F1 World Championships. **DS**

GT | Unipower (GB)

1966 • 77 cu in/1,275 cc, S4 • 67 bhp/50 kW • 0–60 mph/97 kph in 8 seconds • 118 mph/190 kph

This quirky sports car used parts of contemporary British cars mounted on a space frame chassis, including a Mini engine and gearbox. It had independent suspension, with a low weight and low center of gravity, and was just over 40 inches (102 cm) high.

The GT was created by engineer and race-team manager Ernie Unger and designer Val Dare-Bryan. After finishing their prototype in 1965, they ran out of money. A backer was found in Universal Power Drives, a company that made forklift trucks and winches. The name was changed to Unipower GT and the car was launched in 1966. A 60-cubic-inch (998-cc) Cooper-powered version cost £950 ($1,472); the 77-cubic-inch (1,275-cc) Cooper S-engined GT was £1,150 ($1,782).

Technical difficulties slowed delivery, and by late 1968 just sixty had been built. Universal Power Drives lost interest, but money was forthcoming from racing driver Piers Weld-Forester, who presented the Unipower GT Mark 2 in 1969. Weld-Forester entered three works cars for the Targa Florio, Le Mans, and Nürburgring 1,000 kilometers. At Le Mans he reportedly reached 140 mph (225 kph) in practice, but the engine blew shortly into the race. When production of streetcars proved to be difficult once again, Weld-Forester, too, gave up. Only seventy-five of the little GT had been made. **JB**

◁ The Fiat 124 Sport Spider had rally successes in the early 1970s, but was also nifty for noncompetitive driving.

124 Sport Spider | Fiat (I)

1966 • 107 cu in/1,756 cc, S4 • 128 bhp/95 kW • 0–60 mph/97 kph in 8.2 seconds • 118 mph/190 kph

While the staid three-box design of the Fiat 124 sedan (saloon) had not set the world of automotive styling alight, it had been technologically advanced for its time; featuring disc brakes at every corner, modern coil suspension, and perky engines, it had set a new benchmark for low-priced, mass-produced family cars. Fiat utilized this platform to produce the 125 sedan, 124 Coupe, and, prettiest of all, the 124 Sport Spider.

The elegantly styled 2+2 convertible sports car, designed and built by Pininfarina, was well received when unveiled at the 1966 Turin Auto Show. It took another two years for the Spider to arrive in North America, where it was an instant hit; of the 200,000 built, nearly 75 percent were sent across the Atlantic.

In 1971 Fiat acquired Italian tuning specialist Abarth and pooled resources to launch Fiat's first factory-sponsored rally team. A Spider-based works car, the Abarth 124 Rally, was launched in 1972, followed by 400 roadgoing Stradale versions (data given above), required to qualify the car for competition. Powered by a tuned 107-cubic-inch (1,756-cc) engine, the purposeful-looking Abarth Rally had Recaro seats and a rear roll-bar; its fiberglass hardtop, hood (bonnet), and trunk (boot) were painted matte black. Although the car performed well, it was completely outclassed when the Lancia Stratos appeared on the rally scene in 1975.

During its nineteen-year production, various twin-cam engines were installed, ranging from the initial 85-cubic-inch (1,400-cc) to the final 122-cubic-inch (2,00-cc), which was rebadged as the Fiat 2000 Spider. Fiat 124 Sport Spiders in good condition cost around $8,500 (£5,500) today. **DS**

375S | Monteverdi (CH)

1967 • 439 cu in/7,210 cc, V8 • 375 bhp/280 kW • 0–60 mph/97 kph in 6.3 seconds • 161 mph/259 kph

Peter Monteverdi built his first car when he was seventeen years old. In 1961, when he was twenty-seven, he built the first Swiss Formula 1 car, and established his own racing team. He himself drove, but retired after crashing one of his Monteverdi Binningen Motors cars. He then built up a very successful Swiss car distributorship, importing prestigious brands such as Ferrari, Bentley, Lancia, BMW, and Rolls-Royce. In 1967 he founded a new carmaker, Monteverdi, to produce high-performance luxury cars for both racetrack and road. The new company's first car was the 375S.

Monteverdi chose a Chrysler V8 engine to give the car the power he wanted, and with a volume of 439 cubic inches (7,210 cc) it could certainly deliver that. For the bodywork, Monteverdi turned to the Italians, over the border from his base near Basel. He commissioned one of the best Italian designers, Pietro Frua, to produce the ultrasmooth bodywork. From 1969 onward Monteverdi had the cars built in Italy, too, by the coachbuilder Fissore, which had also built Porsches.

The two-seater 375S was launched at the Frankfurt Motor Show in 1967 and was very favorably received. It was a beautiful car that managed to be both stately and sporty, with its potent engine housed in a very classy body. It had power steering and power brakes, and also a built-in radio, which was a feature restricted to luxury cars in those days. The car looked terrific, but sadly did not sell well enough to warrant its continuation, and it was retired from the company's list in 1970, although Monteverdi did introduce redesigned versions in 1972 and again in 1975. His factory in Basel finally closed in 1984. **MG**

Dino | Fiat

I

1967 • 146 cu in/2,398 cc, V6 • 180 bhp/134 kW • 0–60 mph/97 kph in 8.1 seconds • 130 mph/209 kph

For men of a certain age the Fiat Dino Coupe is perhaps most famously known for its cameo appearance in the 1969 movie *The Italian Job*. While the film's producers politely turned down Fiat's offer to use its little sedans (saloons) as the heroes' getaway cars, they were only too happy to cast three black Fiat Dino Coupes as the executive transport of the sharp-suited Mafiosi.

Launched at the Geneva Auto Show in 1967, a year after the Fiat Dino Spider, it was only available on special order. While Pininfarina had built the roadster, this time the bodywork was outsourced to Bertone. This led to a number of stylistic differences between the two versions, but most critics agree that the cleaner lines of the coupe make it the prettier car. It was also more practical; its longer wheelbase allowed comfortable seating for four, rather than the Spider's cramped 2+2.

From 1969 both cars got the 146-cubic-inch (2,400-cc) version of Ferrari's quad-cam V6, a development of the Formula Two race car engine credited to Alfredo "Dino" Ferrari. The same powerplant, in a higher state of tune, was transversely mid-mounted in the Dino 246. Throughout its production, reviews in the motoring press were positive. Many noted that while the coupe was primarily a comfortable luxury grand tourer, it was capable of pinning its occupants back in their seats, as keen drivers raced through its five-speed gearbox. A few journalists criticized its noisy engine, but most thought its Ferrari-like whine was one of its best features.

Today, the few remaining Fiat Dino Coupes that have not rusted away are becoming very collectible. The best preserved examples now start at $25,000 (£16,000) and prices are rising. **DS**

Ro80 | NSU

(D)

1967 • 60 cu in/990 cc • 115 bhp/85 kW • 0–60 mph/97 kph in 13 seconds • 113 mph/182 kph

With its twin-rotor Wankel rotary engine, vacuum-powered semi-automatic gearbox, front-wheel drive, and sophisticated independent suspension, the Ro80 was one of the few cars that was genuinely decades ahead of the rest.

The ultra-advanced German executive sedan (saloon) arrived into a Europe of Morris Minors and Ford Cortinas like a spaceship from Mars. Inexperienced carmaker NSU had bravely created a car packed with technology that leapfrogged all the established rivals. Compared with its contemporaries, the Ro80's slick aerodynamic shape still looks vaguely modern today.

Innovation was everywhere: the gearshift featured synchromesh and a unique automatic clutch—as the lever was shifted, it disengaged the clutch using a vacuum system, saving the need for a left-foot pedal. Meanwhile, the unfamiliar rotary engine was extremely smooth, powerful, and quiet—many said it got quieter the faster it went. The four-door cabin was spacious and light, with large areas of glass and delicate pillars that were also unusual for the time. Under the skin, the car had impressive dual-circuit servo disc brakes, power-assisted rack-and-pinion steering, and handling to put many sports cars to shame.

It was voted European Car of the Year in 1968, but sales were hampered by a high price tag and heavy thirst for fuel. The engine rotors initially proved fragile and the car grew a reputation for unreliability. The Ro80 was axed in 1977 having only sold 37,000 cars. Its poor sales forced NSU into the arms of Audi. But at least some of Ro80 lived on—as the inspiration behind the design of the first Audi 100 in 1982. **SH**

Firebird Trans Am | Pontiac

USA

1967 • 400 cu in/6,561 cc, V8 • 366 bhp/273kW • 0–60 mph/97 kph in 6.5 seconds • 200 mph/325 kph

Launched in 1967—the same year as the Chevrolet Camaro and constructed on the same platform—the Firebird Trans Am was Pontiac's two-door coupe aimed at the pony car market.

Named after and inspired by the Ford Mustang of 1964, new models competing for the custom of predominantly young male drivers needed sports car styling and performance, yet also needed to be compact and affordable. The name "Trans Am" originated from a package of optional extras, which upgraded various mechanical components under the skin. It also meant a boost in power and some exterior design details—such as a rear spoiler—to set the car apart from the crowd.

The collection of extras was officially known as the "Trans Am Performance and Appearance Package," and was named after the Trans Am Series of sports car races that started in 1966. It added $725 to the list price, and

as it was a trademark licensed to the Sports Car Club of America (SCCA), the organization threatened to sue. Pontiac's parent company, General Motors, stepped in and agreed to pay the SCCA a fee of $5 per car sold. The car eventually competed in the Trans Am Series, although initially it could not because the 402-cubic-inch (6,600-cc) engine breached regulations.

The Trans Am kit was first available on the Mark I Firebird and at the beginning proved unpopular because of higher insurance premiums. The second generation, available from 1970 to 1980, was more of a hit, particularly when the famous phoenix decal for the hood (bonnet) was launched. The car also made an appearance in the 1977 movie *Smokey and the Bandit* and its sequel. A modified version of the Mark III car starred as KITT in the 1980s television series *Knight Rider*. The final version lasted until Pontiac eventually killed off the Firebird name in 2002. **RY**

2000GT | Toyota

(J)

1967 • 121 cu in/1,988 cc, S6 • 150 bhp/110 kW • 0–60 mph/97 kph in 8.4 seconds • 135 mph/217 kph

Today Japanese carmakers are renowned for producing some incredible performance machines—from high-tech supercars to rally replicas and stunning roadsters. Things were not always like this. In the late 1960s the Japanese had a reputation for making down-to-earth, reliable cars, but performance machinery was the realm of the Europeans. Toyota set out to change this when they designed the 2000GT. They wanted to prove they could make a sports car as good as anything from the British, Italians, or French. And they did.

The car was actually a collaboration with Yamaha, who at the time were assisting a number of car firms, notably Datsun/Nissan. The basic design was pretty straightforward: a front-engined, rear-wheel-drive, two-seater coupe. But the Toyota's alloy bodywork was something special, with flowing lines and pop-up headlights. There were also driving lights tucked under the nose that gave the GT a distinctive appearance.

The car was heavily influenced by the Jaguar E-Type, but its engineers also studied the Lotus Elan and mimicked its layout of a lightweight body on a separate chassis. The engine began life as a standard Toyota six-cylinder, but Yamaha breathed their magic on it, in the form of an aluminum cylinder head, dual overhead cams, and triple carburetors. The result was a car that changed Europe's opinion of the Japanese and of Toyota in particular. Road testers dubbed it "Japan's first supercar."

A special roadster version appeared in the 1967 James Bond movie *You Only Live Twice,* which was set in Japan. It is alleged they took the roof off because Sean Connery was too tall to fit comfortably in the coupe. **JI**

33 Stradale | Alfa Romeo

(I)

1967 • 121 cu in/1,995 cc, V8 • 230 bhp/169 kW • 0–60 mph/97 kph in 5.5 seconds • 177 mph/278 kph

Only eighteen of these were ever made, making the roadster version even rarer than the Alfa Romeo Tipo 33 racing car on which it was based. Not that drivers of the Stradale (Italian for "road-going") were being exactly shortchanged, with an engine that could race to 60 mph (97 kph) in less than six seconds. That engine was only slightly detuned from the racetrack version, and the Stradale was given a longer wheelbase for more control on the public roads, but otherwise the few who could afford it were effectively getting a racing car capable of 174 mph (278 kph).

The Stradale was also a superb-looking car, the first production car in the world to feature "butterfly" doors, opening outward and upward on either side of the body. The bodywork was designed by Franco Scaglione, an experienced and talented designer who worked on numerous classy cars in his lifetime, including work for Ferrari, Porsche, Maserati, and Jaguar as well as many for Alfa Romeo. The Stradale was one of his finest creations, described by many as being one of the most beautiful cars ever built.

Naturally, as well as being fast and sexy, it was expensive. The asking price when it came on the market was roughly $17,000 (£10,700), making it the world's most expensive car on public sale at the time. You would, of course, have paid rather more for the racing version. In 1969 the model was discontinued, a victim of its own exclusivity. Each of the eighteen that were made was hand-built, and no two were the same. No wonder it featured at number fifteen on the list of the 100 Sexiest Cars compiled by the BBC-TV program *Top Gear* in the United Kingdom. **MG**

The Rover P5 Coupe appealed to a complete cross section of British society—from policemen to the Queen. ⊃

1750 GTV | Alfa Romeo (I)

1967 • 108 cu in/1,779 cc, S4 • 120 bhp/90 kW • 0–60 mph/97 kph in 9.3 seconds • 118 mph/190 kph

They were launched as a trio. The Spider convertible model got the most glory—starring in the 1967 movie *The Graduate* and becoming an icon of the 1960s. The boxier Berlina sedan (saloon) was chosen as the Italian highway police patrol car and appeared in 1969 chasing Mini Coopers in *The Italian Job*. Yet it was the lesser-known GTV coupe that offered the best drive of the three and became an all-time classic.

In fact, the 1750 GTV was one in a series of small, two-door sports cars made by Alfa from 1963 to 1977. They were all officially called the Guilia Sprint but have since become known as Bertone coupes after the Italian styling house that designed their elegant lines. The designer was the celebrated Giorgetto Giugiaro, whose portfolio includes the first VW Golf, Audi 80, and the DeLorean. His drawings for the little Alfa coupes made several design breakthroughs and the use of glass, shape of cabin, and the nature of the front grille proved to be influential for future designers.

If the design of the coupe was beautiful, the engine was even better. It had a lightweight, all-alloy, twin-overhead cam unit that ranged from 78 cubic inches (1,290 cc) to 119 cubic inches (1,962 cc). The 1750 seemed to have the best balance of weight, performance, and economy. They were all four-cylinder, eight-valve units with twin carburetors, except in the United States where regulations enforced the fitting of fuel injection. All the engines were livelier than the figures show and sounded superb. Many drivers of the era found that on a long journey on empty roads, in the days before speed cameras, the GTV lived up to its title of "Gran Turismo Veloces"—or fast grand tourer. **SH**

P5 Coupe | Rover (GB)

1967 • 215 cu in/3,528 cc, V8 • 160 bhp/119 kW • 0–60 mph/97 kph in 12 seconds • 115 mph/185 kph

Having a celebrity endorse your car is something most manufacturers dream of, so Rover must have been delighted when Queen Elizabeth II decided she rather liked the P5. For years it was also the favored transport of British prime ministers, from Harold Wilson through to Margaret Thatcher. It had a certain regal, understated style. It was labeled "the poor man's Rolls-Royce" (ironic considering the Queen bought one), but in a way it was less brash than a Roller. The car was driven not just by royalty and politicians but by business executives, bank managers, and even policemen.

The Mark I version appeared in 1958 as a sedan (saloon) only, badged as the Rover 3 Liter and powered by a straight-six engine. The coupe version, with a lowered roofline, rolled into showrooms in the fall of 1962, with the arrival of the Mark II.

It was not until 1967 that the V8 version appeared—the car that was known simply as the "three and a half liter" and that was so loved by the nation's leaders. Officially this was the P5B, with the "B" standing for Buick. Rather than go down the lengthy and expensive route of designing their own V8, Rover opted to buy in an aluminum engine that Buick had been developing. This put out considerably more power—with less weight—than the six-cylinder and it gave the 5B a character all of its own. The styling was similar to previous versions, but with the addition of fog lights under the headlights, which give the 5B a distinctive profile.

It may have been a symbol of authority but with that V8 burbling away under the hood (bonnet), the P5B carried a knuckleduster in its ministerial briefcase. **JI**

ROVER

3-Liter | Austin (GB)

1967 • 177 cu in/2,912 cc, S6 • 124 bhp/92 kW • 0–60 mph/97 kph in 15.7 seconds • 100 mph/161 kph

The Austin 3-Liter went down in automotive history as one of the British Motor Corporation's biggest sales disasters. Starting as a joint venture project with Rolls-Royce, the Austin 3-Liter was intended to share its platform with the entry-level Bentley Java. But, fearing that the association with the Austin badge might damage its reputation, Rolls-Royce pulled out.

BMC's accountants pressed for cost-cutting designs; the decision was made to reuse the cabin area from the smaller Austin 1800, and graft on a bigger trunk (boot) and a longer front end to house its powerplant. It became derisively known as the "Land Lobster." Its Frankenstein's Monster looks at least gave it a cult following in later years and it did have luxurious comfort levels thanks to Rolls-Royce's early input. Polished wood adorned its interior, and its advanced self-leveling hydrolastic suspension meant the 3-Liter could waft over poorer quality roads with ease. Its C-series engine, borrowed from the MGC sports car, was smooth and powerful, but its heavy weight did not help handling.

Sales of Austin's Land Lobster were dismal. It was costly to run and could not compete with continental or home-grown competition. In the end, just 9,992 cars were made during its short production run. **DS**

Cougar | Mercury (USA)

1967 • 289 cu in/4,736 cc, V8 • 200 bhp/147 kW • 0–60 mph/97 kph in 8.1 seconds • 110 mph/177 kph

Ford had enormous success with their Mustang, which appeared in 1964, and naturally they wanted their subdivisions, such as Mercury, to emulate that without stealing any of the Mustang's thunder. The Cougar that came along in 1967 was based on the redesigned 1967 Mustang, but was different enough to have its own identity. Indeed, it was individual enough for *Motor Trend* magazine to make it Car of the Year in 1967. Rather less impressive was the nickname its startling new grille earned for itself: the electric shaver grille. The grille did look like the top of an electric razor, with its prominent vertical grille bars, but included a newsworthy innovation: retractable headlights.

Early positive publicity for the car proved to be a problem for Mercury, as they knew they would not be able to build enough of them to ensure there was a model in every dealership. Instead they gave a limited number of the cars to one dealer for test marketing. Thirty Cougars were shipped to Principal Motors in Monterey, California, midway between Los Angeles and San Francisco. They sold twenty-nine in the first month and when Mercury rolled out the Cougar fully, they put a big campaign behind it, touting it as "The Man's Car." In fact, the Cougar proved just as popular with women as men, until it was finally phased out in 2002. **MG**

Cosmo | Mazda (J)

1967 • 59 cu in/982 cc • 110 bhp/82 kW • 0–60 mph/97 kph in 16 seconds • 115 mph/185 kph

Mazda had been building motorcycles and trucks since the 1930s but decided to branch out in the 1960s with a sports car. The Cosmo 110S was not like any other car before it: its styling was extraordinary, with slim lines and a very long rear overhang, and under the hood (bonnet) was one of the first uses of a Wankel rotary engine. This new type of powerplant offered smoothness and high revs with the downside of being unfamiliar and using more fuel.

After the initial launch at the Tokyo Motor Show in 1964, Mazda struggled to perfect the Cosmo for production. More than eighty prototypes and test cars were destroyed as the Hiroshima-based designers and engineers tweaked the design. By 1967, the Cosmo 110S finally made it to the showroom with an odd mechanical feature—two spark plugs per cylinder powered by two separate distributors. Nevertheless, the eccentric new grand tourer was considered a "halo" product for the new Mazda brand. To prove the reliability of its engine, two Cosmos were entered for the 1968 Marathon de la Route and one of them came in fourth overall. A total of 1,176 Cosmos were built. Most remain in their home country. Up until 1995, three further series were built, with more conventional styling although the rotary engine remained. **JB**

Gamine | Vignale (I)

1967 • 30 cu in/499 cc, S2 • 21 bhp/16 kW • unknown • 60 mph/100 kph

The Vignale Gamine looks like it should be in a toy shop, perhaps powered by a twelve-volt battery. Yet it is a car for grown-ups, despite its tiny proportions: the wheelbase is only 72 inches (184 cm) long.

Vignale were a firm of Italian coachbuilders who collaborated with carmakers in various countries ranging from Cunningham in the United States and Tatra in the Czech Republic. They also designed bodies for a number of European manufacturers. The 1967 Gamine was the pet project of the company founder, Alfredo Vignale, and was built at his own factory. It apes the style of the 1933 Fiat Balilla Spyder.

The Gamine's mechanics were based on the Fiat 500 Nuovo Sport. Vignale kept the rear-engine layout and the two-cylinder, air-cooled 30-cubic-inch (499-cc) motor from the Fiat. They also retained the 500's steel tube frame. To this they welded an open-top body. Behind the two seats was a metal frame that helped hold up the fabric roof and acted as a roll car. Tucked in behind the front grille were the fuel tank and a spare wheel. It is not known exactly how many Vignale Gamines were built—possibly only 300. The car's slow sales drove Vignale out of business. He was forced to sell out to De Tomaso (owned by Ford) and the name disappeared in 1974. **JI**

Mustang GT500 | Ford

USA

1967 • 427 cu in/7,000 cc, V8 • 355 bhp/261 kW • 0–60 mph/97 kph in 4.8 seconds • 134 mph/216 kph

The Mustang GT500 is such a great car that it would doubtless have been a success even without Hollywood icon Steve McQueen hammering one around the streets of San Francisco in the movie *Bullitt*. But the 1968 movie helped catapult the American muscle car into the minds of car lovers the world over.

The car's story reads like a film script in its own right. American car tuner Carroll Shelby originally asked Chevrolet for some engines. They declined and he turned to Ford instead, and so began the long-running relationship between the two that exists to this day.

When Ford wanted to give their cars a boost they turned to Shelby. After working on Mustangs throughout the early 1960s, he took a slightly different route with the 1967 model. Before then he had turned it into a fierce race car, unsuitable for road driving, but with the GT500 he made it more civilized. Ironically he did this by fitting a bigger engine. The standard car had just been revamped to accept big-block motors so Shelby squeezed in the 428 "Police Interceptor" V8. He fitted this with two huge four-barrel carburetors and an aluminum intake manifold that helped it kick out 355 bhp (261 kW). The GT350 of the year before had been fitted with racing seats and harnesses, but the 500 had a proper cabin with air-conditioning and power steering.

In 2008, on the fortieth anniversary of the film, Ford released a Bullitt Special Edition of their current Mustang. This had a number of performance upgrades but also had the exhaust tuned to sound like McQueen's car. It could not, of course, promise to make the driver as cool as him. **JI**

Ghibli | Maserati

(I)

1967 • 286 cu in/4,691 cc, V8 • 330 bhp/250 kW • 0–60 mph/97 kph in 6.8 seconds • 154 mph/248 kph

The first Maserati from the desk of famous designer Giorgetto Giugiaro, the Ghibli was perhaps the epitome of the Italian brand's work. It offered huge performance and style in abundance. Its sleek design was only 45 inches (116 cm) tall but 18 feet (5.5 m) long. But the svelte lines of the Ghibli masked a hefty kerb weight of 3,520 lbs (1600 kg). This was in part due to the huge V8 that powered it and the primitive live rear axle and outdated leaf-spring suspension. The cabin was typically sumptuous, however, and the splendid styling was up-to-date. It was under the skin that the Ghibli relied on old technology.

The 286-cubic-inch (4,700-cc) V8 engine was based on a racing design dating back to the 1950s but had a power output of 330 bhp (250 kW), impressive by modern standards, let alone in the 1960s. But the car had a ferocious thirst for fuel and was fitted with twin fuel tanks. At the time, speed limits were ill-defined and poorly enforced in Italy, and it was not uncommon for owners to test the limits of their Ghiblis on the Autostradas. A race-prepared version of the Ghibli entered the prestigious 24 Hours of Le Mans race, hitting a phenomenal 191 mph (308 kph) on the Mulsanne straight, although it failed to finish the race.

Options included manual and automatic transmissions, and a few convertibles were made among the 1,274 examples built over a seven-year production run. Notable owners included Sammy Davis Jr. and Peter Sellers. Henry Ford II was so impressed with the Ghibli he reportedly tried to buy the company, but it is hard to imagine such a glamorous machine with a blue oval on it. **RD**

The iconic Chitty Chitty Bang Bang takes to the skies—the 1968 film was based on a novel by Ian Fleming. ▷

Lotus Cortina Mk II | Ford (GB)

1967 • 95 cu in/1,558 cc, S4 • 115 bhp/86 kW • 0–60 mph/97 kph in 11.1 seconds • 108 mph/174 kph

The original Lotus Cortina of 1963 had plenty of modifications that made it significantly different from the standard car on which it was based. Although very exciting to drive, it could be a bit of a handful. The Lotus Cortina Mark II introduced in 1967 was a bit less rarefied, and although a very quick car, it was rather better to drive. Based on the Mark II chassis that arrived in the standard car a year earlier, it was better behaved as a road car than its predecessor, and is judged historically by enthusiasts as the best of the Lotus Cortinas.

Instead of being produced on a special production line elsewhere in Essex, this model was built alongside mainstream Cortinas on the production line at the Dagenham factory. The car's predecessor had some light panels within its bodywork, but this one reverted to normal steel body panels. The twin-cam engine in the Lotus Cortina Mark II was tuned for slightly less power than the first-generation car. The gearbox was not quite as close-ratio as previously, and the car had more of a fast racehorse feel and a bit less of the nervous-natured thoroughbred.

It also looked more discreet, with owners able to choose how flamboyant they wanted the car to look. The first Lotus Cortina had a one-choice striking color scheme of white paintwork, with green stripes running down the body sides most of the way from front to back. Later customers had access to the entire Ford color palette. The change in body shape made the contrasting stripes less suited to curvier body contours, so they did not feature prominently among the cars that were ordered, and are much less often seen. **SB**

Chitty Chitty Bang Bang (GB)

1968 • 183 cu in/3,000 cc, V6 • unknown • unknown • unknown

The most famous movie car of all time would probably be a straight shoot-out between British superspy James Bond's Aston Martin DB5 and Chitty Chitty Bang Bang. Famously christened on screen by wacky inventor Caractacus Potts and his two children—the name relates to the noise the engine makes—it floats and flies its way through the classic family adventure first released in 1968.

The concept was the brainchild of the film's production designer Ken Adam and sculptor Frederick Rowland Emett. Six cars were built for the shoot, including a fully functioning and road-legal version that bore the U.K. number plate GEN 11. Read as Genii, the plural of genie, it refers to a magical person in Arabian folklore. The car was assembled by Alan Mann Racing, based in Hertfordshire and close to the Pinewood Studios where the movie was shot. Power came from a 183-cubic-inch (3,000-cc) V6 engine supplied by Ford and mated to an automatic transmission. Actor Dick Van Dyke, who played Potts, said it had "the turning radius of a battleship."

It was in private ownership in the United Kingdom until 2011, when it was sold at an auction in the United States. The celebrity buyer—who paid close to $805,000 (£512,000) for the car—was *Lord of the Rings* film director Peter Jackson. A second road-going version, which appears on screen briefly, was bought and displayed at the U.K.'s Cars of the Stars Motor Museum in Keswick for a number of years. The center closed in 2011 and the fate of Chitty remains unclear. Another of the original cars is currently on display at the National Motor Museum in the United Kingdom. **RY**

GEN 11

DATSUN
2000

⊂ Datsun produced the Fairlady Sports 2000 as an inexpensive alternative to the Triumph sports car.

Fairlady Sports 2000 | Datsun (J)

1968 • 120 cu in/1,982 cc, S4 • 133 bhp/99 kW • 0–60 mph/97 kph in 8.4 seconds • 120 mph/193 kph

The Datsun Fairlady was the Japanese company's take on the classic British concept of a small, fine handling roadster. The 2000 version came along in the late 1960s, by which time the car had been developed and refined from its early days as a low-powered (36 bhp/27 kW) machine to something altogether more grown-up.

The 1968 Fairlady Sports 2000 had a new body design from its immediate predecessors, with a taller windshield with built in rearview mirror. A padded "safety" dashboard with recessed switches replaced the old flat metal one. However, it was still the same low-cost sports car, aimed squarely at rivals such as Triumph and MG, but with proven Japanese reliability.

Stylistically it was very similar to the Triumph TR5 of the time. The steel body sat on a conventional (i.e., getting old) box-rail chassis with independent front suspension and a live axle at the back.

At the heart of the Datsun was a 122-cubic-inch (2,000-cc), four-cylinder engine running through a five-speed gearbox, something unheard of at the time (many cars in 1968 were then still running on three-speed boxes). You could even get a competition tuning package with dual Mikuni/Solex carburetors that would boost power to 133 bhp (99 kW). That was enough to take the car to 140 mph (225 kph). The Fairlady Sports 2000 was successful on the race track as well as on the road. In the United States, drivers included the Hollywood star Paul Newman. This helped open up the U.S. market to Datsun. However, the car's overall design, like the British marques it copied, was aging rapidly. The model that replaced it—Datsun's legendary Z series—moved the game on significantly. **JI**

2002 | BMW (D)

1968 • 121 cu in/1,990 cc, S4 • 108 bhp/81 kW • 0–60 mph/97 kph in 12.8 seconds • 110 mph/177 kph

The BMW 2002 is credited with creating an entirely new class of automobile: the small performance car. Without the 2002 there might not be any hot hatches or fast sedans (saloons) such as BMW's own 3 Series.

It is also recognized as the car that saved BMW's skin and laid the foundations for the huge commercial giant that the company is today. Prior to the 2002's launch, BMW had been struggling to find its place in the world—more expensive than VW but fighting with tough rivals in the luxury car market.

This began to change with the creation of its "New Class" range of small sedans and coupes. Although these were successful, none caught the public's attention quite as much as the 2002. But it might not have been born at all, were it not for pressure brought by BMW's U.S. importer Max Hoffman. He persuaded the BMW bosses to drop a 122-cubic-inch (2,000-cc) engine from one of their larger cars into the small 1600-2, two-door saloon. The idea was to both boost performance and pass strict U.S. emission controls. The result was a stroke of motoring genius: a small, well-handling car with a hefty amount of power. They called it simply the 2002, or '02 for short.

It was an instant hit in both Europe and the United States. On the track it won the European Touring Car Championship. On the road it was capable of beating many out-and-out sports cars. In the early 1970s a fuel-injected model was available, but overall the car stayed relatively unchanged throughout its nine-year life. Although many see BMW's 1 series coupe as its true heir, the 2002's DNA can be seen in any small, powerful sedan or hatchback. **JI**

504 | Peugeot

(F)

1968 • 109 cu in/1,796 cc, S4 • 82 bhp/61 kW • 0–60 mph/97 kph in 14.9 seconds • 106 mph/170 kph

The new Peugeot family car got off to the worst possible start when its launch in the summer of 1968 coincided with riots, strikes, and political unrest in France. However, within a year it was winning over buyers and was voted Europe's Car of the Year in 1969.

At the time, the rear-wheel-drive, four-door sedan (saloon) was considered a step forward in general quality, ride, visibility, and refinement. Its standard column-mounted, four-speed manual gearshift and sunroof were considered rather sophisticated.

Engines and specifications gradually improved throughout its life, including the introduction of early successful diesels, a powerful luxury V6, and a four-wheel-drive version. Production ended in 1983 by which time more than three million had been built in Europe. Yet the 504 lived on in the rest of the world.

It had become one of the first genuine world cars. Something about its timeless styling, simple design, and rugged construction made it suitable for all sorts of conditions. Versions of the 504 were assembled in France, China, Chile, New Zealand, Egypt, Kenya, Argentina, Nigeria, Australia, and Tunisia. The basic platform was used for a 504 sedan, station wagon (estate), coupe, convertible, and pickup truck.

The 504 had a tough suspension that could take huge undulations in its stride. In Africa it is still a familiar sight as a bush taxi. Its strength and reliability made it a favorite working vehicle in the Far East, where many were built as crew-cab pickups. In 2010 Iran's President Ahmadinejad auctioned his own personal 1977 white Peugeot 504 on state television to raise money for a charity housing project. It raised $2.5 (£1.6) million. **SH**

HK Monaro GTS | Holden

(AUS)

1968 • 327 cu in/5,360 cc, V8 • 250 bhp/186 kW • 0–60 mph/97 kph in 7.6 seconds • 115 mph/185 kph

The Monaro holds a unique place in Australian motoring history and was one of the country's first real "muscle cars." Named after the Monaro region of New South Wales, it was first introduced as a two-door, pillarless coupe in July 1968, and was designed and built during a period of unprecedented social change.

It appealed to the young people of Australia as few cars had before it and was designed for the nation's male youth in particular. The Monaro lost no time embracing them, either when, just a few months after its debut it won Australia's premier road race, the Hardie-Ferodo 500. In fact it did more than win; it dominated, claiming first, second, and third places at the finish. The mythical status that it would go on to achieve had just been given an almighty kick start.

It certainly looked the part with its long, tapered roofline and flared wheel arches. There were three models—standard, GTS, and GTS 327—and Holden's GT versions came with 305-cubic-inch (5,000-cc), six-cylinder, or V8 Chevrolet engines that pretty much blew every other car on the Australian road away.

Although the initial series was discontinued in 1971, it was revived later that year with the GTS 350. Holden phased out the Monaro name in 1979, but the hold the car had gained for itself never lost its marketing muscle. In 2001 it was revived again, with further series unveiled in 2003 and 2004. In 2005, 1,100 limited editions were released, but then that was the end. "Monaro"—an Aboriginal word meaning "high plateau"—was apt. It still stands alone—as the pinnacle of Australian motoring. **BS**

Plus 8 | Morgan

GB

1968 • 215 cu in/3,528 cc, V8 • 161 bhp/120 kW • 0–60 mph/97 kph in 6.7 seconds • 124 mph/198 kph

The last Morgan Plus 8 rolled out of the company's Worcestershire factory in April 2004 and what better way to finish thirty-six years of continuous production than with a fantastic celebration. At the renowned Prescott Hill Climb in nearby Gloucestershire, more than 1,000 Morgans and their owners turned out to honor an icon of British motoring and the end of an era. Its demise was nothing to do with demand for this vintage-styled two-seater. The V8 had been reworked and upgraded so many times that there was no way it could meet new European Union emissions regulations.

The Plus 8 was replaced by the Roadster, and to the untrained eye the pair look remarkably similar. Morgan was not going to tear up its tried and tested formula: it simply designed its old car around a new engine. It bought in the 183-cubic-inch (3,000-cc) unit used in Jaguar's S-Type that was lighter and offered 20 percent more power.

Ironically, it was the death of an engine that led to the Plus 8's production in the first place. In 1966 supply of the Triumph 128-cubic-inch (2,100-cc), four-cylinder unit used in Morgan's visually similar Plus 4 dried up. The answer was Rover's 213-cubic-inch (3,500-cc) V8, shipped in from General Motors, where it was known as the Buick 215. The result was a dynamic new performance flagship that brought the British brand to life and effectively saved the company.

The Plus 8 was first unveiled at the Earls Court Motor Show in London in 1968 and today it holds the record for the longest continuous use of the same powerplant in Morgan's century-long history. It is unlikely ever to be beaten. **RY**

Daytona | Ferrari

1968 • 267 cu in/4,390 cc, V12 • 347 bhp/258 kW • 0–60 mph/97 kph in 5.4 seconds • 174 mph/278 kph

Premiering in 1968, this Italian supercar found global fame more than a decade later, but it was nothing to do with Ferrari. Thousands of miles away across the Atlantic, a 1972 black Daytona was chosen as the weapon of choice for Detective Sonny Crockett, played by Don Johnson, in the first two series of hit U.S. TV crime drama *Miami Vice*.

However, the vehicle used during filming was actually a replica built on a Corvette chassis, and Ferrari bosses were reportedly not pleased with the lack of attention to detail shown by the creator. Close-up shots of Crockett and fellow crime fighter Ricardo Tubbs revealed the seats were pure Chevy. The car was eventually destroyed as part of a story line, and replaced by a genuine white Testarossa—the newest model to wear the Prancing Horse badge.

The car's unofficial name, Daytona, commemorated the Italian brand's 1967 clean sweep of the podium places in the legendary Florida 24 Hour race. Officially it is called the Ferrari 365 GTB/4 and was unveiled to the public at the Paris Motor Show in 1968. Front-engined, with rear-wheel drive and designed by Pininfarina, it was Ferrari's rival to the Lamborghini's mid-engine Miura. On sale for five years, it was replaced by the 365 Berlinetta Boxer. The Daytona's other claim to fame was its role in the barely legal Cannonball Run coast-to-coast race in 1971. Piloted by Le Mans 24 winner Dan Gurney and journalist Brock Yates, the car won the New York to Los Angeles race in just under thirty-six hours. Average speed was 80 mph (128 kph) and Gurney famously commented, "At no time did we exceed 175 mph (280 kph)." **RY**

XJ6 | Jaguar

GB

1968 • 258 cu in/4,236 cc, S6 • 245 bhp/183 kW • 0–60 mph/97 kph in 8.7 seconds • 127 mph/204 kph

When Jaguar unveiled their new XJ six-cylinder luxury sedan (saloon) in 1968, the company's cofounder Sir William Lyons described it as "the finest Jaguar ever." It turned out to also be one of the most important Jaguar's ever, injecting the company with a new vigor that helped it survive the turmoil of the 1970s and 1980s.

The new car replaced most of Jaguar's previous sedans. At launch two different engines options were on offer: a 170-cubic-inch (2,800-cc) and 256-cubic-inch (4,200-cc), straight-six (hence the six in XJ6). Later, in 1972, a 323-cubic-inch (5,300-cc) V12 became available. The 256-cubic-inch (4,200-cc) motor was developed from Jaguar's XK racing engine and could take the car up to 127 mph (204 kph). But this Jaguar was about more than power: it was about traveling in comfort, surrounded by luxury. Across the Mark I XJ range you could specify power steering, leather seats, and air-conditioning (not common on British cars in 1968).

The supple suspension gave the car an impressive ride—a mixture of softness and sportiness. And even by modern standards, the engines offer excellent performance. That said, much of the interior, particularly the clocks and instruments, was already a little outdated in 1968. Overall, the XJ6 was a stunning car. The problem was, having set the bar so high, the Mark I was a pretty impossible act for later models to follow. That is probably why it stayed in production, with relatively small updates, for more than twenty years.

The XJ6 was the last car that Sir William Lyons helped design. It is no exaggeration, however, to say that his legacy lives in on the fact that the XJ range continues successfully to this day. **JI**

Phantom VI | Rolls-Royce

GB

1968 • 411 cu in/6,750 cc, V8 • 200 bhp/147 kW • 0–60 mph/97 kph in 13.2 seconds • 112 mph/180 kph

It was 1925 when the first Phantom I glided smoothly out of the Rolls-Royce works, and the series sailed forth in its stately manner. The Phantom VI was something different, however. It was no longer an exclusive car, but an ultraexclusive one. Rolls-Royce did not do anything as vulgar as simply make the cars and then try to persuade people to buy them. With the Phantom VI you had to order one first, and then the company would build it for you. Fortunately for Rolls-Royce, 374 orders were placed in the twenty-three years that the car was available. If you wanted one, it cost you £8,905 ($14,100).

The customer base for the Phantom VI was predominantly heads of state and royal families. In particular the British royal family is well associated with the car. Queen Elizabeth II was given a Phantom VI by Rolls-Royce for her Silver Jubilee in 1977. It became the Queen's official state car for the next twenty-five years, and is still in use by the royal family today. This was the car that was carrying the Prince of Wales and the Duchess of Cornwall when they were attacked during protests against the rise in university tuition fees in London in December 2010. The car was covered in paint and a side window was smashed. On a happier note, the same car (minus paint) was the one in which Catherine Middleton traveled to her wedding with Prince William on April 29, 2011.

The Phantom VI was phased out in 1991 and the Phantom name did not appear on a Rolls-Royce again until a new series was launched in 2003. Some extra body panels have been built and stockpiled, however, just in case they are ever needed. **MG**

Continental III | Lincoln

(USA)

1968 • 459 cu in/7,538 cc, V8 • 365 bhp/272 kW • 0–60 mph/97 kph in 6.5 seconds • 137 mph/220 kph

The Lincoln Continental Mark III was billed as a "personal luxury car." This is very much an American classification: a two-door automobile that was nearly 18 feet (5.5 m) long. It was intended as a rival to the front-wheel-drive Cadillac Eldorado, which was billed as the "car of the future." It followed (with a gap of several years) the Mark II Continental, which was built in 1956 and 1957. Lincoln (a division of Ford) had tried to make a successor to the Mark II in 1958, but the car died an early death.

The official Mark III finally got them back in the game. It was a big beast, weighing in at nearly two-and-a-half tons (2.54 tonnes). Luckily it had a monster of an engine—Lincoln's all-new 457-cubic-inch (7,500-cc) V8, which produced 365 bhp (272 kw) and was enough to haul it up to a theoretical 137 mph (220 kph). The new engine was also built to be cleaner than ever and meet stringent new U.S. emissions laws.

Although the Continental III was built on the same chassis as the Ford Thunderbird, the Lincoln had a much squarer design. Inside, it was full of luxury touches: there was power to the steering, windows, seats, and brakes. Buyers enjoyed simulated wood aplenty, lots of leather, an eight-track cassette player, and a Cartier clock. One of the most popular options was the vinyl roof, which later became standard. This was a relief to Lincoln as the roof was made in two sections and covering it in vinyl masked the join—a plain painted roof required more work to hide the seam. There was even a nod to the 1950s Mark II: a spare tire bulge in the lid of the trunk (boot), even though the spare was not kept there. **JI**

Espada | Lamborghini

(I)

1968 • 239 cu in/3,929 cc, V12 • 350 bhp/261 kW• 0–60 mph/97 kph in 6.6 seconds • 156 mph/250 kph

Named after a matador's dagger, the wide-tracked, low-slung Espada was a real head turner. With four bucket seats and a well-trimmed interior, the Espada was an "executive express" rather than a sports tourer, and slotted into Lamborghini's lineup alongside the Islero and Miura. Nevertheless, its gutsy 244-cubic-inch (4,000-cc) quad-cam V12 meant the Espada became the world's fastest sedan (saloon) car when the S1 was launched in 1968. Based largely on the 400GT 2+2 platform, it also had fully independent suspension, disc brakes all around, and a five-speed manual gearbox

Despite the 1970s oil crisis, the Espada sold well: 1,217 cars were built during its ten-year production run. When the S3 arrived in 1972 the Espada could be fully loaded with power steering, air-conditioning, and even a three-speed automatic transmission.

Famous owners of the Espada have included the Shah of Iran, the novelist Alistair McLean, and Sir Paul McCartney. McCartney bought his flame red S2 secondhand in 1975 and used it daily while recording with his new band, Wings.

The Espada, like most four-seater supercars of its generation, is not as highly prized by today's collectors as the classic two-seater sports cars. Lamborghini did not produce a workshop manual for it, or give any consideration to how its complex construction might hinder repairs. Like many Italian cars from the 1970s, the Espada also suffers from chronic rust, and restoration costs can be huge. It was rumored that U2 front man Bono spent $40,000 on a two-year restoration of his sky blue S2 Espada; in 2008 it sold at auction for $33,000. **DS**

Islero | Lamborghini

(I)

1968 • 239 cu in/3,929 cc, V12 • 350 bhp/257 kW • 0–60 mph/97 kph in 6.1 seconds • 162 mph/260 kph

Unlike his Italian rivals Maserati and Ferrari, Ferruccio Lamborghini had never been interested in showcasing his cars through motorsports. As a young man Ferruccio had raced a highly modified Fiat Topolino in the 1948 Mille Miglia. After performing well for 700 miles (1,100 km) he lost control and crashed into a roadside restaurant; it seems that he lost his appetite for racing the very same day.

In 1968 Lamborghini launched their new streamlined grand tourer—the Islero. It was perfectly designed for epic transcontinental road trips or simply commuting in style. Largely based on the outgoing 400GT 2+2, the body was restyled by Italian coachbuilders Marazzi to allow a little more headroom for rear passengers. The Islero also had wider arches to accommodate bigger tires, and featured a sloping front end with pop-up headlights, not dissimilar to the Ferrari 365 GTB/4 "Daytona," which had been launched the year before. In 1969 an up-rated Islero GTS was offered with bigger brakes, tweaked suspension, and an engine tuned with parts from the Miura S.

Only 225 Isleros were ever built, five of which came to the United Kingdom in right-hand drive. One of these cars, a silver GTS, had a leading role in the 1969 film *The Man Who Haunted Himself* starring Sir Roger Moore. In 2010 this car, autographed by Moore on the sun visor, was sold at auction for $156,616 (€121,625).

The Islero was named after the infamous Miura bull that killed the Spanish matador Manolete in 1947. To this day Lamborghini continues to appoint each new model a name that references the sport Ferruccio Lamborghini so greatly admired. **SH**

300 SEL | Mercedes

D

1968 • 384 cu in/6,300 cc, V8 • 247 bhp/184 kW • 0–60 mph/97 kph in 2.2 seconds • 400 mph/600 kph

The late 1960s had a strange effect on even the most sober-minded people. The world's most conservative, longest-established carmaker decided to stick a 384-cubic-inch (6,300-cc) V8 in a normal sedan (saloon). The two-ton, four-door family car was transformed. The 300 SEL had performance to test any of the sports cars of the day. It could carry five people at 125 mph (200 kph) in comfort all day, accelerate faster than a Lamborghini, and had a higher top speed than a Ford Mustang. It was as if Mercedes had unwittingly invented the muscle car.

Yet this hot rod was no stripped-out racer—it was packed with wood, leather, and luxury features, such as air suspension, air-conditioning, power windows and sunroof, power steering, and central locking. Rear seat passengers had ample space to spread out, including writing tables with reading lights. Of course, there was the latest audio system—an AM/FM radio with a cassette tape deck plus a powered aerial. *Motor Trend* magazine said, "The 6.3-liter Mercedes is the safest, fastest and most comfortable 4-door sedan made today."

Under the hood (bonnet) was a mass of tubes, wires, and pipework, as Mercedes engineers had struggled to squeeze the fuel-injected engine into the body without any modification. It was a tricky engine for mechanics to work on because there was so little space. In fact, the little 6.3 badge on the right of the lid of the trunk (boot) was the only external clue that this was actually a motoring beast in disguise. Many owners removed this badge to prevent undue attention from traffic police. This was the car that reminded the world that supercar performance is not the preserve of two-door sportcars. **SH**

Scimitar GTE | Reliant

GB

1968 • 182 cu in/2,994 cc, V6 • 135 bhp/101 kW • 0–60 mph/97 kph in 8.9 seconds • 121 mph/195 kph

Reliant started life in 1935 producing three-wheeler delivery vans. Company bosses took the brave move to expand into the sports car market in 1960, with the Sabre fastback coupes. The Scimitar GT, launched in 1964, was an updated version of the Sabre, but it sold poorly. However, Reliant's fortunes were about to change when the station wagon (estate) version, the Scimitar GTE, hit the showrooms four years later. Its shooting-brake design meant that it could comfortably hold four adults and still have plenty of luggage space accessible from its large glass hatchback.

Its lightweight fiberglass body and powerful Ford V6 engine meant the GTE filled a gap in the market for enthusiastic drivers that also needed the practicality of a load-lugging station wagon. It was therefore no surprise that the GTE proved popular with many musicians during the 1970s, including Deep Purple bassist Roger Glover. Equally respected for its predictable handling and sharp performance, the Scimitar GTE was also bought by Motorcycling World Champion Barry Sheene.

Despite Reliant's humble origins, the GTE was an upmarket motor car. At launch the Scimitar sold for £1,759 ($2,787), while the comparable MGC GT sold for £1,337 ($2,119) and Rover's 3500 cost £1,791 ($1,129).

The car gained the Royal seal of approval in 1970 when an airforce-blue Scimitar GTE was bought as a twentieth birthday present for Princess Anne by the Queen and the Duke of Edinburgh. To date, the Princess Royal has owned at least eight GTEs, appreciating the easily accessible trunk (boot) space for her riding gear, and its impressive turn of pace. **DS**

Hilux | Toyota

(J)

1968 • 90 cu in/1,490 cc, F4 • 77 bhp/57 kW • unknown • 81 mph/130 kph

The Japanese pickup has become as much a symbol of the building trade as the paint-splattered radio and low-slung jeans. The Hilux we know today is a rugged muscular beast, as capable of lugging vast amounts of timber as it is of reaching the North Pole driven by the hosts of BBC TV's motoring show *Top Gear*. The program also placed one of the Toyota pickups on the roof of an apartment block and blew up the building. The Hilux survived.

It has not always been like this. When the original Hilux was born in 1968, it was a bit of a weed compared to its rivals. It was a basic rear-wheel-drive truck with a small 91-cubic-inch (1,500-cc) engine and a top speed of 81 mph (130 kph). Over the years the Hilux evolved gradually and each time grew a little more rugged on the outside, and more sophisticated and comfortable on the inside. The engines crept up in capacity, the front end was simplified, and it generally developed more of a tough-guy image.

In 1979 the significant step was taken to introduce a four-wheel-drive version. This is the point at which the Hilux began to take on legendary status, something unheard of for a pickup truck outside of the United States. The technology was pretty basic: the four-wheel-drive model—also called the 4Runner or Surf in some markets—had a solid front axle and leaf-spring suspension.

Today there are no end of options available—two- or four-door cabs, luxury interiors, and multimedia systems. Yet, some things do not change and the Hilux remains the builder's best mate. As it is for the farmer, the hunter, the explorer, and the watersports fan. **JI**

01

A 1969 customized Dodge Charger—dubbed "the General Lee"—starred in the TV show *The Dukes of Hazzard*.

Charger | Dodge (USA)

1969 • 317 cu in/5,210 cc, V8 • 230 bhp/171.5 kW • 0–60 mph/97 kph in 9 seconds • 117 mph/187 kph

With the Confederate flag on the roof and welded-shut doors, the most famous Dodge Charger in history is the General Lee. Featuring in almost every episode of 1980s U.S. TV drama *The Dukes of Hazzard*, scores of the 1969 model were destroyed in various stunts and jumps at an average of more than one per show. The car's other brush with stardom is in the Steve McQueen classic *Bullitt*, taking part in one of the most celebrated and influential chase sequences in movie history.

Both are examples of the earliest production Charger, a mid-sized coupe sold from 1966 to 1978, although it did appear as the name of a concept car in 1964. The showroom model made its public debut during a commercial break in coverage of the Rose Bowl college football game on January 1 1966.

Later that year Dodge went NASCAR racing with the Charger. During testing it acted like an airplane wing and the back end went light, so a trunk (boot) spoiler was added to increase downforce. NASCAR rules meant the production version had to have it too, so the Charger became the first U.S. market road car to feature one. NASCAR driver David Pearson went on to take the Grand National Championship in 1966 with fourteen wins.

The Charger was axed in 1978 and replaced by the Dodge Magnum, but in the 1980s returned as a rather ugly hatchback that did its heritage no favors. The only serious performer was the Shelby Charger developed by racer-turned-designer Carroll Shelby.

Following a 1999 concept car, the name was reborn again as a four-door sedan (saloon) in 2006. It also found its way into Brazilian dealerships as a variant of the Dodge Dart during the 1970s. **RY**

411 | Bristol (GB)

1969 • 383 cu in/6,277 cc, V8 • 335 bhp/250 kW • 0–60 mph/97 kph in 7 seconds • 143 mph/230 kph

In the language of a typical Bristol owner, the 411 could be described as a fine old beast. It was a rare handmade British thoroughbred with a Chrysler V8 under the hood (bonnet)—like a muscle car for the tweed jacket brigade. It was fast enough to challenge the Ferraris of the day, but across seven years of production, only 600 of them found buyers. Nevertheless, the 411 is still considered a sporting classic and has a cult following.

It was built with vintage engineering, however: the box-section chassis came from the Bristol 400, which was taken from a 1930s BMW design. There was a certain atmosphere about the interior with its fine wooden dashboard looking like a piece of dining room furniture, hand-stitched leather seats, and three-spoked leather-wrapped steering wheel with the Bristol badge in the center. The cars used Chrysler's three-speed automatic.

Wealthy British gentlemen would buy their Bristol motor at the smart showroom on Kensington High Street in London, but there was nothing glamorous about the low-rise factory at Filton in North Bristol, where the cars were made alongside an aircraft factory.

There were five generations of the 411, some of which were exported to the United States. Later models added clever self-leveling suspension and even proper seat belts. Some derivations used double pairs of headlights at the front.

The Bristol 411 was one of the fastest four-seaters of the day and the fastest Bristol vehicle to date. It is a period piece from an era when certain buyers did not mind punishing fuel consumption, but wanted exclusive sports cars with a certain British macho charm that has all but disappeared today. **JI**

Indy | Maserati

(I)

1969 • 254 cu in/4,163 cc, V8 • 260 bhp/193 kW • 0–62 mph/100 kph in 7.2 seconds • 154 mph/246 kph

Intended to replace the aging Sebring and Mexico models, Maserati's Indy was designed as a high-speed 2+2. Produced between 1969 and 1975, around 1,000 examples were sold in total, initial versions came with a 256-cubic-inch (4,200-cc) V8, which had two valves per cylinder and twin overhead chain-driven camshafts per cylinder bank.

The elegant coupe body was designed by Giovanni Michelotti of styling house Carrozzeria Vignale, who added their crest to the car's front wings. The shape gave excellent aerodynamic performance and the Indy had an impressive top speed for the era. The name was inspired by the Indianapolis racetrack where Maserati won in 1939 and 1940.

Selling for $18,870 (£12,000) in the United States, the Indy featured a typically luxurious Maserati interior, a small pair of rear seats, and a three-spoke Nardi steering wheel. The leather seats reclined and windows

were electrically operated. The headlights were the pop-up type with a mechanical backup in case they failed. Later cars came equipped with power-assisted steering and air-conditioning, while final cars had a new hydraulic brake system from Citroën.

From 1970 to 1972, Maserati offered the option of a 290-bhp (213-kW) 286-cubic-inch (4,700-cc) engine with Bosch electronic ignition in addition to the original 254-cubic-inch (4,263-cc) engine. This model was sometimes known as the Maserati Indy America. Then, in 1971, Maserati replaced both engines with a 299-cubic-inch (4,900-cc) V8 that also powered the Ghibli SS and gave 320 bhp (235 kW) when installed in the Indy. The top speed of this particular variant was a heady 165 mph (265 kph). These are impressive figures by today's standards, let alone decades ago, when its 14-inch (36-cm) tires and puny brakes struggled to handle the power. **RD**

Mustang Boss 429 | Ford

(USA)

1969 • 429 cu in/7,033 cc, V8 • 375 bhp/280 kW • 0–60 mph/97 kph in 5.1 seconds • 115 mph/185 kph

When top car designer Larry Shinoda was lured to Ford in 1968 to shake up their range of cars, he began a secret project. When asked what he was working on, his enigmatic reply was always "the Boss's car." He did not mean Bruce Springsteen; he meant the Ford president, Semon Knudsen, who had brought him to the company. Shinoda's brief was to build a car that would win the prestigious Trans-Am trophy, and that car became the Boss 302.

The Boss 302 had to have an engine of less than 305 cubic inches (5,000 cc), to comply with Trans-Am regulations, but Ford also wanted a car that could compete in the NASCAR Sprint Cup Series, too. The company was taking no prisoners, and the 429 became a separate project. In the case of NASCAR, rules required that they could only use engines if the identical engine had been in at least 500 cars sold to the general public. Ford was so intent on winning these competitions that it began work on another Boss—the 429—that would go on sale commercially and also compete at NASCAR.

Ford made 859 Boss 429s in 1969, and a further 499 in 1970. Unfortunately, NASCAR success did not follow and the Boss 429 was discontinued. The Boss 302 fared slightly better, winning Trans-Am in its second year, but it too was discontinued. They were both exceptional cars, and because of the short production runs now command high prices at auction. Although the 429s were officially listed as having a power output of "only" 375 bhp (280 kW), they were easily capable of 500 bhp (370 kw). The lower figure had to be given to the public to make the insurance more affordable. **MG**

240Z | Datsun

J

1969 • 146 cu in/2,393 cc, S6 • 163 bhp/120 kW • 0–60 mph/97 kph in 8.3 seconds • 125 mph/201 kph

Nissan was a long-standing carmaker that used the name Datsun in export markets because it sounded less Japanese. Similarly, its range of sports coupes were called Fairladys at home but Z cars abroad. The first of this series was the 240Z, which used a high-revving, six-cylinder engine and a long, sexy body, loosely inspired by British sports cars such as the Jaguar E-Type and MGB. The glamorous-looking car was an immediate success and lifted Nissan's profile to new levels.

As recently as the 1950s, the company had been assembling British Austin cars in Japan under license to gain an insight into the more advanced Western industrial technology. They learned fast. Within twenty years they had completely overtaken the British and launched their Z series, which went on become the best-selling sports car of all time.

The 240Z introduced the sleek, fastback looks with a lift-up tailgate, smooth straight-six, 140-cubic-inch (2,300-cc) power, and independent rear suspension. Its replacement, the 260Z, was effectively the same car with a bigger engine, slightly stiffer chassis, and improved interior. This new 158-cubic-inch (2,600-cc) unit raised the power output from that in the United States, where tighter emission controls meant the bigger unit had to be detuned so it was less powerful. A 2+2 option was also launched with a longer wheelbase. Next came the 280Z in 1975, with an even bigger engine of 170 cubic inches (2,800 cc) and fuel-injection to improve its environmental performance.

All the Z cars are sought-after classics today, but their numbers are few as most fell victim to Datsun's greatest weakness—rust. **SH**

The first Ford Special—a bright orange Capri Vista launched in 1971—was marketed at "those who love life." ⊡

GT | Manic (CDN)

1969 • 78 cu in/1,289 cc, S4 • 105 bhp/78 kW • unknown • 135 mph/217 kph

Canada is not noted as a producer of sports cars, but the Manic GT was probably its finest attempt. It was also one of the last truly homegrown cars to come out of the country.

The car was the brainchild of thirty-two-year-old Jacques About from Montreal, who worked in the public relations department of Renault Canada in the late 1960s. He had been asked to carry out a survey to see if Canadian drivers would be interested in buying the Renault Alpine sports car. The public responded in the affirmative, but, sadly, Renault abandoned any notion of importing Alpines into Canada.

About had an idea of his own, however: to leave Renault and design an Alpine-esque car of his own. The Manic GT—named after the Manicouagan River in Quebec—was therefore born. The car was low to the ground, only just taller than a Lotus Europa. Like the Lotus, the Manic ran on a Renault drivetrain and chassis (from the Renault 10). To this tubular steel chassis a fiberglass body was fixed—not with nuts and bolts but directly bonded. That gave it rigidity, but it made repairs (and restoration) much more difficult.

The 78-cubic-inch (1,289-cc) Renault motor came in three states of tune: 65, 80, and 105 horsepower (48.4/59.6/78 kW). The latter could take the car to 135 mph (217 kph), which made it a serious performer in its day. Unfortunately the inclement Canadian weather did not work well with the nooks and crannies of the Manic's chassis, and few cars lasted more than six or seven years before succumbing to rust. This, combined with cashflow problems, led to the demise of Jacques About's business. **JI**

Capri | Ford (GB)

1969 • 97 cu in/1,599 cc, S4 • 74 bhp/55 kW • 0–60 mph/97 kph in 14.1 seconds • 94 mph/149 kph

There are plenty of British cars from the 1970s and 1980s that are remembered for all the wrong reasons; Austin Allegro and Princess, for example. But there are also those that live long in the memory simply as being quite cool. Like the Ford Capri. The Capri was conceived by Ford's European wing as an attempt to emulate American pony cars such as the Mustang. These were small, well-designed, and affordable cars that also offered sporting pretensions.

As with the Mustang, Ford wanted the Capri to appeal to a wide range of buyers and therefore offered it with a number of engine options at its launch. At the bottom was a 79-cubic-inch (1,300-cc), four-cylinder motor that produced 62-bhp (46-kW). At the other end of the scale was the 122-cubic-inch (1,999-cc), Cologne V6 (built in Germany) that made 85 bhp (63 kW). Sitting between these was the four-cylinder 1.6 that made 74 bhp (55 kW). This mid-range motor took the Capri up to 94 mph (149 kph). The Capri shared many components with the Ford Cortina, including the suspension. This had leaf springs and a live axle at the back and MacPherson struts at the front. The handling was not exactly sports car, but that was not the market that Ford were aiming toward. They were offering a car with a balance of looks, performance, and practicality.

The Capri was a huge success, with 400,000 sold in its first two years. Its looks certainly helped. It had a definite U.S. influence, with elements of the Mustang in the front end and the side profile, with its sculpted flanks and air intakes in front of rear wheels. From almost any angle, the Capri looked good. No wonder Ford called it, "the car you always promised yourself." **JI**

Ford Capri.
Pour ceux qui
aiment la vie.
F O R D
CAPRI 2600 GT

a vie est faite de rêves... et la Ford Capri est la ure de vos rêves les plus fous. C'est un coupé silhouette racée, basse, profilée. Avec sa voie e elle colle à la route. Son moteur est nerveux, direction souple et précise : même dans les combrements, passer les vitesses devient un sir. Et lorsque la route est libre, vous pouvez cer : elle a une formidable tenue de route. Mais c'est aussi une voiture familiale.

Luxueusement confortable. Avec quatre places spacieuses.

Pour la puissance, vous avez le choix entre six moteurs : du 1 300 cm^3 (7 CV) jusqu'au tout nouveau moteur V6 à injection de la nouvelle Capri 2600 RS : 150 ch réels, + de 200 km/h, des accélérations à vous couper le souffle.

Ford Capri, la voiture de ceux qui aiment la vie.
Crédit COFICA - Crédit FORD S.A.

Ford Capri:
à partir de 12940 F*

Ford

917 | Porsche

(D)

1969 • 327 cu in/5,374 cc, F12 • 1580 bhp/1180 kW • 0–60 mph/97 kph in 1.9 seconds • 240 mph/418 kph

Up until the late 1960s Porsche had generally chased class wins with their small-capacity sports cars. However, thanks to a relaxation of the rules governing sports car racing, Porsche saw an opportunity that could allow them to go for the ultimate prize: an overall win at the 24 Hours of Le Mans. In just ten months twenty-five Porsche 917s had to be built to qualify as a "production" sports car. Its 274-cubic-inch (4,500-cc), F12, air-cooled engine was mid-mounted in a space-frame chassis beneath a huge cooling fan. Weight-saving measures were taken to the extreme; even the gearstick knob was made of balsa wood.

Pumping out 580 bhp (426 kw), the 917s achieved an incredible first and second place victory at the 1970 24 Hours of Le Mans, in a race that became known as "The Battle of the Titans." The event provided footage that was heavily used in the 1971 film *Le Mans,* starring Steve McQueen. In 1971 the 917 won again at Le Mans, this time setting a distance record of 3,315 miles (5,335 km), which remained unbeaten until 2010.

In 1973 Porsche set their sights on the popular Canadian-American Challenge Cup. Using an enlarged 329-cubic-inch (5,400-cc) F12 with twin-turbos, the results were mind-blowing. Capable of 1,580 bhp (1,180 kw) for short bursts in qualifying mode, this last incarnation of the 917 could hit 200 mph (322 kph) in 10.9 seconds. Nicknamed the "Turbo Panzer," it dominated the Can-Am race series, and to this day, it remains the most powerful race car ever built.

In 1974 eccentric team sponsor Count Gregorio Rossi had his own 917 race car made road legal. Unsurprisingly, it did not become his daily driver. **DS**

Skyline GT-R | Nissan

(J)

1969 • 121 cu in/1,998 cc, S6 • 160 bhp/120 kW • unknown • 121 mph/195 kph

The name Skyline is synonymous with superpowerful Japanese street cars, even if Nissan has chosen to drop the name from the current GT-R. All the more amazing then that this dynasty began with a relatively plain-looking, four-door sedan (saloon) back in 1969.

The name comes from the Skyline brand of cars, made by the Prince motor company that merged with Datsun/Nissan in 1966—a move encouraged by the Japanese government, which wanted to see larger companies that could compete with the U.S. car giants.

The Skyline GT-R was launched at the Tokyo Motor Show, where it stood next to the Nissan R380 race car. This was to highlight the GT-R's racing heritage as it carried a motor derived from the R380's powerplant. As it turned out, the GT-R became a successful racer in its own right, winning thirty-three races in eighteen months.

The engine was key: a 122-cubic-inch (2,000-cc) DOHC, six-cylinder. It was fed by triple Weber carburetors (later switching to a Lucas fuel injection system) and had four valves per cylinder which, in 1969, was groundbreaking. Peak power came in at a dizzy 7,000 rpm and was fed through a five-speed gearbox to the rear wheels. The suspension was also on the pulse, with a semi-trailing arm set-up all round. At the time many more powerful cars were still running on leaf springs and live axles. The Skyline GT-R had the handling to cope with the strength of the engine.

The interior was nothing special, with no heater or radio, and from the outside it looked like a fairly ordinary four-door sedan. Regardless, the Skyline GT-R dynasty had been born. It was now up to other manufacturers to catch up. **JI**

280SE 3.5 | Mercedes

D

1969 • 213 cu in/3,500 cc, V8 • 197 bhp/147 kW • 0–62 mph/100 kph in 8.4 seconds • 115 mph/185 kph

Very few cars of the era could match Mercedes for quality, prestige, and comfort. With its fast, state-of-the-art engine and subtly modernized smart coupe and cabriolet bodies, the 280SE had the ingredients to woo the wealthy in 1969.

Mercedes's first V8 engine offered a combination of smoothness and sports car performance. It had been produced mainly to answer U.S. critics of the previous six-cylinder engines. With 25 percent more power, it was promoted as "the engine of tomorrow" with new features such as electronic fuel injection and transistorized ignition. Elsewhere on the car there was independent suspension (but not the luxurious air-sprung system), a four-speed automatic transmission, and four-wheel disk brakes, too. These created refined but well-balanced handling and progress.

The 280SE's simple looks have dated well. The old upright Mercedes grille was replaced with a wider lower design, which meant the hood (bonnet) could be lower and the whole body sleeker. It was the first Mercedes with rubber inserts along the bumpers. The previous model's rear fins were replaced by simple curves, while at the front the double headlights remained. The coupe styling is classic—a long two-door body highlighted in chrome, with pillarless side windows and a wraparound rear window. The interior is a leather, chrome, and wood masterpiece. Like the convertible, the coupe had a practical layout, too, with four full-sized seats and a large trunk (boot).

The coupes and convertibles are collectible classics. They were only produced for two years, with less than 5,000 built. Prices of used examples remain sky high. **SH**

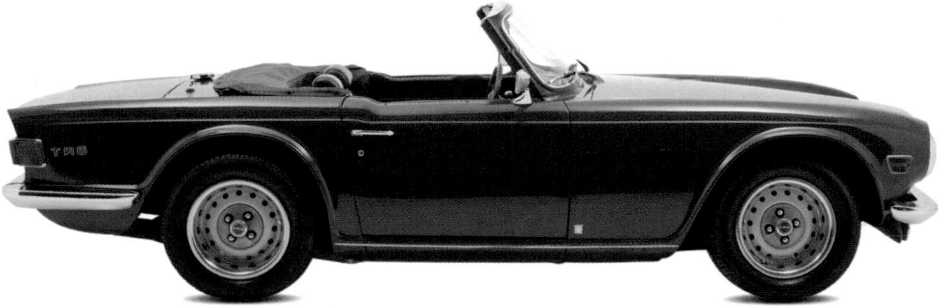

TR6 | Triumph

GB

1969 • 152 cu in/2,498 cc, S6 • 150 bhp/110 kW • 0–60 mph/97 kph in 8.2 seconds • 120 mph/190 kph

The TR6 was one of the most popular small British sports cars ever made. Almost 100,000 were produced and most of them were exported.

In looks, it was not too different from its predecessors, the TR5 and TR4. In fact, the TR6 could be described as dated when compared to cars of the same year, such as the wedge-shaped Lotus Elan. It was only when the TR7 replacement came along in 1976 that Triumph went for a whole new profile.

Parts of the TR6's design were outdated, especially the mechanicals. The body was bolted onto the tubular steel frame, rather than the two being integrated as a unibody or monocoque design. Yet that is not to say it did not perform well. In all markets apart from the United States (due to emission rules), the 152-cubic-inch (2,498-cc), six-cylinder engine was fuel injected, producing 150 bhp (110 kW) and taking the car to 120 mph (190 kph). Later models had the engine detuned to meet even stricter air pollution standards.

The standard four-speed gearbox was available with overdrive, which made it easier to drive on long journeys but also gave more flexibility on twisty roads through the close ratios. It had disc brakes at the front and independent suspension at the rear. The handling was light and precise, in the fine tradition of small British roadsters. The dash was made of veneered wood and was laid out with a full range of classic dials and clocks.

In many ways the TR6 heralded the end of an era—as the last of a breed of masculine, hairy-chested sports cars. The TR7 that followed may have looked more cutting edge, but it lacked the muscle and sharpness of the beloved TR6. **JI**

⊂ A Dino 246GT makes its way through the streets of a Sicilian village during the Targa Florio race on May 16, 1971.

Dino 246GT | Ferrari (I)

1969 • 147 cu in/2,419 cc, S6 • 197 bhp/145 kW • 0–60 mph/97 kph in 7.1 seconds • 146 mph/235 kph

The Ferrari Dino, named in honor of Enzo Ferrari's son, was the company's first mid-engined car. It was also the first Ferrari to be produced in significant numbers. When it first appeared the Dino was considered very daring with its engine aft of the seats—a brave departure for a car intended to be lower-priced and more affordable than Ferrari's usual exotic and astronomically expensive V12 sports cars. The Dino was envisaged as a rival for the Porsche 911.

The 246GT was the best-known Dino. Its name specified that it was a 146-cubic-inch (2,400-cc), six-cylinder model, from the Ferrari custom of using engine size and cylinder count to identify its racing cars, but used this time for a road car. The GT stood for Gran Turismo—Italian for "Grand Tourer".

The Dino 246GT was produced at Ferrari's Modena factory from 1969 until 1974. It was widely praised for its driving caliber and avant-garde design. It is also considered to be one of the best-looking cars of its era. It was so highly regarded that Dino owners included Formula One racing drivers, such as Peter Gethin, who drove for Ferrari and won the 1971 Italian Grand Prix.

The original brochure for the Dino described it as "almost a Ferrari." Enzo did not want to dilute the exclusivity of the Ferrari brand with a downscale model and the Dino did not wear Ferrari badges. Inevitably, however, it became known as the Ferrari Dino.

Dino Ferrari suffered from muscular dystrophy. He was in the hospital when the car bearing his name was in the planning stages, and discussed technical details with engineer Vittorio Dano. Sadly Dino died, at age twenty-four, before the car was produced. **SB**

Rapier H120 | Sunbeam (GB)

1969 • 105 cu in/1,725 cc, S4 • 108 bhp/80.5 kW • 0–60 mph/97 kph in 11.1 seconds • 106 mph/171 kph

One of the most painful chapters in the history of the British motor industry (and there are plenty to choose from) belongs to the long-dead Rootes Group. Only car buffs will have heard of them, but some of their brands are recognizable: Humber, Talbot, Hillman, and Sunbeam. The last name on the list was responsible for the Rapier H120, a stylish, fastback coupe. There was a hint of Americana in the car's profile, not too surprising given that the Chrysler Corporation had a large stake in Rootes. It had a squared-off nose and long sloping rear window that led to a spoilered trunk (boot) lid.

The H120 was the top-of-the-line version of the Fastback Rapier, a four-seater coupe based on the chassis of the Hillman Hunter station wagon (estate). To boost the power of the standard 105-cubic-inch (1,725-cc) engine, Sunbeam turned to a small family-run tuning company called Holbay Engineering (now also defunct). The list of modifications made is exhaustive: Holbay added a new cylinder head, exhaust manifold, high-lift camshaft, and twin Weber carburetors. The H120 also had a close-ratio gearbox with overdrive and a new rear axle to allow a higher top speed.

The aesthetics of the car were also altered, with wider Rostyle wheels (a British style of wheel modeled on U.S. muscle cars), polished sills, a stripe down the side, and a black radiator grille. Ironically, the next version that Sunbeam produced was the lower powered Alpine Fastback, which was much cheaper and was aimed at more budget-conscious buyers.

Production ended in 1976, by which time just 46,000 Alpines and Rapiers had been built. The Rootes Group's days were now numbered. **JI**

Wheel detail from a Ferrari Dino 308 GT4 2+2 coupe, introduced in 1973.

1970–1979

Hai | Monteverdi

CH

1970 • 425 cu in/6,974 cc, V8 • 450 bhp/331 kW • 0–60 mph/97 kph in 4.9 seconds • 180 mph/290 kph

Only two prototypes of this car were ever produced, which does make it just a bit special. The car was built by the Monteverdi company, which was founded by the versatile Peter Monteverdi. He had built his first car in his father's auto repair shop at the age of seventeen, when he took a wrecked Fiat and turned it into what he called the Monteverdi Special. He never lacked confidence, and many years later, with his Monteverdi company, he aimed to build only high-performance luxury cars. His first was the 375S, which garnered good reviews but only modest sales.

Monteverdi's second car was this one—the Hai 450 SS—which was even faster and with better acceleration, as the specifications show. He was really setting his sights on the very top end of the market, trying to compete directly with the likes of Ferrari, Lamborghini, and Maserati. However, he simply did not have the financial clout to compete with the big boys.

The Hai was designed by Italian coachbuilders Fissore, who had undertaken work for Porsche. For Monteverdi Fissore came up with a car that was superbly stylish. It had a look that was both contemporary and also a little otherworldly. The car made its debut at the Geneva Auto Show in 1970 where it drew plenty of admiration but no orders. It was simply too expensive.

The car was shown in several places, but each time it was slightly changed to try and conceal the fact that there was only one in existence. Another prototype was made, but has not survived. When the Monteverdi Hai 450SS with chassis number TNT 101 came up for auction in 2010, it sold for $520,000 (£330,000). **MG**

Junior Zagato | Alfa Romeo

I

1970 • 78 cu in/1,290 cc, S4 • 86 bhp/64 kW • 0–60 mph/97 kph in 11.3 seconds • 109 mph/175 kph

When Alfa Romeo's Junior Zagato was first seen at the Turin Motor Show in November 1969, it was an eye-catching addition to the company's 105/115 series of coupes. That series had been in production since 1963, and every so often Alfa Romeo came up with a twist on the basic model that kept interest alive and sales healthy. The GT1300 Junior came along in 1969 with a top speed of over 100 mph (160 kph), and then in 1970 the Junior Zagato was brought into the range, but was always intended as a high-end limited edition model.

The Zagato name came from the car's body designers, the Zagato engineering and design company of Milan. They were known for car designs that were both stylish and aerodynamic, as well as being ultralightweight. As well as Alfa Romeo they worked for other top names including Maserati, Lancia, Ferrari, Rolls-Royce, and Aston Martin. For the new car, Alfa Romeo took the chassis of their renowned Spider series and, combined with the Zagato body, came up with a two-seater coupe that had all the class and cachet that was expected of Alfa Romeo.

The car's top speed was in excess of the official manufacturer's specification, aided by the stylishly sloping front and the Kammback tail, named after the engineer Wunibald Kamm, who invented a tail that was shaped to reduce turbulence and drag. Zagato had also produced a design that had minimal interference with the driver's all-around visibility; the car also managed to achieve reasonable fuel consumption despite its high-spec. Even though only 1,115 of them were ever made before production ceased in 1972, the Junior Zagato went on to influence car design well into the 1990s. **MG**

Montreal | Alfa Romeo

(I)

1970 • 158 cu in/2,593 cc, V8 • 197 bhp/147 kW • 0–60 mph/97 kph in 7.1 seconds • 133 mph/220 kph

In 1967 Alfa Romeo showed a concept car at Expo 67 in Montreal. It was a sleek 2+2 coupe, with a 97-cubic-inch (1,600-cc) Alfa engine and body styling by Marcello Gandini at Bertone. It caused a sensation, and although the concept had no name, people called it "The Montreal" and the name stuck. By the time Alfa Romeo put the car into production two years later, it had been given a bigger engine. When it was unveiled at the 1970 Geneva Motor Show, the Alfa Romeo Montreal had been upgraded to a 158-cubic-inch (2,600-cc) V8 engine with double wishbone suspension, and a limited slip differential.

The Bertone design made the Montreal a stunning looker. A distinctive feature is the front end, with its four headlights that are covered by unusual grilles. When switched on, the grilles retract to give the light a clear path. Two other notable features are the scooped-out duct on the hood (bonnet) and slatted areas behind the doors. Both of these feature are more cosmetic than functional. The hood duct is blocked off, and merely hides a power bulge above the engine. The slats conceal where air exits the cabin.

The Montreal was in production for seven years, and unusually its manufacture was split between three locations. The chassis was built at Alfa Romeo's factory in Arese, then transported to a Bertone plant near Turin for the body to be fitted; it was then moved to another Bertone center for painting and cabin fitment, before finally going back to Arese for the engine installation. A metallic brown Alfa Montreal features in a 1974 Hollywood movie *The Marseille Contract*, in which it is driven by Michael Caine. **SB**

SM | Citroën

(F)

1970 • 164 cu in/2,700 cc, V6 • 170 bhp/127 kW • 0–60 mph/97 kph in 8.4 seconds • 140 mph/220 kph

The Citroën SM was also known as the Citroën Maserati. SM stood for Sports Maserati because the car was designed as a sports version of the Citroën DS, with a Maserati engine. It was the most dramatically styled car of its era, looking like a wingless aircraft on the ground, at a time when Concorde had just made its first flight.

The SM's futuristic body, with a sharply sloping rear screen and chopped-off tail, was the work of Citroën's chief designer Robert Opron. He had worked on aircraft design in the United States, and the SM reflected that background. The vehicle was unusually aerodynamic for its time, with a remarkably low drag coefficient of 0.26, when a figure nearer 0.35 CD was much more common for most cars. When viewed from above, the Citroën SM's shape resembled a teardrop, with a wide front end tapering further back toward the tail.

At the time of its launch in 1970, the Citroën SM was the fastest front-wheel-drive car on the market. Like the Citroën DS on which it was based, the SM had hydro-pneumatic suspension and self-leveling headlights that turned with the steering. Unusually, it had six square-shaped headlights, a trio of lights on each side, set behind clear panels. This arrangement was then illegal in the United States so the U.S. version of the Citroën SM had four round headlights.

Citroën SM owners included Soviet leader Leonid Brezhnev and author Graham Greene. The car was only produced for four years. In 1974 Citroën went bankrupt and was acquired by Peugeot, who sold Maserati, which had been owned by Citroën, and stopped making the SM. Its end came shortly after the 1973 fuel crisis, when demand for such cars was at a low ebb. **SB**

Gremlin | AMC

(USA)

1970 • 198 cu in/3,258 cc, S6 • 128 bhp/96 kW • 0–60 mph/97 kph in 15.3 seconds • 95 mph/152 kph

Launching a car called the Gremlin on April 1 could be seen as asking for trouble, but the American Motors Corporation did just that in 1970 and went on to sell over 670,000 of them. The AMC Gremlin was the first compact car; the company described it as "the first American-built import." For some time smaller European cars had been imported into the U.S. market, proving that not all American drivers wanted a huge, gas-guzzling monster.

Chevrolet was working on its Vega and Ford on its Pinto, when AMC beat them to the punch with the Gremlin. AMC got in first, and got it right, as the sales figures showed. It became AMC's best-selling passenger car since its Rambler Classic, almost ten years earlier.

What is remarkable is that AMC was one of the smaller companies, with a lot less cash for developing new vehicles. Its designer Richard Teague said that he sketched out the Gremlin on the back of an air sickness bag, about eighteen months before the launch. AMC produced two versions—a two-seater and a four-seater, with the smaller one selling at a modest price of $1,879 (£1,200). Combined with the engine performance, which produced a much faster car than rival models that arrived later, it was little wonder that it went on selling, with refinements, for the next eight years. **MG**

Celica | Toyota

(J)

1970 • 96 cu in/1,588 cc, S4 • 105 bhp/78.2 kW • 0–60 mph/97 kph in 11.5 seconds • 105 mph/168 kph

For thirty-six years and seven generations of development, the Celica was the Toyota's affordable sports coupe, exported around the world and loved by enthusiasts. Always powered by four-cylinder engines, the name is said to come from the Latin word *coelica*, which means "heavenly." It spawned the Celica Supra, which, as the Supra, went on to become one of the best-loved Japanese performance cars of all time.

When Toyota killed the car off in 2006 there was no official explanation. The Mark I car was unveiled at the 1970 Tokyo Motor Show and went on sale in the domestic and North American markets early the next year. It was replaced in 1977 by the Mark II car, best known for being designed by former American child actor David Stollery. The Mark III appeared in 1981 and the next year the first turbocharged version was launched in Japan. Badged the GT-T and powered by a 109-cubic-inch (1,800-cc) gas engine, it formed the basis of Toyota's Group B rally car. The fourth generation in 1985 saw the biggest change to the Celica when it swapped from rear to front-wheel drive. American actor Eddie Murphy advertised the Mark V car, and the Mark VI arrived in 1993 with its double round headlight styling. Six years later the final model appeared, and production ended on April 21, 2006. **RY**

Manta GT/E | Opel (D)

1970 • 115 cu in/1,897 cc, S4 • 102 bhp/76 kW • 0–60 mph/97 kph in 11.2 seconds • 103 mph/163 kph

The Opel Manta appeared in 1970 to rival the Ford Capri, launched a year earlier. Like the Capri, the Manta was a rear-wheel-drive, two-door sports coupe. Both cars were prompted by market research that indicated a desire among car buyers for something a bit less mainstream, and more sporty and interesting.

The Manta debuted at the Paris Motor Show in 1970. Opel had one previous foray into more specialized models with the Opel GT, a two-seater sports coupe. Its successor was the Manta, which was a more practical four-seater car. Its styling was the work of Chuck Jordan, Opel's head of design, who later became design chief at General Motors.

The Manta had a fluid body style fronted by four, small, round headlights and finishing in distinctive circular rear lights on a slightly upswept tail. The side view was very clean-cut, with minimal trim or embellishments, and a notable absence of the quarter-light windows that were a common feature at the time.

Opel's aim was to create a stylish car that still had reasonable back seat room and a good-sized trunk (boot). The Manta was best-known with a 115-cubic-inch (1,884-cc) engine, although other engine sizes were available. During its five-year production run, almost half a million Opel Mantas were built. **SB**

Camaro SS 396 | Chevrolet (USA)

1970 • 401 cu in/6,587 cc, V8 • 375 bhp/280 kW • 0–60 mph/97 kph in 6.2 seconds • 128 mph/205 kph

The first Camaro was built to kick the butt of the Mustang, so its design was dictated by that task. Even though its mission was the same, the 1970 Generation II struck out on its own; Bill Mitchell's design team took inspiration from European exotic coupes, and the result is regarded as a design classic by its many fans.

Chevrolet positioned the new Camaro as an all-around sports car or GT tourer. Virtually every part was new, and it was bigger and heavier. The Mark I convertible had sold poorly, so the new car was strictly coupe only. Mechanically it continued to share Nova underpinnings. The suspension was by A-arms at the front and leaf springs at the rear.

Eight engines were offered; the ultimate SS Camaro had an optional 375-bhp (280-kW) "396" engine with a Holley carb and mechanical valve lifters permitting it to rev higher. A good classic model cost $30,000 (£19,000) upward. The flagship was the Z/28 powered by the 360-bhp version of the 350 engine.

The Camaro's real nemesis was not the Mustang but OPEC. The fuel crisis of the early 1970s brought high gas prices and emissions controls. The 1972 Camaros were the last to offer "big-block" engines and, in fact, only 930 were produced that year. This would also be the last year for the SS until the 1996 model. **LT**

The Blue Flame being prepared for its land speed record attempt at Bonneville Salt Flats, Utah, in September 1970. ▷

Nagari VIII | Bolwell (AUS)

1970 • 302 cu in/4,958 cc, V8 • 220 bhp/164 kW • 0–60 mph/97 kph in under 5 seconds • 130 mph/209 kph

Calculating power-to-weight ratios is a complex business, involving an understanding of rarely considered concepts such as kinetic energy, angular velocity, and "peak" and "actual" values. Essentially it means taking a vehicle's power output and dividing it by its mass (or kerb weight, that is minus driver and cargo) to arrive at a number. The lower the number, the faster the car will go. The 1970 Nagari VIII weighed just 2,160 lbs (980 kg) thanks primarily to its all-fiberglass body (cast in one piece, not in panels as in previous models) and with a Ford V8 under the hood. When the reviewer *Unique Cars* were asked to test-drive it and provide a top speed, they did not come back with a number; they came back with a word: "frightening."

Graham and Campbell Bolwell began building kit cars in 1963 and produced their first Nagari in 1970 before moving to a production series that to this day remains as collectible as anything in Australian motoring. There may not have been a lot of room in the Mark VIII cockpits due to their massive engine, and the pedals were so close together that there was always a good chance the driver would press all three at once, but there have to be some concessions to comfort in return for reveling in the uncommon power it provided.

The Bolwell brothers abandoned carmaking in the 1980s to pursue other interests, but in 2008 they revived the brand with the new Bolwell Nagari. "I was in Canada making wind turbines," Campbell said, "and when I returned thought, 'It's time I built another car.'" Bolwell's latest carbon-fiber, supercharged V6 weighs less than the old Mark VIII and goes from 0-60 mph (97 kph) in under five seconds. Real supercar territory. **BS**

Flame | Blue (USA)

1970 • rocket-powered • 58,000 bhp/42,630 kW • 0–60 mph/97 kph in 1 second • 650 mph/1,046 kph

The first world land speed record was recorded in France in December 1898, when an electric-powered Jeantaud Duc car driven by the grandly named Gaston de Chasseloup-Laubat reached the giddy heights of 39.24 mph (63.15 kph). In 1904 the record was broken in the United States for the first time when Henry Ford's Ford 999 Racer set a new record of 91.37 mph (147.05 kph). From 1929 to the early 1960s, the record stayed in British hands, although most attempts were made on the Bonneville Salts Flats, Utah, in the United States.

It was here in the early 1960s that Craig Breedlove kept breaking his own record in the Spirit of America, pushing the record up to 594 mph (955.95 kph). To drive their car, the builders of the Blue Flame, Reaction Dynamics, hired Gary Gabelich, a one-time delivery driver who had become a racing driver. Gabelich and Blue Flame went for the record on October 23, 1970. (Some sources give the date as October 28, but the Fédération Internationale de l'Automobile, which monitors the event, confirm it was October 23.)

To meet the requirements of the record, the vehicle has to be measured over a Flying Mile, and then back again in the opposite direction to balance out any wind influence; the two speeds are then averaged out. Timing the driving is quite a skill. At one point the rocket-powered Blue Flame was clocked at 650 mph (1,010 kph), but for the record Gabelich averaged 622.407 mph (1001.667 kph) over the Flying Mile and an even faster 630.478 mph (1014.656 kph) for the Flying Kilometer. The record would stand until October 1984. Sadly, Gary Gabelich died in a motorcycle accident in January 1985. **MG**

THE BLUE FLAME

Bug | Bond

GB

1970 • 241 cu in/3,950 cc, V8 • 29 bhp/22 kW • 0–60 mph/97 kph in 23.2 seconds • 78 mph/126 kph

The 1970s was a colorful decade in the United Kingdom: one of the most popular shades for bathrooms was avocado green, and a bright burned orange was the default color for a three-wheeled microcar that arrived on the scene as the decade began. The Bond Bug was styled by Tom Karen of Ogle Design, who was also the man responsible for the look of Luke Skywalker's "Landspeeder" car in the *Star Wars* film, which he created using the chassis of a Bond Bug with the wheels concealed behind mirrors set at forty-five degrees to the ground.

The Bond Bug was produced by Reliant after the Tamworth-based car company bought Bond Cars. The intention was to design a fun car that would appeal to the Swinging Sixties generation growing up and getting mobile. Chief engineer John Crosthwaite designed the chassis, using some of the running gear from a budget model already made by Reliant, the Regal.

The Bug was a tiny two-seater, just over nine feet (2.74 m) long, with a single front wheel and two at the back. The headlights were set into deep grooves in the hood (bonnet). The engine was a 42-cubic-inch (700-cc) unit crammed in at the front, and because of the car's short length it protruded into the passenger area. The standard 700 and 700E models were very basic, but there was also the 700ES, which had better-upholstered seats, extra cabin padding, splash guards, a rubber front bumper, spare wheel, and an ashtray.

The little three-wheeler was only in production for four years, during which time 2,270 were made. It was not particularly cheap, priced just above the four-wheeled, four-seater Mini 850 on sale at the same time. **SB**

Jimny LJ10 | Suzuki

J

1970 • 22 cu in/359 cc, S2 • 21 bhp/15.4 kW • unknown • 47 mph/76 kph

When a U.K. car magazine tested the newly launched Porsche Cayenne SUV, they pitted it against another four-wheel-drive machine, driving them both around a demanding off-road test area. The rival duly hammered the mighty Porsche into the ground. The car was none other than the Suzuki Jimny—a car that proves once and for all that size does not matter, at least when it comes to traversing a plowed field or the side of a Welsh hill.

The Jimny actually dates back to 1970. Suzuki had bought one of its early Japanese rivals, the Hope Motor Company, the year before. They took the firm's two-seater, four-wheel-drive car, rebodied it and put in their own engine. By keeping the two-stroke motor below 22 cubic inches (360 cc) and the overall car length under 10 feet (3 m)—by putting the spare wheel next to the single rear passenger—it qualified for Kei Car status. This kept it exempt from certain Japanese taxes and levies.

The construction was simple, with a ladder chassis and a centrally mounted gearbox that sent propshafts out to the front and rear axles. However, it really was like a miniature Jeep, with true off-road abilities.

Within two years Suzuki had updated it with a liquid-cooled engine and some stylistic changes. Later in the 1970s it began to be sold outside of Japan and its cult status started.

Today the Jimny remains on sale. It still has a ladder chassis and small 79-cubic-inch (1,300-cc) engine but now comes equipped with modern features. Essentially it is a small off-roader capable of embarrassing much more expensive competition. **JI**

El Camino LS6 | Chevrolet

USA

1970 • 402 cu in/6,600 cc, V8 • 450 bhp/331 kW • 0–60 mph/97 kph in 6.6 seconds • 105 mph/169 km/ph

In the late 1950s, farmers in Australia and the United States cried out for dual-purpose automobiles that could take the family to church and the livestock to market with equal ease. Ford answered the call with the Ranchero, while Chevrolet's response was El Camino.

The El Camino started off as a stolid goods wagon that could scrub up for Sundays, but developed over the next decade into a rubber-burning powerhouse. By 1970 there was only the most perfunctory pretense that the Camino was a set of wheels for all the family. Although El Camino retained the bench seat and the deep-twist carpeting up front, and the goods trailer astern, these were no more than light camouflage that made an unconvincing job of hiding the fact that this was really a truck to hurl about in official (and not-so-official) off-road competitions.

The truth began to dawn when one noticed the fat 7-inch (17.7-cm) RWL tires. It became further apparent when the hood (bonnet) was lifted to reveal one of the four V8s that Chevrolet offered on this model. And then when the car was driven, it was crystal clear that the four-speed manual transmission had not been set up in such close ratio for trips to the shopping mall.

Almost as soon as El Camino hit the streets, General Motors decided that, in order to meet increasingly stringent U.S. government emission standards, all its new vehicles from that point should run on unleaded fuel. Chevrolet therefore detuned all its motors and never again produced such a powerful engine, thus assuring El Camino a unique place in history as the last in a long and distinguished dynasty of American muscle cars. **GL**

Chevelle SS | Chevrolet

(USA)

1970 • 396 cu in/6,489 cc, V8 • 325 bhp/243 kW • 0–60 mph/97 kph in 6.8 seconds • 122 mph/195 kph

The 1993 movie *Dazed and Confused* helped make stars out of some of its young actors, including Ben Affleck and Matthew McConaughey, but it was also one of the great car movies of all time. It pays tribute to Dodges and Fords, to Pontiacs and Chevies, and one of its big car stars is Chevrolet's Chevelle SS. McConaughey's character, David Wooderson, drives a 1970 model of the car, which he calls Melba Toast because it soaks up the opposition. It was one of the most powerful production muscle cars ever made, so little wonder that one of the movie's coolest characters should drive one.

The first Chevelle was introduced in 1964 and it was intended to be a very versatile car, with different models ranging from family-friendly and station wagons (estates) through to the muscle cars—the Chevelle SS models. The Chevelles sold well, becoming one of the company's best-selling lines, with more than 76,800 of the SS versions built in 1964.

In 1968 the cars were redesigned, with shorter rears and longer front-ends to create a more fastback look, although sales were down to 57,600 units. By 1970 sales had slipped another few thousand, but the cars built in this year were among the best and most powerful that were made.

It was also something of a swan song for the muscle car, however. After the freewheeling 1960s, the 1970s heralded the beginnings of the health and safety movements. One of the consequences of this was a detuning of muscle car engines, and as a result sales fell. By 1972 only 5,333 examples of the Chevelle SS had been built. David Wooderson bought one of the last of the best of them. **MG**

RRW 97L

⊂ A 1975 publicity shot for the Triumph Stag shows off the car's stylish exterior; mechanically, it was less of a success.

Stag | Triumph (GB)

1970 • 182 cu in/2,997 cc, V8 • 147 bhp/108 kW • 0–60 mph/97 kph in 9.5 seconds • 115 mph/185 kph

In the late 1960s Triumph's director of engineering, Harry Webster, was good friends with the Italian designer Giovanni Michelotti. "Micho," as Webster called him, had already done some design work for the company, and he was given a surplus works Triumph 2000 to adapt as a design concept car. It was intended for display at the Turin Motor Show. The two men agreed that if Triumph liked the result, the company would get first refusal to use it as the basis for a production model.

Michelotti's design adaptation never made it to his Turin show stand. Instead, Triumph adopted it for a sports coupe it planned to roll out as a fast, stylish, and exclusive but better-priced rival for the Mercedes-Benz 280SL. While the car was under development, Triumph merged with Austin-Rover to become part of British Leyland. Webster changed jobs and the project was taken over by Spen King, formerly at Rover.

The Stag was launched in 1970, to general acclaim. Its style was much admired, although the car was soon blighted by reports of mechanical unreliability. This was attributed to poor build quality resulting in engine problems. *Time* magazine subsequently rated the Triumph Stag as one of the worst cars ever made. As a result of the problems, many Stags that have survived to the modern day have been fitted with substitute engines. However, cars with original Triumph V8 engines are the most sought-after by collectors.

The car remained in production until 1977, and during the seven years of its manufacture almost 26,000 were made. A Triumph Stag featured in the 1971 James Bond film *Diamonds Are Forever*. **SB**

Deauville | De Tomaso (I)

1970 • 351 cu in/5,763 cc, V8 • 330 bhp/246 kW • unknown • 143 mph/228 kph

Alejandro de Tomaso was an Argentine businessman who emigrated to Italy. The first cars he was responsible for were the Vallelunga and Mangusta, but his breakthrough came with the 1970 Pantera. A coupe with classic U.S. muscle-car looks, he struck a deal with Ford to sell it through the "blue oval's" North American dealerships. The price paid was his shares in the Italian coachbuilding firm Ghia.

Selling alongside the Pantera was the Deauville. A four-door sedan (saloon) with a striking resemblance to Jaguar's XJ6, it was unveiled at the 1970 Turin Motor Show and featured high-grade Italian leather and suede upholstery. Built on the same chassis as the Maserati Quattroporte III, it was powered by Ford's V8 Mustang engine.

Three generations of the car came and went before the Deauville was axed in the late 1980s. However, over the course of eighteen years of production, less than 250 were made. All were sedans except for a station wagon (estate) version, reputedly built for De Tomaso's wife.

After several years on the shelf, the car's rights were acquired by Italian businessman Gian Mario Rossignolo in 2009, and at the 2011 Geneva Motor Show he debuted an all-new Deauville. Styled as a five-door, hatchback crossover SUV rather than a sedan, he announced plans to put it into production.

Rossignolo hopes to avoid the reliability problems that the brand is perhaps best remembered for. The story of Elvis Presley shooting his gun at a car because it would not start has passed into rock 'n' roll folklore. The vehicle in question was a De Tomaso Pantera. **RY**

Escort RS1600 | Ford

GB

1970 • 95 cu in/1,558 cc, S4 • 120 bhp/88 kW • 0–60 mph/97 kph in 8 seconds • 118 mph/190 kph

This car was conceived as the public road-friendly version of the Escort that Hannu Mikkola drove to victory in the 1970 London to Mexico World Cup Rally. It was the first Ford to carry the "RS" (Rallye Sport) badge and the first car that really put a motorsport element into the small family car range.

Under the hood (bonnet) it featured a Kent engine block (designed by Ford and Lotus) and a sixteen-valve double overhead camshaft (DOHC) supplied by Cosworth, the British high-performance engineering company. These upgrades to the original Mark I Escort demanded significant alterations to the basic two-door shell; they were carried out by Italian stylists Ghia. The main visible difference between the standard production car and the RS1600 is that the latter had slightly longer rear quarterlights, a modification that increased the ease with which the shell and the floor could be joined together. Under the skin, which was specially strengthened, the suspension was beefed up to give sportier handling.

Among a host of features that were innovative at the time were a catalytic converter on the exhaust system, a tilt-and-slide factory-fitted sunroof, tinted glass on the windshield, and central locking. The RS1600 was also one of the earliest production cars to run on unleaded gasoline.

Off-road, the RS1600 swept all before it, winning the East African Safari in 1972 and the British RAC three times running (1972–74), as well as a host of other rallies. The sporty halo model helped the whole Escort range become a successful seller, too. It fast became one of Britain's most popular cars. **GL**

Escort Mexico | Ford

GB

1970 • 97 cu in/1,599 cc, S4 • 87 bhp/64.8 kW • 0–60 mph/97 kph in 10.7 seconds • 99 mph/159 kph

When the Ford Anglia reached the end of its natural life, it was replaced by an all-new car with vastly more advanced styling. The Mk I Escort—with its classic "dog-bone" front grille—was launched in 1967 and became an instant sales hit across Europe.

It was also a hugely successful rally car and the Ford factory team was virtually unbeatable for the next five years. The highlight was victory in the 1970 London to Mexico Rally. Racing between two World Cup venues—London had staged the tournament in 1966 and Mexico was hosting in 1970—the six-week driving challenge covered 16,000 miles (25,749 km) through Western Europe and Central and South America. Finnish driver Hannu Mikkola and navigator Gunnar Palm took the win, with other Escorts finishing in third, fifth, and sixth places. Thrilled Ford bosses launched the Escort Mexico special edition to celebrate. Including tax and delivery charges, it cost $1,800 (£1,150). The "custom pack," which added Recaro sports seats, carpets, and a walnut fascia with clock, was a popular option.

The car filled the gap in the range between the GT and the Twin Cam models, and not surprisingly it became an attractive choice with amateur rally drivers everywhere. The car's straightforward 97-cubic-inch (1,600-cc) engine and durable heavy-duty body have maintained its position as a favorite in classic rallying.

More than 9,000 Escort Mexicos were built before it was killed off in 1974. Its place in history is guaranteed because it marked the start of the British public's ongoing fascination with "fast Fords." Indeed, there has been a monthly magazine in the United Kingdom with that very name since the mid-1980s. **RY**

Challenger R/T | Dodge

(USA)

1970 • 439 cu in/7,206 cc, V8 • 375 bhp/280 kW • 0–60 mph/97 kph in 5.5 seconds • 103 mph/165 kph

Dodge had used the name Challenger before for their 1959 Silver Challenger, a limited-edition model that came only in silver. When they were planning to use the name again ten years later, it was also for a car that had to be something special. They wanted to build the most powerful pony car ever seen—"pony car" being a term that was created after the phenomenal success of the Ford Mustang back in 1964. It described a car that was compact yet powerful, stylish yet not too expensive. In short, it was a kind of dream car.

With a massive 439-cubic-inch (7,200-cc) engine under the hood (bonnet), there was no doubt that the new Challenger would be powerful. The power did not go into producing a supersonic speed; the top speed was impressive enough for road use, but it did give the car some serious acceleration and it could reach its top speed in less than twenty seconds. That figure was for the top-of-the-line model, the R/T (Road and Track). There were no fewer than seven less-powerful engine versions available and a bewildering variety of choices for the buyer: a two-door convertible or two-door hardtop, with three-speed manual, three-speed automatic, or four-speed transmissions. The car's design was by Carl Cameron, the man who had also masterminded Dodge's 1966 Charger, another landmark vehicle for the company.

The many different versions of the Challenger sold a total of 165,437 over the four-year existence of the first generation of Challengers (when the name was resurrected in 1978 it was a rather different vehicle). Of those, it is thought that just forty-four of the special R/T model survive, and they are highly collectible. **MG**

Road-Runner Superbird | Plymouth

USA

1970 • 439 cu in/7,210 cc • 375 bhp/276 kW • 0–60 mph/97 kph in 6.7 seconds • 160 mph/257 kph

Modern racing teams have ranks of aerodynamics experts analyzing wind tunnel data to design bodies that slice through air, while creating downforce to cling like limpets to the road. This idea was novel in the late 1960s, and two of the craziest road cars ever made were the result of Chrysler's early dabbling in this new science. The Dodge Daytona and Plymouth Road-Runner Superbird both started as possibly the most brick-shaped sedans (saloons) on the road, but they sprouted pointy beaks and massive rear wings in order to beat Ford in the prestigious NASCAR race series. Chrysler's Special Vehicles Group called in experts from the aerospace industry and tested the Dodge in a wind tunnel built for Apollo space missions.

Plymouth's Superbird followed the Daytona's lead but had significant differences. It was created for the legendary driver Richard Petty, who gained his nickname "the King" by taking 200 NASCAR wins.

Plymouth needed to sell 1,920 road cars to qualify for NASCAR. The production model was offered with a 440-cubic-inch (7,210-cc) V8, or the 426-cubic-inch (6,980-cc) Hemi. All cars wore a decal of the famous Roadrunner relentlessly pursued by hapless Wile E. Coyote from Warner Bros.'s iconic cartoons. Options included a "beep beep" horn.

Despite its NASCAR success, buyers did not rush out to buy Road-Runner Superbirds, and many dealers stripped off the wings and beaks. Having sold for $4,298 (£2,775) new, classics can fetch $200,000 (£130,000). A blue Superbird called "The King" took to the track in the 2006 Disney-Pixar movie *Cars*, voiced by none other than Richard Petty. **SH**

The iconic chiseled styling of the Range Rover, the work of David Bache, has ensured its status as a design classic. ▷

114 | Zil (RUS)

1970 • 421 cu in/6,900 cc, V8 • 303 bhp/222 kW • 0–60 mph/97 kph in 13.5 seconds • 124 mph/200 kph

The height of luxury in the Soviet era, the Zil-114 was fitted with air-conditioning, electric doors, central locking, and specially tinted windows. It was built only in small quantities and was used almost exclusively for chauffeuring members of the Kremlin Central Committee and their distinguished guests, sometimes along special road lanes reserved only for VIPs in ZILs.

In the USSR it was commonly known in Russian as *chlenovoz,* which can be translated into English as "Politburo taxi." The ZIL company was founded in 1916, but, because of the Russian Revolution in the following year and the ensuing unrest, it was not until 1924 that it produced its first vehicle—a 1.5-ton truck based (without official acknowledgment) on the Fiat F-15. The car's name—an acronym of Zavod Imeni Likhachova ("Factory named after Likhachova," the first director of the plant)—was imposed on the firm by Soviet leader Nikita Khrushchev in 1956.

This outsized Russian limousine superseded the ZIL-111 in 1970. It was basically the same as its predecessor, but had a more powerful engine and modern styling that included a meshed radiator grille and four headlights instead of two. Most ZIL-114s were seven-seaters, but at least one (the 114EA) was specially adapted for the leaders' medical team, with only five seats and room for a stretcher, while another (the 114K) was fitted with a retractable roof hatch so that passengers could stand and wave to crowds.

The most remarkable fact about this great dinosaur of a car was its curb weight, which—at 6,801 lbs (3,085 kg)—is 1,700 lbs (771 kg) more than even the heaviest Maybach. **GL**

Range Rover | Rover (GB)

1970 • 215 cu in/3,528 cc, V8 • 135 bhp/101 kW • 0–60 mph/97 kph in 13.9 seconds • 91 mph/146 kph

The Range Rover made its public debut in June 1970 and was the star of the London Motor Show at Earls Court that fall. It combined two elements for which there was a demand: the rugged, go-anywhere ability for which Land Rover was already renowned with its all-terrain Defender, together with the comforts of a less agricultural car. However, it was not, back then, the luxury vehicle it has since become. The original Range Rover was fairly basic inside, with vinyl seats, a plastic dashboard, and rubber flooring, designed to be washed down with water when it got dirty.

The engineering design team for the Range Rover in the late 1960s was headed by Spen King and Gordon Bashford, who spent six years perfecting the technical formula. They were also responsible for the basic shape of the car, although its iconic chiseled final styling was the work of David Bache. The result was well-received not only in the United Kingdom, but also abroad, including in France, where a Range Rover was exhibited in the Louvre Museum in Paris in late 1970 as "an outstanding piece of modern sculpture."

In 1972, the Range Rover made history when two specially modified cars were used for the British Trans-Americas Expedition. This became the first vehicle-based expedition to traverse the two American continents from north to south, including the roadless swampland and forest of the Darién Gap.

The Range Rover continues to be built at Land Rover's factory in Solihull, West Midlands. The current-generation car is at the pinnacle of luxury "sports utility vehicles" that have been dubbed "Chelsea tractors" by twenty-first-century environmentalists. **SB**

RANGE ROVER
YVB 153H

Hemi Cuda | Plymouth

USA

1970 • 427 cu in/7,000 cc, V8 • 425 bhp/312 kW • 0–60 mph/97 kph in 5.8 seconds • 117 mph/188 kph

In 1968, Plymouth fulfilled a small number of orders from wealthy customers for customized Barracudas with Hemi motors. These engines—in which the roof of each combustion chamber is hemispherical in shape—were the type that first made Chrysler's name. The results were magnificent. However, with their plastic side windows, fiberglass fenders and hood (bonnet), and no exhaust system, they could not legally travel on U.S. highways. The company then decided to work out how the car could be made roadworthy.

Two years later the Hemi Cuda moved into production. It was a high-styled performance pony car that gave a five-fingered salute to the notion that economical was best. A gas-guzzler par excellence, even the most careful drivers could get no more than six miles per gallon out of it.

The car was sold with a wide range of options, including decals, hood modifications, and head-turning 1970s colors, such as Vitamin C (orange), In-Violet, Sassy Grass Green, and Moulin Rouge (red). There was also a convertible model, although only fourteen of the 652 that were built were dropheads. The critical choice was between a four-speed stick shift and automatic transmission; the latter packed a bigger punch and therefore became the version that enthusiastic drivers preferred.

Production ceased four years later. Since then the car has appreciated in value, which is unusual for a vehicle that, in spite of all its distinctive edgings, is basically a souped-up version of an ordinary production car. In the United States, well-preserved models fetch higher prices than Bugattis or Ferraris of the same vintage. **GL**

Monte Carlo | Chevrolet

(USA)

1970 • 349 cu in/5,733 cc, V8 • 250 bhp/187 kW • 0–60 mph/97 kph in 8.6 seconds • 126 mph/202 kph

In 1970 the muscle cars of the United States were at their peak. Pontiac had been selling its Grand Prix since 1962, and was growing with each new generation. Chevrolet's response was the Monte Carlo. It was the idea of Chevrolet's general manager, Elliot M. Estes, who had previously had a successful career heading Pontiac, whose sales increased dramatically under his leadership. Estes worked alongside the company's chief stylist, Dave Holls, to produce a four-person, two-door coupe with some muscle under the hood (bonnet).

It certainly had power and did well on the NASCAR stock-racing circuit. Construction-wise it was a bit of a mongrel, borrowing some of its looks from Cadillac's long-running classic, the Eldorado, and sharing some of the bodywork from Chevrolet's own Chevelle, which came out the same year. This made economic sense, as Chevrolet brought out several new models that year, and if they could share some parts, then it made them cheaper to produce. All they had to do was differentiate them enough, and in this they succeeded.

By the time the Monte Carlo was first shown in the fall of 1969, Estes had left the company and it fell to the new general manager, John DeLorean, to introduce the car. Like Estes, DeLorean had also previously headed Pontiac, where one of the projects he saw through was the Monte Carlo's inspiration, the Pontiac Grand Prix. Despite a strike at the factory where the Monte Carlo was being produced, Chevrolet still managed to make more than 159,000 of them. Soon after the muscle-car market began to collapse, but the Monte Carlo went through several transformations and lived a long and healthy life until 1988. **MG**

Spyder GTS | Puma (BR)

1970 • 96 cu in/1,584 cc, S4 • unknown • unknown • 93 mph/150 kph

High taxes on import cars meant that most Brazilians could only afford vehicles made in the country. Some global manufacturers established factories in Brazil, but there was also a boom in small-scale, homemade cars. Sao Paulo racing enthusiast Rino Malzoni started building race cars in 1964 using a three-cylinder engine in a light fiberglass body. They looked good, won some races, and drove well. The cars started selling so well that a Puma factory was established and they were soon building more than one hundred Pumas a year. Over the next six years the Puma evolved into a two-door coupe based on Volkswagen's (VW) rear-engined, rear-wheel-drive Kharmann Ghia.

In 1970 an even more desirable convertible version was launched, the Spyder GTS. The engine was still the 96-cubic-inch (1,584-cc) unit from VW with added twin carburetors for more power. The Puma Spyder was so successful the company started exporting to North America and Europe. A high-powered coupe was launched in 1973—the Puma GTB. This was a front-engined, rear-wheel-drive two-door using a 250-cubic-inch (4,100-cc) Chevrolet six-cylinder engine.

Strangely, Puma opened a factory in South Africa and while the Brazilian operation closed in the 1990s, the South Africa offshoot is still building Pumas. **SH**

Falcon GT-HO | Ford (AUS)

1971 • 351 cu in/5,752 cc, V8 • 380 bhp/279 kW • 0–60 mph/97 kph in 6.4 seconds • 142 mph/229 kph

The Falcon GT-HO ("HO" stood for "handling options") enabled Ford to achieve one of its biggest Southern Hemisphere ambitions in the 1960s: to get a high-performance car through legislative red tape and on to the roads of Australia. The hottest versions of the Aussie Falcon had been given GT badges since 1967; thereafter every new model had significantly more poke than its predecessor. Phase III was the daddy: it was the world's fastest, four-door production sedan (saloon), and retained that distinction until 1990, when it was knocked off its perch by the Lotus Carlton.

Phase IIIs carved a permanent niche for themselves in racing folklore when they finished first, second, and third in the 1971 New South Wales Bathurst 1000. Their many fans referred to them as Hoeys or Shakers, the latter name inspired by the visible vibration of the air intake scoop on the hood (bonnet) when the engine ran. Not everyone loved this bird of prey: many in the media were horrified that the Falcon should be free to tear up the public highways. The outcry led to a change in racing rules: from 1973 participants in touring car events were no longer required to have the same specs as road-going models. Allowing production models to be modified for the racetrack at last enabled manufacturers to stop making rockets with wheels. **GL**

Nova SS | Chevrolet (USA)

1971 • 349 cu in/5,733 cc, V8 • 210 bhp/157 kW • 0–60 mph/97 kph in 7 seconds • 122 mph/195 kph

Chevy's Nova series began way back in 1962, although it was then called the Chevy II Nova. In 1969 the Chevy II name was dropped, leaving behind the Chevrolet Nova. The Nova SS (Super Sports) first came along in 1966 and was the top-of-the-line car of that year. However, it was sleeker than its mouthful of a name suggested: the Chevrolet Chevy II Nova Super Sport.

In 1968 the Nova SS came alive, and Chevrolet turned it into one of the most compact muscle cars that the industry had ever seen. It was a bold reinvention. The standard engine was 349 cubic inches (5,733 cc), but a massive 396-cubic-inch (6,500-cc) version was also available. It turned the car into a movie star, too, driven by Axel Foley in the first *Beverly Hills Cop* film in 1984.

The 1969 and 1970 models were just as good, only differing slightly in appearance and performance, but the 1971 Nova SS is fondly remembered as the last great Nova. After this, the Nova engines had to be reduced in power due to increasingly stringent driving regulations, and what was once a top-of-the-line car now became commonplace. After 1971 other divisions of General Motors began rebadging the cars and selling them not as their top models but as their entry models. Axel Foley would never have driven one. **MG**

Alfasud | Alfa Romeo (I)

1971 • 241 cu in/3,950 cc, V8 • 63 bhp/47 kW • 0–60 mph/97 kph in 15 seconds • 93 mph/150 kph

The Alfasud takes it name from the fact that it was built in Alfa Romeo's factory in southern Italy (Alfa Sud means Alfa South). The factory was opened as part of an Italian government policy to help a poor region of the country. It was a brave project, with 15,000 unskilled workers being taken on to build the new car.

The Alfasud is widely regarded as one of Alfa's most successful models. It was a pretty-looking car, with bodywork styled by Giorgetto Giugiaro of Turin based Italdesign. It was warmly received both for its styling and its excellent handling, making it much more of a fun drive than many of its rivals. The first Alfasuds were four-door cars, with a two-door model and both three- and five-door hatchback versions following later.

The Alfasud was produced by a design team led by Austrian engineer Rudolf Hruska, who had worked for Porsche and Volkswagen. The team created the car from first draft to finished product in just four years, two years faster than the industry average of the time. They gave it a 73-cubic-inch (1,200-cc) flat-four-cylinder engine, influenced by Hruska's work in Germany.

Production of the Alfasud ended in 1989, after updates in 1977 and 1980. Nearly 900,000 in total were made. There were also another 121,500 of the Alfasud Sprint, a fastback variant, produced from 1976 to 1989. **SB**

3.0 CSL | BMW

D

1971 • 183 cu in/3,003 cc, S6 • 206 bhp/154 kW • 0–60 mph/97 kph in 6.8 seconds • 136 mph/218 kph

Designed to compete in race series, such as the European Touring Car Championship, the BMW 3.0 CSL was a homologation special that was intended to take on the Ford Capri. Developed from the CS and CSI models, CSL stands for "Coupe Sport Light." The lightness was achieved by using thinner steel to build the body, removing some trim parts and much of the soundproofing, and replacing glass side windows with Perspex ones. Doors, hoods (bonnets), and trunk (boot) lids were also constructed from aluminum. Luxuries such as power steering, carpets, and electric windows were also removed. BMW had to build 1,000 to comply with homologation and the first models were only available in Chamonix White and Polaris Silver.

The 3.0 CSL was developed by a special department within BMW, which would later become BMW Motorsport GmbH. While it does not carry the "M" badge, many view this to be the first-ever M car, and it was the first to boast the tricolor motorsport livery.

The car was built by BMW together with Karmann in Osnabrück, Germany. The final versions gave the car its "Batmobile" nickname by adding an outlandish aerodynamic package, which created huge downforce. This included a revised air dam, spoilers, and fins. The huge rear wings were not installed at the factory but were left in the trunk, for customers to install themselves because they were illegal on German roads at the time.

Hans Stuck and Dieter Quester were among the many famous drivers who competed in the 3.0 CSL with tremendous success, winning the European Touring Car Championship every year from 1973 to 1979, apart from 1974 when Ford took the title. **RD**

Bora | Maserati

(I)

1971 • 300 cu in/4,930 cc, V8 • 330 bhp/243 kW • 0–60 mph/97 kph in 6.1 seconds • 177 mph/285 kph

In accordance with Maserati tradition, the Bora is named after a powerful northeasterly wind that blows into the Italian Adriatic, and was the first new model produced after Citroën took control of the Italian supercar manufacturer in 1968.

The Bora was Maserati's first mid-engined, two-seater production car and was built to compete against Lamborghini's Miura, De Tomaso's Mangusta, and Ferrari's 365 GT4 BB. However, the understated styling of the Bora targeted a more refined clientele; Maserati hoped the Bora would be the ideal compromise between the hardcore supercar and a grand tourer. Huge efforts were made to improve sound proofing and minimize engine vibration from its V8 engine; it was also the first Maserati to feature fully independent coil-over suspension to improve its road manners.

Penned by Giugiaro at Italdesign, without the aid of a wind tunnel, the aerodynamic shape and sharp angles wowed the crowds at the 1971 Geneva Auto Show. Giugiaro himself described the Bora as "strikingly sporty but not inordinately aggressive . . . innovative but not revolutionary." Neat design features, such as the brushed steel roof and screen pillars, and the double-glazed engine bay canopy, set it apart from its V6-powered little brother, the Maserati Merak.

From 1974 the Bora's V8 was expanded to 299 cubic inches (4,900 cc), which placed it among the fastest supercars of its generation. A total of 571 Bora were built during its eight-year production run. The lucky few who road-tested it loved its Jekyll and Hyde personality; it combined high levels of refinement, with the stunning performance of a mid-engined supercar. **DS**

This 1971 Ford Mustang Mach 1 advertisement describes how the car's appeal ranged far beyond its innovative design.

Valiant Charger | Chrysler (AUS)

1971 • 162 cu in/2,670 cc, S6 • 302 bhp/222 kW • 0–60 mph/97 kph in 14.1 seconds • 125 mph/201 kph

In the early 1970s the South Australian police purchased twelve Valiant Chargers and adapted them for use as undercover cars. It was a decision loaded with irony because of all the cars on Australian roads of the period none was as conspicuous as the Valiant Charger. *Australian Motoring News* described it as "probably the best-looking car ever made by an Australian manufacturer." To dash any hope of remaining inconspicuous, the police then gave their new acquisitions pink and blue pin-striping. The truth, of course, was that for any Aussie male sitting in a Charger in the early 1970s the last thing they wanted was not to be noticed.

Unlike the Holden Monaro, which barged into the world declaring itself to be "the greatest," the Charger just sashayed into Australia in 1971, promptly won *Wheels* magazine's Car of the Year award, then proceeded to effortlessly embed itself into the Australian way of life. A product of Australia's sexual revolution, it was lauded as a "chick magnet" and was the car of choice in such avant-garde movies as *Alvin Purple* (1973), which kick-started the Australian march onto the international movie scene. It was cheap and powerful, too. With the help of a worked Hemi-6 engine, it grabbed, in 14.4 seconds, Australia's standing quarter of a mile record—and held it for thirty years.

The Valiant Charger was also the subject of one of the greatest TV advertising campaigns in Australian history, which saw average Aussies on the street signaling with a "V" and crying out "Hey, Charger!" as one sped by. That phrase, like the car itself, has become part of Australian culture and national identity. **BS**

Mustang Mach 1 | Ford (USA)

1971 • 301 cu in/4,942 cc, V8 • 141 bhp/105 kW • 0–60 mph/97 kph in 10 seconds • 111 mph/178 kph

Although the Ford Mustang established the style of car that became known as the pony car, the Mach 1 performance model was very much a muscle car.

Ford needed muscle because although the Mustang had hit the ground running, so to speak, after a few years other carmakers had copied, caught up, and passed the Mustang. In 1969 Ford hit back, producing no fewer than seven performance cars, including the Boss 302, Boss 429, and the Mach 1. That was some muscle for car buyers to choose from.

The Mach 1 models came with superior suspension to make the fast ride more comfortable. One small but eye-catching feature was a hood (bonnet) scoop that included tiny turning signals mounted on either side. The car was notable for much more than turning signals, however. The Mach 1 label was proved to be accurate when *Performance Buyer's Digest* magazine tested one at the Bonneville Salt Flats in Utah. It is said to have broken no fewer than 295 United States Auto Club records.

Cool superspy James Bond was probably not too picky about his turning signals, either, when the producers of the 1971 *Diamonds Are Forever* movie got hold of an early version of the 1971 Mustang Mach 1. In the 1974 action movie *Gone in 60 Seconds*, a 1973 Mach 1 was one of the forty-eight cars that had to be stolen by a gang of car thieves. The car was named Eleanor, and it is the only Ford Mustang to ever get a star credit in a movie. It does seem a crime that ninety-three cars were wrecked in the movie's lengthy car chase scene, although it was probably good news for car auction houses. **MG**

Mustang. It's a personal thing.

Like anything that lets you be yourself.

It happens every time. Get into a Mustang and something gets into you.

Is it because Mustang has more rooflines than all its competitors? A choice of six different engines?

Or is it because Mustang offers so many options to select from—so many ways to make it uniquely, totally personal?

Is it something simple, like an instrument panel that gives you organized information for a change?

Is it the proud new profile of this Mach I? Is it the NASA-type hood scoops and competition suspension you get at no extra cost?

No. Mustang is more. It's greater than the sum of its parts. It's something you have to discover. Like yourself.

Your Ford Dealer will help you make Mustang an original creation.

Ford gives you better ideas. (A better idea for safety: buckle up.)

Pantera | De Tomaso

USA

1971 • 351 cu in/5,763 cc, V8 • 350 bhp/257 kW • 0–60 mph/97 kph in 5.2 seconds • 170 mph/273 kph

The Pantera was one of the first and most affordable of supercars in the 1970s. Argentinian Alejandro De Tomaso had sold a major share of his carmaking company, plus the Ghia and Vignale styling houses to Ford, in return for support to build his all-new supercar—the Pantera. The name is the Italian word for "panther" and the badge was an Argentinian flag turned on its side, along with the branding mark of De Tomaso's cattle ranching family.

The two-door, mid-engine, rear-wheel-drive coupe used Ford's then-new 347-cubic-inch (5,700-cc) "Cleveland" V8 mated to a ZF five-speed gearbox with a limited slip differential for more traction. The road car thumped out 330 bhp (243 kW) at launch or 350 bhp (257 kW) in GTS form from 1973, enough performance to easily qualify it for the supercar category.

Race-inspired components included independent suspension, four-wheel power disc brakes, and cast magnesium wheels. The rear trunk (boot) unit was easily removable for engine access and it took plenty of luggage—one of the elements, along with factory air-con, that made the Pantera a practical choice as well as a schoolboy's fantasy. In the United States it gained a reputation for poor reliability, which was not helped when Elvis Presley famously shot his gun at his yellow Pantera after it refused to start.

On the road, the Pantera was a brute. The engine made a shattering snarl, the cabin was cramped, and the driver needed total concentration to keep the skittish beast on its leash. Nevertheless, it stayed on sale until 1993, sprouting spoilers on the way and eventually selling more than 7,000 cars. **LT**

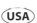

Riviera Gran Sport | Buick

(USA)

1971 • 455 cu in/7,468 cc, V8 • 330 bhp/246 kW • 0–60 mph/97 kph in 7.4 seconds • 120 mph/192 kph

When they were not calling their cars Thunderbirds or Mustangs, U.S. carmakers were fond of using European and especially French names to give an exotic flavor to some of their models. There was, for instance, the Pontiac Grand Prix and the Chevrolet Monte Carlo. Buick was ahead of the game, however, as it first used the Riviera name as long ago as 1949. Back then, and through to 1963, it was only used to describe a style of car, like the Buick Roadmaster Riviera, but from 1963 onward it was a car model in its own right.

The year 1971 saw the third generation of Buick Rivieras, with the usual several styles of car, but this was the year the Riviera got a major makeover. The most striking design change was the introduction of what was known as boat-tail styling. The rear windows were almost flattened, and tapered toward the center of the trunk (boot), making the back of the Rivieras look like the rear of a power boat, and not unlike the front of a modern-day fighter plane.

The Gran Sport version of the Riviera was one of the most impressive cars in the line, with that huge engine giving it immense acceleration power, and although sales of the GS increased to 20,000 over the previous year, Riviera sales generally went down in spite of the exciting revamp the cars were given. It was the beginning of the end for these muscle cars, and in line with other companies, Buick began to detune its hunky engines in line with the increasing demand for more fuel-efficient cars, combined with stricter safety measures. By 1972 only 9,000 Gran Sport models were sold, and although the Riviera name remained, the cars were never the same. **MG**

Miura P400 SV | Lamborghini

I

1971 • 240 cu in/3,939 cc, V12 • 385 bhp/287 kW • 0–60 mph/97 kph in 6.7 seconds • 174 mph/280 kph

At the start of the 1970s, Lamborghini introduced a new, improved version of its Miura supercar. The uprated Miura P400 SV (short for Spinto Veloce, meaning "tuned fast") became available to the wealthy car buyers of the world from 1971. With huge rear wheels 9 inches (230 mm) wide, limited slip differential for extra traction, and optional power upgrades, this has become the version of the Miura most sought after by today's car collectors. At the 2011 Amelia Island Auctions, an SV prototype, originally shown at the Geneva Motor Show, sold for $1.7 million (£1.1million).

At the same time Lamborghini produced an SV Spider prototype, but the model never went into production. That single prototype inevitably became a sought-after classic and eventually ended up in the hands of a rich car collector in Paris.

The Shah of Iran bought a special race-tuned version of the new Miura SV, keeping it under armed

guard at his royal palace in Tehran. The car has had an unusual existence. It was seized from the palace during the shah's overthrow and was eventually sold at auction. Later, the shah's special Lamborghini was bought by Hollywood actor Nicolas Cage for around $500,000 dollars (£320,000).

Lamborghini unveiled the bare chassis of its new V12 midengined sports car at the 1965 Turin Auto Show. Few could have realized that its layout was to set the template for high-performance supercars for generations to come. Even fewer could have believed that the designer Marcello Gandini, then only twenty-seven years old, would craft such a beautiful body for the first 350-bhp (260-kW) Miura P400, which was launched a year later.

By the late 1960s, the Miura had become the must-have car of the superrich and famous. Owners at that time included Frank Sinatra and Miles Davis. **DS**

Merak | Maserati

I

1972 • 183 cu in/3,000 cc, V8 • 190 bhp/142 kW • 0–60 mph/97 kph in 8.2 seconds • 135 mph/217 kph

"Merak," the name of a wind that blows across the Adriatic Sea, was chosen as the moniker for Maserati's new early 1970s sports car. Like the Maserati Junior, it was a lesser version of the Bora designed to tackle other budget supercars of the time, such as the Ferrari 246 Dino and the Lamborghini Urraco.

Giorgetto Giugiaro's elegant coupe design had a new quad-cam V6 engine in the middle, giving the Merak more interior space than the V8-engined Bora. It also had room for a pair of small seats in the rear, and was lighter and better balanced; it had a lower center of gravity, meaning that it handled better, too.

At the time, Maserati was owned by Citroën, with which it shared a number of key components. The dashboard of early Meraks was that of the Citroën SM, as were the brakes, clutch, headlights, and certain suspension components. In return, the Merak's new V6 engine was used in the Citroën SM. When Citroën sold Maserati to DeTomaso in 1975, the Merak's Citroën components were dropped.

In 1976 the SS version of the Merak was launched, with 217 bhp (162 kW) and a lower weight to improve performance. To avoid taxes on larger-engined cars in Italy, Maserati sold a 122-cubic-inch (2,000-cc), 168-bhp (125-kW) version of the V6 called the Merak 2000GT. The Merak failed to equal Lamborghini and Ferrari but remained in production until 1982.

The BBC TV *Top Gear* show bought a Merak for its "Italian Supercar Challenge," paying just £7,000 ($11,000). The fact that the engine had just been rebuilt at a cost of £10,000 ($16,000) did not prevent the Merak from self-destructing during the show. **RD**

X1/9 | Fiat

(I)

1972 • 78 cu in/1,290 cc, S4 • 73 bhp/54 kW • 0–60 mph/97 kph in 12.2 seconds • 100 mph/161 kph

This head-turning little two-seater made an immediate impact. Extraordinarily for a budget sports car, it used a midengine layout that gave it superb handling for the time, even if the performance was only average. Almost 200,000 of Fiat's "baby Ferrari" were made before production ended in 1987. That incredible record shows how much it got right, but unfortunately few have survived; the steel was of such dubious quality and they rusted—everywhere.

In 1969, Italian styling house Bertone had designed a delicate, wedge-shaped sports car with an open roof that was to be called the Autobianchi A112 Runabout. Fiat opted to take it into production as the X1/9, but with a targa roof to comply with tough U.S. safety regulations. The structural rigidity of the new arrangement helped the car's pin-sharp handling.

Rear-wheel drive and the "mid" position of the engine, giving perfect weight balance, also helped. The original 78-cubic-inch (1,290-cc) engine was underpowered and had only four gears, but from 1978 a peppy 91-cubic-inch (1,498-cc) engine and five-speed gearbox boosted performance. From 1980 U.S. buyers could get a 75 bhp (56 kW) fuel-injected option.

Plenty of owners decided that a car with such agile handling deserved more power. Some of those still on the road hide a performance upgrade, such as a Fiat Uno Turbo engine under the hood (bonnet).

All cars had alloy wheels with low-profile tires, tinted windows, and distinctive graphics. Early examples had two soft bags for the compact trunk (boot), made of fabric that matched the seats. From 1982, the model was badged the Bertone X1/9. **LT**

Renault 5
RENAULT 5
RENAULT

(<) A 1970s advertisement for the Renault 5 highlights the car's young and "funky" appeal.

5 | Renault (F)

1972 • 352 cu in/5,782 cc, S4 • 42 bhp/31 kW • 0–60 mph/97 kph in 18.9 seconds • 85 mph/137 kph

To look at the Renault 5 three-door hatchback with twenty-first-century eyes and see it as boxlike and drab is to miss many points that were obvious to the French public in 1972. Straight away, the French knew they were looking at something new, even revolutionary.

Designed to appeal to young female urbanites, the nimble, front-wheel-drive Renault 5 was seen as chic and stylish in a very 1970s kind of way from the moment it rolled off the production line. It possessed a typically "funky" interior, filled with bright colors and a plastic-molded dashboard that enveloped quirky, square-shaped gauges, and it had a rear steeply sloping hatch that opened right down to the fender (bumper). It was one of the first modern hatchbacks.

A new kind of impact-absorbing, strengthened body promised to stay intact in a collision, and reinforced plastic fender bars were embedded into the body rather than protruding from it. Two models were released in 1972, the L and the TL, both of which had folding rear seats, while the TL had reclining front seats and a heated rear window.

In a series of deft strokes, the car's gifted designer Michel Boué, who sadly died prior to its release, had defined all of the essential elements of a new and still-continuing trend in car design. The Renault 5 would become the leader of the so-called "superminis," a British term for automobiles larger than a small city car but not big enough to be considered a small family car.

Two years after its release, the Renault 5's fuel economy, in the wake of the 1973 oil crisis, helped it to become France's best-selling car. It would eventually sell over 5.3 million units worldwide. **BS**

Falcon XA | Ford (AUS)

1972 • 250 cu in/4,100 cc, S6 • 130 bhp/97 kW • 0–60 mph/97 kph in 9.7 seconds • 108 mph/174 kph

One of the more eagerly anticipated cars in Australian motoring history, the Falcon XA, the car that was "Born on the Wind," was a milestone for Ford Australia. It was the first-ever Ford to be designed from the ground up in Australia, and the boldest design the company had ever conceived. Available as a sedan (saloon), and later as a two-door hardtop, it was brought in to help Ford compete with the increasing popularity of Holden's Monaro. But rear-seat hardtop passengers bemoaned the lack of legroom and uncomfortable seats.

For the driver and front-seat passenger, however, the XA had significantly more room than its predecessor, the XY. An impressive list of extras was offered as standard for the first time, including seat belts and air-conditioning in the rear, and power steering. The car was actually hard to steer, but buyers were slow to take up the the power-steering option.

There was a Grand Tourer (GT) version as well, which felt very much at home on the racetrack, where its bulging rear panels were able to take extra width tires. The car was designed to be raced, but it was given touches to make it appeal to the average motorist also, such as improved ergonomics, body styling, more comfortable seats, and a wraparound fascia that gave it the look of an aircraft cockpit. The GT also had a less aggressive look, a heavily chromed grille, a rounded body, and six individual taillights.

The XA's small rear window and very high rear seats made it quite a challenge for the driver to see just how much of the car was behind him. But the benefits far outweighed the criticisms, and the XA was a bold statement of Ford Australia's independence. **BS**

Jensen-Healey | Jensen (GB)

1972 • 120 cu in/1,974 cc, S4 • 140 bhp/104 kW • 0–60 mph/97 kph in 7.8 seconds • 119 mph/192 kph

The Jensen-Healey sports car was unveiled at the Geneva Motor Show in March 1972. Jensen had been in the business of building cars since 1935, but this one was different, a collaborative venture with veteran car boss Donald Healey, whose most famous model was the Austin-Healey 3000. When British Leyland boss Donald Stokes told the then seventy-year-old Cornishman that he was going to shut down the Austin-Healey brand, Healey immediately began plotting to build cars again elsewhere.

The route lay in collaboration with Kjell Qvale, a Norwegian entrepreneur whose San Francisco–based business sold more Austin-Healeys stateside than any other outlet. Jensen Motors, which had built "big Healey" bodies for BMC in the 1950s and 1960s, was up for sale, and Qvale and Healey joined forces to buy it.

The Jensen-Healey, with a 120-cubic-inch (1,974-cc) Lotus twin-cam engine, was designed under the skin by Barry Bilbie, with bodywork styled by William Towns, later famed for his work on the Aston Martin Lagonda. Initially the interior was quite austere, with an all-black or dark brown color scheme and plastic trim. Later versions were enhanced with a woodgrain dashboard and soft padding. Production ceased when Jensen Motors went bust in the mid-1970s. **SB**

J72 | Panther (GB)

1972 • 230 cu in/3,781 cc, S6 • 190 bhp/142 kW • 0–60 mph/97 kph in 6.4 seconds • 114 mph/183 kph

Panther Westwinds of Weybridge, England, has produced a great number of automotive necessities, but it was the J72 that started it all. The car was the brainchild of Robert Jankel, who worked as a fashion designer but had a passion for vintage cars. In his early thirties Jankel restored a prewar Rolls-Royce and took it to Spain. A bullfighter paid him $16,000 (£10,000) for it, and he decided to found an automobile company.

Less than two years later, Jankel introduced the Panther J72. It was inspired by the Jaguar SS100, not just in shape and name but also in its engine; the prototype was powered by a Jaguar V12. At its launch at the 1973 London Motor Show it won the silver medal for coachwork. The car was lavishly built and hand-trimmed with Wilton carpet and Connolly hide.

The J72 had an asking price of around twice that of a contemporary Jaguar, but Jankel knew how to gain publicity and managed to sell more J72s then anyone would have believed. His company was soon building one a week. Contrary to the prototype, most J72s were fitted with Jaguar's straight-six, making the car more than quick enough for respectable performance.

By 1981 a total of 361 was reached, but then a Korean consortium took over. By that time demand had diminished and few sold before the end in 1986. **JB**

911 Targa | Porsche (D)

1972 • 140 cu in/2.3 liter, F6 • 130 bhp/97 kW • 0–60 mph/97 kph in 6.8 seconds • 128 mph/206 kph

Porsche named the Targa version of the 911 after the Sicilian Targa Florio sports-car race, which was discontinued in 1977 because of concerns about the safety of the roads around Palermo. The German manufacturer had chalked up seven victories there between 1956 and 1967, the year in which the 911 Targa was first introduced. The name was appropriate, being the Italian for "shield" or "plate."

The 911 Targa was a halfway point between the soft-top cabriolet and hardtop coupe versions of the iconic rear-engined 911 sports car that had been produced since 1963. Its most immediately striking design features were its manually removable roof panel and its stainless-steel roll bar. The latter was incorporated to satisfy future U.S. safety regulations that never materialized. Removable roof panels had been used before, of course, for example on the 1964 Triumph TR4, when it was called a "Surrey" top.

By 1972 the Targa accounted for about 10 percent of total 911 sales. Its plastic removable rear window was still available, but now 911 Targas came with an optional fixed glass backscreen instead.

Recently the Targa concept has become rare, with makers favoring retractable steel roofs. However, the Bugatti Veyron Grand Sport still has a targa top. **GL**

Nova | ADD (GB)

1972 • various, S4 • various • various • various

The 1970s was the peak of the kit car craze, when enthusiasts took the engine and chassis of a popular budget car and transformed it with a completely new body, usually built from fiberglass.

One of the high points of the era was the Nova kit supercar. Built by Automotive Design and Development (ADD), the Nova was based on the humble Volkswagen Beetle but was styled to rival the Lamborghini Miura and the Ford GT40. The entire roof, windows, and pillars lifted up on struts to allow the driver one of the most stylish entries into a vehicle ever.

The two kit car enthusiasts responsible for the car were Richard Oakes and Phil Sayers, who had built the prototype in less than a year in a Southampton shipyard. Complete bodies, ready to be fitted to the rear-engined Beetle chassis, were offered for sale for just £750 ($1,200). The price even included a set of alloy wheels with Dunlop tires.

In 1975 ADD sold the production rights, after which Novas were sold as the Eagle, Sterling, Purvis Eureka, Totum, Ledl, Défi, Scorpion, Gryff, Sovran, and Tarantula, as well as various unlicensed copies.

The striking looks of the Nova have been popular with movie directors. The kit car appeared in *Cannonball Run II* (1984) and *Death Race 2000* (1975). **JB**

A powerful weapon and a powerful car: Mel Gibson as Mad Max (1979), "the last law in a world gone out of control." ⊡

115 | ZiL (SU)

1972 • 469 cu in/7,695 cc, V8 • 315 bhp/232 kW • 0–60 mph (97 kph) in 13 seconds • 119 mph/192 kph

In the paranoid world of the Soviet Union in the 1970s, a gigantic black armor-plated limo was considered the only reasonable transportation for party leaders and government dignitaries making visits abroad. The monstrous ZiL 115 had steel 1 inch (2.5 cm) thick in places to make it bombproof. Experts calculated that the window glass could withstand bullets from a weapon of up to a .303 caliber.

Amazingly, the ugly, boxy vehicle was not seen as slightly embarrassing and out-of-date by other heads of state, either. Several leaders of Arab and African countries ordered them. East German leader Erich Honecker traveled extensively in the big ZiL, and Soviet leader Mikhail Gorbachev was frequently seen arriving or leaving in one.

The four-door sedan (saloon) needed massive power to move its four-ton weight. A 469-cubic-inch (7,695-cc) V8 did the job and no one cared about the hopeless fuel economy of 10 mpg (24 liters per 100km).

The 115 was a car that would always be driven by a chauffeur. A red button on the dashboard raised a privacy screen between the front and rear seats. The driver relied on the three-speed automatic, power steering, and big hydraulic disc brakes to make progress as smooth as possible for those in the back.

That the ZiL also had a massive trunk (boot) was neatly demonstrated in the James Bond movie *Casino Royale* (2006)—two dead bodies are stored in there.

The big ZiL's days were numbered, however, when the more liberal and colorful leader Boris Yeltsin took over the Russian Federation. He promptly ditched the 115 and ordered a Mercedes 600SEL instead. **SH**

Falcon XB GT | Ford (AUS)

1973 • 347 cu in/5,700 cc, V8 • 600 bhp/441 kW • unknown • unknown

When his family is killed by a vicious motorcycle gang, officer Max Rockatansky dons black police leathers and jumps into a supercharged high-speed pursuit vehicle intent on revenge. This is not just another day in Los Angeles but the start of the hit movie series *Mad Max* (1979–80s), which launched both Mel Gibson's career and one of the best-known cars of the era.

Mad Max's modified black Ford Falcon was meant to be as menacing as possible. The base car was a used limited-edition GT351 hardtop, only sold in Australia in the 1970s. The rear-wheel-drive muscle car was vaunted as "The Great Australian Road Car."

The film crew extensively modified their XB, fitting roof and trunk (boot) spoilers, and a Concorde nose cone that became a popular off-the-shelf extra with Mad Max copyists. The wheel arches were flared to fit wider wheels taken from a van and painted black. A van exhaust system was also fitted. The body was painted gloss black on the upper half, matte black below.

The Falcon also had a supercharger poking from the center of the hood (bonnet). Sadly, this was only for appearance and did not work. It is estimated that a real supercharger would have given the Falcon about 600 bhp (441 kW). Even so, the bikers are no match for Max's Interceptor and they all meet a grisly end.

After filming and promotional appearances, the car was offered for sale, but amazingly there were no takers, so the film mechanic kept it. When *Mad Max* became an hit and *Mad Max II* was started, the same car was reused. For the second film, huge extra fuel tanks were fitted in the rear; by this time, society had broken down and fuel was hard to come by. **SH**

MFP
INTERCEPTOR
MAD
MAX
Produced by
BYRON KENNEDY
Directed by
GEORGE MILLER
With
MEL GIBSON
Music by
BRIAN MAY
Written by
JAMES McCAUSLAND and GEORGE MILLER
From Warner Bros. A Warner Communications Company. © 1979 Warner Bros. Inc. All Rights Reserved.

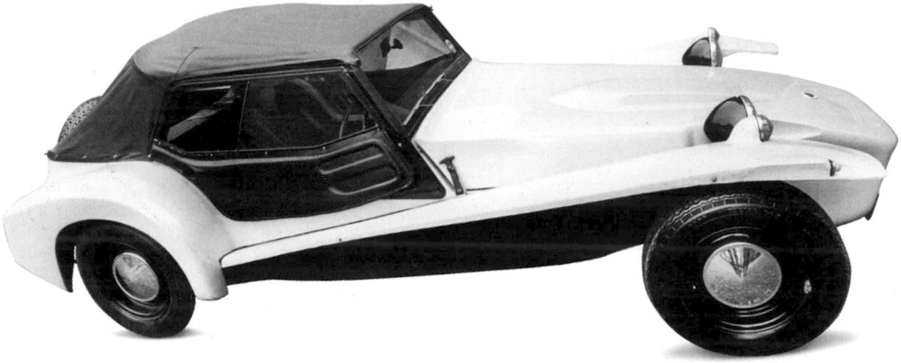

Seven | Caterham

GB

1973 • 95 cu in/1,558 cc, S4 • 125 bhp/93 kW • 0–60 mph/97 kph in 7.1 seconds • 103 mph/166 kph

When the Caterham Seven was launched in 1973, it already had a long history behind it. The low-slung, lightweight, spartan little open-top sports car was essentially a reborn Lotus Seven, a car that had been designed by Colin Chapman and first appeared in 1957. The Lotus Seven was immortalized in the cult 1960s television series *The Prisoner*, filmed in the Welsh village of Portmeirion and starring Patrick McGoohan.

Lotus produced three series of the car, first with Ford engines and then with Lotus's own 95-cubic-inch (1,558-cc). Throughout the 1950s and 1960s, Lotus sold the Seven as a kit car because, under the British tax system at the time, a car sold as a CKD (completely knocked down) collection of parts did not attract the same taxation as a ready-assembled car. This changed in January 1973 when Britain joined the European Economic Community (forerunner of the European Union) and the concession ended.

By then Lotus had stopped making the Seven to concentrate on more profitable and more upmarket preassembled sports cars. The rights to the design and manufacture of the kits were bought by Graham Nearn of Caterham Cars, which had been a main distributor of the Lotus Seven; production resumed under its name.

The Caterham Seven is an open two-seater with minimal luggage space. The bodywork is aluminum and the car's total weight is just 1,135 pounds (515 kg). Early cars had a Lotus engine, but since then the Caterham Seven has been equipped with a variety of engines, including units from Ford, Vauxhall, and Rover.

Because it is so light and fast, the Caterham Seven has always been popular as a racing car. **SB**

Boxer | Ferrari

(I)

1973 • 267 cu in/4,390 cc, V12 • 346 bhp/258 kW • 0–60 mph/97 kph in 5.2 seconds • 186 mph/298 kph

How does a car manufacturer with a name like Ferrari stay at the top of its game? The answer is that it brings out a stunning power car like the Boxer, easily able to race to 60 mph (96 kph) in the time it takes someone to read about it.

In actual fact Ferrari had been faltering a little when it invested in the Boxer. Enzo Ferrari's belief that mid-engined cars were not the way to go—for his company, at least—was costing him some competitive edge. Sure, mounting the engine more centrally did make it trickier for drivers until they got used to the different weight distribution. At last Enzo Ferrari was persuaded to try it with the Boxer.

The first Boxer was the 365 GT4/BB, which was shown at the Turin Motor Show in 1971. Two years passed before it was ready for sale, at the 1973 Paris Motor Show. Only 387 of them were built, a mix of left-hand and right-hand drives, and they were all for the European market. It is only in recent years that some of these have made their way to the United States.

In many ways, Enzo Ferrari was proved right. His company was not accustomed to building mid-engine cars, and it tried innovations like mounting the gearbox under the engine, and mounting the engine longitudinally rather than transversely. Such ideas would have been revolutionary if they had worked. Unfortunately, the cars were difficult to handle and they achieved very little racing success, which did not help to boost sales.

The Boxer, updated in 1976 as the 512BB, stayed in production until 1984, but it was never the raging success that its specifications and looks deserved. **MG**

260Z | Datsun

J

1973 • 158 cu in/2,600 cc, S6 • 165 bhp/123 kW • 0–60 mph/97 kph in 8 seconds • 127 mph/204 kph

Nissan used the Datsun name for cars in export markets because it was thought to sound less intimidatingly Japanese. Similarly, its range of sports coupes, known as the Fairlady at home, were called the Z Series abroad. In 1969, the first of the series, the 240Z, had an advanced 140-cubic-inch (2,300-cc), high-revving six-cylinder engine and a long, sexy body, loosely inspired by British sports cars such as the Jaguar E-Type and MGB. It had a lift-up tailgate and independent rear suspension. The car was an immediate international success and lifted Nissan/Datsun's profile to new levels.

Yet as recently as the 1950s, the company had been assembling British Austin cars in Japan under license. In the process it had gained an insight into advanced Western industrial technology. The Japanese learned fast. Within twenty years they had completely overtaken the British and launched their Z Series, which became the best-selling sports car of all time.

The 240Z's replacement, the 260Z two-seater, was effectively the same car but with a bigger engine, slightly stiffer chassis, and improved interior. The new 158-cubic-inch (2,600-cc) unit raised the power output—except in the United States. There, tighter emission controls meant the bigger unit had to be detuned, so it was actually less powerful than its predecessor. A 2+2 option with a longer wheelbase was also launched.

Next came the 280Z of 1975, which had a 170-cubic-inch (2,800-cc) engine and fuel injection to improve its environmental performance in the United States.

All the Z Series cars are sought-after classics today, but their numbers are few. Most fell victim to Datsun's greatest weakness at the time: rust. **SH**

Khamsin | Maserati

(I)

1973 • 299 cu in/4,900 cc, V8 • 320 bhp/239 kW • 0–60 mph/97 kph in 6.8 seconds • 154 mph/248 kph

In 1972 the Italian design house Bertone showed an interesting prototype at the Turin Motor Show, which is regarded as the fashion showcase of the automotive industry. The car's design was by Marcello Gandini, who would go on to create the sensational-looking Lamborghini Countach. At the Paris Motor Show the following year, Gandini's design study reappeared, this time bearing a Maserati badge. The car went into production shortly afterward and was named Khamsin, for a hot, fierce desert wind that occurs in Egypt.

The Khamsin was a long, sleek, elegant car with a high waistline and a dramatically sloping rear roofline. The long hood (bonnet) accommodated an engine that was set quite far back to allow room in front for the spare wheel to be stored. Then space was freed up at the back to make the trunk (boot) a reasonable size. Another novel aspect of the car's design was a glass panel set below the back window and between the taillights, perfectly positioned to give the driver better rearward vision for reversing.

The car's technical specification included several unusual features. One of them was a type of graduated power steering that gave increased assistance when driving at low speeds; at high speeds, its input reduced to add just a bit more weight to the steering. This kind of variable power steering is common in modern cars but was rare in the early 1970s. The same system was also used in the Citroën SM—Citroën was a major stakeholder in Maserati at the time.

The Khamsin also had hydraulic seats and an adjustable steering column, both innovative at the time. Over nine years, production totaled 430 cars. **SB**

Bagheera | Matra

(F)

1973 • 78 cu in/1,294 cc, S4 • 82 bhp/60 kW • 0–60 mph/97 kph in 12.2 seconds • 116 mph/187 kph

Matra named its new sports coupe after the panther in *The Jungle Book* (1894), and it was certainly a fast-moving, sleek creature. More than that, though, the French car was pushing boundaries of automotive design.

The Bagheera was an early example of siting the engine between the axles to gain a better handling balance. The rear tailgate lifted to allow access to the powerplant behind the passenger seats. The car was also a pioneer in the use of unusual lightweight materials; the aerodynamic body was made of polyester mounted on a tubular steel frame. Even more unusual, there was just one row of three seats, with the driver on one side and two passengers alongside.

The small engine, from the Simca 1100, was enough to give the car decent performance, although a bigger 91-cubic-inch (1,500-cc) unit replaced it in 1975. With wishbone suspension all around, the agile rear-wheel-drive handling was much praised.

Sadly, Matra had not thought about rust resistance. The polyester body was fine, of course, but it seemed to channel water into the steel chassis, which had no rustproofing. Many cars succumbed, and Matra was forced to galvanize its successor, the Murena.

Matra also developed an extraordinary special Bagheera with a unique U8 engine. This comprised two Simca 79-cubic-inch (1,300-cc) engines working together back to back, with the two crankshafts linked by gears and a chain. This 158-cubic-inch (2,600-cc) engine produced 168 bhp (124 kW) and could reach 143 mph (230 kph). The car was given bigger wheels and a longer body. But Matra's parent company, Chrysler, did not support the project and only three were built. **SH**

Robin | Reliant

GB

1973 • 45 cu in/750 cc, S4 • 32 bhp/24 kW • 0–60 mph/97 kph in 22 seconds • 68 mph/109 kph

Manufactured by the Reliant Motor Company and conceived by Ogle Design, the Reliant Robin was a three-wheeled, two-door sedan (saloon), and one of the most unstable cars ever made, thanks to its single front wheel. It was built to replace the successful though staid and equally unstable Reliant Regal, which had been in production since 1962.

The Robin had a fiberglass body over a box-section steel chassis. It was popular with minors who possessed a B1 license to drive motorcycles and quadricycles—and also a car if it weighed less than 1,000 pounds (454 kg) and had three wheels. But beyond its appeal to unlicensed youth and its ability to haul things, this was a car with serious drawbacks.

Even fans of the Robin would stress the importance of trying to avoid going around corners. Wherever possible, drivers would choose to go over a roundabout rather than around it, and indeed always to drive straight ahead. They would also suggest placing a bag of cement on the passenger seat to help balance the car when there was no passenger. Given the reputation of the car, passengers were in short supply, so cement bags presumably did a lot of service.

Every time Reliant Robin owners went out for a drive, the risks equaled those of an extreme sport. In a 2010 episode of the U.K. motoring program *Top Gear*, host Jeremy Clarkson wondered how many people had paid with their lives for the inherent instability of the Robin. He even walked past a headstone in a Sheffield graveyard that read: "Arthur William Hebblethwaite, 29 April 1936–18 October 1981: father, husband . . . Reliant enthusiast." **BS**

Dolomite Sprint | Triumph

GB

1973 • 121 cu in/1,998 cc, S4 • 127 bhp/95 kW • 0–60 mph/97 kph in 8.4 seconds • 118 mph/190 kph

The Dolomite Sprint made its debut in 1973 as a car with a mission. It was introduced as a high-performance halo model of the successful Triumph Dolomite sedan (saloon) designed to do battle with charismatic sports sedans such as the BMW 2002 Turbo. The Dolomite Sprint had a more powerful engine and some modest body tweaks.

Engineering chief Spen King led the team working on the new engine. This was slightly higher in capacity than the standard Dolomite motor, and had a single camshaft and a 16-valve cylinder head. The power unit for the Dolomite Sprint was notable as the world's first truly mass-produced multivalve car engine. In 1974, the year following the car's launch, the design of the new cylinder head was given a British Design Council Award for innovation.

The Dolomite Sprint had the same Michelotti-designed body as the Dolomite, with a few distinguishing embellishments to identify it as the high-performance model. It had the four-headlight format that was reserved for the more upscale models of the Dolomite range. Sporty alloy wheels also gave away the fact that the car was a bit special.

At its introduction, the Dolomite Sprint caused quite a stir, at least partly because of the color scheme chosen for the launch model: mimosa yellow with black stripes, like a wasp with wheels. It looked very rock 'n' roll at a time when David Bowie's *Ziggy Stardust* was the kind of music to be found in the charts. The car was not without its problems, though. The engine was brilliant but underdeveloped and it suffered reliability problems that exasperated owners. **SB**

2002 Turbo | BMW

(D)

1973 • 121 cu in/1,997 cc, S4 • 170 bhp/125 kW • 0–60 mph/97 kph in 6.9 seconds • 131 mph/211 kph

The first BMW Turbo stemmed from a Paul Bracq concept; shown in 1972, this particular model was striking in red with gull-wing doors and a turbocharged engine. It was based on the infamous 130-bhp (97-kW) Tii. BMW engineers added a KKK (Kühnle, Kopp, and Kausch) turbocharger that delivered another 40 bhp (30 kW), bigger brakes, a limited slip differential for better traction, and uprated tires.

It is claimed that this was the world's first turbocharged production car. What is beyond doubt is that the on/off nature of the turbo power delivery made it a real handful to drive. Among the motorsport success it enjoyed was the European Touring Car Championship title with Dieter Quester at the wheel.

The production-ready 2002 Turbo was first shown at the Frankfurt Motor Show in 1973 and it quickly gained notoriety. Cosmetically, the turbo was sensational, with bolt-on wheel arch extensions and front and rear spoilers. Press cars had the words "2002" and "turbo" emblazoned on the front spoiler, written backward, so drivers in front would see exactly what was in their rearview mirror. The German media and safety lobbyists considered this irresponsible and exerted considerable pressure to have them removed. Production cars were delivered without the words, although many owners added them themselves, and there is no denying their retro charm today.

Just 1,672 examples of the BMW 2002 Turbo were built during the two years of production, all with left-hand drive, but only a third of these cars survive today. There is no record of how many of the missing cars ended up in a ditch or crumpled into a tree. **RD**

The Bluesmobile, a police car with magic powers "on a mission from God," performs a miracle in *The Blues Brothers* (1980). ▷

Capri RS 3100 | Ford (GB)

1973 • 188 cu in/3,093 cc, V6 • 146 bhp/109 kW • 0–60 mph/97 kph in 7.1 seconds • 125 mph/200 kph

When the Ford Company's operation in the United Kingdom introduced its first Ford Consul Capri in 1961, it was an immediate success. Building an American car and then selling it in Europe had always been difficult, as had building a European car and selling it in the United States. There were exceptions, but the markets were different and the drivers in each had their definite likes and dislikes, as sales figures made very clear.

The new Consul Capri was a car with a flashy American look—there was certainly a market for them in Britain—but tailored to British roads and much more fuel-efficient than its cousins across the Atlantic. The Consul Capri was, in effect, a Ford Mustang tailored to suit the U.K. driver.

The Ford Capri became a name in its own right in 1969, and by the time the RS 3100 was introduced in 1973 Ford had sold a million of them, a remarkable figure for a British car. The RS 3100 replaced the RS 2600, a high-performance race version of the Capri. It had a bigger engine, as the change of name suggests, and was aimed at the 1974 European Touring Car (ETC) Championship. This Capri was hailed as Europe's fastest touring car at the time.

Being called that was one thing, but competing with Ford's big race rival, BMW, was something else again. BMW had won the 1973 ETC Championship, and Ford wanted the 1974 title for its Capri. It recruited top drivers, including Niki Lauda, and the race with BMW was neck and neck until BMW withdrew from the Championship. Ford went on to win, but not in a Capri. It was another of their race car sets, a Zakspeed Escort, that lifted the trophy. **MG**

Monaco | Dodge (USA)

1974 • 359 cu in/5,898 cc, V8 • 180 bhp/134 kW • 0–60 mph/97 kph in 10.8 seconds • 115 mph/185 kph

When Dodge built its first Monaco back in 1965, it had no idea it was building what would become a legend of the 1980 movie *The Blues Brothers*: the Bluesmobile. It was a 1974 Monaco that brother Elwood Blues bought, telling his brother Jake, "It's got a cop motor, a 440-cubic-inch plant. It's got cop tires, cop suspension, cop shocks. It's a model made before catalytic converters so it'll run good on regular gas."

Dan Aykroyd, who played the part of Elwood and cowrote the script, said he chose the Dodge Monaco because he thought it was the hottest car used by the police in the 1970s. The Monaco was used by both the Chicago city police and the Illinois State troopers in the mid-1970s. In the film's extended car chase, which ends in Chicago and has the car racing under the raised tracks of the El Train, there is a brief shot of the speedometer showing 120 mph (192 kph). This is slightly more than the car's official top speed, but the film's director, John Landis, said there was no trick photography—the car really was being driven that fast through the streets as they were filming.

Thirteen different Monacos were used in the film, together with another sixty cars driven by the pair's pursuants. The film created a new record for the number of cars destroyed during a single movie, a record that remained until its sequel was filmed.

A later model of the car was also used in *The Dukes of Hazzard* TV series, where it stood up well to the crashes and stunts it was asked to perform. The Monaco name was retired in 1978 when the car was replaced by the Dodge St. Regis, and this too continued to be popular as a police car. **MG**

560 | Monica

F

1974 • 339 cu in/5,560 cc, V8 • 280 bhp/206 kW • 0–60 mph/97 kph in 8 seconds • 148 mph/238 kph

Before World War II, France offered several glamorous automobiles from high-class manufacturers such as Talbot-Lago, Delahaye, Delage, and Bugatti. Many were finished in excessive haute couture by such coachbuilders as Franay, Chapron, Saoutchik, and Figoni & Falaschi. By the end of the war, most of those companies had disappeared. The only true postwar French limousine of any importance was the Facel Vega, but that was declared dead after 1964, too.

So perhaps it was not strange that someone came up with the idea of an all-new ultraluxury French four-seater in the late 1960s. The plan came from industrialist Jean Tastevin, who named the car after his wife Monique. With no expertise at all in the automotive industry, Tastevin decided to team up with British car builder, tuner, and racer Chris Lawrence.

It was not the happiest of partnerships, and development of the car took years. Initially Lawrence wanted to have the car fitted with the 207-cubic-inch (3,400-cc) Martin V8 engine, designed and built by his friend, Ted Martin. But with the engine only in its early stages, Tastevin decided to go with the Chrysler 339-cubic-inch (5,560-cc) V8. The body was redesigned several times, but after an incredible twenty-two hand-built prototypes the car finally seemed ready for production around 1974.

That timing could not have been worse—the oil crisis had just hit, killing the market for big, fast, and thirsty cars. Only eight or ten Monica production cars are said to have been built. The last few, plus much of the production machinery, were sold off to a young car dealer named Bernie Ecclestone in the late 1970s. **JB**

Cougar | Mercury

(USA)

1974 • 351 cu in/5,752 cc, V8 • 168 bhp/124 kW • 0–60 mph/97 kph in 8 seconds • 125 mph/200 kph

Ford launched its Mercury Cougar series in 1967 and it became one of the company's best-loved cars, helped by advertising featuring a cougar, or mountain lion, sitting on the hood (bonnet). The animal gave the cars an image of power, speed, and beauty, and they actually provided all three. A big range of Cougars of all kinds was produced over the next few years and the Cougar name gave a touch of class to them all.

The first generation sold until 1970, with some models featuring a huge 427-cubic-inch (7,000-cc) engine. This option continued through a second generation of Cougars, which ended in 1973, and then 1974 saw the Cougar grow even more powerful with a 457-cubic-inch (7,500-cc) option. This would turn out to be the biggest engine seen under a Cougar hood, as from then on the fashion for ever more powerful muscle cars began to wane amid increasingly stringent U.S. government safety regulations and a desire for cars that offered a lot more distance for the fuel they swallowed.

A 1969 Mercury Cougar convertible made it into the movies in style, too, with a bright red model being driven by Diana Rigg in the 1969 James Bond movie, *On Her Majesty's Secret Service*. Alert filmgoers also get glimpses of the 1974 Mercury Cougar in *48 Hours* (1982), *The Blues Brothers* (1980), and *Dazed and Confused* (1993)—although it is hard to find a car that was not featured in the latter film. On TV the car has been used in a wide range of productions, from *Lovejoy* (1986–94) through *T. J. Hooker* (1982–86) to *Seinfeld* (1989–98).

Variations on the Cougar stayed in production for a full thirty-five years. In 2002, the long-running brand was finally deemed tired—and was retired. **MG**

Countach | Lamborghini

(I)

1974 • 315 cu in/5,167 cc, V12 • 449 bhp/345 kW • 0–60 mph/97 kph in 4.9 seconds • 185 mph/289 kph

Ferruccio Lamborghini had reined in Bertone's avant-garde designs for the Espada, but with the replacement for the aging Miura, he let the young stylists go wild. Legend has it that when the design team's boss, Nuccio Bertone, first saw the project's plans he exclaimed, "Countach," the nearest thing to a wolf-whistle in Nuccio's Piedmont dialect. The name stuck, making it the only Lamborghini sports car since the 400GT to be named for something other than bull fighting.

In 1974 the first Countach LP400 (signifying its longitudinale posteriore or longitudinally rear-mounted 244-cubic-inch/4,000-cc engine), was delivered to one lucky Australian customer.

In 2010 *Top Gear* magazine awarded the sleekly designed Countach LP400—with its sharp styling, scissor action doors, and neck-snapping acceleration—first place on its list of the "100 Sexiest Supercars of All Time." But this Lamborghini was never going to age gracefully. The Countach of the mid-1980s, the 5000QV, was seen as a vulgar and bloated status symbol of the tasteless über-rich. Now sporting large air ducts, bulging arches, and ugly slatted side skirts (similar to the Ferrari Testarossa), it also had a huge rear wing and the world's widest rear tires. Nevertheless, it did have a new 315-cubic-inch (5,200-cc) quattrovalve V12, which made it the fastest production road car of 1985.

Despite the Countach's high list price, approaching $100,000 (£61,000) in 1989, 2,042 cars were sold during its sixteen-year run. Later versions are often lambasted by today's critics as cumbersome, cramped, and noisy, but the rarer early cars can cause auction house bidding wars approaching $500,000 (£320,000). **DS**

SV-1 | Bricklin

CDN

1974 • 351 cu in/5,766 cc, V8 • 175 bhp/131 kW • 0–60 mph/97 kph in 8.5 seconds • 117 mph/187 kph

Bricklin is not one of the best-known names in the car world, although Malcolm Bricklin was the founder of Subaru of America. He imported Subaru, Fiat, and many other foreign makes at a time when it was hard to sell them in the United States. By the time he started importing he was already a millionaire, having made his money through running his father's construction supply company and turning it into a franchise operation for do-it-yourself stores. Unfortunately, he did not know as much about the automobile industry and he was destined to lose his money twice over.

The first setback occurred when *Consumer Reports* magazine described the Subaru 360 as "The Most Unsafe Car in America"; sales duly plummeted. It was after this that Bricklin founded Subaru of America and made back his money by again building a franchise operation and then selling his share in the company. It had long been his dream to own a small carmaking business and he sunk his tidy profits into building his first car in Canada. This was the Bricklin SV-1—although there would never be an SV-2.

The "SV" stood for Safety Vehicle. Believing safety to be paramount, he built the car to standards that were way beyond what was legally required in the United States, where he planned to sell the vehicle. Unfortunately, features like the built-in roll cage did not come cheaply, and the car eventually cost a massive £4,700 ($7,490) when it came onto the market.

Bricklin was far better at creating and selling franchises than he was at running a car company. Only 2,854 SV-1s were built before the company went bust, owing £14.5 million ($23 million). **MG**

The chic lines and smooth ride of the Citroën CX were admired by the French business class, 1979.

CX | Citroën (F)

1974 • 143 cu in/2,347 cc, S4 • 166 bhp/122 kW • 0–62 mph in 8.2 seconds • 137 mph/220 kph

The CX was Citroën's last independent fling before a merger with the more conservative Peugeot organization saved it from going bust. It was meant to be an executive car to rival smart six-cylinder BMWs and Mercedes, but the futuristic, aerodynamic body design only had room for a four-cylinder engine.

The car had Citroën's unique self-leveling hydropneumatic suspension, a single-spoke steering wheel, a huge single wiper blade, a concave rear window and one of the most bizarre dashboards of all time, featuring rotating drums instead of instruments. And Citroën did not believe in self-canceling indicators—the driver should cancel them, said its designers.

Nevertheless, the ride was superb, likened by writers at the time to "sailing over the road instead of on it." Rolls-Royce adopted the Citroën suspension under license. Handling was good, too, and the speed-sensitive power steering was unusually sophisticated for the time. Performance was excellent if customers ordered the right engine.

The pioneering turbodiesel engine was the world's fastest diesel at the time. Its smoothness and top speed of 121 mph (195 kph) helped to change European perceptions of diesel engines forever. The 1984 gasoline GTi Turbo was the fastest CX though, and its performance figures are given above.

The CX seemed to appeal to eccentrics. Panamanian dictator Manuel Noriega and East German Communist leader Erich Honecker both used them. Singer Grace Jones built her 1985 "Slave to the Rhythm" video around the car, at one point driving it across a desert into a giant version of her own mouth. **SH**

24-24 | GAZ (SU)

1974 • 337 cu in/5,530 cc, V8 • 195 bhp/145 kW • 0–60 mph/97 kph in 9.8 seconds • 104 mph/168 kph

Few regarded the GAZ 24-24 as a welcome sight. A special limited edition of the more familiar GAZ 24 Soviet sedan (saloon) fitted with a brutally big V8 engine, it was used by the feared KGB secret police. Never made available to ordinary civilians, it was mainly used as a "vehicle interceptor" and security escort car for the limousines of major party officials.

There was little modern or glamorous about the GAZ 24-24. Its aluminum V8, a copy of a 1950s American design, was also used in the Russian Chaika government limousine. The car had a reinforced chassis and suspension, a three-speed automatic gearbox, and power steering. But the 24-24's primitive style and specification made a sober contrast with the era of automotive evolution happening in the West. This archaic lump was launched in the debut year of the Volkswagen Golf and Pontiac Trans Am. Further, the big, growling GAZ became a symbol of overbearing state authority at a time when many were beginning to question the one-party system.

This secretive-looking, rare vehicle with its unusual growling V8 stood out among the old-fashioned cars on the Soviet roads. In satellite states oppressed by Soviet rule, particularly Poland, Belarus, Ukraine, and Mongolia, it gave rise to a popular urban legend, the myth of the "Black Volga." People believed that the mysterious black vehicle suddenly appeared and abducted innocent citizens, especially children. Some told the story to deter youngsters from wandering the streets alone. Others believed that the Black Volga was driven by evil KGB officers intent on kidnapping children to steal and sell their kidneys. **SH**

The rear-engined Lancia Stratos was a car built with ease of maintenance in mind; driver comfort was secondary.

Steamer | Pelland (AUS)

1974 • 67 cu in/1,100 cc, three-cylinder compound engine • 40 bhp/30 kW • unknown • unknown

If it had not been for the discovery of oil and the invention of the internal combustion engine, there is no telling how far steam-powered technology may have come. But oil has always been plentiful and cheap—that is, until 1973, when the Arab oil embargo shocked the West out of its complacency.

The world's first self-propelled road vehicle was a steam-powered three-wheeled wagon invented in 1769 by French engineer Nicolas Cugnot. The 1973 oil crisis led those few who still believed in Cugnot's original vision to start getting busy. One of those people was Peter Pellandine, a car designer formerly of Lotus, who specialized in steam-powered vehicles and kit cars. He went to Australia in 1974 to design and build a steamer for the South Australian government.

Pellandine's response to the oil crisis was a two-seat roadster powered by a high-temperature three-cylinder compound engine. Its fiberglass monocoque body, the construction of which Pellandine had mastered during his early association with Lotus, was bolted to the undercarriage and engine. It had 12-inch (30-cm) wheels in the rear and 10-inch (25-cm) wheels up front, and its tiny engine and fiberglass body made it impossibly light, at just 1,058 pounds (480 kg). The seats were molded onto the body and so could not be adjusted, although the pedal assembly was adjustable. A side air scoop ventilated the rear condenser on the car's rear deck.

The Pelland Steamer, which in our gasoline-starved future may one day be more sought after than a Ferrari Testarossa, has been retired to the National Motor Museum at Birdwood in South Australia. **BS**

Stratos | Lancia (I)

1974 • 147 cu in/2,418 cc, V6 • 280 bhp/209 kW • 0–60 mph/97 kph in 4.1 seconds • 144 mph/232 kph

The Lancia Stratos, nicknamed the "Plastic Dart," was a no-compromise, thoroughbred rally car, built to cope with motorsport's worst conditions. It had a supercar's engine and transmission, taken from the Dino 246 GT, and a striking, wedge-shaped shell styled by Bertone. With wraparound windows resembling a crash-helmet visor, it earned its name after one designer exclaimed that it looked like it had fallen from the stratosphere.

On entering the World Rally Championship in 1974, it took the manufacturer's title three years running. It was so versatile that in 1975 it conquered snow and ice to win the Swedish Rally, and then searing heat and dust to win the East African Safari rally.

Although its fiberglass body sections opened up to allow rally mechanics easy access to its 147-cubic-inch (2,418-cc) powerplant, the cockpit was noisy, poorly ventilated, and so cramped that there was barely enough space to stash away helmets and other safety equipment. Its reclined and offset driving position also took some getting used to. Nevertheless, rally crews loved the Stratos, almost as much as the fans who would camp out at forest stages just to glimpse the little Lancia and listen to the growl of its fire-spitting V6.

To meet motorsport regulations, Lancia was obliged to build 500 roadgoing versions of the Stratos. These "Stradale" variants received the final batch of Ferrari's Dino engines, which were detuned to 190 bhp (142 kW). The crudely finished, short-wheel-base cars were quite a handful, especially in the wet, and many were destroyed in the hands of less talented drivers. Today, they are hugely collectible, with good examples fetching around $300,000 (£200,000) at auction. **DS**

Lafer | MP

BR

1974 • 97 cu in/1,600 cc, S4 • 64 bhp/48 kW • 0–60 mph/97 kph in 20.4 seconds • 87 mph/140 kph

Furniture maker Percival Lafer loved classic British sports cars of the 1940s and 1950s. It was awkward, therefore, that he lived in São Paulo, Brazil, in the 1970s. Undaunted, Lafer set about building his own version of early Morgan and MG cars. The chassis, engine, gearbox, suspension, and steering all came from a Volkswagen Beetle, and he devised an attractive fiberglass two-seater retro-style body to fit on top.

With a 97-cubic-inch (1,600-cc) four-cylinder VW engine mounted in the rear, this was never going to be a high-performance car, but it was certainly a head-turner. It was sought after in both South and North America, and almost 1,000 were exported to Europe, too.

The MP Lafer had the charm of the original roadsters, but modern mechanicals made it more reliable and comfortable. The radiator grille was of course for show only, as the engine was air-cooled and behind the passenger cockpit.

The rear-wheel-drive roadster was promoted with emphasis on its Brazilian home: "From Abingdon to São Paulo, the MG tradition continues," an ad claimed. Buyers were seduced by traditional touches such as the rosewood steering wheel and dashboard, reclining leather bucket seats, and wire-spoke wheels.

The car was available as a kit in the United States, where a methanol-fueled rear-engined version, and even a Ford 140-cubic-inch (2,300-cc) front-engined model, later became available. Almost 5,000 Lafers were sold over a sixteen-year production life. In the 1979 James Bond film *Moonraker*, Roger Moore at the wheel of a white Lafer was pursued through the streets of Rio by a mysterious spy. **SH**

De Ville | Panther

GB

1974 • 258 cu in/4,235 cc, S6 • 190 bhp/141 kW • 0–60 mph/97 kph in 12 seconds • 127 mph/203 kph

A De Ville for Miss De Vil. This car, so obviously styled to look like a Bugatti Royale, will forever be remembered by generations of children as transport for supervillain Cruella De Vil—played by actress Glenn Close—in Disney's 1996 live-action movie *101 Dalmatians.*

Best described as neoclassical in its design, the handbuilt Panther De Ville was aimed at pop stars, celebrities, and Arab princes with more money than taste. The standard car was a four-door sedan (saloon), but it was also available as a two-door coupe or convertible. A one-off six-door limousine was also made. Despite the retro look of the exterior, De Villes were very modern inside and trimmed with the most luxurious fabrics. Often including extras such as drink cabinets, they are now popular for use at weddings and other celebrations.

Only sixty De Villes were ever built, at a factory in Weybridge, South West London, just a stone's throw from the historic Brooklands racetrack. The car was one of a range of vehicles sold by Panther Westwinds, which also included the Lima and Kallista roadsters. All were conceived by Robert Jankel, a former fashion designer who is best known for a Jaguar SS100 copy, the Panther J72. Later in life he became a highly respected creator of specialty vehicles, including armored cars.

The De Ville was powered by either a 258-cubic-inch (4,235-cc) straight-six engine or a 323-cubic-inch (5,300-cc) V12, both of them bought in from Jaguar. The transmission and other mechanical components came from the same source, so the cars were easy to drive and reliable. However, questionable aerodynamics made them more difficult to control at higher speeds. **RY**

Mark I Golf | Volkswagen

D

1974 • 89 cu in/1,471 cc, S4 • 70 bhp/52 kW • 0–60 mph/97 kph in 12.5 seconds • 99 mph/160 kph

Made by Volkswagen (VW), the Type 1 "Beetle" had become the world's biggest-selling motorcar of all time, but by the early 1970s sales in VW's key markets were in decline thanks to the rise of front-engined compact cars from Japan, Italy, and Britain.

VW knew that a radical departure from its traditional designs was required, and in May 1974 it launched the Golf. The water-cooled engine of the front-wheel-drive vehicle was front-mounted. Styled by Italian designer Giorgetto Giugiaro, the compact hatchback had crisp angles and a purposeful look, quite unlike its predecessor.

In 1978 VW began production of the Mark I Golf at its new factory in Westmoreland, Pennsylvania, becoming the first European company to build a car on U.S. soil since Rolls-Royce in the 1920s. The "Rabbit" had the same chassis and body as the European Golf, but had bigger fenders (bumpers) and softer suspension to suit the North American market. Other variants of the Mark I were built at VW plants in Mexico, Australia, and South America; nearly 7 million were made.

Over the next four decades, VW produced seven generations of its best-selling mid-range hatchback. "Golf" is now a byword for Germanic reliability and excellent build quality. Every single version has been nominated for the prestigious European Car of the Year award; the Mark III won the title in 1992. In May 2010 total sales of all Golfs—which have included sedan (saloon), convertible, pickup, and station wagon (estate) version—reached 27 million, making the Golf the world's third best-selling model of all time, just behind the Toyota Corolla and Ford's F Series. **DS**

504 Cabriolet | Peugeot

(F)

1974 • 162 cu in/2,664 cc, V6 • 144 bhp/106 kW • 0–60 mph/97 kph in 9.9 seconds • 117 mph/188 kph

With Peugeot's sturdy, sensible, and reliable 504 family car already a hit in Europe, and gradually becoming a success across much of the rest of the world, Peugeot designers set about adapting the car's rugged build and simple mechanicals into a host of configurations that would maximize its potential. The 504 successfully evolved in several different directions; it was a popular pickup truck in East Asia, a ubiquitous cross-country taxi in Africa, and a smart sedan (saloon) in South America. Back in Europe, it also became a desirable and stylish two-door coupe and cabriolet.

The rear-wheel-drive platform, wide track, and compliant, tough suspension imparted excellent road manners to the 504 coupe and convertible. Particularly when the roof was cut away, the car's lines became rather sleek and elegant. With leather seats, a snug, manual foldaway roof, and distinctive double rectangular headlights, the 504 was now a classic roadster. And unlike smaller sports soft-tops, the 504 still worked as a genuine four-seater with a large, practical trunk (boot).

Shortly after the launch, a fuel-injected 122-cubic-inch (2,000-cc) engine was introduced, followed in 1974 by a smooth and powerful V6. This was later tuned to produce 144 bhp (106 kW)—the figures for this version are given above. But the performance was hardly sporting, even by the humble standards of the mid-1970s. What set the car apart was its roof-down looks. Heads turned as it swooped serenely along a winding open country road in the sunshine, or cruised elegantly along a Riviera promenade. The 504 Cabriolet was an affordable slice of European glamour. **SH**

The 308 GTB is one of the best-selling Ferraris ever released; this 1976 model has been decorated with racing trim. ⊡

Pacer | AMC (USA)

1975 • 231 cu in/3,800 cc, S6 • 95 bhp/70 kW • 0–60 mph (97 kph) in 14.5 seconds • 97 mph/156 kph

The 1975 Pacer was ugly when it first launched, and still makes people point and laugh today. Some have called it a "Flying Fishbowl."

The futuristic shape was highly rounded with a huge glass area. From the back it certainly looked very odd indeed. It was advertised as "the first wide small car." It was true, the Pacer was wider than a Rolls-Royce Silver Shadow but only the length of an average family car—although sadly for AMC, this wasn't a feature that buyers found attractive.

AMC's chief stylist, Richard Teague, began work on the Pacer in 1971, believing there would be more demand for a small-but-spacious car in the future. The plan was to break away from the clichéd boxy styling of many 1970s cars. AMC said the Pacer was the first car ever designed from the inside out, and inside it was very roomy for passengers. But it was the outside that everybody else saw. And the bulbous Pacer often wins polls for the world's worst-looking car ever.

However, the Pacer did drive and handle well, and the ride was good. But it had old-fashioned rear-wheel drive, and after a sudden change of plan the engineers had to hastily redesign the front end to fit an old and thirsty six-cylinder engine instead of the planned modern rotary unit. Another oddity was that the passenger door was wider than the driver's door, to allow access to the back seats.

Despite all this, the Pacer did achieve one major success—as the car in the hit movie *Wayne's World* in 1992. It was a baby-blue Pacer with flame graphics and nonmatching wheels, which the characters called the "Mirthmobile." **BK**

308 GTB | Ferrari (I)

1975 • 178 cu in/2,926 cc, V8 • 255 bhp/190 kW • 0–60 mph/97 kph in 6.7 seconds • 154 mph/246 kph

The 308 is one of North America's best-loved Ferraris, in part because of its starring role in the cult 1980s TV series, *Magnum P.I.* The GTS version made its screen debut with Tom Selleck behind the wheel in 1977 and the lucky lawman got a new car every season. As the entry-point Ferrari, the 308 was the most affordable.

Like all Ferraris, the 308 was assembled at the firm's factory in Maranello, Italy, initially with fiberglass body panels that gave it the very low overall weight of just 2,315 pounds (1,050 kg). Steel was used from 1977 to 1985, a strange decision as the car became substantially heavier and prone to rust. Always mid-engined, it was available with a semi-convertible targa roof or as a Berlinetta coupe.

The latter, badged the 308 GTB, was styled by Pininfarina and made its debut at the Paris Motor Show in 1975. As a two-seater, it was a replacement for the Dino 246, and sister car to the Dino 308 GT4. The design is credited to Leonardo Fioravanti, who penned some of the most widely admired Ferraris of the era, including the Dino and Daytona. The 308 GTB was distinguished by air vents behind the doors that cooled the engine. Cars for the European markets produced 255 bhp (190 kW), but, due to emissions regulations in the United States, U.S. versions were tuned to produce only 240 bhp (178 kW).

The 308 GTS Quattrovalvole premiered in 1982 and also featured a removable targa roof. The whole range was eventually updated and reborn as the 328 in 1985. With more than 20,000 units sold throughout the 1970s and 1980s, the 308 was one of the most commercially successful Ferraris of all time. **RY**

75
75

911 Turbo | Porsche

D

1975 • 182 cu in/2,993 cc, F6 • 260 bhp/190 kW • 0–60 mph/97 kph in 6 seconds • 155 mph/249 kph

The 911 Turbo (also known as the Type 930) was Porsche's first serious attempt to take on Lamborghini and Ferrari. A true supercar, it was born out of Porsche's experimentation with turbocharged race cars, including its Le Mans-winning 917, and the need to build roadgoing versions of the Martini-sponsored Porsche Factory Team cars. A total of 282 hand-built cars were produced in 1975; today, they are among the most highly prized Porsche models.

In the hands of a talented driver, the 911 Turbo was extremely fast and easily capable of keeping up with its Italian rivals. However, it soon gained notoriety as a "widow maker" due to a number of fatal accidents. The short wheelbase, rear engine layout, and extreme turbo lag sent several unwary drivers spinning out of control as they drove too hard mid-corner.

Nevertheless, the aggressively styled 911 Turbo quickly became Porsche's flagship product. Thousands of schoolboys worldwide pinned posters of it to their bedroom walls. Bulging arches, huge rear tires, and the famous "whale-tail" spoiler were added to help traction and stability, while a stiffened suspension and a beefed-up four-speed gearbox were needed to harness the 253 pound-force feet (343 newton meters) of torque.

The 911 Turbo, with its huge price tag, equating to more than $100,000 (£64,000) today, became a symbol of the affluent 1980s and the rise of the Yuppie. Fashion magnate Ralph Lauren owned two black Type 930s for his daily New York commute, explaining that they had "a beauty, and a shape, and a sexiness to them." This was high praise indeed from one of the world's most famous car collectors. **DS**

Princess | Austin

GB

1975 • 135 cu in/2,226 cc, S6 • 110 bhp/82 kW • 0–60 mph/97 kph in 13.5 seconds • 104 mph/167 kph

Britain in the late 1970s and early 1980s was a time of power cuts, industrial disputes, inner-city riots, and even a South Atlantic war. It was against this backdrop that the Austin Princess was born.

In many ways it summed up the country. Part of its design, particularly the aging, underpowered, push-rod engine, harked back to a bygone age. In other ways it was desperately trying to be modern. The striking wedge shape of the bodywork, by the designer of the TR7 sports car, hinted at elements of Italian car design.

When bought with the smaller of its original engines, it took an age to get up to speed, not helped by having only a four-speed gearbox. But once it was moving, the Princess was happy to cruise along all day in comfort. Part of this was due to its clever Hydragas suspension, which replaced conventional springs and dampers with units filled with a mixture of alcohol and water. This innovation gave the hefty Princess a ride quality that compared well with Citroëns, which were then a byword in comfort.

Inside, there was plenty of room for driver and passengers, but the car lacked a hatchback rear end, which hampered its practicality and sales appeal. It was at around this time that vinyl roofs became very popular, and the higher up the model range the customer went, the more shiny the roof plastic became.

The big, slow car was hindered further by poor build quality, and it was eventually replaced by the grandly named but short-lived British Leyland Ambassador. The Princess, like other early 1980s fashions, now has something approaching cult status, though perhaps for the wrong reasons. **JI**

This 1981 TR7 ad comparing the car to a rocket was nothing new; Oldsmobile had done the same for its "88" in 1951.

Seville | Cadillac (USA)

1975 • 347 cu in/5,700 cc, V8 • 180 bhp/132 kW • 0–60 mph/97 kph in 11 seconds • 110 mph/177 kph

This important new Cadillac demonstrated that the "big is best" culture in the United States was losing ground. To launch a smaller Cadillac that was almost 1,000 pounds (450 kg) lighter than the full-sized Cadillac Deville would have been unthinkable a decade earlier. But, importantly for General Motors, the new car was comparable in size to the European cars that were chipping away at Cadillac sales.

The Seville was designed to improve the image of Cadillac, but it was also the first instance of Cadillac engineering one of its vehicles on the basis of components previously used. The chassis was from a Chevrolet and the engine came from an Oldsmobile. The engine in question was the highly successful 347-cubic-inch (5,700-cc) V8, fitted with the Bendix/Bosch electronically controlled fuel injection.

Even the new model's name had been used before. The first Cadillac Seville had been a two-door hardtop version of the 1956 Cadillac Eldorado, but Cadillac had stopped using the name in 1960.

The Seville may have been the smallest car in the Cadillac line, but that did not stop it being the most expensive one. By this time, buyers were learning that a small car also meant better fuel consumption figures, and Seville drivers were finding they could get the unprecedented fuel economy of 23 miles per gallon (10 liters per 100 km). The other large Cadillacs of the time could only achieve mpg in single digits.

The new Seville offered a smooth drive, good performance, and a comfortable ride. It was a successful counter to the rising popularity of luxury imports from Mercedes-Benz and BMW. **BK**

TR7 | Triumph (GB)

1975 • 109 cu in/1,798 cc, S4 • 94 bhp/70 kW • 0–60 mph/97 kph in 12.5 seconds • 106 mph/170 kph

According to the advertisements of the time, the Triumph TR7 was "the shape of things to come." That was a rather ambitious tag for a car with the silhouette of a slice of cheese. The distinctive wedge-shaped body design was the work of Harris Mann, who was also responsible for the wedge-shaped Austin Princess.

While it was under development, the TR7 was referred to within Triumph by the codename "Bullet." Production began at the company's factory in Speke, Liverpool, in 1975. It was first launched on the U.S. market the following January, and the car did not go on sale in its British homeland until May 1976. The U.K. launch was postponed twice because U.S. demand for the TR7 proved so great that Triumph was going flat out to meet it. Customers at home had no choice but to wait impatiently for a chance to buy it.

In 1978 production of the car moved south to Canley, Coventry. Then, in 1980, it was moved again, this time to a Rover factory at Solihull. By that time the TR7 was nearing the end of the road; it finally went out of production in 1981. By then a total of 112,368 hardtop coupe models had been made, and another 28,864 of the cabriolet/roadster.

The TR7 enjoyed television exposure in the mid-1970s as one of several British Leyland cars driven by lead characters in *The New Avengers*, a hit series featuring the exploits of fictional British secret agents. The series starred Patrick Macnee as John Steed and Joanna Lumley as Purdey. Also, in 1978, Coca-Cola and Levi's combined forces with a promotional campaign in which the top prizes were TR7s in red and white livery, with denim upholstery. **SB**

TR7 6 5 4 3 2 1

XJS | Jaguar

GB

1975 • 323 cu in/5,300 cc, V12 • 285 bhp/210 kW • 0–60 mph/97 kph in 7.6 seconds • 143 mph/230 kph

Intended to be the E-Type Jaguar of the 1970s and 1980s, the big XJS was a very different car from the sexy 1960s icon. It therefore had an awkward start in life.

Traditional, tweedy fans were dismayed by the XJS's gaudy image. It was not the lithe, agile sports car they were expecting, and its thirsty V12 fitted badly with the world fuel crisis. Critics pointed out that, while the hood (bonnet) and trunk (boot) were enormous, the two-door 2+2 cabin was very cramped. The distinctive rear-window pillars were so wide that German authorities would not give it approval for sale, citing the dangers of restricted visibility.

Yet this was an appropriately smug grand tourer for the disco generation, and it ditched tradition in favor of instant glamour. As the *Daily Telegraph* reported, "Its role was to stand valiantly outside a nightclub while its owner swayed under a glitter ball in a flared suit." But its striking looks appealed strongly to TV producers. It figured prominently in popular long-running shows of the day, such as *Columbo*, *Falcon Crest*, *Dallas*, and *Knots Landing*. It was also the car used in the 1970s by Simon Templar in the TV series *Return of the Saint*, and by Gareth Hunt's character Gambit in *The New Avengers*.

Slowly, over its long, twenty-one-year production run, the "big cat" was improved in looks and engines. The XJS brand benefited from the introduction of sleeker cabrio and sporty XJR-S versions.

Gradually the car became a more acceptable sight in the golf-club parking lot. That slow acceptance has continued right up to today. The XJS is now considered a glorious period piece and is lusted after by collectors willing to pay high prices at auction. **SH**

Beta Montecarlo | Lancia

(I)

1975 • 122 cu in/2,000 cc, S4 • 120 bhp/88 kW • 0–60 mph/97 kph in 9 seconds • 112 mph/180 kph

Superficially an exotic supercar, the Montecarlo was a rather humble machine beneath its glamorous skin. It was designed as a big brother to Fiat's perky little X-19 sports car, and if it had been promoted under a major brand's name, perhaps it would have preempted the success of the mid-engined Toyota MR2 almost a decade later. As it was, the Pininfarina-designed Beta Montecarlo was instead given to Lancia, under which it became a little-known niche car.

The mechanical layout was new to Lancia. The twin-cam engine was placed sideways in the monocoque chassis, just in front of the rear wheels. The car was available as both a hardtop and a targa top.

The looks of the new Montecarlo, stylish and aggressive, implied great speed and handling. Sadly, those looks were deceptive; performance was distinctly average. It was claimed that Pininfarina designed the Montecarlo after the Ferrari Dino 246 of the 1970s, but, if it did, this car had none of the Dino's performance. The model built to U.S. specifications, called the Scorpion, was even more pedestrian. To meet emission controls, the mid-engined Lancia was given a smaller and slower 107-cubic-inch (1,756-cc engine).

All versions handled well, though, thanks to that mid-engined balance and the car's radial tires, alloy wheels, sporty suspension, and wide wheelbase. Roadholding and steering were superb for the period.

But all Lancias of the period were prone to disastrous rust. The Montecarlo disintegrated quickly, and not many remain on the road today. But the model survives in one way: as Herbie's girlfriend Giselle in the 1977 Disney movie *Herbie Goes to Monte Carlo*. **BK**

The Porsche 924 looked good but customers wanted more power, which led to the 1979 turbocharged variants. ⊃

Cosworth Vega 75 | Chevrolet (USA)

1975 • 121 cu in/1,994 cc, S4 • 110 bhp/82 kW • 0–60 mph/97 kph in 10.3 seconds • 117 mph/187 kph

When Chevrolet introduced its Vega in 1970, it was well received and even chosen as *Motor Trend* magazine's "Car of the Year." But the car went on to suffer from engineering problems and safety concerns; there were numerous design changes and—always the ultimate horror for a car company—recalls to the factory.

The car failed to shake off its reputation for unreliability, so in 1975 Chevrolet tried a rescue package by bringing out the Cosworth Vega 75. This, it hoped, would be a kind of supercar that would be dynamic yet utterly reliable, and would transform the Vega's fortunes. As a high-performance car with a limited production run it would be, Chevrolet fervently hoped, eminently desirable.

The U.S. carmaker worked with Britain's prestigious Cosworth Engineering to develop an engine that was virtually hand-built, each one signed by its maker. The association meant that the always-impressive name of Cosworth was allowed to appear on the car.

Cosworth built 5,000 of the engines, but only 3,508 cars were ever made. They certainly looked eye-catching; the 1975 models had black and gold bodies and a range of interiors—some black, some white, with dashes of gold here and there. In 1976 several new exterior and interior colors were added to the line.

The Cosworth Vega was a decent-enough car and did not suffer from the mechanical problems that had blighted the main Vega series. But it was not special enough to set the world alight or overturn the Vega's tarnished image. Production was stopped in 1976, and the stock of autographed engines was never used up. The whole Vega series was retired in 1977. **MG**

924 | Porsche (D)

1975 • 121 cu in/1,984 cc, S4 • 125 bhp/93kW • 0–60 mph/97 kph in 9.5 seconds • 126 mph/203 kph

The Porsche 924's flowing lines, pop-up headlights, and predictable handling eventually spawned a new generation of affordable sports coupes the world over.

Despite sales of more than 150,000, the 924 was never intended to bear the Porsche badge. Volkswagen (VW) had originally commissioned Porsche to design a sports coupe as a flagship for its Audi line. However, following the 1973 oil crisis, VW scrapped those plans. Porsche bought back the design and in 1975 launched the 924 as a replacement for its aging 914.

The 924 was to be Porsche's first water-cooled and front-engined production car, and it borrowed several styling cues from the 928, which was already under development. Although the 924's 121-cubic-inch (1,984-cc) engine was related to the one used in VW's LT vans and the AMC Gremlin, performance was fairly brisk by the standards of the day. But it was the car's fabulous handling that really started to win over the skeptics; near-perfect 48/52 weight distribution also helped traction to the rear-driven wheels and braking.

Some aficionados dismiss the little 924 as a "poor man's Porsche," but it was not a cheap car; when it first arrived in the United States, it cost more than the 210-bhp (160-kW) Chevrolet Corvette. It still proved extremely profitable for the German brand, accounting for 65 percent of Porsche sales across North America in the late 1970s. Eventually, customer demand for greater power was met by turbocharged variants and Porsche's own 152-cubic-inch (2,500-cc) powerplant.

But perhaps the ultimate 924 was the "giant killing" 375-bhp (280-kW) Carrera GTR race car that, in 1982, battled to a class win in the 24 Hours of Le Mans. **DS**

450 SEL 6.9 | Mercedes-Benz (D)

1975 • 421 cu in/6,900 cc, V8 • 286 bhp/213 kW •
0–60 mph/97 kph in 7.5 seconds • 140 mph/225 kph

Despite its being more than double the price of the top Cadillac, plenty of wealthy buyers craved this big new Mercedes. Actress Sophia Loren even had one converted to carry her dogs in the back.

The flagship car was packed with new technology. It had antilock brakes, and was the first Mercedes with hydro-pneumatic self-leveling suspension using fluid-filled struts. Handling and comfort were superb, and the ride height could be altered by up to 2 inches (5 cm) through a dash-mounted control. The fuel-injected engine had electronic ignition, a dry oil pan normally found only in race cars, sodium-filled valves like those of aircraft engines, and maintenance-free hydraulic valves.

The interior was austere in luxury terms. Velour was standard, though leather seats were an option. Neither the mirrors nor the front seats were power-adjustable, but a powered rear seat was optional. Rear-seat passengers had special lighting in the rear roof pillars to enable them to read. With its lofty price, total sales of 7,380 during its six-year life span were considered good.

And the car had a certain menace, too. In the 1998 action film *Ronin*, a 450 SEL performed a series of dramatic stunts in the course of a high-speed car chase through French mountains with Robert de Niro as a pistol-toting passenger. **SH**

Pony | Hyundai (ROK)

1975 • 97 cu in/1,597 cc, S4 • 71 bhp/53 kW •
0–60 mph in 14.4 seconds • 96 mph/154 kph

In the early 1960s, the Republic of Korea's three biggest exports were clothing, plywood, and wigs. Today, Korea is the world's fifth-largest car producer, with 70 percent of its output being exported. This automotive revolution was triggered in 1975, when the Hyundai Pony was launched at the Turin Motor Show.

Hyundai Motors was founded in 1967, and initially produced cars in partnership with Ford and General Motors. When it decided that it wanted to build its own car, Hyundai hired a team of British engineers to oversee the project; styling was outsourced to Italdesign-Giugiaro, and engines were bought in from Mitsubishi.

The Pony was not Korea's first homegrown car, but it was the most successful. When it reached European markets in 1976, it began to dominate the lowest priced sectors. In 1984 it became Canada's best-selling motorcar; over 25,000 were sold in that year alone, five times more than Hyundai had predicted. In its fifteen-year run the car was sold as a five-door hatchback, a sedan (saloon), a station wagon (estate), and a pickup.

But the Pony's significance mostly lies in the way it helped Korean carmakers to break into new markets. In 2008 a blue Mark 1 Pony went on display at the National Folk Museum of Korea in recognition of the part it played in the story of the Korean motor industry. **DS**

Chevette HS | Vauxhall (GB)

1976 • 139 cu in/2,279 cc, slant 4 • 135 bhp/101 kW • 0–60 mph/97 kph in 8.5 seconds • 117 mph/188 kph

The Vauxhall Chevette was a small, British-built hatchback largely intended for the domestic market. Its modern styling and spritely performance attracted younger drivers, and it was the best-selling car of its type until rivals arrived from Ford and British Leyland.

To boost interest in the Chevette, Vauxhall decided to race a sporty version of the car in international rallying. The Chevette HS was launched in early 1976. With a sixteen-valve 139-cubic-inch (2,279 cc) four-cylinder engine mated to a close-ratio five-speed gearbox, it proved to be extremely quick, especially on tarmac. Bigger brakes and beefed-up suspension were added, and aerodynamics were improved by a front air dam and a small rear spoiler. Wide alloy wheels were added under new wheel arches to complete the rally-car look.

To qualify for competition, a statutory 400 road-legal production models had to be built. Most of these were painted silver, like the rally cars, and featured lurid tartan interiors. While the HS was huge fun to drive, a lack of refinement and a high purchase cost (double that of the basic Chevette) made it difficult to sell.

Yet the HS was a great rally car. With three respected drivers—Tony Pond, Pentti Airikkala, and Jimmy McRae (father of Colin)—behind the wheel, the HS took British Open Rally Championship titles in 1979 and 1981. **DS**

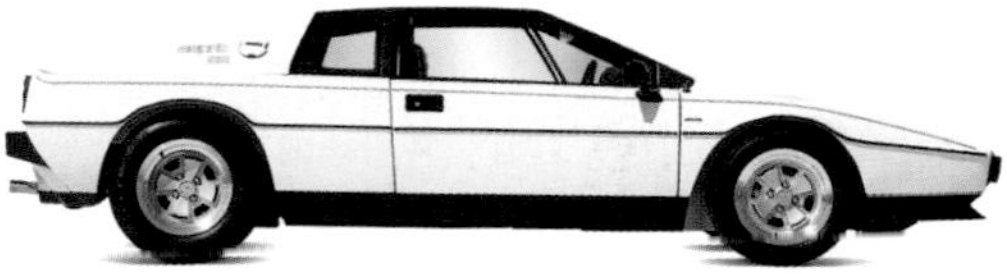

Esprit | Lotus (GB)

1976 • 120 cu in/1,973 cc, S4 • 160 bhp/119 kW • 0–60 mph/97 kph in 6.8 seconds • 137 mph/221 kph

Many exotic cars have featured in James Bond films, but few are as memorable as the Lotus Esprit driven by Roger Moore in 1977's *The Spy Who Loved Me*. In one of the best movie car chases of all time, the Esprit escapes by converting into a submarine and diving underwater, its wheels retracting and fishlike fins emerging.

First seen as a design study at the Turin Motor Show in 1972, and officially unveiled at the Paris Motor Show in 1975, the Esprit began in production in 1976. Exposure in the Bond film gave it huge publicity around the world.

The Esprit was conceived to replace the Lotus Europa. The team behind it was led by Mike Kimberley (later to become chief executive) and Tony Rudd. The car was powered by a Lotus Type 907 engine, mounted longitudinally behind the passenger compartment, and it had race car–style inboard rear brakes.

The original idea for the name of the car was "Kiwi," but that did not fit the Lotus tradition of model names starting with the letter "E," so Esprit was chosen instead. The body shape was by Giorgetto Giugiaro; it was the first of his famous polygonal "folded paper" designs, and the Esprit was widely praised for its gorgeous looks.

Four generations of the Esprit eventually appeared, until production ceased in 2004. More than 10,600 had been made. **SB**

Mark II Escort RS2000 | Ford

GB

1976 • 122 cu in/2,000 cc, S4 • 110 bhp/81 kW • 0–60 mph/97 kph in 8.9 seconds • 110 mph/177 kph

In the days before hot hatchbacks, young European men squealed their tires and impressed the girls in small sporty sedans (saloons), and among the kings of the go-faster-stripe posse was Ford's Escort RS series. "RS" stood for Rally Sport. It was a badge that Ford Europe had introduced in 1970 on a version of the Mark I Escort 1600. This was the first Ford to feature a twin-cam sixteen-valve engine.

The Mark II Escort, which appeared in 1975, marked the final fling for rear-wheel-drive Escorts. Sporty versions of this more modern, angular generation continued to be badged as "RS." The RS2000 was launched in 1976 with the 122-cubic-inch (2,000-cc) Pinto engine used in Ford's bigger Cortina range. The car came with a unique polyurethane "droop snoop" front spoiler that gave it an instantly recognizable character.

But there was nothing sophisticated about this two-door Escort. Even in the mid-1970s it did not seem well equipped. The suspension was independent at the front with an anti-roll bar, but was just old-fashioned leaf springs at the back. There was only a four-speed manual gearbox, drum brakes at the rear; fuel economy was poor at 25 mpg (9.4 liters per 100 km).

What passed as extra features in those days were very minimal. Front sports seats, green-tinted windows, and a glove box were about the sum of the luxuries on offer. But of course the RS2000 came complete with flashy alloy wheels and—most important of all—a broad stripe that ran the length of the car.

Escort enthusiasts were rewarded in 1980 by the appearance of the third-generation model, with front-wheel drive and hatchback styling. **SH**

Golf GTI Mark I | Volkswagen

D

1976 • 97 cu in/1,600 cc, S4 • 108 bhp/80 kW • 0–60 mph/97 kph in 9 seconds • 110 mph/177 kph

To replace the "Beetle," which had been produced since World War II, Volkswagen (VW) went to Italy. World-renowned car designer Giorgetto Giugiaro of the ItalDesign studio drew the body of the new car, and his sharp, angular hatchback design seemed modern, chic, and exciting. The 1974 VW Golf was an instant hit.

A small group of VW engineers began working on a sporty version of the new front-wheel-drive hatchback in their spare time. They toned down their original rather extreme ideas until their bosses accepted the concept. In 1975, just a year after the standard Golf was launched, "the fastest ever Volkswagen" was revealed at the Frankfurt Motor Show.

The world had seen a few rally-bred specialist hot-hatches before, but this was very different. The GTI was the first mass-market model to have such modern but popular sporting appeal. The Motor Show crowds remarked the details that made the GTI clearly different from the standard Golf: a chin spoiler, black side stripes, black plastic wheel-arch kits, and a fine red pinstripe around the front grille. Inside there was a smile-raising golf ball serving as a gear knob, and the seats were covered in racy tartan fabric. The car was only available in the three-door format.

The engine had been tweaked, of course. There was now fuel injection, and larger valves to increase power. At the time its performance seemed very exciting, and suddenly it was the car everyone was talking about. Its fame spread across the world and it was a huge sales success. VW had an unexpected hit on its hands, and most other manufacturers paid the GTI the ultimate compliment by trying to copy it. **BK**

Lima | Panther

GB

1976 • 139 cu in/2,279 cc, S4 • 109 bhp/81 kW •
0–60 mph/97 kph in 7.6 seconds • 112 mph/180 kph

Founded in 1972, the British-based Panther company produced cars based on older classics and given more powerful engines. The Lima of 1976 was an open-top two-door sports cabriolet that conjured up a 1930s British racer. Indeed, its Vauxhall Magnum engine provided speeds and acceleration that would be perfectly at home on the racetrack. Other parts of the Magnum were used in the car, too, and Vauxhall also provided the transmission. The styling of the lightweight fiberglass body had a look of a Bugatti.

About 600 of this first series were built from 1976, until a second series was introduced in 1978. With an engine of similar size, these had some cosmetic changes, including a walnut dashboard. Some 300 of this model were built between 1978 and 1982. The company had collapsed in 1980 but was bought by a Korean businessman. Although he built a new factory, the Panther name eventually disappeared in 1990 when his company went out of business.

Fewer than 900 Limas were produced in all. Because of their rarity, they do not often come up for auction, but when they do, they sell for surprisingly modest amounts. In 2009 a 1979 Panther Lima roadster was auctioned by Bonhams and sold for only €8,050 ($10,700/£6,700). **MG**

Accord | Honda

J

1976 • 97 cu in/1,600 cc, S4 • 68 bhp/51 kW •
0–60 mph/97 kph in 13.8 seconds • 102 mph/164 kph

The arrival of the Accord sparked a revolution. It seems like an ultranormal family car today, but in 1976 it set new standards. It was designed with the engine sideways in the front powering the front wheels, as the Austin Mini had done many years before. This meant no driveshaft running to the back axle and no engine taking up valuable passenger space. So despite its small overall dimensions, the Honda had class-leading space inside. Add in the folding rear seats and there was the potential for a huge cargo area.

The fuel-efficient little Honda was launched one year after the first global energy crisis. It also arrived in America with more standard equipment than anything in its class, with new gadgets such as intermittent wipers and an AM/FM radio. It seemed practical, handy, and modern compared with its rivals. U.S. buyers started abandoning their wallowing great Cutlasses and Monte Carlos for the cheery and cheeky Accord.

By 1979 there was a four-door Accord sedan (saloon), and in 1982 the Accord became the first Japanese car to be built in the United States, when Honda opened its Ohio factory. The range grew in size and body styles; there was soon an elegant coupe and a stationwagon (estate). And within in a few years most cars being built in the world were front-wheel drive. **SH**

Alpina 2002Tii A4S | BMW (D)

1976 • 121 cu in/1,997 cc, S4 • 168 bhp/125 kW • 0–60 mph/97 kph in 7.4 seconds • 125 mph/201 kph

In 1965, Burkard Bovensiepen began a new business venture, Alpina, making tuning parts for BMW. Starting with carburetors and cylinder heads, he gradually became recognized as a manufacturer in his own right. The BMW Alpina 2002tii A4S was one of Alpina's earliest cars, and today it is one of the rarest.

In 1976 BMW was offering a turbocharged version of its new 3-Series model; Alpina took the already potent motor and fettled it further. Alpina's 2002Tii A4S sported distinctive blue and green decals down the flanks, a front bib spoiler with a large Alpina logo, and a black rubber trunk (boot) spoiler. The model was available as a two-door sedan (saloon) marketed as a coupe, and a three-door touring version. It ran on 13-inch (33-cm) wheels and was certainly striking.

Under the skin it had a dog-leg four-speed manual gearbox (modern Alpinas being almost exclusively automatic) and rear-wheel drive. The engine delivered 168 bhp (125 kW) as standard, although examples exist with 200 bhp (149 kW) and more. The car was safe only in the hands of the most experienced of drivers, for its tail-happy behavior and potent engine meant that a rare car quickly became rarer. It performed superbly in motorsport, and the years following its launch saw Alpina's best-ever results in many events. **RD**

Kyalami | Maserati (I)

1976 • 254 cu in/4,163 cc, V8 • 226 bhp/198 kW • 0–60 mph/97 kph in 6.4 seconds • 149 mph/240 kph

The Maserati Kyalami, named for the Kyalami Grand Prix Circuit in South Africa, endured a long and complex evolution. At the 1972 Turin Motor Show, carmaker DeTomaso had shown off its "Longchamp" model, designed by Tom Tjaarda. When ownership of the Maserati company fell into DeTomaso's hands, the car was relaunched as the Kyalami, appearing under its new name at the 1976 Geneva Motor Show.

After a reworking of the original design by Maserati's Pietro Frua, the new Kyalami was lower, wider, and longer than the Longchamp, and now shared many mechanical components with its stablemate, the Quattroporte. Initially powered by a 254-cubic-inch (4,163-cc) V8, and later by a 299-cubic-inch (4,900-cc) V8 with either five-speed manual or three-speed automatic transmission, the Kyalami offered high performance, excellent driving characteristics, and great comfort for the era.

The Kyalami cost $33,000 (£21,189), making it an expensive alternative to established rivals such as the Mercedes-Benz SL. The price, combined with its angular looks, resulted in unspectacular sales—in fact, only around 200 examples were made. It was a rare car at the time it was made, and is rarer still today due to a scarcity of parts and high ownership costs. **RD**

Niva | Lada

SU

1977 • 103 cu in/1,700 cc, S4 • 80 bhp/59 kW • 0–62 mph/100 kph in 17 seconds • 90 mph/145 kph

The likable little Niva was Lada's first model not to be based on an old Fiat. Its basic and boxy body, four-wheel-drive system, and surprisingly adept suspension were all Russian designed. Production of the small utility vehicle started in 1977 at the Togliatti plant, which was then the biggest car factory in the world with more than 185 miles (300 km) of assembly lines. The Niva has been such a worldwide success it is still being built today (in Ukraine and Kazakhstan).

The recipe is fairly basic: the Niva is cheap, simple, and rugged. It's old fashioned and uncompetitive on the road, but as an off-roader it's one of the best, with a low center of gravity, high ground clearance, narrow thick tires, permanent four-wheel-drive, and high and low ratio gearboxes. The Niva even comes with a twenty-one-piece tool kit for roadside repairs.

The simplicity means that many models have been converted or tuned for performance, including a Ferrari mid-engined rally version and a turbocharged Niva that did well in the grueling Paris–Dakar race. One has even been converted to drive completely underwater.

Nivas were built to handle the worst that Siberia had to offer and have coped with extreme terrains all over the world. Several Nivas have driven to the North Pole, and they've also been used at Russian bases in Antarctica. In 1999 three Nivas drove higher than Everest Base Camp to 18,786 feet (5,726 m) in the Himalayas, a new world record for vehicle altitude. This record stood until 2005, when specially prepared Volkswagen Touaregs reached an altitude of 19,948 feet (6,080 m) in Chile. **SH**

SC100 Coupe | Suzuki

J

1977 • 59 cu in/970 cc, S4 • 47 bhp/35 kW • 0–60 mph/97 kph in 16.5 seconds • 89 mph/143 kph

This pert little runabout was the export version of the Cervo SS20 (based on Giorgetto Giugiaro's Fronte Coupe), with which Suzuki had broken into the mini sportscar market in Japan in 1977. Suzuki modified the Cervo for export, replacing the original three-cylinder engine with a rear-mounted 59-cubic-inch (970-cc) four-cylinder F10A power unit. Its engineers applied extra weight to the front end to even out the car's balance. They also substituted square headlights for the original round ones, and moved the indicator lenses from the bumper to the front grille. Officially named the SC100 Coupe, this car was marketed in Britain (where the only available option was the GX) from 1978 as the Suzuki Whizzkid.

In the late 1970s, many Europeans perceived Japanese cars as inferior to native brands. Suzuki tried to overcome market resistance to the Whizzkid by stacking it with appealing extras. These included a heated rear window, independent all-round suspension, reclining seats, and push-button radio. It was priced about the same as the much less well-equipped Mini.

Between the Whizzkid's introduction and the end of production in 1982, Suzuki's British import agents, Heron, sold 4,696 units. The little car was comparably successful in the Netherlands, Hong Kong, South Africa, New Zealand, and several Latin American countries.

Today the Whizzkid is something of a retro icon, distinguished as the first Suzuki to hit the British Isles. Another factor to its lasting appeal is its extreme frugality—it returned 57 mpg (4 liters per 100 km) on long journeys and 42 mpg (5.6 liters per 100 km) on a combined cycle. **GL**

Gamma Coupe | Lancia

(I)

1977 • 152 cu in/2,500 cc, F4 • 140 bhp/104 kW • 0–60 mph/97 kph in 9.4 seconds • 120 mph/193 kph

The little-known Lancia luxury two-door was one of the most elegant car designs of the 1970s. Its simple but subtle lines were penned by Italian styling house Pininfarina, creating a sleeker version of the 1976 Gamma Berlina sedan (saloon). Fiat had by now taken over Lancia and the brand was to be positioned as the prestige one of the group. The Gamma was the flagship for the whole Fiat empire and was designed to be distinguished, with a well-appointed interior.

The body shapes were confusing to buyers, however. Although it was called the coupe, it had an extending trunk (boot) beyond the rear window. Meanwhile, the so-called sedan had a sloping fastback. There was no doubting that the coupe was the prettier of the two, although the sedan sold more than twice as well. Both versions were front-wheel drive.

With the 152-cubic-inch (2,500-cc) engine the coupe had grand touring pace rather than sports car performance, and independent suspension geared toward to comfort rather than precision handling. The lightweight alloy engine was an unusual "flat-four" design, allowing the hood (bonnet) to be lower. It was large for a four-cylinder unit. The horsepower rating was fairly humble, but it developed plenty of torque, or pulling power.

Sadly the coupe was hampered by fuel thirst and a lack of six-cylinder versions to challenge its German rivals. Like all Lancias of the time it suffered badly from rust. Its reputation was also blighted from the start by an early problem with the power steering pump. The Gamma Coupe lived on for seven years, but fewer than 7,000 cars were sold in that period. **SH**

Lagonda | Aston Martin

GB

1977 • 325 cu in/5,341 cc, V8 • 310 bhp/232 kW • 0–60 mph/97 kph in 7 seconds • 140 mph/225 kph

When Aston Martin introduced the Lagonda in October 1976, it was the first production car in the world to have a digital instrument panel and computer-controlled features. At the time this was almost a space-age luxury. Other indulgences that came as standard on this high-end car included air-conditioning, power steering, power brakes, power windows, and power door locks. Mind you, when buyers were paying £32,620 ($51,600) they probably expected a little bit of luxury. They were also treated to a very high-performance car with impressive acceleration and top speed.

The Lagonda was designed by William Towns, who had worked his way up from designing car seats and door handles to working on the Hillman Hunter. He then moved to Aston Martin and was one of the main people involved in the Lagonda. It was his final triumph at the company, as he then left to do lucrative work in industrial design, although he did some freelance work on several more cars, including the Jensen-Healey.

Towns's design was for a very strange-looking wedge-shaped car, and people either loved it or hated it. In 2011 *Bloomberg Businessweek* voted it one of the fifty ugliest cars from the last fifty years. It was certainly different, though, and enough people loved it for it to attract plenty of advance orders. This is what Aston Martin needed, as despite its big name it was rather low on funds in the 1970s, and was in want of a financial success. Although it was previewed in 1976 and launched in 1977, the first owners didn't get their hands on cars until 1979. It was a success, however, and stayed in production until 1990. **MG**

99 Turbo | Saab (S)

1977 • 122 cu in/2,000 cc, turbocharged S4 • 143 bhp/107 kW • 0–60 mph/97 kph in 8.9 seconds • 124 mph/200 kph

With the success of Abba and Bjorn Borg, all things Swedish were suddenly cool—that's when Saab launched the 99 Turbo. It was one of the first mass-produced turbocharged cars. Other manufacturers had tried the idea on specialist performance cars, but Saab was the first to bring it to the mass market. The new Saab was a humble four-cylinder family car that could now outrun the six-cylinder BMW 528. It was a breakthrough for turbocharging—and for Saab itself.

Yet the turbo idea had been a desperate last resort. The 99 range was already a decade old, and was being outclassed by bigger-engined rivals. Saab didn't have the budget to develop a new model, but was in danger of falling foul of new Californian emissions controls. So Saab tried using turbo technology that it was already familiar with from its aircraft-making division. Engineers were worried about overwhelming the engine so they used a smaller, lighter turbo than other carmakers. The effect on performance was stunning, with an immediate improvement of around 40 percent. The power output may sound humble today, but it was immediately 33 bhp (24 kW) more than the market-leading BMW 320. Moreover, the main effect was on torque, or pulling power. The little Saab now had world-beating mid-range punch—the all-important overtaking power. **SH**

Rancho | Matra (F)

1977 • 87 cu in/1,442 cc, S4 • 80 bhp/59 kW • 0–60 mph/97 kph in 14.9 seconds • 90 mph/145 kph

The launch of the Range Rover in 1970 had created a market for off-roaders that drove like a car but looked capable of climbing a mountain. Matra wanted to join that market but didn't have the same expertise. So it used what it had to hand: a Simca 1100 pickup, some fiberglass, and a Chrysler Alpine engine.

Thanks to the magic of designer Antonis Volanis, the humble Simca was made to look like it could tackle a jungle expedition. But really it was just a box stuck on the back of a supermini's chassis. Contrasting colored moldings, strips, and rails, plus metal bull bars and light guards, helped make it look more macho. The pickup's chassis was stretched and the ground clearance raised, but inside was a basic hatchback engine, four-speed manual gearbox, and front-wheel drive. Matra didn't have the budget for a 4x4 version.

Optional extras included a front-mounted electric winch, sump guard, and spare tire on the roof. There was a soft-top version and a "luxury" model with alloy wheels and metallic paint. More importantly, with two extra seats in the luggage area, the Rancho could carry six—making it a precursor to the first people carriers.

It cost just over half the price of a Range Rover, so, although it struggled to even climb a speed bump, the Rancho sold twice as well as Matra was expecting. **SH**

4104 | ZiL (SU)

1978 • 469 cu in/7,695 cc, V8 • 309 bhp/230 kW • 0–60 mph/97 kph in 12.1 seconds • 121 mph/195 kph

The debut of the ZiL 4104 was timed to coincide with the 1978 Communist Party congress, and it proved to be all that party officials had come to expect from the makers of their limousines since the 1930s. It had a big, 469-cubic-inch (7,695-cc) V8 engine that produced the necessary horsepower to propel its 3.3-tonne weight. It still had ZiL's traditional, boxlike proportions, but this time there were a few nods to Western styling with side moldings in its exterior panels, and chrome trims over its wheel arches. There was also a new, fully chromed grille, and its headlights and indicators—which in previous models had been packed together—were now separate. Sure, the changes to its aesthetic appeal were incremental and improving at the rate of Soviet democratic reforms, but at least it was progress.

The build of ZiL cars was as good as the very best custom-made coachwork in the West. Dashboards and trims were made from Karelian birchwood and seats were leather. Each car was extensively road tested before delivery to eliminate any "bugs," and was fastidiously logged and maintained during its period of service.

Although manufacture of ZiL limousines has long ceased, there have recently been calls for their return, with some Russian Armed Forces officials complaining about having to drive around in "foreign" Mercedes. **BS**

3000S | TVR (GB)

1978 • 182 cu in/2,994 cc, V6 • 142 bhp/106 kW • 0–60 mph/97 kph in 7.7 seconds • 125 mph/201 kph

In 1972, TVR's new boss, Martin Lilley, launched the M-Series of sports coupes; the engine options ranged from a weedy 97-cubic-inch (1,600-cc) four-pot, to the lusty 182-cubic-inch (2,994-cc) V6 from Ford's Capri. In 1978 the convertible 3000S model was added to the line up, with a detachable soft-top roof that was stowed in the trunk (boot).

With superlight bodywork, plenty of torque and fully independent suspension, the 3000S did well in motorsport. In the 1979 British Racing Drivers Championship, a race-prepared 3000S won every one of the twenty-two races it entered that season.

Just 258 models were built in the 3000S's short two-year production run. Some sixty-seven of these were left-hand-drive export versions, mostly destined for North America. Costing $10,000 (£6,390), the 3000S was considerably cheaper—and far quicker—than the recently launched Porsche 924, and it should have sold well in the United States. However, problems with American emission regulations resulted in the final twenty-five cars being impounded and shipped back to Blackpool.

Today, the 3000S is a highly sought-after modern classic, and good examples can command prices upward of £10,000 ($15,700). **DS**

M1 | BMW

(D)

1978 • 210 cu in/3,453 cc, S6 • 273 bhp/204 kW • 0–60 mph/97 kph in 5.8 seconds • 160 mph/260 kph

BMW has only ever made one mid-engined car, and the M1 is it. It was an exotic supercar, a long, low, rear-wheel-drive model with a 210-cubic-inch (3,453-cc), straight-six-cylinder engine behind the seats. Like so many of the best-looking cars of the 1970s, its bodywork was styled by leading Italian designer Giorgetto Giugiaro.

The idea behind the BMW M1 was to produce what is known as a "homologation special." To comply with some categories of motorsport, regulations stipulate that any car intended to compete in a racing series has to have been manufactured in sufficient numbers as a road car. So the M1 was scheduled for a limited production run for the road to qualify it for the track.

The car started out as a collaboration between Lamborghini and BMW. The German company commissioned Lamborghini to develop the chassis, build prototypes, and produce the vehicle. But the project was ill-fated. Lamborghini ran into financial problems when only seven prototypes had been made, and BMW was forced to take control and bring the project back in-house. The production run lasted three years, during which time 455 cars were made. It remains one of BMW's rarest models.

The M1 was sensational both in looks and performance. As a road car, it was well-endowed with a power output of 273 bhp (204 kW). Tuned and turbocharged as a racing car, its peak power output reached 850 bhp (634 kW). Racing M1s competed in a support series that ran alongside Formula One, the Procar BMW M1 Championship. The series lasted only two years, and produced two champions: Niki Lauda in 1979 and Nelson Piquet in 1980. **SB**

928 | Porsche

D

1978 • 329 cu in/5,397 cc, V8 • 345 bhp/257 kW • 0–60 mph/97 kph in 5.4 seconds • 168 mph/270 kph

Nicknamed the "Land Shark," the sleek 928 was Porsche's second model to feature a water-cooled engine at the front instead of air-cooled powerplants at the rear. However, this time they gave their car some real muscle. Porsche's own 274-cubic-inch (4,500-cc) V8 engine was continually enlarged, culminating in the epic 329-cubic-inch (5,397-cc) GTS before production ended in 1995.

Winning the prestigious European Car of the Year Award in 1978, the Porsche 928 remains to this day the only sports car to hold this title. Its avant-garde design featured sculpted polyurethane bumpers to aid aerodynamics; it was also the first ever car to feature a moving instrument binnacle, and rear passengers were even treated to their own sun visors and air-conditioning. These luxuries meant the 928 was heavier than the 911 it was intended to replace, although its extra horsepower, perfectly balanced 50/50 weight distribution, and clever rear-steering suspension meant that performance on track was equally matched.

However, the lure of the quirky old 911 was too strong for most Porschephiles. Nevertheless, the 928 attracted a large number of customers who enjoyed its predictable road manners and welcomed the cabin's creature comforts. More than 80 percent were specified with automatic gearboxes, and by the time a few additional boxes had been checked off on the options list, it could cost about the same as three Porsche 924s.

The beautiful bodywork of the 928 places it among the world's greatest car designs. It is even rumored that Apple founder and design guru, Steve Jobs, was influenced by the shape of his own "Land Shark" when styling the first Macintosh computers in 1981. **DS**

L'il Red Express | Dodge

(USA)

1978 • 359 cu in/5,899 cc, V8 • 225 bhp/167 kW • 0–100 mph/160 kph in 19.9 seconds • 120 mph/192 kph

Launched in 1980, the Dodge Ram is one of the world's best known pickups. Prior to its debut, the U.S. brand's truck range was the D Series. It arrived on the scene in 1961, but the third-generation model (1972–80) showcased a more rounded look. It was during this era that Dodge introduced a number of design-led special editions, including perhaps the most famous American truck of all time, the L'il Red Express.

It was only available during 1978–79, a time when U.S. legislation was impacting the power and emissions of new cars. But trucks weren't affected, so Dodge created a headline-grabbing hot rod with a modified V8 that could outrun most muscle cars of the day. *Car and Driver* magazine pitched it against a Chevrolet Corvette and Pontiac Firebird Trans Am, and found the L'il Red Express was quickest to 100 mph (160 kph).

There was no mistaking it for anything else. Obviously only available in red, and with its name emblazoned on both doors in gold paint, it featured perforated steel exhaust stacks and wooden flatbed cladding. Dodge sold the truck under its "Adult Toy" banner. Preempting what would later be marketed as a "lifestyle" pickup, the L'il Red Express was aimed at drivers who wanted a practical vehicle in their personal lives, not just for work. Inside, a red or black bench seat was standard, though individual chairs were an option.

The L'il Red Express wasn't the only special-edition D series of the time—others included the Warlock, the Adventurer, and, with arguably the most over-the-top name of any vehicle ever, the Macho Power Wagon. It just edges out Dude Sport Trim Package, available on the 1969 D Series, for silliest badge. **RY**

RX-7 | Mazda

J

1978 • 169 cu in/1,146 cc, rotary • 100 bhp/75 kW • 0–62 mph/100 kph in 11.4 seconds • 112 mph/180 kph

Almost all the cars in this book have an engine that uses pistons and cylinders to create power. The RX-7 sports car series is one of very few cars that uses a "rotary engine." The concept was invented by German engineer Felix Wankel in 1929, but it was not used in a car until the 1950s. German carmaker NSU was the first to begin using the idea, which was then licensed to Japanese manufacturer Mazda, who became the greatest proponents of the idea.

In a rotary engine combustion takes place inside a circular chamber and drives a triangular rotor around. The engine is compact, light, creates smoother power, and allows higher revs, but uses more fuel and has a less attractive exhaust whine. Mazda had begun using this unusual engine in small sports cars like the Cosmo, a sequence of RX cars, and even their pickup trucks.

The new RX-7 was the first rotary-engined car to make a big impact internationally. Its engine was rated at only 69 cubic inches (1,146 cc), although it's hard to compare rotary engine sizes with normal units. The long, low, two-door 2+2 sports car was still lively enough for the era, however, thanks to the engine's 100 bhp (75 kW) output. It had a slinky, aerodynamic body with pop-up headlights, and the engine was mounted behind the front axle, which gave better handling balance. Mazda called it a "mid-front engine." With this unusual power plant, Mazda claimed its new car was ahead of its time compared to rival coupes.

The RX-7 was continually upgraded through more powerful generations until it was replaced by the RX-8 in 2002. And that, of course, was powered by a rotary engine, too. **SH**

Rocket | Budweiser

USA

1979 • liquid-fueled rocket • unknown • 0–497 mph/800 kph in 10 seconds • 739.6 mph/1,190.27 kph

In the 1970s Hollywood movie director Hal Needham began a project to create the world's fastest car, simply "because it would be nice to make a bit of history." With sponsorship from Budweiser and the help of engineer William Frederick, his team built a long, thin, three-wheeled vehicle with a liquid-fueled rocket engine.

Initial trials showed that the Rocket would not meet the regulations to tackle the Land Speed Record; these require cars to maintain the speed for a distance in two directions and most regulations require the vehicle to use four wheels. Even more alarmingly, they indicated that the Rocket was not quite fast enough. The team responded by changing their target to breaking the sound barrier . . . and buying six Sidewinder missiles from the U.S. Navy. For each speed run, a Sidewinder was now bolted behind the driver's cockpit. The driver could "fire" the missile when he reached top speed to give the final thrust necessary to push the speed beyond the sound barrier.

In December 1979, on a dry lake at Edwards Air Force Base in California, the Rocket was recorded reaching a speed of Mach 1.01 by USAF monitoring equipment. Needham's friend, stunt man Stan Barrett, was the driver; a disk in his neck was ruptured by the G-force of the acceleration. The Rocket traveled so fast that both rear wheels left the ground and Barrett was close to losing control of it. Because the speed trials were not conducted under strict FIA rules, the team's claim was never officially recognized. It has been a subject of fierce controversy ever since. **SH**

Bulldog | Aston Martin

GB

1979 • 323 cu in/5,300 cc, V8 • 700 bhp/522 kW • unknown • 191 mph/307 kph

Dreamed up in an era when flat surfaces and sharp edges were the height of fashion, the Bulldog is a world away from the flowing and dynamic lines that are associated with modern Aston Martin cars.

A concept designed to preview an all-new supercar, it debuted in 1979 with talk of a production run limited to a handful of examples. It was styled by William Towns, the man behind the 1974 Aston Martin Lagonda, which had what critics kindly referred to as "an unconventional look." But the Bulldog was something else entirely.

With its gullwing doors and two-tone silver finish, comparisons with the De Lorean DMC-12 of the same era are inevitable. There were a number of other unusual styling cues, not least the five headlights mounted centrally on the front of the car and midway up the hood (bonnet). It was also extremely low to the ground, with a roofline of just 3.6 feet (1.1 m). The angular exterior lines continued into the cabin, which was all brown leather and carpet, with state-of-the-art digital instrumentation and a TV monitor to show the rear view.

The Bulldog was no show-pony though, and its top speed was verified by Aston Martin at 191 mph (307 kph). There were always claims—never proved—that it could go much faster, and as a production vehicle it could have challenged for speed records. But it never came to pass, and the one completed car stands as a testament to the company's grand ambitions. It was reputedly sold for £130,000 ($200,000) and spent some time in America. Its current whereabouts are unknown. **RY**

3000ME | AC

GB

1979 • 182 cu in/2,994 cc, V6 • 136 bhp/102 kW • 0–60 mph/97 kph in 8.5 seconds • 127 mph/203 kph

In 1904 in London, a wealthy butcher named John Portwine backed the Weller brothers, who were talented car engineers, and the resulting union eventually became AC Cars, one of the more unusual of the smaller car manufacturers. In 1929 the company went under and was bought by the Hurlock family; they were haulers and wanted the AC factory mainly for storage. However, they allowed the servicing of AC vehicles to continue, and in 1930 William Hurlock had a car built for himself. He liked it and agreed that it should go into limited production, mainly using pieces left over from the previous business.

The Hurlock family still ran AC Cars in the 1970s, which by then was focusing on luxury cars, although a mainstay of their business was building invalid carriages for the British government, who provided them cheaply to people with disabilities. Luxury cars weren't selling well in the early 1970s, and MD Derek Hurlock wanted a more modest mid-engine sports car to revive the company's fortunes. The 3000ME was the choice and it debuted at the 1973 London Motor Show (though as the ME3000). It got a good reception, but wasn't ready to go into production until 1976—the same year that the lucrative government contract to build invalid carriages came to an end.

At the same time, the British government introduced stringent new safety regulations, which affected all car manufacturers, and it was literally a case of back to the drawing board as AC Cars redesigned the 3000ME. It was all too much for the ailing company, and after only seventy-one cars had been sold, the plug was pulled on it. **MG**

Mustang III | Ford

(USA)

1979 • 170 cu in/2,800 cc, V8 • 134 bhp/98 kW • 0–60 mph/97kph in 11.2 seconds • 180 mph/290 kph

The third-generation Ford Mustang was the first four-seater in this iconic sports line. It was taller and longer, too, and demonstrated an enduring feature of car lines—that they grow bigger. A disconsolate Ford stockholder once famously asked Henry Ford II, "Why can't you just leave a small car small? You keep blowing them up and starting another little one, blow that one up and start another one. Why don't you just leave them?" The motor mogul gave an equivocal answer, but his designers kept enlarging cars, charging more, and introducing smaller models underneath them.

The Mustang had been in production for fourteen years when Ford decided to turn it into a four-seater. They used the large "Fox" platform previously used on the Fairmont and the Mercury Zephyr twins that had appeared the year before.

An increase in passenger numbers was not all that could be accommodated in this great new package: among the many extra benefits were more trunk (boot) space and a bigger engine bay for easier access during servicing and maintenance. There was a choice of a coupe (notchback) or hatchback (fastback) body and a choice of entry level or Ghia trim. All had a more European look with less traditional Mustang styling.

There was a range of engines carried over from the Mustang II, including a 140-cubic-inch (2,300-cc) four-cylinder, a 170-cubic-inch (2,800-cc) V6, and a 201-cubic-inch (3,300-cc) straight six. However, the V8 was most popular. The model of choice was the King Cobra, which was available in any color, although most of the 5,000 units produced were red. Many were individualized with wild bodywork patterns applied to order. **GL**

The crossover SUV concept of the 1979 AMC Eagle confused the company's executives, but proved popular with buyers.

F50 | Daihatsu (J)

1979 • 152 cu in/2,500 cc, S4 • 43 bhp/49 kW • unknown • 65 mph/105 kph

This no-nonsense, four-wheel-drive, two-seater jeep was a pioneering mini SUV. It was a direct descendant of the Daihatsu Taft, which was introduced in 1974 as the first many off-roaders built by the Japanese brand. The Taft was a reworking of the familiar Willy's Jeep concept, with similar round headlights, raised hood (bonnet), and folding windshield. These originals had been lightweight and, with only 61-cubic-inch (1,000-cc) engines, more than a little underpowered for their purpose.

The new F50, however, was the real deal: with a 152-cubic-inch (2,500-cc) diesel engine beneath the hood and improved transmission, this was a 4x4 that really was up for off-road exploits. Among its numerous attractions was the height of the body above the top of the tires, as well as its tight turning circle. Sadly, on-road performance wasn't up to much—the F50 could only hit 65 mph (105 kph) at best, and took an eternity to reach that speed. It came in hard- and soft-top versions, and there was also a choice between pickup and trayback/flatback bodies.

The F50 was so successful that within a year it had been updated as the F60, which was basically identical but had a deluxe 170-cubic-inch (2,800-cc) diesel and an optional fifth gear. Eventually they were replaced by the bigger and more robust Rocky/Rugger/Fourtrak line.

Most of the F50s kept going, however, and—although their undercarriages have had some rust issues (which is not entirely surprising in view of the terrain in which most of them operate)—many are still in regular use now. **GL**

Eagle | AMC (USA)

1979 • 256 cu in/4,200 cc, S6 • 110 bhp/82 kW • 0–60 mph/97 kph in 15.2 seconds • 88 mph/140 kph

What do you get when you cross a compact car body style from one part of your company with the 4x4 powertrain and off-road expertise from another? The answer for American Motors Corporation (AMC) was a series of vehicles that launched a new automobile category—the crossover SUV.

The respective "donors" were the AMC Concord and the underpinnings from the Jeep division. The man credited with this motoring mash-up is Jeep engineer Roy Lunn. History books record the response from Gerald C. Meyers, AMC's chairman at the time, as "What the hell is it?" The answer was America's first four-wheel-drive car, rather than a truck. When the 1979 energy crisis struck, even Meyers could see its merit as a sensible blend of the opposing sides of his business.

Available as a sedan (saloon), coupe, or station wagon (estate), Eagle sales were brisk from the off. All versions offered a comfortable ride on the highway, with enough traction for light off-road use. That's the dictionary definition of today's crossovers manufactured by almost every mainstream brand. AMC tried a variety of body styles over the years, including a liftback and hatchback. In the early 1980s there was even an authorized convertible conversion, the Sundancer, engineered by a Florida company.

By the time the last Eagles were sold in early 1988, almost 200,000 had found homes. AMC had become part of Chrysler Corporation and the Eagle named soldiered on with a number of vehicles that failed to match the original concept's success. Chrysler bosses finally pulled the plug on Eagle in 1998, but the cars remain a popular choice on the used market. **RY**

AMC 80
AMC 80

Cortina Mk V | Ford

GB

1979 • 121 cu in/1,993 cc, S4 • 101 bhp/74 kW • 0–60 mph/97 kph in 10.5 seconds • 106 mph/171 kph

Picking up the long-running Cortina saga again . . . the boxy Mark II had been replaced by an American-influenced Mark III, then came the more conventional Mark IV and the first upmarket Ghia trimmed model. All had been successes, establishing the Cortina as the U.K.'s consistently best-selling car. There were years when one-in-seven new British cars was a Cortina. Each generation was more successful than the last. The final incarnation, the Mark V, continued that legacy.

Officially titled the "Cortina 80," the new model was a classic design with sharper lines than the out-going model. The car was essentially just a revamp of the previous version, but looked bigger, wider, and more modern. There was more glass, narrower pillars, a wider grille, and a flatter roof. This was what British families thought the family car for the 1980s should look like.

The Cortina by now had quite an elaborate line: there were two- and four-door sedans (saloons), a five-door station wagon (estate), a pickup truck, and a convertible. The engine range was enormous, too: from 79 cubic inches (1,300 cc) to 140 cubic inches (2,300 cc) in Europe, to 250 cubic inches (4,100 cc) in Australia.

It was built in Dagenham in the United Kingdom, as well as in factories in Australia, Taiwan, and South Korea. It was very closely related to the Taunus, which did the same job for Ford across the rest of Europe.

Finally, after twenty years and more than 4.3 million models, the Cortina was gracefully retired in 1982. The Sierra that replaced it was a leap forward in styling and technology, but such was the affection for the old Cortina that conservative buyers still clamored to snap up the last few models left on forecourts. **SH**

Sunbeam Lotus | Talbot

GB

1979 • 132 cu in/2,172 cc, S4 • 150 bhp/112 kW • 0–60 mph/97 kph in 6.6 seconds • 121 mph/195 kph

In 1978, Chrysler was in financial meltdown and sold its European holdings to Peugeot. After much deliberation, Peugeot gave its newest acquisition the name "Talbot," and applied it to the Chrysler Sunbeam: a front-engined, rear-wheel-drive hatchback that Chrysler had produced in 1976 with help from the British government. The car was renamed the "Talbot Sunbeam," but the first models left the motoring world yawning. However, a new version—the TI—released in 1979 and modified with a 132-cubic-inch (2,172-cc) Lotus sixteen-valve engine with a new five-speed gearbox, would leave a different impression. It was one of the first discreet but seriously rally-bred hot-hatches.

Peugeot always intended to enter the resurrected Talbot in rallying, and had created the Talbot factory team to make it happen. Its standard 150 bhp (112 kW) engine was further tuned to produce 240 bhp (177 kW), and rear brakes changed from drum to disc. The new engine powered the light, 2,116-pound (962-kg) Talbot as though it were a thoroughbred, and in its inaugural season a Talbot raced to fourth place in the 1979 Rallye San Remo.

Its progression in the rallying world continued with a win in Portugal in 1980, and a one–three–four finish in the Lombard-RAC rally, the United Kingdom's leg of the World Rally Championship. In 1981 a Talbot achieved the ultimate accolade by winning the World Rally Championship, eleven points ahead of Datsun and a whopping thirty-seven points ahead of Ford's stable of high-achieving Escorts. The Talbot rally program was discontinued by Peugeot in late 1981 in favor of the new Group B Peugeot 205 4WD T16. **BS**

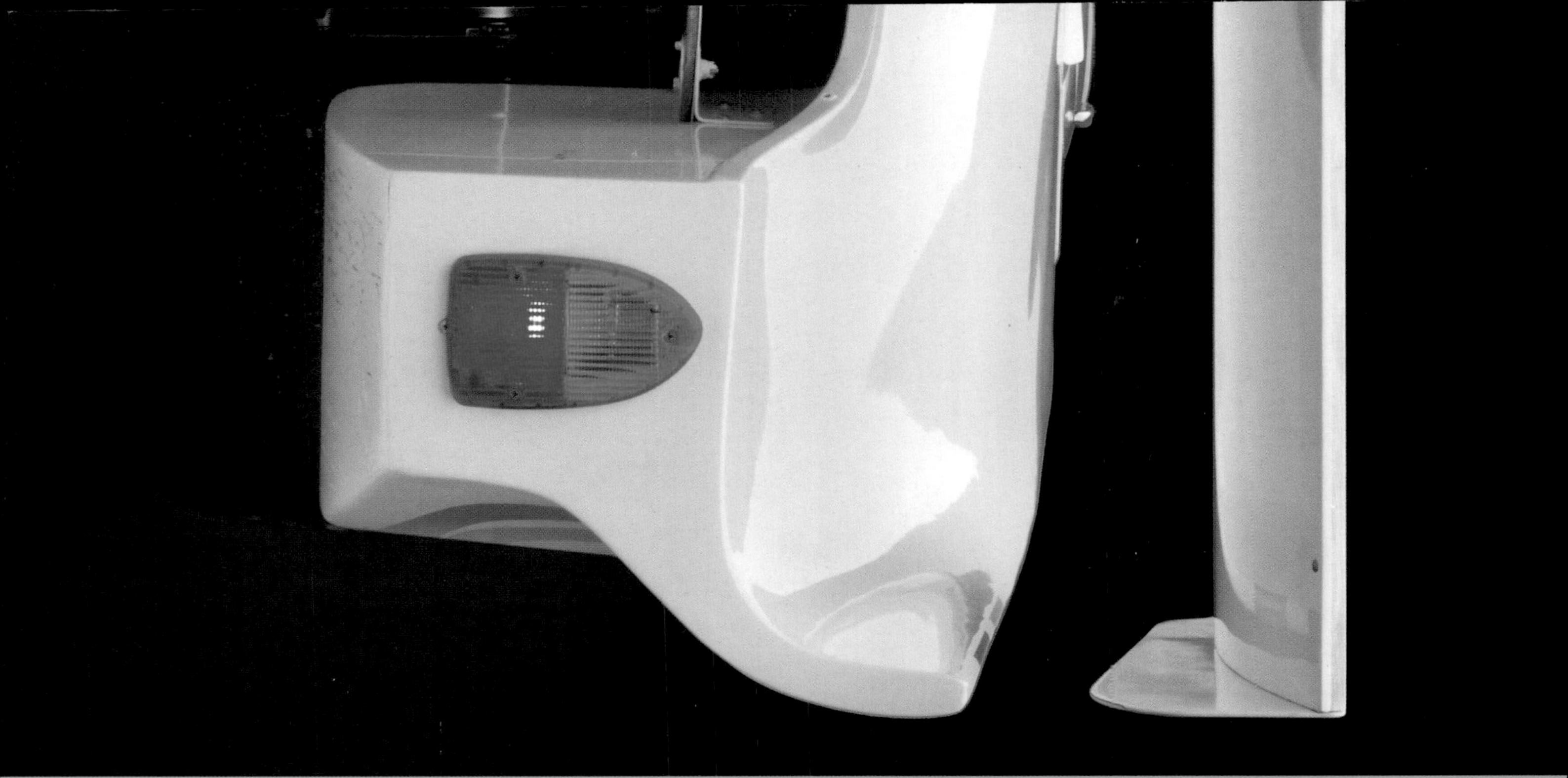

The racing credentials of the 1984 Jaguar GTP XJR-5 are evident even from the car's rear.

1980–1989

Piazza Turbo | Isuzu

J

1980 • 122 cu in/2,000 cc, S4 • 148 bhp/110 kW • 0–60 mph/97 kph in 8.4 seconds • 130 mph/209 kph

The Piazza was an early attempt by General Motors to create a global sports car to rival contemporary Japanese successes like the Toyota Celica and Mazda RX-7. However, bad planning and hurried development meant the Isuzu was always fighting a losing battle.

Italian designer Giorgetto Giugaro had been hired to draw a three-door coupe. He described it as a combination of his best ideas, but in fact it was a mix of several old designs he had hanging round the studio. The car was built by GM's Japanese subsidiary Isuzu, but Isuzu was—and still is—best known as a truck manufacturer. Isuzu bosses were excited about their new car and hurried it into production.

In most countries the new wedge-shaped Isuzu was called the Piazza; in the United States it was the Impulse. According to rumor that was because U.S. buyers would think it sounded too much like "pizza." In Australia GM used another subsidiary name to badge it the Holden Piazza. In Canada it was the Asuna Sunfire.

The first Piazza used rear-wheel-drive and a choice of weedy 122-cubic-inch (2,000-cc) engines. In its base form it was rather bland and unexciting, and sales were disappointing. From 1985 a turbocharged version added much-needed zip (figures given above).

Lotus was later brought in to help improve the car's much-criticized handling. They worked on all the Piazzas but made most changes to U.K.-imported cars, which were badged "Handling by Lotus." The second-generation Piazza, launched in 1990, was a front-wheel-drive hatchback, but by then the damage had been done. GM didn't even try selling the new car in Australia or the United Kingdom. **SH**

M535i | BMW

(D)

1980 • 210 cu in/3,453 cc, S6 • 215 bhp/160 kW • 0–62 mph/100 kph in 7.2 seconds • 130 mph/219 kph

The first product from BMW's motorsport division is, today, something of a hidden gem. Despite lacking the badging that makes an M5 stand out as something special, the M535i was actually the first mainstream creation from the "M" department. It was the quickest car that BMW made at the time. *BMW Car* magazine later affirmed "BMW Motorsport became a serious driving force with the arrival of the M535i."

Based on the E12 Type 5 Series BMW, the Motorsport division installed a fuel-injected 210-cubic-inch (3,453-cc) straight six-cylinder engine, more commonly found in the larger (and heavier) 6 and 7 Series cars. It had a close ratio dog-leg gearbox, limited slip differential, and uprated brakes that struggled to rein in the now very speedy car. The cabin was equipped with leather Recaro seats and there were practical touches like heated doorlocks. Externally there were Motorsport decals but the M535i was, like all subsequent M cars, a subtle brute. It wasn't cheap, however, and just 1,410 cars were ever produced.

With its "M" engineering (despite the lack of "M" badge) it was very much a driver's car. An armful of oversteer awaited anyone with a heavy right foot and, like other cars of the era, it made do without ABS. *Autocar* magazine tested one some years after launch. They reported, "Compared to a modern sports saloon [sedan] it feels light and immediate, with its barely assisted steering and taut damping."

Despite its interesting heritage, the M535i is now something of a bargain, and a worthy modern classic. Examples in Tunis beige with the optional corduroy-clad seats are a unbeatable slice of the 1980s. **RD**

FIAT
Fiat Panda

◁ The Fiat Panda, launched in 1980, was a pleasingly simple alternative to the heavily accessorized cars of the era.

Panda | Fiat (I)

1980 • 45 cu in/750 cc, S4 • 34 bhp/25 kW
0–62 mph/100 kph in 23 seconds • 78 mph/125 kph

The first Fiat Panda was a refreshingly basic, cheap, and practical car, launched at a time when manufacturers were packing cars with technological gadgets and heavy, power-sapping luxuries. Giorgetto Guigiaro's design was like a box on wheels. The engine range started with a tiny two-cylinder 39-cubic-inch (652-cc) unit and reached its peak with a humble 61-cubic-inch (1,000-cc) powerplant. Performance figures for the popular 45-cubic-inch (750-cc) version are given above.

The Panda was a great success, however, thanks to simple practical details like rear seats that could fold into a bed or be removed to create a small van. Seat covers and door trim could be taken off for washing and a simple, folding, full-length canvas sunroof was available. It was even fun to drive—on little winding roads though, not on motorways.

Improvements slowly arrived, along with a rugged 4x4 model, a 79-cubic-inch (1,300-cc) diesel, a "Selecta" model with continuously variable transmission, and an early electric version. The original Panda remained in production until 2003, clocking up 4.5 million sales.

The Panda also helped boost the Spanish car industry. The Seat Panda had been produced under license in Spain, but when the agreement ended, Seat started building their own popular version called the Marbella, as well as a topless version called the Pandita.

Meanwhile, back in Italy, Fiat launched a second generation of Panda in 2003. This was a more modern small car, built in Poland. It shared the cheeky charm of the original but not its simplicity—nor its unruly build quality. The new Panda has also been a sales success, with more than two million sold in eight years. **SH**

Golden Spirit | Zimmer (USA)

1980 • 255 cu in/4,183 cc, V8 • 112 bhp/84 kW
0–60 mph/97 kph in 16 seconds • 93 mph/149 kph

When the Zimmer company produced its first cars, it was safe to say that noone had ever seen anything like them before. They were retro-style neoclassic automobiles that were gloriously over the top. The sketch for the first Zimmer car was allegedly done on a napkin by Paul Zimmer, the company's founder.

Zimmer was a fascinating and energetic character, who had started the Zimmer Manufacturing Company in the 1950s, which provided factory-built houses. It made so much money by the 1970s that Paul Zimmer decided to reinvest some of his profits by starting several subdivisions, which were as much for fun as for business. As Paul Zimmer enjoyed driving an Excalibur, a retro-styled classic sports car, he decided he would set up a company to create cars along similar lines. The result was that car designed on a napkin, the Golden Spirit, which first appeared in 1980 and cost $75,000 (£47,600).

Zimmer's car company was as successful as his other ventures, and the annual revenue reached $13 million (£8.25 million). It was a huge amount for an independent carmaker with, initially, just one model. In 1985 a second car, the Quicksilver, was launched. Between them the two cars sold around 180 models a year.

Production ceased in 1988 when Paul Zimmer suffered a heart attack, and within a year all Zimmer companies had closed. Paul Zimmer eventually recovered, but he had lost everything; he died several years later. In 1998, Art Zimmer—no relation to Paul—bought a 1987 Zimmer and decided to restart the company with an updated version of the Golden Spirit, keeping true to the original design. **MG**

Corvette C3 | Chevrolet

(USA)

1980 • 349 cu in/5,733 cc, V8 • 190 bhp/142 kW • 0–60 mph/97 kph in 7.8 seconds • 137 mph/219 kph

The Corvette was one of Chevrolet's best-loved cars, and it was continually reinvented through several generations. For 1980, one of the major changes was in its weight. By using lightweight doors and hood (bonnet), and even thinner glass, this version of the Corvette was about 250 pounds (113 kg) lighter than its predecessor. Design changes were fairly minimal, although the tiny split grille was deeply recessed and is where the parking lights were placed. The car was also made more attractive to buyers by including as standard several of the optional features on the 1979 model, such as power windows, the exterior sports mirrors, the stylish tilting telescopic steering wheel, and air-conditioning.

Chevrolet had had a record year for its Corvettes in 1979, shifting some 53,807 of them, and that still remains their best year ever. The following year, 1980, did not quite match that,

with only 40,506 sold, but the Corvette itself was an improvement in many ways on the year before. It got a better top speed by a good 15 mph (24 kph), and shaved almost a second off its 0–60 mph (0–97 kph) acceleration time. These results were partly due to a redesign of the bumper covers, in which they were integrated with aerodynamic spoilers, which reduced the drag considerably.

Improvements do not always convert into sales, however, and the Corvette C3 was retired in 1982, when sales were down to 25,407. Chevrolet marked the retirement with a special Collector Edition, the first Corvette with a hatchback rear. Although an excellent car, the 1980 Corvette model can be found at modest prices when it comes up for sale, with cars selling in 2011 for an average of just over $12,000 (£7,600). **MG**

Murena | Matra

(F)

1980 • 134 cu in/2,200 cc, S4 • 142 bhp/104 kW •
0–62 mph/100 kph in 8 seconds • 131 mph/210 kph

This little-known French coupe from the early 1980s had several claims to fame. For starters, the Murena had an unusual three-seat layout, with the driver and two passengers sitting in a row; the middle seat could fold down to become a wide armrest. To counter the rust that plagued its predecessor, the Bagheera, it was the first production car with a fully galvanized steel chassis. The body was made of twelve fiberglass and polyester panels so, rarely for cars of the era, rust was not an issue.

Designer Antonis Volanis had drafted a two-door mid-engine design with rear-wheel drive. The big glass tailgate lifted to allow access to the 97-cubic-inch (1,600-cc) or 134-cubic-inch (2,200-cc) engine. The sleek, aerodynamic body had the lowest drag factor of any mid-engined car up till that date. Handling was superb, but most reviewers wanted more power.

So Matra introduced a faster "S" version of the 2.2 engine (figures above). Almost 11,000 Murenas were built, of which 480 were "S" models. A handful of special "4S" cars were also made, with a sixteen-valve version of the 134-cubic-inch engine that produced 180 bhp (132 kW) and a 140 mph (225 kph) top speed. However, Matra's factory in France only had one production line, so when a deal was made to build the new Renault Espace, the Murena was abandoned forever. **SH**

Beaufighter | Bristol

(GB)

1980 • 359 cu in/5,898 cc, V8 • 170 bhp/127 kW •
0–60 mph/97 kph in 7 seconds • 140 mph/224 kph

The Beaufighter name was first used in 1939, on a fighter plane made by the Bristol Aeroplane Company. The end of the war saw the retirement of the bomber and also the start of Bristol Cars, a separate division that grew out of the airplane makers. The Bristol Beaufighter car came along in 1980, emerging from the company's 400 series, which ran between 1947 and 1975.

Injecting a little variety and punch into the series, the Beaufighter was effectively the Series Three version of the 412. Outwardly it was virtually identical, the only noticeable difference being a double headlight arrangement at the front. If you name a car after a fighter plane you might expect something a little special under the hood (bonnet), but the Beaufighter's engine was slightly smaller and less powerful than the 412's. Bristol did manage to squeeze the same top speed out of it, however. Although its official top speed was 140 mph (224 kph), the Beaufighter has frequently been reported as being capable of 150 mph (240 kph).

The Beaufighter bomber was a bulky number, so the name was an odd choice for a handsome and zippy little sports car. They were designed, like the 412s, by Zagato of Italy, and had the same targa tops. It was a design that didn't date, either, as the cars stayed in production until 1993. **MG**

Seville | Cadillac (USA)

1980 • 368 cu in/6,036 cc, V8 • 145 bhp/108 kW •
0–60 mph/97 kph in 12.7 seconds • 111 mph/178 kph

The Seville name first entered the Cadillac lexicon in 1956 when it introduced its Eldorado Seville model, which was the hardtop version of the company's top-of-the-line car at that time. The name Seville then vanished in 1960, until the Cadillac Seville came in as a model in its own right in 1975, when it was marketed as "Cadillac's first small car." It sold well enough, but not brilliantly, though the 1978 model was notable for its unique new Cadillac Trip Computer, called the Tripmaster. It gave a digital rather than needle reading for both the speedometer and the fuel gauge.

In 1980 it was time for a new Cadillac Seville, and it was the rear of the vehicle that got a lot of attention. It was given a classy sloping style reminiscent of British Daimlers, and the inside of the trunk (boot) caught the eye, too. That also sloped, at the same angle as the rear window—sometimes it's these small but unusual features that appeal to buyers. The new Seville design came from veteran General Motors designer Bill Mitchell. He was in his late sixties when he worked on the new Seville, and it had been forty-two years since he designed one of his first great cars, the 1938 Cadillac Sixty Special. Mitchell had lost none of his skills and the Seville was to be one of his final design successes, selling almost 200,000 until it was retired in 1985. **MG**

Fleetwood Brougham | Cadillac (USA)

1980 • 368 cu in/6,036 cc, V8 • 150 bhp/112 kW •
0–60 mph/97 kph in 13.2 seconds • 104 mph/166 kph

Early Cadillac Broughams used Fleetwood bodies. Later came the Cadillac Fleetwood as a separate car, with a Brougham as a body style. Then, as if things weren't complicated enough already, in 1947 the Cadillac Fleetwood Brougham arrived. A new series of Fleetwood Broughams was launched in 1977. Still, confusing or not, the cars sold—and that's the bottom line.

When the Fleetwood Brougham was announced in 1976, it was Cadillac's top model. That's even though it was near identical to the less-exclusive Sedan de Ville. Outside you had to look carefully at the hubcaps and the hood ornament to be able to spot the difference, although Fleetwood Brougham buyers did get more luxurious interiors in return for their extra money.

For 1980, the Brougham (by now in its eleventh generation) was redesigned again. It got a more boxlike look, and a classier roof line, making it one of the most visually appealing versions. It also had a kick to its performance. Cadillac further brought out a two-door Brougham that same year, adding yet another to the bewildering number of models available. In 1987 the Fleetwood part of the name would be dropped, and it would continue as just the Cadillac Brougham again. It would stay in production until 1992—making seventy-six years of assorted Cadillac Broughams! **MG**

The De Lorean may not have been a commercial success, but it found fame as the time machine in *Back to the Future* (1985).

Strada/Ritmo Cabrio | Fiat (I)

1981 • 91 cu in/1,500 cc, S4 • 83 bhp/61 kW • 0–60 mph/97 kph in 11.2 seconds • 103 mph/166 kph

In Italy it was the Fiat Ritmo. In Britain and the United States it was the Strada. In Spain it was the Ronda. But everywhere, it was a distinctive-looking hatchback range with a popular cabriolet offshoot. It was one of the first lines to use completely automated assembly.

Today, the car looks strangely angular. The cabriolet is particularly boxy and awkward. It's a sign of how fashions change that the Strada was seen as a chic, stylish car in the late 1970s and early 1980s. The line had been designed by one the most famous Italian styling houses, Bertone. It was successful, staying in production for a decade and selling 1.8 million cars. The basic car was a three- or five-door front-wheel-drive hatchback with 67-cubic-inch (1,100-cc), 79-cubic-inch (1,300-cc), and 91-cubic-inch (1,500-cc) gasoline engines, and 103-cubic-inch (1,700-cc) diesel. A more sporting model appeared later—the 105TC. This had a 96-cubic-inch (1,585-cc) twin-cam engine and livelier performance. Tuning specialists Abarth got in on the act, too, and produced the hottest versions. The 130TC could reach 121 mph (195 kph).

There was a less successful sedan (saloon) version called the Regatta, a station wagon (estate) called the Regatta Weekend, and, in 1981, an interesting cabriolet. This two-door, four-seater soft-top version was not just designed by Bertone, but built by it, too. It was a cheaper rival to the Golf Cabriolet in an era when there were few soft-top versions of standard production cars. It retained the window pillar and incorporated a roll-over bar. Bertone reinforced the floor to ensure the body was stiff enough without a roof. The Cabriolet sold better than expected, with more than 4,000 cars finding buyers. **SH**

DMC-12 | De Lorean (GB)

1981 • 173 cu in/2,849 cc, V6 • 156 bhp/116 kW • 0–60 mph/97 kph in 10.5 seconds • 110 mph/177 kph

The DeLorean DMC-12 was the dream of one man: John DeLorean. He was the Detroit-born son of a Ford car company worker, who took a master's degree in engineering and went to work for General Motors. He started at Pontiac, before rising rapidly through the ranks to head first Chevrolet, then GM's entire Car and Truck Division. He resigned from GM in 1973 and began pursuing an ambition to build his dream car.

DeLorean decreed that the car should be "fun to drive, safe to operate, and long lasting." He was interested in new construction materials, and set up a Composite Technology Corporation to develop them. Colin Chapman of Lotus was involved in engineering the car, and Giorgetto Giugiaro styled it. Northern Ireland was chosen as the site for the factory to build it.

The project was fraught with problems. When the factory opened in 1981 it attracted IRA protesters. This was at the height of the Troubles in Northern Ireland, and the plant had to be shut several times over safety fears. Early cars were so badly made that DeLorean had to set up correction centers in the United States to repair them before delivery to customers.

There was big demand for the car in the United States, but the problems led to cash-flow difficulties and the company went bust, put into receivership in 1982. Around 8,500 DeLoreans had been made.

The DeLorean may have been ill-fated, but it was a celebratory masterpiece of one man's ambition. It was sensational-looking, with gull-wing doors and a stainless-steel body that was left unpainted. The car was later immortalized as a time machine in the 1985 film *Back to the Future* starring Michael J. Fox. **SB**

DMC

VH Commodore | Holden (AUS)

1981 • 201 cu in/3,298 cc, S6 • 134 bhp/100 kW • unknown • unknown

The 1980s were challenging for Holden. They began with the closure of its factory in New South Wales. The company was still feeling the effects of the 1979 recession, and the increasingly popular Ford Falcon was closing the sales gap on its Commodore. Nevertheless, production of Commodore continued undaunted, with the VH following on from the VB (1978–80) and the VC (1980–81). The changes to the VH (1981–84) may have seemed subtle, but it was lucky that the V-series was still being produced at all, given the bleak outlook the Australian manufacturing sector was facing at the time.

The competition between the Commodore and the Ford Falcon saw the VH given a new horizontally slatted grille. It also had a lower, wider look, thanks to its redesigned front lights. The mechanical specifications were mostly inherited from the VC, but there was the option of a five-speed manual transmission with the 115-cubic-inch (1,900-cc) and 152-cubic-inch (2,500-cc) models. The VH also signaled the start of the age of computerized components in mass-produced Australian cars, with the introduction of a trip computer, electronic spark selection, and seat height adjustment.

The rivalry between Holden and Ford continues to this day—with the Commodore and Falcon still the weapons of choice. **BS**

BiTurbo | Maserati (I)

1981 • 121 cu in/1,996 cc, V6 twin turbo • 180 bhp/134 kW • 0–62 mph/100 kph in 6.5 seconds • 135 mph/217 kph

Maserati's BiTurbo capitalized on a mix of modern angular styling and turbocharged performance, and created huge interest in 1981. Hundreds of workers were employed on new production lines designed to make 7,000 BiTurbos a year . . . and yet the final product came twenty-eighth in the 2004 BBC book *Crap Cars*.

Maserati took a trusted V6 engine and added a pair of turbochargers, believing forced induction would be a fuel-efficient way of creating more power. Owners overlooked the manual's advice and failed to let the engine and turbos cool before switching off after driving, so critical components overheated and seized. It was easy to over-rev the engine, too. Maserati fitted a black box to record engine rpm—the data must have come in handy when fending off warranty claims.

As Italian workers went on strike, quality plummeted further. Cars went up in flames as catalytic converters overheated, and American customers started filing expensive claims against Maserati.

Buyers could choose fuel-injected or carburetor-fed BiTurbos, and 121-cubic-inch (1,996-cc) or 152-cubic-inch (2,500-cc) versions. For all its foibles, the BiTurbo was an interesting alternative to its German rivals, although it was far from Maserati's finest hour. Ownership was a tough labor of love. **RD**

Capri 2.8i | Ford

(D)

1981 • 170 cu in/2,792 cc, V6 • 160 bhp/118 kW • 0–60 mph/97 kph in 7.9 seconds • 130 mph/209 kph

The 1978 Ford Capri Mk III sold poorly in the United States, continuing a decline in sales that started with the 1974 MK II. U.K. sales, however, pointed to a lingering interest in high performance Capris, aided, perhaps, by the cars' starring role in the television series *The Professionals* (1977–83). This prompted the decision to press ahead with developing the next incremental version of the long-running line, the 2.8 Injection, or 2.8i.

The push for the development of the 2.8i came from Bob Lutz, head of Ford Europe. Realizing the car was being left to suffer a slow death, Lutz directed research to begin on one final, and much beefier, model. The car was developed in Germany, at Ford's Dunton Research & Engineering Center, and premiered at the 1981 Geneva Motor Show. The first Capri to have a fuel-injected engine since the RS2600 in 1970, the 2.8i reinvigorated the Capri name with its 170-cubic-inch (2,792-cc) "Cologne" V6 engine. Sales in Britain alone topped 3,600 in its first year, dwarfing Ford's own projection of 500.

The decision to keep the Capri brand alive for a couple of years longer than originally planned enabled Ford to recoup some of the development costs of the soon-to-be-released Ford Sierra, and also allowed the Ford Capri to end its production life on a much-deserved high. **BS**

Fiesta XR2 | Ford

(USA)

1981 • 97 cu in/1,598 cc, S4 • 84 bhp/63 kW • 0–60 mph/97 kph in 9.6 seconds • 103 mph/166 kph

Until the early 1980s, Ford had nothing that could really compete with Volkswagen's hugely successful Mk1 Golf GTI. After testing the "hot-hatch" market with the Fiesta Supersport, Ford finally launched a counterattack in December 1981 with the XR2. Powered by the engine used in the American Ford Fiesta, it was mildly tuned to help the XR2 break the 100 mph (161 kph) barrier. It also borrowed some styling cues from its American cousin, including round headlights and indicators mounted on the fender (bumper). The sporty look was completed with 13-inch (33-cm) "Pepper Pot" alloys, wheel-arch extensions, and large decals across its flanks.

While the XR2 looked the business, it was around a second slower to 60 mph (97 kph) than the Golf GTI and had a lower top speed. However, it handled well, thanks to its lowered suspension, fatter tires, and rear anti-roll bar; but most importantly, it cost £1,000 ($1,600) less. The XR2 gained a cult following and was loved by armies of "boy racers" across the United Kingdom and Europe. By 1984, when the MkII was launched, more than 20,000 first-generation XR2s had been sold in Britain alone.

Today, an original XR2 is a rare beast; middle-aged Ford fanatics, keen to recapture their misspent youths, will pay handsomely for cherished examples. **DS**

David Hasselhoff and his 1980s *Knight Rider* costar Kitt, an artificially intelligent Pontiac Firebird Trans Am. ⊡

900 Turbo 16S | Saab (S)

1981 • 121 cu in/1,985 cc, S4 • 170 bhp/125 kW • 0–60 mph/97 kph in 9 seconds • 124 mph/200 kph

Swedish manufacturer Saab had been a pioneer in the field of turbocharging with its trendsetting 99 Turbo. So when the Saab 99 was replaced by the 900, it was logical that a new Turbo version would follow.

The Saab 900 Turbo APC was the first model to use a turbo in combination with a sixteen-valve cylinder head. Another novel feature was the APC (Automatic Performance Control) system: an electronic turbo boost control system that made the turbo engine suitable for all kinds of gasoline that were available on the various markets.

Despite the massive turbo lag of the engine, it didn't take long before the Turbo became a success. Performace was exciting for the time, and in 1983 one out of any three 900s sold was a Turbo. From 1988 onward, the 900S was also available on the European markets. That model used a "low-pressure turbo" to get rid of much of the notorious turbo lag. The 900 Turbo 16S, available from 1989, came with a characteristic aerodynamic body kit that consisted of spoilers and the typical three-spoke aluminum wheels.

Swedish police used 900 Turbos for many years, but Saab's most coveted 900 Turbo came to life in three spy novels of the early 1980s, as James Bond's personal car. In the books Bond refers to it as "the Silver Beast." After its fictional appearance in the books, Saab actually built a copy of the car, complete with armor plate and bulletproof glass. The promotional vehicle came with gadgets such as digital head-up display, a remote text-messaging system, and a filter to neutralize deadly gas entering the car's passenger cabin, with oxygen masks under the seats. **JB**

Firebird Trans Am | Pontiac (USA)

1982 • 304 cu in/4,998 cc, V8 • 145 bhp/107 kW • 0–60 mph/97 kph in 7 seconds • 110 mph/177 kph

GM premiered the first Pontiac Firebird in 1967, and over the next fifteen years a succession of new models followed, equipped with a variety of four-cylinder, six-cylinder, and V8 engines. In 1982, as part of the Firebird's third-generation release, GM borrowed the Trans Am name from the Sports Car Club of America, who first coined the phrase in 1966, agreeing to pay them $5 (£3) for every car sold with the Trans Am name.

The 1982 Firebirds came with a four-cylinder standard, six-cylinder S/E luxury, or the Trans Am high-performance Chevrolet V8 (Pontiac had ceased production of its own V8). All were light and aerodynamic. In fact, everything on the new Firebirds was designed to lower drag, from their new low-slung front ends and cone-shaped side-view mirror housings to their finned aluminum wheels and retractable headlights. Even the windshield was sloped at a sleek 60 degrees, lower than any windshield in GM history. What emerged was a menacing-looking car, with elongated front turn-signals that looked eerily like deep-recessed eyes (that is until Pontiac began tarting it up with odd-looking "screaming chicken" decals and out-of-place scoops). No wonder that it was a modified black 1982 Trans Am that was chosen to become David Hasselhoff's robotic, talking Kitt in the popular 1980s television show *Knight Rider*.

Road & Track magazine labeled the standard four-cylinder Firebird "one of the twelve best cars in the world." How much better, then, would a Trans Am be with either a 304-cubic-inch (4,998 cc) or 349-cubic-inch (5,735 cc) Chevrolet V8 under the hood (bonnet), to take one of the world's twelve best cars a few notches higher? **BS**

Spider | Alfa Romeo

I

1982 • 122 cu in/2,000 cc, S4 • 126 bhp/94 kW • 0–60 mph/97 kph in 9 seconds • 125 mph/201 kph

The Spider had been a 1960s icon long enough—it needed upgrading. The early 1980s was the era of rampant safety legislation and the beginning of tighter emission control. Tradition wasn't cool.

So the new Spider was forced to change with the times, like a 1960s playboy swapping his paisley shirt for a 1980s *Miami Vice* suit. What happened to the Spider was indicative of that era of automotive history.

Pininfarina was still making the Spider for Alfa. It "refreshed" the rear-wheel-drive design with the style features of the day—extended rubber fenders (bumpers) and a rubber rear spoiler. In the engine, carburetors were replaced with Bosch fuel-injection systems. Reliability improved, if not performance.

Underneath, the Spider was still a classy roadster with a screaming twin-cam engine, wood-rimmed steering wheel, crisp five-speed manual gearbox, enjoyable handling, and a sense of Riviera style . . . but there was also a feeling it was clinging to past glories.

It didn't help that Alfa introduced a "Graduate" model in some markets. Like other short-lived publicity exercises at the time, it tried to capitalize on the car's brief moment of fame in the 1967 Dustin Hoffman film. The Graduate Spider was an entry-level model with vinyl seats, wind-up windows, and steel wheels. And by 1986 Alfa purists were choking on their carbonara as Spiders were now available with a plastic body-kit of go-faster lower skirts and boy-racer bumpers.

By the early 1990s, the Spider had run its course and was rarely seen or talked about. Alfa knew they had to go back to the drawing board and invent a completely new Spider—which, thankfully, they did. **SH**

911 Cabriolet | Porsche

(D)

1982 • 182 cu in/2,994 cc, F6 • 201 bhp/150 kW • 0–60 mph/97 kph in 6.4 seconds • 146 mph/235 kph

When the Porsche 911 Cabrio made its debut at the 1982 Geneva Auto Show, it was hard to believe it had been seventeen years since the end of the company's beloved 356, which had fallen victim in 1965 to the then-growing preference for closed-body comfort and practicality. After years in the convertible wilderness the Cabrio was an instant success for Porsche, selling over 4,200 units in its first year and remaining in the Porsche catalog ever since.

It was the fastest production Cabrio of its time, able to reach the same top speed as a coupe—though this was debated—thanks to its innovative folding roof, half of which was reinforced around steel struts to maintain rigidity and so cope with the sort of buffeting 146 mph (235 kph) winds can deliver. The roof design also meant less "wind noise," the bane of partially deaf convertible owners everywhere. There was virtually no "body rattle" either—that other consequence of driving cars without a roof—with only minimal reinforcement required to maintain its coupelike integrity.

The years prior to the convertible resurgence typified by the Porsche Cabrio were a difficult period for "ragtops." Mooted U.S. legislation said to require roll-bars and other forms of "roll-over" protection led some to predict the end of convertibles for the world's number one market. Such fears, however, proved unfounded. Not only would the Cabrio continue, it would do so with frequent upgrades and aggressive marketing, thanks to one of its most ardent admirers, Porsche chairman Peter Schutz. Schutz preferred its steady 9,000-unit-per-year sales to the ups and downs of those "other" Porches, the 928 and 924. **BS**

Robots and multiwelders work on the bodyshells of a row of Ford Sierras at a Ford factory, May 1984. ▷

BX | Citroën

F

1982 • 115 cu in/1,900 cc, S4 • 160 bhp/118 kW • 0–60 mph/97 kph in 7.4 seconds • 123 mph/198 kph

Peugeot and Citroën merged in 1976. Their first major joint project was a medium-sized family car. Using the same base, Peugeot designed the 405 sedan (saloon), while Citroën came up with this odd boxy contraption.

The BX once again demonstrated Citroën's eccentric principles. The body was made of plastic and the suspension was an unusual hydro-pneumatic self-leveling system. The ride height could be raised as if the car was on stilts to get through flood water or over uneven ground. It was designed by Italian Marcello Gandini, who also created the Lamborghini Countach, Fiat X-19, and Lancia Stratos.

There was a wide choice of engines. Some markets had small 67-cubic-inch (1,100-cc) units; in others, Citroën's new diesels broke through old prejudices and became bestsellers. The cheap and spacious station wagon (estate) version was popular everywhere, and there was even a four-wheel-drive model.

Buyers liked the low price, good fuel economy, and lavish equipment list. The suspension may have been unusual, but it offered great handling and a comfortable ride. It also meant the BX won worldwide awards for being the finest tow car. In all, almost 2.5 million BXs were sold between 1982 and 1994. The ultimate version was the BX GTi sixteen-valve, which had sports car performance (figures given above).

Citroën entered the heavily modified BX4TC in Group B rallying. It had a 128-cubic-inch (2,100-cc) turbo engine but similar suspension to the standard cars. Citroën had to build 200 of them to qualify for the rally series, but only sold sixty-two. The rest were scrapped, making the 4TC a valuable collector's item today. **SH**

Sierra | Ford

UK/D

1982 • 122 cu in/2,000 cc, S4 • 125 bhp/93 kW • 0–60 mph/97 kph in 10 seconds • 119 mph/192 kph

For a mainstream family car with unexciting technical specifications, the Sierra caused outrage at its release. The aerodynamic curvy body had clearly been launched slightly ahead of its time. The press and public ridiculed the shape, dubbing it "The Jellymold" or "The Spaceship." Conservative buyers called for the return of its boxy predecessor, the ultraconventional Cortina, while avant-garde designers flocked to see the Sierras displayed almost as works of art at London's Victoria and Albert Museum.

Yet within a few years the Sierra's shape started to seem pretty normal. Sales boomed. It became the tenth most popular car ever in the United Kingdom. In fact, its shape became so commonplace and copied that by the end of its production run a decade later "Sierra" was often used to mean boring and mundane.

Underneath this huge swing in public perception was a capable and versatile rear-wheel-drive vehicle. Unusually, the Sierra line was launched only in hatchback and station wagon (estate) forms. Ford believed that sedans (saloons) were past their sell-by date. But, like the futuristic bodyshape, they overestimated buyers' ability to embrace big changes.

Eventually the Sierra line grew to include three- and five-door hatchbacks, station wagons, the Sapphire sedan, all-wheel-drive versions, muscle cars like the Cosworth and XR4i, and the P100 pickup. Engines ranged from a 79-cubic-inch (1,300-cc) to a 200 bhp (150 kW) turbo in the RS Cosworth. A more typical Sierra engine of the time would be the 122-cubic-inch (2,000-cc) twin-cam from a 1989 2000E, the performance figures for which are above. **SH**

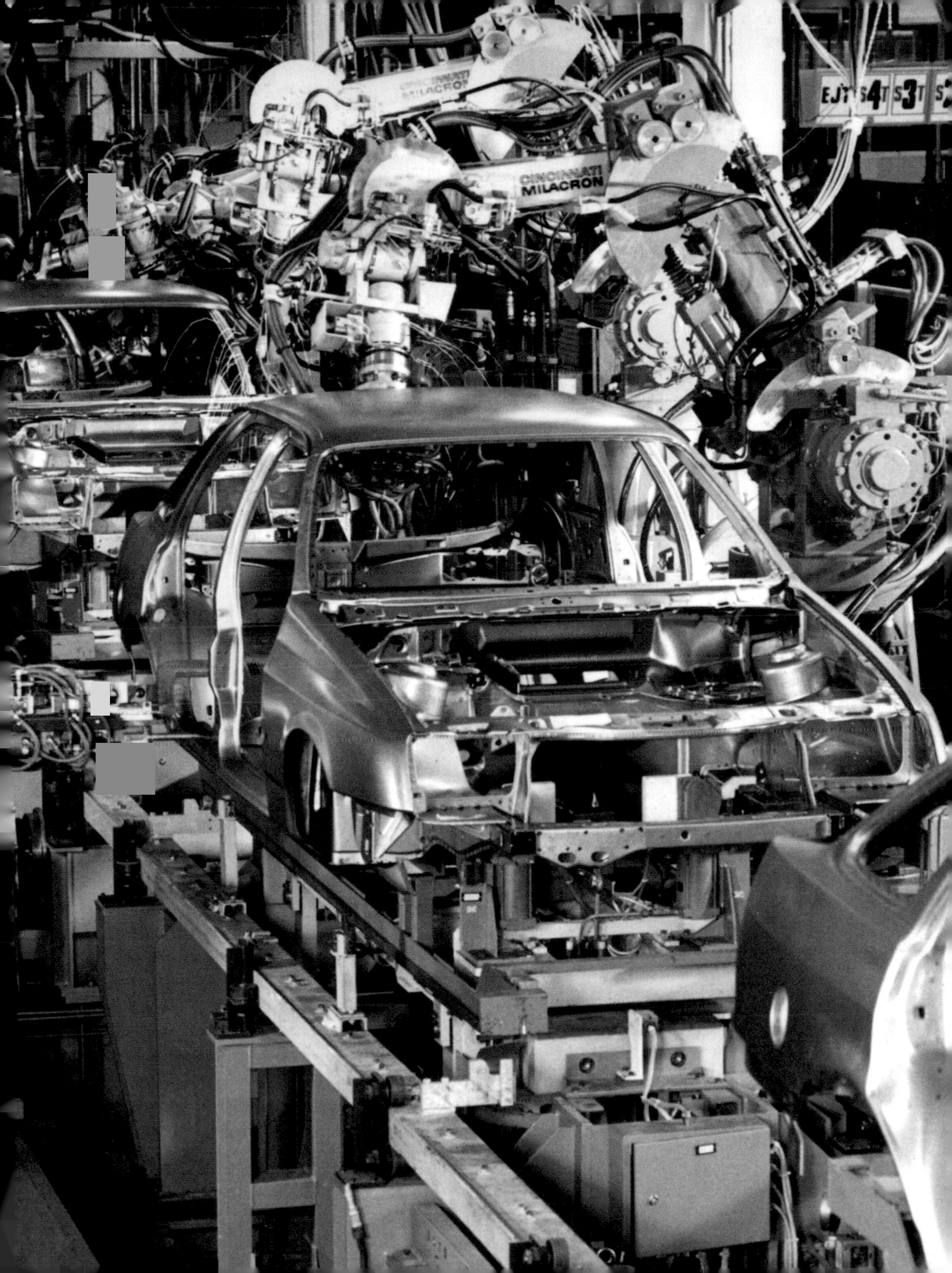
CINCINNATI
MILACRON
CINCINNATI
MILACRON

SD1 Vitesse | Rover

GB

1982 • 215 cu in/3,528 cc, V8 • 190 bhp/142 kW • 0–60 mph/97 kph in 7.6 seconds • 133 mph/214 kph

The Rover SD1 was the first product from British Leyland's "special division 1." It was a svelte five-door liftback, well-appointed and popular despite (at times) questionable quality. The car was designed by David Bache and Spen King, and won the European Car of the Year title in 1977. What particularly distinguished the SD1, though, was its fuel injected 215-cubic-inch (3,528-cc) V8 engine. Originally a Buick design, the V8 gave the previously sedate Rover 190 bhp (142 kW) and helped the SD1 become something of a motoring icon.

Depending on trim level, the SD1 was very well equipped and offered more gadgets than buyers in this sector had previously been accustomed to. Owners got electric mirrors, windows, sunroof, and door locks; cruise control; leather seats; headlight washers; trip computer; and a four-speaker stereo. These are common features now but were considered luxurious in the early 1980s. A clever design meant that the dashboard was largely symmetrical, allowing Rover to make both left- and right-hand-drive cars without extra costs. Wood & Pickett offered an SD1 with further bespoke fittings, including locks controled by a security keypad on the b-pillar. The SD1 was sold with Union Jack decals in the United States.

The SD1 earned a reputation as a driver's car, competing successfully in sedan (saloon) car racing throughout Europe and, despite its bulk, rallying, too. Racing driver Raymond Mays said his own (road) car was the best he'd ever had. Over 300,000 SD1s of all types were built. When British Police forces learned that the SD1 Vitesse was going to be replaced by the unlovely Rover 800, they stockpiled cars for later use. **RD**

944 | Porsche

D

1982 • 151 cu in/2,479 cc, turbocharged S4 • 250 bhp/186 kW • 0–60 mph/97 kph in 5.5 seconds • 162 mph/261 kph

When Porsche sales started to flag in the early 1980s, the German carmaker realized that it had to put some sparkle back into its entry-level model, the 924. The 924 was by now under attack from a new breed of sporty hot hatches from the likes of Volkswagen and Ford.

Building on the 924's wonderfully balanced chassis, Porsche ditched the lackluster 122-cubic-inch (2,000-cc) engine, which it had shared with the VW LT van, and fit its own 151-cubic-inch (2,479-cc) water-cooled four-cylinder. Designers also decided to give the car a more aggressive and purposeful stance; taking styling cues from the Carrera GTR that had campaigned at Le Mans, the car was given flared wheel arches and a wider track.

The new steroid-pumped 924, now sporting a proper Porsche powerplant, was relaunched as the 944 and marketed as a completely new product in an attempt to take the brand upmarket. The plan worked brilliantly, especially in the United States, where a whopping 16,618 cars were sold in 1984 alone.

In the affluent 1980s, the 944 found favor with rich urban professionals who wanted the kudus of that famous Porsche badge. Keener drivers also appreciated the car's fantastic handling, thanks to its 49/51 weight distribution. In 1984, *Car & Driver* magazine described it as "the best handling production car in America."

Over time the 944's motor was enlarged to 183 cubic inches (3,000-cc), to create the largest four-cylinder production engine of its time. However, most consider the turbocharged variants that first arrived in 1985 to be the greatest 944s ever built, and they are the most sought after by Porsche fans today. Performance figures for the 1988 Turbo S model are shown above. **DS**

Santa Matilde 4.1 | Cia. Industrial Santa Matilde

BR

1982 • 250 cu in/4,100 cc, S6 • 171 bhp/157 kW 0–60 mph/97 kph in 7.7 seconds • 128 mph/206 kph

Brazilian engineering factory boss, Humberto Duarte, was tired of waiting for his new GM Puma GTB to arrive. So he asked his daughter Ana Lidia to try designing a new Brazilian sports car. The result was this pioneering, rear-wheel-drive, fixed-head coupe. Ana's unique styling was based on no other car and stayed in production for twenty years. It has since become a collectable classic in South America.

The body was made of reinforced fiberglass and used well-tuned versions of a Chevrolet straight-six engine with a new exhaust and carburettor. The engine and some of the chassis components came from the Chevrolet Opala, a mid-size car sold by GM Brazil. When the Santa Matilde, or "SM," was revealed at the 1976 Sao Paulo Motor Show, it was considered one of the most luxurious cars in Brazil. Reaction was good enough for the car to go into production near Rio de Janeiro.

There was a 152-cubic-inch (2,500-cc) turbo version, but the powerful 250-cubic-inch (4,100-cc) was the faster and more desirable car. Standard features included powered windows, radio-cassette, leather seats, and air conditioning. There were disc brakes all round but the gearbox was a basic four-speed manual and the cabin was cramped for tall adults. The rear seats were so small as to be almost useless. Nevertheless, there were contemporary safety features like rubber fenders (bumpers) on retractable steel frames and progressively deforming structure for collision protection.

In 1984 a convertible version was launched and in 1991 the SM got a minor facelift, including square headlamps. However, the essential body designed by Ana remained in production until 1997. **SH**

Thunderbird | Ford

(USA)

1983 • 301 cu in/4,942 cc, V8 • 130 bhp/97 kW • 0–60 mph/97 kph in 9.6 seconds • 121 mph/195 kph

The Thunderbird premiered in 1955 as a classic sports coupe, a gorgeous two-seat V8 runabout that perfectly captured that era of carefree American motoring. It evolved into a boxier four-seater in 1958, and then into the charismatic "Jet Bird" of 1964, with its elongated hood, before losing its way in the 1970s with a series of lazy—more like sleazy—bloated, tanklike models that fairly trashed the proud Thunderbird name. Something had to be done; and, in 1983, something was.

The '83 Thunderbird was as much of a departure from its forbears as any new model in recent American history. Nobody outside Ford saw it coming. Gone was the ponderous bulk and hard-edged squareness of its "luxurious" 1970s predecessors. In their place was a brazenly aerodynamic new T-bird, with exciting new flourishes like a slicked-back sixty-degree windshield and cowl doors with drip rails that slashed cabin noise when traveling at high speed. It was slimmer too, losing a few inches in width and reducing its drag coefficient to a Teflon-like 0.35. Barely a vestige of any 1970s T-bird could be seen. It was a monumental change of direction. The '83 T-birds were beautifully detailed and finished to a standard that hadn't been seen in the series for over ten years.

The Thunderbird was back and all was forgiven. Almost 122,000 1983 models went out the doors of Ford dealerships across America that year, an astonishing 250 percent increase in sales over the previous (albeit recession-hit) year. The brand had at last come of age, and brought to Ford a new era of fit, finish, and drivability that would pave the way for even better Thunderbirds to follow. **BS**

Escort XR3i | Ford

(GB/D)

1983 • 97 cu in/1,596 cc, S4 • 105 bhp/78 kW • 0–60 mph/97 kph in 8.5 seconds • 120 mph/193 kph

The third-generation Escort introduced a new front-wheel-drive and hatchback model in direct competition to the popular Volkswagen Golf and the new Vauxhall Astra. Its sharp styling and well-trimmed interiors earned it the 1981 European Car of the Year award.

Ford had a long tradition of offering performance versions of its mainstream cars, which started in 1962 with the Lotus Cortina. Its first offering with the MkIII Escort, the XR3, was an instant hit: 11,581 were sold that first year in the United Kingdom alone. With its distictive "clover leaf" alloy wheels, boot spoiler, and sporty decals, thousands of "boy racers" aspired to own one.

However, despite its good looks, Ford's new hot hatch had rather tepid performance figures in comparison to the seminal Golf GTI. It wasn't until the revised XR3i was revealed in January 1983, that Volkswagen gained a serious rival. Built in Saarlouis, Germany, the XR3i received a Bosch fuel-injection system, improved suspension, and a better geared five-speed box to transform the Escort into a real driver's car (see performance figures above).

As the Escort received major styling revisions in 1986, 1992, and 1995, the XR3i gained bigger body kits and styling tweaks to keep it looking fresh. However, it always remained the cut-price alternative to the hottest GTIs from Peugeot and Volkswagen; while the Golf gained a reputation for solidity and had an upmarket appeal, the XR3i was the working-class hero, beloved by the blue-collar motorist after low-budget thrills. But not everyone bought their own XR3i to enjoy a blast around the local back roads—in the late 1980s the sporty little Ford was Britain's most stolen car. **DS**

Sierra XR4i | Ford

(GB/D)

1983 • 170 cu in/2,792 cc, V6 • 150 bhp/110 kW • 0–60 mph/97 kph in 7.7 seconds • 129 mph/208 kph

The "Jellymold" Sierra had been given a rough reception by conservative buyers longing for the return of the popular but boxy Ford Cortina. Within a year however, Ford started to win over the doubters.

The sporty XR4i, launched in 1983, was the start of that process. This new Sierra used a three-door body but with a spectacular rear spoiler. It was powered by the big fuel-injected V6 engine from Ford's successful Capri. Performance was brisk, although handling was often tricky. Nowadays, the XR4i is a collectible period classic. A popular DIY modification is to add a turbo to boost power over 200 bhp (147 kW).

The XR4i was replaced by the XR4x4 in 1985. This was a five-door hatchback with permanent four-wheel drive giving more secure road manners. The car was powered by the same 170-cubic-inch (2,792-cc) V6, meaning it took almost a second longer to reach 60 mph (96 kph) from a standstill. Meanwhile, Ford launched an XR6 version in South Africa with a 183-cubic-inch (3,000-cc) V6 and a XR4 in Argentina with a 140-cubic-inch (2,300-cc) V6.

As part of a global master plan, Ford then sent a version of the XR4i from Europe to the United States, where it was badged the Mercur XR4Ti. It was given a turbocharged 140-cubic-inch (2,300-cc) engine, as Ford hoped to repeat its European sales success back home. But the 130 mph (210 kph) Mercur didn't sell well.

Strangely, however, Ford then sent an XR4Ti back to Europe, where race driver Andy Rouse used it to win the U.K. Saloon (Sedan) Car Touring title in 1985. Technical feedback from his race team helped Ford develop the next generation of Sierra, the Cosworth. **SH**

Quattro | Audi

D

1983 • 130 cu in/2,144 cc, S5 • 197 bhp/147 kW •
0–60 mph/97 kph in 7.1 seconds • 143 mph/230 kph

The Audi Quattro has acquired legendary status as the car that put rally performance onto the road. It was the first high-performance four-wheel-drive car, named after the Italian word for "four." In the hands of world class rally drivers such as Hannu Mikkola, Stig Blomqvist, and Michele Mouton, it did sensationally well in rallying, winning a total of eight world rallies.

The Quattro began with a proposal from one of Audi's leading chassis engineers, Jorg Bensinger. He noticed that a Volkswagen Iltis 4x4 military vehicle could outperform much more powerful cars in the snow, so suggested equipping a performance car with all-wheel-drive. His idea was picked up by Audi's director of predevelopment, Walter Treser.

The first Quattro appeared in 1980, but it was the 1983 A1 version, introduced in response to new rally regulations, that really gave the car liftoff on the international motorsport scene. It debuted at the Monte Carlo Rally, driven by Mikkola. He won the event, and went on to more victories in Sweden and Portugal.

The Quattro enjoyed a resurgence of popularity when a red 1983 model was used as the character DCI Gene Hunt's car in the 2008–2010 BBC television series *Ashes to Ashes*. It also featured in a poster campaign by Labour for the 2010 British general election. **SB**

M635CSi | BMW

D

1984 • 210 cu in/3,453 cc, S6 • 286 bhp/213 kW •
0–62 mph/100 kph in 6.5 seconds • 158 mph/255 kph

The 6 Series BMW was, like the 3.0CS that preceded it, a graceful design. Its sleek coupe shape was penned by Paul Bracq, and although it had reasonable performance, it lacked the bite that the sharklike styling promised.

First shown at the Frankfurt Motor Show in 1983, the M635CSi finally got the engine it deserved with the 210-cubic-inch (3,453-cc) straight-six that also powered BMW's M1. It gave a healthy 286 bhp (213 kW) and the car was soon dubbed "the Bavarian Ferrari." The CSi hit 100 mph (160 kph) in just 15.6 seconds.

Other high-tech trickery was also employed, such as uprated suspension and damping, and the option of self-leveling rear suspension. Many found their way to the United States, badged as an M6. Buyers there loved the blend of performance, styling and reliability. With slightly less power than the European versions, thanks to the fitting of a catalyst for emissions reasons, they had ugly rubber fenders (bumpers) added. On the inside they offered features such as nappa leather with the option of a dedicated air-conditioned drinks chiller.

A total of 5,855 models were made. Among these were a few rare after-market versions with their tops chopped off to make a convertible—but such butchery of one of BMW's most beautiful designs should have seen the perpetrator thrown to the sharks. **RD**

Espace | Renault (F)

1984 • 121 cu in/1,995 cc, S4 • 103 bhp/77 kW • 0–62 mph/100 kph in 10.7 seconds • 112 mph/181 kph

The Renault Espace was designed as a practical and modern replacement for the awkward Talbot Rancho. The concept was designed by Chrysler, then had involvement from Simca, who were swallowed up by Peugeot Citroën (PSA). It was given to Matra to manufacture, but PSA got cold feet and passed it to Renault, which sold it as its own product.

Seating seven, the Espace claimed to be the world's first MPV. Its boxy shape provided cavernous space for its occupants. The body was fiberglass and the chassis galvanized steel, meaning the Espace was far less likely to rot than other station wagon (estate) cars. After a slow start the Espace became a popular seller, inspiring MPV offerings from other manufacturers.

In 1995, to celebrate ten years of production, Matra built a one-off Espace, called simply the F1. Powered by a mid-mounted 800 bhp V10 engine more commonly found in F1 cars and with carbon-fiber bodywork, the Espace F1 was capable of 0–124 mph (0–200 kph) in a terrifying 6.9 seconds.

In 2003, after three successful Espace models built by Matra, Renault decided to take over building it with the Espace IV. Matra instead built the Avantime, a futuristic oddity that failed to sell. Eventually, Matra was reduced to making electric bicycles for one. **MG**

288 GTO | Ferrari (I)

1984 • 174 cu in/2,855 cc, V8 • 394 bhp/294 kW • 0–60 mph/97 kph in 3.8 seconds • 190 mph/304 kph

The figures above show that this is no ordinary car. How do you get 190 mph out of a 174-cubic-inch (2,855-cc) engine? And how do you get it to 60 mph (96 kph) in less than four seconds? It's only possible if you're like Ferrari, and can produce a Formula One car that is also street-legal. GTO stands for Gran Turismo Omologato, Omologato being the Italian word for "homologation".

Ferrari wanted to compete in and win the new 1982 Group B races, and to do this they could only enter a car if at least 200 were produced and sold commercially. They built 272 of their new pride and joy in 1984–85, but as only they and Porsche entered the Group B races the cars were designed for, the competition was abandoned and all 272 288 GTOs went on sale to the public. It was the first street car capable of doing over 186 mph (300 kph).

Some of its astonishing power was due to the longitudinal mounting of the engine toward the rear of the car. It also had high-mounted side mirrors, and a double set of headlights that had to be powerful enough to illuminate a racetrack at night in the rain while traveling at top speed.

With such a small production run, 288 GTOs don't come on the market very often. When one did in 2011, however, it was sold for $750,000 (£476,000). **MG**

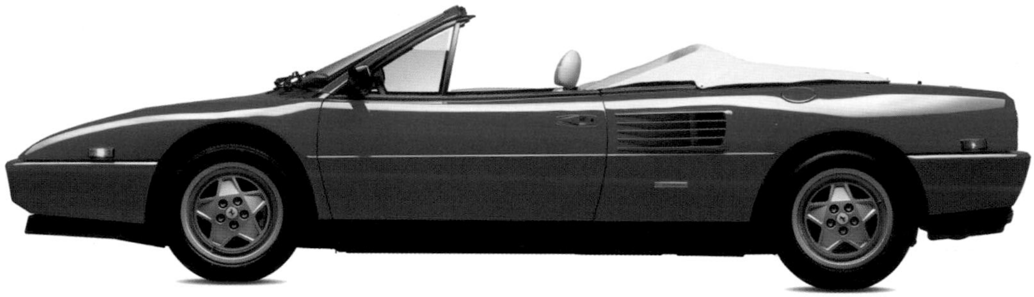

Mondial Cabrio | Ferrari

I

1984 • 207 cu in/3,405 cc, V8 • 295 bhp/220 kW • 0–60 mph/97 kph in 7.5 seconds • 158 mph/254 kph

Pininfarina designed the Mondial coupe, which was named after the Mondial 500 races of the 1950s. This two-door 2+2 was launched in 1980 and was presented as a practical and usable Ferrari. With an eye on the U.S. market, Ferrari unveiled a cabriolet version in 1984. It was the only four-seat, mid-engined convertible car ever mass-produced. The design was simply the coupe without its roof, but this created a pretty car, ideal for cruising on sunny boulevards.

Like the coupe, the cabriolet had a tubular steel chassis and all-around independent suspension. It was powered by a V8 engine that came in varying capacities, offering up to 300 bhp (224 kW). It kept the coupe's two rear seats, but they had to be mounted more closely together. This made it even more cramped in the rear, so it was only suitable for children.

The Mondial Cabrio was the first convertible Ferrari since the Daytona model of the 1970s. Despite having excellent handling, the Cabrio wasn't widely regarded as a driver's Ferrari by many. "Among the Ferrari cognoscenti," said *Road & Track* in its 1990 road test, "some see the Mondial Cabriolet as a concession to the times. Other Ferrari folks, however, consider it the most useful car out of Maranello."

The Mondial was recently picked by *Time* magazine as one of the worst cars of all time, for being underpowered and unreliable. The transistor-based electronic system was certainly notoriously troublesome. In general, however, the Mondial is seen as one of the more affordable Ferraris, and from the driver's seat, the Cabrio version feels like Florida in August, even if you're in Manchester in March. **RD**

Corvette C4 | Chevrolet

USA

1984 • 349 cu in/5,733 cc, V8 • 205 bhp/153 kW • 0–60 mph/97 kph in 6.8 seconds • 150 mph/240 kph

With the retirement of each model in their popular Corvette series, Chevrolet knew they had to come up with another winner to keep the line going. The C3 model finished production in 1982, and sales had been falling despite it being an excellent car. How would the C4 resurrect interest in the name Corvette? There wasn't a Corvette available for 1983, but Chevrolet did build no fewer than forty-three prototypes of the next generation in order to test and refine it.

By the time the 1984 model was ready to roll, Chevrolet had made the design sleeker and upped the power yet again, for a top speed that could easily beat anything the Corvette had done before. It was the first all-new Corvette since 1968. It was shorter and lighter, and about 25 percent more aerodynamic. It had to be, in order to meet tough new U.S. government requirements for fuel efficiency. There were new safety rules, too, and the C4 was given a collapsible steering wheel, to protect the driver in the event of a head-on collision. To protect the front-seat passenger in these days before airbags, the glove compartment was replaced by a padded area.

Chevrolet also worked directly with Goodyear to produce tires for what they wanted to be the best-handling sports car ever built. They attempted to achieve this by developing tires from those used by Formula One cars in rainy conditions, which not only performed well at high speeds, but also looked good. The price of the new Corvette when it came out was $21,800 (£13,800), and it restored sales levels to what they had been a few years earlier. It then stayed in production until 1996. **MG**

Testarossa | Ferrari

I

1984 • 301 cu in/4,943 cc, F12 • 385 bhp/287 kW • 0–60 mph/97 kph in 4.8 seconds • 180 mph/288 kph

Testarossa means "redhead" in Italian, and the name refers to the car's red-painted cam covers. However, for many people, it may as well mean "testosterone." The Testarossa launched in a blaze of glory in 1984 as the fastest production car in the world, a real supercar, and it remained as such for the next eleven years.

Its origins date back to 1982 when the Italian car design company of Pininfarina, which had produced dozens of stellar designs for companies such as Rolls-Royce, Chevrolet, Jaguar, MGB, and Alfa Romeo, as well as Ferrari, was commissioned to come up with the dream car. It was taken for granted that it would have a twelve-cylinder engine, be capable of 180 mph (288 kph), have the most luxurious fittings, yet also be as practical as possible and come with plenty of luggage space for the jetset traveler.

The Testarossa's stunningly sleek body was designed in a wind tunnel for aerodynamic perfection,

and lightweight aluminum was used wherever stronger and heavier material was not needed. It was slightly bigger than the Boxer, and looked very different. One notable feature was the driver's single rearview mirror, which was mounted high on the A-pillar on stalks. This was moved to a more conventional position on cars for the U.S. market, while another rearview mirror was later added on the passenger's side for safety reasons. The car went on sale in 1984 for £62,666 ($100,000) and stayed in production until 1991, when it was replaced by the 512 TR. Over 7,000 models were built during that time.

As well as being a hit with the public, the car, not surprisingly, became a movie and TV star, too. Most notably, Ferrari gave two Testarossas to the producers of the 1980s TV series *Miami Vice*, and specially made them in white to stand out in night scenes. **MG**

205 T16 | Peugeot

F

1984 • 108 cu in/1,775 cc, turbocharged S4 • 450 bhp/336 kW • 0–60 mph/97 kph in 4.5 seconds • unknown

Rallying's Golden Age arrived in 1982 with the introduction of Group B; with virtually no restrictions on power output or vehicle construction, the only real requirement was that 200 road-going versions of each rally car had to be built. The motorsport divisions of several major manufacturers put their best experts on top secret missions to build fire-spitting, all-wheel-drive rally cars. Capable of over 400 bhp (298 kW) thanks to the lack of restrictions on turbocharging technology, most used superlight body work, and mid-mounted their engines to improve handling.

Peugeot came late to the party in 1984 with its T16 (so called because of its turbocharged, sixteen-valve engine), and initially couldn't quite match the pace of the dominant Audi Quattros. However, after further development, and with the talented Salonen and Kankkunen behind the wheel, Peugeot won the 1985 and 1986 WRC Constructors' and Drivers' titles.

Nicknamed "L'Enfant Terrible," the short-wheelbase car was a handful to drive. Nevertheless, it had armies of fans who yearned for their own road-going version. These 200 homologation specials also had turbocharged engines in place of a back seat, but they were detuned to a less lethal 200 bhp (149 kW). Despite looking outwardly similar to the ordinary road car, the only part the T16 shared was the windshield frame.

When Group B rallying ended, Peugeot adapted the T16 for the Paris–Dakar endurance rally. Covering 8,000 miles (13,000 km) through barren North African deserts, it won in 1987 and 1988, before being retired and put out to stud. Its offspring, the 405 T16, clearly inherited the racing gene, but that's another story... **DS**

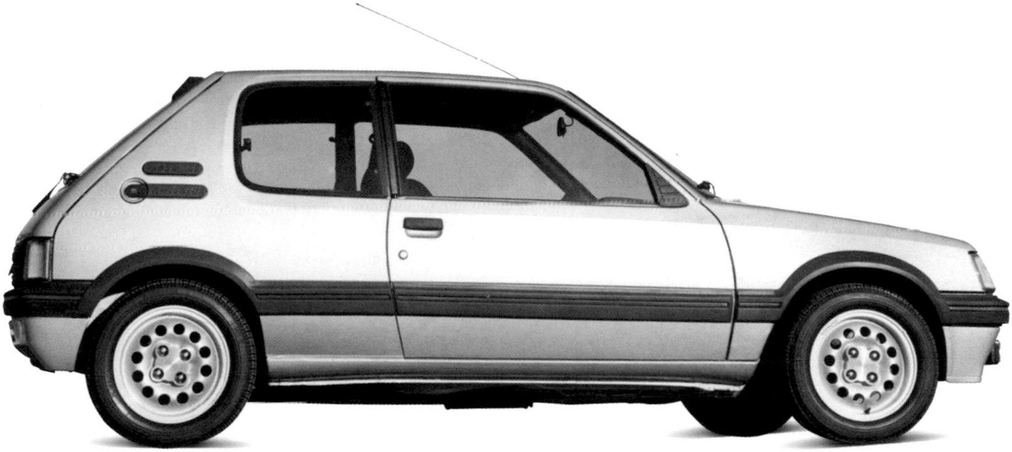

205 GTI 1.6 | Peugeot

(F)

1984 • 96 cu in/1,580 cc, S4 • 115 bhp/86 kW • 0–60 mph/97 kph in 8.7 seconds • 122 mph/197 kph

The Peugeot 205 GTI was arguably the most dynamic hot hatch of the 1980s. While the Volkswagen Golf GTI might have set the template a decade earlier, it had already started to bloat in its MkII guise. The French alternative was far more nimble and purposeful.

High bolstered seats, red carpets, and a leather-trimmed steering wheel and gear knob added to the sense of occasion. Exterior styling was carried out in house by Peugeot and still looks fresh today. Subtle aerodynamic additions, red pinstriped trim, and tasteful eight-spoke alloy wheels set it apart from lesser models.

On its U.K. launch the 205 GTI cost £6,520 ($10,330), notably less than similar offerings from Ford, Volkswagen, and Vauxhall. Nevertheless, the 205 repeatedly came top in hot-hatch group tests, with journalists praising its superior handling above all else. *Autocar* declared that "the 205 GTI sets new standards for responsiveness. It has tremendous front-end grip and traction, very little body roll in hard cornering." Peugeot achieved this through stiffer springs, uprated dampers, front anti-roll bars, and beefed-up suspension mounts. The car was also very light at just 1,870 pounds (850 kg).

However, the GTI could bite back if pushed too hard; lifting off the throttle midcorner upset its balance, sending drivers spinning into the nearest hedge. Lacking the security devices found on other vehicles, GTIs also became attractive to car thieves. Additionally, their low value meant many deteriorated as they passed through a series of cash-strapped owners. It is becoming increasingly difficult to find early GTIs in good, original condition. Today, they are highly sought after, so if you do stumble across one, buy it. **DS**

Fiero GT | Pontiac

USA

1984 • 152 cu in/2,500 cc, S4 • 92 bhp/68.6 kW • 0–60 mph/97 kph in 11.6 seconds • 103 mph/168 kph

As a strikingly designed mid-engined two-seater coupe, you might think the Fiero would be treading on the toes of General Motor's more famous sports car, the Corvette. But GM bosses realized there was a gap in the market for something that looked the part, yet featured a sensible four-cylinder engine offering decent fuel economy at an affordable price. The result was the Fiero, a cut-price Corvette for commuters. Despite a disappointing critical reaction because of its miserly power output, it sold well. The factory in the Michigan city of Pontiac initially couldn't meet demand and in five years more than 370,000 Fieros were sold.

Beneath its skin the car was staunchly traditional, built around an extremely solid steel chassis. But its plastic body panels—famed for their ability to pop back into shape after low-speed impacts—were radical at the time. The mid-engined layout was chosen because it offered the best weight distribution, and the car was later offered in notchback and fastback body styles. In 1985 a larger V6 engine became available.

The Fiero was axed in 1988. One reason was a GM forecast that two-seater sales were going to decline, but the decision also coincided with mass media coverage about engine fires in the original 1984 model. The cause was blamed on oil leaking onto hot components and combusting. In 1990 a concept car was designed and publicly shown, but never put into production.

The Fiero is now a cult car, highly collectible and prized by enthusiasts for its convertibility. Those detachable body panels sparked a craze for Ferrari and Lamborghini look-alikes, and more recently it has become popular as an aftermarket electric vehicle. **RY**

Mantula | Marcos

GB

1984 • 215 cu in/3,532 cc, V8 • 155 bhp/116 kW • 0–60 mph/97 kph in 6 seconds • 139 mph/224 kph

British company Marcos had a mixed history in its attempts to build competitive sports cars. Cofounder Frank Costin left the company after only two years, although he left the "Cos" part of his name joined to that of the other founder, Jem Marsh. In 1968 Marcos had brought out two versions of its Mantis car, but the company then folded in 1972. Marsh started Marcos up again in 1982, and the 1984 Mantula was its first major new car.

The Mantula used a Rover 215-cubic-inch (3,532-cc) engine, and as well as the factory models it came in kit form, as had earlier Marcos cars. The engine was lighter than previous Marcos engines, and this time the Mantula had a fighting chance when competing against better-known sports cars like the Morgan. It had an impressive top speed and a zippy acceleration, too.

It was a handsome car, looking not unlike a scaled-down version of the classic Jaguar E-Type, and the interior had been updated from the Mantis. However, the Mantula was always going to be a limited-production car, and only about 170 of them were built from its launch in 1983 to its retirement in 1992. Alongside the Mantula, Marcos produced two variations. The Martina was essentially a less expensive version of the Mantula, while the Marcos Spyder, which arrived in 1986, was the Mantula convertible model.

The Mantula has maintained its popularity with car buyers and there is an active fan base. The cars can be picked up reasonably cheaply at auction, with prices for good models around $16,000 to 19,000 (£10,000 to 12,000). **MG**

350i | TVR

GB

1984 • 215 cu in/3,528 cc, V8 • 197 bhp/147 kW • 0–60 mph/97 kph in 6.5 seconds • 134 mph/216 kph

By the late 1970s, Blackpool-based sports-car builder TVR was looking to inject some sparkle back into its model lineup. Although cars like the TVR Taimar and 3000S had been great in their own ways, the basic body style had changed little since the mid-1950s.

An all-new model called the Tasmin was unveiled at the Belgian Motor Show in January 1980. Styled by former Lotus designer Oliver Winterbottom, the car's distinctive wedgelike shape was inspired by Lotus supercars, the Esprit and Eclat. Early Tasmins used Ford's trusty V6 borrowed from the Capri, but under the new leadership of millionaire entrepreneur Peter Wheeler, the "Wedge" was given some real grunt courtesy of Rover's all-aluminum 215-cubic-inch (3,528-cc) V8.

The revamped Tasmin eventually became known as the TVR 350i. Tubular exhaust manifolds and a sports exhaust system gave the 350i a deep resonant growl that announced the arrival of one serious sports car well before it came into view. Owners of the "Blackpool Bomber," both past and present, tell the same story: weekend drives were carefully planned to take in as many road tunnels as possible, just to get the full aural experience of that glorious V8.

While that lovely exhaust burble was to become a TVR trademark, so was the car's rapid turn of pace and much improved handling. When *Car Magazine* road-tested an early prototype in September 1983, they commented that it "not only sounded like a dragster, it took off like one." Suitably impressed, the journalist concluded, "the £14,800 [$23,220] 350i gave me more undiluted motoring entertainment than any car I've driven since a Ferrari 275GTB/4 over a decade ago." **DS**

MR2 Mk 1 | Toyota

(J)

1984 • 96 cu in/1,587 cc, S4 • 112 bhp/84 kW • 0–60 mph/97 kph in 8 seconds • 127 mph/205 kph

In the early 1980s, Toyota was best known for its line of sensible family cars. But planning was in hand for a small, fun, economical model that would appeal to keen drivers and add a touch of glitter to the company's offerings. A project had been ongoing since 1976, but its gestation was slow as alternatives for the engine position and the type of drive were tested. Akio Yoshida led the development, and prototypes were tried out in both Japan and America. Formula One driver Dan Gurney helped with some of the testing in California.

It was not until 1983 that the car neared production readiness. All the lengthy studies of various options and the extensive testing had resulted in a small rear-wheel-drive, mid-engined sports car. At that year's Tokyo Motor Show, the MR2 was revealed. The car inevitably received huge publicity as it was to be the first mass-produced, mid-engined car from a Japanese manufacturer. It went on sale the following spring.

The MR2 name derived from "Mid-ship Runabout Two-seater," in recognition of its mid-mounted engine. At least, that was the original explanation, although the company later said that the R represented rear-wheel-drive. Somewhat inevitably over the years it has acquired the nickname of "Mister Two." But the name has also fallen victim to the vagaries of translation. In the French language, MR2 is pronounced "em-air-deux," and sounds very like a swear word. So for the French market the car was rebadged as the Toyota MR.

The MR2 owed its success to being an affordable, fun-to-drive little sports car, with handling honed by Lotus suspension engineer Roger Becker. After three generations of the MR2, production ended in 2007. **SB**

M3 | BMW

D

1985 • 140 cu in/2,302 cc, S4 • 197 bhp/147 kW • 0–60 mph/97 kph in 6.9 seconds • 146 mph/235 kph

Paul Rosche, technical director of BMW M GmbH, was the designer of the engine fitted to the BMW Brabham Formula 1 car, which won the World Championship for Nelson Piquet in 1983. He was assigned the project of homologating the BMW E30 3 series for Group A Touring Car racing, in competition with rivals fielded by Mercedes-Benz. He came up with what was to be the first of many fabulous BMW M3s.

Rosche's M3 was launched at the Frankfurt Motor Show of 1985. Germany's *Sport Auto* magazine promptly made it the "Sporting Sedan (Saloon) of the Year." The only exterior body panels it shared with the standard Model 3 Series were the hood (bonnet), roof, and sunroof. The body had distinctive, boxy, flared wheel arches to accommodate a wider track and bigger wheels. The dog-leg gearbox had first gear down and to the left. The engine was a straight four-cylinder chosen for its low weight and strength. Rosche managed to extract 235 bhp (175 kW) from this engine in later EVO models.

The M3 was a big hit in motorsport, winning the twenty-four-hour endurance races at Nürburgring, Spa, and Guia, and even the Tour de Corse on gravel, where its rear-wheel-drive configuration put it at a disadvantage with four-wheel-drive competitors such as Ford's Sierra Cosworth.

The car was only available in left-hand drive and sold for $36,800 (£23,000) when new, but was very well received. The first M3 quickly became a cult classic for its heritage and performance. Later M3s had six- and eight-cylinder engines, but many consider the original four-cylinder E30 M3 the best of all. **RD**

328 | Ferrari

I

1985 • 194 cu in/3,185 cc, V8 • 266 bhp/199 kW • 0–60 mph/97 kph in 5.1 seconds • 163 mph/261 kph

For the 328, Ferrari turned again to Pininfarina, designer of the body of the Testarossa. Although it was barely a year old, that sports car was already a legend. The Italian design company could hardly be expected to top the car for Ferrari, as not every car can be outstanding, but the manufacturer did need a top replacement for its 308 model. It was to be called the 328: "32" for the size of its 3.2-liter (194-cubic-inch/3,185-cc) engine, and "8" for the number of cylinders.

Like the 308, the 328 came in two body styles: the GTB and GTS. The GTB stood for Gran Turismo Berlinetta, which had a fixed roof, while the GTS was the Gran Turismo Spyder, with a removable roof. With more luxurious and spacious interiors than the 308, both performed better, had better road holding, and were better designed. The 328 was marginally taller than the 308, but such were its sleek looks and flatter shape that it seemed to look smaller and speedier. Once again, Pininfarina had produced a classic.

In 1986 Ferrari built two special versions of the car, the GTB Turbo and GTS Turbo. These were designed for the Italian market and the engines were brought down below 2 liters to bring them into a cheaper tax band. However, turbocharging the engines resulted in very little reduction in performance levels.

Ferrari built 7,400 of its 328 in the four years before the 348 took over in 1989, with the removable-top GTS model outselling the GTB by a factor of almost four to one. The 328 became Ferrari's most successful model up to that point. They are still highly desirable cars, and good examples have sold recently for prices in the region of $60,000–80,000 (£38,000–51,000). **MG**

Metro 6R4 | MG (GB)

1985 • 182 cu in/2,991 cc, V6 • 410 bhp/306 kW • 0–60 mph/97 kph in 3.2 seconds • 120 mph/193 kph

In October 1980, British Leyland had unveiled the Austin Metro as its potential successor to the original Mini. When, just a month after the Metro's launch, British Leyland retired its TR7 V8 from international rallying, it seemed logical that its Group B rally car program should showcase its newest model.

The Group B project was entrusted to Williams Grand Prix Engineering, which in early 1984 unveiled the prototype MG Metro 6R4 (six-cylinder, rally prepared, four-wheel drive). In the classic red and white livery of the Monte Carlo–winning Mini Coopers, the 6R4 had little in common with the mainstream Metro. It featured a mid-mounted V6 engine within a space-frame chassis and integral roll cage. Its lightweight body panels were made largely of fiberglass and aluminum. Huge spoilers, bulging wheel arches, and air scoops completed the Metro's transformation from a bland little hatchback to a rally-honed monster. The obligatory 200 road-going examples were called the 6R4 Clubman.

The 6R4 was never truly competitive on the world rally stage; the best WRC result it ever attained was third place in its debut appearance at the 1985 British Lombard RAC rally. Nonetheless, the car still has a huge cult following in Britain and draws large crowds at exhibitions and rallies. **DS**

Uno Turbo | Fiat (I)

1985 • 83 cu in/1,372 cc, S4 • 116 bhp/85 kW • 0–60 mph/97 kph in 7.7 seconds • 130 mph/209 kph

The hot hatch was the king of the streets in 1980s Europe. No-one could ever describe 1984's Fiat Uno as hot—it had been designed by Giorgetto Giugiaro as a small, practical family car—but Fiat's sporting specialists Abarth saw possibilities. The single-overhead cam engine was given a turbo, multipoint fuel injection, and electronic ignition, and tuned to a decent 116-bhp (85-kW) output. The hot Uno also had a more aerodynamic body and independent suspension, tweaked to handle the extra power. Even so, it could not quite match the handling prowess of hot-hatch rivals from Peugeot and Renault.

Still, the Uno Turbo had good straight-line speed for the price and was fun to drive. It was gradually improved, gaining more power, more features, and a better interior. There were disc brakes all around, plus a crisp five-speed manual gearbox. Some models had leather seats, trunk (boot) spoilers, a chrome exhaust tailpiece, alloy wheels, and antilock brakes.

The Turbo engine also proved to be highly tunable, and many have been customized by enthusiasts or adapted for the track. Some claim that the little Fiat can be tuned to produce more than two-and-a-half times its original factory power output. More than 250 bhp (184 kW) in a Fiat Uno? Now that *is* a hot hatch. **SH**

Celica | Toyota
(J)

1985 • 122 cu in/1,998 cc, S4 • 148 bhp/110 kW • 0–60 mph/97 kph in 8.5 seconds • 131 mph/210 kph

The 1985, fourth-generation Celica was all new. The main mechanical changes were front-wheel drive and a new 122-cubic-inch (1,998-cc) engine, while the body was redesigned for a more rounded and sleeker look.

In Japan it was followed in 1986 by the "ultimate Celica," the GT-Four, which was Toyota's top-of-the-line car for the next few years. This had a turbocharged version of the new 122-cubic-inch engine and all-wheel drive, and it served as the company's official rally car while it remained in production. Most Celicas were built in Japan and then fine-tuned in the United States, but the GT-Four was readied for rallies by Toyota Team Europe at its base in Cologne, Germany.

The first generation of the GT-Four was known as the ST165. It competed in its first rally, the Tour de Corse, in 1988, but had to wait until the 1989 Rally Australia to secure its first victory. The second generation, the ST185, came along in 1989; its most successful year was 1992, when it won five events, including the Safari Rally, and the World Rally Championship (WRC) drivers trophy. In 1993 and 1994 it won both the WRC manufacturers trophy and the drivers trophy. The next generation, the ST205, won the 1996 European Rally Championship. So the GT-Four probably was Toyota's "ultimate Celica." **MG**

Delta S4 | Lancia
(I)

1985 • 107 cu in/1,759 cc, S4 • 394 bhp/294 kW • 0–60 mph/97 kph in 3.2 seconds • 153 mph/245 kph

Lancia's Delta S4 was built as a Group B rally car, a replacement for its earlier 037 model, which had won the Constructors trophy for Lancia in 1983 but had not been able to compete with the likes of Audi and Peugeot. The Delta S4 won its first race, the 1985 RAC Rally, driven by Finnish ace Henri Toivonen.

The Delta 4 was one of the most high-tech cars ever built, its sole purpose being to win races. It was named the Delta to link it with Lancia's commercial Delta series, although the cars had little in common except the name and a similar look. Its engine was both supercharged and turbocharged; the supercharge operated at lower speeds until the turbocharge kicked in. The result was a phenomenal rate of acceleration; independent tests produced even more impressive results than the official factory figures, indicating it could achieve 0–60 mph (97 kph) in just over two seconds.

After its 1985 winning debut, it went on to take the 1986 Monte Carlo Rally, the Rally Argentina, the European Rally Championship, and the Olympus Rally. Tragically, in the Tour de Corse that year, the car plunged into a ravine and both driver Henri Toivonen and codriver Sergio Cresto burned to death. The Delta S4 was retired soon afterward. It is considered to be the greatest car never to win a world title. **MG**

Turbo R | Bentley

GB

1985 • 412 cu in/6,750 cc, V8 • 295 bhp/220 kW • 0–60 mph/97 kph in 7.5 seconds • 136 mph/217 kph

When Bentley first introduced the Turbo R at the 1985 Geneva Motor Show, the company regarded the high-performance model as the ultimate successor to its popular Mulsanne Turbo. The "R" stood for "roadholding."

Bentley originally intended to make the two cars available side by side for a while, but with favorable early reviews and sales of the new Turbo R surpassing expectation, production of the Mulsanne was stopped sooner than anticipated. Even so, Bentley had sufficient stock of the Mulsanne in hand to keep both cars available for the next few years.

The new Turbo R at first inherited the Mulsanne's big turbocharged engine, but very soon a more powerful engine was used to achieve even better speed and acceleration figures. The Turbo R also had a retuned suspension, which made for a major

improvement over the Mulsanne, which had been criticized for not entirely providing the smooth ride expected of a car of its class. The Turbo R was also the first Bentley fitted with alloy wheels, a surprising move from a fairly staid company. The car did appear much sportier as a result, but the look did not go down well with traditional Bentley buyers.

In 1989 a revamp, which included small design changes such as the square headlights being replaced by round ones, made the Turbo R look sportier yet. The car continued in production until 1997, when it was replaced by the Bentley Turbo RT.

Only 7,230 Turbo Rs were built thoughout its twelve-year lifespan, and it proved to be one of the company's best-selling models. Today, good ones can be picked up for a very modest $20,000–25,000 (£13,000–16,000), less than 20 percent of their cost when new. **MG**

Bus it!
25
VICTORIA
Bus it!

‹ A Sinclair C5 is driven through London in a commuter race held by the *Daily Mail* newspaper during the 1989 transport strike.

C5 | Sinclair (GB)

1985 • 250-watt electric motor, 12-volt battery • 0.33 bhp/0.25 kW • unknown • 15 mph/24 kph

Sir Clive Sinclair made his name with the first low-priced domestic computer, the ZX80, produced by his company Sinclair Research, based in Cambridge. His next product, the ZX Spectrum, became Britain's best-selling home computer. Then came his big idea for personal transportation: the Sinclair C5, an electric tricycle with one front and two rear wheels.

The C5 was a plastic-bodied, battery-powered, electric vehicle with an open-sided driving seat, no roof, and steering via a handlebar between the driver's knees. It was just 5¾ feet (175 cm) long and 2½ feet (79 cm) tall. Being slow, it could be driven on British roads without a license. The Hoover company at Merthyr Tydfil in Wales was contracted to make it.

The quirky little single-seater car was given a big launch on January 10, 1985, at London's Alexandra Palace but was greeted with more mirth than admiration. During a televised testdrive in the grounds of the launch venue, the C5 lifted a wheel and almost tipped up as it tried to negotiate a small roundabout.

The press was not convinced, and neither were the public. The tiny vehicle felt much too vulnerable to be mixed with traffic, its roofless design was clearly unsuited to the notoriously changeable British climate, cold weather shortened its battery life, and it was suspected of being inherently unstable. It was also considered costly at $640 (£399) plus delivery charge.

It was a sales disaster. Despite promotional help from Stirling Moss, demand flopped and the run lasted only seven months. In August 1985, Hoover announced the shutdown of production after just 17,000 models; two months later, Sinclair Vehicles went bust. **SB**

Saga | Proton (MA)

1985 • 92 cu in/1,500 cc, S4 • 90 bhp/67 kW • unknown • unknown

When Malaysia's Prime Minister Mahathir Mohamad decided to develop his country's own car industry, things moved pretty fast. Within two years of the Proton company being established, the first vehicles were rolling off the production line near Kuala Lumpur. Within a year Proton had produced 10,000 cars.

While the Proton Saga did not embody state-of-the-art technology, Malaysia seemed to have jumped from nowhere to become a major car-producing nation. Less than two decades later, Proton had bought the Lotus company, is exporting cars to fifty countries, and is involved in Formula 1 and Indycar racing.

The car that started it all was the humble Proton Saga (or Proton MPI as it is known in some countries). Uprated versions of the Saga are still sold today. The Saga was based on the Mitsubishi Lancer, which at the time was an average small modern car from Japan. At first Proton worked with Mitsubishi, which part-owned Proton until it was bought out by Malaysian interests. Two engines were available, the 79-cubic-inch (1,300-cc) and 92-cubic-inch (1,500-cc), and two body styles, a hatchback and a sedan (saloon).

A Malaysian lottery was held to select the lucky citizen entitled to select the name of the new national car. The old soldier who won promptly christened the car the "Saga," named for a Malaysian tree.

While being chosen largely for its very low price elsewhere, the Saga was the source of much national pride back home. The first car built was presented to the Malaysian National Museum, and Mr. Mahathir drove another Saga across Penang Bridge to open the museum officially in 1985. **SH**

V8 Zagato | Aston Martin

GB/I

1986 • 326 cu in/5,341 cc, V8 • 430 bhp/316 kW • 0–60 mph/97 kph in 4.9 seconds • 186 mph/300 kph

Virtually all Aston Martin models are highly desirable to collectors, but the most collectible of all has to be the DB4 GT with a body styled by Italian house Zagato. Between 1960 and 1963, only nineteen were built and today they do not sell for less than a million dollars. In the mid-1980s, Zagato noted this demand for the classic and began to think there was a strong market for a modern resurrection.

Zagato showed nothing more than a drawing at the 1985 Geneva Motor Show, but it attracted more than fifty orders and started production of the Aston Martin V8 Vantage Zagato. This had the production V8 Vantage as its base but with a makeover in aluminum. The new design was said to be an angular take on the DB4 GT Zagato of the 1960s, including a squared-off grille. The big bulge in the hood (bonnet) was not liked by everyone but was needed to house the twin Weber carburetors.

Like the DB4 GT Zagato, the V8 Vantage Zagato was shorter and 10 percent lighter than the production car on which it was built. A year after the first drawings were shown, the car was launched in the middle of the "supercar price boom." Just fifty-two were built, after which Zagato launched a more expensive roadster version; another thirty-seven of that roadster followed. **JB**

Alpine GTA | Renault

F

1986 • 150 cu in/2,458 cc, V6 • 200 bhp/147 kW • 0–62 mph/100 kph in 5.8 seconds • 155 mph/250 kph

Built at the separate Renault Sport factory in Dieppe, northern France, the Alpine GTA was Renault's attempt to build a Porsche-beating supercar. The two-door coupe succeeded in almost everything—except sales. The Alpine was certainly fast enough. The 150-cubic-inch (2,458-cc) V6 turbocharged engine of the big Renault 25 luxury sedan (saloon) pushed this smaller plastic and fiberglass-bodied car to 155 mph (250 kph). The engine sat sideways at the back, driving the rear wheels, and there was sophisticated sports suspension, with antilock brakes as standard. For the first time, the polyester body parts were cut to shape by a robot using a high-pressure water jet. Levels of luxury were fine, too; the interior was swathed in black leather, and the car featured gadgets, such as remote-control central locking.

What let down the coupe were its awkward looks and badge snobbery. The design had class-leading aerodynamics, but its lines were not as glamorous as rivals from the United States, Japan, Italy, or Germany. Only 7,000 Alpine GTAs were sold in the nine-year production run. In 1991 the GTA was replaced by the Alpine A610, which looked very similar and also had a rear-mounted turbocharged V6, enlarged to 183 cubic inches (3,000 cc). But in five years only around 800 cars were sold and manufacture ended in 1995. **SH**

412 | Ferrari (I)

1986 • 302 cu in/4,943 cc, V12 • 318 bhp/237 kW • 0–60 mph/97 kph in 6.3 seconds • 149 mph/239 kph

Ferrari began its 400 series in 1976, and after ten years it was time for a makeover. All the more so because the car had been described by Britain's best-known motoring journalist Jeremy Clarkson as "awful in every way" on his BBC TV show *Top Gear*. The Ferrari 412 was a much better car, though, with a bigger engine and better acceleration and top speeds than its predecessor. It was the first Ferrari to have an antilock braking system (ABS). Effective ABS systems had been around since the early 1970s, but they were only now becoming more widespread.

The 412 remained in production only until 1989, by which time Ferrari had built 576 of them. One of these models gathered quite a cult following after it appeared at the start of the 2007 movie *Daft Punk's Electroma*, where it can be seen with the number plate HUMAN. *Daft Punk's Electroma* tells the story of two robots who want to become human. That car went up for sale on eBay in 2011, auctioned by the EMI Group with other music-related items to raise funds after the Japanese tsunami disaster. It sold for almost $42,000 (£26,500), less than Jane Birkin's handbag, which went for $163,000 (£103,000), but more than Katy Perry's cupcake trampoline stage prop, which sold for $5,075 (£3,200). **MG**

560SEC | Mercedes-Benz (D)

1986 • 339 cu in/5,549 cc, V8 • 238 bhp/175 kW • 0–60 mph/97 kph in 6.8 seconds • 155 mph/248 kph

The Mercedes 560SEC was produced for only five years, from 1986 until 1991, but it was a big hit with drivers. Despite its being only one of many Mercs that were being sold at that time under their Special Class, or Sonderklasse, label, this particular model built up a loyal following and still has a big fan base.

The 560SEC was one of the W126 series of Mercedes cars, the W126 referring to the chassis and the 560 to the engine size. The W126 series first came out in 1979, although the cars were in development for six years before that. Mercedes wanted to be absolutely sure to retain the status and success built up by the preceding W116 series, which had become the best-selling luxury sedan (saloon) in the world. Specifically, the company knew that it had to improve the model's fuel efficiency, update its safety features, and offer a car that guaranteed an even smoother ride than the one before it.

Several versions were made available when the new W126 series was launched at the International Motor Show in Frankfurt in 1979. The SEL variants were the long-wheelbase models, while in 1981 the new coupes were introduced as the SEC models. After the 560SEC came out in 1986, drivers bought 74,000 of them over its five-year run, enough to make up 40 percent of Mercedes' worldwide sales. **MG**

The 1986 Lamborghini LM002 was a radical departure from the sleek designs of the company's sports cars.

Charger GLH-S | Shelby (USA)

1986 • 135 cu in/2,212 cc, S4 • 146 bhp/109 kW • 0–60 mph/97 kph in 6.5 seconds • 124 mph/200 kph

It may be an awful thing to say, but anyone who took a nice-looking car like a Pontiac Firebird Trans Am or a Ford Mustang, and drove it not too fast into a wall, then reversed and drove it into the wall again would end up with a car having a front end much like the Shelby Charger GLH-S. Not that looks are everything, thank goodness, and the above analogy is, of course, a poor one because the GLH-S has straight front-end panels that are not the product of an accident; it just seems that way. The interior, too, was an ergonomic disaster. The truth is that the GLH-S was one particularly ugly automobile. Fortunately, good looks were not what the GLH-S was all about.

The Shelby Charger GLH-S was a modified Dodge Omni GLH, another so-called muscle car built for speed and not for looks and one of the few genuine performance cars ever made by Chrysler. Dodge's GLH designation, meaning "Goes Like Hell," was apt. The Omni's Turbo I engine had been given a radical overhaul; an intercooler extracted excess heat from the turbocharged engine, which was capable of producing 146 bhp (109 kW), with acceleration of 0–60 mph (97 kph) in just 6.5 seconds. And it could do a quarter-mile (0.4 km) in 15.7 seconds, faster than a Nissan ZX.

Because only 500 were made, the GLH-S did not meet the minimum production quota of 1,000 needed for SCCA competition. Pontiac Trans Ams and Ford Mustangs could all breathe a sigh of relief. If the "Goes Like Hell-Shelby" had encountered either one of them over a standing quarter-mile in 1986, it would have been the power-packed, pug-ugly Shelby Charger GLH-S that would have had the last laugh. **BS**

LM002 | Lamborghini (I)

1986 • 315 cu in/5,167 cc, V12 • 444 bhp/331 kW • 0–60 mph/97 kph in 6.9 seconds • 125 mph/200 kph

Nicknamed the "Rambo Lambo," the LM002 was unlike any other Lamborghini ever seen. A massive sports utility vehicle (SUV), not a sleek and stylish sports car, it was a bit like a Hummer before Hummers existed.

Lamborghini had begun work on developing an SUV, which they codenamed "Cheetah," way back in 1977. The company was hoping to sell it to the U.S. armed forces, but the prototype was destroyed by the military in the course of testing, and the project came to nothing. In 1981 Lamborghini began work on turning the Cheetah into a more commercial model, the LM001, but this was found to have serious handling problems and only one prototype was made.

Deciding that the vehicle's handling problems were due to having the engine at the rear, Lamborghini engineers moved the engine forward, at the same time replacing the LM001's V8 with a V12. The resulting vehicle more than made up for the previous disappointments, and was first shown at the 1986 Brussels Auto Show. It was aimed at both the military and personal markets. The rugged SUV was luxuriously kitted out with leather seating and a top-of-the-line stereo built into a roof console.

Pirelli was commissioned to come up with two types of special tires exclusively for the LM002. One type was for general use; the other was designed for use in desert conditions. The latter could cope with extreme heat, the demands of a heavy vehicle traveling at high speed, and could be used when deflated, without being damaged. Colonel Gaddafi, the former Libyan leader, is said to have bought a hundred LM002s for use by the Libyan military. **MG**

Lamborghini
LM002

M5 | BMW

(D)

1986 • 209 cu in/3,420 cc, S6 • 286 bhp/213 kW • 0–60 mph/97 kph in 6.2 seconds • 153 mph/246 kph

Modern BMW M-Series cars are largely made in the same factory as the German manufacturer's more mundane machines. The original M5, however, was a bespoke machine, developed and built by the same race engineers that worked on BMW's motorsport products, and their know-how clearly shows. With the chassis of the BMW 535i and a modified 209-cubic-inch (3,420-cc), twin-cam, twenty-four-valve, straight-six engine from the BMW M1, the Bavarian machine had huge performance. Revving to 6,500 rpm, it produced a heady 286 bhp (213 kW) and sounded great, too.

BMW was careful to ensure that the M5 did not overshadow its other, more mainstream, cars. The performance figures it quoted were suspiciously conservative, perhaps to avoid upstaging its more expensive M635CSi. Alpina and Hartge offered further tuning options, and the same engine was capable of delivering an unbelievable 900 bhp (670 kW) when turbocharged for Group 5 racing elsewhere in the BMW group. And there was more to this car than just the engine. For those able to keep it pointed in the desired direction of travel, the M5 was a thoroughly rewarding machine to drive. Today it is one of the rarest "M" cars ever made, with just 2,145 examples originally built.

Rumor has it that Jeremy Clarkson, the BBC's *Top Gear* host, once helped tow a friend with a stricken M5 in London. Securing the tow-rope to his own car, and what he thought was the M5's tow-hook, he got quite some distance before realizing he was only towing the M5's oil cooler, which had parted company with the rest of the car. The motorsport men at BMW who hand-built it would not have been amused. **RD**

RS200 | Ford

GB

1986 • 110 cu in/1,803 cc, S4 • 250 bhp/186 kW • 0–60 mph/97 kph in 6.1 seconds • 140 mph/225 kph

The regulations of the Group B rally class demanded that at least 200 cars be built to a road-legal specification for a vehicle to be allowed to compete. And so the RS200 was born. Unveiled at the Turin Motor Show of 1984 and styled by Turin coachbuilder Ghia, this mid-engined turbocharged coupe was designed to be a motorsport monster. It had a dramatic rear-roof spoiler to increase downforce, and power upgrades that took output to 650 bhp (485 kW) were available to buyers.

Production started in 1986 and a successful race career began immediately. A car took third place in the Rally of Sweden, but at the very next event, the Rally of Portugal, tragedy struck. In one of the worst motorsport accidents for years, an RS200 left the route at speed, killed three spectators, and injured many more. After more major accidents involving the RS200 and other Group B cars, the series was canceled after just one season. Ford was left with an expensive problem, but rather than scrap the whole project and write off the cost, it commissioned engineering firm Tickford to convert its 200 cars from stripped-out racers to luxurious, high-revving road-ready machines. These went on sale for $70,000 (£45,000) each.

Owners found the ride to be surprisingly supple, given the RS200's heritage, and the car was spectacularly grippy through corners. But the cabin was cramped and engine noise was a constant—the RS200 was never meant to be a road car. So, while the model did plenty to raise the profile and performance credentials of the blue oval, Ford subsequently admitted that it had lost millions on the project. **RY**

The 1986 Ford Sierra RS Cosworth was the model that finally won enthusiasts round to the Sierra's futuristic shape. ▷

Challenge | Sbarro (CH)

1986 • 303 cu in/4,973cc, V8 • 350 bhp/257 kW • 0–60 mph/97 kph in 5 seconds • 196 mph/315 kph

One of the highlights of the Geneva Motor Show each year is Swiss-born Franco Sbarro's stand, invariably displaying some of the wildest vehicles imaginable. The 1985 show was certainly no exception to that rule; in that year, Sbarro unveiled the Challenge.

And wild it was. With an extreme wedge shape, scissor doors, and a virtually flat windshield, it looked like nothing that had ever seen before. The shape proved extremely slippery, too, and with a drag coefficient of just 0.26 it was more aerodynamic than most supercars for years to come.

The Challenge was also pretty impressive in its specifications. Its turbocharged V8 engine, from Mercedes-Benz, drove all four wheels and gave it a top speed of more than 200 mph (322 kph). Among its other innovations were rotating wiper blades, air brakes in the shape of wings at the rear, inboard televisions in the doors, and a video player plus a camera instead of rearview mirrors.

The Challenge may have looked like a designer's fantasy that would certainly never become reality, but in fact it did reach production. In 1986 and 1987, Sbarro built several cars, which were known as Challenge II and Challenge III. Unlike the 1985 show car, these were powered by Porsche six-cylinder "boxer" engines and came with two-wheel drive only. They were offered for sale at 320,000 Swiss francs ($350,000/£220,000) and ten are said to have found their way to customers.

Sbarro, who founded his own design school, has continued to build eccentric cars and display them at the Geneva show. To this day he mentions the Challenge as one of his all-time favorite designs. **JB**

Sierra RS Cosworth | Ford (B/GB)

1986 • 122 cu in/2,000 cc, S4 • 204 bhp/150 kW • 0–60 mph/97 kph in 6.2 seconds • 145 mph/233 kph

By 1986, Ford's blobby "spaceship" Sierra was becoming more popular, but it was the RS Cosworth version that sealed its acceptance among enthusiasts. Much of the technical development, including suspension and aerodynamic tweaking, derived from racing the U.S. Merkur XR4Ti version of the Sierra. The new car's power came from a 122-cubic-inch (2,000-cc), twin-cam, sixteen-valve turbo specially developed from Ford's Pinto engine by Cosworth. Power could be easily tweaked up to 300 bhp (221kW) for track use.

The car, built in Ford's factory in Genk, Belgium, had the body of a standard three-door, rear-wheel-drive Sierra. After speed testing at Italy's Nardo circuit, Ford decided to add the large rear spoiler wing to combat aerodynamic lift. To keep costs low, the car was only offered in black, white, or blue. It had Recaro sports seats and a turbo boost gauge, but otherwise much of the interior resembled that of a standard Sierra.

For just $25,000 (£16,000), buyers could reach supercar speeds while enjoying fairly normal fuel consumption for the time: 24 mpg (12 liters per 100 km). The only problem for most buyers lay in the cost and difficulty of insuring such a fast machine.

Two years later, in 1988, Ford launched a second-generation "Cossie," a four-door sedan (saloon) with slightly softer suspension settings but the same engine: this was the Sierra Sapphire RS Cosworth.

Then, in 1990, a third incarnation was revealed. The Sierra Sapphire RS Cosworth 4x4 was given four-wheel drive to enable Ford to compete in rallies. Power was increased to compensate for the added weight, so its performance remained much the same. **SH**

D784 SNA

959 | Porsche

(D)

1986 • 174 cu in/2,847 cc, F6 • 450 bhp/336 kW • 0–60 mph/97 kph in 3.9 seconds • 197 mph/317 kph

By 1981, many Porsche engineers felt that the design of its rear-engined air-cooled 911 was anachronistic and nearing the end of its production life. But, in a last-ditch attempt to see what still could be got out of the aging platform, the 911 was used as a test-bed for a variety of technical innovations; it was these that led to the 959.

To conform to international rally regulations, Porsche's decision to try out the new model on the racetrack necessitated a production run of more than 200 roadgoing examples; the new 959 would not qualify for Group B rallying without them. By the time the first production cars arrived, the all-wheel-drive 959 had become a technological tour de force; this was now more of a mobile automotive laboratory than a rally car. Powered by a race-proven 174-cubic-inch (2,847-cc) flat-six engine, the car had computer-controlled torque delivery to individual wheels that allowed it to hit 60 mph (97 kph) in less than four seconds.

Although racing the Porsche 959 had become of secondary importance, the car performed brilliantly in the grueling Paris–Dakar endurance rally, taking first and second places in 1986. In the same year, a one-off track-focused variant took a class win at Le Mans.

Customers had to wait another year before they could collect their road-going version. Capable of 197 mph (317 kph), the 959 was the fastest production car of 1987. Despite its list price of more than $780,000 (£500,000) in today's money, Porsche barely recouped half of the 959's production costs. Nevertheless, it was worth every penny; without it, the much-loved 911 may not have survived.

Considered by many as a modern design classic, a silver 959 owned by Ralph Lauren went on display at the Boston Museum of Fine Arts in 2005. Other famous owners have included actor Jerry Seinfeld and Microsoft founders Bill Gates and Paul Allen. **DS**

Undeniably a fun car, the Saab 900 convertible also expressed a reserve and sophistication that was particularly Swedish. ▷

5 GT Turbo | Renault

(F)

1986 • 85 cu in/1,400 cc, S4 • 118 bhp/88 kW • 0–60 mph/97 kph in 7.5 seconds • 125 mph/201 kph

In the 1980s manufacturers vied to transform their little front-wheel-drive hatchbacks into rally-style performance cars. This usually meant adding body kits, wider wheels, and tuned engines. The most prized hot-hatch feature was the exciting new turbo.

From the cheeky little Renault 5, launched in 1972, the carmaker ignored the fact that much of it derived from the ancient Renault 4 and created one of the first hot hatches: the Gordini/Alpine. The engine was of a venerable push-rod design, but with a bit of expert coaxing, it could just top 100 mph (161 kph).

The second-generation Renault 5 was a new hot-hatch variant: the GT Turbo. Its engine was still the 85-cubic-inch (1,400-cc) unit from the 1950s, but this time with a turbo added. At just 1,874 pounds (750 kg), the car was light, so performance was genuinely hot. The car had the obligatory overlarge body additions, too—chunky, plastic side skirts, fenders (bumpers), and arches. It was certainly fast, but it had chronic turbo-lag; a press on the accelerator would be followed by a mild increase in revs, then a sudden, belated surge of power as the turbo whizzed into life.

Earlier, Renault had launched a Renault 5 Turbo (not "GT"). This was a more serious contender, with a mid-mounted turbo engine and a rally-style body. Drive was rear-wheel, unlike all the other front-wheel-drive Renault 5s. At the time of its launch, this was France's most powerful production car. A wide-wheeled Renault 5 Turbo featured in a long chase sequence with James Bond in 1983's *Never Say Never Again*. Bond, in a dinner jacket, rides a modified Yamaha motorbike but cannot catch the Renault. **SH**

900 Convertible | Saab

(S)

1986 • 122 cu in/2,000 cc, S4 • 185 bhp/136 kW • 0–60 mph/97 kph in 7.7 seconds • 143 mph/230 kph

The Saab 900 had been launched in 1978 and even then it was just an updated version of the 99, which dated back to the 1960s. The 900s were premium front-wheel-drive sedans (saloons) with character, great handling, and unusual features that gave them a cult following. But the basic Saab design was getting very long in the tooth by 1986.

Saab's U.S. wing suggested that a convertible might restore some glamour to the line and boost sales. Big U.S. car builders were not producing cabriolets at the time, and it was an idea that would not have come naturally to the conservative Swedes.

A Michigan coachbuilder was employed to build prototypes and eventually the two-door drop-head went into production at a factory in Finland. The plan was to produce just 2,000 flagship cars a year, but the public's response was far more enthusiastic than Saab had imagined. With its spacious, four-seat interior and sturdy folding fabric roof, the car was an instant classic. The 900's long hood (bonnet) and stumpy rear end definitely looked more sleek and exciting without a roof. Soon there was a three-year waiting list; by 1992 Saab was selling more than 10,000 convertibles a year.

Saab became part of General Motors in 1989. The second-generation 900, based on the Opel Vectra, lacked some of Saab's unique character. Fans mark this as the beginning of the end of their brand's identity. However, the 900 convertible soldiered on with its old platform until 1995. Most 900 convertibles used the hottest 122-cubic-inch (2,000-cc), sixteen-valve turbocharged engine. Figures for the second-generation turbo model are given above. **SH**

SAAB
900 S
SAAB 900

Croma Turbo D i.d. | Fiat (I)

1986 • 116 cu in/1,900 cc, S4 • 93 bhp/69 kW •
0–60 mph/97 kph in 12.5 seconds • 112 mph/180 kph

For years diesel engines were considered noisy, dirty, and slow compared to gasoline ones. The little-known Croma D i.d. played a vital part in the process of improving the image of diesel. It was also the first production car to feature direct injection. Today, all diesel cars have it, but Fiat's Croma was a pioneer.

The Croma line was unremarkable apart from this distinction. It was one of the "Type Four" cars—the others being the Saab 9000, Lancia Thema, and Alfa Romeo 164—built on a shared platform. The other three were upmarket executive cars, with Fiat's big family diesel being the mass-market version.

The Croma was Fiat's first big car, with frontwheel drive and a sideways-mounted engine, and when sales proved to be sluggish Fiat stopped making big cars for a while. The Croma came with the usual array of engines, from a 98-cubic-inch (1,600-cc) petrol to a 153-cubic-inch (2,500-cc) V6.

The heart of this trendsetting diesel version was its sophisticated injectors. They squirted diesel right into the cylinders, rather than into a preliminary ante-chamber as in all previous diesels. That does not sound like much of a change, but it made the whole combustion process much more efficient. Diesel became more powerful, economical, and therefore attractive. **SH**

205 GTI 1.9 | Peugeot (F)

1986 • 116 cu in/1,905 cc, S4 • 130 bhp/97 kW •
0–60 mph/97 kph in 7.6 seconds • 123 mph/198 kph

By the mid-1980s a new wave of more powerful hot hatches, such as the Ford Escort RS Turbo and the Vauxhall Mark II Astra GTE, began to appear. Peugeot's response was to fit a bigger, fuel-injected 116-cubic-inch (1,905-cc) powerplant into the 205 GTI to create what many believe is the greatest hot hatch ever built.

While the new engine gave only 15 bhp (11 kW) more, it gained a keener throttle response and a lot of low-down torque. The Little Pug gained all-around disc brakes and bigger, 15-inch (38-cm) alloy wheels. Uprated springs and dampers and thicker antiroll bars were also added to complement the power gains. Inside, the car was trimmed in half leather. With a basic price of $11,820 (£7,460), the new GTI was excellent value and considerably cheaper than its nearest rival, Volkswagen's Golf GTI 16v.

In 1988 *Car* magazine pitched the Peugeot GTI against the Lotus Esprit Turbo, costing $47,500 (£30,000), on a trans-European road test. The journalists involved all agreed that the supercar was not superior.

As the flagship model of the 205 range, the GTI brought the Peugeot brand some much-needed kudos. In 1990, *Car* magazine declared the 205 to be its Car of the Decade; by the time production finally ended in 1998, over 5 million 205s had been built. **DS**

Sierra Cosworth RS500 | Ford (GB)

1987 • 122 cu in/2,000 cc, S4 • 224 bhp/166 kW • 0–60 mph/97 kph in 6.1 seconds • 154 mph/248 kph

In the late 1980s, Group A race regulations stipulated that manufacturers had to produce and sell 500 road-going versions of any cars competing on the track.So in 1987, in an attempt to create a dominating car for the circuit, an even hotter version of the Ford Sierra RS Cosworth was produced in small numbers. The RS500 was a success, becoming a multiple race winner, with road-going versions becoming sought-after collectors' classics. This most special of the Sierra Cosworth family was faster, more powerful, and more expensive than any other Sierra. It cost almost $6,250 (£4,000) more than the standard Sierra Cosworth.

The fine tuning was handled by Tickford, a United Kingdom–based motorsport subsidiary of Aston Martin. With tweaks like more fuel injectors, a heftier fuel pump, and a strengthened block, Tickford tuned the engine for extra power. The RS500 had bigger and better brakes, stiffer suspension, and upgraded aerodynamics. In place of fog lights, it had ducts for a front-mounted intercooler that fed cold air to a new, larger turbocharger. Color choice was limited; of the cars sold, fifty-six were white, fifty-two blue, and 392 black. Fewer than half of them remain on the road today, so they are much prized, especially the white and blue examples. Prices can reach over $40,000 (£25,000). **SH**

Thema 8.32 | Lancia (I)

1987 • 179 cu in/2,927 cc, V8 • 212 bhp/158 kW • 0–60 mph/97 kph in 6.8 seconds • 149 mph/240 kph

The Lancia Thema was a large sedan (saloon) related to the Alfa Romeo 164, Fiat Croma, and Saab 9000. The otherwise unassuming boxy sedan had been in production for a few years before it got a memorable engine transplant. The 179-cubic-inch (2,927-cc) V8 used in the Ferrari 308 and Mondial Quattrovalvole was shoehorned under the hood (bonnet) of the Thema. The 8.32 (from "8" cylinders and "32" valves) was born.

There was already a hot Thema in the lineup: the 2.0 turbo, which accelerated more quickly but could not match the muscle of the Ferrari-engined 8.32. Lancia's brochure vaunted the Ferrari association, stating, "It has all the temperament of the prancing horse." The engine cover read "Lancia by Ferrari."

The Thema 8.32 had a number of unusual technical features. It was the first example of a transverse-mounted V8 in a front-wheel-drive car. The chassis, brakes, and suspension were all reworked to cope with the extra power. Lancia worked on the interior, too, adding luxurious Alcantara trim and neat touches such as radio headphone jacks in the rear seats. Visually the 8.32 was very similar to its more modestly powered siblings, but it had a discreet spoiler the driver could deploy electrically, perhaps to help passersby locate the source of the glorious Ferrari engine sound. **RD**

The Jeep Wrangler reconciled dreams of rugged exploration with the humdrum reality of suburban shopping trips.

260 | Venturi (F)

1987 • 174 cu in/2,849 cc, V6 • 260 bhp/194 kW • 0–60 mph/97 kph in 5.2 seconds • 167 mph/269 kph

New sports cars do not often result from two people working for a manufacturer suddenly deciding to team up, leave, and start for themselves.

In the case of Venturi, however, that is just the way it happened. Claude Poiraud and Gérard Godefroy gave up their engineering jobs at Heuliez, a manufacturer of concept cars and niche vehicles in the Loire, France. Their ambitious idea was to build a GT car of their own to rival Ferrari and Porsche. And when they came up with a beautifully proportioned sports car, it was clear that their plans should be taken seriously.

The car was initially launched as the MVS (for Manufacture de Voitures de Sport), but that rather dull name was soon replaced by Venturi. The car's mid-placed six-cylinder engine, sourced from Renault, was replaced after some years by a more powerful version, now supercharged and good for 260 bhp (194 kW).

Despite having good press, strong demand, and great results on the track, Poiraud and Godefroy decided to sell the company in 1994 when manufacture had reached a peak. Venturi had even developed its own "Gentlemen Drivers Trophy."

The new owner of the factory, which employed a workforce of over 400, was Scotsman Hubert O'Neill, who primarily focused on racing. He introduced standard carbon ceramic brakes on his Venturis—a world first. The cars went to Le Mans several times, but the company was sold once again in 1996 to a Thai firm. A double turbo was now introduced, but slow sales led to bankruptcy in 2000. Once again it was sold, this time to Monegasque millionaire Gildo Pallanca Pastor, who currently focuses on electric power. **JB**

Wrangler | Jeep (USA)

1987 • 256 cu in/4,200 cc, S6 • 112 bhp/82 kW • 0–60 mph/97 kph in 12 seconds • 88 mph/141 kph

The Wrangler is the Willys Jeep of World War II updated for the modern sports utility vehicle generation. The thirty-year-old four-wheel-drive military vehicle was updated by Chrysler in the 1980s with more power, more comforts, and more styling. It was designed to appeal to new buyers who were not even alive when the original Jeeps were driving ashore on D-Day.

This new Jeep still had rugged looks and off-road ability, but, as it was more likely to be driving to the shopping mall than climbing over shell holes, it was gentrified with more sophisticated suspension, a wider track, and lowered ground clearance.

The Wrangler came either as a soft-top convertible or with a removable hardtop. By the mid-1990s the Jeep had features never dreamed of for the original Willys: rear seat belts, antilock brakes, and an optional automatic gearbox. It was still popular with hardcore off-roaders, but now it had a new following at beaches, festivals, and city centers.

Off-road ability remained its strength, though, thanks to big, grippy tires, underbody protection, steep approach and departure angles, and a roaring low-range gearbox. There are holes in the floor for hosing out the hard plastic interior after an expedition in the wilds, and it can wade through water 20 inches (50 cm) deep. Compared to many of the new breed of "soft-roaders," though, the Wrangler's short wheelbase, loud and drafty cabin, and tepid performance made it an unlikely choice for regular commuting.

The Wrangler was built in Ontario, Canada, until 1992, when production shifted back to the United States and the original Willys factory in Ohio. **SH**

BFGoodrich OFFICIAL
OFFICIAL
WWW.JEEPWORLD.CO.UK
PRESS
J33P JW

Allante | Cadillac

USA

1987 • 250 cu in/4,100 cc, V8 • 170 bhp/127 kW • 0–60 mph/97 kph in 9.3 seconds • 122 mph/196 kph

For more than half a century, Cadillac was seen as the number one automobile of luxury in the United States. Then in the 1960s and 1970s, it started losing its status to more sophisticated imports. By the 1980s, the time had come for Cadillac to create something new and exciting to stay competitive. If Cadillac were to compete with Jaguar and Mercedes, it needed to call in a European designer and renowned coachbuilder. The Allante was designed and built in Italy by the master craftsmen at the Italian Pininfarina design studio. They created a real Italian-American luxury car that combined streamlined Italian bodywork and a classic U.S. V8 engine.

Cadillac milked the situation for publicity. The firm announced that the Allante bodies were being built in Italy and flown by specially equipped Boeing 747s to a Michigan Cadillac factory, where bodies were then mated to the chassis and engine. The Allante was

called the "Flying Italian Cadillac" and a product of "the world's longest assembly line." To get the model into the public eye, actor Larry Hagman was given an Allante, and so was his character J. R. Ewing in the popular TV show *Dallas*.

The Allante was Cadillac's first venture into the luxury two-door roadster market; the model sold from 1987 until 1993. It was a front-wheel-drive, luxury two-seater, with a removable hardtop and fabric soft-top. Billed as GM's "passenger car flagship," it featured a full arsenal of electronic luxuries, such as ten-way power-adjustable leather seats, state-of-the-art digital instruments, and a Bose hi-fi system.

But at $54,700 (£34,500) it was expensive—more than double the price of the Cadillac De Ville—and its performance was not exciting. Around 21,000 examples were built during its production run, but that was roughly half what Cadillac was hoping for. **BK**

Galant | Mitsubishi (J)

1987 • 122 cu in/2,000 cc, S4 • 237 bhp/177 kW • 0–60 mph/97 kph in 7.3 seconds • 143 mph/230 kph

The Galant had been a cheap but boring Japanese family car since 1967, evolving through several generations and usually trailing the rest of the world's fashion and technological trends by about five years.

In 1987 Mitsubishi was determined to celebrate the Galant's twentieth birthday with a whole new product. It launched a sixth-generation Galant—also called the Eterna, ZX, Dodge 2000GTX, and Eagle 2000GTX—that was suddenly a world-class contender.

The standard front-wheel-drive 98-cubic-inch (1,600-cc) and 122-cubic-inch (2,000-cc) models were smart sedans (saloons) with an unbeatable reputation for reliability, but it was the top-of-the-line models that really started turning heads. They featured a state-of-the-art four-wheel steering system that was designed to give better cornering above 30 mph (48 kph).

The GTi-16v version was swift and tidy to drive, but the VR-4 model with four-wheel drive and a turbocharged engine was the star of the line (its performance figures are given above). This hot Galant won three major rallies before its engine and drive system were switched to the smaller and more suitable Mitsubishi Lancer. The turbocharged Lancer became a serious rally contender too, sparking the high-performance Evo series that continues today. **SH**

Grand National GNX | Buick (USA)

1987 • 231 cu in/3,791 cc, V6 • 276 bhp/206 kW • 0–60 mph/97 kph in 5.5 seconds • 125 mph/200 kph

Buick's Grand National cars are noted for many things, one of which is their striking all-black appearance. They were a variant on the Buick Regal series, and first appeared in 1982. The name came from the NASCAR Grand National racing series—Buick had won the Manufacturers Cup in both 1981 and 1982. Those first Grand National cars were actually gray, not black. Just 215 Buick Grand Nationals were made in 1982. They were great cars and got a lot of attention, but Buick did not repeat the Grand National in 1983.

In 1984 the Grand National returned, but was painted black. It looked stunning and this time Buick built 2,000 of them. In 1987 the Grand National hit its peak, particularly with the GNX (Grand National Experimental) model. This was the ultimate Grand National, and cost $29,900 (£18,900). Although it was rated 0–60 mph (97 kph) in 5.5 seconds, in some tests it achieved it in 4.7 seconds. Its top speed was some 20 mph (32 kph) higher than claimed by the factory.

Only 547 GNXs were built. Many were specifically bought by collectors with the intention of keeping them rather than driving them, as if they were bottles of fine wine. As a result, they are eminently desirable among today's collectors, who expect to pay in excess of $50,000 (£32,000) for a GNX with low mileage. **MG**

Corolla | Toyota

1987 • 79 cu in/1,300 cc, S4
0–60 mph/97 kph in 12.8 s

By 1987 the Toyota Co… becoming the world's best-selling c… into its sixth generation, there were sporty mod… were surprisingly fun to drive, and all Corollas had vastly improved handling and ride. The looks were more modern. Some even had pop-up headlights; others featured a new liftback style that was halfway between a coupe and a station wagon (estate).

The Corolla Mark VI was more refined mechanically: all were front-wheel drive, with a few four-wheel-drive versions. Engines stretched from a humble 79-cubic-inch (1,300-cc) version to a typical 1980s screaming hot hatch available only in Japan that had a supercharged 98-cubic-inch (1,600-cc) engine producing 162 bhp (121 kW). Around the world there were two- and four-door Corolla sedans (saloons), three- and five-door hatchbacks, a coupe, the liftback, and a station wagon.

Toyota's factory in California had been supplemented by a new one in Canada, and the sixth-generation Corolla was being built in nine different countries. It was rebadged in the United States as the Geo Prism, and in Australia as the Holden Nova.

Most importantly, buyers loved the reliability of the Corolla. It was simply the world's first ultradependable, long-lasting, and easy-to-own family car. **SH**

… drive versio… fiery Delta Integrale wa… did Lancia sell all 5,000 of the cars it … produce, it ended up selling a total of 44,296 o…

The sixteen-valve version was the star, winn… the first rally it entered in 1989 and carrying on… dominate the sport. In 1990 and 1991, Lancia won b… the drivers and manufacturers world titles. Lancia's … consecutive manufacturers world titles is still a recor…

For road users the Integrale was a formidab… performer. A slight bump hinted that there w… something extra crammed beneath the hood (bonn… of the 1980 European Car of the Year. And wider whe… in bulging wheel-arches suggested the purpose of t… version of the Italian three-door hatch.

The Integrale was at heart a practical hatchba… that became a supercar with a dab of the throttle. … big rival at the time was the similarly endowed Au… Quattro. There was not much to distinguish the… certainly in driving and performance, except that t… Lancia was around half the price of the Audi. **SH**

8 | Audi

D

38 • 256 cu in/4,200 cc, V8 • 276 bhp/206 kW • 0–62 mph/100 kph in 6.8 seconds • 155 mph/250 kph

e range-topping Audi V8 was a deliberate attempt create an upmarket aura to confront established rman rivals Mercedes and BMW, and it worked. The was a large, luxurious four-door sedan (saloon) th a powerful V8 engine, the Audi Quattro's four-heel-drive system, and a state-of-the-art four-speed tomatic transmission (and later, a six-speed manual). early use of galvanizing to prevent the body from sting allowed Audi to introduce what seemed like an credible ten-year anticorrosion warranty.

The thirty-two-valve, four-overhead-camshaft, all-uminum V8 engines were advanced for the era. At st there was a 220-cubic-inch (3,600-cc) V8, which as essentially formed out of two Volkswagen Golf GTi ngines. This was joined by a more powerful 256-cubic-ch (4,200-cc) version, whose figures are given above.

The look of the car followed the design of the Audi 100 series, with minor changes such as a new grille, fenders (bumpers), and lights setting a more exclusive tone. The interior was made as luxurious as possible, with heated leather seats as standard and walnut trim, wool carpet, and an eight-speaker Bose hi-fi system.

The V8 was available as a long-wheelbase version, too, and Audi considered building a station wagon (estate) model, or "Avant" in Audi-speak. Indeed, one V8 Avant was built, for the wife of Audi boss Ferdinand Piech. That car is now displayed in the Audi museum in Ingolstadt, Germany. The museum also houses motorsport versions of the V8 that won the German Touring Car Championship in 1990 and 1991. These are rare examples of track cars retaining their production model's incongruous, walnut-trimmed interiors. **SH**

164 V6 | Alfa Romeo

I

1988 • 183 cu in/3,000 cc, V6 • 228 bhp/170 kW • 0–62 mph/100 kph in 7 seconds • 152 mph/245 kph

Executives looking for a new company car in the late 1980s had plenty of fine established options from Germany, plus an exciting newcomer from Italy. The elegant and roomy 164 luxury sedan (saloon) was the first big front-wheel-drive Alfa Romeo. It was also the last new car developed by the company before it was swallowed up by Fiat.

Fitted with a wonderful-sounding V6 engine, the sharply styled 164 had exciting performance to match its sporty handling. The interior was luxurious, with features such as automatic climate control and heated and electrically adjusted seats with leather upholstery. There was also high technology on offer, including antilock brakes, electronically controlled suspension for an optimum comfort and roadholding balance, and hydraulic engine mounts for smoothness.

The 164 was one of the jointly developed "Type 4" cars, along with the Fiat Croma, Lancia Thema, and Saab 9000. While the others were so similar they could interchange body parts, Alfa preserved a degree of independence by hiring designers from Pininfarina to make the 164's galvanized body distinctively sleeker and more aerodynamic.

The 164 was Alfa's first big-car success for decades, selling more than a quarter of million. *Autocar* magazine described it as "a German car with personality." Sadly, it was also like a German car with Italian electrics. Its extraordinarily complex wiring loom included three linked onboard computers and a unique grid pattern of buttons on the dashboard. Predictably, owners experienced plenty of annoying electrical problems with their prestigious Alfa. **SH**

The Ferrari F40, with its undiluted race-car characteristics, was sadly impaired by most countries' statutory speed limits.

F40 | Ferrari (I)

1988 • 179 cu in/2,936 cc, V8 • 471 bhp/352 kW • 0–60 mph/97 kph in 3.6 seconds • 201 mph/322 kph

Ferrari's F40 was the successor to its 288 GTO model. The company again turned to the Italian design gurus at Pininfarina to produce a car that would be worthy of the Ferrari name; this time the car would be called the F40 in commemoration of Ferrari's fortieth anniversary. Pininfarina's general manager, Leonardo Fioravanti, rose to the challenge; he announced that his firm would produce a car to give Ferrari owners the closest possible thing to a race car that they could drive on the roads. The top speed and acceleration figures above show that Pininfarina did indeed give Ferrari something rather special. For overtaking, the car could accelerate from 40 to 70 mph (64 to 112 kph) in just two seconds.

This was not only the most powerful Ferrari ever built, it was also the most expensive. It was initially expected to be priced at about $280,000 (£177,000), but when it eventually appeared the price had rocketed to roughly $400,000 (£250,000).

The Ferrari F40 was primarily conceived as a race car; consequently, it featured the latest aerodynamic design. But as it was to be driven on the road, stability rather than sheer power had to be a factor. It is one thing to flip a car or lose control on a racetrack, but quite another to do it on a twisting public main road.

Over its five-year lifespan, 1,315 Ferrari F40s were built, all of them in the striking red shade of *rosso corsa* (racing red). The F40 was to be the last car for which Enzo Ferrari himself was responsible—the company founder died in 1988 at the age of ninety. His instruction to the team had been to build a car that was the best in the world. They did, and it was a fitting tribute to the great man. **MG**

V8 | Giocattolo (AUS)

1988 • 304 cu in/4,987 cc, V8 • 300 bhp/220 kW • unknown • 160 mph/257 kph

The Australian automotive landscape is littered with broken dreams, and one of these was a fledgling 1980s automotive company based in the seaside town of Caloundra on Queensland's Sunshine Coast. Giocattolo Motori was the joint creation of car enthusiast Paul Halstead and Formula 1 engineer Barry Lock. In two years of promise and innovation, the pair designed and manufactured fifteen Alfa Giocattolo V8s. The Giocattolo (Italian for "toy") would be a typical Australian hybrid, consisting of an otherwise reputable, two-seat, front-wheel-drive Alfa Romeo Sprint with a few tweaks, such as—potentially—the replacement of its engine with an Alfa V6.

When the Alfa V6 proved costly to import, Halstead and Lock went looking for a suitable replacement; this turned out to be the Australian-made Walkinshaw Group A 304-cubic-inch (4,987-cc) Holden V8. They then redesigned the Sprint as a mid-engined car to improve its weight distribution, aiming for a perfect union of engine and chassis. When the engine was further upgraded to Group B status, Giocattolo at last had a car to be reckoned with. But the engine was not the only refinement. Kevlar wheel arch extensions followed, as did F1-standard suspension and brakes, and a luxurious, handcrafted interior.

New government legislation—ironically designed to foster growth in the domestic car industry—then forced Halstead and Lock to purchase the entire Alfa from Italy, not just the bodies. The two had come up with the right car—Australia's first supercar—but at the wrong time. Unable to make the car economically, Giocattolo was forced into liquidation in 1989. **BS**

Reatta | Buick

USA

1988 • 231 cu in/3,791 cc, V6 • 165 bhp/123 kW • 0–60 mph/97 kph in 9.5 seconds • 125 mph/200 kph

When it was launched in 1988, the Reatta was the first two-seater that Buick had produced since 1946, and the only sports car it had in its line. The car was unusual in that it had its maximum speed restricted electronically to 125 mph (200 kph); an alarm system was triggered when the driver reached that speed, although it could be overridden. Other electronic features included its ECC, or electronic control center, an advanced, touch-screen control system that operated the radio, diagnostics, and heater/air-conditioning. There was also a trip computer.

The luxurious and handsome car was built by hand, with Buick's engineers lavishing attention on its every detail. Initially it was offered as a hardtop coupe; a convertible option came out in 1990. At first Buick had high hopes for what was a sporty new venture and hoped to sell 20,000 a year, but the initial sales were disappointing and in the first year it sold fewer than a quarter of that amount. It was thought that the advanced electronic gadgets were putting off typical Buick buyers, who were usually older and more conventional in their habits, and that younger buyers tended to see any Buick as a plodding "dads' car."

For 1990 and 1991 Buick removed some of the electronic controls and returned to a more traditional dashboard look, dispensing with the trip computer completely in the process. But it didn't work. Although 1989 sales had been better, at just over 7,000, and in 1990 better still, at 8,515, it was still nowhere near the numbers needed to make the car economically viable. Buick decided to return to its core market, dropping the Reatta completely in 1991. **MG**

Corrado | Volkswagen

D

1988 • 175 cu in/2,861 cc, VR6 • 190 bhp/140 kW • 0–60 mph/97 kph in 6.3 seconds • 146 mph/235 kph

Like its predecessor, the Scirocco, the Volkswagen Corrado was seen by many as the budget, and more practical, alternative to Porsche's entry-level 924 and 944 sports cars. The four-seater coupe was based on the Mark II Golf platform and built under contract by Karmann. It received a variety of powerplants during its eight-year production run, including normally aspirated 110-cubic-inch (1,800-cc) and 122-cubic-inch (2,000-cc) versions and a supercharged 110-cubic-inch G60. In 1992 the much lauded twelve-valve VR6 engine was used to create a fine front-engined sports coupe.

Marketed as the Corrado SLC (Sports Luxury Coupe) in North America, this export model received the smaller 171-cubic-inch (2,800-cc) lump, while the European VR6 got the "full-fat" 177-cubic inch (2,900-cc). This flagship version also had uprated steering and suspension components from the Mark III Golf, and required wider arches and a raised hood (bonnet) to accommodate its new six-cylinder.

Utilizing a single cylinder head, the VR6 used a staggered overlapping configuration to fit all six cylinders into a compact engine block. Its super-smooth power delivery, and great low-down torque, made the car an instant hit. While the car remained docile at low revs around town, it could also embarrass many a sports car, at twice the price, if it was required to do so.

The British motoring magazine *Car* listed the Corrado among its Twenty-five Cars You Must Drive Before You Die. BBC TV *Top Gear* host Richard Hammond has said that the VR6 version will become a classic, a status aided by its great styling, fantastic performance, and small production numbers. **DS**

405 Mi16 | Peugeot

F

1988 • 116 cu in/1,900 cc, S4 • 158 bhp/116 kW • 0–60 mph/97 kph in 8.2 seconds • 134 mph/216 kph

Peugeot's Mi16 sedan (saloon) was a discreetly sporty version of its 405 family-car line that quickly gained a cult following. The sixteen-valve engine was tuned to give it a level of performance that was considered exceptional for a four-door sedan at the time.

The whole front-wheel-drive 405 series, Europe's Car of the Year in 1988, was known for its balance and fine handling. But this lightweight Mi16 version was even better thanks to sporty lowered and stiffened independent suspension all around. There were alloy wheels and a discreet body kit with a slim trunk (boot) spoiler, front skirts, and side sill extensions for better aerodynamics and sportier looks.

High powered for its time, the engine was a stock Peugeot/Citroën unit upgraded with twin overhead camshafts, electronic fuel injection, and four valves per cylinder. The Mi16 got a sportier five-speed manual gearbox and all-around powered disc brakes with an antilocking system, too. A few Mi16s—the Mi16x4s—had four-wheel drive with a transmission from the Lancia Integrale. The extra weight slowed this all-wheel-drive Mi16 slightly but made it very surefooted.

A revamp of the line in 1992 changed the engine to a slightly weaker 122-cubic-inch (2,000-cc) unit and introduced a Mi16 Le Mans version in a special-edition red with distinctive leather and suede seats.

A very rare top-of-the-line T16 model was made available in left-hand drive only. This was a turbocharged four-wheel-drive Mi16 with a sizzling maximum power of 220 bhp (162 kW). The 0–60 mph (97 kph) acceleration figure was around seven seconds. A fleet of sixty were built for the French police. **SH**

Civic CR-X | Honda

J

1988 • 98 cu in/1,600 cc, S4 • 157 bhp/117 kW • 0–60 mph/97 kph in 7.9 seconds • 131 mph/211 kph

It may be only a small Japanese two-door hatchback with front-wheel drive and a high-revving engine, but something about the cheeky character of the Honda Civic CR-X has bestowed cult status upon it. Years after its disappearance from showrooms, the CR-X is still a sought-after modern classic.

The compact coupe evolved through various guises. In the United States it started as a two-seater, in Europe as a 2+2. The boxy first generation offered engines from just 79 cubic inches (1,300 cc). The sexier, curvier second incarnation from 1988 reached a peak when it was given Honda's new free-revving 98-cubic-inch (1,600-cc) VTEC engine.This advanced unit used variable valve timing to increase power at high revs while keeping low fuel economy. With pin-sharp steering, fine roadholding, and precise handling, the CR-X was the first choice for many a driving enthusiast on a tight budget.

By the late 1980s the CR-X was scooping awards around the world: *America Road & Track* magazine called it one of the best ten cars of all time, and a CR-X single-model track race series was begun in the United Kingdom. The CR-X was also an easy car to live with. It had legendary reliability and low running costs, and its large glass tailgate made it a practical day-to-day hatchback. The rear seats folded flat to increase space.

In 1992 Honda introduced a third-generation model with a changed body shape and a targa-top option. Sometimes called the Civic del Sol, this CR-X had more power but less handling precision. Buyers saw that it lacked the character of the earlier models and sales slipped. It was withdrawn in 1997. **SH**

With the new 1989 Discovery line, Land Rover was determined to uphold its reputation for off-road performance. ⊡

XJR-S | Jaguar (GB)

1988 • 366 cu in/6,000 cc, V12 • 329 bhp/245 kW • 0–60 mph/97 kph in 6.5 seconds • 158 mph/253 kph

In 1984 race driver and car builder Tom Walkinshaw had won the European Touring Car Championship at the wheel of the big Jaguar XJS luxury coupe. Another XJS had triumphed in the U.S. coast-to-coast Cannonball Run in a record time, and XJSs were regularly winning Touring Car races in Australia. The big cat was showing its sporting potential everywhere, but a road-going sporty version of the car was still unavailable.

In the United Kingdom, owners could uprate their cars thanks to Walkinshaw's TWR company, which was selling XJS body and suspension kits. Finally, Jaguar took the hint and commissioned TWR to build a special high-performance XJR-S supercar for road use. The special cars were given a striking body kit of lowered front and rear aprons and side skirts, new alloy wheels, and a trunk (boot) spoiler. The cars had a well-equipped interior swathed in leather and walnut. TWR also modified the suspension, steering, and brakes. Options included race brakes and a lowered ride height.

The 323-cubic-inch (5,300-cc) engine was soon replaced with a 366-cubic-inch (6,000-cc) one that could produce 329 bhp (245 kW). Top speed was limited to 158 mph (253 kph). Customers could choose either a coupe or convertible body style. All were hand-built and featured a numbered plaque on a door kick plate.

According to the XJS-R brochure, the concept was simple: "To combine traditional Jaguar values—craftsmanship, comfort, power, and refinement—with performance that matches or exceeds that of the world's most illustrious sporting coupes." With TWR's help, Jaguar succeeded; the XJR-S stayed in production until 1993 and a total of 1,130 cars were sold. **SH**

Discovery | Land Rover (GB)

1989 • 214 cu in/3,500 cc, V8 • 152 bhp/113 kW • 0–60 mph/97 kph in 11.8 seconds • 101 mph/163 kph

The market for off-roaders was changing fast. Land Rover had already produced the big, luxurious Range Rover and the rough-and-ready original Land Rover, but it needed something between the two to rival the new wave of Japanese sports utility vehicles.

The Discovery was based on the Range Rover's chassis but had a less overpowering presence. It looked more functional than a Range Rover, more comfortable than a Land Rover. The company had realized it did not have much sense of contemporary style, so it employed the Conran Design Group on the interior. The award-winning creation by Conran was very innovative: the light-blueclad interior included a Land Rover fabric holdall as part of the center console that could be removed and used as a shoulder bag. There were clever touches such as map slots above the windshield, handholds incorporated into head restraints, and remote radio controls. The twin-panel sunroof was stored in a bag behind the backseats.

Initially the "Disco" was powered by a 214-cubic-inch (3,500-cc) V8 or a 153-cubic-inch (2,500-cc) turbodiesel. An underpowered 122-cubic-inch (2,000-cc) gas-engined version was briefly available, and Prince Philip of the British royal family was often seen driving one. The Discovery had permanent four-wheel drive, manual-locking center differential, and high ground clearance.

A TV commercial showed Japanese mountaineers struggling to follow in the tracks of a mysterious vehicle. Finally reaching it by means of a helicopter, they wipe snow from its nose to reveal the Land Rover badge. "Land Rover Discovery: It already has its followers" was the pointed slogan that followed. **SH**

Favorit | Skoda

CS

1989 • 79 cu in/1,289 cc, S4 • 67 bhp/50 kW • 0–62 mph/100 kph in 17 seconds • 92 mph/148 kph

The long-standing Czechoslovakian auto industry had suffered a lingering demise under Communist rule. Its cars of the 1970s and 1980s were a long way below the standard of Western products, and the Skoda car became a humorous stereotype for comedians.

As Czechoslovakia began to change, so did its cars. The ancient, rear-engined, rear-wheel-drive Estelle was replaced in 1989 by a thoroughly modern, well-designed, and well-built car. In this year, the Czech "Velvet Revolution" changed the country from Stalinism to democracy, and the Favorit was to change the image and the fortunes of the Skoda company.

It was a five-door, front-engined, front-wheel-drive hatchback designed by the Italian styling house Bertone, which had previously drawn up Lamborghinis and Ford Mustangs. Perhaps Skoda bosses knew that it was a historic car for the brand, because they named it Favorit after a beloved Skoda luxury sports sedan (saloon) originally produced in 1936, in the pre-Communist era.

Within a year Skoda was allied to the Volkwagen (VW) Group and by 1994 the Favorit was relaunched as the Felicia. Within six years Skoda was topping customer satisfaction surveys across western Europe.The car was quickly upgraded each year as VW's influence grew.

By 1994 a Skoda Favorit was competing in the FIA World Rally Championship. The motoring world was shocked when the little Skoda won the 2-liter (122-cubic-inch/2,000-cc) category despite having only a 1.3-liter (79-cubic-inch/1,289-cc) engine. And most satisfying of all for Skoda was that among the rivals it beat to first place were the cars entered by its Volkswagen parent company. **SH**

S-Cargo | Nissan

J

1989 • 91 cu in/1,487 cc, S4 • 72 bhp/54 kW • unknown • unknown

It was one of the oddest vehicles ever produced by a mainstream manufacturer: a retro minivan with cartoonlike looks. In fact, the Nissan S-Cargo has been called the ugliest car ever built, but it also has a cult following. The name is a pun; although it can be taken as standing for "small cargo, " it sounds like *escargot*, the French word for a snail, which it actually resembles.

The design was inspired by the Citroën 2CV, particularly the van version that was popular in Japan. Like the French van, the S-Cargo featured bug-eyed headlights, a single-spoke steering wheel, and a big, round, central speedometer. Only available in right-hand drive, it had a three-speed automatic gearbox with the shift mounted high on the dashboard. Snail-like power came from a 91-cubic-inch (1,487-cc) petrol engine. Many components were shared with the Nissan Sunny.

Features included air-conditioning, removable rear seats, and a large flat top to the dashboard for map-reading and paperwork. Eccentric options included an oval window on each side and an electric canvas roof.

The vehicle proved popular with Japanese buyers and 12,000 were produced over three years for the home market. They spread gradually to other countries but only as gray imports. Some are sought by collectors as distinctive commercial vehicles.

Regardless of its comical looks, the S-Cargo does the work of a small van. It can haul loads of up to 660 pounds (300 kg) and has a large tailgate and low cargo floor for easy loading. The big side panels have often been used for commercial signage, and it has also been used as a mobile billboard by big companies like Kentucky Fried Chicken and McDonald's. **SH**

TC | Chrysler (USA)

1989 • 135 cu in/2,213 cc, S4 • 160 bhp/119 kW •
0–60 mph/97 kph in 10.2 seconds • 131 mph/210 kph

In the 1980s Chrysler was restored to financial health by its chairman, Lee Iacocca, but its automobiles were doing little to excite its customers, much less attract new ones. Iacocca contacted his friend Alejandro de Tomaso, who had taken over Maserati in 1975 but had failed to develop the firm's U.S. market. Chrysler was after some glamour, a "grand touring" luxury convertible; Maserati needed money after its heartbreakingly awful Biturbo. What the two companies came up with was the Chrysler TC—which provided nothing of either.

Apart from the go-nowhere styling there was a disastrous two-year delay before production actually began. The logistics alone were mind-boggling. The transmission and tires came from Germany, ABS brakes from France, cams from Florida, wiring from Spain. By the time everything got to Italy and the first of the turbocharged Chrysler-designed, Maserati-engineered engines were fitted into the handcrafted Italian bodies, and the products shipped back to the United States, the TC was already yesterday's car. It looked much too much like Chrysler's run-of-the-mill LeBaron, which ended up being produced first and making the TC look like some odd kind of afterthought—a derivative, but at twice the cost. **BS**

Golf G60 Rallye | Volkswagen (D)

1989 • 108 cu in/1,763 cc, S4 • 160 bhp/119 kW •
0–60 mph/97 kph in 7.4 seconds • 132 mph/212 kph

In 1986 few rallying fans even realized that there was a second-division contest going on for production cars. After seven class wins, Volkswagen (VW) took the Group A title in its two-wheel-drive Golf GTI 16v. Yet, VW bosses still wanted to showcase their products in top-flight rallying, and in 1988 work began on the four-wheel-drive Golf G60 Rallye. Based on VW's Mark II Golf, the Rallye received a unique eight-valve, 108-cubic-inch (1,763-cc) supercharged powerplant, which just crept inside the engine-capacity limits set by the FIA.

By the time the car was ready for its first World Rally Championship season in 1990, the rules had changed. The Rallye would now be competing against more powerful turbocharged cars. To remain competitive, the Rallye's engine was frequently pushed beyond its limits, and team mechanics were rumored to be changing the car's supercharger more often than its tires. The VW Rally Team finished the season in a lowly seventeeth place. But more than 5,000 160-bhp (119-kW) road-going examples of the Rallye were built to qualify the Golf for competition. At twice the price of a standard VW GTI, they were well equipped with Recaro seats, electric windows, and high-quality sound systems. Today, the Golf G60 Rallye is among the most desirable of all classic Volkswagens sought by collectors. **DS**

SZ/RZ | Alfa Romeo (I)

1989 • 183 cu in/3,000 cc, V6 • 207 bhp/154 kW •
0–60 mph/97 kph in 6.9 seconds • 155 mph/250 kph

In the late 1980s the giant Fiat Group was desperate to recapture attention for its once-great subsidiary Alfa Romeo. What it came up with was one of the most extraordinary cars in the history of Alfa Romeo.

The SZ, or Sprint Zagato, was a plastic-bodied, limited-edition, rear-wheel-drive super coupe in an age when most people wanted a hot hatchback. Little wonder, then, that Italians dubbed the space-age machine "Il Mostro"—the Monster. Its looks were certainly head-turning, if not pretty. But for some it was a dream machine; the SZ was fast and handled superbly. Available only in Alfa red, the SZ was really a track car for the road. Its alloy engine was a 183-cubic-inch (3,000-cc) V6 tuned by Alfa's racing engineers, and its suspension was based on the Alfa 75 competition car.

Only 1,000 were built, all with a numbered identification plate on the dashboard. In 1992 a convertible version appeared, the brutal-looking RZ, or Roadster Zagato. This is even rarer; only 278 were built.

After the SZ and RZ, Alfa went back to producing mass-market cars. It switched back to Pininfarina from the rival Zagato styling house, even though Zagato had had little to do with either model. But whatever the world thought of them, Alfa had achieved one thing: people had sat up and taken notice again. **SH**

XM V6 | Citroën (F)

1989 • 182 cu in/2,975 cc, V6 • 197 bhp/147 kW •
0–62 mph/100 mph in 8.6 seconds • 146 mph/235 kph

Europe's 1990 Car of the Year (beating the Mercedes SL) was the quirky new Citroën XM executive's car. Often likened to a slab of cheese in design, it sold more than a third of a million examples before disappearing in 2000.

The low, pointed nose and big, glassy rear meant rear passengers sat higher than those in the front, and there was a big tailgate for access to the huge trunk (boot); the station-wagon (estate) version claimed to have the world's biggest trunk. The enormous interior boasted strange switchgear, a foot-operated parking brake, and a single-spoke steering wheel.

To dispel buyers' recollections of old, rusty, underpowered, and wallowy Citroëns, the XM was crammed with advanced features such as an electronically controlled suspension, a galvanized body, and powerful, multivalve engines. Best of all was the twenty-four-valve V6 version, which combined a floating ride quality with fast and refined progress. Extra leather and wood veneer adorned the cabin, and heated seats, climate control, and air-conditioning were added to the standard specification. The U.S. flagship version was marketed as the XM Vitesse.

British suspension guru Dr. Alex Moulton owned an XM V6 from new and often spoke out in praise of the efficiency of its "hydropneumatic" system. **SH**

Celica | Toyota

J

1989 • 122 cu in/1,998 cc, S4 • 158 bhp/118 kW • 0–60 mph/97 kph in 7.6 seconds • 132 mph/212 kph

The fifth-generation Toyota Celica had a "super round" shape, claimed by Toyota to add strength without making the car any heavier. The curvy style was strikingly different at the time and was soon adopted by designers used by other manufacturers.

Although Toyota produced a range of engines for the new Celica, not all of them were available in every market. In the United Kingdom, for example, the car was only offered with a 122-cubic-inch (1,998-cc) motor, either as the front-wheel-drive liftback model (figures are given above) or as the range-topping four-wheel-drive GT-Four. In the late 1980s and early 1990s, Toyota was riding the crest of a wave in the World Rally Championship (WRC), using a full-blown works GT-Four. This helped to give the Celica brand a reputation for superior performance.

The GT-Four road car was turbocharged up to 222 bhp (165 kW), with a full-time four-wheel-drive system and a viscous-coupling center differential that distributed the power between the front and back wheels. For the European market, an antilock braking system was standard for the GT-Four, as were luxury touches (for the time) such as electric windows. There would later be a Carlos Sainz special edition, named after Toyota's Spanish WRC driver.

But the standard front-wheel-drive models were also popular and seen as offering good performance at a relatively low cost. In particular, their handling was good, thanks to independent suspension all around.

The Celica of the early 1990s achieved something rare in car manufacture: a connection between success in world motorsports and showroom appeal. **JI**

Taurus SHO | Ford

(USA)

1989 • 182 cu in/2,986 cc, V6 • 220 bhp/162 kW • 0–60 mph/97 kph in 7 seconds • 143 mph/230 kph

The success of the Taurus SHO (Super High Output) was a great surprise to the marketing department at Ford. Originally intended to be a limited-production model spanning three or four years, the SHO proved such a hit with consumers—selling more than 15,000 units in its first year alone—that Ford decided to order more engines and beef up production. Ten years and three generations later, the series finally came to an end in 1999 after selling more than 106,000 units.

The SHO was the "muscle car" of the Taurus range and the fastest four-door sedan (saloon) in the history of U.S. motoring, thanks to a twenty-four-valve V6 engine, built in collaboration with engineers at Yamaha. The engine was originally developed to fit into a canceled mid-engined Ford sports car designed to compete with the Chevrolet Corvette and Nissan's Z series. Ford remained contracted to purchase the engines after the sports car's demise, so the SHO was nominated as the Yamaha V6's new home.

The SHO was never intended to match the phenomenal sales of the sedate, family-friendly 140-bhp (103-kW) Taurus, which had been clocking up sales across North America in the hundreds of thousands. It came with side skirts, performance suspension, and a five-speed gearbox (no automatic was available), and was definitely a car for the enthusiast, despite only being available as a sedan. It had antilock brakes all around, inboard fog lights, V-rated tires, roll bars, and side-bolsters on its front bucket seats. Featuring regularly on the covers of U.S. auto mags, it appeared on several critics' Top Ten lists. Many saw it as not unlike a BMW—but at a fraction of the cost. **BS**

Director Tim Burton stands atop the Batmobile during filming of his 1989 *Batman* movie at Pinewood Studios, England. ▷

Dakota | Shelby (USA)

1989 • 318 cu in/5,211 cc, V8 • 175 bhp/130 kW • 0–60 mph/97 kph in 5 seconds • unknown

The Shelby Dakota originated as the rather plain Dodge Dakota pickup, a midsized (by U.S. standards) truck powered by a V6 engine. All changed dramatically for the humble Dakota in 1989 when legendary tuner and modifier Carroll Shelby had a look at it. Like Clark Kent turning into Superman, the Dodge Dakota was transformed into the fastest production pickup available at the time.

The first thing to go was the Dakota's engine, which was replaced by a 318-cubic-inch (5,211-cc) V8. This would be the first rear-wheel-drive V8 vehicle that Shelby had built since the 1960s. There was no room left in the engine bay for an engine-driven fan, so he fitted an electric one. The air-intake system had to be reworked, using a snorkel air filter from a muscle car.

New technology was employed in the Shelby Dakota, too. Its four-speed automatic gearbox, an all-new design from Chrysler/Dodge, was one of the most complex the company had produced. There was an antilock braking system on the rear wheels. The suspension was carried over from the standard pickup, but with gas-charged shock absorbers. The Shelby had unique alloy wheels, and there were also body changes, such as a different front fender (bumper) and, of course, a big stripe down the side. Inside, the Shelby logo appeared in the center of the steering wheel and on the dashboard, as well as in the fabric of the seats.

The overall performance of the truck was good by pickup standards. Its acceleration matched that of the Chrysler Neon sedan (saloon) and the Shelby Dakota could generally look after itself out on the open road. But only 1,500 were built in the truck's one-year run. **JI**

Batmobile | Warner Bros. (USA)

1989 • jet turbine • unknown • 0–60 mph/97 kph in 3.7 seconds • 330 mph/531 kph

Tim Burton's 1989 movie *Batman* introduced a much darker superhero than the world was expecting, and the caped crusader needed a car to match his new, brooding image. The Batmobile driven by Michael Keaton did not disappoint. Disregarding the fact that it was built on a humble Chevrolet Impala chassis, the vehicle was every Gotham City villain's worst nightmare. The menacing Art Deco–styled machine was designed by British movie artist Anton Furst, who won an Oscar for it before tragically committing suicide.

The Batmobile itself was remarkably armed and equipped. To make quick turns, it fired grappling hooks and used them as anchors to fling itself around corners. It also had a central pivot that, lowered to the ground, enabled the car to twist itself through 180 degrees. Two Browning machine guns were housed in the fenders (bumpers), and a side-mounted "Bat Disk" ejector released fifteen disks per second. Oil-slick dispensers and smoke machines stood ready for deployment, and the aircraft-style cockpit featured voice control.

In the 1992 follow-up film, *Batman Returns*, also directed by Tim Burton, the same Batmobile had a special mode in which the wheels and side panels disengaged from the body, leaving a thin, missilelike capsule that could squeeze through tight alleyways. The vehicle was then retired, but remains the most popular Batmobile of all the versions made.

Amazingly, in 2011 an American racing specialist built a working replica of the 1989 Batmobile using a Boeing turboshaft aircraft engine to drive the rear wheels. The car was completely road legal. **SH**

Elan M100 | Lotus

GB

1989 • 97 cu in/1,588 cc, S4 • 165 bhp/123 kW • 0–60 mph/97 kph in 6.5 seconds • 136 mph/219 kph

For many, the Elan M100 is the forgotten Lotus, sandwiched in the history books between the last V8 Esprit, and the launch of the Elise. However, a privileged few remember it as being one of the best-handling front-wheel-drive cars ever built. It was the first all-new model that Lotus had produced since 1975; developed in conjunction with General Motors, the Elan M100 was brought to market in just three years, thanks to a $55 million (£35 million) development budget. The Elan remains the only front-wheel-drive sports car that Lotus has ever built, and it has also been the most controversial. At the time Lotus fans were horrified by the configuration; many worried that a softer, less engaging model would alienate loyal customers. But while some still dismiss the M100 as "not being a proper Lotus," it has generated a cult following among the few that have driven them.

Most of these Elans received the sixteen-valve turbocharged 97-cubic-inch (1,588-cc) Isuzu engine, which could push the fiberglass-bodied car to 60 mph (97 kph) in less than seven seconds. Sales brochures announced that the chassis and robust mechanicals were designed to "allow 100 percent of its owners to use 90 percent of its performance 90 percent of the time."

Octane magazine agreed that the M100 was "conclusive proof that sports cars can be front-wheel drive, as Lotus once again leads the pack in handling technology." But sadly, in the same year as the Elan M100 was launched, the Japanese carmaker Mazda unveiled its own tribute to the original Elan in the form of its retro-styled MX-5. The cheaper, rear-wheel-drive Mazda was less predictable, but it was more entertaining. In the end, only 4,655 Elan M100s were built. **DS**

Escort RS Cosworth | Ford

GB

1989 • 122 cu in/1,993 cc, S4 • 217 bhp/162 kW • 0–60 mph/97 kph in 6.2 seconds • 137 mph/220 kph

Many carmakers boast that a model they introduce is a rally car or a race car for the road, but often their claim is no more than that—a boast. The Ford Escort RS Cosworth was an exception—the Real Deal.

In the late 1980s Ford wanted to build a car to compete in the World Rally Championship. The class it was aiming at was Group A, based on production-derived cars. At the time Ford did not have a turbocharged, four-wheel-drive, road-going Escort to turn into a rally car, so it built one specifically, based on the engine, transmission, and suspension of the Sierra Cosworth. Ford then wrapped this machine in the body of a Mark V Escort, although most of the body panels were actually quite different.

The engine was a turbocharged, 122-cubic-inch (1,993-cc) unit. The first batch of cars, built for approval for rallying, had a large Garrett T35 turbo. This developed considerable turbo-lag (a delay before spinning up to speed), which was less of an issue in rallying than it was on the road. Once approval had been given to the rallying model, a less powerful but smoother turbo was put in the road cars, making them easier to drive.

In rallying the car immediately proved its worth, coming second in the Monte Carlo Rally of 1993. On the road it was a razor-sharp tool with the reputation of a "hooligan car": huge power, four-wheel drive, incredible handing, and outrageous looks. Apart from some garish color schemes, the looks were dominated by a vast whale-tale rear spoiler. With later cars the spoiler became something that buyers could opt out of. It comes as no surprise that most rally-aware road-going purchasers chose to keep it. **JI**

R. McCLELLAND
BBS
YOKOHAMA
CONVERSION
TECHNIQUES

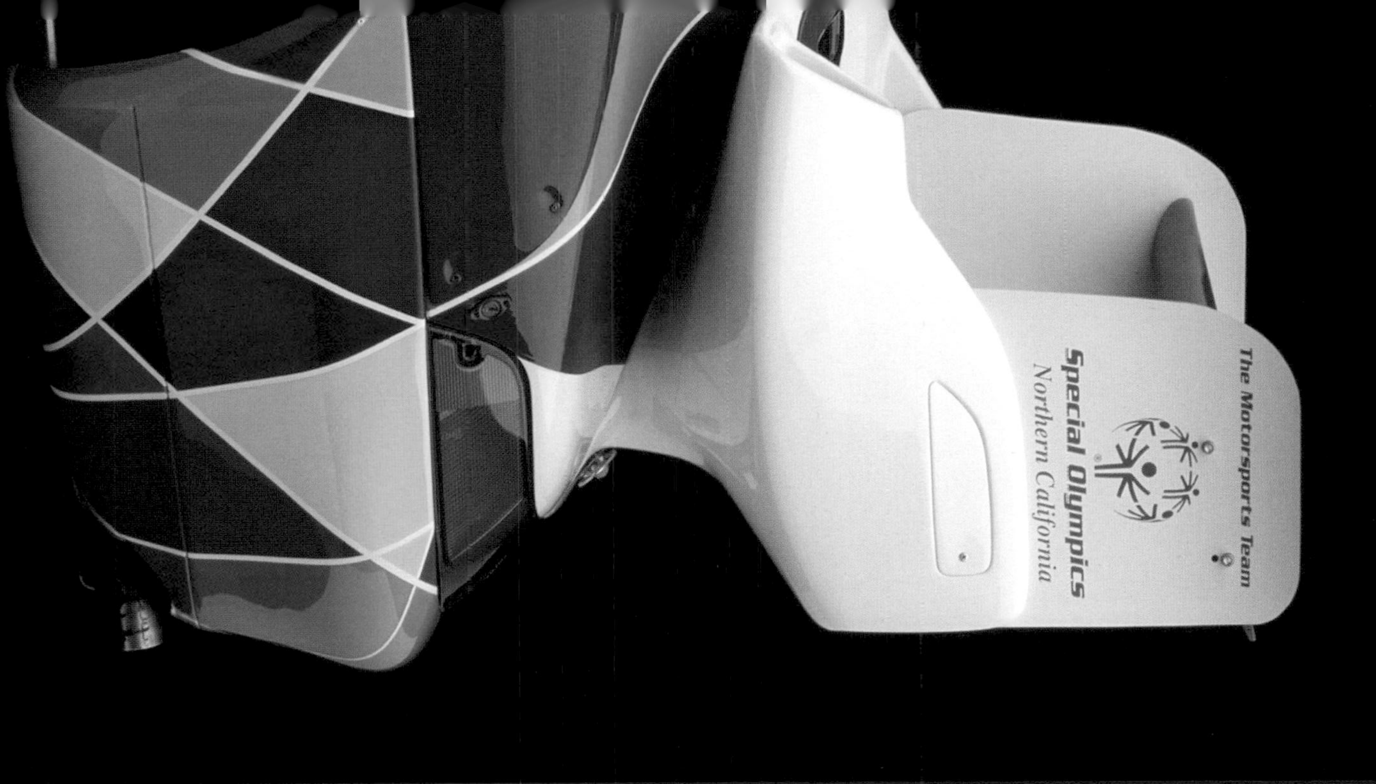

A multicolored 1997 Porsche 911 GT2—the GT2 was the racing version of the 911 Turbo.

1990–1999

The Lamborghini Diablo was famous for its striking looks, but it packed a punch with its performance too. ⊡

Tempest | Jankel (GB)

1990 • 409 cu in/6,700 cc, V8 • 535 bhp/399 kW • 0–60 mph/97 kph in 3.89 seconds • 200 mph/322 kph

Robert Jankel built lavish Bugatti Royale lookalikes, streamlined two-seaters with six wheels and 488-cubic-inch (8,000-cc) engines, plus Vauxhall-powered Lima roadsters. But when Porsche launched its 959 hypercar, Ferrari announced its F40, and Jaguar the XJ220, Jankel decided to come up with a similar super sports car.

He based his quest for power and luxury on the Corvette C4. Much of that car's original body was thrown away and replaced by Kevlar and fiberglass panels that were handmade and attached to a racing chassis. The "Tempest by Robert Jankel," as the result was officially named, came in the shape of a convertible with a detachable hardtop.

Under the hood (bonnet) now lay a supercharged and water-injected V8 engine that was designed by a Los Angeles company for drag racing. It produced a massive power output and Jankel claimed it could do a sprint through 0–60 mph (97 kph) in 3.3 seconds. That proved to be a bit optimistic, but with it's actual 3.89 seconds acceleration time it nevertheless made it into the 1992 *Guinness Book of World Records* as the fastest road car of its time for that particular sprint.

Thanks to the combination of Jankel's typically high level of finish and trim and its £130,000 ($207,000) price tag, the Tempest actually seemed cheap compared to its competitors. Only available as right-hand drive, it remains unknown exactly how many Tempests were built—but there must have been several. When the power steering pump of the cars proved to become noisy in 2000 (that's ten years after the Tempest was launched), owners could have them replaced under warranty. **JB**

Diablo | Lamborghini (I)

1990 • 348 cu in/5,700 cc, V12 • 492 bhp/367 kW • 0–62 mph/100 kph in 4.5 seconds • 202 mph/325 kph

The Diablo is one of the most famous supercars of all time. In addition to its performance, which is still sensational today, it was designed to be the greatest head-turner on the road—and it succeeded.

It was the fastest production car in the world at the time, but it was the aggressive, futuristic looks that made it the motoring icon of a generation. The low body with a big tail wing, the scissor-opening doors, the exotic alloy wheels, the huge air scoops down either side, and the pop-up headlights all contributed to an image of sheer glamorous indulgence.

Yet the design process had been controversial. Marcello Gandini drew up the first plans. The new owners of Lamborghini, Chrysler, looked at his drawings and immediately called in their Detroit design team to "soften" the shape. Gandini, who had designed the Diablo's two predecessors, was furious. He took his more angular original design to Cizeta, to use for its new car being financed by musician Gorgio Moroder and built by former Lamborghini staff.

Meanwhile, Chrysler paid for the Diablo's finishing touches and it was launched to world acclaim. Its design has certainly aged better than Gandini's Cizeta. In its eleven-year production run, almost 3,000 Diablos were built—an impressive total for a hand-built supercar costing around $150,000 (£100,000).

Over the years, the Diablo gained four-wheel drive, increased power, and a removable roof. Mechanically, though, it was never very advanced. It had none of the technical finesse of Porsche—it simply had a big, thunderous, twelve-cylinder engine right behind the driver's head. For most owners, that was enough. **SH**

Silhouette | Oldsmobile

USA

1990 • 191 cu in/3,129 cc, V6 • 120 bhp/88 kW • 0–60 mph/97 kph in 9.6 seconds • unknown

The Oldsmobile Silhouette was, along with the Chevrolet Lumina APV and Pontiac Trans Sport, one of the latests version of the "minivan," which had its U.S. origin in the Chrysler Mini-Max of the 1970s (although the ubiquitous Volkswagen vans had been around since the mid-1950s). It first appeared in 1990 as GM's "luxury" offering, but almost immediately customers complained about the amount of light being reflected off its expansive dashboard. The long dash also affected visibility—it stretched 4 feet (1.2 m) from driver to windshield, making it impossible to see the corners of its sloping nose. The van's stretched proportions reflected the considerable debate within GM as to how these new vans should look, and various alterations in following series bore out just how much of a work in progress the Silhouette continued to be.

Labeled "Dustbusters" because of their frontal resemblance to a brand of vacuum cleaner, sales of U.S. minivans rarely ever rose above sluggish. They were, however, functional. The Silhouette's internal bucket seats were in a 2+3+2 configuration that offered several ride choices. Options included power-operated sliding side doors that automatically retracted if they met an obstruction when closing, a traction control system, and child seats in the second row. It also came with composite plastic body panels that would bounce back into shape after (very) minor dings.

The Silhouette had to cope with some harsh critics that included the Insurance Institute, which gave it a poor safety rating. For whatever reason, it failed to capture a significant market share and the final model rolled off the GM assembly line in March 2004. **BS**

454 SS Pickup | Chevrolet

USA

1990 • 454 cu in/7,440 cc, V8 • 230 bhp/169 kW • 0–60 mph/97 kph in 7.2 seconds • 120 mph/193 kph

In 1990 Chevrolet started to tinker with the time-honored image of the American pickup truck. It took a short-boxed, lightweight C1500 two-wheel-drive cab and gave it a 454-cubic-inch (7,440-cc) V8 engine cooled by a heavy-duty radiator with separate coolers for the oil and transmission fluid. The engine was so large it almost filled the C1500's engine compartment, and what it did to the humble pickup was turn it into a power-packed machine.

The V8 engine of Chevrolet's 454 SS pickup had enough torque to challenge the Mustang GT in the 0–60 mph (97 kph) acceleration stakes. Not content with simply installing a new engine, Chevrolet also added a forward roll bar, quick-ratio steering, a front stabilizer bar, and the sort of luxurious internal features normally found in a luxury passenger car, such as high-back reclining red bucket seats, cruise control, and tinted windows.

The SSs were generally finished in Onyx Black, which only added to their aura of meanness, although the only external hint to high performance was the black-out grille and slotted chrome wheels.

Considering its high center of gravity, the SS handled exceptionally well on the open road. It did not seem to matter that its carrying capacity, at a touch under 1,100 pounds (500 kg), was somewhat less than other pickups, and, of course, its V8 engine made it very thirsty. Its value never really took off as expected, either. But it could cruise comfortably at high speed all day long, unlike every other pickup on the road. Most importantly, going to work was never so much fun as it was in Chevrolet's new working-class "muscle truck." **BS**

900 Carlsson | Saab (S)

1990 • 121 cu in/1,985 cc, turbocharged S4 • 185 bhp/136 kW • 0–60 mph/97 kph in 8 seconds • 130 mph/209 kph

To spice up the image of their 900 series, Saab launched the sporty Carlsson model. The car honored Saab's link with Swedish racer and two-time Monte Carlo Rally winner, Erik Carlsson, who had appeared in two James Bond novels, teaching 007 advanced driving skills.

All Carlssons were based on the standard 900 three-door hatchback, but could be distinguished by their alloy three-spoke wheels with low profile tires, aerodynamic body kit, twin chrome exhaust pipes, and discreet "Carlsson" logo and stripes. It only came in black, red, or white, with leather seats, steering wheel, and gear knob. Options were limited, but build quality was good. The dashboard had new dials and instrumentation, and the upmarket features included a steel sunroof, heated front seats, and tinted windows. The engine was a tuned version of an existing sixteen-valve turbocharged 121-cubic-inch (1,985-cc) unit with electronic fuel injection; the gearbox was a five-speed manual.

Performance was swift rather than blistering, but mid-range acceleration was impressive and the special sports suspension provided excellent handling. Road testers criticized the stodgy gearchange and harsh ride, but the Carlsson was generally well received. Just 600 Saab 900 Carlssons were produced from 1990 to 1992. They are now sought-after classics. **SH**

LS400 | Lexus (J)

1990 • 244 cu in/4-liter, V8 • 250 bhp/190 kW • 0–60 mph/97 kph in 6.7 seconds • 155 mph/250 kph

The first Lexus took the luxury car world by storm. Toyota had created a whole new brand and spent $1 billion (£630 million) developing a car to take on Mercedes, Jaguar, Cadillac, and BMW. They made 450 prototypes and test-drove them for 1.7 million miles (2.7 million km) until they were satisfied. The end car was so good, it outsold all those established brands within a year.

The LS400 had the usual luxury basics: a V8 engine, rear-wheel drive, and a plush sedan (saloon) body. What set it apart was the quality of each part and the way it was built. It pioneered features like a powered tilt-and-telescopic steering wheel, power adjustable seat belts, and an auto-dipping rearview mirror. The dashboard had a holographic digital display and a memory system that recalled your seat, belt, mirror, and steering wheel settings. It was also faster, smoother, and quieter than its rivals; the new V8 linked seamlessly to an electronically controlled four-speed automatic gearbox. Handling was comfortable rather than inspiring, but Lexus correctly judged that was what prestige buyers wanted.

When Cadillac bought and disassembled an LS400, it concluded that GM simply didn't have the capability to build such a car. The only weakness reviewers could find was its bland looks. The LS400 beat the old school at everything—other than character and style. **SH**

3000GT/GTO | Mitsubishi (J)

1990 • 183 cu in/3,000 cc, twin-turbo V6 • 320 bhp/239 kW • 0–60 mph/97 kph in 4.7 seconds • 155 mph/249 kph

This Asian muscle car seemed to arrive from outer space. It boasted virtually every trendy technological feature of the time, including four-wheel drive, four-wheel steering, active aerodynamics, and electronically controlled suspension. Even the exhaust was adjustable from sports to touring mode.

The sleek body originally featured pop-up headlights and automatically adjusting front and rear spoilers, but the pop-ups were replaced with fixed projector beam lights in 1994. Under the hood (bonnet) of the most expensive models was a smooth twenty-four-valve V6 engine with twin turbos, but confusingly the car was available with different engines in different markets at different times; some had a single overhead cam version, some a twin. And power outputs varied greatly, from a 160 bhp (119 kW) first-generation model in North America to the fire-breathing final VR-4 model in all markets. But all that gadgetry made the car heavy. It was fast, but worked better as a grand tourer rather than a sports car.

The rather cramped 2+2 was called the GTO in Japan, but Mitsubishi thought that might offend Ferrari and Pontiac fans in Europe and America so rebadged it as the 3000GT for export. It was also sold by Chrylser in the United States as the Dodge Stealth. **SH**

190E Evolution 1 | Mercedes (D)

1990 • 150 cu in/2,463 cc, S4 • 232 bhp/171 kW • 0–60 mph/97 kph in 7.3 seconds • 143 mph/230 kph

The 190E Evolution 1 was Mercedes' response to the release of BMW's M3 Sport Evolution, and was built for one purpose—to race. You could tell an Evo 1 instantly, by its wider wheel arches and inner wings, built to house racing wheels, more responsive steering, and the largest rear spoiler ever fitted to a Mercedes.

Under the hood (bonnet), the engine was that of the standard 190—save for the tweaking of things such as compression ratios, cam timings, and valve clearances that boosted the power from 195 bhp (143 kW) to 232 bhp (171 kW). The Evo 1 was faster than the stock 153-cubic-inch (2,500-cc) sixteen-valve engine, and handled superbly thanks to its stiffer springs and shocks. An all-new approach to suspension included a "ride-height" adjuster, which allowed the driver to change the car's road clearance by flicking a switch.

As the name suggests, the Evo 1 wasn't the end of things. The Evolution 2 came with bespoke 17-inch (43-cm) wheels and one of the most outrageous body kits ever given to a production car. Sure, the looks of the two cars took some getting used to for the Mercedes traditionalist, but they did their job—matching BMW's M3 in every department, attracting the attention of a younger crowd, and proving that "staid" Mercedes could produce a mad, bad car when it needed to. **BS**

Sunny/Pulsar GTI-R | Nissan

J

1990 • 122 cu in/2,000 cc, turbocharged S4 • 227 bhp/169 kW • 0–60 mph/97 kph in 5.6 seconds • 144 mph/232 kph

In some countries it was the Sunny, in others it was the Pulsar, but wherever it was, this one of the most macho hot hatches of its era. It was only produced to allow Nissan to enter the World Rally Championships (WRC), so was a race-bred rally car for the road.

The specifications were serious: permanent four-wheel drive and a turbocharged 122-cubic-inch (2,000-cc), sixteen-valve twin-cam engine. It looked, handled, and performed like a professional racer. All over the world, young men clamored to buy the new super hatch.

They loved the GTI-R's impressive-looking body kit, with louvered air intakes on the hood (bonnet), hefty rear spoiler, and deep front skirts. The chassis and suspension were race-tuned and the brakes were big ventilated discs with an antilock system. The black-swathed cockpit had deep bucket seats, air-conditioning, and a sports steering wheel. The Nissan slogan above a dark menacing photo of a black GTI-R face-on was: "Even standing still, it's still moving."

Nissan had to sell 500 homologated cars to enter the WRC, but the car was so popular that it ended up selling around 15,000. On the rally circuit, however, the GTI-R wasn't such a success. In fact, it never won a race. Various excuses were used at the time—the Dunlop tires were blamed, as was the inefficiency of the turbo intercooler in hot weather. A more likely problem was the constant political wrangling between Nissan's Japanese HQ and its European-based rally team.

The final humiliation for the GTI-R came when Scot Colin McRae won the British Rally Championship, not in the four-wheel-drive super rally car . . . but in Nissan's front-wheel-drive Sunny GTI. **SH**

MX-5/Miata/Eunos | Mazda

J

1990 • 98 cu in/1,598 cc, S4 • 114 bhp/85 kW • 0–60 mph/97 kph in 8.6 seconds • 116 mph/187 kph

The best-selling sports car of all time is a simple, lightweight, two-seater roadster. There was nothing new about this traditional formula of a soft-top and rear-wheel drive, but Mazda got everything exactly right where so many had tried and failed before.

The little car was developed by a partnership of Japanese, American, and British designers. It had more than a passing resemblance to a 1960s Lotus Elan, complete with retro pop-up headlights. And it handled like a dream thanks to perfect 50:50 weight balance, accurate steering, and double wishbone suspension.

Options included a removable hardtop, plus the normal folding soft-top, a stereo system with speakers in the seat headrests, and leather upholstery. But that's about it. The MX-5 wasn't a luxurious supercar, more a cheerfully updated MGB or Austin-Healey Sprite.

It had the same populist charm, too. The MX-5 wasn't expensive and had a tremendous reputation for reliability. It became a huge sales success, both as a cool cult car and a mass-market triumph. Enthusiastic owners' clubs sprang up all over the world, and thanks to the superb handling, it was popular on tracks, too.

The first car was called a Miata in the States, an MX-5 in the U.K., and a Eunos Roadster in Japan. The 98-cubic-inch (1,598-cc) engine was soon joined by more powerful versions, including a 167 bhp (125 kW) range-topping 122-cubic-inch (2,000-cc). The latest generation is more luxurious and, although it may have lost the pop-up lights, it is still very popular. Today, the MX-5 continues to increase its *Guinness World Records* sales figure for the best-selling sports car ever. In 2011, this stood at 900,000. **LT**

MR2 Mk II | Toyota

J

1990 • 122 cu in/2,000 cc, turbocharged S4 • 242 bhp/180 kW • 0–60 mph/97 kph in 6.2 seconds • 145 mph/233 kph

The first Toyota MR2 had been an innovative sports car with angular styling and a low price tag, but the bigger, heavier second generation seriously upped the game. The new model added a sexy supercar-style body and more powerful engines. Sales boomed as the curvy, low-slung Toyota was dubbed a "poor-man's Ferrari."

The MK II kept its straight four-cylinder engine behind the two seats and provided similar, if not quite as accurate, handling. And it still offered the chance to own a sports car for the price of an ordinary family car.

The exact models varied in different markets; options available included faster turbocharged engines and a "T-bar" two-piece glass targa top. Most boasted a rear spoiler and leather interior. The figures above are for the Japanese turbo GT version, the fastest production model; other versions offered much lower top speeds and acceleration in return for more affordable and practical ownership. Europe and the United States generally received milder tunings and more economical, greener engines, but many Japanese turbocharged cars were independently exported to enthusiasts.

Owners also had a range of body kits and uprated engine options. An MR2 MC8-R racing version was built for Le Mans, with a 600 bhp (450 kW) twin-turbo 244-cubic-inch (4,000-cc) engine, while more conventional versions performed well in the Japanese Touring Car Championship.

Within its lifespan, the MR2 MkII received many revisions, most notably to the suspension. It was eventually replaced in 2000 with the third-generation MR2, a less head-turning roadster that some nevertheless dubbed "the poor man's Boxster." **SH**

NSX | Honda

(J)

1990 • 194 cu in/3,179 cc, V6 • 276 bhp/206 kW • 0–60 mph/97 kph in 4.4 seconds • 168 mph/270 kph

The Honda NSX is considered to be Japan's first supercar. Its designers had set the Ferrari 348 as its performance benchmark, but the NSX needed to be less expensive without compromising Honda's legendary reputation for reliability.

Hand-built by 200 handpicked engineers, the NSX was the first production car to utilize an all-aluminum body. To ensure its balance was absolutely perfect, Honda called on the services of Formula 1 drivers to fine-tune its chassis. Satoru Nakajima carried out grueling endurance tests at the Suzuka F1 circuit, while the car's excellent handling was largely due to Ayrton Senna's recommendations to stiffen the suspension.

Only a year after the NSX reached North America, it was crowned *Automobile* magazine's Car of the Year. Keen drivers loved the car's impeccable handling and its everyday practicality. F1 car designer Gordon Murray drove an NSX for seven years; Ayrton Senna owned two.

The design was refreshed several times in the NSX's lifespan, and its high-revving VTEC V6 was eventually enlarged to 195 cubic inches (3,200 cc). In 2003 the NSX-R had its final makeover, and was given a fitting send off with a blast around the Nürburgring. It lapped the 13-mile (21-km) Nordschleife circuit in 7 minutes, 56 seconds, exactly the same time as the new Ferrari 360 Challenge Stradale with 50 percent more horsepower.

The NSX makes a cameo appearance in Quentin Tarantino's 1994 movie *Pulp Fiction*. When the services of the fast-talking Mr. Wolf are requested, he famously replies, "That's thirty minutes away. I'll be there in ten." As his silver NSX screeches into the shot, we can see it actually took just 9 minutes, 37 seconds. **DS**

Lotus Carlton | Vauxhall

GB

1990 • 221 cu in/3,615 cc, S6 • 377 bhp/281 kW) • 0–60 mph/97 kph in 5.2 seconds • 177 mph/285 kph

In a repeat of the collaboration between Ford and Lotus in the 1970s, General Motors and Lotus joined forces in the late 1980s to work on a high-performance version of the Opel/Vauxhall Carlton. The Vauxhall Lotus Carlton appeared in 1990 to a rapturous reception.

It was a monster of a sedan (saloon), breathing Lotus magic onto a standard car to transform it into the fastest four-door sedan in the world at that time, with a top speed more than two-and-a-half times the British legal limit. Modifications to the Carlton started with an upgraded engine and added twin turbochargers. Lotus gave the car bigger brakes and modified suspension, a limited-slip differential, and larger wheels.

Under its skin the Carlton was transformed, like a muscle man pumped up on steroids. But external differences were limited, to keep the car discreet and to avoid a hike in its insurance premiums. A rear spoiler was added, air intakes were cut into the hood (bonnet), a modest body kit was installed with wider wheel arches, and small Lotus badges adorned the car's front and rear. The Lotus Carlton was sold in only one color, Imperial Green, which was a very dark shade of British racing green that appeared almost black in dull light.

Enthusiasts loved the Lotus Carlton, but so did the criminal fraternity. It became a notorious target for car thieves and joyriders, and because the car was so fast—quicker than any police car at the time—stolen Lotus Carltons became almost impossible to catch.

GM planned to build a total of 1,100 Lotus Carltons, but that target didn't anticipate the recession that hit Europe in the early 1990s. Production ended in December 1992, 150 cars short of expectation. **SB**

300ZX | Nissan

(J)

1990 • 183 cu in/3,000 cc, turbocharged V6 • 300 bhp/224 kW • 0–60 mph/97 kph in 5 seconds • 155 mph/250 kph

The 1990 second-generation 300ZX marked a big change in the long-running Z Series of sports cars. The old 1980s styling was banished, and a sleek new design emerged. For once this wasn't the work of a famous Italian design team—it was the work of a computer.

Nissan had used the Cray supercomputer in Seattle to design an all-new sports coupe, in one of the first applications of Computer Aided Design (CAD) software to a production car. The body was lower, shorter, and wider, but the wheelbase was longer—this was an era when wheels were increasingly heading for the corners of cars generally. In 2010 *GQ* judged the 300ZX one of the most stylish cars of the previous fifty years.

The high technology didn't end with the design—the car offered four-wheel steering (for more precise cornering) and variable valve timing (for better engine response). The power steering was speed sensitive and drivers could adjust the all-independent suspension settings between "touring" and "sport."

Meanwhile, the interior was black, simple, and efficient. Most cars had a Bose hi-fi system, automatic climate control, air bags, and powered seat adjustments. The twin turbo two-seater version had supercar performance (see figures above), with a limited top speed of 155 mph (250 kph). There was a 2+2 option and, for the first time in the Fairlady Z/Z-Car series, Nissan offered a cabrio version.

American actor Paul Newman drove a Nissan 300ZX to win a Trans Am race at Lime Rock in the United States. Other wins for the car followed, including first place in the 24 Hours of Daytona and first in its class at the 24 Hours of Le Mans race. **SH**

Despite its cutting-edge technology and lavish launch party, the EB110 was unable to revive Bugatti's fortunes. ⊳

Super Saphier | Jehle (LI)

1990 • 397 cu in/6,500 cc, V12 • 1,000 bhp/746 kW • 0–60 mph/97 kph in 3.1 seconds • 249 mph/400 kph

One of the strangest-looking supercars of all time, the Jehle Super Saphier was produced in a small workshop in the tiny European country of Liechtenstein. Jehle was a specialist engineering company founded by Xavier Jehle, which mainly built the bodies for commercial trucks. It also worked on tuning De Tomaso sports cars. Eventually the two strands of the business merged, and Jehle decided to produce its own performance car.

The Saphier had a unique wedge-shaped plastic body with no conventional doors. Instead, the whole windshield and both side-window panels lifted up together to allow the driver and passenger access. This panel could be removed altogether for a very open-top driving experience. The engine was placed behind the two seats, driving the rear wheels. There were pop-up headlights and a rear glass hatch to reach a luggage area above the engine. Inside, a futuristic set of controls on the center console was marked by a grid of square buttons of different colors.

The basic version sat on the chassis of a VW Beetle; higher-powered models used Jehle's own aluminum chassis. The basic model used a 75 bhp (56 kW) four-cylinder VW Golf engine. Then the power leapt up. By 1991, an extraordinary output of 1,000 bhp (746 kW) was claimed for the 397-cubic-inch (6,500-cc) engine of the "Super Saphier." If true, this would have been one of the first 1,000 bhp cars ever produced.

The Saphier's ultimate development was the Artemis. This had a modified plastic body with two chunky wings housing massive air scoops at the rear, and unique golden reflective windows. Only three were built and of those just one sold—to an Arab prince. **SH**

EB110 | Bugatti (F)

1991 • 214 cu in/3,499 cc, turbocharged V12 • 553 bhp/412 kW • 0–60 mph/97 kph in 3.4 seconds • 213 mph/343 kph

Romano Artioli was a self-made multimillionaire who grew rich by selling Ferraris and Suzukis. He decided to invest his wealth in reviving the once-famous Bugatti brand with a quite incredible supercar: the EB110. The name came from the initials of company founder, Ettore Bugatti, and the launch date, 110 years after his birth. It was a hugely ambitious project.

Artoli built a new factory to make the EB110. In technical terms, the car was cutting-edge: the chassis was built by aircraft manufacturer Aérospatiale, the sixty-valve V12 engine was boosted by four turbos, the drivetrain was four-wheel drive, and the bodywork featured active aerodynamics. The engine could be admired through a clear cover. Scissor doors opened to a luxurious cabin. Bugatti held a launch event for the EB110 in Paris, inviting a select 1,800 guests and opening 1,000 bottles of champagne to celebrate. The price for the car was an eye-watering $500,000 (£316,000).

Bugatti then released a more extreme version, the EB110ss, with power up to 603 bhp (450 kW). F1 driver Michael Schumacher bought one in yellow, but later crashed it. Perhaps this was an omen for Bugatti. Artioli stretched himself financially with the purchase of Lotus cars and plans for a four-door model. Only around 150 EB110 cars were sold and the company went bankrupt.

This wasn't quite the end of the car, though—Dauer of Germany and B-Engineering of Italy both attempted to launch cars based on the EB110. The Bugatti name also lived on, eventually becoming part of VW and producing the similarly groundbreaking Veyron. Perhaps Artioli's dream of reviving Bugatti did come true, albeit not in the way he wanted. **RD**

Griffith | TVR (GB)

1991 • 241 cu in/3,950 cc, V8 • 240 bhp/179 kW • 0–62 mph /100 kph in 5.2 seconds • 158 mph/254 kph

The Griffith was the creation of TVR's eccentric owner, Peter Wheeler. It was intended as a spiritual successor to the TVR Griffith, which enjoyed sporting success in the 1960s. Using his outgoing S model as a starting point, Wheeler's new Griffith had a robust, triangulated steel spaceframe chassis, a wider track, wishbone suspension, and was clothed in fiberglass panels.

Modern styling and huge performance made the Griffith an instant hit. The price was a very competitive $39,000 (£24,802). More than 300 orders were taken at the launch alone, and over 3,000 were eventually made. These were TVR's golden years, and the Griffith has a cult following even today. TVRs are famous, however, for their design quirks. The Griffith's door handles were recessed behind the door, the bumpers were smoothed into the shape of the body, and the rear registration plate was backlit to remove the need for any superfluous lumps or bumps in its curvy profile. Even the petrol filler cap was hidden in the boot.

The launch model had a V8 engine originally developed by Rover, which in turn was based on a Buick design. It received a number of modifications throughout its use in the Griffith. Owners loved the sound and performance of the V8, but lively rear-wheel-drive handling made it a car only for the bravest. **RD**

Syclone | GMC (USA)

1991 • 262 cu in/4,300 cc, V6 • 280 bhp/206 kW • 0–60 mph/97 kph in 4.3 seconds • 126 mph/203 kph

Designed for racing, not working, the GMC Syclone was the first pickup to break the 200 mph (322 kph) barrier when it flew at a tick over 210 mph (338 kph) at the Bonneville Salt Flats in Utah in 1990. It had a 305-cubic-inch (5,000-cc) V6 engine tweaked to produce a frightening 549 bhp (404 kW), and had to be slowed with the help of a parachute. It was a remarkable feat considering it had the aerodynamics of a house brick.

The Bonneville Syclone and the "kinder, gentler" production version that followed the next year were high-performance versions of GMC's Sonoma pickup truck. The production Syclones had a 262-cubic-inch (4,300-cc) Vortec V6 engine and a liquid-intercooled turbocharger that gave out a still-scary 280 bhp (206 kW). In September 1991, a Syclone raced a Ferrari 348ts over a standing quarter mile and won by 0.4 seconds. They also had a braking challenge—the first production truck to have all-round antilock brakes won that, too.

As a truck it might have been wanting, considering that the owner's manual forbade carrying loads over 500 pounds (227 kg) or risk damaging the drivetrain due to the already lowered suspension. But who cares? GMC had succeeded in creating a sports car that looked like a truck, and brought a smile to the face of a generation of good ol' boy, Deep-South truckers. **BS**

780 Coupe Turbo | Volvo

(S)

1991 • 174 cu in/2,849 cc, V6 • 200 bhp/150 kW • 0–60 mph/97 kph in 8.7 seconds • 132 mph/213 kph

The publicity photo showed two models walking from a manor house to a white car. He wore a mustache, blazer, and silver tie clip; she wore a white blouse, high-waisted cream trousers, and blonde mullet hairdo. This was Volvo trying to be classy—and failing. The 780 Coupe was Volvo's big step into competing with the top German brands, but the car was about as stylish as the models that advertised it.

Yet it wasn't a bad car. The Turbo version had serious performance, the body lines had been drawn by Bertone, and the luxurious interior was Volvo's best yet. The 780 Coupe had been launched in 1985, but the fastest version, with 200 bhp (150 kW), was released only in Italy at the end of its production run in 1991. It was Volvo's most powerful model to date.

The Coupe was loaded with goodies: electric glass sunroof, massive audio-cassette system, heated seats, and elaborate climate control. The spec list was long, including leather seats, antilock brakes, self-leveling suspension, birch trim, and a limited-slip differential.

But there was no disguising the dated rear-wheel-drive platform, soggy handling, and high price. Even the body started to look old-fashioned while the car was still on sale. And sadly, the entire 780 Coupe line only sold 8,500 worldwide in five years of production. **SH**

RX-7 | Mazda

(J)

1991 • 80 cu in/1,308 cc, twin-rotor, twin-turbo • 276 bhp/206 kW • 0–60 mph/97 kph in 5.3 seconds • 153 mph/246 kph

The final generation of Mazda's rotary-engined sports coupe was perhaps the best. Mazda was now considered a high-tech innovator, and the rear-wheel-drive RX-7 was one of its showcase cars. It had a twin-rotor Wankel engine, which featured a pioneering twin sequential turbocharger that allowed an increase in power without the associated "turbo lag." Power was raised over the four years it was in production; figures for the final 276 bhp (206 kW) version are given above.

Reviewers heaped praise on the little Mazda. It was *Motor Trend* magazine's Import Car of the Year, *Playboy*'s Car of the Year, and *Road & Track* magazine called it the "most exhilarating sports car in the world." The weight distribution was almost a perfect 50:50 on each axle, giving the RX-7 unbeatable handling on the road. Different markets received different versions, including a two-seater, a 2+2, and a convertible.

In many countries, sales of the RX-7 suffered because of its cramped interior and high thirst for fuel, which could often be under 20 mpg (14 liters per 100 km). In 1992 Mazda tried to stimulate sales in the United Kingdom by cutting the price to £25,000 ($39,000) from £32,000 ($50,000). Amazingly, they tracked down and refunded the difference to those who bought the car before the price cut was announced. **SH**

Despite its design pedigree and powerful engine, the 1991 Cizeta-Moroder V16T failed to achieve commercial success. ⊡

Gold Label | Jankel (GB)

1991 • 409 cu in/6,700 cc, turbo V8 • 296 bhp/221 kW • 0–60 mph/97 kph in under 5 seconds • over 150 mph/241 kph

The man behind Panther cars had been the London-based engineer Robert Jankel, who produced luxurious retro roadsters in the 1970s. After Panther went bankrupt, Jankel moved into specialist coachbuilding at a workshop in Surrey. At first he created custom models for luxury brands, such as Bentley, Mercedes, Jaguar, Range Rover, and Rolls-Royce, for whom he built more than one hundred Silver Spur limousines. Then, in 1991, Jankel made the Gold Label—his own new and exclusive grand-touring roadster. It is now one of the world's rarest cars.

The design was slightly clunky, particularly the front end and the sloping radiator grille, but the bodywork was top quality, handmade in aluminum by Janke's team. Jankel's contacts in the exclusive car brands enabled him to buy luxury components. So the Gold Label was given a turbocharged Bentley engine and gearbox, with an overdrive that allowed ultra-relaxed cruising. It was said to drive at 70 mph (113 kph) at only 2,100 rpm.

Jankel targeted his buyers with a high-end luxury specification. The Gold Label had just two seats, which were from Recaro. The interior was trimmed in Rolls-Royce–quality Connolly leather, with matching Wilton carpet. The mohair soft-top roof with cloth headlining was power-operated and stored in a special cover. Standard features included electric seats, windows, and mirrors, and a sophisticated entertainment system.

Jankel only ever managed to build two of his exclusive Gold Labels, however. One—in blue—was sold to the oil-rich Sultan of Brunei. The location of the other remains unknown. **SH**

V16T | Cizeta-Moroder (I)

1991 • 366 cu in/6,000 cc, V16 • 540 hp/403 kW • 0–60 mph/97 kph in 4.5 seconds • 204 mph/328 kph

One of Italy's most promising supercar projects of the late 1980s/early 1990s was the Cizeta-Moroder V16T. The car was developed by a group of former Lamborghini engineers, led by the talented Claudio Zampolli, who'd teamed up with an unlikely partner: music composer Giorgio Moroder. He'd previously won three Oscars and two Grammy awards for his film music—and he was a car nut, too. For the car's body design, Marcello Gandini was employed; cars that he had previously drawn included the Lamborghini Miura, Lancia Stratos, and Lamborghini Countach.

And then there was the power plant. It was based on two V8 engines put together, making it a transversely mounted V16, with dazzling specifications. The price tag was impressive, too: $300,000 (£200,000) in 1991. The newborn supercar builder did manage to sell several though, including to the royal family of Brunei, who bought a handful of the cars. But when a financial crisis hit the wealthier parts of the world shortly after the car's launch, it soon became very difficult to sell more. Cizeta-Moroder made loss after loss. The planned target to build a car a week was never made, and wasn't helped by its virtually unknown name. To make things worse, Zampolli and Moroder split up and the car was renamed Cizeta V16T. In 1995 the company had to close its doors, by which time a reputed eight cars had been built.

However, there proved to be a few people still longing for a V16T, and some years after the company's downfall another three cars were completed. One, a unique roadster named the "Cizeta V16T Spyder TTJ," was sold for just under $850,000 (£540,000). **JB**

B2 TCW

⟨ The limited-edition Nissan Figaro was so popular that a lottery had to be held in Japan for prospective buyers.

Figaro | Nissan (J)

1991 • 61 cu in/998 cc, turbo S4 • 75 bhp/56 kW • 0–60 mph/97 kph in 12 seconds • 106 mph/171 kph

The Figaro always seemed destined to become a classic. It was launched to celebrate Nissan's fiftieth year of production under the slogan "Back to the future."

The tiny 2+2 retro convertible was built in limited numbers (20,000) for one year only, but public demand was so great it had to be sold by lottery in Japan. Winning tickets changed hands for prices far above the car's asking price of about £10,000 ($16,000).

The body was modeled on cars of the 1950s and 1960s—but much smaller, giving it a likable charm. There was an easily folded soft-top that slid into the trunk, white leather seats with contrasting piping, white steering wheel, and groovy pastel color schemes. The car featured plenty of chrome, both inside and out, at a time when few cars used it. Even the wheel hubs were distinctively white.

Underneath the retro wrapping, however, this was a modern small Japanese car. It was mostly based on the contemporary Nissan Micra, although without Nissan badging. So the Figaro came with standard hatchback features like air-conditioning, power steering, CD player and electric windows. The engine was small—a 998-cc turbocharged unit—and there was a standard three-speed automatic gearbox. This meant moderate performance to match the relaxed handling. It was a fun car rather than a sports car.

Some car journalists ridiculed the femine cuteness of the Figaro. In the U.K., *Top Gear* called it "a suburban Noddymobile." They missed the point, of course, and the owners who still run the reliable, stylish little roadster have had the last laugh as Figaro values have stayed very high. **SH**

Typhoon | GMC (USA)

1991 • 262 cu in/4,300 cc, turbo V6 • 280 bhp/209 kW • 0–60 mph/97 kph in 5.3 seconds • 124 mph/200 kph

There was a time when off-road utility vehicles like the Land Rover, G Wagon, and Landcruiser were slow, lumbering things. It was assumed that was the price you paid for off-road ability, and their wealthy owners were content to trundle along in the slow lane.

Then the Typhoon blew in and overturned that slow SUV stereotype in an instant. It started a fashion that has led to today's high performance SUVs, such as the Porsche Cayenne and Cherokee SRT8. And it suddenly made SUVs cool.

It was a standard boxy-looking two-door GMC Jimmy, but with a 4.3-liter turbo V8 under the hood (bonnet). Power went through a four-speed automatic transmission to all four wheels. Drivers learned to shift into "Drive," hold the footbrake down, accelerate until the revs were bursting, then release the brake. The big old-fashioned SUV would take off like a rocket—the quarter mile came up in just 14.1 seconds.

This performance rivaled the Ferraris and Mustangs of the day and left the previous SUV champion, the Jeep Cherokee, trailing in its dust. The Typhoon's mid-range acceleration was "among the fastest we have ever recorded," gasped *Car & Driver* magazine. Brakes were beefed up and suspension stiffened, but they couldn't make it handle like a sports car so GMC limited its top speed to 124 mph (200 kph).

The downside of all this on-road ability was that the Typhoon was a useless off-roader. And owners were told not to use it to tow anything. The almost 5,000 buyers of the Typhoon weren't worried, though—they were too busy having fun surprising sports car owners pulling away from stop signs. **SH**

Cappuccino | Suzuki

J

1991 • 40 cu in/657 cc, turbocharged S3 • 64 bhp/47 kW • 0–60 mph/97 kph in 8 seconds • 87 mph/140 kph

Kei cars are a unique Japanese category of tiny vehicles that get big tax and insurance reductions. The idea was originally to encourage Japan's car industry; today, it's more relevant that buyers don't need to own a parking space in order to buy a kei car.

The kei category has created some strange vehicles, but the Suzuki Cappuccino isn't one of them. It was simply a normal roadster that had been shrunk. The tiny two-seater car only measured 129.7 inches (329.5 cm) long and 54.9 inches (139.5 cm) wide. It weighed just 1,598 pounds (725 kg). That low weight meant that the 657-cc turbocharged engine powered the rear-wheel-drive roadster in a lively way on smaller roads and around town—but it was still limited on motorways.

Roof panels could be removed to alter the car from a closed coupe to targa-top or full convertible. The panels could be stored in the tiny trunk—although they would use up what is a miniscule luggage space.

At first the Cappuccino was only sold in Japan. In response to pleas from dealers it came to Europe in limited numbers from 1993, costing around $18,600 (£12,000). It was upgraded until its demise in 1997; specifications on later models included speed-sensitive power steering, optional three-speed automatic transmission, and antilock brakes. Some owners tried increasing performance by fitting a large motorcycle engine, tuning or "chipping" the existing unit. Up to 150 bhp (110 kW) was possible with a new turbocharger.

Like the Austin-Healey Sprite and MG Midget that inspired its design, the cheeky-looking Cappuccino has a cult following. Even BBC *Top Gear*'s Jeremy Clarkson called it "the perfect car for summer in the city." **SH**

Cinquecento | Fiat

(I)

1991 • 68 cu in/1,108 cc, S4 • 53 bhp/40 kW • 0–60 mph/97 kph in 13.4 seconds • 93 mph/150 kph

It was the cool new city car from Fiat. With a cheeky design and trendsetting mechanical brio, it was like a little slice of Italy on wheels—except that the small angular hatchback was never produced in Italy. The Cinquecento was a product of Poland.

This was the first Fiat built entirely at the old FSO factory in Tychy. It had originally been built to make a Polish version of the Fiat 126. When the old state motor industry was privatized, Fiat stepped in and bought the factory outright. Since then Tychy has built all the Cinquecentos, Siecentos, new Pandas, and new 500s for Europe. Some experts say the improvement in Fiat's build quality dates from the switch to this factory.

Today, the Cinquecento looks like an average three-door hatch, but in 1991 Giorgetto Guigiaro's design was considered very new and stylish. It was a more advanced machine than any previous Fiat minicar. The engine was in the front for a change, and it drove the front wheels, too. Independent suspension gave it good handling, galvanized panels kept rust at bay, and disc brakes and crumple zones racked up safety points.

Engines ranged from a 43-cubic-inch (704-cc) unit up to the lively fuel-injected 68-cubic-inch (1,108-cc) "FIRE" engine used in the Cinquecento Sporting. This version had lowered suspension, close-ratio gearbox, alloy wheels, and anti-roll bars. Inside there were sports seats and a leather steering wheel. It wasn't very fast, but it was fun, cheap, and economical.

Other Cinquecento versions had full-length canvas sunroofs and there was even a pioneering electric version, the Elettra, that sold relatively well in wealthier parts of Europe despite a high price tag. **SH**

Brooklands | Bentley

GB

1992 • 412 cu in/6,750 cc, V8 • 300 bhp/221 kW • 0–60 mph/97 kph in 10 seconds • 127 mph/205 kph

The Brooklands was Rolls-Royce's response to difficult economic times: a budget Bentley costing around a mere £100,000 ($150,000). The Mulsanne and Bentley Eight were dropped and the Brooklands took their place. It was meant to be a more driver-oriented luxury car, but it had an old-fashioned normally aspirated engine, old-fashioned angular design based on an old-fashioned platform—and even an old-fashioned name.

Brooklands was the racetrack where Bentley made its name in the 1930s. It wasn't a name that inspired confidence in the new car's modernity: the Brooklands circuit, in Surrey, England, hadn't hosted a race since 1939 and had since become a museum. In fact, the interior of the Bentley was like a mobile museum. It was quiet, comfortable, and traditional, with acres of polished wood and a swathe of cream leather.

It had an ancient Rolls-Royce engine under the long hood (bonnet). The drive went to the rear wheels as before, but there was a new sporting-style gearshift on the center console controlling the electronic four-speed automatic transmission. Despite the name there was actually plenty of new technology—micro-computers controlled the self-leveling suspension, air-conditioning, and instrument displays.

It was roomy and well built, but the price was still high and the performance distinctly average. In the end, the Brooklands totalled about 1,400 sales during its five-year production run.

Volkswagen took over Bentley the next year, and resurrected the Brooklands name in 2008 for the Bentley Brooklands Coupe—a roomy two-door turbocharged supercar with a 184 mph (296 kph) top speed. **SH**

Camry | Toyota

J/USA

1992 • 153 cu in/2,500 cc, V6 • 158 bhp/118 kW • 0–60 mph (97 kph) in 9.8 seconds • 124 mph/200 kph

It took the Toyota Camry fourteen years to conquer America. It was launched to an import-phobic market in 1983 and by 1992 had been enlarged and refined to meet American tastes. By 1997 it was the best-selling car in the United States—and it still is today.

Its predecessor, the old rear-wheel-drive Corona, was a rank outsider in U.S. car buyers' eyes. It was something cheap, odd, and unfamiliar from Japan. Its front-wheel-drive replacement in 1983 was bigger, more powerful, and more comfortable, but the new Camry only sold 50,000 in the United States that year.

Gradually the Camry package was fine-tuned. Engines grew, refinement blossomed, luxury evolved. The Camry was becoming a very smooth, quiet, and well-equipped car. Technology was increasing and the car was becoming more desirable. It was better built than anything from Detroit and that meant the promise of reliable and durable motoring.

By 1992 there was a bigger Camry that could be bought with a smooth 183-cubic-inch (3,000-cc) V6, automatic gearbox, and, most importantly of all, was built in the United States. The new Kentucky Toyota plant turned out as many Camrys as it could while the American public made it its fifth best-selling car that year.

Toyota kept adding more power, more luxury, and more space, until by 1997 the Camry was America's top seller. And it remained so for the next three years. It was the biggest seller in the United States again in 2002, and it has been top of the sales charts ever since. For the last three years the Camry has also been top of the list of all-American cars because more than 80 percent of its parts are now made in America—more than any other car. **SH**

RV8 | MG

GB

1992 • 241 cu in/3,946 cc, V8 • 190 bhp/140 kW • 0–60 mph/97 kph in 6.9 seconds • 136 mph/219 kph

The MGB was dead, long live the MGB! The RV8 celebrated the thirtieth anniversary of the affordable MGB roadster that had been popular with flat-cap wearers everywhere in the 1960s. It was created by Rover Group's Special Products team, and the marketing blurb described it as "what the MGB would have become if it had stayed in production" (rather than being killed off in 1980). The tragedy is that if the MGB had survived, it might well have ended up as messed with as this.

The RV8 was based on the Heritage bodyshell that was developed to help enthusiasts restore their rusting originals, but a tubbier body kit was added, along with lots of luxury touches to justify the outrageous price of £25,440 ($30,000). This was close to the price of a Morgan Plus 8 or TVR Chimaera.

A Range Rover–sourced V8 was forced under the hood (bonnet), but it kept rear brake drums, leaf springs, and a live axle. So much power in a Fred Flintstone–like chassis made cornering an adventure.

What enthusiasts wanted in 1992 was a new MG sports car to take on the car the Rover Group should have built—the 1989 Mazda MX-5. The RV8's enthusiastic reception from buyers (if not magazine road testers) finally nudged Rover to get on with it. The MGF arrived in 1995, but too late to save the company.

In all, 1,982 RV8s were produced; 1,583 going to Japan. A large number were reimported to the United Kingdom or imported to Australia, as the cars fell foul of increasingly stringent emissions regulations. Today, reimports tend to be cheaper in the United Kingdom, but there are reports that two long sea voyages encouraged rust. **LT**

Viper | Dodge

(USA)

1992 • 488 cu in/8,000 cc, V10 • 400 bhp/300 kW • 0–60 mph/97 kph in 4.6 seconds • 180 mph/290 kph

It was a retro, full-blooded sports machine taking cues from old Jaguars and Cobras to create a muscle car for a new generation. The first Viper was just a very stripped-out two-seater—with no roof or side windows. Edmunds.com explained the first car's appeal: "This wasn't some sort of alternate-fuel vehicle pointing the way to a diminished future, but a beast looking to feast on fossil fuel and fry rubber."

For 1992, this 180-mph (290-kph) machine seemed extraordinary. Some questioned whether it was even legal to build such a thing. Forget mid-engined supercars with gadgets to control the stability and traction; there wasn't even an antilock braking system. As one Chrysler boss explained at the time, the Viper's process was simple: "It makes great gobs of power and puts it through enormous wheels."

The fiberglass body looked like something rather rude. There was a side-mounted exhaust, a one-piece nose that stretched to the horizon, giant air scoops, and big wheels with very wide tires. Who needed external door handles anyway? And the only weather protection was a soft cover meant for keeping the car in a garage.

The Viper was dodgy to handle at the limit and numerous legs got scalded on the hot side pipes. But it had what it needed: a big, powerful non-turbocharged engine, all-independent suspension and a manual gearbox, and big discs at each wheel to do the braking.

The Viper has evolved since then, but original idea is still going strong. The 25,000th Viper was bought by American race driver Kurt Busch. As *Car and Driver* concluded, "This Viper is one of the most exciting rides since Ben Hur discovered the chariot." **SH**

850CSi | BMW

(D)

1992 • 342 cu in/5,600 cc, V12 • 375 bhp/279 kW • 0–60 mph/97 kph in 8.1 seconds • 147 mph/237 kph

This was BMW's new flagship line—a large two-door high-tech, high-performance coupe. It was available with a 244-cubic-inch (4,000) V8 engine in the 840ci, and with a 342-cubic-inch (5,600-cc) V12 producing 375 bhp (279 kW) in the line-topping 850Csi. It was designed by Klaus Kapitza, who also worked on less exciting products such as the Ford Escort and Sierra. His plans were drawn with the help of computer-aided design systems, which were still unusual at the time.

The BMW 8 Series debuted at the Frankfurt Motor Show in 1989. It almost seemed like BMW's first supercar. Its technical innovations included an electronic throttle, four-wheel steering, and the first use of a six-speed manual gearbox with a V12 engine in a roadcar. However, the 850Csi was no lightweight racer; it was a luxuriously appointed grand tourer, lavishly and expensively equipped inside with electrically adjustable leather seats, electric steering column,

electric sunblind, electric sunroof, and climate control. The beautiful exterior included pop-up headlights and frameless doors. Contemporary U.S. TV commercials for the 8 Series said, "experience the unexpected"; such cryptic gibberish didn't deter the buyers, though. Famous owners included boxer Oscar de la Hoya.

BMW briefly planned an even more powerful version of the 850 Csi, called the M8, tuned to 550 bhp (410 kW). However, only one was made. It was locked away with other rare BMW prototypes in their "Giftschrank" or "quarantine" area, and has rarely been seen by the public.

The 8 Series may have been a step too far for BMW. The market for large, expensive, thirsty, and overtly luxurious coupes was not good at the time of the recession and Gulf War. Just over 30,000 were sold worldwide in seven years, so BMW dropped its flagship altogether in 1999. **RD**

Renault was initially hesitant about the Twingo's design, but its fun, fresh look immediately appealed to buyers.

Hyena | Lancia (I)

1992 • 122 cu in/2,000 cc, S4 • 250 bhp/186 kW • 0–60 mph/97 kph in 5.4 seconds • 143 mph/230 kph

In the 1980s Lancia had made name and fame in the international rally championship with their notorious Delta HF Integrales. In fact, that car still won rallies as late as 1992, over a decade after it was introduced. The ultimate variant, however, was realized when Zagato supervised a makeover that year for the Lancia Hyena.

The Hyena came in the shape of a compact coupe based on Integrale underpinnings. The idea for the car was dreamed up by Dutch Lancia dealer and Zagato fan Paul Koot, as early as 1986. Koot contacted the Italian coachbuilder with his plan, and while Zagato wasn't in the healthiest of financial states around that time, it decided this might be a money spinner.

Koot assisted throughout the process of design and development and the car was launched in Brussels in January 1992. The process of building the Hyena was rather complicated, as the cars were shipped from Lancia's factory in Italy to the Netherlands to get rid of their bodywork and interiors. Next they were transported back to Milan, where a new lightweight aluminum body was fitted at Zagato's. After that they once again returned to the Netherlands to be finished.

With some 440 pounds (200 kg) less weight than the standard Delta, better aerodynamics, plus plenty of power from its turbocharged engine, the Hyena wasn't just a pretty face but a seriously fast car, too.

Zagato approached Lancia to have 500 Hyenas built, but Lancia refused, so Zagato and Koot decided to do it themselves. The one hundred cars they planned never materialized, though. Just twenty-six Hyenas were built, making them one of the more desirable and collectible of modern Lancias. **JB**

Twingo | Renault (F)

1992 • 73 cu in/1,200 cc, S4 • 55 bhp/41 kW • 0–62 mph/100 kph in 13.7 seconds • 94 mph/151 kph

The first Twingo was a cutting-edge city car with a small engine, cheeky looks, and modern interior. Today it seems fairly ordinary, but at the time it was a risky design—it appeared very contemporary and likely to only appeal to young buyers. Renault's head of design, Patrick Le Quement, had seen the dull Renault 9 and 11 fail miserably, so he famously told his bosses that "the greatest risk is not to take any risks."

The little Twingo was considered almost revolutionary in design terms. Some of the features seemed almost toylike. The public's instant reaction was positive, with a surge of sales proving the risk was worth taking. Ironically it was middle-aged buyers who were most taken with the Twingo's charm.

The basic layout was a two-door, front-wheel-drive hatchback, with a sloping hood (bonnet) line from bumper to roof and wheels right in each corner of the body. It was only built in left-hand drive.

The use of internal space was pioneering; the rear seat slid to allow either more boot space or legroom. Somehow, in a car that was smaller than the Clio hatchback, there was more space than in the grand Renault 25 luxury sedan (saloon). Reviewers were amazed by the uncluttered interior that featured a central instrument panel, with no dials in front of the driver, only a row of warning lights.

To keep the price low, the only optional extra available was color. A Twingo came in pastel shades previously unused on production cars, like green, pink, and light brown. With deliberate contrariness, Le Quement insisted that white, the most popular car color in France at that time, was not available. **SH**

XJ220 | Jaguar

GB

1992 • 213 cu in/3,498 cc, V6 • 542 bhp/404 kW • 0–60 mph/97 kph in 3.6 seconds • 200 mph/320 kph

During the 1980s there was a group of people in Jaguar's engineering department that met informally as The Saturday Club. It was headed by chief engineer Jim Randle, and the group began planning a concept car intended to suit a new motor racing category, the "Group B" supercar formula. They made by hand a shape for the chassis, and a body style was created for it by Jaguar's chief designer, Keith Helfet. The concept was given the code name XJ220.

To show the world what Jaguar was capable of, the XJ220 concept was given an airing on its stand at the British Motor Show in Birmingham in 1988. The reaction to it was rapturous, and it was the unrivaled star of the show. Encouraged by the excitement the car generated, Jaguar began work on turning it into a limited-run production model.

The result was a mid-engined supercar produced by Jaguar in collaboration with Tom Walkinshaw Racing. It had a 213-cubic-inch (3,498-cc) twin-turbocharged V6 engine and was built in Oxfordshire. A modified model clocked a top speed of 217 mph (350 kph), and held the record as the world's fastest road car until it was later beaten by the McLaren F1.

Soon after production began in 1992, a press launch was staged at an Austrian racetrack. One of the journalists who attended was a man from the *Guardian* newspaper. Driving the car at high speed, he missed a gearshift and wrecked the gearbox of a $620,000 (£400,000) car. The story made headlines around the world.

In the two years the XJ220 was produced, a total of 281 cars were made. Famous owners have included Elton John and the Sultan of Brunei. **SB**

Rocket | Light Car Company

GB

1992 • 65 cu in/1,070 cc, S4 • 171 bhp/127.5 kW • 0–60 mph/97 kph) in 3.8 seconds • 150 mph/240 kph

The Light Car Company's (LCC) only product was the extraordinary Rocket car, created by the racing car designer Gordon Murray. The formula was ingenious. Murray reckoned that if the car was light enough, the engine wouldn't have to be very big. So he managed to keep the Rocket's weight down to an amazing 840 pounds (381 kg) and used a tuned motorcycle engine to power it. He was right; performance was shattering and handling was superb.

It looked like a small 1950s grand prix car. Despite the small size and a weight that made even a Caterham seem portly, the Rocket came with all the technology a driving enthusiast needed: fully independent suspension all around, coil springs and adjustable shock absorbers, and four-wheel racing-quality disc brakes. The rear-mounted engine drove the rear wheels.

It was road legal, but it was one of the least practical cars ever built. There was no roof, doors, windows, windshield, or luggage space. Drivers would usually wear raincoats, gloves, hats, earplugs, and goggles. Under a rear cover, there was a tiny passenger seat for occasional use. The passenger's legs had to squeeze either side of the driver's seat. The power was so awkward to apply that there was a low ratio section of the sequential gearbox for stopping and starting, then a high ratio for cruising, making a total of ten gears.

It was built at a small workshop in the Oxfordshire countryside by a team that included several former Formula 1 engineers. At around $59,000 (£38,000) it was so cheap that LCC probably lost several thousand on each one of the forty they sold. Nevertheless, it has since been relaunched and is still on sale at the time of writing. **SH**

Arnold Schwarzenegger uses his Hummer H1 to aid him with a political campaign in Sacramento, California, 2005.

Roadster | Panoz (USA)

1992 • 305 cu in/5,000 cc, V8 • 305 bhp/227 kW • 0–60 mph/97 kph in 4.3 seconds • 140 mph/225 kph

It was America's version of the classic Lotus Seven, which meant it had to have more of everything. The original Lotus doctrine was to make everything ultralightweight. Panoz followed that to its logical conclusion; it used lightweight aluminum for both its body, and (eventually) its chassis, too. This made it America's first "aluminum intensive vehicle."

And, being an American car, it scrapped the idea of a small four-cylinder engine or even a motorcycle power plant. Instead, the Panoz used the big growling 5-liter V8 engine from the Ford Mustang.

Car designer Freeman Thomas was employed to draw up something far more interesting than the old Lotus and Caterham long box that hadn't changed for decades. Thomas was used to unconventional cars, having designed the new Beetle for VW and the first Audi TT. His plan for the new roadster was a glamorous updating of the Seven concept—like a Caterham that had been working out and now had muscled curves. It was short, squat, and wide, with wheels right in each corner. And it looked like it meant business.

The spec was simple: the big V8 was matched to a five-speed gearbox and rear-wheel drive. As many parts as possible were sourced from Ford, keeping buying and running costs low. The fat tires and sports suspension meant superb grip and handling.

In 1996 the updated "AIV" Roadster was launched. It had the new aluminum chassis and a more powerful Ford V8, with a bulging hood (bonnet) air scoop. A few of these cars came with a supercharger, for presumably insane performance that hasn't been recorded. The figures above are for the standard AIV Roadster. **SH**

H1 | Hummer (USA)

1992 • 397 cu in/6,500, V8 • 194 bhp/145 kW • 0–60 mph/97 kph in 17.8 seconds • 83 mph/134 kph

We have Arnold Schwarzenegger to thank for the Hummer H1. He fell in love with the military Humvee when it shot to stardom in 1991's Operation Desert Storm, and he just had to have one.

The Humvee, or M998 Series High Mobility Multi-Purpose Wheeled Vehicle (HMMWV) was made by AM General for the U.S. Army and wasn't street legal. Arnie did manage to get one, but continued to campaign for a civilian version—and he had plenty of support. In a road test of the H1, *Motor Trend* wrote, "[The] Modern chariot of the military, the AM General HMMWV has become a mechanical symbol of freedom. The mere sight of one conjures patriotic spirit and forces a smile."

AM General launched the civilian Hummer in 1992 and Schwarzenegger bought the first two off the line. Starting at $93,650 (£59,806), the line included a soft-top, a four-door hardtop SUV, a pickup truck, and the collectible Alpha Wagon. It became known as the H1 when GM launched the H2 in 2003.

Driving it on road was like piloting a large commercial truck. The interior was spartan and surprisingly cramped. Off-road, however, it was superlative, capable of clambering over a 22-inch (56 cm) obstacle, climbing a 60 percent side slope, and fording 30 inches (76 cm) of water.

By 2008 no one much felt like cheering when discussing foreign wars, and gas prices were starting to smart. The financial crash hit the auto industry hard and Hummer's global sales fell from 66,261 in 2007 to 37,573 in 2008. The next year, Hummer became a victim of GM's bonfire of the brands. Will it be back? It's doubtful. Used H1s sell for less than half their price new. **LT**

REFORM 1
TIE-DOWN

968 Club Sport | Porsche

D

1992 • 182 cu in/2,990 cc, S4 • 240 bhp/179 kW • 0–60 mph/97 kph in 6.1 seconds • 160 mph/257 kph

The 944 was Porsche's best-selling model. Originally, the German brand had simply intended to refresh the 183-cubic-inch (3,000-cc) version to extend sales into the 1990s, but engineers got so carried away that over 80 percent of the car's key mechanical components ended up being replaced or upgraded. So Porsche decided to relaunch the heavily revised car as the 968.

They gave the car a new streamlined look and better-equipped cabin than the outgoing 944. The recessed headlight design was borrowed from its bigger brother, the 928, to create a new corporate family "face" and brand identity for Porsche.

The 182-cubic-inch (2,990-cc) water-cooled power plant was the largest four-cylinder production engine of its generation, and capable of monumental torque. Clever variable-valve-timing gave the 968 almost as much power as the hottest 944 Turbos, but its power delivery through all six gears was instantaneous and not hampered by the turbo-lag of its predecessor.

Road handling and balance of all 968 variants was superb, honed from the original 924 platform over twenty years of development. Near-perfect weight distribution and tweaked suspension earned the Club Sport version *Autocar & Motor*'s Car of the Year Award. This stripped-out, track-focused Porsche sold for around £30,000 ($47,000) in the United Kingdom, £5,000 ($7,800) less than the standard car. It threw away luxuries like rear seats, electric windows, central locking, and its air bag to save around 110 pounds (50 kg). A favorite among track day enthusiasts, today the 968 is becoming increasingly rare and is now a highly sought-after modern classic. **DS**

M3 | BMW

D

1992 • 182 cu in/2,990 cc, S6 • 282 bhp/210 kW • 0–60 mph/97 kph in 5.9 seconds • 160 mph/250 kph

The original BMW M3 had proved to be an instant classic. When the E30 3 Series model that car was based on was replaced with the new E36 model, it only seemed right that BMW make an M3 version of that one, too. Expectations were high as it was launched at the Paris Motor Show. The brochure confidently stated, "The letter M is BMW's pledge to supreme performance in technology and on the road."

Initially available only as a coupe, the M3 had a quick-revving straight six-cylinder engine with double variable camshaft control (VANOS in BMW-speak), developing 282 bhp (210 kW) with six-speed manual transmission and rear-wheel drive. The car was bigger than the previous model, though, and despite the extra power it didn't perform quite as crisply as the original four-cylinder M3.

This version was the first M3 to be made in right-hand drive. Various specials were built for road and track use, including the M3 Evo that gave 316 bhp (236 kW) via a complex (and occasionally troublesome) sequential manual gearbox.

Two years after its launch BMW extended the line, offering the M3 as a cabriolet and a four-door sedan (saloon)—a first for an M3. The four-door was born partially in order to fill a gap in BMWs lineup, as they were without an M5 (based on the larger 5 series) for nearly three years.

Despite perhaps lacking the sparkle of the original M3, it was more user-friendly and nearly 70,000 examples were built. Their popularity when new meant that they subsequently became the most affordable of the famous BMW "M" cars to buy used. **RD**

zoom

‹ Although it may look like a Smart car, the Renault Zoom concept car preceded that vehicle by six years.

Zoom | Renault (F)

1992 • electric • 34 bhp/25 kW • 0–60 mph/97 kph in 6 seconds • 75 mph/121 kph

Concept cars allow manufacturers to display ideas for the future, which make it into production or not depending on the reaction they get. Renault's 1992 Zoom is one of the most innovative and exciting concept cars of the last twenty years. It was a small two-door, two-seater city car shown at the Paris Motor Show six years before anyone had heard of the Smart car.

The Zoom was certainly a glimpse into the future; the engine was a 35 bhp (25 kW) electric motor with a 93-mile (150-km) range for emission-free motoring. The doors opened in a "beetle-wing" scissor action to reduce space. The interior was futuristic considering that this was the year the first Hummer was launched, *Wayne's World* was filling movie theaters, and Whitney Houston was at the top of the charts. Inside the Zoom there was a special console between the wide bench seats, housing a "communications center" with a hands-free mobile phone system and satellite navigation. The front and rear glass extended high over the passengers, forming a light, airy cabin trimmed in new zany colors. A CD audio system was built into the steering wheel.

The most innovative system was the adjustable wheelbase. At speed the rear wheels would swivel into an elongated position behind the car to improve stability. For parking, they could be tilted forward to reduce the wheelbase and make it easier to fit into small spaces. The bodyshell was made of a self-healing composite material colored during its manufacture so it would never need painting.

Sadly the Zoom never made it into Renault showrooms, but many of its features have since appeared on production cars. **SH**

Calibra Turbo 4x4 | Vauxhall (D/UK)

1992 • 122 cu in/2,000 cc, turbocharged S4 • 201 bhp/150 kW • 0–60 mph/97 kph in 6.4 seconds • 152 mph/245 kph

The Calibra was a two-door coupe version of Opel's unexciting Vectra family car. It looked cool and attracted a cult following, but at launch it had the same engines and handling as its rather average sedan (saloon) sisters.

The gorgeous fastback design by American Wayne Cherry was so sleek that the Calibra was found to be the world's most aerodynamic car, and it remained so for the next ten years. It was badged a Chevrolet, Vauxhall, Holden, or Opel, depending on the country it was in, and sold almost a quarter of a million.

The original Calibras came with an eight- or sixteen-valve 122-cubic-inch (2,000-cc) engine, but in 1992 a high-performance four-wheel-drive turbo model arrived, and in 1993 a smooth, refined 153-cubic-inch (2,500-cc) V6 was added. Slight changes in body details meant that these faster Calibras sadly had more average aerodynamic drag figures.

Nevertheless, the Calibra Turbo was much more sophisticated than a standard Vectra. It had a sporty six-speed manual gearbox, sixteen-valve twin-cam engine, and technically complex all-wheel-drive system developed by Steyer-Puch-Daimler. The stiffer and lower suspension improved the handling. So it was a four-seater with all the practicality of a Vectra but with very swift performance and sports car handling.

However, many buyers experienced problems with the fragile four-wheel-drive system. The transfer box was found to be so sensitive that owners were advised to keep all their tire-tread depths within 0.08 inches (2 mm) of each other and change all the tires at the same time. This meant that if there was a puncture in one tire, owners often had to buy a whole new set. **SH**

4/4 | Morgan

GB

1993 • 110 cu in/1,796 cc, S4 • 114 bhp/84 kW • 0–60 mph/97 kph in 8.3 seconds • 112 mph/180 kph

The Morgan 4/4 was the Morgan Motor Company's first ever four-wheeled vehicle. Introduced in 1936, it has been in continuous production ever since—making it the world's longest-running production vehicle. 4/4 means "four wheels, four cylinders," and this designation was about all that remained the same as the 4/4 evolved over the decades to include two- and four-seat versions and drophead coupes, all powered by innumerable four-, six- and, eight-cylinder engines of ever-increasing horsepower.

In 1993 the Morgan 4/4 was given its most powerful engine to date—a Ford 1800 Zetec four-cylinder engine that generated 114 bhp (84 kW). This took it from a standing start to 60 mph (97 kph) in just over 8 seconds. (Morgan has never produced its own engines, preferring Ford components whenever possible.) The elegant 4/4 was suddenly transformed into a reasonably mean performer, and when road tested it drew the comment, "Boy, does this chassis communicate, yapping away like Ruby Wax. . ."

Morgans change slowly. The rate of production is still about nine cars a week, the same number as in the early 1920s. Waiting lists are long—about five years—and its curves have a worldwide patent that prevents a Morgan from ever being copied. The 1993 4/4, like all Morgans before it and since, possessed a sort of antiappeal. It wasn't always comfortable, nor was it always practical, and sometimes it wasn't even weatherproof. But it handled like a classic sports car should, without the aid of power-assisted devices, and offered its driver an affinity with the road that was at best a hit-or-miss "option" in other, more expensive sports cars. **BS**

Camaro Z28 | Chevrolet

USA

1993 • 350 cu in/5,733 cc, V8 • 275 bhp/205 kW • 0–60 mph/97 kph in 6.5 seconds • 150 mph/241 kph

The Camaro was Chevrolet's great survivor, having faced extinction over three generations. First there was the oil crisis, which had eliminated the Camaro SS. In 1975 the car's third generation was announced, but it didn't hit the road for seven years. In the late 1980s a sales slump again had executives talking, this time about turning it into a front-wheel version of Chrysler's sedate Lumina sedan (saloon). Then in 1993, just as it was looking as though the Camaro had irretrievably lost its way, it remembered who it was.

The '93 Camaro couldn't have done more to reassert everything that the name had stood for, and it became the standard by which other sports coupes were measured. Its supersleek design was sheathed in dent-resistant plastic panels made from a mixture of polyester resin and chopped-up fiberglass. It had dual air bags and antilock brakes, and a redesigned suspension system that replaced the bone-rattling rides of previous Camaros with a softer one that didn't sacrifice handling. And for those who believe prestige is everything, it returned, unmodified, to once again pace the Indianapolis 500 for the first time since 1982.

There was no money for the Camaro's usual midgenerational update. In desperation, Corvette and Cadillac parts were scrounged by GM's own engineers, who were determined to keep it going. Declining sales, however, led to the series being halted in 2002. The fifth generation Camaro didn't appear until 2009.

Incidentally, the name Camaro had no actual meaning. When a GM executive was once asked what it meant, the reply was 'a small, vicious animal that eats Mustangs'. **BS**

Supra Mk4 | Toyota

J

1993 • 183 cu in/2,997 cc, twin-turbo S6 • 320 hp/239 kW • 0–60 mph/97 kph in 4.9 seconds • 155 mph/200 kph

When Toyota launched the Mk4 Supra, the car took a serious step forward in terms of performance. It had begun life as the offspring of the Celica, but by this time the Supra was a car in its own right—although it did share mechanical parts with the Lexus Z30 Soarer.

The Mk4 lost the sharp, angular design of the previous model and wore a more bulbous, rounded body. That effect was enhanced by the new car being slightly shorter and wider.

There were two new engines. Both were 3-liter, six-cylinder units, but one was fitted with twin turbos. For the European and American markets, this produced 320 bhp (239 kW), while the Japanese version made slightly less. The two turbos worked in tandem, with the second coming in at higher revs to reduce turbo lag and give a more instant response to throttle input.

The turbo Supra had a six-speed manual gearbox, although an automatic was available. It also had more potent brakes. The new car made more use of aluminum in the chassis and suspension as well as lightweight materials elsewhere to trim any excess flab. That gave the Supra near-supercar performance. Although the car's top speed was limited to 155 mph (200 kph), an unrestricted version can reach over 180 mph (290 kph).

The Supra Turbo has become a stalwart of the drifting and drag racing fraternity. The ease with which more power can be teased out of the standard engine also made it a hit with tuners. A 700 bhp (520 kW) example was the star of the 2001 movie *The Fast and The Furious*. You could have one just like it, if you had $70,000 (£44,000) to spare. **JI**

Impreza Turbo | Subaru

J

1993 • 119 cu in/1,944 cc, F4 • 208 bhp/155 kW • 0–60 mph/97 kph in 5.8 seconds • 137 mph/220 kph

Think of a Japanese car with a rallying pedigree and real credibility on the road. Chances are you thought of the Subaru Impreza Turbo. Subaru had built cars since the 1950s, but the Impreza Turbo was the one that made them a household name outside of Japan. The car's engine and drive system were key to this. The engine was a 2-liter boxer, with two rows of cylinders opposing each other, lying flat. This made for a punchy yet compact unit and is now a Subaru trademark.

In the 1993 Impreza Turbo the engine produced a healthy 208 bhp (155 kW)—not bad for a car with a wheelbase of only 88 inches (2.2 m). The transmission system was full-time four-wheel drive with a center viscous coupling that split the power between the front and rear wheels. There was also a limited-slip differential at the rear for more traction. The suspension, particularly on the higher-spec WRX models, was performance tuned.

What this resulted in was a car with stunning real-world performance. The Impreza Turbo was not just fast in a straight line but handled like, well, a rally car. Grip levels were phenomenal and on a twisty road a well-driven Impreza could keep up with virtually anything.

Meanwhile, as the road car was gained a cult following, the Impreza WRC was stacking up rally win after rally win. To mark this, Subaru created a number of special editions for the road, including cars honoring the late drivers Colin McRae and Richard Burns.

On top of its performance, the Impreza Turbo was a car you could live with every day. Time and time again Subaru come out top in reliability surveys. Fast, agile, and well made; it's no wonder it's become a legend. **JI**

LISTER STORM

THE SUPERCAR FOR THE REAL WORLD

🅒 This simple advertisement for the 1993 Lister Storm belies the car's eye-watering £220,000 ($350,000) price tag.

Storm | Lister (GB)

1993 • 427 cu in/6,996 cc, V12 • 546 bhp/407 kW • 0–60 mph/97 kph in 4.1 seconds • 208 mph/335 kph

Small British tuning specialists Lister became known in the 1980s as experts in increasing the size of their customers' Jaguar XJS engines. Using this engineering expertise, Lister boss Laurence Pearce decided to jump on the growing supercar bandwagon of the early 1990s and create the company's own supercar.

After two years in development the Lister Storm was unveiled. With their trademark twin-supercharged, bored-out 427-cubic-inch (6,996-cc) Jaguar V12 driving the rear wheels through a high-performance Getrag six speed gearbox, the it was acclaimed as the world's fastest four-seater sedan (saloon) at the time.

It had a lightweight aluminum honeycomb chassis with aluminum and carbon-fiber body panels. The monstrous engine was pushed back almost into the cockpit to help balance the weight distribution. It was a 2+2, which made it unusually practical in the supercar class. It even had a sizable trunk. The Storm's luxury features included a fully leather-trimmed interior, air-conditioning, hi-fi system, and electric seats.

The body styling, however, was fairly eccentric, and the handmade car struggled to compete with the luxury and build quality of its rivals. At £220,000 ($350,000), the price was stratospheric. Only four road-going cars were ordered, of which three survive.

Having built road cars, Lister was allowed to create another six race versions of the Storm to compete in the 24 Hours of Le Mans race and international GT championships. Lister finally won the FIA GT World Championship in 2000, with factory driver Jamie Campbell-Walter taking the driver's championship and Lister bagging the constructor's title. **SH**

F150 Lightning | Ford (USA)

1993 • 351 cu in/5,751 cc, V8 • 250 bhp/179 kW • 0–60 mph/97 kph in 7.6 seconds • 110 mph/177 kph

"A Mustang GT with a cargo bed"—that was how Ford described their F150 Lightning when it came out in 1993. They had turned one of their stalwarts, which just happened to be a pickup truck, into a performance car.

The F150 has been the best-selling truck in America for thirty-four years. In 1993 Ford introduced the Lightning version to compete with Chevrolet's 454 SS sports truck. Neither manufacturer created this niche for performance pickups in the car market—that accolade most likely rests with the Shelby Dakota.

However, the F150 Lightning was undoubtedly the most successful vehicle of its kind. Motor-racing champion Jackie Stewart helped tune the chassis of the single-cab pickup. The center of gravity was lowered and the chassis was stiffened. The engine was particularly special—a 351-cubic-inch (5,751-cc) V8 with the cylinder head from Ford's GT40 Le Mans car. It produced 250 bhp (179 kW), which ran through an automatic gearbox that maximized the change-up point in each gear.

The Lightning had a special air-intake manifold, alloy wheels, electrically adjustable bucket seats, and a limited-slip differential for extra traction. The result was a truck with a straight-line performance to match many European sedans (saloons). It look less than 8 seconds to reach 60 mph (97kph); the top speed was limited to 110 mph.

But even more surprisingly, the Lightning could handle. The work on the chassis had paid off, because it could tackle corners at speeds unheard of in a normal pickup. The downside was a rock-hard ride. And the choice of colors—red or black. **JI**

Celica | Toyota (J)

1993 • 122 cu in/2,000 cc, turbocharged S4 • 251 bhp/187 kW • 0–60 mph/97 kph in 6.1 seconds • 148 mph/238 kph

By the early 1990s, the Celica had become an enduring and familiar global badge. The new sixth generation was perhaps the most beautiful of all, with exotic curves, distinctive headlights, and a pert, purposeful rear end. It was available as a two-door coupe, three-door liftback, or a convertible. All versions were front-engined, with a range of engine sizes to choose from, and most were front-wheel drive, although a four-wheel-drive version was also available.

After twenty-two years the Celica had evolved into a popular mainstream sports coupe. It was the modern grand tourer for the era and was backed by Toyota's world-class build quality and reliability.

Toyota claimed this Celica was faster, more powerful, safer, and more spacious than any previous model. It was lighter, but also more rigid, with improved handling from redesigned MacPherson strut suspension.

Top of the line was the most powerful Celica to date—the GT-4. The four-wheel-drive coupe had been consistently improved with feedback from Toyota's factory team in the World Rally Championship. It had a turbocharged engine producing a hefty 251 bhp (187 kW) for the Japanese version, slightly less for export models. Performance figures for the Japanese GT-4 are given above. **SH**

Fleetwood 75 | Cadillac (USA)

1993 • 350 cu in/5,733 cc, V8 • 185 bhp/138 kW • 0–60 mph/97 kph in 10.5 seconds • 127 mph/204 kph

Cadillac's Fleetwood series had a long and distinguished history. It had only been a series in its own right since 1985, but the Fleetwood name goes way back. Henry Fleetwood was a coachbuilder in seventeenth-century England, and out of this grew the Fleetwood Body Company of Fleetwood, Pennsylvania, which was bought by Cadillac in 1925. Fleetwood was considered one of the best bodywork companies in the United States, and from 1925 onward it worked exclusively for Cadillac.

The Cadillac Fleetwood 75 was distinguished by the fact that at 225 inches (571 cm), bumper to bumper, it was the longest production car ever built in the United States. The car could not really compete with similar specification models that were being imported from Europe, however. It mainly sold because it was cheaper, although at $30,000 (£19,000) it was hardly a bargain. The model was also a weighty car and, if not exactly ugly, it was fairly plain and unexciting. Nevertheless, many U.S. drivers want their cars plain and unexciting, as long as they are big, and this second generation of Cadillac Fleetwood remained the longest production car ever, right through until Cadillac ceased production of the model in 1996, after selling more than 90,000 of them. **MG**

Clio Williams | Renault

F

1993 • 122 cu in/1,998 cc, S4 • 145 bhp/233 kW • 0–60 mph (97 kph) in 7.8 seconds • 134 mph/215 kph

The Clio Williams was a lightweight hatch that made up for a modest power output with fabulous handling characteristics. The original Clio had won the European Car of the Year title in 1991, and Renault cashed in on its ties with the Williams F1 team by using their name on this model. There was no input from Williams, despite a plaque on the dash of launch models.

Buyers quickly snapped up the cars in what was supposed to be a limited-edition run. All were the same striking shade of blue and had gold-colored alloy wheels. They were built on a basic Clio platform with uprated gearboxes and suspension, and had a wider front track. These changes transformed the handling, the uprated engine gave more go, and the Williams name added a touch of glamour. Its relatively low price meant it was, and still is, a common sight on track days throughout Europe. It came sixth in a Car of the Decade feature by *Evo* magazine.

However, the exclusivity of these first cars was soon threatened. The Williams I had become a victim of its own success. Renault seized on the demand and launched a second model, then later a third. Original buyers were outraged. Aside from some updated safety features and a sunroof, little had been changed. Total production was a not-so-exclusive 12,100. **RD**

Impreza WRX | Subaru

J

1993 • 150 cu in/2,457 cc, F4 turbo • 320 bhp/236 kW • 0–60 mph/97 kph in 4.8 seconds • 158 mph/254 kph

In the world of motorsport, Subaru is to rallying, what Ferrari is to Formula 1. However, unlike the Italian brand, Subaru's ascent has been largely due to a single model—the brilliant Impreza WRX. In the early 1990s, following changes to the World Rally Championships (WRC) regulations, Subaru began development of a purpose-built rally car to replace the ageing Legacy RS. In 1993 the factory-prepared Impreza 555 rally car started to impress on the WRC stages. Within a year, motorsport fanatics were lining up to get their hands on the turbocharged all-wheel-drive production version—the WRX. Between 1995 and 1997 the Subaru World Rally Team took three successive manufacturers' titles. Colin McRae also became the first Briton to take the driver's championship in 1995.

While the WRX was the company's best seller, the more serious (and wealthier) driver could have the in-house tuning company, Subaru Technica International (STI), tweak the engine and suspension to create a rally-bred supercar that would outperform exotic machines costing four times the price.

The WRX has been repeatedly face-lifted over the years, although not always successfully. But drivers love the Impreza for its power delivery and unrelenting levels of grip, not for its looks, comfort, or economy. **DS**

Guarà | De Tomaso

(I)

1993 • 281 cu in/4,600 cc, V8 • 305 bhp/227 kW • 0–60 mph/97 kph in 4.8 seconds • 172 mph/277 kph

Alejandro De Tomaso's 1970s heyday as a motor manufacturer lay far behind him. But in the early 1990s, as new supercars were springing up everywhere, it seemed as though it was time for the Argentinian to come up with a fresh sports car of his own. The result was unveiled at the 1993 Geneva Motor Show and was christened the De Tomaso Guarà, after a South American wild dog.

But under its supercar skin, the new De Tomaso wasn't as new as you might have thought. A 1991 Maserati prototype—the Barchetta Stradale—was used as a base. That base consisted of a strong tubular chassis and was now mated to a BMW V8 engine that was placed in the middle. Like the Maserati it was based on, the Guarà's body was designed by Carlo Gaino and was made of fiberglass and carbon fiber.

Three variants were offered for sale: a Coupe, a Barchetta, and a Spider, of which only the last retained its BMW engine. The Coupe and Barchetta soon used a Ford V8 engine with 305 bhp (227 kW), or even 430 bhp (316 kW) when the supercharger option was chosen. The new engine could not be fitted to the Spiders because of the folding roof that needed extra space.

Sadly, the car didn't become the success De Tomaso had hoped for. The company was taken into receivership in 2004, which spelled the end for the Guarà. During all those years some fifty Coupes are said to have been built, plus ten Barchettas and just five Spiders. One year before bankruptcy, Alejandro De Tomaso died at the age of seventy-five. Several attempts to revive his brand have been undertaken since, but so far without success. **JB**

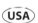

Aurora | Oldsmobile

USA

1994 • 244 cu in/3,995 cc, V8 • 250 bhp/186 kW • 0–60 mph/97 kph in 8.6 seconds • 135 mph/217 kph

In the 1980s and 1990s, Oldsmobile had a serious PR problem. Everyone thought of its cars as the vehicles their fathers drove. GM spent years looking for a model that would revitalize its image and kick-start a new surge of interest in the brand. Then, when it did finally come up with a concept—and a very good one—in the form of the Aurora full-size sports sedan (saloon), it stripped the car of almost all Oldsmobile references and badging and instead gave it a stylized letter "A," which didn't refer to anything in particular except GM's own uncertainty regarding the Oldsmobile name.

The result of a lengthy period of research, the first glimpses of the Aurora could be seen in the Tube Car, a 1989 concept car that would form the basis of the Aurora's styling. Tube Car features such as its frameless windows, full-width taillights, and contoured look all found expression in the new Aurora. It was like no other Oldsmobile seen before, and went on to influence the styling of other Oldsmobile models for years to come.

Powered by a 244-cubic-inch (3,995-cc) V8 the Aurora was a luxury performance sedan that should have been everything GM had been looking for. It received widespread praise from the motoring press. It had dual-zone climate control, walnut accents throughout its interior, power seats with leather inserts, and driver and passenger air bags. A modified version of its impressive engine was used in the Indianapolis Racing League by GM's racing division, and its new unibody frame proved so strong in tests that it disabled GM's stress-testing machine. Although first year sales were strong, they soon fell away, and the Aurora proved not to be the answer to Oldsmobile's ills. **BS**

The Ferrari F355, shown here in its 1995 incarnation, perfected the balance between a Formula 1 race car and a road car.

Vertigo | Gillet (B)

1994 • 256 cu in/4,200 cc, V8 • 420 bhp/309 kW • 0–60 mph/97 kph in less than 3 seconds • unknown

Former racing driver Tony Gillet was making a living importing Dutch Donkervoort sports cars into Belgium when he decided to create his own supercar. The result was the Vertigo, an ultralightweight hand-built sports coupe with an engine at the front driving the rear wheels. It's still for sale, although it has evolved since 1994, powered by a series of increasingly high-performance engines. Gillet cars have proved popular with wealthy European buyers, including the "French Elvis" Johnny Halliday and Prince Albert of Monaco.

The first generation of the car was a peculiar mix of open track design and sleek road coupe. It used a 134-cubic-inch (2,200-cc) Ford Cosworth engine, which was tested at 3.27 seconds for the 0–62 mph (100 kph) sprint. This figure allowed the Vertigo to briefly claim the title of the world's fastest production car. A Gillet Vertigo was chosen as the official pace car for all the 1995 Belgian Pro Car championship races, and it also acted as a pace car in the 1995 Monaco Grand Prix. The car uses an F1-style carbon and alloy honeycomb chassis that only weighs 128 pounds (58 kg), but is very rigid and strong.

The latest version, the Vertigo.5 Spirit, uses a Maserati V8 engine, sequential gearbox, and a closed-body design with supercar-style butterfly doors. It still only weighs 2,094 pounds (950 kg), though.

A paltry total of twenty-six cars have been sold since 1994, making the Vertigo one of the rarest production cars on the market. Ironically, more are owned digitally by console game players than by real owners, as the Vertigo appears as a choice for players of Need for Speed, Gran Turismo, and Forza Motorsport. **SH**

F355 | Ferrari (I)

1994 • 213 cu in/3,495 cc, V8 • 375 bhp/279 kW • 0–60 mph/ 97 kph in 4.6 seconds • 185 mph/298 kph

If ever there was a Formula 1 racing car disguised as a street car, it was the Ferrari F355. Its engine had titanium alloy con rods that had only ever been used on F1 racing cars. Instead of a clutch pedal there was the option of a tiny finger-operated shift behind the steering wheel, just as in F1 racers. But it was the 355's five-valves-per-cylinder that was its greatest unseen advantage and which gave it its real power—three for intake plus two for exhaust was an equation that translated into better breathing efficiency, higher revs, higher intakes, and a 7-second faster circuit around Ferrari's private testing track at Maranello than its predecessor, the "nervous at the limit" F348.

Two models were available upon debut, a coupe and a targa-topped GTS (a convertible would be released the following year). Although the lovely "cheese-slicer" side grilles of the Testarossa were gone, the Pininfarina-designed body was given lovely rounded edges and included air intakes for its rear-mounted engine that were as much functional as they were gorgeously sculptural.

But it was those F1 touches that set the F355 apart. It had an underbody tray for additional downforce and electronic damping for velcrolike cornering. It was also easier on its driver's body, with a lighter clutch than a typical Ferrari and a slicker six-speed gearbox.

The F355 may have been succeeded by the F360, but it was not bettered. It became the most successful Ferrari in history, selling over 11,200 units in its five-year production run, and without any significant alterations. Because when Ferrari gets something right the first time, there's nothing left to improve. **BS**

FTO | Mitsubishi

J

1994 • 122 cu in/2,000 cc, V6 • 168 bhp/125 kW • 0–60 mph/97 kph in 7.3 seconds • 130 mph/209 kph

Customer power can be a wonderful thing. When Mitsubishi first built the FTO coupe, it was meant for the domestic Japanese market only. But it became hugely popular as an independent, gray import into the United Kingdom, Ireland, and New Zealand (all countries that share right-hand drive with the Japanese). Eventually Mitsubishi changed its mind and sold it officially.

The name means "Fresh Touring Origination" and nods to the FTO being more of a GT car than an out and out sportser. There was a limited engine choice: either a 110-cubic-inch (1,800-cc) four-cylinder or a 122-cubic-inch (2,000-cc), twenty-four-valve V6. The FTO won Japan's Car of the Year in 1994—the first sports car to do this since the Mk1 MR2 a decade before.

This then prompted a GPX Special Edition, with the V6 power taken to 197 bhp (147 kW) with variable valve timing. The power went through a five-speed manual or an automatic transmission to the front wheels. The latter used clever electronics that adapted to the user's driving style and could even recognize road gradients.

The rounded bodywork divided opinion between funky and ugly, but there was no denying the sophistication of the chassis setup. McPherson struts at the front were coupled with a sophisticated multilink rear suspension to give precise handling. The engine did need to be revved hard, in true Japanese style, before it delivered much of its power, but the reward for all that effort was a fast, capable coupe.

The feeling at the time of its launch was that this was a car that Europe was crying out for. But by the time Mitsubishi got round to officially importing it, there were better home-grown rivals already on offer. **JI**

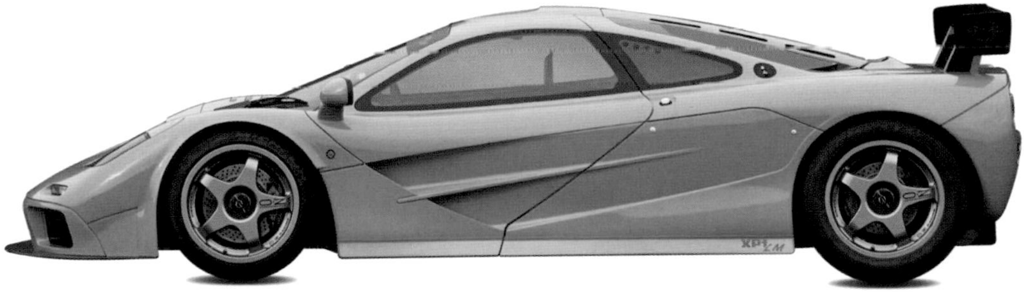

F1 | McLaren

GB

1994 • 370 cu in/6,064 cc, V12 • 618 bhp/461 kW • 0–60 mph/97 kph in 3.1 seconds • 241 mph/388 kph

McLaren is well known globally for its Formula One team, and for six years in the 1990s it was also the manufacturer of an ultraexotic supercar for the road. The McLaren F1 began production in 1992 and ended in 1998, by which time 102 cars had been made.

The F1 grew from a concept conceived by McLaren chief engineer Gordon Murray, who convinced his boss Ron Dennis to back the project. Peter Stevens, one of Britain's most renowned car designers, was hired to do the exterior styling work. He penned a shape that resembles a wingless jet fighter plane at ground level.

The car is notable for having three seats across the cabin, with the driver set slightly forward in the middle and room for a passenger on either side. The doors unusually pivot forward and upward to allow access to the cabin. The Fl was built using hugely expensive lightweight materials, including carbon fiber, Kevlar, titanium, magnesium, and even gold.

The engine is a 370-cubic-inch (6,064-cc) V12, built by BMW's Motorsport division under the direction of Paul Rosche. It is a sophisticated design and produces a staggering power output. Contemporary reactions to the car were in awe of its performance. In 1998 an F1 became the fastest road car in the world, topping 242.95 mph (391 kph) with its engine rev limiter removed.

Because of the car's astronomical price—over £600,000 ($960,000)—all those who bought a road-going McLaren car were extremely wealthy. An F1 owned by Rowan Atkinson, famous for his Mr. Bean and Blackadder characters, hit the headlines worldwide when he lost control and crashed it, in one of the most expensive road crashes ever involving a single car. **SB**

Mustang GT | Ford (USA)

1994 • 302 cu in/4,942 cc, V8 • 215 bhp/158 kW • 0–60 mph/ 97 kph in 6.7 seconds • 135 mph/217 kph

Around 22,000 of Ford's inaugural 1964 Mustang were sold on the first day of the model's launch. It became one of the most famous automobiles in the world, and in 1994 it was time to celebrate, and come up with a thirtieth anniversary special edition.

It had a lot to live up to, but the first major redesign in fifteen years delivered almost everything Mustang aficionados were hoping for. It sat on a version of the Fox chassis that had underpinned every Mustang since 1979, only now it was significantly stiffened to improve the car's handling. But its 302-cubic-inch (4,942-cc), V8 engine, though more refined than the '93 version, delivered 10 bhp (7 kW) fewer and had to be worked on by the driver to achieve that optimum Mustang grunt. Fans didn't much like the fact it lacked the punch of its rival, the Camaro, to the tune of 60 bhp (44 kW).

Nevertheless, everyone knew that this was the best Mustang in years. *Motor Trend* named it their 1994 Car of the Year, and nothing would spoil Ford's high-profile thirtieth anniversary parties—including one soirée at the Charlotte Motor Speedway, where President Bill Clinton arrived in his own Mustang. The Camaro may have had more horses under the hood (bonnet), but the Mustang had the only horse that mattered: that timeless thoroughbred emblazoned on its grille. **BS**

Ram V10 | Dodge (USA)

1994 • 488 cu in/7,997 cc, V10 • 300 bhp/220 kW • 0–60 mph/97 kph in 7.8 seconds • unknown

When the designers at Dodge were drawing up a new look for the 1994 model Ram, they asked customers what they wanted. The reply they got back was: "A pickup that looks like a big-rig truck." So the new Ram got a nose that looked like it had come off an eighteen-wheeler. Dodge knew this might not appeal to everyone, but at least it would be instantly recognizable.

There was a range of engines on offer, starting with a 238-cubic-inch (3,900-cc) V6 and even including a diesel. But the one that caught the most attention was the new addition to the line-up—a 488-cubic-inch (7,997-cc) V10. This had come from Dodge's Viper supercar, and been developed with expertise from Lamborghini. At the time the Italian firm was owned by Chrysler, the Dodge parent company. The V10 had been designed for use in trucks and the Lamborghini engineers were called in to recast the iron block and head in aluminum. The Ram was built on a ladder-type chassis and the rear end was a primitive live axle, rather than independent. So this was never a vehicle that was going to be able to corner like a sports car. However, what it did have was vast reserves of pulling power.

In 1994 Dodge sold almost a quarter of a million Rams. They had raised the bar in the world of muscular trucks to a whole new level. **JI**

A8 | Audi

(D)

1994 • 256 cu in/4,200 cc, V8 • 295 bhp/221 kW • 0–62 mph/100 kph in 7.3 seconds • 155 mph/250 kph

Audi's A8 was the first production car with an aluminum body to reduce weight, avoid corrosion, and increase structural rigidity. There were long-wheel-base versions, a line of smaller engines, and front-wheel-drive models, but the star of the line was the Quattro (figures above). This used the punchy all-aluminum thirty-two-valve V8 engine.

The A8 was a luxury prestige sedan (saloon), so of course the interior was coated with leather and wood. Audi's interiors were already among the best, and this spacious cabin easily hit the quality mark. Audi had built its brand image on its use of technology so there were gadgets everywhere, including heated seats that had powered adjustment in fourteen different directions. Other standard features included a Bose hi-fi, dual-zone climate control, plenty of air bags, and a first-aid kit. More driver-oriented "sport" trim models got lowered and stiffened suspension and sports seats.

The A8 was sleek but conservative, with a hint of excitement in the racy alloy wheels. It was proof that Audi could make a luxury sedan to compete with the best of its rivals. To emphasize the point, in 1996 Audi produced the S8 Quattro model—the latest version of which has supercar credentials, with 512 bhp (382 kW) and 0–62 mph (100 kph) acceleration in 4.2 seconds. **SH**

RS2 | Audi

(D)

1994 • 136 cu in/2,226 cc, S5 • 315 bhp/232 kW • 0–60 mph/97 kph in 4.8 seconds • 163 mph/262 kph

Taken from the German *Renn Sport* or "racing sport," the Audi RS range was the company's high performer of the 1990s. The cars were designed and engineered at the Audi AG facility near Stuttgart, and the first model was a five-door, five-seat station wagon (estate) that was a joint venture between Audi AG and Porsche—the Audi RS2 Avant. Porsche had recently transformed the unexciting Mercedes W124 sedan (saloon) into the dynamic Mercedes 500E, and Audi wanted Porsche to do the same for its S2.

Porsche lost no time getting to work on the S2's engine. They added a KKK turbocharger, gave it a larger intercooler, more aggressive camshafts, and larger fuel injectors, and Audi's straight five-cylinder engine was instantly evolved. The S2 then got the Porsche 911's braking system, its 17-inch (43-cm) wheels, its Dunlop high-performance tires, and a sports-tuned suspension that brought the A80 body 1.6 inches (4 cm) lower to the ground. The RS2 still had Audi's Quattro four-wheel-drive unit and Audi's procon-ten safety system with its array of cables and wires that would "pull" the steering wheel away from the driver in the event of an impact.

The very new, very fast RS2 became a worldwide hit, and is generally credited with establishing Audi as a maker of quality, practical, high-performing cars. **BS**

Spider | Alfa Romeo

(I)

1995 • 183 cu in/3,000 cc, V6 • 218 bhp/160 kW • 0–60 mph/97 kph in 6.8 seconds • 146 mph/235 kph

The motoring world was amazed when Alfa Romeo unveiled its new Spider and GTV coupe counterpart at the 1995 Geneva Motor Show. It was a radical change from the classic Duetto Spider design that it had repeatedly revamped over the previous thirty years.

The old-world charm was gone and replaced by a modern, aggressive muscularity. The new front-wheel-drive car had a stubby nose with short overhangs, a steeply raked windshield, and a chunky, purposeful rear. These styling cues had all emerged long after the original program of Spiders had been designed.

The most distinctive feature of the body design was a diagonal slash running from the front fender (bumper) to the back of the trunk (boot). Pininfarina's designers were clearly intent on ignoring the past and bringing the Spider concept up to date.

Another sign of the times was that the Spider was now made by part of the Fiat Group, for whom economy of scale was a byword. In consequence, the Spider was built on a platform shared with other small cars made by the group, such as the Fiat Tipo hatchback.

There were tweaks for the Spider's benefit, of course. It was given Alfa's stiffest ever convertible chassis and a sporty new rear suspension. The choice of engines ranged from a 110-cubic-inch (1,800-cc) Twin Spark with two spark plugs per cylinder to a mighty, line-topping V6 (performance figures are given above).

Alfa Romeo had extended its Spider line and reintroduced its open-top two-seater to a new generation. But the new car was greeted in a different way from the lovable original, with many viewing it as merely the cabrio version of the GTV. **SH**

Barchetta | Fiat

(I)

1995 • 110 cu in/1,800, S4 • 129 bhp/96 kW • 0–62 mph/100 kph in 8.9 seconds • 120 mph/200 kph

Fiat's "little boat," as Barchetta translates, was essentially a spider version of the popular Punto hatchback. However, it was given a look and character of its own. It had a front-mounted, sixteen-valve engine and front-wheel drive. It was the first Fiat engine to use variable-valve timing, giving the Barchetta a sportier performance. The design had numerous retro touches, recalling past Alfa Romeo and Fiat roadsters. A prototype coupe version was built by Italian styling house Maggiora; it looked like a U.K. car from the 1960s, but wasn't approved for production. Another prototype, built by the rival team at Stola, was a roofless racer with a 122-cubic-inch (2,000-cc) engine from the Fiat Coupe Turbo. This 1950s-style design had a 167 mph (270 kph) top speed and acceleration of 0–62mph (100k ph) in 5.8 seconds. Again, sadly only one car was made.

Fiat concentrated on the two-seater roadster but only produced left-hand-drive versions, which limited its appeal in Japan and the United Kingdom. But with its light body, the Barchetta was fun to drive—the Punto's agile chassis and all-around independent suspension proved to be up to the job. Cornering was a real pleasure.

The two-door soft-top was fairly well-equipped for its humble price. There were air bags, five-speed manual gearbox, antilock brakes, and a decent audio system. Some cars came with alloy wheels, leather seats, and air-conditioning. A hardtop was an optional extra.

The little Fiat starred in a BBC *Top Gear* Christmas Special in 2010, when an old used model drove one of the "three wise men" hosts to Bethlehem. The other cars used were more expensive: a Mazda MX-5 and a BMW Z3—but the Fiat proved most reliable. **SH**

Integra Type R | Honda

(J)

1995 • 110 cu in/1,797 cc, S4 • 187 bhp/139 kW • 0–60 mph/97 kph in 6.2 seconds • 145 mph/233 kph

In 2006 the British magazine *Evo* ran a group test to determine the best front-wheel-drive car ever made. The fifteen finalists included older classics, such as Peugeot's 205 GTI and the Lotus M100 Elan, and newer models like Mini's John Cooper Works GP. After several punishing track sessions, the final verdict was unanimous: the Honda Integra Type R was, by some margin, the winner. One journalist exclaimed, "It's a car as sweet and all-consuming as any I've experienced, at any price . . . Forget the accolade of greatest front-wheel-drive car. The Integra Type R ranks as one of the truly great drivers' cars of any kind."

The first Integra was launched in 1985, and was a familiar sight in the United States as the entry-level model of the upmarket Acura brand. The brand did not reach Britain until 1997.

The third-generation Integra was the first Honda to sport the Type R badge. At 9,000 rpm, the Type R's normally aspirated VTEC engine could put out an incredible 187 bhp (139 kW). Honda's engineers beefed up the Integra's chassis with thicker steel plate, and added front and rear strut braces to cope with the power gains. To further improve handling, the suspension was lowered 0.5 inch (15 mm) and the car was put on a crash diet; thinner glass, racing seats, and lightweight alloy wheels were used, and most of the sound proofing was removed.

"R" stood for "racing," and Honda wanted to showcase its high-performance products on tracks around the world. The Type R's huge success in touring-car races was some compensation for the fact that Honda lost money on every single sale. **DS**

Coupe 20v Turbo | Fiat

(I)

1995 • 122 cu in/1,998 cc, S5 • 220 bhp/160 kW • 0–60 mph/97 kph in 6.5 seconds • 155 mph/250 kph

American designer Chris Bangle later found fame and controversy by restyling the entire BMW lineup. But first he made his name at the Fiat Group by designing one of the most striking high-performance cars of the early 1990s. With sharp wheel-arch diagonals and bulging front headlights, the Fiat Coupe was ahead of its time in looks, having a distinctive angular style that did not take hold elsewhere for at least another five years.

The impressive interior was designed by Italian stylist Pininfarina, which also built the car at its factory just north of Turin. The design featured a body-colored metal strip that ran around the inside of the doors and along the dashboard.

Mechanically, this first sporty Fiat in a decade was a scorcher. In the twenty-valve turbo version, performance was venturing into supercar territory. It was one of Europe's fastest front-wheel-drive cars of the era and the quickest car Fiat had ever built.

The Coupe was also a practical choice, with two usable rear seats and a surprisingly large trunk (boot). The equipment was not bad for the time, too: there were antilock brakes, leather seats, twin air bags, and air-conditioning. The Turbo's five-speed gearbox was later uprated to a six-speed unit.

The car soon had a cult following, and in 1998 Fiat cashed in with a special limited-edition 20v Turbo model—the LE. This had an even more aggressive body kit, plus red Recaro racing seats, a red starter button, red brake calipers, and a more rigid chassis for even sportier handling. The LE cars were individually numbered. Formula One champion Michael Schumacher was rumored to have bought the first example. **SH**

MGF | MG

GB

1995 • 110 cu in/1,796 cc, S4 • 143 bhp/107 kW • 0–60 mph/97 kph in 7.2 seconds • 130 mph/209 kph

Although the MG emblem appeared on line-topping versions of British Leyland's family sedans (saloons) and hatchbacks, the last true MG (a bronze-yellow MGB Roadster, to be precise, had rolled out of the factory gates in October 1980. The newly formed Rover Group had flirted with the idea of a new production sports car since the early 1980s, but it was not until the launch of the Mazda MX5 in 1989 proved that there was still a lucrative market for affordable, sporty, two-seater convertibles that the MGF development program was finally given the go-ahead.

The MGF was developed on a shoestring budget, with Rover's engineers ransacking spares departments for most of its vital components. Innovative designers reversed the Metro's subframe to cradle the mid-mounted K-Series engine, and the Hydrogas suspension system (first used on the Austin Allegro) did a great job of soaking up the bumps. Parts of the Rover 200 and 400 were used to keep down costs, and the car's body styling was carried out in-house.

When the MGF was launched in March 1995, it was well received by the motoring press, which praised the handsome bodywork and forward-thinking design. Road testers loved the way the 110-cubic-inch (1,796-cc) VVC (variable valve control) K-Series engine would spring into life beyond 4,000 rpm, while the well-balanced chassis was almost impossible to spin.

The MGF was an instant hit, becoming the United Kingdom's best-selling sports car for the next six years. While some would argue that it was kept in service too long in its TF and Chinese reincarnations, the original MGF was a worthy rival to the ubiquitous MX5. **DS**

Sport Spider | Renault

F

1995 • 122 cu in/1,998 cc, S4 • 148 bhp/110 kW • 0–60 mph/97 kph in 6.5 seconds • 131 mph/211 kph

Renault unveiled the Sport Spider at the 1994 Geneva Motor Show. It was intended as a halo car for the rest of its line—something exciting to add sportiness to its portfolio of conservative cars. The Spider was certainly exciting. In fact, it went into limited production as both a racing car and road car for those happy to brave whatever the weather threw at them in the exposed cabin. Renault called it a "single-seater for two."

With the 122-cubic-inch (1,998-cc) engine of the sporty Renault Clio Williams transferred to the back of a chassis related to the flyweight Lotus Elise, the Spider had plenty of punch. The brakes came from Alpine's powerful A610. The panels were plastic, and Renault saved further weight by dropping creature comforts such as a heater, roof, and windshield. A clever design forced hot air through vents to act as a wind deflector where the windshield would have been. However, for the 200 Sport Spider buyers in rainy Britain, a conventional glass windshield was included in the $39,000 (£25,000) asking price. The U.K. *Independent* newspaper called it "raw, masochistic fun."

The Renault Sport Spider had only a very short production run; just ninety-nine were built for track use, with an additional 1,541 sold to private buyers for use on the road. Renault's model was undercut and outperformed by the Lotus Elise, which, although it offered the windshield and roof generally missing from the Spider, was still considerably lighter and generally performed much better on the road. What the Elise lacked, though, was the Spider's unique windshield-free driving experience of raw wind in the hair and insects in the teeth. **RD**

Azure | Bentley

(USA)

1995 • 413 cu in/6,761 cc, V8 • 450 bhp/330 kW • 0–60 mph/97 kph in 6.3 seconds • 150 mph/241 kph

An anonymous craftsman took around fifteen hours to stitch by hand its leather-clad steering wheel. The internal wood veneers along its doorframes and dashboard were hand-cut to a thickness of 0.02 inches (0.6 mm). The car was so colossal that it required a 7-feet (2.1-m) long Pininfarina-designed and manufactured convertible roof to emerge from the trunk (boot) to cover it. And the chassis subframes were held together by a pair of carbon-fiber crucifixes that brought everything together to make the new Bentley Azure three times tighter in the body than the model that it was built to replace.

When it was made, the Azure was the biggest, most expansive, and most expensive four-seat luxury convertible in the world. Built on the Continental R coupe's platform, it was seriously long at 17.5 feet (5.3 m) and weighed a tanklike 5,754 pounds (2,610 kg). It required every last cubic centimeter of its V8 twin-turbo to pull it along . . . and every last bit of patience on the part of its well-heeled new owners who had to wait over twelve months for delivery. Only nine were completed by the end of its first full year of production (and just 251 in all).

Just because it was a Bentley doesn't mean it was without its imperfections. Film director Michael Winner test-drove an Azure and much preferred his own '75 Bentley Corniche. "In my Bentley the seat feels like a lounge chair. This feels like an office chair. And look at the wood. It's like something out of an Ikea catalog," he said. Perhaps it's true that only a Bentley owner can be another Bentley's critic. For the rest of us, though, the envy rolls on... **BS**

A4 | Audi

(D)

1996 • 153 cu in/2,500 cc, V6 • 148 bhp/110 kW • 0–60 mph/97 kph in 9 seconds • 131 mph/210 kph

Audis were boxy-looking, efficient but boring cars. The mid-range 80 Series, for example, was not bought for its style, image, or status. But that changed with the arrival of its successor, the A4. The name alone sounded more chic and modern, and the sleek, rounded design was immediately exciting and contemporary.

At around this time, Audi was deliberately moved upmarket by the Volkswagen Group so the two brands could focus on different markets. It worked: Audi was soon elevated to the level of BMW and Mercedes in buyer perception, helped by the slogan *Vorsprung durch Technik*, represented in the United States as "innovation through technology." Audi had used the slogan for many years, but with the launch of the A4 it became a major feature of all their advertising and it still is today.

Despite all the marketing and style, there was not a lot new about the A4. It used many parts from the old A80 and shared a platform with other Volkswagen Group vehicles. Many of the same old engines were mounted at the front to drive the front wheels, or, in some special "quattro" versions, all the wheels. There was a sedan (saloon), marketed as a "compact executive" car and an Avant station wagon (estate). The second and third incarnations of the A4 included a cabriolet version, too.

Gradually the line was given extra technological pizzazz. These Audi firsts included an engine with five valves per cylinder, an early version of tiptronic semiautomatic transmission, and a four-wheel-drive turbodiesel sports sedan with the latest direct fuel injection; its performance figures are given above. **SH**

Cerbera | TVR

GB

1996 • 273 cu in/4,475 cc, V8 • 440 bhp/328 kW • 0–60 mph/97 kph in 3.9 seconds • 193 mph/311 kph

In mythology, Cerberus was the monstrous, three-headed hellhound that guarded the gates to the Underworld. Adapted, the name was appropriate for this savagely powerful sports car, which would bite its less talented pilots if pushed too hard.

The TVR Cerbera was the first hardtop built under TVR's new leadership, and the first to be powered by its own engine. The Cerbera was designed as a four-seater coupe, with a passenger seat that could be slid forward to create an unusual 3+1 configuration.

When BMW bought the Rover Group in 1994, TVR was worried that its supply of 214-cubic-inch (3,500-cc) V8 powerplants might dry up. To protect its new model lineup, TVR had an entirely new 256-cubic-inch (4,200-cc) V8 designed by Formula One race engineer Al Melling. In a clever piece of viral marketing that reinforced TVR's "bad boy" image, TVR owner Peter Wheeler told reporters at the car's official press launch that the new, F1-inspired "Speed Eight" engine was just too powerful for a lightweight road car.

The Speed Eight was later enlarged to a 273-cubic-inch (4,475-cc) engine, which can be identified by its wonderful popping and banging exhaust notes. In its "Red Rose" high-performance specification, TVR created one of the most powerful normally aspirated V8s ever made; its performance figures are given above.

The ultimate Cerbera was the 470-cubic-inch (7,700-cc) "Speed Twelve" GT1 race car. No accurate record of this car's power output was ever made as it destroyed TVR's dynamometer at the first attempt. Priced at $295,000 (£188,000), only one road-going version was sold. **DS**

XK8 | Jaguar

GB

1996 • 244 cu in/3,996 cc, V8 • 290 bhp/213 kW • 0–60 mph/97 kph in 6.5 seconds • 155 mph/246 kph

The XK8, Jaguar's first true sports car since the E-Type, was a joint development between Jaguar and its recently acquired parent company, Ford. However, it was not at all some kind of Jaguar/Ford hybrid when it came to parts. Granted, the development was made possible only by the collaboration, but the hardware of the successor to the XJS coupe was all Jaguar, from its alloy 244-cubic-inch (3,996-cc) V8 engine—the first V8 for a company famous for its V6 and V12 engines—to the unashamedly E-Type-looking radiator grille and the power bulge in its hood (bonnet). The only Ford-supplied part to be found anywhere was a microchip in the car's ignition key.

More agile than the XJS, the XK8 still could not be called a true sports car. It was more a heavyweight that enjoyed grand touring, a beast that preferred a more sedate way of getting places. This was a quality motor car, and the search for the very best components took designers to Japan for its air-conditioning and to Germany for the electronically folding canvas top of the convertible that would follow. The ride comfort of the XK8 was extraordinary in any weather, thanks to a traction control system and antilock brakes, and the ride was so quiet that the loudest noise passengers were aware came from the tires.

The XK8 would become the best-selling sports car in Jaguar's history. In time it would lose its premium-price status. An early-model coupe can now be bought for less than $15,800 (£10,000), and yet a 1996 XK8, with its Connolly leather interior, walnut trim, and Jaguar pedigree, remains as desirable now as it was then. It is just that the car is a lot more affordable now. **BS**

Boxster 3.4 | Porsche

D

1996 • 207 cu in/3,386 cc, F6 • 310 bhp/228 kW • 0–60 mph/97 kph in 4.7 seconds • 170 mph/274 kph

By the mid-1990s Porsche sales were starting to dip as its limited model lineup got longer in the tooth. Its two front-engined coupes, the 968 and 928, were both based on designs first penned in the early 1970s; the air-cooled 911 could trace its origins back to the 1960s. If Porsche were to survive, it needed to inject some sparkle back into the brand.

The company's savior came in the form of a new entry-level mid-engined sports car. The first Porsche to be known by a name rather than a number, the Boxster got its moniker from its flat-six boxer engine and roadster body style. The motoring press were astounded by the little two-seater's poise and handling; BBC TV *Top Gear* host Jeremy Clarkson described its roadholding as "balletic." However, some journalists were disappointed by the lack of power delivered by the water-cooled 153-cubic-inch (2,500-cc) engine, and Clarkson went further by famously claiming that "it couldn't pull a greased stick out of a pig's bottom."

Porsche answered its critics by adding the 195-cubic-inch (3,200-cc) Boxster S to its lineup in 2000. This car went on to win a clutch of awards, ranging from Car of the Year from Canada's *Le Guide de l'Auto* magazine and the U.S. TV show *MotorWeek*, to the Most Sex Appeal award of *American Women Motorscene* magazine.

Despite a major facelift in 2009, the Boxster has retained its fine, understated exterior styling. However, unlike most of its drivers, the Boxster continues to lose weight as it matures, thanks to clever use of exotic metals and composite materials. While handling remains sublime, the latest 207-cubic-inch (3,386-cc) Boxster S has more grunt than an early 911 Turbo. **DS**

Elise | Lotus

GB

1996 • 110 cu in/1,796 cc, S4 • 118 bhp/88 kW • 0–60 mph/97 kph in 5.8 seconds • 125 mph/201 kph

The Lotus Elise perfectly encapsulates all the ingredients that Lotus cars have always been famous for. Stylish, light, rapid, and nimble, it is judged by many to be the finest-handling car of its generation. Named after the granddaughter of Italian businessman Romano Artioli, who was chairman of Lotus at the time of the car's launch, it is a mid-engined, rear-wheel-drive, slightly raw two-seater fun car with a hand-finished fiberglass body on a bonded extruded aluminum chassis. The car is strong but lightweight, and relatively inexpensive to make.

Production began in 1996 at Hethel in Norfolk, where Lotus is based and has its own test track. The car was designed by chief engineer Richard Rackham and head of design Julian Thomson, both widely regarded as having done a great job in devising such a rewarding car to drive.

As soon as it appeared, the Elise was praised for its serene ride and limpetlike handling. It is much lighter than most, weighing only 1,600 pounds (725 kg), which explains the very rapid, race-car-pace of acceleration in a road model with a 110-cubic-inch (1,796-cc) Rover K-Series engine. The car's braking behavior, cornering prowess, and good fuel economy all benefit from the lightweight body structure. The principle of combining a lightweight body with a mid-range engine had been established years ago by Lotus founder Colin Chapman, who died some fourteen years before the Elise first appeared.

The Elise Series 1 stayed in production until 2001, and this unalloyed original is viewed by many enthusiasts as the best. A Series 2 model was introduced in 2002 and remains in production today. **SB**

Esprit V8 | Lotus

GB

1996 • 214 cu in/3,506cc, V8 • 350 bhp/257 kW • 0–60 mph/97 kph in 4.8 seconds • 175 mph/282 kph

Giorgetto Giugiaro is an Italian automobile designer famous for his "folded paper" designs of the 1970s. His work includes the angular DeLorean DMC-12, the Maserati Merak, and this new Lotus Esprit V8, a wedge-shaped fixed-head coupe.

The Esprit was a twenty-year-old series by the time U.S. emissions laws began to draw a noose around the neck of its high-emission, four-cylindered versions. The laws forced the introduction of a cleaner, twin-turbocharged, entirely Lotus-developed V8 that would take the car to an entirely new level of performance.

Giugiaro's beautifully angled Lotus had been given a supercar engine to match its supercar looks. Gearbox problems that had bedeviled earlier models were rectified, and now the Esprit could legitimately saddle up its horsepower alongside the Ferrari F355 and Porsche 996. It is amazing what a bit of tinkering and a whacking big engine transplant can do.

The car had continued to seem contemporary despite its creeping age, and there was still that renowned Lotus handling thanks to its all-around coil springs, anti-roll bar, and rack-and-pinion steering. Of course, the interior continued to be an ergonomic challenge to enter and exit, and drivers with large feet found the footwell annoyingly restrictive.

But power was what the new Esprit was all about, to the point that the engine's performance was actually "wound back" to protect a suddenly vulnerable Renault transaxle. Power like that at least made it easier to live with the brand's age-old issues of reliability, expressed by an annoying Lotus acronym that would not go away: "Lots Of Trouble, Usually Serious." **BS**

550 Maranello | Ferrari

(I)

1996 • 334 cu in/5,474 cc, V12 • 485 bhp/357 kW • 0–60 mph/97 kph in 4.2 seconds • 199 mph/320 kph

After a quarter of a century of Ferrari producing its array of red supercars—from the Testa Rossa to the 512M—all with their engines placed firmly behind their drivers, along came the 550 Maranello two-seat Grand Tourer. It was Ferrari's answer to those who claimed a front-engined V12 could not possibly possess the same performance as a mid-engined sports car. Sergio Pininfarina, for one, disagreed, "Ferrari returned to the front-engined configuration because the progress of technology allowed us to reach the same level of performance as a mid-engined design."

The Maranello had a new 334-cubic-inch (5,474-cc) V12 engine able to produce almost 500 bhp (357 kW) at 7,600 rpm. Highly impressive, but for once Ferrari's biggest leap forward was not the engine. A new control system called ASR was fitted that could sense traction loss and immediately reduce engine power in the event of even a hint of rear-wheel slippage. If things really got out of hand, ASR would intervene to activate the car's ventilated disc brakes' antilock mechanism. Of course, drivers wanting real fun in the Maranello tend to follow Jeremy Clarkson's advice and turn it off.

The interior maintained the pure Ferrari layout of a tachometer and speedometer either side of the steering column, and tell-tale chrome shift gate with wafer-thin gearstick and metal knob on top. Custom-fitted luggage was available to help when packing the car's typically small trunk (boot), just as the car's ASR was there to assist drivers with its speed.

On October 12, 1998, in Marysville, Ohio, a 550 Maranello set a new production-car speed record of 189 mph (304 kph) over a 62-mile (100-km) course. **BS**

Berlingo | Citroën

(F)

1996 • 122 cu in/2,000 cc, S4 • 89 bhp/66 kW • 0–60 mph/97 kph in 12.7 seconds • 98 mph/158 kph

The Citroën Berlingo's claim to fame is that it was a pioneering crossover between a family car and a commercial van. Indeed, there is a Berlingo version without windows that *is* a van. Even as a car, it has a lot going for it. It is practical, roomy, and durable, with a light and airy cabin. Unpretentious, unconventional, and inexpensive, the Berlingo may not impress the neighbors, but it is the ultimate small people carrier.

Citroën tried hard to make the Berlingo cool when it was launched. In some countries it was painted in jazzy colors and called the "Multispace." It had a full-length sunroof and bright striped seats like deckchairs, but these did not drive the sales. People bought it for the practicality of two doors that slid open to reveal roomy rear seats that could be folded completely flat or removed altogether to create an enormous load space.

Engines have ranged from a 85-cubic-inch (1,400-cc) gasoline to a 122-cubic-inch (2,000-cc) diesel. Different versions have it powered by liquid gas or electricity. The electric version has a 38-bhp (28-kW) electric motor, a top speed of 59 mph (95 kph), and a range of 59 miles (95 km). To save battery power, the heater is separate and driven by gas. The Citroën Berlingo Electrique has become a familiar sight in France as it is used by the French post office. **SH**

GT | Keinath

(D)

1996 • 183 cu in/3,000 cc, V6 • 210 bhp/157 kW • 0–60 mph/97 kph in 7.8 seconds • 130 mph/210 kph

Even late into the 1990s, Horst Keinath of Gersthofen in southern Germany considered the Opel GT to be his dream car. Such was his passion for the car that Keinath decided to build one to his own specification. He was convinced that fellow enthusiasts would buy it.

The GT that Keinath launched in 1996 shared only its looks with the original car. It had a tubular chassis mated to a fiberglass bodyshell that was almost 9 inches (23 cm) wider than the Opel version. Under the hood (bonnet) was the V6 engine from the Opel Omega, which would deliver enhanced power to the baby coupe's rear wheels. The car's interiorcer was also a lot more more luxurious than that of its forebear, with full leather upholstery and plenty of electronic gadgetry. But few bought into Keinath's dream.

Keinath is thought to have built thirty-eight GTs before his company went bankrupt. One of the cars included a GM 348-cubic-inch (5,700-cc) V8, while another one got a Mercedes-Benz V12 engine, which would have made it truly alarming to drive. Keinath did not give up, though, and came back to unveil the convertible Keinath GT/R and the Keinath GTC, a further development of his dream coupe. Meanwhile, the GT was given a new lease on life when the rights to produce it were bought by a Chinese firm. **JB**

156 | Alfa Romeo (I)

1997 • 195 cu in/3,200 cc, V6 • 247 bhp/184 kW • 0–60 mph/97 kph in 6.3 seconds • 155 mph/250 kph

Alfa Romeo, by now part of the giant Italian Fiat Group, tried to be a little more mainstream with the launch of its compact executive line in 1997. For too long Alfa had built exciting but unreliable sports cars. This was its attempt to steal sales from the BMW 3-Series.

Styled more conservatively than usual, the 156 was an attractive range of front-wheel-drive, four-door sedans (saloons) and station wagons (estates). With 680,000 sales, it was a major success for the brand. Yet Alfa could not help introducing some oddities into the car. The front license plate was offset to one side, a mahogany steering wheel was an option, and the rear doors appeared to have no handles.

The engine range was wide, but even the humblest diesel achieved 117 mph (188 kph); all the cars could reach 60 mph (97 kph) in less than 10.5 seconds.

The 156 GTA, launched in 2001, was very different from the standard 156. The GTA's twenty-four-valve 195-cubic-inch (3,200-cc) V6 was an enlarged and tuned version of the classic Alfa 183-cubic-inch (3,000-cc) V6. There was an optional Formula-1-style semiautomatic paddle-change gearbox. The GTA's lowered and stiffened sports suspension was specially built, and its brakes and steering seriously uprated. Alfa had turned its 156 into a 155-mph (250-kph) supercar. **SH**

V70 T5 | Volvo (S)

1997 • 142 cu in/2,319 cc, S5 • 241 bhp/177 kW • 0–62 mph/100 kph in 7.1 seconds • 152 mph/245 kph

Volvo had become known as the purveyor of big, safe, boxy station wagons (estates) to the middle classes, so it was astonishing when the Swedish company launched a fire-breathing, turbocharged version of its biggest, boxiest car. No sedan (saloon) version of this top-of-the-line station wagon was launched.

The key to the V70 T5's performance was its straight five-cylinder, fuel-injected gas engine. Made of light alloy, it had a double overhead camshaft layout and a high-pressure turbocharger. This engine gave the big front-wheel-drive wardrobe-carrier a mid-range acceleration to embarrass many sports cars. It was a popular choice as a motorway patrol car.

Extra features included a stability and traction control system, a leather-covered interior, and alloy wheels. The car also included famed safety features such as side-impact protection, antiwhiplash front seats, dual-stage air bags, and inflatable side curtains. At the time it was a unique vehicle—a very rapid station wagon ideal for transporting a family on long journeys.

In 2000 it received a minor revision, including a new engine. The size was increased to 146 cubic inches (2,400 cc), continuously variable valve timing was added, and power rose to 260 bhp (191 kW). The new model could hit 60 mph (97 kph) in 6.8 seconds. **SH**

◁ Thrust SSC races across the Nevada desert in 1997 to become the first land vehicle to break the sound barrier.

Thrust SSC | SSC Program (GB)

1997 • two turbojets • 110,000 bhp/82,000 kW • 0–100 mph/161 kph in 4 seconds • 763 mph/1,228 kph

At the time of writing, the Thrust SSC (SuperSonic Car) is the fastest land vehicle in the world. It has held the land speed record since October 1997, when it reached 763 mph (1,228 kph) in the Black Rock Desert in Nevada. It was the first time a land vehicle had exceeded the speed of sound.

The Thrust has two Rolls-Royce turbojet engines from the British version of the F-4 Phantom II fighter aircraft. These supply the equivalent of the power of 145 Formula One racing cars. The British-built vehicle is 54 feet (16.5 m) long and weighs 10.5 tons. Fuel economy is low at 0.04 mpg (5,500 liters per 100 km). Thrust SSC is now displayed at the Transport Museum in Coventry, England.

The driver for the record-breaking run was RAF Wing Commander Andy Green, a jet pilot who also captains the RAF's toboggan team on the Cresta Run. Green also holds the land speed record for a diesel vehicle—in the JCB Dieselmax (328.7mph/529kph).

The project was headed by engineer and adventurer Richard Noble. He is now working on an even more formidable machine, the Bloodhound SSC, and plans to use the power of a jet engine and a rocket in an attempt to reach more than 1,000 mph (1,600 kph). Rival projects are the North American Eagle, a U.S./Canadian jet-powered vehicle, and the Silver Bullet, an Australian rocket-propeled machine.

The Thrust, however, is not technically the fastest car in the world because it does not use its wheels to drive; they merely steer. The fastest wheel-driven vehicle is currently the U.S.-built Vesco Turbinator, which achieved 470 mph (757 kph). **SH**

Alpina B10 V8 | BMW (D)

1997 • 282 cu in/4,619 cc, V8 • 340 bhp/253 kW • 0–60 mph/97 kph in 5.9 seconds • 175 mph/282 kph

BMW has, with its M-Series cars, always delivered high-performance models. But for customers who prefer vehicles with major quantities of power delivered in a less heavy-handed manner than an "M," specialist company Alpina of Bavaria had just the thing in 1997. The Alpina B10 V8 is a classic example of its work.

Starting with the E39 variant of BMW's M5 series, Alpina created a new engine block and crankshafts and created a 282-cubic-inch (4,619-cc) V8 with a whopping 340 bhp (253 kW). Unlike the manual BMW M5, which was based on the same E39 model, the transmission in the Alpina B10 V8 was an automatic system from ZF. The choice reflected the less frenetic driving characteristics of Alpina products.

The production process was seamlessly integrated into BMW's own production line. Alpina negotiated an agreement with BMW stipulating that any example of the Alpina B10 V8 would be covered by the same warranty that BMW dealerships offered.

In addition to the big, torquey engine, Alpina installed a luxury wood and leather trim in its corporate color. The B10 thus had blue instrument dials and seats embossed with the Alpina logo, and was only available in Alpina's patented blue paint scheme.

The Alpina was a subtle tool for demolishing long journeys on derestricted autobahns. If owners could afford the $100,000 (£63,500) list price, they could also afford the V8's 20-mpg (14 liters per 100 km) thirst.

Evo magazine wrote, "It's wickedly quick when you're in the mood for entertainment or feel like blowing off steam, relaxing and refined when all you want to do is mosey home." **RD**

Corvette C5 | Chevrolet

USA

1997 • 347 cu in/5,680 cc, V8 • 345 bhp/257 kW • 0–60 mph/97 kph in 4.7 seconds • 181 mph/291 kph

As many a car designer will tell you, making a convertible version of an existing hardtop car can lead to problems. As well as keeping out the rain, that metal roof helps to maintain the rigidity of the car. Without it, the car can flex and twist. Either that, or you end up adding so much extra metal to compensate that it weighs more than the original.

Not so the Corvette C5. Chevrolet designed it as a convertible from the start, building in a clever, preformed box chassis that did not need a roof to make it stiff. Just as well, because the C5 was powered by a huge, 347-cubic-inch (5,680-cc) V8 that produced 345 bhp (257 kW). The front-mounted engine sent its power through to a rear-mounted gearbox, spreading the weight evenly across the car. There was a choice of an automatic transmission or a six-speed manual gearbox. Curiously, even the manual would sometimes automatically shift from first to fourth.

The body design was more curvy than that of the previous C4, which had been sharp and angular. It also made extensive use of composite materials, which were both strong and light (as well as being cheaper to produce).

The C5 had an unusual mix of old and new technology: leaf-spring suspension joined a drive-by-wire throttle and even a head-up display. But what really mattered the most to any would-be owner was the amount of muscle under the hood (bonnet). The C5 could compete on that score with some of the best cars in the world, with a 0–60 mph (97 kph) time of just 4.7 seconds. The starting price for such power was $38,995 (£24,912).

A Corvette C5 convertible was used as the Pace Car at the 1998 Indy 500 race. For many potential buyers, that was the best advertisement that the C5 could have had. **JI**

Prowler | Plymouth

USA

1997 • 215 cu in/3,523 cc, V6 • 214 bhp/157 kW • 0–60 mph/97 kph in 7.2 seconds • 118 mph/180 kph

How did the Plymouth Prowler ever qualify for *Time* magazine's list of the Fifty Worst Cars of All Time? Perhaps there was something the eye could not see, some flaw only encountered when behind the wheel?

Chrysler's engineers were given a free rein to create a head-turning hot-rod, and what they came up with was unquestionably that. It had open, Indy-like front wheels with exposed suspension, a raked, aggressively tapered profile, and a Prowler-purple aluminum body to keep the weight down. Demand was so feverish that bidding wars broke out between prospective buyers for the 312 examples produced in its first year.

Shortcomings soon presented themselves, however, when buyers started poking around. Those looking in the cockpit would exclaim, "Where is the gear stick?" Looking under the hood (bonnet), it would be an incredulous, "Where is the V8?" Lesser shocks followed. When the top was folded back inside the rear-hinged trunk (boot), there was about enough space left over for a few good books; it was so small that Plymouth offered an optional "trunk-trailer." The fat rear tires sought out every imperfection on America's aging roads, and there were those out-of-place, ineffective-looking front "fenderettes" (bumpers), added to satisfy interfering Federal bureaucrats.

Models were upgraded to 253 bhp (173 kW) in 1998, giving a truer hot-rod-like performance, but the Prowler still lacked a V8 and manual transmission. Purists remained displeased, thinking that its looks towered above its purpose. But was it really one of the Fifty Worst Cars of All Time? *Time* magazine surely was just grinding some personal grudge. **BS**

CLK GTR | Mercedes-AMG

D

1997 • 365 cu in/5,986 cc, V12 • 612 bhp/456 kW • 0–60 mph/97 kph in 3.8 seconds • 214 mph/345 kph

When the International Touring Car Championship folded in 1996, Mercedes' luxury-car subsidiary, AMG, was suddenly left without a showcase. A new one was soon found: the FIA GT Championship. The entry requirement for any car was that a minimum of twenty-five examples of that car should be produced. Mercedes did not have a car, so to ensure the AMG team could participate in the first race of the 1997 season, FIA officials moved the deadline by which the production cars had to be ready. It was moved from before racing started . . . to December 31, 1997.

AMG hurriedly got to work. It designed and built its first two CLK GTRs in only 128 days, just in time for the first round of the championship. There, the CLK began poorly, losing the first three rounds to McLaren. AMG officials decided not to race at Le Mans, but take advantage of the enforced layoff to improve the CLK and close the gap on McLaren. The decision proved a wise one. Mercedes-AMG proceeded to dominate the remainder of the season, winning both the driver's and constructor's titles and having its driver, Bernd Schneider, crowned World Champion.

The CLK GTR's carbon-fiber monocoque chassis was vaguely reminiscent of the CLK road car, but a very confined, almost claustrophobic cockpit inflicted a like-it-or-not upright driving posture. And getting out through its gull-wing doors was only funny if one happened to be a bystander when one pulled up.

The remainder of the twenty-five road-going examples required were produced in 1998 and 1999. The CLK GTR's exclusivity and rocketlike performance made it one of the great supercars of the 1990s. **BS**

The Ferrari F50 certainly looked like a top performer, but it only matched its rivals rather than leaving them in the dust. ▷

VehiCross | Isuzu (J)

1997 • 214 cu in/3,500 cc, V6 • 215 bhp/160 kW • 0–60 mph/97 kph in 8.8 seconds • 115 mph/185 kph

It was a futuristic vision—an aggressive-looking, sporty off-roader that could turn heads *and* conquer the toughest terrain. With its black plastic-clad lower half, chrome wheels, and sporty body shape, Isuzu's concept vehicle at the 1993 Tokyo Motor Show was like a cartoon version of an off-roader.

The VehiCross was such a hit that Isuzu decided to launch it as a full production model. The industry expected the usual watered-down version of a concept car, but what it got was this avant-garde sport utility vehicle. Behind the scenes, Isuzu had used avant-garde management, and the finance department was not allowed to interfere. The company even rejected the practice of using customer clinics to appraise the design in case its ideas were diluted.

It was launched with an exterior that was brave and inspiring, while the compact crossover showcased much of Isuzu's technological prowess. A cutting-edge computer-controlled four-wheel-drive system, using twelve sensors all over the vehicle, ensured a high level of traction over all surfaces. The advanced suspension had a damping system with heat-expansion chambers for better handling both on and off-road. High ground clearance and a low-ratio gearbox ensured serious off-road driving.

The VehiCross had good performance thanks to a hefty 214-cubic-inch (3,500-cc) twenty-four-valve V6 with a variable induction system that maximized power across a wide rev range. There was plenty of muscle for tackling muddy hills and overtaking on the road, too. So when it entered the Paris–Dakar rally in 1998 few were surprised at the outcome . . . it won. **SH**

F50 | Ferrari (I)

1997 • 287 cu in/4,698 cc, V12 • 513 bhp/382 kW • 0–60 mph/97 kph in 3.7 seconds • 194 mph/312 kph

With the F50, Ferrari succeeded like never before in taking the principles, the form, the mechanics, and the high-tech specifications of Formula One and embodying them in a street car. The F50 was constructed to the same tolerances as an F1 racer, with weight considerations seldom applied to even the best road vehicles: examples include an aeronautically designed rubberized fuel tank; a wholly carbon-fiber chassis; a gearbox housing made from magnesium alloy; and an electronic control unit to minimize body roll. It had magnesium alloy wheels and cam covers, titanium hubs, and Nikasil (a matrix silicone-carbide) liners in its crankcase.

Gone were all the commonly accepted definitions of styling, too. Infinitely more seductive "F1 styling" involved space-age plastics such as Kevlar and honeycombed Nomex for its exterior panels, which formed a seamless, sweeping expanse of red all the way from the front air intakes to the rear spoiler.

But for all of this unbridled innovation, many saw the F50 as a failure. A new-model Ferrari is expected to set performance records as a rite of passage, but the F50 never did so. At the launch Ferrari made no press cars available, but *Car and Driver* magazine gained the permission of one F50 owner to do some acceleration runs at a test track in Dublin, Ohio. When these were done, the owner asked, "Was it as quick as other supercars?" The reply: "Faster than a Dodge Viper, half a second quicker than a Lamborghini Diablo."

Pity the poor Diablo owner. In the world of the supercar, there is always something else a little bit faster. And it is usually red. **BS**

Prius | Toyota (J)

1997 • 91 cu in/1,497 cc, S4, plus electric motor • 58 bhp/43 kW • 0–60 mph/97 kph in 12.7 seconds • unknown

The 1997 Toyota Prius was a key point in automobile history. Indeed, the Prius was dubbed by *Time* magazine as one of the most important cars of all time. Even its name was significant. It came from the Latin word for "prior" or "before," suggesting that the car is a predecessor of things to come.

The Toyota Prius is the world's first hybrid car, sold at below-cost price to show Toyota's commitment to green technology. To some, it is a leap toward clean and efficient motoring. To others, it is a symbol of how some people will buy anything if they think it projects the right image. And that is all down to the car's engines, because—being a hybrid—it has two forms of propulsion. In slow traffic an electric motor does the work, powered by nickel-metal hydride batteries. A 91-cubic-inch (1,497-cc) gasoline engine kicks in when the driver needs more power for acceleration, while also charging the batteries. Even the brakes play their part, using recovered energy to charge the batteries further.

The technology is undeniably clever, but from the car's launch opinion was divided over whether it really was as green as Toyota claimed. Nonetheless, the car quickly attained iconic status with Hollywood stars rushing to be seen driving one. In 2003 five Priuses were even used as limousines at the Academy Awards. **JI**

Forester | Subaru (J)

1997 • 122 cu in/2,000 cc, F4 • 123 bhp/90 kW • 0–60 mph/ 97 kph in 7.9 seconds • 123 mph/198 kph

Few knew what to make of the new Subaru Forester when it launched. Some called it a hatchback, others an off-roader or a sports sedan (saloon). The only thing that was certain was that it was a lot of fun to drive.

The Forester was developed on the same platform as the Impreza, had the engine of the Outback, but was styled more like a Legacy. Its four doors and big tailgate made it seem like a hatchback, but its performance made it more like a sports car. The Subaru "soft-roader" had the permanent four-wheel drive and the low- and high-ratio gearboxes of a proper mud-plugger, but its cross-country abilities were restricted by limited ground clearance and standard road tires.

The Forester came in turbo and nonturbo versions (figures for the S-Turbo version are given above), but there were no diesels. The engine is a flat-four boxer design with pistons placed horizontally either side of the crankshaft, making it smoother than a standard one and capable of fitting into a lower front end.

A lower center of gravity helped the Forester's handling, too. It was more agile on tarmac than other sport utility vehicles, and felt more rugged and durable than other station wagons (estates) or hatchbacks. To emphasize its practicality, it even included a washing-up bowl on top of the spare wheel. **SH**

406 Coupe V6 | Peugeot (F)

1997 • 183 cu in/3,000 cc, V6 • 190 bhp/140 kW • 0–60 mph/97 kph in 7.6 seconds • 146 mph/235 kph

Peugeot called in Italian design house Pininfarina to draw the lines of the coupe version of its popular medium-sized family sedan (saloon). The result was a beautifully styled, elegant two-door.

Rumors were that Pininfarina's Lorenzo Ramaciotti (designer of the Ferrari 456 and 550 Maranello) had already pitched the design to Ferrari in a bid to tempt them to build a budget supercar. That failed, so the French carmaker got it instead.

There was a range of engines, but the obvious line-topper was the twenty-four-valve, direct-injection V6. Handling was fine, with good grip and precise steering. Only the bland, plasticky interior deprived the car of a leap into a higher class. At least the interior was spacious, and, unusually for a coupe, there was ample room in the back. Equipment levels were lavish: alloy wheels, digital air-conditioning with climate control, a CD autochanger, rain-sensitive wipers, trip computer, leather seats, side air bags, an auto-dipping rearview mirror, headlight washers, speed-sensitive steering, and a Brembo four-piston braking system.

The 406 Coupe V6 had to wait for the 2002 movie *Le Boulet* (*Dead Weight*) for a major role. It featured in a dramatic chase through central Paris involving a cop on a motorcycle. It escaped, naturally. **SH**

R390 | Nissan (J)

1998 • 214 cu in/3,500 cc, V8 • 641 bhp/478 kW • 0–60 mph/97 kph in 3.1 seconds • 217 mph/350 kph

When Nissan decided to return to motorsport in 1995, the 24 Hours of Le Mans race was at the top of its priority list. The R390 GT1 was developed for it with help from the United Kingdom. The car's lines came from draughtsman Ian Callum, who had only just finished the Aston Martin DB7. Under the gorgeous bodywork lay a massively powerful V8 engine designed by Nissan in cooperation with race chief Tom Walkinshaw.

But to homologate for Le Mans, Nissan needed to prove that at least one similar car had been created for the road. The first Nissan R390 was immediately one of the most exciting road cars in existence. It was painted a metallic bright blue color, came with a red leather interior, and was road-registered in Japan. Nissan never sold this one-off road-going special. In fact, the company still holds it in a hidden lockup.

But when a demanding European customer became aware of the existence of this car, he asked Nissan for one to join his extraordinary collection of supercars. Money was not an issue. Nissan decided to give it a go and thus built a second road car. This one is still privately owned by the man who commissioned it, and who prefers to remain anonymous.

In all, that brings the total of Nissan R390s built—including the R390 GT1 Le Mans cars—to eight. **JB**

TT RS
2 TTS

⊲ The unmistakable shape of the Audi TT was applauded by design critics, and proved popular with customers, too.

TT | Audi (D)

1998 • 151 cu in/2,480 cc, S5 • 335 bhp/250 kW • 0–60 mph/97 kph in 4.6 seconds • 155 mph/249 kph

The Audi TT gets its name from the famous Isle of Man Tourist Trophy motorcycle race, which has been running since 1904. In the 1950s NSU (which later merged with Auto-Union to form Audi) had dominated the competition. The German company, in commemoration of its motorcycling heritage, had launched the rotary-engined NSU 1000 TT in 1965.

Thirty years later, at the Volkswagen Group Design Center in California, the TT moniker was revived for a sporty 2+2 concept car; this was unveiled at the 1995 Frankfurt Motor Show. Although it was based on the Golf Mark IV platform, its elegant, Bauhaus-inspired design was considered avant-garde. Sweeping exterior curves and uncluttered styling were matched on the inside by a snug, ergonomic cockpit; brushed-aluminum detailing gave the impression that this was a car built by engineers, rather than robots.

Audi's sports coupe was considered a masterpiece of modern industrial design. Following the car's debut, thousands flocked to their local Audi dealers to put down deposits. By the late 1990s, the TT had become a must-have fashion accessory. However, the Bauhaus movement's guiding principle that "form follows function" did not strictly apply to the high-priced TT. It had the looks and plenty of power, but its handling was disappointing, especially when compared to its nearest rivals, the Porsche Boxster and the Honda S2000.

In 2006, the Mark II TT was launched. The new version finally combined both form and function, and Audi won the highly prestigious World Design Car of the Year award in 2007. Performance figures for the range-topping TT RS are given above. **DS**

Niva | Chevrolet (RUS)

1998 • 104 cu in/1,700 cc, S4 • 82 bhp/61 kW • 0–60 mph/97 kph in 17 seconds • 87 mph/140 kph

When General Motors signed a joint venture contract with Russian company AvtoVAZ (formerly VAZ), its mission was to replace the Lada Niva, a motoring icon that had been on sale for more than thirty years.

The idea was to build a car that offered off-road capacities similar to Russia's favorite four-wheel-drive, but with more comfort. General Motors (GM) decided to retain the old Niva's base, as its mechanicals had more than proved themselves, not least on Russia's tough tundra. The body and interior, however, were completely renewed, and the crude 104-cubic-inch (1,700-cc) four-cylinder gas engine was given a revamp.

The end result was a car—badged as a Chevrolet rather than a Lada—that was still able to ford 2 feet (0.6 m) of water and climb 45-degree gradients. Its looks, however, were something else, as the new Niva certainly did not have the rocky appearance of its predecessor. The lines were rounded, and had more in common with Asian "soft-roaders" than the hardcore 4x4 the Niva used to be.

But before the new Niva went on sale, there were more mountains to be climbed. After the concept was shown in 1998, everything remained silent for a long time. It turned out that GM-AvtoVAZ had problems with production of the new car. A planned 110-cubic-inch (1,800-cc) engine was canceled, and it took until 2001 before the car found its way to showrooms.

In Russia and Eastern Europe, the Chevrolet Niva is now slowly replacing the Lada Niva, but exporting it to Western countries remains problematic. Even a facelift carried out by Italian design house Bertone in 2009 failed to boost its appeal. **JB**

A 2002 advertisement for the Smart Fortwo entices buyers with a convertible version of the diminutive city car. ▷

Indigo 3000 | Jösse Cars (S)

1998 • 183 cu in/3,000 cc, S6 • 204 bhp/152 kW • 0–60 mph/97 kph in 6.5 seconds • 155 mph/250 kph

The Jösse company was set up in 1997 in Arvika, a country town in southern Sweden, in order to build a classic roadster powered by a big Volvo engine. The car Jösse designed, the Indigo 3000, was a traditional open-top two-seater with rear-wheel drive.

Apart from its modern technology, it could have been an Austin-Healey from thirty years before. The Indigo 3000 had lightweight composite body panels on a rigid space frame chassis made of galvanized welded steel. It was fitted with power steering, electric heated and adjustable wing mirrors, automatic headlights, and an adjustable seat and steering wheel. There were disc brakes all around, although an antilock braking system was only an optional extra.

The all-aluminum engine, a nonturbocharged Volvo straight-six, produced plenty of power. With twenty-four valves and multipoint fuel injection, it produced very fast acceleration, an inspiring noise, and a top speed that was limited to 155 mph (250 kph).

Everything was closely linked to Volvo. Designer Hans Philip Zackau had worked on the Volvo 850 hatchback. The five-speed manual gearbox and rear suspension was from a Volvo 960, the steering column from a Volvo 850, and the seat base from a Volvo S40.

The Jösse team marketed its roadster as an affordable high-performance car with an emphasis on safety; there were roll-over bars behind each seat to protect occupants, and the sills were built high to give protection against side impacts.

Sadly, Jösse only built forty-eight before the company disappeared, so the Indigo 3000 is now a very rare sight, even on the roads of southern Sweden. **SH**

Fortwo | Smart (D)

1998 • 61 cu in/999 cc, S3 • 84 bhp/62 kW • 0–60 mph/97 kph in 13.8 seconds • 92 mph/148 kph

The Smart car is like a Swatch watch: cheap, colorful, and a bit funky; it was also sold—initially—from a transparent box. In fact, SMH, makers of the Swatch, worked with Daimler-Benz to create the Smart, but creative differences during the model's early life led to Daimler buying out SMH's shares in the project.

The car was dreamed up at the Mercedes-Benz design center in California. It was planned to be a two-person city car for the future, able to sip fuel and grab parking spaces too small for other drivers. In 1998 it went on sale from 600 glass "Smart towers" across Europe, where it was displayed as if in a vending machine. Marketing insisted on using lower-case type for the small car, so officially it is a "smart."

With 61 cubic inches (999 cc), the Smart was never going to be fast. It is fun for the city and lively in small roads, but struggles to keep up with traffic on highways. The main complaints are its noise, hard ride, and jerky semiautomatic gearbox. Even so, it has proved popular as an economic city car, one that has indeed turned out to be amazingly easy to park.

By its tenth birthday in 2008, more than a million Smarts had been sold in thirty-seven countries. Autosport entrepreneur Roger Penske sold 45,000 in the United States from 2007 to 2011 when his dealer network had exclusive rights.

Smart has kept up a relentless series of models, such as the Roadster and Roadster Coupe of 2003 to 2005, and the Brabus. The Electric Drive of 2011 delivers 87 mpg (3.3 liter per 100 km). Singer Robbie Williams' Brabus-tuned "Crossblade" cabrio version was used in advertising promotions for the brand. **LT**

smart
>>Less CO_2. More O_2.
What a breath of fresh air. Now you can enjoy all that oxygen knowing your smart cabrio has the lowest CO_2 emissions of any convertible. And while you soak up the solar power, you can revel in the fact that the cabrio's fuel consumption is a measly 57.6mpg. Even the remotely operated hood saves you using too much energy. How cool is that?
Great minds think smart.
smart - a brand of DaimlerChrysler

KX51 KHP

Multipla | Fiat

I

1998 • 116 cu in/1,900 cc, S4 • 120 bhp/88 kW • 0–60 mph/97 kph in 12.2 seconds • 110 mph/177 kph

The world did not know what to make of the strange people carrier that Fiat launched in 1998. It was proudly displayed at the Museum of Modern Art in New York, and the BBC's *Top Gear* program voted it Family Car of the Year for four consecutive years. But it also judged the Multipla "the world's ugliest car." When Simon Cowell appeared on the same car show, he said the Multipla looked like "it had a disease."

The object of all this comment was a humble people carrier that dared to be different. It was unusually short and wide, with two rows of three seats inside. It was crammed with clever new design touches that led to a very practical vehicle, but it still attracted as much derision as desire. The way the windshield met the broad, flat hood (bonnet) was certainly a unique design feature. Other parts of distinction included a bulbous, glassy rear end, long wing mirrors on stalks, and sidelights on a strip at the back of the hood. Yet original U.K. models bore a Fiat sticker on the rear window that said, "Wait until you see the front."

The interior was surprisingly spacious considering that the multipurpose vehicle was based on a three-door Bravo hatchback; it had room for six adults and their luggage. With its rear seats removed, the Multipla had the capacity of a medium-sized van. It performed reasonably and handled tidily thanks to the wide stance, although it was tricky to park in narrow streets.

Subsequent versions of the Multipla were progressively normalized. The Multipla is still awkwardly wide and still seats six in two rows of three, but now looks similar to rival people carriers. *Top Gear* declared, "Now you look boring as well as a bit stupid." **SH**

Cube | Nissan

J

1998 • 110 cu in/1,800 cc, S4 • 122 bhp/90 kW • 0–60 mph/97 kph in 10 seconds • 105 mph/169 kph

The design was reputedly inspired by a 1950s refrigerator. No wonder the Nissan Cube is one of the most distinctive vehicles on the road. It certainly has the boxiest design this side of a panel van.

Strangely, the tiny Nissan people carrier has gotten more and more eccentrically cuboid since its launch. The original Cube was based on the Nissan Micra hatchback and seemed to be just a high-roofed variant of that car. It was mainly sold in Japan. The second generation arrived in 2002, sporting rounder, more toylike looks and a unique wraparound rear window on one side only. The third generation, from 2008, was the first to be officially exported, and it soon found a cult following in the United States and Europe.

The Cube continued Nissan's tradition of micro-retro-oddity cars, like the Figaro and S-Cargo. It fell into the category of "love it or hate it." Style guru Stephen Bayley praised it as "an amusing affront to convention," while the *Los Angeles Times* called it "a box of ugly."

The reality was more mundane. The Cube was really a small hatchback with space for five tall adults and a load bay accessed by a side-hinged door. It was fun to drive, lively around town, and spacious, although sliding the rear seats backward would eat up most of the trunk (boot) space. But the Cube is well equipped, with a large glass sunroof, alloy wheels, and navigation system. Performance and fuel economy are average.

There is an electric version, and an electric part-time four-wheel-drive option. Some Cubes have manual gearboxes, some automatic, and some have a continuously variable transmission. Figures are given above for the most powerful version. **SH**

Drivers wanted.®

‹ Volkswagen's New Beetle was available in all the colors of the rainbow, as evidenced by this 1999 advertisement.

New Beetle | Volkswagen (D)

1998 • 121 cu in/1,984 cc, S4 • 115 bhp/86 kW • 0–60 mph/97 kph in 10.9 seconds • 115 mph/185 kph

The Volkswagen (VW) New Beetle was unmistakably an evolution of its Porsche-designed forefather, and it inherited a number of design details. Like the old air-cooled Bugs, it featured separate wings, sloping headlights, large rear "elephant foot" light clusters, and the same rounded profile. Unlike its ancestor, this Beetle was based on the water-cooled Mark IV Golf.

A wide range of powerplants were available, but mechanically the New Beetle was not particularly groundbreaking. However, its shape was a refreshing change at a time when vehicle design had become rather stale. Available in a wide pallet of vivid colors, including lime greens, acid yellows, and bright oranges, it was an instant hit with style-conscious drivers. In 2003 sales further increased when the convertible New Beetle was launched.

Not all the news was good. Although the German brand had been famed for its excellent quality standards, many of these Mexican-built New Beetles were plagued by electrical and mechanical problems. Interior trim was brittle, and the convertible had various issues with hood (bonnet) and window mechanisms.

When production ceased at the end of 2010, around 1,164,000 cars had been sold worldwide, with an estimated 75 percent of owners being female.

In North America, the announcement that a second-generation new Beetle was on its way was made during the last episode of *Oprah's Favorite Things* in November 2010. In a clever piece of showmanship, VW staff then gave all 275 members of the studio audience keys to their very own New Beetle, to be collected from dealerships the following year. **DS**

TD 2000 Silverstone | TD Cars (MAL)

1998 • 122 cu in/2,000 cc, S4 • 130 bhp/96 kW • 0–60 mph/97 kph in 6.7 seconds • 112 mph/180 kph

The Silverstone looks like a British sports car from the 1930s, but is actually a modern lightweight fiberglass body mounted on a steel chassis and powered by a twin-cam Toyota engine. In all respects other than nostalgia, it is a better car than the original.

The Silverstone was designed to capture the best of the period charm of the 1936 MG TA Midget. This MG was the sort of car driven by mustachioed RAF pilots, reveling in the glamour of wire wheels, leather seats, and a wooden dashboard and steering wheel. The Malaysian retro replica uses burr walnut for the dashboard, red leather upholstery, a wood-rimmed steering wheel, traditional sidescreen "curtain" windows, and black-on-white dials. There is even a side-opening hood (bonnet), spare wheel mounted on the trunk (boot) lid, tonneau cover, luggage rack, optional two-tone color scheme, and a stainless steel bar on which to mount to mount motoring badges.

Thankfully, the car is not entirely true to the original. There are decent disc brakes all around, and safety features such as a collapsible steering wheel, third brake light, roll-over bar, and side impact bars. Modern features include a CD/radio system with powered aerial, immobilizer, and air-conditioning.

The drive is still sent to the rear wheels, but through a modern Japanese three-speed automatic or five-speed manual gearbox. Other improvements include electronic fuel injection and modern independent double-wishbone sports suspension.

How do the two compare? Well, from a standstill the MG TA reached 60 mph (97 kph) in twenty-three seconds. The TD 2000 takes just 6.7 seconds. **SH**

Accord Type R | Honda (J)

1998 • 134 cu in/2,200 cc, S4 • 220 bhp/162 kW • 0–60 mph/97 kph in 6.9 seconds • 142 mph/229 kph

The Honda Accord Type R was not easily distinguished from the rest of the Accord line. There was no visible clue to the stiffened independent sports suspension, the uprated brakes, or the limited-slip differential. The dual exhaust system and the lightweight close-ratio six-speed manual gearbox were invisible, and there was no way of knowing whether the engine under the hood (bonnet) was the 134-cubic-inch (2,200-cc) VTEC unit. In fact, on most models the only indication was a tiny red "R" on the front grille and rear trunk (boot) lid.

In the United States the Accord line was a bestseller, but in Europe it was seen as an expensive and bland alternative to home-grown vehicles. The four-door front-wheel-drive sedan (saloon) was comfortable and reliable, but was only loved by the sedate.

So the Type R—with its high-revving VTEC virility—was quite a shock. The car was stripped out to make it lighter, with the rear power windows and sunroof being ditched, and the trim minimized. Inside the car were Recaro sports seats, a leather-trimmed Momo steering wheel, and a stubby short-throw gearlever.

The Type R was only sold in Europe, and had a short, five-year production life. But the Accord Type R did its job—it made Europe appreciate that the family-sized Honda was not just for families. **SH**

Seville STS | Cadillac (USA)

1998 • 278 cu in/4,565 cc, V8 • 300 bhp/221 kW • 0–60 mph/97 kph in 6.8 seconds • 135 mph/217 kph

The 1997 and 1998 Cadillac Sevilles appear almost as twins when viewed from afar. The styling of the 1998 Seville STS was unremarkable, a little wider than its predecessor, a little shorter, a little rounder; an evolution more than a revolution. But the great thing about Cadillac's new four-door sedan (saloon) was its Northstar V8 engine, one of the best anywhere in the world according to those who know. It did not require fuel injection, and only needed servicing once every 100,000 miles (160,000 km).

The STS also had a Performance Algorithm Shifting device, or PAS, which anticipated a corner and selected the proper gear before the car even started to turn into it. Add that to its "road sensing suspension," which self-adjusts as the car passes over the bitumen, and there is barely anything left for the driver to do but steer.

On the downside, the automatic gearbox was frustratingly slow. The STS was also a front-wheel-drive car in a rear-wheel-drive world, even if Cadillac's own surveys suggested that consumers cared little which set of wheels the drivetrain was connected to.

The STS was Cadillac's first foray into Europe and the best Cadillac to date, yet sales were poor. It just proved too big and fuel-hungry for European tastes, and lacked the quality of Mercedes and BMW. **BS**

Racing Puma | Ford (USA)

1999 • 102 cu in/1,679 cc, S4 • 155 bhp/116 kW • 0–60 mph/97 kph in 7.8 seconds • 130 mph/209 kph

Ford's Puma ST160 concept was a "rally-car-inspired" version of its diminuitive sports coupe, first showcased at the Geneva Motor Show in 1999. Buoyed up by positive feedback, Ford decided to produce a limited run of 1,000 Racing Pumas in partnership with Tickford Engineering in the United Kingdom.

Part-assembled Pumas, all painted the same Ford Racing Blue, were shipped to Tickford, where their standard interiors were stripped and replaced by blue Alacantra trim, Sparco racing seats, and a three-spoke steering wheel. With Ford's new 102-cubic-inch (1,679-cc) sixteen-valve Sigma engine (developed in partnership with Yamaha), and a Janspeed sports exhaust, performance was up nearly 30 bhp (22 kW) on the standard Puma. Motoring journalists described the Racing Puma as the best-handling front-wheel-drive car they had ever driven, and ranked it alongside Honda's Integra Type R and the Lotus M100 Elan.

However, outsourcing the convoluted production process to Tickford made the car ridiculously expensive—even at $36,000 (£23,000), Ford lost money on every one sold. Struggling to shift unsold cars from its showrooms, Ford cut the production run to just 500 U.K. cars. Today, the very rare Racing Puma is highly sought after by Ford fanatics. **DS**

Celica | Toyota (J)

1999 • 109 cu in/1,794 cc, S4 • 188 bhp/140 kW • 0–60 mph/97 kph in 7.2 seconds • 140 mph/225 kph

In 1999, the seventh and final generation of Toyota's Celica sports coupe appeared. The Celica Mark VII was given a sharp new design with a stubby tail, air-scoops on the hood (bonnet) and beneath the front fender (bumper), and more aggressive slants for its headlight "eyes." The car looked fast, but this was a Celica for the road rather than rallying.

Only 109-cubic-inch (1,794-cc) engines were available, but with different power outputs across the globe. The high-revving VVT-i engine, with variable valve timing and multipoint fuel injection, was the best performer. Figures for the European version are given above; it was slightly detuned for North America.

The Celica had always scored as a sensible choice due to its long service intervals, reasonable running costs, safety features, and depreciation. These factors certainly counted for more than the rear-seat space, which was only suitable for children. However, the big glass liftback gave access to a large luggage area that could be increased by folding down the rear seats.

The Celica Mark VII was competing in a tough marketplace. Rivals such as the Mazda RX-8, Chrysler Crossfire, and Nissan 350Z were stealing its sales, so finally, after thirty-six-years, the Celica series was brought to a conclusion in 2006. **SH**

DB7 Vantage | Aston Martin

GB

1999 • 362 cu in/5,935 cc, V12 • 420 bhp/309 kW • 0–60 mph/97 kph in 5 seconds • 184 mph/296 kph

The DB7 was the first Aston Martin to be developed in collaboration with the Ford Motor Company, which became Aston's owner in 1988. The model debuted at the Geneva Motor Show in 1993. It came on a Jaguar XJS floorpan (Ford also owned Jaguar), and the architectural purity of its engine drew from that of the 1995–97 Jaguar XJR. On the outside there was an odd sense of déjà vu as well, most obviously in its shape; the new DB7 could, from a distance, almost be mistaken for Jaguar's new XK8. Yes, there were unquestionable similarities, but the new DB7 was still the start of a series that would be nothing other than pure Aston Martin.

In 1999 the DB7 and its convertible cousin were succeeded by the DB7 Vantage and Vantage Volante (convertible). Vantage was Aston Martin's term for "performance," with all Vantage models of the past having engines significantly tweaked for maximum power. This time, however, the upgrading was taken one step further with the new Vantage model being the first production Aston ever to be fitted with a V12 engine. This represented a massive increase in power over the 1993–98 models, and the new car required suitably upgraded Brembo brakes and a significantly modified chassis and suspension system to help it cope with its new-found muscle.

The interior had all the usual refinements buyers would expect in an Aston—leather, wood, suede, and great instrumentation—but it was the DB7's handling that proved to be its most significant leap forward. The car left behind forever the tell-tale wobbles of the past and finally became something that all Aston lovers could be proud of when taking corners. **BS**

SC-5A | Strathcarron

GB

1999 • 73 cu in/1,200 cc, S4 • 125 bhp/93 kW • 0–60 mph/97 kph in 5.6 seconds • 125 mph/201 kph

The Strathcarron SC-5A was a small ultralightweight sports car dreamed up by Ian McPherson, a motoring columnist and author of two spy novels who was to inherit the title of Lord Strathcarron in 2006. The car debuted at the Geneva Motor Show in 1999. It was a composite-bodied two-seater originally powered by a mid-placed 73-cubic-inch (1,200-cc) Triumph Trophy motorcycle engine producing 125 bhp (93 kW). The bike's six-speed sequential gearbox was used, too.

The SC-5A made plenty of appearances at track events. The small, spartan roadster with no roof, doors, or heater won many admirers. Its high-revving engine was seriously quick and, with a sophisticated suspension setup, it handled very neatly.

The Strathcarron company's idea was to sell around fifty cars a year from 2000 onward, but a sudden change in U.K. legislation caused problems just after its launch. Suddenly the SC-5A was not road-legal. Hastily, the design was changed, and the bike engine was replaced by Rover's K-series unit. But when that was eventually done, further clouds appeared, this time of a financial nature; by 2001, with just seventeen cars built, the company had run out of money.

Selling the project seemed the only possibility left, and that is exactly what happened. In 2002 the rights to build the car were taken over by Javan Smith, who later offered the car for sale as the Javan R1. The shape remained virtually unchanged, but once again a new powerplant was fitted into the car. Smith managed to have it fitted with a 220-bhp (164-kW) Honda VTEC engine, which gave the car a better power-to-weight ratio than many a supercar. **JB**

The 1999 Pagani Zonda was a pivotal model in the history of supercars, combining power and beauty as never before. ⊡

Insight | Honda

(J)

1999 • 61 cu in/995 cc, S3 plus electric • 67 bhp/50 kW • 0–60 mph/97 kph in 10.6 seconds • 112 mph/180 kph

Which was the first production auto hybrid to go on sale worldwide? Most people would say the Toyota Prius, but it was actually the Honda Insight, which went on sale in Japan and key global markets in 1999. The Prius launched in Japan two years earlier, but did not go global until 2001. The Insight of 2000 was awarded an impressive U.S. Environmental Protection Agency (EPA) rating of 70 mpg (4 liters per 100 km) on the highway, and 61 mpg (4.6 liters per 100km) in the city.

At its launch in 1999, Honda challenged several U.S. automotive magazines to an economy run. The staff of *Car and Driver* came up with an ingenious cheat and rigged up a Ford Excursion with a large box behind it, in which the Insight could be driven in a nearly drag-free aerodynamic environment. They won, achieving 121.7 mpg (2.3 liters per 100km) at an average speed of 58 mph (93 kph). In the real world, the figures were not quite so impressive. With CVT (Continuously Variable Transmission) automatic and air-con, the EPA rating dropped to 57/56 mpg (4.9/5 liters per 100 km).

The Insight, whose gas engine switched with a 13-bhp (10-kW) electric motor, was too radical in design. Honda had reckoned its most receptive market to be stylish city-dwelling early adopters, who would want a car that made a statement. The teardrop-shaped Insight was cute and chic, with spats over its rear wheels to improve aerodynamics, but it was only a two-seater and it had very little storage space.

The roomy Prius sold in the millions, while the Insight struggled and was dropped in 2006. A new generation arrived in 2009, but it had become a conventional-looking, practical hatchback. **LT**

Zonda | Pagani

(I)

1999 • 365 cu in/5,987 cc, V12 • 740 bhp/552 kW • 0–60 mph/97 kph in 3 seconds • 233 mph/375 kph

When, in 1992, Argentinian entrepreneur Horacio Pagani set up shop under the noses of Ferrari and Lamborghini, few would have believed that he would change perceptions of what a supercar should be.

Pagani and Formula One legend Juan Manuel Fangio worked on early designs for a mid-engined sports car that would be thrilling to drive and beautiful to look at. Pagani was determined to make his car an automotive art form, with a lavishly quilted interior, bespoke instruments, and chromed switchgear. Fangio was willing to lend his name to the car on condition that it was powered by a Mercedes engine. Unfortunately, Fangio died before the finished car was unveiled at the 1999 Geneva Motor Show. As a mark of respect, the car was renamed "Zonda," after the warm winds that blow across the Argentinian Andes.

Aerospace technology featured in the Zonda's lightweight construction, and it also inspired the cars aesthetics; the driver's bubble canopy is set well forward like a fighter jet's, and the four exhaust pipes are clustered together like the barrels of a Gatling gun.

Around 140 cars were built during the twelve-year production run. Perhaps the greatest was the Zonda R track car, which smashed the Nürburgring lap record in June 2010 with a time of six minutes, forty-seven seconds. Its performance figures are given above.

Top Gear magazine was unstinting in its praise of Horacio Pagani as "the da Vinci of car builders—a rare genius whose mastery of the balance between poise and power, looks and aerodynamics, modernity and classical design has created arguably the purest driving machine on the planet." **DS**

TT Roadster | Audi

D

1999 • 120 cu in/1,968 cc, S4 • 168 bhp/125 kW • 0–60 mph/97 kph in 7.5 seconds • 140 mph/225 kph

Launched just one year after the coupe, the Mark I Audi TT Roadster was assembled at the same factory, in Győr, Hungary. Despite some bad press regarding its stability at high speed and minor electrical glitches, waiting lists were long for what had become the most desirable drop-top of the late 1990s.

The Bauhaus-inspired design of the TT was credited to the U.S. design team of J Mays and Freeman Thomas, who also worked together on Volkswagen's New Beetle. Although the convertible version lacked a little of the tin-top's elegant simplicity, it still looked good. Performance and handling were only slightly dented in comparison to the coupe, but then few people bought this car expecting it to behave like a stripped-out track racer. For this reason, many customers specified one of the more frugal powerplants from the Audi list for their TT. Many Mark I TT Roadsters received the 180-bhp (134-kW) 110-cubic-inch (1,800-cc), while the Mark II was available for the first time with a 120-cubic-inch (1,968-cc) turbo-diesel (performance figures shown above).

The better-handling Mark II is longer and wider than its predecessor, but the rear seats are still tiny. However, the powered roof can take quick advantage of any break in the weather, and is stowed away in under twelve seconds. The TT has always sold well in North America and southern Europe as an interesting, cut-rate alternative to the BMW Z4 and Mercedes SLK.

The TT Roadster has become a design icon. It remains the default choice of the fashion-conscious motorist looking for a stylish, well-built, open-top tourer with the added kudos of the Audi brand. **DS**

S2000 | Honda

J

1999 • 122 cu in/2,000 cc, S4 • 247 bhp/184 kW • 0–62 mph/100 kph in 6.2 seconds • 150 mph/241 kph

To celebrate its fiftieth anniversary, Honda built a tidy two-seater with one of the most powerful 122-cubic-inch (2,000-cc) nonturbo engines ever made. It was a lightweight, twin-cam, sixteen-valve unit incorporating many advanced technologies developed in racing.

The Honda engine included featuress such as variable-valve timing, which allowed it to produce more of its power in a wider range of driving situations. It worked right up to a screaming motorcycle-style 9,000-rpm redline; its maximum power of 247 bhp (184 kW) came at 8,300 rpm, the sort of revving that would blow most 122-cubic-inch (2,000-cc) engines apart. No wonder, then, that the Honda unit won the International Engine of the Year title five times.

Apart from that perky little powerplant, the Honda S2000 had precise powered steering, huge amounts of grip, and exciting rear-wheel-drive handling. It was an enthusiast's dream, with a six-speed close-ratio sports gearbox, limited-slip differential for improved traction, and high-quality double wishbone suspension. The S2000 was particularly highly rated for its reliability and build quality. It won the Premium Sports Car class in the JD Power Vehicle Ownership Satisfaction Study for three years and never left the top three spots.

Even so, the Honda roadster—successor to the S500, 600, and 800 of the 1960s—lacked some of the lovable personality that was making the Mazda MX-5 such a worldwide success at the same time.

Midlife revisions added traction control, tweaked suspension for a more reliable grip, and a power hood (bonnet) that closed in six seconds. Yet buyers started to drift away, and production stopped in 2009. **SH**

GORGEOUS commands
a second look.
JAGUAR.CO.UK
JAGUA
DIESE
THE S-TYPE TWIN TURBO DIESEL
Beauty cannot be measured by one thing alone. Only the
perfect combination of poise and good looks stops everyone in their tracks.

◁ The elegant retro styling of the Jaguar S-Type is used as a key sales feature in this advertisement from the early 2000s.

S-Type | Jaguar (GB)

1999 • 183 cu in/3,000 cc, V6 • 240 bhp/177 kW • 0–60 mph/97 kph in 8 seconds • 141 mph/267 kph

The design of the S-Type deliberately recalled Jaguar's motoring heritage in an attempt to break into a market dominated by German badges. The rounded rear window, four separate headlights, and retro grille were reminders of the Jaguars of the 1960s, as was the name. But under the classic styling was a modern international car built in Jaguar's old Castle Bromwich factory in England . . . and in Taiwan in Asia.

The four-door executive Jaguar shared its platform with the Ford Thunderbird and Lincoln LS. This was a rear-wheel-drive sports sedan (saloon) for the new century, created by British car designer Geoff Lawson. The car was intended to take sales from BMW, Audi, and Mercedes, so it came with a wide range of engines, from a 153-cubic-inch (2,500-cc) V6 to a 256-cubic-inch (4,200-cc) V8. There was even a 165-cubic-inch (2,700-cc) twin-turbo V6 diesel version that had appeared in a Citroën and a Land Rover. Figures above are for the 1999 183-cubic-inch (3,000-cc) V6 automatic. A supercharged S-Type R later joined the line, boasting a sporty body kit, a 256-cubic-inch (4,200-cc) V8, and a 0–60 mph (97 kph) acceleration of just 5.3 seconds.

All S-Types had a classy feel to match the styling inside and out. The ride was quiet and comfortable, and the handling refined. Engines were smooth and powerful. The interior had the Jaguar ambience, often of wood and leather, but always with a traditional layout and good level of equipment: cruise control, automatic headlights, electric driver's seat, and heated mirrors. But the tradition only went so far; instead of being standard, the Jaguar hood (bonnet) ornament, the leaping Jaguar statuette, was just an option. **SH**

Skyline GT-R R34 | Nissan (J)

1999 • 164 cu in/2,688 cc, S6 • 276 bhp/206 kW • 0–60 mph/97 kph in 5.2 seconds • 155 mph/250 kph

The last to bear the name Skyline, the R34 was the fifth incarnation of Nissan's classic performance car. Its eventual replacement would simply be called the GT-R.

While the engine was the same as the previous, fourth-generation model, the new car was shorter, with less of a front overhang. Its nose was subtly different, too, taking a small step toward the totally new look that the GT-R was to assume a few years down the line.

In the cabin was an LCD screen that displayed information such as oil and water temperature, turbo pressure, torque split, and even throttle position.

The 164-cubic-inch (2,688-cc), six-cylinder, twin-turbo engine produced 276 bhp (206 kW). At least on paper it did. Many owners of standard cars reported higher readings, and tuning shops found it easy to tease a lot more from the Nissan motor. It is a testament to the strength of the R34's engine and transmission that they could handle that unplanned-for horsepower.

Although the R34's engine was much the same as that of the previous model, it had been refined further for a smoother performance. That is not to say that the R34 was not every bit as much of a hoodlum as any previous Skyline GT-R. The car starred in the 2003 movie *2 Fast 2 Furious* but proved too good for the camera. Because the director needed it to step out its back end in true Hollywood style, he had the R34's front driveshaft disconnected, making it two-wheel drive. The Skyline GT-R R34 really was too good to be true.

An R34 V-Spec (Victory Specification) model carried the ATTESA system to control the car's four-wheel-drive transmission and distribute the torque to each wheel according to its level of grip or slip. **JI**

The 2010 Audi E-tron concept car features an electric motor for each of its four wheels.

2000–PRESENT

The BMW Z8 left critics confused, but it was still stylish enough to be used by James Bond in *The World Is Not Enough* (1999). ⊡

ML 55 AMG | Mercedes-Benz (D)

2000 • 332 cu in/5,439 cc, V8 • 342 bhp/252 kW • 0–60 mph/97 kph in 6.9 seconds • 150 mph/241 kph

When the Mercedes-Benz ML 55 AMG off-roader was released in 2000, it was immediately the fastest, best-handling sport utility vehicle in the world. At its heart was a fabulous AMG-tuned aluminum 332-cubic-inch (5,439-cc) twenty-four-valve V8 engine.

Technology improved handling beyond that of the standard M-Class. The AMG's stability-control software could sense a loss of traction and intervene with targeted braking to set the vehicle back on to its intended course. The AMG was also the first SUV to have both front- and side-mounted air bags with occupant detection mechanisms.

The new model was spacious and well-equipped, of course. The interior was leather and walnut, with fine seats and gadgets to play with. The car's overall finish, however, was not Mercedes' best. The engine and chassis modifications may have been refined to a fault in Germany, but the final assembly was completed in the United States, at Mercedes' M-Class factory in Tuscaloosa County, Alabama.

In the BBC television auto show *Top Gear*, an imperfection in the AMG's external panel work was highlighted when host Jeremy Clarkson inserted his fingers in between the rear fender (bumper) and the taillights. That hopeless panel gap was typical of the less than perfect finish of the AMG and led to cruel but well-deserved jokes about the "Alabama Mercedes."

Overall, though, the ML 55 AMG was a huge hit. A high-performance variant of the Mercedes 320, it offered the kick of a sports car, the refinement of a luxury sedan (saloon), and the muscle to match the best off-road 4x4s of its era. **BS**

Z8 | BMW (D)

2000 • 302 cu in/4,941 cc, V8 • 400 bhp/298 kW • 0–60 mph/97 kph in 4.8 seconds • 155 mph/249 kph

In the 1999 James Bond movie *The World Is Not Enough*, a BMW Z8 driven by Pierce Brosnan ended up being sliced in half by a tree-cutting helicopter. But it was a measure of the new BMW's glamour and kudos that it even made it that far. Of the 5,703 made, all were hand-finished and roughly half were exported to the United States. *Friends* actor Matt Perry managed to crash his, happily not fatally or into a helicopter.

The BMW Z8 was the production variant of the Z07 concept car that was shown at the 1997 Tokyo Motor Show. Intended to evoke and celebrate the classic BMW 507 of 1956, it was originally designed by Henrik Fisker in California as a styling exercise.

There was nothing historical about the performance, though. Powered by the V8 from the BMW M5, the Z8 had modern acceleration figures to complement its classic styling. BMW only made it with a six-speed manual gearbox, although the Alpina firm offered a version with an automatic.

The swoopy body hid a number of technical innovations, such as taillights and turn lights powered by neon tubes, turn indicators hidden in the side vents to render them invisible when not in use, and run-flat tires. To avoid cluttering the classic cabin, most of the modern equipment was modestly located behind covers. Each car was sold with a matching hardtop.

Car and Driver magazine tested the car and found that it out-accelerated the contemporary Ferrari 360 Modena. Other reviewers were confused by it. Was it a luxury car, or a modern classic, or a supercar? Maybe *Bimmer* magazine best summed up the Z8 by calling it "the civilized supercar." **RD**

M3 | BMW

D

2000 • 198 cu in/3,246 cc, S6 • 338 bhp/252 kW • 0–60 mph/97 kph in 5.1 seconds • 155 mph/249 kph

Every time BMW introduced a new generation of its 3-Series compact executive line, a high-performance M3 model would follow. The M3 that was unveiled at the 2000 Paris Motor Show was spawned by the E46 3 Series. It had a lot to live up to but featured all the expected extras, like an uprated suspension and brakes, plus a limited-slip differential for extra traction. More excitingly, this M3 featured an engine that had the highest specific output (for its time) of any normally aspirated (nonturbo) BMW engine.

Available with either a six-speed manual or a sequential manual gearbox from Getrag, the rear-wheel-drive M3 quickly won many awards for its performance. Drivers enthused about the huge power delivered via a beautifully balanced chassis, although a brake upgrade was the first modification for regular trackgoers. Like nearly all German cars of the era, the M3 had a speed restrictor in place, but given a suitable stretch of empty autobahn and the restrictor removed, the M3 could hit an incredible 191 mph (307 kph).

Buyers could choose from a coupe or convertible (with a fabric roof). Whatever body style buyers chose, they found themselves at the wheel of one of the great BMWs. But it was to be the last six-cylinder M3, because future models had an eight-cylinder engine. **RD**

Impreza P1 | Subaru

J

2000 • 122 cu in/1,994 cc, F4 • 280 bhp/208 kW • 0–60 mph/97 kph in 4.8 seconds • 155 mph/250 kph

In 1999 Subaru U.K. had a problem on its hands. British drivers were desperate to get their hands on Japanese-market high-performance versions of the Impreza and unofficial importers were having a field day, leaving Subara dealers annoyed. Not only that, the "gray" imports were not subject to the same level of approval testing as official imports.

So Subaru got in touch with Prodrive, the British company responsible for running their rally team, who came up with the Impreza P1. The power output of the boxer engine was boosted to 280 bhp (208 kW), which reduced the 0–60 mph (97 kph) acceleration time from 6.3 to 4.8 seconds. The car's already excellent suspension was tuned specifically to suit British roads.

The Impreza P1 only came as a two-door sedan (saloon). Its front and rear spoilers were designed by Peter Stevens, the man who designed the Subaru "555" World Rally Championship cars and the McLaren F1. There was also antilock braking, quicker steering, a shorter gearchange linkage, plus OZ alloy wheels.

Of course, Impreza owners are a sharp bunch and would have smelled a rat if the car had been anything less that excellent. There was no need to worry. At times ragged, at times sublime, the P1 was a true performance car for the road. **JI**

LE Defender | Land Rover (GB)

2000 • 241 cu in/3,950 cc, V8 • 182 bhp/136 kW • unknown • unknown

Throughout the action-packed 2001 adventure movie *Lara Croft: Tomb Raider*, the heroine (Angelina Jolie) is seen at the wheel of a modified Land Rover LE Defender. Painted dark gray and reinforced with checker plate aluminum, the Landie had a V8 with automatic gearbox, and was beefed up with a roll cage, roof rack, a snorkel for river crossings, winches, and safari lights.

Two 110 High Capacity Pick-Ups were custom-made for filming by a team of ten men at Land Rover's special vehicles operation. Each cost $175,000 (£110,000) and took 500 man-hours to build. One of them is now on permanent display at the Heritage Motor Centre Museum in Warwickshire, England.

Land Rover built 250 Tomb Raider LE Defenders to commemorate the vehicle's big-screen appearance. They were only sold at U.K. dealerships and were powered by Land Rover's five-cylinder turbo-diesel. Painted the same Bonatti gray with blackened roofs, they bore special plaques and expedition accessories to complete the *Tomb Raider* look.

Tomb Raider was a fantastic opportunity for Land Rover to showcase its vehicles to a younger audience. Other Land Rovers used in the movie eventually included two Discoverys and a V6 Freelander; even Lara's arch-enemy drove a Range Rover. **DS**

X5 Le Mans | BMW (D)

2000 • 366 cu in/5,999 cc, V12 • 700 bhp/522 kW • 0–60 mph/97 kph in 4.6 seconds • 173 mph/278 kph

The X5 Le Mans was the centerpiece of BMW's stand at the 2000 Geneva Motor Show. It was a one-off concept car designed to showcase the ultimate on-road potential of BMW's new Sport Activity Vehicle (SAV).

Earlier that spring, BMW had taken a standard X5 off its production line in South Carolina and shipped it to Germany; upon its arrival, a team of twelve BMW engineers installed a cast-alloy 366-cubic-inch (5,999-cc) V12 powerplant, borrowed from its 1999 Le Mans–winning sports car. Without speed restriction, this engine could pump out 700 bhp (522 kW) and deliver a monumental amount of torque. Wherever possible, weight-saving aluminum and carbon fiber replaced standard items, and four bucket seats were fitted. Apart from the 20-inch (51-cm) racing alloy wheels and a 1.18-inch (30-mm) drop in the suspension, the only other external modifications were the enlarged front air intake and the huge power bulge in the hood (bonnet).

BMW enlisted Hans Stuck, its veteran touring car and test driver, to take the Le Mans around the legendary Nürburgring circuit in Germany. Over two days, Stuck threw the SAV around the "Green Hell," watched by the motoring press and BMW management. His best time of seven minutes, fifty seconds was faster than BMW's Z8 sports car. **RD**

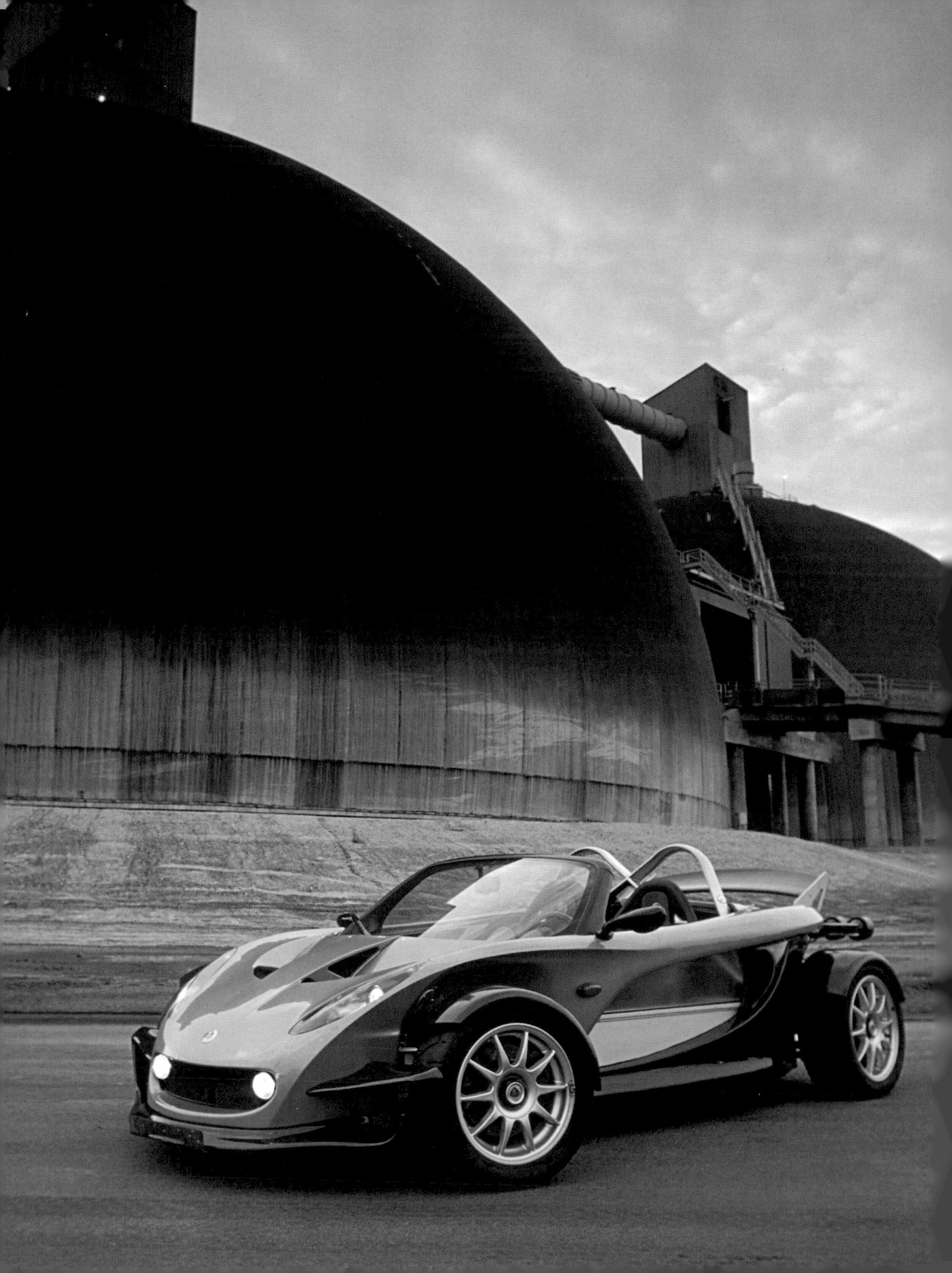

Ⓒ The futuristic lines of the Lotus Elise 340R are highlighted by sinister, brooding nuclear containment buildings.

Elise 340R | Lotus (GB)

2000 • 110 cu in/1,796 cc, S4 • 187 bhp/139 kW • 0–60 mph/97 kph in 4.4 seconds • 130 mph/209 kph

The Lotus Elise 340R was the brainchild of four automotive journalists from the U.K. magazine *Autocar* and a team of Lotus design engineers. The challenge was to create a stripped-down, track-focused machine that would give Lotus's most demanding customers the ultimate driving experience. With a target performance of 340 bhp (254 kW) per tonne (2,200 pounds)—hence its name—and a $55,000 (£35,000) price tag, the British carmaker had Caterham's Superlight R in its sights.

With no wings, roof, or doors, the 340R's fiberglass shell barely covered half of the car's exposed aluminum body tub and cockpit. Formula One–inspired front winglets and a large rear spoiler added huge downforce and allowed the car to corner at gut-wrenching speeds. Wheels and suspension components were left exposed, giving the Lotus a futuristic, pared down style, similar to the naked motorcycles made popular by the Ducati Monster.

The 340R was powered by a tweaked version of the Rover VHPD (Very High Power Derivative) 110-cubic-inch (1,796-cc) engine used in the Lotus Exige. *Evo* magazine exulted, "The 340R is like an Elise turned up to eleven . . . The chassis composure when really pushed is beyond brilliant; it's close to unbelievable." In 2009 *Evo* gave the 340R second place on its list of the 100 Greatest Driver's Cars; the little Lotus was pipped at the post by the $670,000 (£425,000) Pagani Zonda F.

Although the 340R cannot quite beat the astounding performance figures of Caterham's hottest Superlights, most agree that it is more rewarding to drive. After glowing early press reviews, Lotus sold all 340 production cars before they were even built. **DS**

Megabusa | Westfield (GB)

2000 • 79 cu in/1,300 cc, S4 • 178 bhp/131 kW • 0–60 mph/97 kph in 3 seconds • 148 mph/238 kph

In the last fifty years, the Lotus Seven has inspired many track, kit, and street cars. The Westfield Megabusa took the car in yet another direction by fitting a motorcycle engine. Using a small, light but very powerful, high-revving powerplant from a motorcycle can secure incredible speed and agility at a low price.

Westfield chose the sixteen-valve, 79-cubic-inch (1,300-cc) engine from the Suzuki Hayabusa GSX 1300R bike, and linked it to Suzuki's six-speed sequential gearbox to drive the rear wheels. It was a bike engine that could scream all the way to 10,000 rpm in each gear. The no-frills, precolored fiberglass body weighed only 970 pounds (440 kg), so performance was staggering. Ironically, this car can overtake most bikes.

Westfield is a family company based in the West Midlands, England. It makes sports cars and has sold more than 12,000 kits and fully completed cars since it began in 1982. Westfield creations have included a V8-powered Lotus Seven–styled car and an electric sports car project. It has also produced an XTR2 racer kit using the same Suzuki bike engine as the Megabusa with a more substantial track-style body and rear wing.

The Megabusa is officially meant for both road and track, although its practicality is severely limited in everyday usage. The track-day intentions of this machine are obvious in its options list, which includes a roll cage, four-point racing harnesses, and a quick-release steering wheel for easier access. Owners do happily use them on the road, but there are no doors, heater, or roof, and a windshield is an optional extra. Yet at around $34,000 (£22,000), this car is one of the world's high-performance bargains. **SH**

Tuscan | TVR

GB

2000 • 220 cu in/3,605 cc, S6 • 350 bhp/261 kW • 0–60 mph/97 kph in 3.7 seconds • 158 mph/254 kph

The striking Tuscan was one of the last models from TVR, the small, independent sports carmaker based in Blackpool in England. The third car from TVR to bear the Tuscan name, it was also one of their wildest models.

The Tuscan was the first TVR to be powered by a TVR engine; called the "Speed 6," it was offered as a 220-cubic-inch (3,605-cc), then a 244-cubic-inch (4,000-cc), with claimed power outputs of 350–400 bhp (261–298 kW). *Evo* magazine said it delivered "the kind of honest-to-goodness normally aspirated thump that makes every squeeze of the throttle a vivid, sensory kaleidoscope." The car was available as a coupe, targa, and convertible, at prices starting at $63,000 (£40,000).

TVR already had development of the Speed 6 underway when BMW bought Rover, potentially threatening their previous source of engines. The development of the Speed 6 was accelerated, and TVR's media-savvy boss Peter Wheeler did not miss an opportunity for some patriotic PR when he stated, "I don't want anything German in my car." Perhaps no one told him the fuel pump and coil pack came from Bosch.

In typical TVR fashion, safety equipment was sparse. The company told the *Telegraph* newspaper that the car was safer without traction control, air bags, or an antilock braking system because it encouraged drivers to take greater responsibility for their driving.

In the 2001 movie *Swordfish*, John Travolta and Hugh Jackman use a Tuscan to escape dozens of hit men in black SUVs. The actors take turns driving, shooting, and swapping one-liners in this major chase scene. Sadly, TVR did not benefit much because the car was unavailable in the United States at the time. **RD**

Exige | Lotus

GB

2000 • 211 cu in/3,456 cc, V6 • 345 bhp/257 kW • 0–60 mph/97 kph in 3.8 seconds • 172 mph/277 kph

The Exige has been referred to as the aggressive, wayward brother of the Lotus Elise. Featuring an aerodynamic hardtop roof, bigger spoilers, and a lot more horsepower, the Exige has always been a minimalist, superlightweight machine designed to give the ultimate driving experience.

The original Exige, based on the Series-1 Elise, used a Rover VHPD (Very High Performance Derivative) 110-cubic-inch (1,800-cc) mid-mounted engine. Capable of 192 bhp (143 kW) in its highest state of tune, this car quickly became the ultimate track-day weapon. Today, Series-1 Exiges are fast becoming collector's items, thanks to their fragile bodywork and limited production numbers.

Designers of the Series-2 Exige focused on its aerodynamics to give the new model nearly eight times the downforce of the standard Elise. And the awesome S260 version squeezed 257 bhp (192 kW) from its 110-cubic-inch (1,800-cc) Toyota powerplant; it could hit 60 mph (97 kph) in just four seconds.

In 2012 Lotus announced that the new Series-3 Exige S would deliver "raw performance, mind-blowing agility, and unparalleled ride and handling." Now with a longer wheelbase than the Elise, and the Lotus Evora S's 214-cubic-inch (3,500-cc) V6, this car had Lotus fans bristling with excitement. Weighing 2,380 pounds (1,080 kg), the new Exige S is an extremely rapid sports car; its performance figures are given above.

The Exige R-GT is a highly modified version built to compete with its German and Italian rivals on tarmac stages of the World Rally Championship, including the Monte Carlo and San Remo rallies. **DS**

GTR | Ultima

GB

2000 • 384 cu in/6,300 cc, V8 • 534 bhp/398 kW • 0–60 mph/97 kph in 2.6 seconds • 231 mph/372 kph

Ultima is a low-volume manufacturer of supercars based in Leicestershire, England. The GTR is its multiple record-breaking car, designed by Ted Marlow and Lee Noble (who later went on to form Noble Automotive).

Key ingredients for super performance are low weight and high power. The GTR comprises a tubular space-frame chassis and composite body panels; its Chevrolet LS3 384-cubic-inch (6,300-cc) V8 engine is mated to a five-speed Porsche G50 transaxle. The engine delivers 534 bhp (398 kW) as standard, but many are tuned to yield a monumental 1,000 bhp (745 kW).

The car is a collation of race-bred components: AP Racing provides the brakes, Intrax the suspension, and the door locks are from the humble Fiat Panda; they were "the lightest we could find," according to Ultima. The gull-wing doors open to reveal optional leather seats and safety harnesses. This is a road-legal car, but there are few concessions to comfort.

And so to the numbers for which this car is famous: at the time of writing, the Ultima GTR holds the records for the fastest 0–60 mph (97 kph) time—2.6 seconds; fastest 0–100 mph (160 kph) time—5.3 seconds; fastest 30–70 mph (48–110 kph) time—1.8 seconds; fastest 0–100–0 mph (0–160–0 kph) time—9.4 seconds; and fastest 100–0 mph (160–0 kph) time—3.6 seconds.

Ultimas are raced in various series around the world. *Car and Driver* magazine said, "We could gush on forever, but the bottom line is we'd sacrifice plenty for a day of track time in the GTR." The GTR is available as a factory-built car, and also as a kit of components starting from $109,000 (£70,000), so now any home mechanic could build a world-beating car. **RD**

VX220 | Vauxhall

GB

2000 • 134 cu in/2,196 cc, S4 • 145 bhp/108 kW • 0–60 mph/97 kph in 5.6 seconds • 135 mph/217 kph

The mid-engined, low-slung Vauxhall VX220 was styled by an Australian, designed in Germany, and built in England. General Motors (GM) collaborated with Lotus to develop a successor to the popular Series-1 Elise, as new E.U. safety regulations meant Lotus was unable to continue its production beyond the year 2000.

In exchange for GM's investment, Lotus agreed to build an Opel-powered sister car to the new Series-2 Elise. Initially designated the Lotus Type-116, it became known as the Opel Speedster in Europe and the Vauxhall VX220 in the United Kingdom.

GM was hoping that a lightweight, Elise-based sports car would help to spice up Vauxhall's image, and when the very first press cars were sent out to motoring journalists in 1999, the reviews were glowing. The VX220 had more grunt than the "rev happy" Elise, and safety improvements included an air bag and an antilock braking system. However, it was its handling that put it into a class of its own.

At launch the VX220 sold for $36,700 (£23,490), almost exactly the same price as the new Elise. Unfortunately, the Lotus outsold the GM car by a ratio of five to one. It appeared that the lure of that famous badge was just too strong. In Britain Vauxhall could not quite shake off its staid public image, despite general agreement that the VX220 was a better package. Only 5,267 normally aspirated cars were eventually produced before production ceased in 2004.

In December 2009 *Evo* magazine declared the model to be among the ten greatest cars of that decade, one journalist declaring, "The first time you see a VX220 in daylight, you forget to breathe." **DS**

KE02 EWW

(‹) James Bond's V12 Vanquish performed well on ice, but its real claim to fame was its "Vanish" invisibility technology.

Vanquish | Aston Martin (GB)

2001 • 362 cu in/5,935 cc, V12 • 465 bhp/335 kW • 0–60 mph/97 kph in 4.3 seconds • 190 mph/305 kph

Aston Martin has made many iconic cars over the years, but the Vanquish was the one that helped boost the company into the twenty-first century. And once again it was a connection to a certain fictional secret agent that played a part in the car's success.

The Vanquish was designed by Ian Callum, who had previously worked at Ford and would later go on to design the all-new Jaguar XK (which bears some resemblance to an Aston). The striking bodywork was a blend of ultrahigh technology mixed with traditional skills and craftsmanship. The main structure was made out of aluminum, with carbon fiber and steel elements bonded to it. There was sufficient room inside to make it available as either a pure two-seater or a two-plus-two with a pair of modest rear seats.

Although Aston Martin, backed by its then-parent Ford, had developed a state-of-the-art manufacturing process for the Vanquish, the body was still finished by hand. The Vanquish would be the last Aston Martin to be made in this way. It was also the final model to roll out of the Newport Pagnell factory, which had been in operation for nearly fifty years.

Beneath the slippery body was a normally aspirated 362-cubic-inch (5,935-cc) V12, developed by Ford in the United States. The alloy forty-eight-valve unit produced 465 bhp (335 kW) at 6,500 rpm. Through the electronic, paddle-controlled gearbox, the Vanquish could reach just short of 190 mph (305 kph).

The car's profile was boosted by appearing as James Bond's personal transport in the 2002 movie *Die Another Day*. The cool, brutish lines of the Vanquish reignited the public's affection for the Aston brand. **JI**

XTR2 | Westfield (GB)

2001 • 79 cu in/1,299 cc, S4 • 170 bhp/127 kW • 0–60 mph/97 kph in 3.1 seconds • 160 mph/257 kph

Westfield's XRT2 derived its name from "Extreme Track & Road 2002." It was one of a new generation of megalight motorcycle-engined sports cars primarily aimed at the hardcore track-day enthusiast.

Devoid of any creature comforts, the open-cockpit car was built around a lightweight space-frame chassis. Its fiberglass shell, styled like a small Le Mans race car, was fitted with a huge rear wing to increase downforce. In racetrack specification the car tipped the scales at an incredible 904 pounds (410 kg), less than half of the Lotus Elise, or one-third of the Mini Cooper S.

Power came from Suzuki's "Hayabusa" GSXR-1300R sports bike engine, mated to a six-speed sequential gearbox. With a little tweaking, upward of 180 bhp (134 kW) was achievable. To get the best out of the compact little powerplant, the car needed to be revved hard, right up to its 11,000-rpm redline, because it had very little low-down torque. While this driving style was great on track, the road-legal XTR2 was not ideal for most people's everyday commute.

Perhaps the most amazing thing about Westfield's superlight sports car was its price. In 2002 a starter kit, for building the basic chassis in a home garage, retailed for £6,000 ($9,470). The finished car cost around £20,000 ($31,580), and could be built in a week.

Developing a mind-blowing 460 bhp (338 kW) per tonne (2,205 pounds), Westfield had created a track weapon—Ferrari's F40 only produced 440 bhp (324 kW) per tonne. In 2002 the BBC's *Top Gear* test driver, "The Stig," drove the 79-cubic-inch (1,299-cc) XTR2 around the Dunsfold aerodrome track in a faster time than the 445-cubic-inch (7,300-cc) Pagani Zonda. **DS**

Clio V6 | Renault

(F)

2001 • 180 cu in/2,946 cc, V6 • 227 bhp/169 kW • 0–60 mph/97 kph in 7.5 seconds • 146 mph/234 kph

The standard Renault Clio is, despite its European Car of the Year award, a rather sedate small car commonly found outside supermarkets and libraries. In 2001, however, Renault decided to use the Clio as a base for an extreme one-make race series. It added an (almost) inappropriate amount of power and created the hottest of hot hatches: the Clio V6.

It was a radical overhaul. The Clio V6, as the name implied, was powered by a twenty-four-valve, 183-cubic-inch (3,000-cc) V6, which had variable-valve timing and more than twice the power the chassis was originally designed for. The brakes were of a type found on TVR and Morgan models. The rear seats were ditched, replaced by the engine, and the original front engine compartment became redundant. One of the drawbacks was the shift in weight, 66 percent going to the rear of the car, making it a real handful to drive quickly. Another consequence of the unusual configuration was a huge turning circle.

Despite a small net for storage, it was no longer at home outside the supermarket. Phase One models of the V6 were built by TWR in Sweden, their bespoke bodies coming from Valet in Finland, and according to *Practical Performance* car magazine had "bullfrog looks and bulldog bite."

Phase Two cars had a power hike, with Porsche's help, to 255 bhp (190 kW). Recognizing that it had created a monster, Renault increased the track and wheelbase. The Phase Two retained all the screaming performance of the original, but was more readily kept under control. An *Evo* magazine reviewer commented, "I can trust the mad mutant Clio at last." **RD**

Avantime | Renault

(F)

2001 • 180 cu in/2,946 cc, V6 • 210 bhp/156 kW • 0–60 mph/97 kph in 8.6 seconds • 137 mph/220 kph

As the new century dawned, the team at Renault was doing some blue-sky, out-of-the-box thinking about luxury. Someone said, why must a limousine always be a sedan (saloon)? Maybe a big, light and airy one-box coupe would be a great idea? People nodded wisely.

When the car was revealed at the 1999 Geneva Motor Show, Renault design chief Patrick Le Quement talked about the revolutionary "Coupespace" concept. Journalists merely wrote down "minivan." The price was high at $40,000 (£27,000), but Renault optimistically planned to sell 2,000 units a year.

The Avantime's upside-down boat shape certainly turned heads. Unique double-hinged pillarless doors gave access to the front and rear seats, and a "grand air" button opened all the windows and an enormous glass sunroof simultaneously to create the illusion of being in a convertible—though still a minivan. Power sunshades prevented occupants from baking like brie.

If the "limousine" was picking up VIPs, its load area, at 18.7 cubic feet (530 cubic liters), was big enough to take their pile of Louis Vuitton luggage. Unfortunately, the VIPs themselves were unlikely to enjoy the drive, because the rear was not all that comfortable.

Yet it was surprisingly good to drive. The 183-cubic-inch (3,000-cc) V6 or 122-cubic-inch (2,000-cc) turbo both gave punchy performance. The six-speed box was smooth and slick, although the armrest could get in the way of the driver's elbow. It was more taut and nimble than Renault's Espace, but it was no sports coupe.

The Avantime did not change luxury cars as we know them, and was withdrawn in 2003. But style guru Stephen Bayley said it was "outstandingly innovative." **LT**

The Saleen S7 was a supercar in every sense of the word—superfast, superlight, and superexpensive. ⊡

ZT-260 | MG (GB)

2001 • 281 cu in/4,601 cc, V8 • 260 bhp/190 kW • 0–60 mph/97 kph in 6.2 seconds • 155 mph/218 kph

MG-Rover engineers created an ambitious concept car—the MG ZT XPower 500—based on the popular but dated Rover 75 sports sedan (saloon). It was not designed for production, just to showcase what MG could do with the chassis. But the concept was received very favorably, so MG pressed ahead on a limited budget. The result was the MG ZT-260.

The new model was visually almost identical to its aging sibling, the 75, apart from quad exhaust pipes. Under the skin, MG and its engineering partner ProDrive had extensively reworked the 75. The car was changed from front- to rear-wheel drive and a Ford Mustang 281-cubic-inch (4,601-cc) V8 was shoehorned in. There was even a station wagon (estate) version.

Competitively priced at £28,495 ($45,000), the MG ZT-260 looked as if it could be driven by an old lady but was a muscle car in disguise. *Auto Express* magazine called it "a truly remarkable car, especially given MG's limited development budget compared to rivals."

In 2003 a modified version became the world's fastest nonproduction station wagon with a run at the Bonneville Speed Week Nationals in Utah. The car's V8 engine was bored out to 366 cubic inches (6,000 cc) and supercharged to produce a startling 765 bhp (570 kW). It was also given a limited-slip differential for more traction. It hit a top speed of 226 mph (361 kph).

When MG-Rover went out of business in April 2005, the Bonneville speed record car was auctioned off.for just £30,000 ($48,000). The public were left wondering what might have happened had MG-Rover been as adventurous with its other products as it had been with its remarkable ZT-260. **RD**

S7 | Saleen (USA)

2001 • 427 cu in/7,000 cc, V8 • 550 bhp/410 kW • 0–60 mph/97 kph in 3.8 seconds • 201 mph/322 kph

Some say that the Saleen S7 was the first U.S. supercar. Former racing driver Steve Saleen's creation was certainly a supercar in looks; it was also the fastest U.S.-built production car when it launched and the third-fastest in the world. And with a top speed of 248 mph (399 kph), the S7 was not just fast, it was one of the most technically advanced road cars of its time.

The body was made of carbonfiber, a very strong, lightweight material made from polymers reinforced with fibers of carbon. This sat on a honeycomb-construction chassis of steel and aluminum. The whole car weighed just 2,750 pounds (1,247 kg). The huge engine, set behind the cockpit, was a normally aspired (nonturbo) unit that powered the Saleen to complete a standing quarter-mile (0.4 km) in 11.75 seconds, reaching 126 mph (203 kph). Huge air scoops were incorporated to cool the engine. At 160 mph (257 kph) the car generated its own weight in downforce.

At launch, the S7 was the only U.S. street-legal car with more than 500 bhp (373 kW) on tap. With time 500 bhp has become less extraordinary, so the S7 has had to evolve. In 2005 its new engine produced 750 bhp (559 kW), with a new top speed of 248 mph (399 kph) and a 0–60 mph (97 kph) time of just 2.8 seconds. And the price of enjoying all this big-time speed? That was big too: almost $600,000 (£400,000).

Next, Saleen produced a "competition package" that raised power to 1,000 bhp (746 kW). In the 2008 movie *Iron Man*, there was an "S7 competition" in which acceleration was reduced to just 2.6 seconds for the 0–60 mph (97-kph) dash. The top speed is believed to have been at least 250 mph (402 kph). **SH**

Aero 8 | Morgan

GB

2001 • 268 cu in/4,398 cc, V8 • 325 bhp/242 kW • 0–60 mph/97 kph in 4.3 seconds • 170 mph/270 kph

The Aero 8 was an ultrasophisticated supercar with an aluminum chassis and coachwork, built by hand by the Morgan family business in Malvern, England. The car's styling, however, harked right back to 1936.

Seeing the Aero 8 for the first time at the Geneva Motor Show in 2000, motoring journalists said a lot of unkind things about the car. It looked cross-eyed because the headlights were mounted on the inner wings. And it was expensive, costing at least £56,000 ($87,000); the coupe version cost almost double that.

The Aero 8 was Morgan's first new car since 1948. The company had started by making three-wheeler sports cars, and previously the biggest change in its history had been adding a fourth wheel in 1936. It was third-generation family proprietor Charles Morgan who gave enthusiasts the Aero 8 roadster (or Aeromax coupe, or SuperSports with a targa roof), all being the first Morgans to abandon a wooden frame.

A 268-cubic-inch (4,398-cc) BMW V8 under the hood (bonnet), which rose to 293 cubic inches (4,799 cc) in 2008, gave the lightweight car effortless performance, and the Aero 8 proved excellent fun to drive or race. Several have competed well on the track, including two finishes at the 24 Hours of Le Mans Race.

The cabin is still handmade, using ash hardwood, and the buyer can choose from eighty different colors of leather. From 2006, the "bug eye" Beetle headlights were replaced by MINI headlights supplied by BMW.

Celebrity owners include host Richard Hammond of BBC TV's *Top Gear*, comedian and deejay Paul O'Grady, and Mr. Bean comedian and historic race-car enthusiast Rowan Atkinson. **LT**

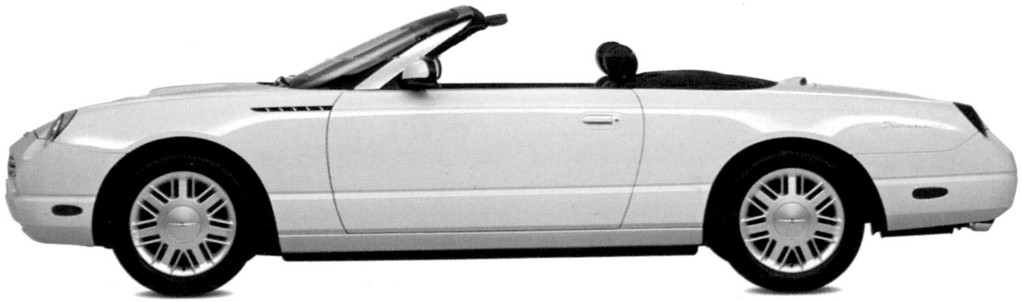

Thunderbird | Ford

(USA)

2001 • 240 cu in/3,933 cc, V8 • 252 bhp/188 kW • 0–60 mph/97 kph in 7.6 seconds • 146 mph/235 kph

Nostalgia may not be what it used to be, but that did not stop Ford from resurrecting the ghost of its old Thunderbird when it relaunched the car in 2001. The T'Bird hadn't actually been out of production for long—only a year, in fact—but it had been a fair while since it had looked anything like the 1955 original.

Back then, Ford called it the first "personal car," a mass-market vehicle with luxury touches and a touch of sporting performance. Over the years it had become less distinctive, bordering on the downright ugly.

The reborn Thunderbird was originally shown as a concept at the 1999 Detroit Motor Show. Full production started in September 2001. The new car had a design described as "retrofuturistic," which possibly means that it looked like a car of the future, as drawn by someone in the late 1950s.

Beneath the largely plastic body was a Lincoln LS or Jaguar S-Type (they shared the same platform). This made the 2001 Thunderbird 11 inches (27.5 cm) longer than the original 1955 car.

Only one engine was available: a 240-cubic-inch (3,933-cc) V8 running through a five-speed automatic gearbox. Some U.S. drivers considered this too small, as the two-seater Thunderbird weighed almost as much the previous four-seater model. The car was only available as a convertible, although a removable hardtop could be purchased separately; this was a weighty beast in itself and required two people to lift it.

Some new versions of old cars gel with the public (the BMW Mini is a prime example), but the revamped Thunderbird never quite clicked. Trading on past glories was not enough; it was discontinued in 2005. **JI**

Murciélago | Lamborghini

(I)

2001 • 396 cu in/6,496 cc, V12 • 661 bhp/493 kW • 0–60 mph/97 kph in 3.1 seconds • 212 mph/342 kph

This all-wheel-drive flagship Lamborghini was named after a famous fighting bull that refused to die; after surviving nearly thirty sword wounds from the matador El Lagartijo, the bullfighter spared the beast's life.

Following in the footsteps of its flamboyant forefathers, the Countach and Diablo, the Murciélago sported the same scissor-action doors and aggressive angular styling. It was the first new model from the Italian brand in eleven years, and the first to be launched under Audi's new ownership. As its CEO announced at the press launch, "Murciélago embodies the pure, unadulterated values of our brand. It is truly extreme, uncompromising, and unmistakably Italian."

The Murciélago was the last full production Lamborghini to use the legendary quad-cam V12, as originally fitted to the 350 GT in 1964. Heavily modified, and enlarged to almost twice its original capacity, the new 378-cubic-inch (6,200-cc) supercar could propel its occupants to 60 mph (97 kph) in around 3.5 seconds, and go on to more than 200 mph (322 kph).

In 2009 Lamborghini unveiled the ultimate version of the Murciélago (performance figures are shown above). The 396-cubic-inch (6,496-cc) LP 670-4 Super Veloce lost 200 pounds (91 kg) thanks to extensive use of carbon fiber. This was a supercar for those who liked to be seen. *Car and Driver* magazine described it as a "wonderfully brutal, raucous thrill ride." Despite the ostentatious styling, the writers concluded, "When that free-revving V12 is spinning at about 5,000 rpm, roaring from deep within its throat, and there's a shiver running through every part of the car, you can assign the driver whatever cheap showiness you like." **DS**

C8 | Spyker

NL

2001 • 256 cu in/4,200 cc, V8 • 400 bhp/298 kW • 0–60 mph/97 kph in 4.5 seconds • 190 mph/300 kph

The historic Dutch car and aircraft maker's name of Spyker had lain dormant since 1925. In 2000 it was resurrected by two Dutch entrepreneurs: Victor Muller, who is also chairman of Saab, and car designer Maarten de Bruijn. They launched just one exotic model, the two-seater C8 supercar, and it is still produced today in various forms. The Spyker company is now owned by wealthy American enthusiast Alex Mascioli.

The original C8 design included classic supercar elements such as rear-wheel drive and doors that opened in a scissoring up-and-over style. Most distinctive were the prominent aircraft-style air-intake tubes on the flanks and on the roof of the coupe versions. Track versions boasted power of up to 600 bhp (450 kW). The car's looks earned it prominent roles in the 2006 movie *Basic Instinct 2* and 2007's *War*.

The Spyker firm has evolved a unique personalized ownership process to woo ultrawealthy car buyers. Each car, identified by its chassis number, is given a customized specification by its new owner. The information is recorded on the car's build sheet, which is updated when any new work is done to it. The sheet is available to owners on a personalized Web page. Every body panel and component of the Spyker C8 is numbered to identify it as belonging to the car's chassis number. Uniquely, owners may follow the assembly process of their Spykers by means of a dedicated webcam system within the factory itself.

Today's Spyker C8 Aileron has all the features that have kept the C8 at the forefront of the supercar world. The model has a high-powered Audi V8 mounted amidships in a light, hand-built aluminum body. **SH**

RS6 Avant | Audi

(D)

2002 • 256 cu in/4,200 cc, V8 • 450 bhp/331 kW • 0–60 mph/97 kph in 4.4 seconds • 155 mph/250 kph

The RS6, at the top of the Audi A6 line, had unique engines and technology and was handbuilt in limited numbers by the separate, high-performance Quattro company. It came either as a sedan (saloon) or an Avant station wagon (estate). The Avant version, which unusually was launched first, was one of the fastest station wagons ever built.

Specifications were far from just a stiffened suspension, bigger brakes, and smaller steering wheel. The RS6 was Audi's technological showcase. Both body versions had permanent four-wheel drive, tiptronic semiautomatic transmission, and Audi's Dynamic Ride Control system, which used adaptive shock absorbers to maintain stability and counteract roll in fast corners. The enormous, sophisticated brakes dealt with the huge power output from the forty-valve aluminum V8, whose 155-mph (250-kph) top speed is limited.

In 2004 an RS6 Plus version, released in Europe only, had even more power, thanks to engine tuning from Cosworth. It was only available as an Avant and had a top speed of 174 mph (280 kph). In 2008 a second-generation RS6 produced 571 bhp (426 kW); top speed was 170 mph (274 kph). RS6 cult followers refer to this powerful car wearing Audi's interlocking-circles symbol as the "Lord of the Rings." **SH**

XC90 | Volvo

(S)

2002 • 269 cu in/4,400 cc, V8 • 311 bhp/232 kW • 0–60 mph/97 kph in 6.9 seconds • 130 mph/209 kph

The XC90 was Volvo's first ever off-roader. It looked like a pumped-up station wagon (estate). But it is a sign of how well Volvo knew its customers that the chunky car was its best-selling vehicle worldwide within two years.

The ingredients for a successful crossover vehicle were understated luxury and prestige, plus a dose of rugged efficiency and practicality. Of course, the Swedes were experts at building station wagons, and they included seven seats and plenty of storage space.

Big SUVs generally roll in corners and wallow over undulations much more than a station wagon. With the industry's first antiroll stability system, the XC90 does not suffers these problems as badly as many rivals.

Being a modern Volvo, safety features are well trumpeted, too, with a patented front crumple-zone system to protect from impact and minimize injury to pedestrians. There is also a rollover protection system including high-strength steel roof reinforcment. The XC90 has been awarded the highest safety ratings.

Figures are given above for the range-topping 4.4-litre V8, an engine manufactured by Yamaha.

The XC90 has an unlikely claim to movie fame as a star of the 2009 comedy blockbuster *3 Idiots*. This was Bollywood's highest grossing film to date and caused demand for the big Volvo to soar across India. **SH**

Leon Cupra R | Seat (E)

2002 • 110 cu in/1,800 cc, S4 • 207 bhp/154kW •
0–60 mph/97 kph in 6.7 seconds • 150 mph/241 kph

Seat had become established in the Volkswagen (VW) empire. The plan seemed to be for it to become the firm's sporty arm, a little like Alfa Romeo's role within Fiat.

The Leon hatchback line had been launched in 1998, as a derivation of VW's Golf Mark IV and Audi A3. It was given sportier, more youthful looks, bright colors, and some hotter hatch versions to generate interest. The Leon Cupra, for example, had a turbocharged 110-cubic-inch (1,800-cc), twenty-valve engine, or, in some countries, the 171-cubic-inch (2,800-cc) VR6 engine with four-wheel drive.

The launch of the Cupra R in 2002, however, showed that Seat had ambitions to build the hottest hatch available. Seat engineers had modified the standard Cupra R as though preparing for a race: it was given a new engine management system, new inlet and exhaust systems, an extra turbo intercooler, better brakes, lowered ride, firmer shock absorbers, better steering, and more agile suspension.

How good was it? When, in 2010, the readers of *Autocar* magazine were invited to vote for the best hot hatch of all time, the Cupra R came a creditable seventh, beating the Renault 5 GT Turbo, Mini Cooper S, Citroën Saxo VTS, Renault Clio Williams, and, most impressively, its parent company's VW Golf GTi 16v. **SH**

Aerio/Liana | Suzuki (J)

2002 • 97 cu in/1,586 cc, S4 • 105 bhp/77 kW •
0–60 mph/97 kph in 11.3 seconds • 109 mph/175 kph

This small, undistinguished family vehicle became one of the world's best-known racetrack cars after it appeared in a feature, "Star in a Reasonably Priced Car," on the BBC TV program *Top Gear*. For seven series of the show, celebrities from all over the world thrashed it around the *Top Gear* test circuit in Surrey, England.

Suzuki had launched the Aerio, or Liana as it was badged in Europe (the name means "Life in a New Age"), hoping to win sales with its low running costs. However the Aerio was chosen by *Top Gear* as a representative of the bland mediocrity of many modern cars. The program's car was worth $15,000 (£9,995) and was standard apart from a roll cage and racing seats, both added for safety. Each guest practiced before making several attempts to lap the track in the fastest time.

The Liana endured considerable abuse. Actor Sir Michael Gambon almost turned it over at a spot henceforth named "Gambon Corner." One of the front wheels fell off when singer Lionel Ritchie drove it, and actor/singer David Soul managed to destroy two gearboxes. In all, the car covered 1,600 laps and its tires and brakes were changed 100 times; it needed six new clutches, two new hubs, driveshafts, wishbones, struts, gear linkages, and one replacement wing mirror. **SH**

The power and beauty of the 2002 Ferrari Enzo made the car a fitting tribute to the company's founder.

Enzo | Ferrari (I)

2002 • 366 cu in/5,998 cc, V12 • 651 bhp/485 kW • 0–60 mph/97 kph in 3.1 seconds • 220 mph/350 kph

The Ferrari Enzo has become the benchmark by which all other supercars are measured. When it was launched in 2002, rival manufacturers claimed to have cars that were faster or more exclusive, but it was nearly always pictures of the outrageously styled Enzo that young boys pinned to their bedroom walls.

Named after Enzo Ferrari, the company's founding father, the Enzo was built at a time when Scuderia Ferrari and the hugely talented Michael Schumacher completely dominated Formula One (F1). Under the Enzo's carbon-fiber bodywork, a normally aspirated V12 powerplant propelled the car to 100 mph (161 kph) in just 6.6 seconds. An F1-style semiautomatic paddle-shift gearbox, carbon-ceramic brakes, and a computer-controlled rear wing enabled the Enzo to lap the Nürburgring in less than seven and a half minutes. A red "race" button activated savagely quick gearshifts, stiffened the suspension, and relaxed the traction control. The Enzo also featured "launch control," as used on F1 cars until the mid-1990s before it was banned.

When *Evo* magazine reviewed Ferrari's new flagship in 2003, it was simply blown away: "Steel yourself and wind it out to six- or seven-tenths and the result is mesmerizing. Staring wide-eyed through the Enzo's huge windscreen, every other car on the road appears to be moving as though ploughing through treacle. Nothing I've driven disguises its speed so surreally and yet gives such a satisfying hit of involvement . . . The Old Man would be proud."

Only 400 Ferrari Enzos were ever built; the first British import, in a vivid Modena Yellow, was bought by veteran rock legend Eric Clapton. **DS**

62 | Maybach (D)

2002 • 336 cu in/5,500 cc, V12 • 543 bhp/405 kW • 0–60 mph/97 kph in 5.4 seconds • 155 mph/250 kph

The Maybach company aimed to produce "private jets for the road." It was styled as an überluxury brand above Mercedes to lure super-rich buyers away from the recently rejuvenated Rolls-Royce and Bentley.

Wilhelm Maybach worked with Gottlieb Daimler in the late nineteenth century to build the first automobiles powered by internal combustion. He and his son Karl set up on their own in 1909, building engines for Zeppelin airships and later a series of graceful, custom-built luxury cars.

Daimler bought the then-dormant Maybach name in 1960 and it was finally resurrected in the twenty-first century for the Maybach 62 and 57—named after their lengths in tenths of a meter. The S model stood for "Special," and a Laudaulet Convertible was launched in 2009 for $1,380,000 (£880,000).

Sadly, the reborn Maybach 62 and its 57 sibling never lived up to the historic originals. Where the new Rolls-Royce Phantom was designed from scratch, the Maybach's heavy body sat on an aging Mercedes S-class platform and did not deliver the superlative driving experience its $375,000 (£240,000) price demanded. All the attention was focused on the sumptuous rear, with its individual reclining seats and air-driven back-massage function.

The faux art deco styling, diffused lighting, and optional rear curtains made the Maybach feel like a funeral car, but the hip-hop community loved it. Stars such as P Diddy owned or rapped about it; Kanye and Jay-Z customized one in a video. But the brand never made a profit, and was dropped for 2013. By then, most hip-hop stars had already defected to Bugatti. **LT**

7 Series | BMW

D

2002 • 152 cu in/2,497 cc, S6 • 228 bhp/170 kW • 0–60 mph/97 kph in 8.1 seconds • 147 mph/237 kph

The luxury BMW 7 Series sedan (saloon) was a step away from its conservative predecessors. Known within BMW as the Type E65, it was much less traditional, with striking exterior styling and a gadget-laden, high-tech interior. Designer Chris Bangle attracted criticism for the rear of the car, sometimes called the "Bangle butt," although it was actually designed by Adrian van Hooydonk, who later went on to succeed him.

Early models featured an innovative i-Drive system. By controlling all the equipment via a single knob, this removed the clutter of conventional switchgear. Of the 700 functions of i-Drive, 270 could be operated by voice recognition, but frustrated owners called it "i-Distract." Later options included infrared night vision for the driver and digital television for passengers.

Like most BMWs of this era, the 7 Series was an excellent driver's car, despite its luxurious fittings. Diesel engine options included a 183-cubic-inch (3,000-cc) straight-six and 269-cubic-inch (4,400-cc) V8. Gasoline options included a 183-cubic-inch straight-six, 269-cubic-inch V8, and 366-cubic-inch (6,000-cc) V12. There was even an experimental hydrogen-fueled model. The 7 Series also featured Dynamic Drive, an active antiroll system that ensured flat cornering without overly loading the suspension. An Alpina B7 version delivered 186 mph (300 kph).

Heads of state and African despots could order the Type E67 bulletproof version with carbon-fiber reinforced armor plating. Made in Germany, Thailand, Mexico, Egypt, and Russia, face-lifted models had revised i-Drive controls and toned down exterior styling, and the same excellent driving dynamics. **RD**

Escalade EXT | Cadillac

USA

2002 • 366 cu in/6,000 cc, V8 • 345 bhp/254 kW • 0–60 mph/97 kph in 8.4 seconds • 108 mph/174 kph

Cadillac's first-generation Escalade in 1999 had been a rushed and clumsy reworking of the General Motors Yukon Denali, and the luxury carmaker's first attempt to make a sport utility vehicle (SUV). Cadillac said it was the "most acclaimed luxury SUV ever," but it was not very acclaimed at all. However, the Mark II Escalade, from 2002, was a much more interesting model.

This Texas-built SUV had the basics right for the U.S. market: it was big, with room for eight passengers, and powerful, with two chunky V8 options, a 323-cubic-inch (5,300-cc) and a 366-cubic-inch (6,000-cc) (the figures for the latter are given above). Cadillac did not say so, but the 366-cubic-inch is a close relation to a unit found in one-ton Chevy trucks. Instead, sales staff crowed that the engine created "the world's most powerful SUV," as it had 3 hhp (2 kW) more than the Mercedes ML55 AMG; they omitted that the AMG was much faster. Buyers could choose all-wheel drive, or just admit that they were never going to drive off-road and settle for the cheaper rear-wheel-drive version.

Inside, the Escalade's leather-covered cabin was brimming with gadgets and luxuries, including hands-free voice-activated phone capability, Internet-based information screen, 250-watt Bose hi-fi, and heated front- and second-row seats. Perhaps as a result of having all that kit, the Escalade was then the most commonly stolen vehicle in the United States.

The surprise for Escalade drivers was the handling. The big Caddy SUV had nimble reflexes and its active suspension system was very effective. "We were shocked at how the Escalade drives much 'smaller' than it really is," said *Motor Trend* magazine's reviewer. **SH**

Crossblade | Smart

(D)

2002 • 600 cc, S3 • 70 bhp/52 kW • 0–60 mph/97 kph in 16.5 seconds • 85 mph/135 kph

Founded by motoring giant Mercedes-Benz and fashion group Swatch, Smart had the right ingredients to start an exciting new brand. A new factory on the French-German border was opened in 1997 to produce these innovative city cars. But it is hard to imagine what they were trying to achieve when they butchered a Smart car to create the unique Crossblade.

Removing the door panels, roof, and much of the windscreen left one of the most bizarre-looking cars of the decade. It was designed to let fashion-conscious drivers see and be seen; singer Robbie Williams bought one before he could even drive.

The Crossblade had a Brabus-tuned 70-bhp (52-kw) engine fettered by a jerky, semiautomatic transmission. The standard Smart was at home making short trips around the city, but the Crossblade had only a tiny perspex screen and its owners dared not venture out unless the sun was shining. Owners also complained about the door bars jamming shut, although climbing out would have been easy.

The car, weighing much the same as the conventional Smart, was safer than it looked. Smart's clever "tridion" steel body, air bags, stability package, and limited top speed meant drivers were more at risk of getting a fly in their eye than a crash-related injury. Available only in left-hand drive, the Crossblade sold new for $25,000 (£16,000); only 2,000 were made during the twelve months it was in production.

At the time, Smart claimed: "No other manufacturer of production cars has a comparable competitor to the Smart Crossblade." That is perhaps because no-one other than Smart could really see the point of it. **RD**

Ram SRT10 | Dodge

USA

2002 • 8,275 cc, V10 • 510 bhp/372 kW • 0–60 mph/97 kph in 5.2 seconds • 154 mph/248 kph

The Dodge Ram is more than a truck; it is an American icon, like apple pie, a stetson, or a loaded shotgun. And the most iconic Ram is the SRT10, which borrowed the Viper's 8.3-liter V10 engine from 2002 to 2007.

In February 2004, NASCAR driver Brendan Gaughan drove an unmodified SRT10 into the Guinness World Records as the world's fastest production pickup: it achieved a top speed of 154.587 mph (248.783 kph) over a flying kilometer. Chrysler was delighted that it had trumped Ford's 146-mph (235-kph) SVT Lightning.

At the launch of the SRT10 Quad Cab in 2006, Dan Knott of the Chrysler Group said, "We wanted to offer customers not only the boldest, baddest, fastest pickup truck in the world, but also the boldest, baddest, fastest pickup truck with two rows of seating and towing capability." It could tow 8,150 pounds (3,696 kg).

The SRT10 rode on big, 22-inch (56-cm) forged aluminum wheels; the race-inspired seats had suede panels, and the Quad Cab version had rear entertainment for the kids. The truck's base price was $22,425 (£14,500), but buyers could easily double this with accessories. And anyone worrying about the 9-mpg (31 liters/100 km) gas consumption really did belong in the market for a Ram.

In 2008 the center of Detroit was closed to allow Chrysler executives to play at cowboys, driving longhorn cattle between the skyscrapers as part of the launch of the latest Dodge Ram truck. But financial storm clouds were gathering even as the Chrysler men celebrated, and soon the V10 was being withdrawn. In 2011, as a sign of the times, the company began to test a fleet of Ram plug-in hybrids. **LT**

The sedate pose of this Nissan 350Z in 2004 provides no hint of the car's blistering performance credentials.

Burton | Burton (NL)

2002 • 37 cu in/602 cc, S4 • 29 bhp/21 kW •
0–60 mph/97 kph in 13 seconds • 87 mph/140 kph

This retro roadster from the Netherlands was based on an unlikely technological source, the Citroën 2CV. The Burton's body is mounted on the chassis of the ancient French people's car, and power is provided by the 2CV's humble 602-cc engine.

The Burton company was established by two colorful car-mad brothers, Dimitri and Iwan Göbel. Big fans of the 2CV, they opened a specialist workshop in the Netherlands, repairing and tuning 2CVs; they then built their own pickup versions. The Burton sports cars followed, as both complete cars and DIY kits. Burton is now the country's largest sports car manufacturer.

The Burton's fiberglass body is inspired by prewar sports cars such as early Bugattis and Alfa Romeos. Promotional videos show drivers in leather helmets and goggles. Reusing parts from 2CV donor cars keeps construction and running costs very low; completed cars are available from around $13,500 (£8,500).

There is a coupe version with gull-wing doors, and a soft-top roadster. The car weighs a third less than the 2CV so performance is more lively and handling more exciting. Burton tunes the engine with bigger cylinders, racing camshafts, electronic ignition, and a lighter flywheel, and performance is boosted significantly.

An even more economical derivation is the new electric-powered Burton roadster. It has the same body shape but with a small 16 kW battery and an electric motor instead of a gas engine. The Burton Electric weighs only 1,631 pounds (740 kg). It can operate over a range of 87 miles (140 km) with a top speed of 75 mph (120 kph). Burton claims that the price of a full battery charge is about four euros ($5.50/£3.50). **SH**

350Z | Nissan (J)

2002 • 214 cu in/3,500 cc, V6 • 309 bhp/227 kW •
0–60 mph/97 kph in 5.5 seconds • 155 mph/250 kph

Chunky, macho, and aggressive, like a beefed-up Porsche, Nissan's new "Z" car updated the appeal of its long-lasting sports car series for the modern generation. The two-door, two-seater still had the basics, of course: more speed than expected of a reliable car costing the same as a smart family sedan (saloon); pin-sharp, rear-wheel-drive handling; and a sexy interior with leather sports seats, purposeful dashboard, and plenty of Z logos. And in true Z car style, it was packed with desirable features, including six air bags, climate control, CD autochanger, and xenon headlights.

The 350Z reintroduced a sporting series that had started in 1969. After the 300ZX there had been a gap of four years before this fifth-generation Z car launched, but for sports car enthusiasts it was worth the wait—this was the most appealing Nissan sports car ever. The performance was blistering, and the sounds and feel of the car were raw and exciting.

A roadster followed the launch of the coupe, and a special "Track" model was also added. The 350Zs started winning races and were tuned by specialists. The engine was officially uprated for even hotter performance; its figures are given above.

The 350Z GT-S Concept was revealed at the British Goodwood Festival of Speed in 2006. It featured a supercharger that could be switched on and off with a dashboard-mounted button. With 383 bhp (285 kW), its performance was Porsche-destroying. There were suggestions that it might be offered as a special upgrade kit, but, perhaps due to unfavorable economic conditions, the supercharged car did not reappear. **SH**

Z4 | BMW

(D)

2002 • 182 cu in/2,979 cc, S6 • 335 bhp/250 kW • 0–60 mph/97 kph in 4.8 seconds • 155 mph/249 kph

The BMW Z4 was a rear-wheel-drive, two-seater sports car that followed hot on the wheels of the BMW Z3. First unveiled at the 2002 Paris Auto Show, its angular bodywork looked quite different to the softer curves of the Z3 roadster it replaced. Many, though not all, liked the sharp, modernist styling from American automobile designer Chris Bangle, who had originally joined BMW in 1992, and whose styling was now being used across the BMW model range. *Automobile* magazine was certainly a fan, giving the Z4 roadster its prestigious Design of the Year Award in 2002.

While the Z3, first introduced in 1996, had sold well, especially in North America where it was built, it was never highly regarded as a driver's car. The Z4 was a different animal, however. The chassis was three times stiffer than its predecessor's and an advanced multilink rear suspension had been set up to improve handling dramatically. A range of lusty six-cylinder powerplants

was available to go under the long hood (bonnet), although a four-cylinder version was also available to the more frugally minded buyer. The gearbox was a six-speed manual. The performance of the aggressively styled Z4 was soon noticed and, nicknamed the "Land Shark," it gained recognition as a serious rival to the Porsche Boxster and the Honda S2000.

In 2009 the second-generation Z4 was introduced. This model merged the earlier roadster and coupe into a single model, thanks to an electrohydraulic retractable hardtop that could be raised or lowered in just twenty seconds. While the hardtop's extra weight slightly dampened the cars on-track abilities, the face-lifted Mark II Z4 was applauded for its good looks, build quality, and comfort. *Automobile* magazine again came out in support, describing the new Z4 as having a "cohesive, coherent shape that is at once beautiful and elegant, expressing power and performance." **RD**

CS | Lexus

J

2002 • all electric 47 battery • 671 bhp/500 kW • unknown • 70 mph/123 kph

Director Steven Spielberg, a Lexus owner, had asked the Japanese carmaker to dream up a concept car to use in his 2002 science fiction movie *Minority Report*.

The result was the CS, a radical electric sports car incorporating a combination of the Japanese motor industry's long-term seed ideas, most sophisticated motor sport technologies, and wildest fantasies of the wackiest designers. Some of their craziest ideas have since become commonplace, such as parking assist systems, dashboard computers, and auto self-diagnosis.

The CS was built on a carbon-fiber and titanium chassis with color-impregnated, carbon composite body panels that changed color at the driver's voice command. Actor Tom Cruise drove the car throughout the movie, which was takes place in the year 2054. The "smart recharging" electric motor was powered by forty-seven batteries and produced a hefty output of 671 bhp (500 kW), so the two-seater could drive at 70 mph (113 kph) for long periods between charges. Cruise used voice commands for most controls and needed no keys—a DNA-recognition entry and ignition system was built-in. The car also featured an "auto valet" control that allowed it to drop off the owner at a desired location, park itself for recharging, and arrive for owner pickup at the commanded location.

The titanium double-wishbone suspension included adaptive variable suspension and speed-sensitive automatic height control. The computerized ceramic disc brakes had a built-in regeneration system to recharge the batteries, and the tires adjusted their traction automatically to suit road conditions. **SH**

Streetka | Ford

(E)

2003 • 97 cu in/1,597 cc, S4 • 94 bhp/70 kW • 0–60 mph/97 kph in 12 seconds • 108 mph/174 kph

Ford's Ka, introduced in 1996, was a hit because of its striking "new edge" styling combined with excellent handling. It was easy to park, frugal, and fun.

In 2003 Ford created two more powerful versions, the Sportka for men (advertised as "the Ka's evil twin") and the two-seater open-top Streetka for women; the latter was advertised with the help of Kylie Minogue. Both versions came with a 97-cubic-inch (1,597-cc) engine and a chunky body kit.

The Streetka had a light and simple top that could be opened or closed with one arm. Ford worked hard to make its body as stiff as possible and so the little soft-top dealt with bumpy roads better than many more expensive cabriolets. The standard Ka's excellent handling, precise steering, and tenacious grip were preserved intact.

All versions of the Streetka came with remote central locking, alloy wheels, electric windows, and a CD player, so buyers were not short-changed on equipment. The 1.6i Luxury version came with leather seats and a few more nice visual goodies.

The Streetka's image as a "woman's car" wasn't necessarily a bad thing if you were a woman. If your ride was a Mini Cooper or an MX-5, a boyfriend or husband was likely to try muscle his way into it. If you had a Streetka, he wouldn't want to be seen in it at all.

When Ford helped to promote the *Thunderbirds* movie in 2004, it brought out a special edition, called the Streetka Pink, in the same shade as Lady Penelope's FAB 1 Rolls-Royce. Women tempted to buy a used model should really love pink and want to keep it forever. They will probably never be able to sell it again. **LT**

The narrowed eyes and wide mouth of the 2003 Dodge Viper ZB take their styling cues from the car's reptilian namesake. ▷

Desert Runner | URI (ZA)

2003 • 183 cu in/3,000 cc, S4 • 107 bhp/80 kW • unknown • unknown

This hardcore 4x4 was originally built by Ewart Smith, a goat farmer in Namibia, for driving around the Kalahari desert. Entrepreneur Adriaan Booyse saw it on Smith's farm, bought the rights, set up Uri (which means "jump" in Namibian), and began building the Desert Runner as an ultimate third-world utility vehicle. A new factory has opened near Pretoria in South Africa to cope with growing demand.

The Desert Runner is designed to cope with the worst terrains found in Africa. It is made from steel tubing 0.1 inch (3 mm) thick, clad with 0.06-inch (1.6-mm) sheet metal to create a very strong framework. The tailgate and doors can be removed completely for loading awkward items. Zinc primers and industrial top coats provide thorough rust protection; industrial polyurethane is used to treat the whole underbody, loading bay, engine compartment, and interior.

Heavy mechanical components are placed at the rear for improved traction, while long travel suspension all around provides double the ground clearance of a normal 4x4. The engines and gearbox come from Toyota pickups, for which there are many spares in Africa. Buyers can opt for either 122-cubic-inch (2,000-cc) or 183-cubic-inch (3,000-cc) turbodiesel, or 134-cubic-inch (2,200-cc) or 146-cubic-inch (2,400-cc) gasoline units.

The lack of frills keeps the cost low and the weight down to 3,718 pounds (1,690 kg). The rugged build ensures that a lifespan of around 200,000 miles (300,000 km) is both achievable and surpassed many times. All manner of major recovery equipment and tools can be fitted to the vehicle, including shovel, fender (bumper) jack, and spare wheels. **SH**

Viper ZB | Dodge (USA)

2003 • 506 cu in/8,300 cc, V10 • 500 bhp/370 kW • 0–60 mph/97 kph in 3.8 seconds • 193 mph/310 kph

At the time of writing, Dodge's new Viper is the fastest, most powerful production car in the United States.

With a huge engine under its long hood (bonnet), the Viper ZB was aimed right at the Chevrolet Corvette. It was still a hairy-chested muscle-car experience, but it had better build quality. The convertible roadster version had a decent folding roof.

Chrysler was now part of the Daimler-Benz empire, and the European influence showed. The Viper still looked fabulously exciting, but it had a more international styling. Unexpectedly, the designer of this all-American hot-rod was Osamu Shikado, a former Toyota designer responsible for the Corolla and Camry. His lines for the Viper were considered more elegant but almost too pretty for a muscle car. So Osamu was overruled about normalizing the Viper's exhaust pipes, which stayed in their traditional place at the sides, albeit mostly hidden by the sills.

The new car was shorter than before, but with a wheelbase extended by pushing the wheels further into the corners of the body. Chrysler's Street and Racing Technology (SRT) team improved the chassis too, making it lighter but more rigid. The Viper Mark III was thus more refined to drive but tackled corners with as much drama. A coupe version was introduced later, retaining its predecessor's distinctive double-bubble roof shape. The SRT team even worked on tuning the sound of the new car. Previously the side pipes only handled the outlet from one side of the V10, so the car sounded like a straight five-cylinder unit from either side. Now the exhausts were mixed, so passers-by got the full V10 orchestra from either side pipe. **SH**

SSR | Chevrolet

(USA)

2003 • 325 cu in/5,326 cc, V8 • 300 bhp/291 kW • 0–60 mph/97 kph in 7.7 seconds • 126 mph/203 kph

Retro-futurist style was big in the 2000s. The Plymouth Prowler hot rod had kicked things off in 1997, followed by the millennium lead-sled PT Cruiser in 2000. Chevrolet's SSR (Super Sport Roadster) of 2003 looked like a chrome-laden 1950s pickup, but it had the powertrain of a rear-wheel-drive V8 sports car and a two-piece power-retractable hardtop. For anyone wanting the looks of a classic truck without overfamiliarity with towing services, it was perfect.

The concept was created by the man behind the fifth-generation Camaro, General Motors (GM) design chief Ed Welburn. It appeared at the Detroit Auto Show in 2000 and the public loudly demanded a production model; GM duly obliged in 2003.

The production SSR sat on a modified version of the Trailblazer platform. It was two-wheel drive only, with 19-inch (48-cm) aluminum wheels in front, 20-inch (51-cm) at rear. Independent front and five-link rear suspension gave the handling a sporty flavor, but the 350-bhp (257-kW), 348-cubic-inch (5,700-cc) Corvette V8 struggled to get the 4,700-pound (2,132-kg) truck shifting with any vigor. For 2005, a 400-bhp (294-kW), 366-cubic-inch (6,000-cc) engine with an optional six-speed manual transmission was a welcome upgrade.

The cabin could seat two in comfort or squash in a third for short journeys. The seats were leather, but most blingy touches were optional. The sticker price was a thumping $41,500 (£26,000) and production was always limited, so Chevrolet sold only 25,000 between 2003 and 2006. But the retro theme has not died, and the SSR has an enthusiastic following; maybe we will see another cute convertible sports truck. **LT**

Fulgura | Laraki

MA

2003 • 335 cu in/5,493 cc, V8 • 920 bhp/677 kW • 0–62 mph/100 kph in 3.2 seconds • 247 mph/398 kph

The first Arab supercar was designed and produced in Casablanca, Morocco. The young Moroccan designer Abdeslam Laraki had started by creating luxurious yachts for wealthy customers. Using his knowledge of the tastes of the world's super-rich, Laraki produced two now-forgotten supercars between 2002 and 2008.

The Fulgura was the Laraki company's first attempt. The concept version appeared at the 2002 Geneva Motor Show, and the "production" model was shown a year later, with a Mercedes engine replacing the original Lamborghini unit. The car was based on a Lamborghini Diablo frame, with its quad-turbo Mercedes-Benz 366-cubic-inch (6,000-cc) V12 engine fitted longways just behind the seats to drive the rear wheels. On top of this, Laraki fitted a new, sleek, lightweight carbon-fiber body with a total curb weight of only 2,534 pounds (1,152 kg). The car cost more than $500,000 (£320,000).

A slightly redesigned version was unveiled in 2004 with a choice of Mercedes V8 or V12 engines. In 2005 Laraki claimed the engine could now produce 671 bhp (494 kW), and in 2007 it produced a concept version with a claimed output of a staggering 920 bhp (677 kW). Its figures, quoted above, are manufacturer's estimates and are not independently tested.

The second Laraki car, the Borac, was a grand tourer. The engine was mounted at the front and there were two small rear seats. The Borac used the Fulgara's Mercedes engine but without turbocharging.

Fully specified models were built as prototypes but it seems that Laraki's super-rich clients failed to buy. Sadly, both cars have since faded into history. **SH**

Copen | Daihatsu

J

2003 • 79 cu in/1,300 cc, S4 • 86 bhp/64 kW • 0–62 mph/100 kph in 9.5 seconds • 110 mph/170 kph

Japan's "kei car" small-vehicle category has lead to some strange and interesting cars over the years as Japanese manufacturers have tried to benefit from their government's tax advantages.

Daihatsu's Copen was a tiny, retro-styled, two-door sports car with a retractable aluminum roof. In Japan it was fitted with a turbocharged 40-cubic-inch (659-cc) three-cylinder engine to meet kei restrictions. This version could accelerate from 0 to 60 mph (97 kph) in 11.7 seconds and reach 90 mph (145 kph). Many other countries got a later version fitted with a 79-cubic-inch (1,300-cc) engine from the Daihatsu Sirion instead. This was a sophisticated unit using variable valve timing and twin-overhead camshafts and it gave a more spritely performance (figures given above). Both versions were front-engined, front-wheel-drive cars.

The hardtop folded and disappeared into the surprisingly spacious trunk (boot) in about twenty seconds at the press of a button. The interior was smart but cramped, with leather seats and steering wheel. The car weighed just 1,873 pounds (850 kg) so handling was sharp. The features list included air-conditioning, antilock brakes, and alloy wheels, but it failed to disguise the fact that the Copen was so small that many drivers felt like they were driving a car for children. One British reviewer even called it the car "that took Toytown by storm."

Nevertheless, it was cheap to buy and run and could provide an impressive smiles-per-mile ratio. As a city car it was head-turning and fun to drive. The little Copen developed a cult following, and used values have stayed remarkably high as a result. **SH**

Roadster | Smart

(D)

2003 • 42 cu in/689 cc, S3 • 80 bhp/60 kW • 0–60 mph/97 kph in 10.9 seconds • 109 mph/175 kph

Jens Manske's team at Smart wanted to build on the success of the standard Smart car, so it was decided to use the same technology to create a simple, lightweight, affordable sports car. Intended to invoke the driving experience of modestly powered classics such as the MG Midget, the Smart Roadster offered open-air motoring wrapped up in a reliable, modern package. Smart's philosophy was to "reduce to the max."

The Roadster, based on a slightly stretched Smart, had a targa-style convertible roof and a much lower center of gravity. The same Mercedes-developed, turbocharged "suprex" engine, with two states of tune available, powered the rear wheels, but it would not trouble many speed cameras. The gearbox was also retained, a clumsy six-speed semiautomatic that required a special technique to get anything like a smooth gearshift from it. This, and the fact that the chassis offered more grip than feedback, was the Roadster's Achilles heel.

Costing $18,000 (£12,000), the Smart weighed 1,738 pounds (790 kg). It offered driving fun at sensible speeds, but it was so slow, for a sports car, that BBC *Top Gear*'s Jeremy Clarkson stated, "It has exactly the same top speed as Henry VIII." *Top Gear* magazine still named it as its 2005 "Fun Car of the Year, however.

German tuning company Brabus built a prototype Roadster with two of the original three-cylinder engines built together to make a new V6 with two turbos. With 215 bhp (160 kW), it had the same power-to-weight ratio as a contemporary Porsche 911. But this missed the "less is more" point of the Roadster. Thankfully, it never made it to production. **RD**

FULL THROTTLE
FULL THROTTLE
Suspension

The off-road prowess of the 2003 Hummer H2 bespeaks its military origins, but its looks tend to antagonize nature lovers.

H2 | Hummer (USA)

2003 • 366 cu in/6,000 cc, V8 • 316 bhp/232 kW • 0–60 mph/97 kph in 10.4 seconds • 93 mph/150 kph

The Hummer H2 has the honor of being named both North American Truck of the Year in 2003 and one of *Time* magazines Fifty Worst Cars of All Time in 2011. What a difference a financial meltdown can make.

The Hummer began as the military Humvee, much celebrated during the first Iraq War. Arnold Schwarzenegger led a campaign to persuade its maker, AM General, to produce a civilian version from 1992. The success of this beast persuaded General Motors (GM) to buy the rights in 1999 and develop a more suburban model aimed, in particular, at female buyers. Based on the good old Chevy Tahoe chassis, the H2 re-created the Humvee's wide, threatening stance and mouth-full-of-braces grille.

With a starting price of $48,800 (£31,000), some drivers in Michigan were no doubt disappointed not to get a gun turret, but owners were offered astonishing off-road ability and an undeniable presence. The H2 could also probably tow a house if necessary. Drawbacks included its trucklike drive, cramped cabin, and the V8's 10-mpg (28.2-liters/km) thirst.

H2s were soon lining up next to Chevy Suburbans and Lincoln Navigators outside malls all over the United States. GM produced variants including pickups and the smaller H3, and Hummer became a brand in its own right. Hummers were a big hit with all lovers of bling, and many were radically customized. But others were vandalized by activists who saw it as an arrogant, militaristic destroyer of the planet.

Sales plummeted when gas prices rose after the financial crisis of 2008, so GM axed it. Used H2s are now available for around $15,000 (£9410). **LT**

SV | MG (GB)

2003 • 281 cu in/4,601 cc, V8 • 320 bhp/239 kW • 0–60 mph/97 kph in 5.3 seconds • 165 mph/265 kph

MG Rover was looking for a "halo" product to add some shine to its aging lineup of models. The assets of independent Italian carmaker Qvale became available, and were snapped up by cash-strapped MG Rover, which hoped that the Qvale Mangusta might serve as its new model as it was already selling in the U.S. market. The Mangusta had originally started life as the De Tomaso Bigua and had been bought by Qvale when De Tomaso ran into financial trouble.

Code-named MG X80, the Mangusta was reworked by British designer Peter Stevens. Expensive carbon-fiber bodywork was assembled from more than 3,000 individual pieces. The lightweight steel chassis had integrated rollover bars built to FIA racing specifications. Lights were borrowed from Fiat, and the engine from Ford, the 281-cubic-inch (4,601-cc) V8 delivering performance to match the styling's promise. Priced from £65,000 ($100,000), the MG SV was an ambitious project for a company already on the brink.

Yet in 2004 an even hotter version was released: the SV-R. Powered by a highly tuned 305-cubic-inch (5,000-cc) V8 with 385 bhp (287 kW), its top speed was a claimed 175 mph (281 kph). MG intended to offer further upgrades capable of up to 1,000 bhp (746 kW). *Evo* magazine, which tested the standard SV, warned, "It'll willingly give you enough rope to hang yourself."

A convoluted production process and financial difficulties in the twilight years of MG Rover meant that only around seventy-five examples of these cars were ever delivered. The demise of MG Rover in 2005 was not the end for the car, though. In 2007 a company called MG Sports and Racing bought the rights to the SV. **RD**

M3 CSL | BMW (D)

2003 • 198 cu in/3,245 cc, S6 • 355 bhp/265 kW • 0–62 mph/100 kph in 4.5 seconds • 155 mph/250 kph

The BMW M3 was already a huge hit, but obsessive BMW engineers felt they could do better. A tweaked version called the M3 CSL was developed for limited markets only. The CSL (Coupe Sport Leichtbau) was not only lighter, but even more power had been wrung from the M3's straight-six engine—with modifications to the air intake, valves, and camshaft timing, an extra 17 bhp (13 kW) was gained. The car was only available with BMW's semiautomatic SMG gearbox for the quickest shifts.

BMW applied its typical attention to detail, ditching the stereo and air-conditioning, although buyers could have them fitted for free if they preferred. There was extensive use of carbon fiber in the body. BMW even went to the huge trouble of using thinner steel in the exhaust and thinner windshield glass to save a further few grams. Although the 240-pound (110-kg) overall weight saving may not seem much, BMW had worked on the location of weight within the car, cleverly lowering the center of gravity to improve handling.

The limited run sold almost instantly. For buyers with a race license, BMW removed the 155-mph (250-kph) speed limiter. The effort to make what may seem like small changes had made a big difference. BMW's obsession turned the already potent M3 into a supercar slayer in CSL form. **RD**

VX220 Turbo | Vauxhall (GB)

2003 • 122 cu in/1,998 cc, S4 • 197 bhp/147 kW • 0–60 mph/97 kph in 4.6 seconds • 150 mph/242 kph

Despite getting rave reviews, the VX220 was being outsold by its Lotus-badged stablemate by five to one in 2002. Unfairly perceived as a poor man's Elise, it also lacked the kudos of the Lotus. General Motors realized that its car needed a serious makeover.

A 122-cubic-inch (1,998-cc) turbocharged engine from the Astra GSi was fitted into the little sports car; it gained a 38-percent power increase. Weighing only 2,050 pounds (930 kg), thanks to its aluminum chassis, the VX now had a power-to-weight ratio to match a Porsche 911. The 0–60 mph (97 kph) sprint took less than five seconds, but it was the power delivery beyond that point that most impressed early test drivers.

The VX220 Turbo cost just £25,500 ($40,000) when it was launched. BBC TV *Top Gear* host Jeremy Clarkson declared that nothing in its price range came close in terms of performance and sheer fun, and it was awarded *Top Gear*'s Sport Car of 2003.

Only 1,940 cars were built before production ceased in 2005. Sadly, many of these cars have since been crash damaged beyond repair, and they have become increasingly rare. For these reasons, MSN Cars suggested in 2011 that the VX220 Turbo was among the ten best potential investments for any shrewd car collector, and was a definite future classic. **DS**

Gallardo | Lamborghini (I)

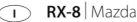

2003 • 303 cu in/4,961 cc, V10 • 493 bhp/366 kW • 0–60 mph/97 kph in 4.1 seconds • 192 mph/309 kph

In 1998 Lamborghini was sold to the Volkswagen (VW)/Audi group. There were already plans afoot for a new car, the "Baby Lambo," and under VW's ownership this was developed fully and launched in 2003. It was called the Gallardo, named for a famous breed of fighting bull.

Though not the first Lambo made under the new German owners (that was the Murciélago), the Gallardo was significant because it showed how determined VW was to expand and strengthen the company's lineup. This car was 4 inches (10 cm) shorter than the Murciélago and powered by a V10 engine, rather than a V12. It produced 493 bhp (366 kW) that ran through a four-wheel-drive system with a viscous coupling. The system adjusts the amount of power going to the front and back wheels depending on load and grip. Buyers could choose between a conventional six-speed gearbox or an electronic one with paddle shifters.

The new car was more drivable than previous Lamborghinis, but it lost none of the brand's "supercar" status. Indeed, it has become the biggest- selling Lamborghini to date, with 10,000 built in its first seven years. The Gallardo platform has also been used for the Audi R8 supercar, although that originally had a V8 engine to to prevent it from competing with its Italian cousin. It is now available with the same V10 motor. **JI**

RX-8 | Mazda (J)

2003 • 79 cu in/1,300 cc, twin-rotary • 228 bhp/168 kW • 0–60 mph/97 kph in 6.4 seconds • 146 mph/235 kph

Mazda's RX-8 took over the rotary engine mantle from the RX-7. The new car had the same lively performance and well-balanced handling as its predecessor, but it was different in crucial ways. Not only was it cheaper, it was bigger, too. The RX-8 had two small, chunky, rear-hinged "suicide" doors behind the normal wide front ones. These gave access to small rear seats that had limited head and foot room, although definitely more than the unusable old 2+2. It also had a bigger cabin, fat wheel arches, and arrowhead front end.

Inside the engine, the sequential turbochargers of the old car were dumped in favor of a return to a more predictable, normally aspirated performance. Various states of engine tune were available in different countries, depending on their emission requirements. Figures for the U.K. configuration are given above.

The RX-8 was warmly received by British reviewers, but sadly it also suffered from the RX-7's weaknesses: tiny luggage space and high fuel consumption. A crippling depreciation added to the running cost.

Mazda tried hard to emulate the long-standing success of its smaller MX-5 with a series of special editions, body kits, and even a hydrogen-powered version, the RX-8 RE. But time caught up with the RX-8 and production ground to a halt in 2012. **SH**

Phantom | Rolls-Royce

GB

2003 • 412 cu in/6,749 cc, V12 • 453 bhp/338 kW • 0–60 mph/97 kph in 6 seconds • 149 mph/240 kph

In 2003 Rolls-Royce became cool again. The stodgy, wallowy old Seraph was banished and in its place stood a brutalist, slab-sided monster with small headlights and close to a cartoon of the classic upright grille.

The price at launch was £250,000 ($300,000). Naturally every sheik and oligarch wanted one, but so did almost every rapper and football star. The Phantom became one of the most customized cars ever. While Rolls-Royce likes to stress the car's British heritage, and the location of its factory on the estate of the car-mad Earl of March at Goodwood in southern England, the company had been a subsidiary of BMW since 1998, and its mighty V12 and most innards were German.

The engine is a development of the direct-injection, all-alloy, forty-eight-valve V12 that powers the BMW 760iL. Peak power is 453 bhp (338 kW), and peak torque is 531 pounds per foot (718 Nm); delivered through a ZF six-speed automatic gearbox.

The car is a gorgeous machine to drive: powerful, creamy smooth, and sumptuous. Its aluminum space frame and panels aid stiffness while reducing weight. Air springs protect the occupants from the worst roads. The steering is light but precise, and the Roller feels far smaller than it looks. Cameras are placed on the long nose for seeing around corners.

Rear passengers enter via rear-hinged "coach doors" that close at the touch of a button. There is an umbrella inside one door. Once inside, passengers can bury their toes in a soft sheepskin rug.

A final touch of perfection: the "RR" badge in the center of the steering wheel always remains upright because it is mounted on an independent bezel. **LT**

SLR McLaren | Mercedes-Benz

(D)

2003 • 332 cu in/5,439 cc, V8 • 626 bhp/467 kW • 0–60 mph/97 kph in 3.6 seconds • 208 mph/334 kph

The Mercedes SLR McLaren is a true supercar: a blend of cutting-edge technology and high art. In an Anglo-German collaboration between Mercedes and McLaren, the cars are assembled at the Formula One team's technical center at Woking in England.

The car was inspired by the 1955 Mercedes-Benz 300 SLR Uhlenhault, which was driven to victory in the Mille Miglia in Italy by Sir Stirling Moss. The new SLR was a fresh design, built around an entirely carbon-fiber body and an aluminum frame. The engine is a hand-built aluminum supercharged V8. Originally the engine was to be at the nose of the car, but McLaren moved it 40 inches (1 m) back to achieve better balance; the SLR is technically front-mid engined.

The motor produced 626 bhp (467 kW), driven through the rear wheels via a sophisticated semiautomatic five-speed gearbox. The drivers are able to select how much control they want over the transmission, and even decide at what level of rev count the automatic system should change up. There are also three manual settings.

The rest of the car's mechanicals were equally well thought out: double wishbone suspension, carbon disc brakes, and a sophisticated rear spoiler. The latter, as well as rising into place at high speed, can be adjusted further at the flick of a switch; under heavy deceleration it also acts as an air-brake.

As astonishing as the original SLR McLaren was, Mercedes and McLaren went on to produce several special versions, including a "Stirling Moss" limited-edition roadster with its power boosted to 640 bhp (480 kW). The SLR line was discontinued in 2009. **JI**

A bird's-eye view of the 2003 Porsche Carrera GT shows its mighty V10 engine framed by the rear hood (bonnet). ▷

Cayenne Turbo | Porsche (D)

2003 • 275 cu in/4,500 cc, V8 • 450 bhp/336 kW • 0–60 mph/97 kph in 5.3 seconds • 165 mph/266 kph

When Porsche announced it was building a sport utility vehicle (SUV), the brand's fans were aghast. "Wait until you drive it," was Porsche's response. When they did, the Cayenne Turbo soon won them over. Drivers got a commanding view of the traffic ahead for the first time, yet still had the power to overtake almost anything in front of them. *Autocar* magazine tried the Turbo model and gasped, "It's a car of staggering ability."

Weighing two tons and almost 5 feet 10 inches (170 cm) high, this was never going to be another Porsche 911, but the Cayenne's performance was extraordinary for an SUV. On-road handling was flawless, thanks to front and rear setups of double wishbone, air springs, and an anti-roll bar. No one expected the four-door Porsche to be a heroic mud-plugger, though—it is strictly limited to slippery car parks and sandy boat slipways. But it was the start of a new breed of vehicle, the high-performance crossover.

Porsche was too small a company to fund such a new development single-handedly. The Cayenne, supported by Volkswagen, shared about 60 percent of its parts with the Taureg. But some of the most character-building components were Porsche's own, including the high-performance V8 engine and the sophisticated six-speed semiautomatic gearbox.

The ride height is adjustable, and the suspension has different settings for normal, comfort, and sport. The main criticism has been of its rather anonymous looks and its thirsty engines. In 2009 Porsche produced an unlikely answer to the Cayenne's fuel economy problem—a diesel version. Fans grumbled again, but the turbodiesel's performance won them over. **SH**

Carrera GT | Porsche (D)

2003 • 350 cu in/5,733 cc, V10 • 604 bhp/450 kW • 0–60 mph/97 kph in 3.5 seconds • 205 mph/330 kph

Porsche doesn't really do supercars. Although the first 911 Turbo, and the 959 rally car, were awesome machines for their time, Porsche has tended to focus on sports cars with a high degree of everyday usability rather than all-out performance.

The Porsche Carrera GT was a completely different animal. It was penned on an entirely fresh piece of paper, and, despite some similar design features, was not constrained by the 911's platform. This time the inspiration came from its LMP2000 Le Mans project. But, not wishing to be outdone by its German rival Audi, Porsche pulled the plug on this race car program and decided to put its energies, technology, and budget into a road-going supercar instead.

Powered by a 350-cubic-inch (5,700-cc) V10 unit, originally built for the Footwork Formula One team, the car's lightweight chassis and bodywork were made entirely of carbon fiber. As a nod to the GT's Le Mans heritage, the six-speed manual had a gearshift knob made of wood, just like the Porsche 917's. The large rear spoiler deployed upward on two carbon-fiber stanchions when the car hit 70 mph (110 kph).

Only 1,270 Carrera GTs were built up to 2006, with around half being exported to the United States. Obvious rivals to the Carrera GT were the Ferrari Enzo and Pagani Zonda. TV shows, magazines, and Web site forums were ablaze with debate as to which really was the greatest supercar of them all. But after a 2004 *Autocar* group test, the magazine declared that "when the voices settle, the verdict will remain unequivocal: the Carrera GT is the best supercar ever made, and probably the most exciting road car in history." **DS**

Carrera GT

Crossfire | Chrysler

USA

2003 • 195 cu in/3,200 cc, V6 • 215 bhp/160 kW • 0–60 mph/97 kph in 6.4 seconds • 155 mph/250 kph

It looked like an brawny old muscle car reborn, a rear-wheel-drive two-seater with a hot V8 under the hood (bonnet) that seemed built to tackle the Mustangs and Camaros of the 1970s. Yet the Crossfire was a twenty-first-century car, the product of a troubled partnership between Chrysler and Mercedes.

Designed by American Eric Stoddard, who later moved to Hyundai, it was based on an aging Mercedes SLK platform and engine. Its combination of U.S. and European sports-car design was characterized by distinctive side vents and a retro boattail rear. The sporty intent was signaled by big wheels, a pop-up rear spoiler, and center-exit dual exhausts.

This slightly confused but characterful car inherited the rigid build of the SLK, which was built in the same factory in Germany. However, the SLK was replaced in 2004, leaving the Crossfire as a relic of the previous generation. Some Americans felt like they were being treated like an emerging East Asian manufacturer, just making a European brand's hand-me-downs.

Stability control, an antilock braking system, and traction control helped to generate plenty of grip but did not improve the stodgy steering and uncomfortable ride. Likewise, electric-powered leather seats, dual-zone climate control, and a 240-watt stereo could not disguise the plasticky and cramped interior.

A Crossfire convertible soon followed, then a hot-blooded supercharged SRT-6 version, with 330 bhp (246 kW), capable of 0–60 mph (97 kph) in 4.8 seconds. But sales never really took off. Fewer than 100,000 sold worldwide, Mercedes and Chrysler divorced in 2007, and so ended production of the Crossfire. **SH**

Quattroporte | Maserati

(I)

2004 • 256 cu in/4,201 cc, V8 • 394 bhp/294 kW • 0–60 mph/97 kph in 5.6 seconds • 167 mph/269 kph

As the name states, the Quattroporte was a four-door sedan (saloon) from Maserati. The model launched in 2004 was the fifth generation of this car and was designed by Italian styling house Pininfarina. A luxurious sports sedan, the Quattroporte was unveiled at the Frankfurt Motor Show in September 2003 and made its U.S. debut at the 2003 Pebble Beach Concours d'Élégance. Classic Maserati styling cues included an oval-shaped grille, triple porthole vents in the wings, and an almond-shaped clock in the dashboard. *GQ* magazine placed it twenty-first among its Most Beautiful 100 Things in the World awards in 2003.

Those stunning looks hid some supercar muscle. The launch model had a 395-bhp (294-kW) 256-cubic-inch (4,201-cc) V8. *Auto Express* magazine said it had "one of the most glorious soundtracks of any production car."

The transmission, however, came in for much criticism. Called DuoSelect and based on a design from sister brand Ferrari, the gearbox could give awkward gearshifts that did not suit the limousine nature of the Quattroporte. Maserati eventually replaced it with a conventional six-speed automatic gearbox from German manufacturer ZF in 2007.

Prices started at $120,000 (£75,000) for the 256-cubic-inch (4,201-cc) V8 model. A later Sport GT S model offered 433 bhp (323 kW). France's *L'Automobile* magazine awarded it Best Luxury Car of 2008, although it never won any awards for fuel economy or emissions. Predictably, nineteen examples of the Quattroporte were purchased by the Italian Government, and surely there could be no finer way to arrive at a official state banquet. **RD**

T6 Roadster | Caresto

S

2004 • 177 cu in/2,900 cc, S6 • 330 bhp/246 kW • unknown • unknown

Caresto is at the forefront of Sweden's booming hot-rod scene. Its founder is development engineer Leif Tufvesson, formerly of Volvo and supercar maker Koenigsegg. Basing hot-rod supercars on normally sedate Volvos is a habitual automotive joke with Caresto. This sensational-looking retro racer, based on a Volvo XC90, is one of its most successful creations.

The small team working in a workshop in rural southern Sweden put a standard Volvo engine in the back of the T6, powering the rear wheels via a four-speed sequential Volvo gearbox. On top of this machine they placed a handmade aluminum body and a removeable polycarbonate roof on a hand-formed tubular steel frame. The lines are simple and striking.

For this model, Caresto used the twin-turbo straight-six engine from the biggest Volvo production car. The engine is mounted just behind the two leather bucket seats. As the car weighs only 2,370 pounds (1,075 kg), the performance is stunning but unquantified—Caresto has not published performance figures for its cool two-seater.

The Caresto T6 is appointed with fine-quality components and feaures, including full hand-stitched Scottish leather trim, antilock braking system, and alloy wheels. Technical sophistication abounds: to help keep the engine cool, the rear deck-lid raises up automatically at a preset temperature. The high-performance suspension has specially fabricated A-arms all around with carbon-fiber leaf springs.

Hot Rod magazine called the multiaward-winning T6 one of the "most spectacularly crafted hot rods to ever grace the pages of this or any other magazine." **SH**

T4 | Troller

BR

2004 • 183 cu in/3,000 cc, S4 • 161 bhp/120 kW • unknown • 93 mph/150 kph

The T4 was inspired by the Willys Jeep and keeps close to the simple, lightweight concept of the original while adding some modern features of its own. Troller is a Brazilian off-road vehicle manufacturer and is a subsidiary of Ford. The T4 is its flagship vehicle. It is considered a local, cheaper, and more rugged rival to Ford's Wrangler, another evolution of the Willy's Jeep.

The T4 has a hefty Brazilian-built 183-cubic-inch (3,000-cc) turbodiesel engine with common-rail fuel injection. It has permanent four-wheel drive and a five-speed manual gearbox. The two-door fiberglass body is classically styled and sits on a rigid rectangular tubular steel chassis. Fiberglass is used for its low cost, low weight, and freedom from rust. The equipment list includes leather seats, air-conditioning, power steering, powered mirrors and windows, and alloy wheels.

The T4 includes a removable hardtop, a small tailgate where the spare wheel resides, roof rails and an exhaust "snorkel chimney" carrying emissions up to roof level—this allows the T4 to drive through deep water that would swamp a normally-positioned exhaust pipe. The T4 also has very accommodating approach angles at both ends, meaning it can tackle sudden steep inclines without fouling its fenders (bumpers).

The T4 has competed in many rallies, including the formidable Paris–Dakar event. It has proven so popular in Africa that Troller has opened a factory in Angola. In December 2009, a Brazilian TV news helicopter filmed a Troller T4 driving through deeply flooded streets of São Paulo, water covering its hood (bonnet) and surging up its windshield. The T4 looked so capable that Troller has since used the footage in a TV commercial. **SH**

DB9 | Aston Martin

GB

2004 • 362 cu in/5,935 cc, V12 • 469 bhp/350 kW • 0–60 mph/97 kph in 4.6 seconds • 186 mph/300 kph

While the Vanquish is remembered as the last car built at Aston Martin's fifty-year-old Newport Pagnell factory, the DB9 was heralded as the first to come out of the company's new Gaydon facility in Warwickshire.

The DB9's immediate predecessor, the DB7, had been based on the Jaguar XJS, which harked back to another era in sports-car design. But 2004 marked a turning point for Aston Martin, which at that time was owned by Ford. There had been heavy investment in new designs and technology, and the DB9 was all new. It was the first car built on the VH aluminum platform that would also be used for cars like the V8 Vantage.

Why did Aston Martin skip a number, going from DB7 to DB9? Not only did that reinforce the huge leap forward in technology, but it avoided any confusion over the engine configuration. Calling it DB8 may have led people to think it was powered by a V8 rather than the same V12 as the earlier Vanquish.

The DB9 was designed by Ian Callum shortly before he left for Jaguar, where he penned the XKR. The two cars do bear some mutual resemblance and compete in the same area of the car market: the grand tourer.

Robots were involved in parts of the assembly process of the DB9—unlike previous models—particularly bonding of the aluminum body panels. The car blended traditional Aston Martin qualities with cutting-edge technology, such as a redline that varied according to factors such as mileage and engine temperature. The V12 engine can take it up to 186 mph (300 kph) and it can cruise easily all day at twice the legal limit—in any country. And it was even crash-tested by the engineers at Volvo. **JI**

Titan | Nissan

J

2004 • 339 cu in/5,552 cc, V8 • 305 bhp/227 kW • 0–60 mph/97 kph in 7.2 seconds • 115 mph/185 kph

There are certain things that define the United States, and one of them is the belief that bigger is better. From burgers to buildings, size always matters.

This possibly explains why mammoth pickups are so popular in the country. Patriotism may also play a part: the most popular pickups in the United States are all made by U.S. companies. Toyota tried to crack the market, but the U.S. brands prevailed. Maybe those Japanese trucks were just not big enough.

So when Nissan joined the fight, it made sure it did so in style, with the mighty Titan. Two things may have helped in its acceptance and sales; it is made at the Nissan factory in Canton, Mississippi, and it is around 19 feet (6 m) in length.

The 339-cubic-inch (5,552-cc) V8 engine did not do it any harm either, and most agreed that in the muscle contest with its U.S. rivals it came out on top. The U.S.-made V8 engine also had the benefit of Japanese technology: the big lump packs four valves per cylinder, compared to the two valves of some rivals.

Although the Titan comes in only one overall size, the pickup is served up in different versions. There is the King Cab, with rear seats but no rear doors, and the Crew Cab, with more rear space and a full complement of doors. While the Crew Cab is larger at the expense of the load space behind it, its rear-space comfort suggests a dual use of the Titan, as a family vehicle as well as a load hauler.

Such features quickly endeared the Titan to the U.S. motoring press and public alike. Nissan had pitched into one of the hardest-fought areas of the U.S. car market and had given the local boys a bloody nose. **JI**

RSQ | Audi

D

2004 • unknown • unknown • unknown • unknown

It is the year 2035. A policeman played by Will Smith speeds around Chicago in a two-door, two-seat coupe that somehow is instantly recognizable as an Audi.

Audi had dabbled with product placement before, but for the 2004 movie based on Isaac Asimov's science fiction story *I, Robot*, Audi went one stage further; it created a whole new car for the film. Audi designers, with just ten weeks to design the RSQ, managed to reach a plausible compromise between present and future. The vehicle had to be fantastical while including as many of Audi's recognizable styling cues as possible. This would ensure the maximum marketing benefit of appearing in an epic blockbuster.

So, despite the wild, fiberglass body shape, the front end of the car has an almost normal Audi look, with a trapezoid grille and an Audi badge. On the back, four interlocking Audi rings glow red. More than that, the car has styling links with the later TT and R8, suggesting that the RSQ actually influenced Audi's future production designs.

The RSQ is a mid-engined coupe whose most noticeable feature is its spherical wheels. It also has reverse-hinged butterfly doors (similar to cars from Lamborghini, controlled by Audi), fully functioning autopilot, and a color-changing luminescent paint job.

Inside, Will Smith could use a U-shaped "wheel" that automatically folded out from the dashboard. When the car was on autopilot, the wheel folded back into the dashboard. And one feature was actually available on contemporary Audis. Sharp-eyed filmgoers could clearly see Smith use Audi's trademark Multi Media Interface dial and screen. **SH**

Mark III La Joya | Bufori

(MAL)

2004 • 162 cu in/2,656 cc, V6 • 172 bhp/127 kW • 0–62 mph/100 kph in 6.7 seconds • 137 mph/220 kph

Bufori is a small family company that makes hand-built cars inspired by 1930s U.S. coupes. In 1986 Gerry Khouri began building three special sports cars in his garage in Sydney, Australia, one for himself and one for each of his two brothers, Anthony and George. The result was such a success that the trio went into business in Kuala Lumpur, Malaysia, with a small specialist factory producing up to 300 cars a year.

The Bufori company name is an acronym of "beautiful, unique, fantastic, original, romantic, and irresistible." The La Joya—Spanish for "the jewel"—was its fifth model. Bufori marketing is never understated, and the company claims the La Joya to be "one of the most unique and luxurious cars on the planet."

The two-seater may have retro styling, but it is totally up-to-date with a strong, lightweight mix of carbon fiber and Kevlar, and a quad-cam V6 driving the rear wheels via an automatic Tiptronic gearbox. The high-tech features list includes an antilock braking system, parking sensors, traction control, voice-activated Bluetooth, and tire-pressure monitoring.

But what really sets the car apart are the finishing touches. The cabin has Persian silk carpeting, a French-polished walnut dashboard, and twenty-four-carat-gold-plated instruments. A solid gold hood (bonnet) emblem is an optional extra and customers can choose gemstones to be mounted anywhere on the vehicle.

Though the La Joya has a traditional long hood, the engine is mounted just ahead of the rear axle. This gives the car ideal balance. With race-style double wishbones and adjustable shock absorbers, the La Joya has handling to match its lively performance. **SH**

612 Scaglietti | Ferrari

(I)

2004 • 348 cu in/5,700 cc, V12 • 533 bhp/397 kW • 0–62 mph/100 kph in 4.3 seconds • 196 mph/315 kph

It was one of the least likely police cars in the world. Ferrari had painted a 612 Scaglietti in dark blue, with a white horizontal stripe and the word "police" on the hood (bonnet). It even had a row of lights on the roof. But no police force had suddenly gone supercar crazy. Instead, it was part of an international promotional stunt by the prancing-horse brand. The 612 police car was driven by real police officers leading a parade of Ferraris across the United Kingdom as part of the brand's sixtieth anniversary relay in 2007.

Unusually for Ferrari, these cars were true four-seaters. The large two-door grand touring coupe had a 348-cubic-inch (5,700-cc) V12 engine (shared with the 575 Maranello) under the hood at the front, sending the drive to the rear wheels. The sleek body with deeply scalloped sides was made from aluminum welded onto an aluminum chassis. Buyers could choose a six-speed manual or a six-speed paddle-shift semiautomatic. There was awesome speed on demand and sporty handling, but for once this was a Ferrari that was easy to drive around town and edge forward in traffic.

The car's name refers to Carrozzeria Scaglietti, the famed Italian coachbuilder responsible for many of Ferrari's track cars in the 1950s. The 612 was built at the former Scaglietti factory at Modena, Italy. Ferrari had wanted to honor aging coachbuilder Sergio Scaglietti despite that fact that he had not worked with Ferrari in seventeen years. "I found out two hours before the presentation that the car's name was Scaglietti," the eighty-three-year-old told the media. "They called me and said to be sure to make it to the introduction of 'my car.' I was flabbergasted." **SH**

M400 | Noble

GB

2004 • 181 cu in/2,968 cc, V6 • 425 bhp/317 kW • 0–60 mph/97 kph in 3.2 seconds • 187 mph/301 kph

There is a long history among sports-car makers in the United Kingdom of borrowing engines from other manufacturers, often American, and slipping them into a nimble, agile chassis. As far back as the 1930s, Allard was doing it with V8s.

Noble kept up this tradition by appropriating the 181-cubic-inch (2,968-cc) V6 engine from the Ford Mondeo ST220 and putting it into the steel frame chassis of its M400. The result was then wrapped in a fiberglass body that was reminiscent of a Lotus.

Before it went into the car, the Mondeo engine was thoroughly reworked by the Noble engineers (who were based in Leeds although the production cars themselves were made in South Africa). Just to start with, the engineers fitted two turbochargers, new pistons, and new fuel-injection systems. The upgraded engine put out 425 bhp (317 kW) to drive a car that weighed only 2,337 pounds (1,060 kg).

One car magazine managed to reach 100 mph (161 kph) from standstill in 7.52 seconds, while another took it way past its official top speed to 202 mph (325 kph). The high power-to-weight ratio of 400 bhp per ton (hence the name of "M400") helped, as did the aerodynamics. The M400 was developed as a track car, with huge levels of grip and high corner speeds, but a number have been used as road cars. These are not the most practical of beasts, and usually can be heard coming from a long way off.

Noble has now sold the rights to the M400 to what used to be its U.S. importer, 1G Racing. That company has relaunched it as the Rossion Q1, with a more luxurious interior and a 450-bhp (336-kW) engine. **JI**

SLK | Mercedes-Benz (D)

2004 • 110 cu in/1,800 cc, S4 • 161 bhp/120 kW • 0–60 mph/97 kph in 7.9 seconds • 143 mph/230 kph

The Mercedes SLK belongs to one of the purest breeds of car: the small, light, and potent two-seater roadster. The name comes from the German term *Sportlich, Leicht und Kurz,* or "sporty, light, and short." The car was first introduced in 1996 to take on the Porsche Boxster and BMW Z3. At the time it was the only one that could operate as both a roadster and a hardtop. It had a clever folding metal roof with five hydraulic chambers to slide it backward and stack it neatly away in the trunk (boot).

The 2004 model had a Formula One–inspired nose that was also influenced by Mercedes' 2000 concept car, the Vision SLA. There was also a new line of engines, from a 110-cubic-inch (1,800-cc) supercharged four-cylinder to the mighty 330-cubic-inch (5,400-cc) V8 that went into the SLK AMG, which served for a while as the Formula One safety car.

Features on board included the Airscarf system, which delivered a stream of warm air to the necks of driver and passenger. For a convertible, that was a stroke of inspiration; the system even adjusts itself as the road speed and ambient temperature change.

But the SLK was mainly designed to deliver driving fun, and it did this in spades, picking up a number of awards along the way. Even the entry-level model (figures given above) has good, sporty performance. **JI**

Roadster | Morgan (GB)

2004 • 181 cu in/2,967 cc, V6 • 204 bhp/166 kW • 0–60 mph/97 kph in 4.9 seconds • 134 mph/216 kph

"If it ain't broke, don't fix it": that well-known saying must be pinned up on the wall at the Morgan Motor Company headquarters. The Morgan Roadster was launched in 2004, but at first glance it bore a remarkable likeness to previous cars from the venerable British firm.

That is because it was basically a Morgan Plus 8, which began life in the late 1960s. There was one key difference, however: the choice of engine. Gone was the old Rover V8, to be replaced by a more modern and lighter Ford 183-cubic-inch (3,000-cc) V6.

The wire-wheeled Roadster stays true to Morgan's values: driver and passenger are exposed to the elements and flung down the road at great speed. The car has a steel chassis, upon which is an ashwood frame. The steel and aluminum body is then built around this.

The suspension was actually already dated when the Roadster's predecessor, the Plus 8, was launched. The rear has leaf springs, while the front features sliding pillars, where the wheel assembly and stub axle move up and down in a frame. This may look like a conventional suspension wishbone, but it is fixed in place. Add in some primitive drum brakes at the rear and Morgan's choice of the 204-bhp (166-kW) Ford V6 looks quite brave. But then, a cushy ride has never been the top priority of Morgan buyers. **JI**

C55 AMG | Mercedes-Benz (D)

2004 • 332 cu in/5,439 cc, V8 • 362 bhp/270 kW •
0–60 mph/97 kph in 6.2 seconds • 155 mph/250 kph

On the surface, the Mercedes C55 AMG was a comfortable, luxury sedan (saloon), but under the skin it had elements of pure muscle car. The 332-cubic-inch (5,439-cc) Mercedes V8 engine was thoroughly revamped by tuning specialists at AMG. The normally aspirated nonturbocharged unit packed a hefty punch, with 362 bhp (270 kW) on tap at only 5,500 rpm.

The rear-wheel drive could easily have been a recipe for fun and games, particularly on wet corners, but the C55 AMG was packed with electronics to keep the chassis in line for a comfortable and serene ride.

The five-speed automatic gearbox had a number of modes, including manual (with paddle shifts). Pleasingly, this would hang onto each gear, even when drivers hit the rev limiter, unlike others that override the supposedly manual controls. Turn off the ESP system and there was a direct link between the right foot and that big V8. It was enough to smoke tires and fire the car forward in the blink of an eye. On a slippery road things could get out of shape, but this was when the car's electronics could still kick in and rectify matters.

The C55 AMG's big rival was the legendary BMW M3, similarly equipped with a V8. Most reviewers decided that the Mercedes was a brilliant car, but the Beemer just nudged it as a driver's tool. **JI**

G 55 AMG | Mercedes-Benz (D)

2004 • 332 cu in/5,439 cc, V8 • 476 bhp/350 kW •
0–60 mph/97 kph in 5.6 seconds • 130 mph/209 kph

The Mercedes G-Wagen is a rugged, down-to-earth off-roader that is used by military forces and government agencies the world over; even the Pope has one. So what better way to mark its twenty-fifth anniversary than by shoehorning in a supercharged 332-cubic-inch (5,439-cc) V8 engine, pumping out 476 bhp (350 kW)?

At its restricted top speed of 130 mph (209 kph), occupants would find conversation difficult because of the wind noise. The G55 has the aerodynamic properties of a concrete block that has been flung from a catapult. At lower speeds, at least they would have been able to enjoy the roar of that mighty AMG V8, blasting through the exhausts that exited just in front of the rear wheels.

The ride on the road could not be described as supple, although visibility was good as a result of the high ride position and large windshield area. Steering on the tarmac was also surprisingly direct for such a big vehicle. Most G55 AMGs would probably never stray off the tarmac, which was a shame because, as with all G-Wagens, it handled brilliantly in the mud.

The truth is, most buyers were not interested in crossing deserts; they just wanted to know they had the most powerful 4x4 available. English international soccer star Wayne Rooney bought one. **JI**

Evo VIII FQ-400 | Mitsubishi

J

2004 • 122 cu in/1,997 cc, S4 • 405 bhp/302 kW • 0–60 mph/97 kph in 3 seconds • 175 mph/282 kph

To call this car by its full title—the Mitsubishi Lancer Evolution—is akin to hearing a television interviewer refer to a rock star by his real name. Just as Bono is simply Bono, the Evo is not referred to as anything else. If the world of cars were a bar, then this four-wheel-drive Japanese rocket would be the bad boy, spilling drinks and starting a fight. It would steal your girlfriend.

The FQ-400 is the baddest of the bad. Mitsubishi has never confirmed or denied the rumor that the name stands for a common expletive followed by "quick," but that would be a fair description of the car.

The "400" refers to the power output: just over 400 bhp (302 kW) from a 122-cubic-inch (1,997-cc) straight four-cylinder unit. That is a big step up from the non-FQ Evo VIII's 276 bhp (202 kW). The engine also produces more than 200 bhp (149 kW) per liter, which is claimed to be the highest power output for any production road car. To get to this figure, Mitsubishi handed a standard Evo VIII over to three British companies: Rampage Tuning, Flow Race Engines, and Owen Developments. The engine block is new, as are the pistons. There is a tailor-made Garrett turbo and a new stainless-steel exhaust manifold. The full upgrade list covers virtually every aspect of the car's mechanics.

In common with all Evo models is the FQ-400's raft of clever electronics that stops the car from getting totally out of shape. Among them is the Active Yaw Control, which sends different power to each wheel; this can bring even the Evo FQ-400 back into line.

Drivers who like their performance smooth and sophisticated had better go elsewhere. But if you like to hang out with the bad boys, strap yourself in. **JI**

Cayman | Porsche

(D)

2005 • 207 cu in/3,387 cc, F6 • 295 bhp/220 kW • 0–60 mph/97 kph in 4.8 seconds • 171 mph/275 kph

Envious observers have been heard to mutter that the Cayman was for people who could not afford a 911. Perhaps they had never driven one. The Cayman was a Boxster with a metal roof and a practical hatchback. The jelly-mold shape was reminiscent of the gorgeous Porsche 356, and the simple sweep of its rear fenders (bumpers) evoked James Dean's 550 Spyder.

Porsche claimed that the roof, plus an extra crossbeam, gave double the torsional rigidity of the Boxster. This allowed the engineers to stiffen the suspension for even better handling.

The Cayman S arrived first (its figures are given above); it returned 18 mpg (16 liters per 100 km) in the city, 26 mpg (11 liters per 100 km) on the highway. A base model arrived a year later with a 245-bhp (180-kW) 165-cubic-inch (2,700-cc) engine, returning 20 and 29 mpg (14 and 9.7 liters per 100 km) respectively. On paper, the S alone sounded underpowered, but this car was not about growling, stomping grunt; its forte was grip, precision, and balance, the result of its low weight and strong mid range torque. The metallic note of the flat-six engine, plus the whirring of belts and accessory pumps coming from under the mound behind the seats, were like music to the ears of aficionados.

The ride was supple, even with those firmer springs, and the adjustable shock absorbers of the optional electronic Porsche Active Suspension Management system ironed out the bumps.

Yes, it was around $10,000 (£6,300) cheaper than a 911, and only slightly more expensive than the Boxster, but the Cayman was pure Porsche. For usable performance every day, it was the perfect choice. **LT**

◁ The 2005 Bugatti Veyron is a masterpiece of engineering—as you would hope, given its wallet-busting price tag.

Veyron EB 16.4 | Bugatti (F)

2005 • 488 cu in/7,993 cc, W16 • 987 bhp/736 kW • 0–60 mph/97 kph in 2.5 seconds • 254 mph/408 kph

The Veyron is about excess and—let us be honest—showing off. Bugatti's owner, Volkswagen (VW), was showing what it could do if money was no object.

VW bought the venerable but long-defunct brand in 1998. The Veyron's chief designer was VW's Hartmut Warkuss, and the exterior was designed by Jozef Kaban.

Before the Veyron, the most famous Bugattis were nimble racers such as the Type 35 in the 1920s, or the opulent Type 41 Royale of 1927. The car is named after Pierre Veyron, who won the 24 Hours of Le Mans in 1939 driving a Type 57. The "EB" is for Ettore Bugatti, and "16.4" refers to sixteen cylinders and four turbochargers.

Any description of this car tends to become a list of ludicrous numbers. *Automobile* magazine observed that if you drove the Veyron at top speed, you would run out of gas in twelve minutes. *Top Gear's* James May noted that at maximum speed the engine consumes 9,900 gallons (45,000 liters) of air per minute, as much as a human breathes in four days.

At 140 mph (220 kph), hydraulics lower the car, while a wing and spoiler deploy to provide 770 foot pounds (3,425 Nm) of downforce. To achieve maximum speed, the driver must turn a key: the wing and spoiler retract, the front air diffusers close, and ground clearance drops to 2.6 inches (6.5 cm). In 2010 the 1,184-bhp (883-kW) Super Sport model became the fastest road-legal production car in the world, having achieved 269.80 mph (434.2 kph).

So who drives a car costing $1,300,000 (£812,500)? Pop impressario Simon Cowell has one, as does model Katie Price (aka Jordan). Beyonce bought one for Jay-Z's birthday. Clearly, it is not for shy types. **LT**

Haval H3 | Great Wall (CN)

2005 • 122 cu in/2,000 cc, S4 • 128 bhp/95 kW • 0–62 mph/100 kph in 12 seconds • 112 mph/180 kph

China's motor industry has been slow to start producing its own vehicles. The Haval—also called the Hover, Hafu, or the X240 in some markets—is the first sign that the country is about to become a serious contender on the world stage. Great Wall has already opened a factory in Bulgaria, and it has said it wants to open one in the United States, too.

After its birth in 1976, Great Wall initially built trucks. When it moved into passenger vehicles, the Chinese company leaned heavily on foreign brands by using some of their obsolete parts. The chassis of the Haval comes from the Toyota 4Runner, its design strongly resembles an Isuzu Axiom, and its entry-level engine comes from the Mitsubishi Galant. However, Great Wall has also launched a Haval with its own 171-cubic-inch (2,800-cc) common-rail diesel engine. The latest H3, called the H5, looks better and is better specified.

All Havals offer a basic recipe of four-wheel drive or rear-wheel drive, five-speed manual transmission, front independent suspension, and disc brakes all around. Typically, foreign buyers are seduced by very long warranties, including free servicing and roadside assistance. Brand-awareness promotions have included entering Havals in the 2011 Paris–Dakar Rally.

Strangely, Great Wall also produces a stretched limousine version of the Haval that has proved surprisingly popular, particularly in export markets. The Hover Pi is 22 feet (6.9 m) long and is powered by a 146-cubic-inch (2,400-cc) Mitsubishi engine. The first Hover Pi was given to President Fidel Castro of Cuba.

Great Wall's Havals have plenty of potential. In Italy a version that can run on liquid gas is sold. **SH**

Corvette C6 | Chevrolet

USA

2005 • 366 cu in/6,000 cc, V8 • 400 bhp/298 kW • 0–60 mph/97 kph in 4.2 seconds • unknown

New body, new engine, new suspension: it is a wonder they kept the same name. This sixth generation was not just a revamp of the Corvette, it was a complete rethink.

Chevrolet called it a "Corvette for the twenty-first century." The C6 kept the time-honored layout of front engine, rear transmission, and rear-wheel drive, but everything else was new. It was 5 inches (13 cm) shorter, but had a longer wheelbase. The wheels were pushed out to the corners to maximize the stance for better handling, as well as create more room inside.

The cabin was refined in a bid to capture sales from the better-finished European rivals. That was only partially successful, though, as the quality of materials and switchgear could not match the best imports.

The C6's body had evolved into a more aerodynamic shape, making it the slipperiest Corvette ever. Exposed headlights made the front look more potent; it was the first 'Vette since 1962 without pop-ups. Airflow was improved to generate more high-speed downforce at the stubby rear end.

The independent suspension system made the C6 more agile and gave it a more comfortable ride. Gearboxes were improved, and brakes enlarged. And performance was the new car's crowning glory. The 366-cubic-inch (6,000-cc) engine produced 400 bhp (298 kW), enough to do a quarter mile (0.4 km) in 12.9 seconds, reaching almost 110 mph (177 kph).

The new C6 was the platform to launch even hotter Corvettes. The Z06, with a 427-cubic-inch (7,000-cc) engine, soon joined the ranks. And the C6 ZR1, with a supercharged 378-cubic-inch (6,200-cc) V8, was the most powerful Corvette ever. **SH**

Plus 4 | Morgan

GB

2005 • 122 cu in/1,999 cc, S4 • 200 bhp/149 kW • 0–60 mph/97 kph in 6 seconds • 135 mph/209 kph

All Morgan sports cars are hand-built by craftsmen at the company's factory in the Malvern hills, England. The styling of its core models have changed little over the last hundred years, and Morgan is the last independent, family-owned motor manufacturer in the world.

Reintroduced in 2005, the new Morgan Plus 4 is faithful to the design of the 1950s original, but has modern mechanical underpinnings. Powered by Ford's 122-cubic-inch (1,999-cc) Duratec, the Plus 4 pushes out 145 bhp (106 kW) in standard trim; its lightweight construction gives the retro-styled roadster a better power-to-weight ratio than a Mark IV Golf GTI.

With its traditional design and perky performance, the Morgan Plus 4 has a large cult following. This is a car for the motoring enthusiast who enjoys taking the scenic route home whenever possible. BBC *Top Gear* magazine commented, "As fine a British institution as cold showers, and about as comfortable, the Morgan Plus 4 is an antiquated indulgence that you shouldn't want but absolutely will the second you step aboard."

In 1962 the original Plus 4 Super Sports race car took a class win at the 24 Hours of Le Mans race. To honor this famous victory, a modern version of the Super Sport was added to the model lineup in 2011. To a new 200-bhp (149-kW) powerplant, performance exhaust, and uprated sports suspension were added quirky period accessories including twin dash-mounted stopwatches, a racing-style filler cap, and race number roundels on the doors and hood (bonnet).

Costing £49,995 ($78,476), only sixty Super Sports (performance figures are given above) were built to represent the Plus 4's sixth decade in production. **DS**

575 Superamerica | Ferrari

I

2005 • 348 cu in/5,700 cc, V12 • 533 bhp/397 kW • 0–60 mph/97 kph in 4.3 seconds • 199 mph/320 kph

Boasting a top speed of just a shade under 200 mph (320 kph), the Ferrari 575 Superamerica was marketed as "the world's fastest convertible." The Superamerica was a special limited-edition version of the 575 Maranello, which in turn was an updated 550M, a model that dated back to the mid-1990s. This was an aging platform by Ferrari standards, and the Superamerica was a last fling. Even so, it turned out to be a truly exotic convertible that gave the series one last breath of fresh air.

Literally, the driver could press a button and the roof performed a unique gasp-inducing trick. The whole roof pivoted 180 degrees on its rear pillars until it was lying flat across the rear deck. This took just seven seconds and, as well as looking very cool indeed, had the benefit of leaving the luggage space underneath intact. The rear window also pivoted, turning into a wind-blocker for the occupants.

The rotating roof was made of steel and light-sensitive laminated glass. When the roof was in place, drivers could switch the glass from clear to dark blue to shade the interior. The rotation and the type of glass had never been seen before on a production car.

As if that was not enough to lure buyers, this sexily sculpted two-seater had a power boost from the earlier coupe model, too. The cylinder head and pipework were tuned to produce another 24 bhp (19 kW).

Fast and looking like a dream, the Superamerica revived a name that Ferrari had last used in the 1960s in a blatant attempt to break into the U.S. market. It was different this time; everyone wanted a Superamerica, but Ferrari stubbornly only built 599 of them. **SH**

Solstice | Pontiac

USA

2005 • 145 cu in/2,384 cc, S4 • 177 bhp/132 kW • 0–60 mph/97 kph in 7.4 seconds • 120 mph/193 kph

This cute little roadster from General Motors (GM) was the twin brother of GM's Saturn Sky, and both cars were expected to steal customers from the evergreen Mazda MX-5. The twins shared the same mechanical package, but the Pontiac's styling followed the curvy Solstice concept shown at the 2002 Detroit Auto Show. The Sky's edgier design came from the 2003 VX Lightning concept, which spawned the Opel GT in Europe.

GM's new strategy at this time was for Pontiac to relaunch as the group's performance division, and this affordable little roadster fit in perfectly. In 2006 it cost just $19,420, (£12,350), while the more upscale Sky started at $23,995 (£15,300). The third-generation MX-5 Miata was in the middle, at $20,435 (£13,000).

It may have been small, but the Solstice was immediately recognizable as a Pontiac from the front, thanks to the split grille and badge, reinforced by the wide-track stance that Pontiac had used for many years as a big part of its advertising thrust.

On the road the Solstice was no fireball, but it was quick enough and its ride and handling were smile-worthy. Like the Miata, it was at its most fun on a favorite twisty road or local racetrack, but it just was not as sharp and balanced as the pesky Japanese roadster.

The flying buttresses looked great when the roof was up, and the line was tidy when it was stowed. The trouble was, a degree in origami was needed to achieve this, and the roof took up half the small trunk (boot). The Miata's roof was stowed in seconds.

When the financial crisis hit, it was not just the Solstice but the entire Pontiac brand that bit the dust, along with Saturn and the Sky. Game to the Miata. **LT**

The 2005 Maserati MC12's air intakes, aerodynamic curves, and rear spoiler testify to extensive wind-tunnel testing. ⊳

Roadster | Leopard (PL)

2005 • 364 cu in/5,967 cc, V8 • 405 bhp/302 kW • 0–62 mph/100 kph in 4 seconds • 155 mph/250 kph

The Leopard is a hand-built retro supercar produced in small numbers in the unlikely surroundings of Mielec in Poland. But there is nothing retro about the Leopard's supercar performance. Cars of yesteryear never reached 62 mph (100 kph) in less than four seconds with a limited top speed of 155 mph (250 kph).

The car was created by Polish nuclear technology entrepreneur Zbysław Szwaj, an enthusiastic fan of classic roadsters, and his son Maxel, who worked as an automotive designer for Rover in Coventry and Porsche in California. What they produced was a high-quality, traditionally styled high-performance roadster incorporating the latest technology.

The Leopard has a classic rear-wheel-drive layout, but the engine is an all-aluminum V8 from General Motors, also used in the Corvette. The gearbox is a manual six-speed used in the Dodge Viper, and the precision hydraulic power steering comes from the British maker of steering systems for Morgan cars.

Everything reeks of money-is-no-object quality. Expensive components are used throughout, including a Momo steering wheel, Brembo brakes, and a custom-made Swedish Setrab radiator. The Leopard's body is handcrafted aluminum, the exhaust is stainless steel, the well-balanced chassis is tubular steel, and the wheels are custom-made lightweight alloy.

The most expensive car ever produced in Poland, with prices exceeding $150,000 (£100,000), the Leopard has a limited clientele. A maximum of twenty-five cars a year drive out of the factory. King Carl XVI Gustaf of Sweden has bought one, as has the Twentieth Century Fox movie studio in the United States. **SH**

MC12 | Maserati (I)

2005 • 366 cu in/5,998 cc, V12 • 0–60 mph/97 kph in 3.8 seconds • 205 mph/330 kph

Maserati built just twenty-five of the MC12 for track use, a further twenty-five for customers, and five other development cars that never reached the road. All were blue and white. With a staggering list price of €600,000 ($800,000/£500,000), it was a very rare track toy for a lucky few. *Car and Driver* magazine said, "You'd be extremely lucky to get one, and luckier yet if you could find a use for it that justified its acquisition."

Maserati began what became the MC12 as a project to go racing in the FIA GT championship. Frank Stephenson and Giorgetto Giugiaro worked on the styling of the car, although the majority of the drivetrain, chassis, and other major components were sourced directly from the Ferrari Enzo.

The V12 engine, mounted at 65 degrees, was lifted directly from the Enzo, along with the six-speed semiautomatic gearbox. Externally, there were no shared components with the Enzo other than the windshield, although the MC12 was actually 12 inches (30 cm) longer than the Ferrari. The 19-inch (48-cm) wheels were unique to the MC12, which also had Pirelli tires rather than the Enzo's Bridgestones. The MC12 had color-coded center-lock wheel nuts: red on the left of the car, and blue on the right.

The MC12 sported a targa-top roof, although the detached roof could not be stored in the car. The interior shared little with its Ferrari cousin, being carbon-fiber coated with a unique gel; it featured Maserati's trademark oval analogue clock. The MC12 won in its first race at Zhuhai in China, and competed in the Italian GT series, too, although it was penalized for its size/weight at the American Le Mans series. **RD**

Mark LT | Lincoln

USA

2005 • 330 cu in/5,409 cc, V8 • 300 bhp/224 kW • 0–60 mph/97 kph in 8.8 seconds • 101 mph/162 kph

"The Mark LT takes luxury to a place it has never really been before—the truck market," said Darryl Hazel, president of Lincoln Mercury at the 2005 North American International Auto Show. "This is a Lincoln designed for people who need a truck, but want all the trappings of a luxury vehicle."

Lincoln was relaunching itself with a new modern look for its range of cars and sport utility vehicles (SUVs). It was thought that a fancy truck flagship might just draw new buyers to what had become a "granddads' choice" brand. The top-specification Ford F150 and Dodge Ram had actually been offering plenty of luxury equipment before this; what was missing was a truck with a luxury-brand badge and a lot more chrome.

The Lincoln Mark LT had proper truck credentials because it sat on the F150's chassis and used the same V8 engine. Also, it could tow 8,900 pounds (4,037 kg) if drivers were willing to get its shiny wheels dirty. However, the styling followed the Lincoln Aviator and Navigator SUVs. A chrome waterfall fell from its nose, there was a hefty chrome band wrapped right around it, and the wheels were thick-spoked chrome-plated 18-inch (46-cm) monsters. The comfortable cabin boasted real ebony accents, soft Nudo leather, and plenty of sound insulation.

The LT sold poorly in the United States, possibly because it could not compete with the much-loved F150. It was withdrawn in 2008. But customers in Mexico went crazy for it, and a new model was launched there in 2010. Since its demise, the F150 Lariat and Platinum and Ram Laramie have piled on the luxury, and the LT is credited with kicking off the luxury-truck trend. **LT**

Exelero | Maybach

D

2005 • 366 cu in/6,000 cc, V12 • 700 bhp/522 kW • 0–60 mph/97 kph in 4.4 seconds • 218 mph/351 kph

The Exelero is one of the most extraordinary cars ever built. It is a one-off, two-seater luxury limousine weighing over 2.5 tons that can reach supercar speeds.

The only Exelero in the world was unveiled in Berlin in 2005. The price tag was $8 million (£5.2 million), and Maybach has been trying to sell it ever since.

American billionaire rapper Brian "Birdman" Williams claimed he bought it in 2011 (he already owns a Bugatti Veyron and a Maybach Landaulet), but at the time of writing the money had not changed hands and the car was still for sale.

The Exelero was built as a joint project with the U.S. tiremaker Fulda as a test and promotional vehicle. Its body was loosely inspired by Fulda's test vehicle from the 1930s, which itself was based on a Maybach. Previously, Fulda had cooperated with Porsche on a 600-bhp (441-kW) modified car to show off the company's high-performance tires.

The Exelero was put together in Turin after Mercedes engineers had worked on their V12 to increase output. The final test at the Nardo circuit in southern Italy proved that they had done their job. The huge car was clocked at 218 mph (351 kph), a world record for a limousine on standard road-going tires.

The car is a mix of vulgar, retro, and aerodynamic styling. Riding on air suspension, it has three manually activated spoilers to combat rear-end lift. Inside is a cocoon of leather and carbon fiber. The two occupants get rigid sports seats with five-point racing harnesses.

The Exelero has been described as everything from "a monster" to "voluptuous," with one reviewer even judging it "the perfect transport for Darth Vader." **SH**

Alpina B5 | BMW (D)

2005 • 268 cu in/4,398 cc, V8 • 493 bhp/368 kW •
0–60 mph/97 kph in 4.5 seconds • 195 mph/314 kph

The BMW Alpina B5 was a monstrous engine crammed into a modest 5-Series saloon. One of the most extreme road-going models ever made by specialist Alpina, the B5 was as easy to live with as a standard 5-Series car—which is almost as amazing as its performance.

Taking the V8 from the BMW 545i, Alpina reworked it extensively and added a supercharger and intercooler. The power of 493 bhp (368 kW) trumped exotica like the Ferrari F40, which made do with a mere 478 bhp (356 kW). Unlike its cousin, the BMW M5, the B5 had peak power available at low engine speeds, and its automatic gearbox meant that it was less stressed. *Autocar* magazine said, "Movement feels controlled, deliberate, and usable even if you are brave enough to turn the traction control off."

Most of the high-performance parts that make the Alpina so potent actually came from the BMW parts bin. The car was assembled on the 5-Series production line and was even available as a station wagon (estate) with the quality and reliability unchanged. In keeping with other Alpina models, the B5 had a plush wood-and-leather interior featuring liberal use of its logo. The exterior carried its distinctive pinstripes, and Alpina badges replaced the BMW ones—although most other road users only got to see a blur. **RD**

Evo IX FQ360 | Mitsubishi (J)

2005 • 122 cu in/1,997 cc, S4 • 360 bhp/268 kW •
0–62 mph/100 kph in 3.9 seconds • 157 mph/253 kph

Although the Mitsubishi Evo is synonymous with the World Rally Championship, the factory team actually pulled out of top-flight Group-A competition in 2005. The Evo IX, therefore, represents the last of Mitsubishi's rally-bred lineage before the all-new Evo X in 2008.

The Evo IX's turbocharged 122-cubic-inch (2,000-cc) all-wheel-drive formula was tried and tested. Its huge rear spoiler, exposed radiator, and cavernous exhaust were the first clues that this was no cooked version from Mitsubishi's family-car lineup. There were also the lightweight aluminum panels, the uprated springs and shock absorbers, massive Brembo brakes, and the computer-controlled four-wheel-drive system.

On paper, the range-topping FQ360 might have seemed a step backward from the Evo VIII FQ400 it initially replaced; however, the new car delivered more torque, and packed a bigger mid-range punch, thanks to some fettling from Mitsubishi's in-house tuner, Ralliart. *Car* magazine was particularly impressed by the FQ360: "It's an absolute belter. Utterly driver-centric, unfeasibly fast, with incredible body control, excellent damping, and superb steering."

Priced at around $55,000 (£35,000), the Evo IX FQ360 was a little more expensive than the hottest Impreza, but 40 percent cheaper than BMW's M3. **DS**

F430 | Ferrari (I)

2005 • 262 cu in/4,300 cc, V8 • 483 bhp/360 kW • 0–62 mph/100 kph in 4 seconds • 196 mph/315 kph

Former racing driver Jason Plato conducted the first-ever TV review of the new F430. He drove every other Ferrari model, then swooped around the country roads near Maranello, Italy, in a yellow F430. After hurling it around a test track, Plato announced he liked it so much he was going to buy one then and there.

What was it about the new entry-level Ferrari that was so irresistible? First, the F430 looked totally desirable; a curvy two-seater coupe or convertible that epitomized everything about Ferrari. Then there was the engine: a symphonic growl of a superb V8 under a glass window behind the seats. It was a shared Ferrari and Maserati design, and Ferrari's first departure from the Dino-bred V8 engine in more than fifty years.

The F430 also introduced two industry firsts. The car's electronic differential was developed by Ferrari to optimize traction in Michael Schumacher's Formula One car; it was its first use in a production car. The other first was the steering-wheel-mounted commutator switch (known in Italy as the *manettino*). This allowed drivers to adjust the car's dynamic systems to suit the conditions. It could be used to switch to "sportier," "track," or "snow and ice" settings for the gearbox, throttle, suspension, and e-differential. Brave drivers could even use it to switch all the driver aids to "off." **SH**

STS-V | Cadillac (USA)

2005 • 269 cu in/4,400 cc, V8 • 469 bhp/350 kW • 0–60 mph/97 kph in 4.8 seconds • 165 mph/266 kph

It was a fast, powerful, luxurious, and smooth executive express with hot-rod performance. Cadillac had realized it was losing ground to its rivals, so for the first time the Caddy engineers supercharged their thirty-two-valve, quad-cam Northstar V8 and unleashed the STS-V. The "V" was the flagship of the STS range, distinguished by a lower front end, a power bulge in the hood (bonnet), and a bigger grille to let in more cooling air. Aerodynamic tinkering, including a bigger rear spoiler, made the range-topper more slippery.

The supercharger added 120 bhp (88 kW) to the power of a normal STS V8. In days gone by that would have rocketed the Caddy to the top of the class, but contemporary sports sedans (saloons) regularly packed 500 bhp (373 kW) under the hood. Nevertheless, the STS-V had performance and handling to tackle the Europeans. The technical specification was up to par, with bigger wheels, tires, and brakes, plus electronic antilock, stability, and traction controls. Rear-parking assist, lane departure alert, and a blind-spot warning system were also standard.

The STS-V matched the world's best, but its main downfall was its faster and more exciting younger brother, the CTS-V. This was a little less spacious, but was also $20,000 (£13,000) cheaper. **SH**

Sport | Range Rover

GB

2005 • 305 cu in/4,997 cc, V8 • 510 bhp/380 kW • 0–60 mph/97 kph in 5.9 seconds • 140 mph/225 kph

In the 1970s, Range Rovers were primarily designed as practical off-roaders for use by active rural folk. Early cars had few creature comforts, but they had a useful trunk (boot) and their rubber mats, plastic dashboard, and vinyl seats could be hosed down should anyone need to spruce it up for a trip into town.

Thirty-five years later the original "mud-plugger" has evolved into a high-end luxury sport utility vehicle (SUV), beloved by wealthy professionals. However, that does not mean that this city slicker is any less capable than its dung-spattered forefather.

The Range Rover Sport's chassis comes from its utilitarian brother, the Discovery, but in a modified and shortened form. The standard ride height of 6.8 inches (17.2 cm) would cause the Sport to ground itself on a rutted farm track, but with a flick of a switch the car lifts to its off-road height of 8.9 inches (22.7 cm). Even then, the car has one more party trick should it "belly out": its air suspension automatically extends to its full height of around 11 inches (28 cm), lifting it out of trouble.

Land Rover's patented Terrain Response system also has settings to cope with snow, mud, sand, and boulders; electronically adjustable differentials, traction control, and hill-descent programs make the Range Rover Sport a very capable off-roader. Even so, in reality, most examples will live out their days in the urban jungle rather than the tropical variety.

True to its name, the Sport's roadholding, aided by that same electronic trickery and air suspension, is surprisingly good. In the case of the range-topping 305-cubic-inch (5,000-cc) supercharged V8-driven model, performance figures are simply astonishing. **DS**

H3 | Hummer

(USA)

2005 • 211 cu in/3,460 cc, S5 • 220 bhp/160 kW • 0–60 mph/97 kph in 11 seconds • unknown

With the arrival of the H3 in 2005, Hummer had become the edgiest brand within the General Motors (GM) stable. There were hopes that it would carve out a niche in global markets, and it was built in Louisiana, South Africa, and Russia.

The target owner aspired to the Hummer's macho image but also wanted something smaller and cheaper that occasionally achieved two-digit fuel economy. Where the H2 took up half the street, the H3 was dwarfed by Chevy Suburbans and GMC Yukons; it had only two rows of seats, plus disappointing luggage space. Yet, despite sharing the Chevrolet Colorado's platform and having only a straight five-cylinder engine under the flat, square hood (bonnet), the H3 retained its essential "Hummerness." The wide stance, toothy chrome grille, and narrow side windows were signature touches, and its off-roading ability certainly did not shame its bigger brothers.

Electronically controlled four-wheel drive allowed a switch from high to low ratios at the touch of a button. Short overhangs and good approach and departure angles allowed it to scrabble up steep slopes and clamber over rocks. It could even drive through 24 inches (61 cm) of water at less than 5 mph (8 kph). And it could tow 4,500 pounds (2,041 kg).

The first model achieved 14 mpg (20 liters per 100 km) in the city, 18 mpg (16 liters per 100 km) on the highway, but its performance was sluggish. So, in 2007 its power was increased to 239 bhp (176 kW).

By 2010 Hummer had become a symbol of excess, so even the baby Hummer faced the GM firing squad, along with Oldsmobile, Pontiac, and Saturn. **LT**

The 2005 Gumpert Apollo, built for the racetrack, is not the most comfortable babe magnet a playboy might choose. ⊡

Mustang GT | Ford (USA)

2005 • 281 cu in/4,600 cc, V8 • 300 bhp/224 kW • unknown • unknown

Ford's Mustang of 2005 was all-new but with a clever, "retro-futuristic" design that captured the best of the past. The Mustang Mark V came as a coupe or a convertible. Both versions, with their trademark long hood (bonnet), galloping horse logo in the center of the grille, and stumpy rear deck, looked the part and drove as well as their illustrious forebears.

The new car's suspension was more sophisticated and featured lighter components. The result was a great ride with sharp, sporty handling. Drive went to the rear wheels as usual, but the wheelbase was increased by pushing the wheels right to the corners of the body; the cockpit was correspondingly spacious.

The GT version had a smoothly powerful 281 cubic-inch (4,600-cc) V8 with variable valve timing. It produced 300 bhp (224 kW), coincidentally double the power rating of the first Mustang of 1964. It had the biggest brakes ever fitted to a mainstream Mustang, with an antilock braking system and traction control.

The cabin continued the retro theme. Depending on the model and trim, equipment lists included keyless entry, a 1,000-watt hi-fi, and leather seats. Drivers could even select the backlighting color for their dashboard instruments at the press of a button: white, blue, green, and orange were available. Another option was a red-leather interior with red floormats.

The Mustang had, of course, been an icon of American sports cars since 1964, always with a macho styling, chunky engine, and rear-wheel drive. The 2005 model was a completely new car, but it retained the line's traditions. The Mustang had been made faster, more agile, and better looking than ever. **SH**

Apollo | Gumpert (D)

2005 • 254 cu in/4,163 cc, V8 • 641 bhp/478 kW • 0–62 mph/100 kph in 3.1 seconds • 224 mph/360 kph

Even in the context of street-legal race cars, the Apollo is considered sizzling hot. Its twin-turbo Audi V8 (from the RS6) comes in three states of tune: "Street Plus" with 641 bhp (478 kW); "Sport" with 690 bhp (515 kW); and an "R" race version that offers 789 bhp (588 kW).

The "base" version is capable of 224 mph (360 kph) and can drive from a standstill to 120 mph (200 kph) in 8.9 seconds. Acceleration of the "R" version from 0 to 60 mph (97 kph) is ridiculous at around two seconds.

All Apollo models have a racing level of specification: the huge brakes have eight-piston calipers, the Formula One–inspired six-speed gearbox is sequential, and huge air scoops provide cooling for the brakes and engine. This is a supercar for track enthusiasts wishing also to use their car on the road. It is not pretty, but it has the classic components of a modern superfast car: a mid-engine and rear-wheel drive for balance, an alloy tubular frame, and fiberglass or carbon-fiber panels for low weight.

Of course, it is just a two-seater; occupants have to clamber in via spectacular gull-wing doors. There is little sense of luxury. The cabin is swathed in Alcantara mock suede and leather, but the gadgets are largely limited to a start button, four-point racing harnesses, and a fire extinguisher. The race version comes with free Nomex racing overalls and racing helmet.

The Apollo is the creation of former Audi engineer Roland Gumpert, working at Altenburg in eastern Germany. In 2008 his car appeared on BBC *Top Gear*. With "The Stig" at the wheel, the Apollo S achieved the program's record for the fastest lap time until beaten by the Bugatti Veyron Super Sport. **SH**

Sagaris | TVR

GB

2005 • 244 cu in/4,000 cc, S6 • 380 bhp/283 kW • 0–60 mph/97 kph in 3.7 seconds • 185 mph/298 kph

TVR's dramatically styled "Blackpool Ferrari" was tested by BBC *Top Gear*'s Jeremy Clarkson, who started by saying it looked like "it has been designed by a lunatic then hit with an axe." The body was aerodynamic but also featured heavy air vents, both real and fake. The roof on the driver's side was made higher to allow the wearing of a crash helmet, and the twin exhausts poked out at right angles to the sides of the car.

TVR was an independent British sports carmaker based in the northwest of the country. Since 2006 its ownership, status, and location have changed repeatedly and its present situation is unclear.

The Sagaris cost only about £50,000 ($77,000), making it one of the cheapest ways to reach 185 mph (298 kph). Like all TVRs, it was a loud, fast, basic muscle car with a head-turning fiberglass body and a hefty engine. Reviewers found it to be one of the loudest cars ever tested. TVR did not believe in safety equipment, claiming it encouraged driver negligence, so the Sagaris has no traction control, air bags, or even antilock brakes. Yet the car turned out to be one of the first TVR models to have predictable handling as well as brutal straight-line speed. With just two turns from lock to lock, steering was extremely responsive.

Like all TVRs, the car had quirks in its design, such as a button on the dashboard that acted as a door handle, and instrument lights that dazzled the driver. And the traditional TVR problem of inconsistent build quality remained. Clarkson's verdict, as he roared around the test track in the Sagaris, was only just heard above the noise of the engine. He yelled, "It smells of glue, and bits of the body are falling off." **SH**

300C SRT8 | Chrysler

USA

2005 • 370 cu in/6,059 cc, V8 • 425 bhp/317 kW • 0–60 mph/97 kph in 4.9 seconds • 165 mph/265 kph

The 300C was the kind of car American enthusiasts thought had disappeared. It was not a modern-retro interpretation of a classic, like the Mustang or Camaro, but it evoked powerful U.S. sedans (saloons) of the past.

The 300C's high beltline, curving fenders (bumpers), and big wheels gave it a powerful, hunkered-down look, while its chunky chrome grille told drivers exactly what was coming up behind. The interior, clothed in high-quality materials, was simple but elegant. Some of the mechanicals came from Chrysler's partnership with Daimler (Mercedes), but in classic American style it was a rear-wheel-drive with a powerful Hemi V8.

A Hemi had powered the 1950s Chrysler 300, as well as muscle cars such as the Dodge Charger and Plymouth Cuda. This Hemi was not the same engine, but its name plucked at heartstrings. The new 340-bhp (254-kW), 345-cubic-inch (5,700-cc) Hemi powered the car from 0 to 60 mph (97 kph) in 5.6 seconds.

Then Chrysler handed the 300C to the SRT (Street and Racing Technology) team. This gang of crazy hot rodders worked in a kind of clubhouse creating cars they wanted to drive. Out went the puny standard V8, and in went a bored-out 370-cubic-inch (6,100-cc), delivering 425 bhp (317 kW). By 2012 a 392-cubic-inch (6,400-cc) V8 gave 465 bhp (347 kW).

This car not only took the fight to European super-sedans, it did so at an affordable price. Suspension tweaks lowered and stiffened the chassis, so the SRT8 handled its power and weight well. And the stability-control system even allowed *Dukes of Hazzard*–style tail-wagging if the urge got too much. **LT**

M6 | BMW

D

2006 • 305 cu in/4,999 cc, V10 • 500 bhp/373 kW • 0–62 mph/100 kph in 4.4 seconds • 155 mph/249 kph

The original BMW 6-Series cars of the 1970s and 1980s were graceful machines with straight-six engines and classy coupe styling. When BMW relaunched the "6-Series" name in 2003, it followed the format of rear-wheel drive and coupe bodies, but, compared to the original, these were tech-heavy, bloated beasts. The M6 of 2006 was the pinnacle of the range and one of the most expensive models. BMW's slogan at the time claimed it was "the ultimate driving machine."

The V10 engine that powered the M6 came from its M5 sibling. Capable of an earth-moving 500 bhp (373 kW), it won ten Engine of the Year awards in various categories over three years. With the speed limiter removed, it was capable of 205 mph (330 kph). BBC *Top Gear* described the acceleration as "like you've stepped on a bomb." Transmission was either a manual six-speed or a seven-speed semiautomatic. Using BMW's i-Drive system, the driver could alter gearshift speed, shock absorber settings, and engine configurations. A head-up display gave speed, revs, and navigation information. The seats even had electrically powered bolsters that automatically hugged the driver. It was said that the M6 packed enough computing power to make 200 million calculations a second.

Despite its aluminum suspension, doors, and hood (bonnet), carbon-fiber roof, and plastic trunk (boot) lid and wings, the M6 was heavier than the big Porsche Panamera. It handled well but lacked the sporty feel of the original 6-Series. Tellingly, *Autocar* magazine said the best 6-Series model was the diesel convertible. The M6 might have been the "ultimate machine," but it was not quite the "ultimate driving machine." **RD**

Spider V6 Q4 | Alfa Romeo

I

2006 • 195 cu in/3,200-cc, V6 • 260 bhp/191 kW • 0–62 mph/100 kph in 7 seconds • 146 mph/235 kph

The latest in the long line of iconic Alfa Spiders has all the ingredients of a classic roadster: strikingly beguiling looks, an easy-to-use soft-top roof, and a throaty, powerful V6. It also has a swift power mechanism for the folding roof (it takes just twenty-five seconds), four-wheel-drive for extra traction and roadholding, and a hill-holder function for starting on steep gradients. The Pininfarina-designed Spider range now also includes a fast 200-bhp (147-kW) diesel and a more economical 134-cubic-inch (2,200-cc) gas engine with front-wheel drive, but the big V6 is the most classy act of the trio.

The Spider is not just a ragtop Alfa Brera; the Spider's chassis is shorter and sits closer to the ground. The styling is distinctive, too. There is an Alfa family nose with the familiar badge and grille, but then the uncluttered lines sweep back past muscular wheel arches and a steeply raked windshield to create a purposeful dynamic shape.

Drivers squeeze into the cramped cabin of soft leather and aluminum, press the start button, and hear the roar of the twenty-four-valve V6. A stubby gear lever controls the six-speed, close-ratio manual gearbox. Gadgets include dual-zone climate control, steering-wheel-mounted audio controls, satellite navigation, and a Bluetooth mobile phone system.

The aluminum engine has twin overhead camshafts, variable valve timing, and direct fuel injection into the combustion chamber. Its sound may be as Italian as pasta, but it is actually built in Australia by General Motors. The V6 Q4's powerplant is more than capable of powering this surprisingly heavy convertible to respectable speeds. **SH**

Lacetti | Chevrolet (USA)

2006 • 110 cu in/1,800 cc, S4 • 120 bhp/90 kW • 0–60 mph/97 kph in 9.5 seconds • 120 mph/194 kph

There is one field that certain carmakers excel at: badge engineering. That is, taking one company's car and renaming it another as an exercise in branding.

The Chevrolet Lacetti, for example, is actually a Daewoo. In 2003 that Korean firm decided to rebrand its cars as Chevys for certain European markets. The official corporate line was that "Daewoo has now grown up enough to become Chevrolet." The name Chevrolet was thought preferable to Daewoo.

The Lacetti was a medium-sized hatchback and in truth it was not a bad car. The 110-cubic-inch (1,800-cc) engine offered decent performance, although it could get noisy when worked hard. It did not handle as well as the best in class, but then it also cost a whole lot less.

But the Lacetti's real claim to fame is that in 2006 it was picked by BBC's *Top Gear* to replace the Suzuki Liana for its "Star in a Reasonably Price Car" slot, in which celebrities took it around the program's track. When, in 2010, the Lacetti's time on *Top Gear* expired, it received a form of Viking burial, being crushed by the weight of an industrial chimney that was being demolished.

The Lacetti may not be the greatest car in the world, but it is a prime example of selling into different markets. It is available across the world under more than twenty different names and brands. **JI**

Z4M Coupe | BMW (D)

2006 • 198 cu in/3,246 cc, S6 • 343 bhp/252 kW • 0–62 mph/100 kph in 5 seconds • 155 mph/249 kph

Although BMW's Z3 roadster had sold well (around 280,000 in a seven-year production run), it was never highly praised by top drivers due to its soft suspension and floppy chassis. However, around 20,000 people bought Z3s with a proper metal roof. The Z3 Coupe was three times stiffer than its wobbly soft-topped sibling, and it was utterly brilliant in M-Sport specification. In 2000 the Z3M Coupe was *Top Gear* magazine's Driver's Car of the Year. The highly acclaimed Z4 roadster was launched at the Paris Motor Show in 2002, but it was another four years before customers could get their hands on the tin-topped M-Sport version. Fortunately, it was easily as good as the Z3M Coupe before it.

While the original Z3M Coupe was not exactly pretty, its successor was. Its stylish "double-bubble" roof (as seen on Zagato-bodied race cars from the 1950s) allowed headroom for crash helmets, while its integrated rear spoiler planted the rear-driven wheels when traveling at speed.

When *Evo* magazine put the car through its paces at the Belgian Grand Prix circuit, it was hugely impressed: "The Z4 really flies, fizzing through the gears with angry purpose and piling on speed in relentless, pulse-quickening style . . . The M Coupe almost quivers with intensity and sharp-edged urgency." **RD**

John Cooper Works GP | MINI (GB)

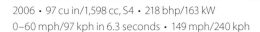

2006 • 97 cu in/1,598 cc, S4 • 218 bhp/163 kW
0–60 mph/97 kph in 6.3 seconds • 149 mph/240 kph

The newly reborn MINI was an instant success when launched by new owner BMW in 2001. The sportiest production version, the supercharged Cooper S, was aimed at the enthusiast. Dealer-installed John Cooper Works (JCW) tuning parts offered a further upgrade.

However, with the second-generation MINI imminent, designers wanted to use the Cooper S platform to create the ultimate supermini. This semi-race-prepared limited edition was called the GP, and only 2,000 were assembled at the Bertone factory in Italy. All were finished in Thunder Blue metallic paint (with a Pure Silver roof), with distinctive red door mirrors; each car's production number was also inscribed on the roof, along with a plaque in the cabin.

Rear wipers, sound deadening, and even the rear seats were removed to save around 90 pounds (41 kg). Body-hugging front seats were installed, and a rear strut brace stiffened the chassis. The GP's suspension was dropped and lightened, the brakes were uprated, and the underside was paneled to improve airflow. Further tuning unleashed 218 bhp (163 kW) from the tiny engine. In 2006 *Evo* magazine was to comment, "Not a single horsepower is wasted, the chassis uses every ounce of grip . . . It's clinically efficient but incredibly good fun." **DS**

D12 Peking to Paris | Spyker (NL)

2006 • 366 cu in/6,000 cc, W12 • 500 bhp/373 kW •
0–60 mph/97 kph in 5 seconds • 185 mph/298 kph

One of the world's first sports utility vehicle (SUV) supercars, the Spyker D12 is a luxury, high-performance, all-terrain crossover vehicle named for a Spyker that came second in a daring Peking-to-Paris cross-country endurance rally in 1907.

The prototype shown to the world in 2006 was like nothing else, combining styling of sports cars with off-road features. The body and chassis are made of aluminum and sit high above enormous 24-inch (61-cm) ten-spoke alloy wheels. The cabin is opulent, spacious, and light, thanks to a full-length glass roof with distinctive stainless-steel roof rails. The rear doors are hinged at the back, the front nose has an aggressively gaping grille, and the pert rear end has delicate round light clusters.

Power comes from the Audi W12 engine, which is like two V6 engines side by side. This high-performance unit powers the D12 through a six-speed paddle-shift sequential gearbox and permanent four-wheel-drive system. The whole thing sits on air-suspension and uses carbon-ceramic racing brakes. The D12 is large, but its road performance shames many sports cars. It has impressive off-road abilities, too, thanks to its high ground clearance and four-wheel drive. Prices have been quoted at around $310,000 (£200,000). **SH**

RS4 Avant | Audi

D

2006 • 269 cu in/4,200 cc, V8 • 414 bhp/309 kW • 0–62 mph/100 kph in 4.9 seconds • 155 mph/250 kph

The original RS4 Avant Quattro, which in Audi-speak means a station wagon (estate) with four-wheel drive, was introduced in 2000. It was powered by a 165-cubic-inch (2,700-cc) turbocharged V6 engine developed in the United Kingdom by Cosworth.

The second-generation RS4 was launched in 2006, this time with a massive 256-cubic-inch (4,200-cc) engine, four-wheel drive, and the options of sedan (saloon) or cabrio body versions, too. It was the station wagon that seemed the most extraordinary car, though. It combined sports-car performance and handling with a cargo bay of 47.8 cubic feet (1,354 liters) when the rear seats were folded flat.

A sophisticated but naturally aspirated all-aluminum thirty-two-valve V8 engine with variable valve timing produced a limited 155-mph (250-kph) maximum speed. BBC TV's *Top Gear* called this V8 "one of the best engines in the world."

The station wagon sits lower than a normal Avant and has a beefier body styling. There is a six-speed manual gearbox and four-wheel drive is permanent. Press the "sport" button and all the car's responses sharpen up for a more exhilarating drive.

Specification is high throughout the car, in keeping with the lofty price tag. There is a 190-watt Bose ten-speaker sound system, plus Recaro front seats, starter-button ignition system, and the steel body is fully galvanized to prevent rusting.

At the time of writing, a new RS4 Avant is planned, with even more power from the V8 and a seven-speed gearbox. Rumors suggest that, once more, the RS4 will be available only as a station wagon. **SH**

C70 | Volvo

S

2006 • 153 cu in/2,500 cc, S5 • 230 bhp/132 kW • 0–62 mph/100 kph in 7.4 seconds • 146 mph/235 kph

Volvo's Mark II C70 coupe convertible replaced the Mark I version, which had a conventional folding fabric roof. The second generation retained the appeal of the first version—its premium build quality, spacious four-seat interior, and refined, comfortable ride—while adding the glamour of a high-tech roof mechanism. With the roof in place, this Volvo looks like a stylish two-door coupe. When the sun comes out, the metal roof folds away at the touch of a button to reveal a neat, open-top four-seater.

The roof action is amazing to see. The roof appears to split into three panels, before sliding back behind the rear seats in about thirty seconds. It is not the first roof to fold away automatically like this, but it is one of the most stylish. The trend for metal convertible roofs has enabled manufacturers to produce a new type of open-top car—a convertible that is practical to live with all year round, whatever the climate. Trunk (boot) space is halved with the roof stowed, however.

The C70's interior features Volvo's most recent design touches, including a thin, floating center console, to create a neat, contemporary look. If there are only two people on board, there is a wind deflector that fits over the rear seats for draft-free motoring, at the same time turning the car into a two-seater.

The C70 is not a high-performance sporting range; instead, the engines and handling are best suited to relaxed fast cruising. Volvo's emphasis on safety continues with features such as a blind-spot warning system and the world's first door-mounted curtain air bags, which work even with the roof down. The C70 could be the safest convertible ever. **SH**

The SSC Ultimate Aero TT could reclaim the world speed record for production cars, surrendered by SSC in 2010. ⊡

Commander | VEPR (UA)

2006 • 238 cu in/3,900 cc, S4 • unknown • unknown • 87 mph/140 kph

Big Hummers seem puny compared to the VEPR Commander, Ukraine's macho multipurpose off-roader. Local world champion heavyweight boxer Vitali Klitschko drove the monster 4x4 to promote it at the press launch in Kiev. He is 6 feet 7 inches (201 cm) in height but fit in easily—it is enormous. A massive 16½ feet (5 m) long, the vehicle is more than 12 inches (30 cm) longer than the Hummer H1, weighs more than 3 tons, and can carry more than fifteen passengers.

Details about the VEPR vehicle are scarce, due to its military and security applications. The Commander was actually based on a military vehicle already in production, called the Chainmail. Two other versions are produced, one for hunting in extreme conditions, the other fully armored for heavy-duty security duties. Electronic counter measures are available for countering guided missiles.

The Commander is assembled at Kremenchuk in central Ukraine and costs more than $70,000 (£45,000) in that country. Designed to deal with the worst terrains in Siberia, it features tire pressures that are adjustable to fit the ground conditions, adjustable ground clearance—between 12 and 24 inches (30 and 60 cm)—and closed drum brakes that function in 5 feet (1.5 m) of water. The transmission is manual and suspension is independent all around. The vehicle is mounted on a stainless-steel frame and is capable of carrying a two-ton payload.

The Commander is more than a huge, primitive tractor, having a smart leather interior, air-conditioning, and a heating system that runs independently of the engine. Its fuel consumption is surprisingly modest. **SH**

Aero | SSC (USA)

2006 • 384 cu in/6,300 cc, V8 • 1,287 bhp/960 kW • 0–60 mph/97 kph in 2.8 seconds • 257 mph/414 kph

In 2007 the Aero from SSC (formerly Shelby SuperCars) was clocked at 257 mph (414 kph) on a closed-off 4-mile (6.4-km) single-carriageway road in Texas. This made it the fastest production car of all time. Amazingly, the car was driven by a seventy-one-year-old with no racing experience who refused to wear a crash helmet. The Aero's record lasted for three years, until the Bugatti Veyron Super Sport, backed by the huge resources of Volkswagen, reached 268 mph (408 kph) in 2010. SSC's next version, the Ultimate Aero TT, was slightly lighter and more powerful. The maker claimed it could reach 273 mph (439 kph), although that has yet to be verified. The Chevrolet V8 engine is adapted to produce enormous power, while the body is ultralight and aerodynamic.

The car itself is a mid-engined, rear-wheel-drive, luxurious two-seater with scissor-action "butterfly" doors. Use of titanium and carbon fiber keeps the weight down. The latest Aero has a new "AeroBrake" system, a spoiler that rises up to 8 inches (20 cm) when the brake is pressed to slow the car.

SSC cars are the creation of a small team of engineers working with enthusiast Jarod Shelby in a garage behind his house in Washington State. (Jarod is no relation to American Cobra guru Carroll Shelby.)

At the time of writing, SSC's new car is being unveiled. Called the Tuatara, it is an even more powerful version of the Aero, boasting an extraordinary 1,350 bhp (993 kW). The price is huge, too, at around $1.3 million (£850,000). Its projected top speed is 276 mph (444 kph). The world production car speed record faces another U.S. challenge. **SH**

MT900S | Mosler

USA

2006 • 427 cu in/7,000 cc, V8 • 600 bhp/450 kW • 0–60 mph/97 kph in 3.1 seconds • 179 mph/288 kph

When millionaire *Star Wars* producer/director George Lucas looks for a new car, it has to be something pretty special. So when the first street-legal Mosler MT900S ever sold was delivered to his ranch in California, the motoring world began to pay more attention to this small independent U.S. supercar builder.

Mosler Automotive, founded by economist and former Democrat presidential candidate Warren Mosler, is based in Florida. It has built small numbers of high-performance cars for more than twenty-five years. Many are used on the track only.

The MT900 series was launched in 2001 and only a handful were sold in the decade of production. The MT900R was a racing version that achieved several track victories. Lucas's all-black MT900S was an upgraded road-going model that looked like the sort of futuristic machine Darth Vader would drive. It was built to a classic supercar formula, with a big supercharged Corvette V8 mounted between the axles to drive the rear wheels. It had a carbon-fiber chassis, body, and wheels, and used a six-speed manual gearbox and a limited slip differential for extra traction. The scissor-action doors evoked a *Star Wars* spaceship. Lucas specified the all-black interior and added a twelve-CD hi-fi system with carbon-fiber speaker enclosures.

A standard MT900S cost around $189,000 (£120,000), but for an optional extra $50,000 (£32,000) buyers could specify the Photon model, in which magnesium, titanium, and carbon fiber reduced the weight to 1,980 pounds (898 kg). One Photon was imported into the United Kingdom. Details of its enhanced performance figures are unknown. **SH**

V8 Speedster | Caresto

S

2006 • 269 cu in/4,400 cc, V8 • 340 bhp/250 kW • unknown • unknown

Award-winning Swedish car creator Leif Tufvesson's Caresto V8 Speedster is, he says, a whole new category of car: the "sport rod." The Speedster is built for fans of unique head-turning cars, but, unlike traditional superpowered hot rods, it also has high-performance roadholding and handling. It also has exemplary build quality and a touch of luxury.

There is very little normal in the car. The engine, for example, is a stock unit from the Volvo XC90 that has been converted to run on carbon-free ethanol as well as gas. The Speedster's body is hand-built from aluminum and carbon fiber on a tubular steel frame. The suspension can be lowered or raised to suit road conditions, and the rear deck lid rises automatically to cool the engine at a preset temperature. The composite hardtop is removable. There are three built-in rearview cameras. Many of the styling details are made by computerized milling of solid aluminum, including the wheel spindles and the headlight housings.

The car appeals to the heart as well as the head, with a previously unthinkable throaty roar from the rear-mounted Volvo V8, and a fine reek of leather from the two beautifully finished leather bucket seats.

The Volvo steering wheel is surely a joke from Tufvesson, however—that wheel was never designed to pilot such a wild machine. The six-speed sequential gearbox is another product from Volvo.

No performance figures have been released, but with a hefty V8 driving such a lightweight two-seater body, the Speedster is likely to live up to its name.

Caresto is building only six Speedsters, and those have a price tag of around $330,000 (£212,000). **SH**

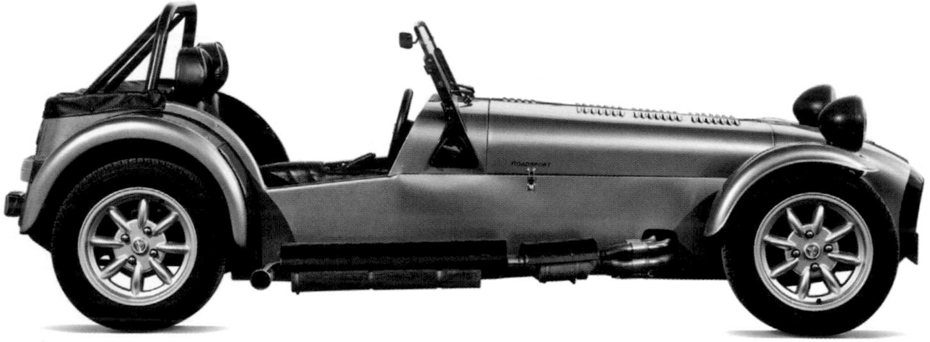

7 CSR | Caterham

GB

2006 • 140 cu in/2,300 cc, S4 • 260 bhp/191 kW • 0–60 mph/97 kph in 3.1 seconds • 155 mph/250 kph

Fabulous sports-car performance is simply not enough for some drivers. They prefer to strap themselves into the equivalent of a rocket and light the blue touchpaper. That is what the Caterham 7 CSR is all about. This extreme evolution of the fifty-year-old Lotus Seven is an eye-watering motoring experience, thanks to a simple formula; put a Cosworth sixteen-valve racing engine into a tiny plastic body shell weighing just 1,267 pounds (575 kg), and the result is predictably explosive. The tiny two-seater can accelerate from a standstill to 100 mph (161kph) in 8.9 seconds. BBC *Top Gear* described driving the "Cosworth-engined bath-tub" as akin to "wrestling wild animals to death."

The 7 CSR is the latest generation in Caterham's long process of gradually refining its spartan, high-performance cars. Its handling is more agile than that of a supercar with race-carlike grip, and the unpowered brakes and steering are simple and ultraresponsive.

But age-old Lotus Seven problems remain. The steering is heavy at low speeds, the roof is a primitive pop-stud affair that is awkward to erect, and the trunk (boot) is tiny. And the 7 CSR's aerodynamics are crude compared to a newly designed supercar; there are performance and handling problems as the airflow causes the car to lift on its suspension at high speeds.

The 7 CSR can be purchased as a kit, like previous Caterhams, but the company advises against this due to the complexity of the car. The basic model costs around £37,000 ($57,000), but that lacks extras, such as a roof or doors, that some might consider indispensible. As a reviewer at *Auto Express* magazine pointed out, "It's not cheap for a toy." **SH**

Tramonto | Fisker

(USA)

2006 • 336 cu in/5,500 cc, V8 • 610 bhp/455 kW • 0–60 mph/97 kph in 3.6 seconds • 202 mph/325 kph

The Fisker Tramonto (which means "sunset" in Italian) is a beautifully styled supercar with performance to match. It is produced by a small team, based in a tiny workshop in southern California, who simply rebody the Mercedes SL55 AMG.

If the customer wants even more power than AMG provides, a high-performance package is available. Danish specialist Kleeman tunes the engine to produce a hefty 610 bhp (455 kW), and the car is fitted with all the corresponding technical upgrades needed to cope with the extra output, including high-performance brakes, suspension, and an exhaust with four stainless-steel catalytic converters. A new custom-made computer engine-control unit is also installed.

The Mercedes body is removed and the interior stripped out. A new lightweight carbon-fiber and aluminum body is then fitted. Car designer Henrik Fisker, who formerly worked with Aston Martin and BMW, created the styling. His lines are exclusive and elegant, with a shorter rear than the base car's, and a long, swooping hood (bonnet). The more aggressive nose is inspired by the F-22 Raptor fighter jet.

Inside, all surfaces are retrimmed in hand-stitched Italian leather (alligator and ostrich hides are options), and milled aluminum replacements are used for all detailing and switchgear. Computer-assisted design systems, scanners, and mills enable every switch and button to be re-created in the new material.

The Mercedes retractable hardtop, air bags, active suspension system, and crash protection zones remain in place, making complex retesting of the vehicle by U.S. government authorities unnecessary. **SH**

XKR | Jaguar

GB

2006 • 305 cu in/5,000 cc, V8 • 542 bhp/405 kW • 0–62 mph/100 kph in 4 seconds • 186 mph/250 kph

Jaguar's XK series of grand tourers has cruised the world's treelined boulevards since 1996, after it replaced the grand old XJS series. The XK8 was Jaguar's first ever eight-cylinder model. A supercharged superfast version appeared in 1998, called the XKR.

In 2006 a new generation of XK cars was given a strikingly muscular, menacing, and modern shape. The new car had "immense visual energy," claimed Jaguar. With a 174-mph (280-kph) top speed, the new "R" version had performance to match; the figures above are for the fastest option, the 305-cubic-inch (5,000-cc) supercharged V8, which was introduced in 2011.

The XKs come as coupes or convertibles. They all have four seats, although the rear ones are just for children. The standard versions are comfortable high-speed tourers for long-distance motorway excursions.

The R versions are aimed at driving enthusiasts. Their performance is combined with a sportier suspension and better brakes. Springs and shock absorbers are upgraded, and the computer controlling the suspension is reprogrammed. An active exhaust system keeps the noise quiet during cruising but turns up the volume for hard acceleration. The XKR sounds like "someone dropped the London Philharmonic's percussion section down a lift shaft," reported the *Daily Telegraph*.

The R's features include adaptive around-the-corner headlights, stability control, and keyless entry and starting. There are iPod/USB interfaces, an air-quality sensor, front-park assist, and powered, heated wing mirrors that dip automatically. Options include everyday motoring essentials such as a satellite radio and a heated steering wheel. **SH**

Corvette Z06 | Chevrolet

USA

2006 • 428 cu in/7,000 cc, V8 • 505 bhp/376 kW • 0–60 mph/97 kph in 3.6 seconds • 199 mph/320 kph

Under its long, menacing hood (bonnet), the Z06 has an engine layout of good old Chevy simplicity, but this was not just another big lump of brute force. This time Chevrolet used the best it could get from the GM stable. Inside the special V8 were race-bred components such as titanium connecting rods and inlet valves, sodium-filled exhaust valves, pistons made of a special high-tolerance aluminum alloy, and a crankshaft of forged steel. There was also a "dry-sump" oil system, normally only found on race cars.

Called the LS7, the engine made this version of the Corvette the fastest and most powerful production car General Motors had produced. The LS7 was hand-built at the General Motors Performance Build Center in Michigan. It was also used in the Holden W427 muscle car, the fastest production car ever built in Australia.

The Z06's supercar performance was also helped by a lightweight body made of aluminum panels sitting on a bespoke structure of carbon fiber, magnesium, and aluminum. Other weight saving measures included a floor that was made of a balsa wood and carbon fiber composite, and a cradle for the engine that was made of magnesium. Along with its light alloy wheels, the whole car weighed just 101 pounds (46 kg) more than a Volkswagen Golf GTI. Not bad for a 428-cubic-inch (7,000-cc) V8 road-eating monster.

Performance was sensational. The quarter mile (0.4 km)was achieved in just 11.8 seconds, with a final speed of 122 mph (196 kph). It was no surprise that the Z06 was chosen as the official pace car for both the 2006 Daytona 500 and the Indianapolis 500 races. **SH**

GT | Ford

USA

2006 • 330 cu in/5,410 cc, V8 • 550 bhp/410 kW • 0–60 mph/97 kph in 3.6 seconds • 212 mph/341 kph

Remaking one of its greatest cars is a dangerous move for any company, but when Ford wanted to mark its centenary, it took the brave step of announcing to the world that it would be producing a replica of its classic GT40 racer. This was the model that won Le Mans four times in a row during the late 1960s, and which only came into existence when Henry Ford II demanded a car to beat Ferrari, having been snubbed by them as a potential buyer of the Italian firm.

For legal reasons, Ford was not able to use the GT40 name again, so the new car became known simply as the Ford GT. It may have looked like the original, but this was an entirely new design.

The space-frame chassis was aluminum, as were the body panels. The latter were formed using "hyperplastic" technology: the metal is heated until it loses its rigidity and can be shaped more easily. The 330-cubic-inch (5,400-cc) V8 engine was also

aluminum and produced 550 bhp (410 kW) at 6,500 rpm. Power was fed to the rear wheels through a six-speed manual gearbox and limited slip differential for more traction. To cope with all this power, the car was given an advanced suspension setup, with yet more use of aluminum. Racing-specification Brembo brakes took care of hauling everything to a stop.

The GT's performance was as impressive as the technology used to make it. The speed of 60 mph (97 kph) was reached from a standstill in just 3.6 seconds and the car's top speed was a staggering 212 mph (341 kph).

The GT went on sale from just under $140,000 (£88,000) although a few early cars went for much more. Ford had planned on building 4,500, but production actually stopped just short of 4,100. Most people would agree that Ford's gamble had paid off; the GT was a fine tribute to the 1960s legend. **JI**

599 GTB Fiorano | Ferrari

I

2006 • 366 cu in/5,999 cc, V12 • 612 bhp/457 kW • 0–60 mph/97 kph in 3.6 seconds • 205 mph/330 kph

Ferrari claims that its GTB (Gran Turismo Berlinetta) was designed "to increase driving pleasure, to guarantee performance, and to ensure comfort, ergonomics, and safety." Named for its engine displacement, it also commemorates the Fiorano test track as used by Ferrari's Formula One race and road car teams.

The elegantly styled Pininfarina bodywork aimed to balance "sportiness and sophistication." By mounting the lusty V12 up front, the designers created a spacious two-seater; with its bespoke luggage carefully stowed away, the 599 becomes a usable grand tourer. However, the purposeful stance, quad exhausts, and carbon-fiber-trimmed cockpit hint that this is a sports car with serious racing pedigree.

When launched, the 599's normally aspirated 366-cubic-inch (5,999-cc) engine was the most powerful ever fitted to a Ferrari road car. Trickle-down technology from Formula One also inspired Ferrari's new "SuperFast" six-speed paddle-shift gearbox; in "Race" mode the gear changes are completed in a savagely quick 100 milliseconds.

Reviews in the motoring press were universally positive. *Auto Express* magazine exclaimed, "The 599 GTB can rightly claim to be one of the world's best-ever supercars. Simply amazing in so many ways." *Evo* magazine named the Fiorano as its 2006 Car of the Year, and it was BBC TV *Top Gear*'s Supercar of the Year.

Famous 599 GTB owners have included actor Sylvester Stallone and veteran rock star Rod Stewart. Portuguese soccer player Cristiano Ronaldo bought a second one after he ricocheted his first through a road tunnel near Manchester. **DS**

C16 | Callaway

USA

2006 • 378 cu in/6,200 cc, V8 • 700 bhp/515 kW • 0–60 mph/97 kph in 3.2 seconds • 210 mph/338 kph

For thirty years, former race-driving teacher Reeves Callaway had sold extra performance packages for standard sports cars from his headquarters in Connecticut. He then set about turning one of his most popular conversion kits into a whole new car with a whole new name—the Callaway C16.

This company flagship is not just a bolt-on package but a supercar in its own right. The C16 is based on the Corvette C6 but turns that standard sports car into a 210-mph (338-kph) fire-breathing street race car.

Callaway's conversion of the C6's engine was the starting point. He then added a supercharger and changed many of the components, including the camshafts, valves, and pushrods. The result is eye-watering performance, although the cost is also supercharged, way up into Ferrari's pricing territory.

The Callaway C16 can be ordered as a coupe, convertible, or a completely roofless "speedster" with a slippery, retro look. The interior is built in Callaway's German workshop, next door to an Audi factory. A team of former Audi specialists ensure that build quality is exemplary. Many surfaces are finished in hand-stitched soft leather. All cars are sold direct by Callaway and have an impressive five-year warranty.

Callaway has also rebuilt the car's suspension with adjustable shock absorbers, added a new, stiffer chassis, and seriously beefed up the brakes. The body has a sleek, classic look with a retro grille. Even the carbon-and- magnesium wheels are specially made by Callaway, who claims they are 40 percent lighter than any aluminum wheels. Little of the Corvette is left in the C16, but, with performance like this, who cares? **SH**

◀ Pope Benedict XVI waves to pilgrims from his Mercedes M-Class Popemobile during a visit to Munich in 2006.

Popemobile | Mercedes-Benz (D)

2006 • 336 cu in/5,500 cc, V8 • 388 bhp/285 kW • 0–60 mph/97 kph in 6 seconds • 155 mph/249 kph

The official transport of the head of the Catholic Church has certainly evolved since the 1970s, when he was simply carried on a chair on papal attendants' shoulders. It costs an estimated $300,000 (£200,000), weighs five tons, and outperforms many sports cars.

The current Popemobile is a heavily customized Mercedes M-Class sport utility vehicle fitted with serious security features after a 1981 assassination attempt. Pope Benedict XVI's car has a half-inch (13-mm) steel bomb guard underneath and lightweight kelvar cabin armor. Its bulletproof plastic glass is 3 inches (8 cm) thick, and it has run-flat tires and a separate air supply in case of gas or chemical attack. Despite its nonaerodynamic shape, the vehicle has a reported top speed of 160 mph (257 kph), although it more typically cruises at 6 mph (10 kph).

Entering through a rear tailgate door, the Pope ordinarily sits in a normal rear passenger position, but during parades he is raised by hydraulic motors into the glass turret to be seen by crowds. Glass side panels are lowered when security conditions allow. The interior is trimmed in white leather and contains built-in religious icons. The personalized license plate, "SCV 1," signifies the Pope's position in the Vatican City State.

Mercedes is working on a hybrid-engined M-Class Popemobile to set a greener example on papal visits. An all-electric vehicle was rejected as too slow to escape an emergency situation in good time.

In Mexico and the Philippines, devout local Catholics made pilgrimages to see a display of old Popemobiles in order to feel spiritually close to the Holy Father without the expense of journeying to Rome. **SH**

HSV Maloo R8 | Holden (AUS)

2006 • 364 cu in/5,965 cc, V8 • 400 bhp/298 kW • 0–60 mph/97 kph in 5.1 seconds • 168 mph/271 kph

To many Australians, the "ute" is as much of a symbol of their country's motoring culture as a pickup truck is to denizens of the United States. Both are rugged, practical machines, often powered by pretty hefty motors. But the two things are not the same: unlike a pickup, a ute is designed to be just like an ordinary car up front, with the practicality of a load-bay at the rear. That gives it the benefit of a low center of gravity and makes it more drivable.

Just as well, because Holden's Maloo R8 is a true performance car lurking beneath the skin of a load carrying workhorse. The Maloo has been in production since 1990 and is billed as a performance coupe utility. The R8 is based on the ordinary Holden Utes that sell extremely well Down Under, but it comes from Holden Special Vehicles (HSV), the company's performance division. The standard V6 is taken out and replaced by a 366-cubic-inch (6,000-cc) V8, as used in the Chevrolet Corvette LS2. This produces 400 bhp (298 kW), running through a six-speed manual gearbox to the rear wheels.

The R8 has independent suspension all around, unlike the many U.S. pickups that still rely on leaf springs and a live axle. This hands the Australian the crown when it comes to handling. The brakes are taken as seriously as the suspension, fortunately.

In June 2006 a standard Maloo R8 became the world's fastest pickup/ute, breaking a record set by a Dodge Ram. The R8 managed 168 mph (271 kph).

Maloos compete against V8 sedans (saloons) on Australian racetracks. A well-driven one would give a car like a BMW M5 a fair run for its money . . . and carry a load of bricks home afterward. **JI**

Monaro VXR 500 | Vauxhall

(AUS)

2006 • 364 cu in/5,965 cc, V8 • 493 bhp/298 kW • 0–60 mph/97 kph in 4.9 seconds • 190 mph/271 kph

This car was well traveled even before it had left the showroom. The engine, a hefty 366-cubic-inch (6,000-cc) V8 originally designed for the Chevrolet Corvette, was shipped from the United States to Australia. Holden then dropped it into the Monaro muscle car, which was shipped to the United Kingdom. It then went to the U.K. tuner Wortec, who bolted on a Harrop supercharger. The finished item was then sold through a single dealership in Kent, England.

But it was worth all that shipping and boxing. Badged as a Vauxhall (like Holden, a part of General Motors), the Monaro VXR 500 put out an astonishing 493 bhp (298 kW). It had a shorter gearshift linkage added to its six-speed manual transmission, which helped it on its way to 60 mph (97 kph) in less than five seconds. The top speed was 190 mph (306 kph). Thankfully, upgraded AP brakes and an adjustable suspension package were available to keep the car in check. The VXR 500 actually looked the same as a standard Monaro—understated and fairly subtle compared to some of its competitors.

But the sound from the tailpipes was unlike anything else. This was of course a U.S. V8 married to Australian engineering and some clever British know-how. The result was a bark that made people's hair stand on end, even those who were not car enthusiasts.

The VXR 500 could also shred tires, thanks to the monstrous amount of torque on offer. There was traction control, but that had not been upgraded from the standard car and could struggle to keep on top of things. When all is said, this was a bad boy's car. And everyone loves a bad boy. **JI**

CX-7 | Mazda

J

2006 • 138 cu in/2,260 cc, S4 • 244 bhp/182 kW • 0–62 mph/100 kph in 8 seconds • 130 mph/209 kph

"Why choose between performance, power, and practicality?" asked Mazda's writers, suggesting that here was the perfect vehicle that could provide all three. "This innovative Sports Crossover offers you the best of all worlds, by combining the road presence, practicality, and high seating position you would expect from a luxury crossover SUV with drive characteristics more attuned to a sports car."

In some parts they were right—for once, this was not just hype. The Mazda CX-7 has dynamic ability to match its sporty good looks. It is an agile 4x4 with lots of equipment and internal space, and a selection of fast engines. The fastest CX-7s are available in Japan and the United States; the figures for the gas turbo version are given above. Other markets have a turbodiesel that gives less performance but better economy.

All models come with an electronically controlled four-wheel-drive system and stability control. The crossover vehicle surprised journalists at its launch, however, with its slick, sporty handling on the road. One reviewer said driving the CX-7 offered "the thrills of an MX-5 in the body of an SUV."

Perhaps the off-roading ability was compromised by the sporting credentials, but the CX-7's practicality was also limited by having to make a hefty SUV-style body fast and nimble. The luggage room, for example, is average, more than most people carriers but less than a station wagon (estate). The back seats fold flat to create a good, vanlike space, though.

The fuel economy, insurance costs, and CO_2 output figures are pretty poor, pointing to high running costs, again a consequence of that added performance. **SH**

Brera V6 | Alfa Romeo (I)

2006 • 195 cu in/3,200 cc, V6 • 260 bhp/190 kW • 0–62 mph/100 kph in 7 seconds • 155 mph/250 kph

The Brera was a modern, sexed-up version of the Alfa Romeo classic sports coupes and roadsters. The headline model, the V6, had the performance and features to tackle rivals from Porsche and BMW.

The V6 used Alfa's quad-cam twenty-four-valve 195-cubic-inch (3,200-cc) engine, with sophistications such as variable valve timing and direct injection to create more power. Alfa's engineers baulked at directing 260 bhp (190 kW) through the front wheels alone; that could cause all sorts of handling problems. So initially they opted for a permanent four-wheel-drive system that could send up to three-quarters of the power to the axle that needed it most. The result was very surefooted handling on varied surfaces.

Later, a front-wheel-drive version of the V6 was also offered. This was slightly slower off the mark because it had less traction from a standstill, but had a slightly higher top speed because it lacked the weight of the all-drive system. Its figures are given above.

The Brera range was designed by famed Italian stylist Giorgetto Giugiaro and built by independent sports specialists at Pininfarina. It was available in coupe and convertible forms. The coupe has two small seats in the rear only suitable for children; the Spider convertible is purely a two seater. **SH**

Latigo CS | Fisker (USA)

2006 • 342 cu in/5,600 cc, V10 • 648 bhp/477 kW • 0–60 mph/97 kph in 3.9 seconds • 205 mph/330 kph

Danish car designer Henrik Fisker revived the long-lost art of coachbuilding to create this stunning two-door coupe. Underneath the Latigo's elegant body there is a standard BMW 650i or M6.

The Latigo was first revealed at the 2005 Frankfurt Motor Show in Germany, as BMW designers looked on. They must have felt humbled, because the Fisker body took Chris Bangle's smart but unexciting creation and turned it into something far more desirable and exotic.

The Latigo process is this: a customer's BMW 6-Series car has its body removed and interior stripped out. Fisker replaces the skin with panels of sophisticated lightweight race-bred materials such as carbon fiber and aluminum. The interior is completely retrimmed with new, buttery-soft leather. Buyers even have the option of a leather-lined luggage bay.

Bigger 20-inch (51-cm) Fisker-forged wheels are fitted and the suspension stiffened for sportier handling. Fisker can also fit a BMW V10 engine, enlarged and tuned to produce 648 bhp (477 kW). All this may double the price of the original car, but with a new 205-mph (330-kph) top speed, the standard BMW 2+2 coupe or convertible has been transformed into one of the world's fastest four-seaters—and one of the best-looking cars seen anywhere. **SH**

S65 AMG | Mercedes (D)

2006 • 366 cu in/6,000 cc, V12 • 603 bhp/444 kW • 0–60 mph/97 kph in 4.2 seconds • 155 mph/250 kph

When Mercedes handed its basic S65 to sports tuning subsidiary AMG for a bit of a sporty upgrade, the result was the S65 AMG. The big luxury car was transformed, not only into the highest-powered sedan (saloon) AMG had ever created, but into the world's most powerful production sedan.

The conservatively designed S-Class was given more purposeful and aerodynamic AMG bodywork, and improvements were made to components like the suspension, brakes, fuel supply, and cooling system. But it is the brutal power of the engine that sets the AMG S-Class apart. The manufacturer's figures given above are understated. Owners report that the car was actually faster on the road. The S65's maximum speed was electronically limited to 155 mph (250 kph), but AMG offered an option to reset the limit to 186 mph (300 kph). It could go faster still if it was allowed. In addition, a simple electronic tweak could boost power even higher, to a dizzy 740 bhp (544 kW).

The thirty-six-valve powerplant actually has so much torque, or pulling power, it has to be limited electronically. All that grunt makes for stupendous mid-range performance. *Evo* magazine likened the sensation of pressing the accelerator pedal in the big limousine to "an out-of-body experience." **SH**

Cee'd | Kia (ROK)

2006 • 97 cu in/1,591 cc, S4 • 123 bhp/92 kW • 0–60 mph/97 kph in 10.4 seconds • 119 mph/191 kph

From 2010, celebrities let loose on the BBC TV *Top Gear* test track for its "Star in a Reasonably Priced Car" challenge found themselves behind the wheel of a Kia Cee'd 2. Tom Cruise took a corner on two wheels, but could not knock Matt Le Blanc from his top placing.

The Cee'd took over from the Chevrolet Lacetti, and the Suzuki Liana before that. Stephen Kitson, communications director at Kia Motors (UK) said, "The last time *Top Gear* paid us any attention, I think they tried to build one of our cars out of washing machines, so this is a quite a step forward in their understanding of just how Kia has changed."

The Europe-only Cee'd's main attraction was still its extremely reasonable price and a seven-year warranty. Kia called the car "futureproof" because this guaranteed good residual values. True, its 97-cubic-inch (1,591-cc) gas engine was gutless and noisy, and the benchmark VW Golf and Ford Focus did just about everything better, but the Cee'd was designed and built in Europe, it looked stylish, and overall it offered good value.

Buyers could chose between a three- or five-door hatchback or a station wagon (estate). There was also the possibility of a smaller, 85-cubic-inch (1,396-cc) gas engine, preferred by *What Car?* magazine, or a 96-cubic-inch (1,600-cc) diesel. **LT**

The 2007 Lexus IS-F was a mean-looking machine from a stable better known for stately thoroughbreds than mustangs. ▷

One | Carver (NL)

2007 • 40 cu in/660 cc, S4 • 65 bhp/48 kW • 0–60 mph/ 97 kph in 8 seconds • 115 mph/185 kph

The Carver One was a brave attempt to create a unique three-wheeler sports car that tilted into corners like a motorcycle. The cabin could tilt up to forty-five degrees, depending, not on the road speed of the vehicle, but on the speed and force with which the steering wheel was turned. This hydraulically powered "automatic balancing system" was said to give total stability in all situations.

A single motorcycle wheel steered at the front, while the back wheels were slightly smaller. The engine was small, too, but its turbo and sixteen valves gave reasonable performance. An optional upgrade took power up to 85 bhp (63 kW) and the top speed up to a wobbly 141 mph (227 kph).

The vehicle had a smooth five-speed, lever-change gearbox plus reverse, and a proper steering wheel, not a handlebar. The passenger sat behind the driver. A removable roof added to the experience. Road-test reports were mixed. Some reviewers found the Carver exciting, others were disconcerted by its inappropriate leaning—going slowly around a roundabout at forty-five degrees, for example.

In Europe the Carver One could be driven on a car license but was taxed as a motorcycle. Among its attractions were said to be easy maneuverability and parking in cities and low fuel consumption, but the Carver did not come cheap; at around $47,000 (£30,000), it cost as much as a new Lotus sports car. Sales were slow and the Dutch maker was soon beset with financial problems. A U.S. company has bought the rights to the leaning three-wheeler technology but has yet to put a vehicle into production. **SH**

IS-F | Lexus (J)

2007 • 305 cu in/5,000 cc, V8 • 416 bhp/311 kW • 0–60 mph/ 97 kph in 4.9 seconds • 168 mph/270 kph

Lexus had made luxury cars, quiet and smooth cars, high-tech cars, and hybrid cars. But it had never made a hardcore hot rod until the IS-F.

Toyota's luxury division realized that it could never compete with the iconic German brands unless it had some sort of high-performance heritage. So Lexus engineers took the big V8 from the LS600 limousine and squeezed it into the front of its smallest car, the IS sedan (saloon). Of course, some tweaks were necessary along the way: the cylinder head and some pipework were tickled by Yamaha Racing team specialists, and some of the software settings were maximized. The result was a compact, four-door car with a 416-bhp (311-kW) powerplant on board.

The IS-F was Lexus's answer to the BMW M3, and the bland, standard body of the IS was restyled to say just that. The aerodynamic and styling changes made the car look like "a clenched fist of aggression," according to *Evo* magazine. The body was lowered, the hood (bonnet) bulged, and there were new fenders (bumpers), skirts, and air scoops. It even had fake quad exhausts poking from the back.

Inside, the normal Lexus cozy ambience gave way to four sporting bucket seats, aluminum panels, and a race-style, eight-speed, steering-wheel paddle-shift semiautomatic gearbox. There were also forged aluminum wheels, six-piston Brembo brakes, electric steering, and a multimode stability system.

The IS-F had sizzling acceleration accompanied by an inspiring bellow of power. In corners it had grip, and in normal driving, it was poised and comfortable. Lexus at last had the muscle car it had wanted. **SH**

A10 | Ascari

GB

2007 • 305 cu in/5,000 cc, V8 • 625 bhp/466 kW • 0–60 mph/97 kph in 2.8 seconds • 220 mph/350 kph

Strap into the race-style seat, buckle the five-point harness, and press the red start button: the big V8 booms into life directly behind. Press the go pedal and the Ascari leaps for the horizon. Flicking through its whining six-speed sequential gearbox, the A10 can reach 100 mph (160 kph) in just 5.8 seconds. Few supercars perform more quickly than that.

The Ascari is powered by a V8 taken from the BMW M5, but with improved variable-valve timing to boost its output to 625 bhp (466 kw). The body, made of five pieces of carbonfiber glued together, weighs just 2,822 pounds (1,280 kg). BBC TV *Top Gear* host Jeremy Clarkson thought its performance was "eye-swivellingly, unbelievably brilliant."

Yet this mid-engined, rear-wheel-drive supercar was made in the unlikely setting of leafy Banbury in Oxfordshire, England. The brainchild of Dutch billionaire racing enthusiast Klaas Zwart, the A10 was conceived to celebrate the tenth anniversary of his company. It was a road-going version of his KZ1-R, which competed in the Spanish GT Championship. Both cars were designed by former-Formula 1 creator Paul Brown. Cost was about $650,000 (£350,000).

The A10 has no luxuries: no air-conditioning, soundproofing, or audio system. Instead it features a serious roll-cage, race-tuned suspension, and a knob for altering the front-to-rear brake balance.

Zwart has also built the Ascari Race Resort, a racetrack in southern Spain that includes re-creations of famous corners from circuits of the world. There is a luxury hotel, supercar-owner membership scheme, and a performance-driving training academy. **SH**

Leon FR TDI | Seat

(E)

2007 • 116 cu in/1,900 cc, S4 • 168 bhp/125 kW • 0–62 mph/100 kph in 8 seconds • 133 mph/214 kph

Seeing a diesel car taking the checkered flag in a touring car championship made many car buyers consider diesel for the first time. Diesel family cars had been followed by diesel hot hatchbacks, diesel executive cars, and finally even diesel sports cars. Diesel success on the track was the last frontier.

The Volkswagen-Audi Group (VAG) had long been at the forefront of promoting the benefits of diesel engines—a broader power band, increased torque, and fuel efficiency. VAG diesel cars had already achieved one notable success on the track with a special track car, the Audi R10 TDI, which won the 24 Hours of Le Mans Race in 2006.

The Leon front-drive hatchback from Seat, VAG's Spanish division, was another small step in diesel's progess. The FR TDI version had the group's 116-cubic-inch (1,900-cc) common-rail turbodiesel engine and was a hot hatch with sports suspension, sporty bodywork, and alloy wheels. Yet it could return 57 mpg (4 liters per 100 km) and was a practical family car. Little wonder it became the best-selling version of the Leon..

Seat was the first carmaker to enter the World Touring Car Championship with diesel-powered cars. The Leon FR TDI entered soon after its launch in 2007, halfway through the season, and achieved three wins and seven podium places in ten races.

Two race-prepared Leon FR TDIs were entered for the 2008 season of the World Touring Car Championship. The diesel-powered Leon won the manufacturer's title, and its French driver, Yvan Muller, took the driver's title. The next year Gabriele Tarquini repeated the double win for the Leon FR TDI. **SH**

i30 | Hyundai

ROK

2007 • 97 cu in/1,582 cc, S4 • 129 bhp/93 kW • 0–62 mph/100 km in 10.9 seconds • 122 mph/196 kph

Korean manufacturers Hyundai and Kia started by producing cars that they hoped would sell purely on price. Once the two sister companies got a foothold on the world stage with those cheap and cheerful models, they began a gradual shift upmarket.

With the i30, Hyundai showed the world that Korea could build a car as good as any produced in the West. It was a comfortable, refined, and well-equipped mainstream five-door hatchback; it was excellent value, good to drive, and promised world-class reliability. It even looked modern and rather cool.

Underneath its contemporary and spacious body, the i30 was closely linked to Kia's well-received Cee'd. Of the mix of engines, the diesel figures are given above. Top-specification i30s had a leather-covered steering wheel, alloy wheels, six airbags, and an electronic stability system. Discreet blue illumination lit the instruments, the air-conditioning also cooled the glovebox, and the stereo system played mp3.

Hyundais are sold with a five-year warranty and values of the i30 are expected to hold up well over time—another first for Korea. A BBC *Top Gear* reviewer was typically blunt: "Either someone has slipped something into my drink, or this is a Korean car you might actually want to buy," he said. **SH**

Q7 | Audi

D

2007 • 366 cu in/6,000 cc, V12 • 493 bhp/368 kW • 0–62 mph/100 kph in 5.5 seconds • 155 mph/250 kph

The Q7 off-roader was Audi's first-ever sport utility vehicle (SUV). It was a big unit then, and it continues to grow. The dimensions overflow most parking spaces and make town driving uncomfortable, yet it has been classed as a "soft-roader," being better suited to driving on the road than off.

For cross-country travel, the Q7 has Audi's well-tried Quattro four-wheel-drive system, plus an air suspension with adjustable ground clearance. But buyers were more excited about the level of luxury and technology on board—from an early iPod-compatible audio system to Audi's first blind-spot detection system. An eight-speed Tiptronic semiautomatic gearbox is standard. Options include a voice-control system, auto-dimming lights, and parking cameras. Latest models have the Audi Connect interactive online information service, with a color touch screen on the dashboard and Wi-Fi connection through the cabin.

The Q7 has been built with a wide variety of engines. The figures above are for the biggest: the turbodiesel V12. This is a unique engine in any passenger car and was derived from Audi's R10 race car. The Q7 V12 has uprated suspension, plus tires and brakes to cope with the extra power; it is now considered the best-handling version. **SH**

Fighter T | Bristol (GB)

2007 • 488 cu in/8,000 cc, V10 • 1,012 bhp/755 kW • 0–60 mph/97 kph in 3.4 seconds • 225 mph/340 kph

Bristol's supercoupe entered the 1,000-bhp (746-kW) club when a turbocharger was fitted to its Viper V10. The top speed was limited to 225 mph (340 kph), but potentially exceeds 270 mph (435 kph).

Bristol is a small, independent British supercar builder that used to make aircraft. The aircraft heritage is clear in the company's pioneering management of wind flow. The Fighter's exhaust pipes, for example, run within the sills so as to not disturb the smooth underbody. Bristol claimed the front air intake was positioned to provide extra boost to the engine above 200 mph (322 kph).

The Fighter coupe had two gull-wing doors and a distinctively tall cockpit—Bristol said it could accommodate a driver 6 feet 7 inches (200 cm) tall. The brown leather-covered interior was spacious and well finished. The engine was in the front, so there was room for luggage in the back.

The Fighter was fast enough, but the T version's enormous power output is owed to twin turbochargers and engine tuning. The torque, or pulling power, was particularly high, so the six-speed manual gearbox had to be redesigned to take the strain. This meant that the Fighter T could reach 60 mph (97 kph) in first gear in less than 3.5 seconds. **SH**

Golf W12-650 | Volkswagen (D)

2007 • 366 cu in/5,998 cc, W12 • 641 bhp/478 kW • 0–60 mph/97 kph in 3.7 seconds • 202 mph/325 kph

For more than thirty years the Wörthersee GTI festival in Austria has attracted an annual pilgrimage of European Volkswagen (VW) fanatics. As a little thank you to its loyal customers, VW often chooses this event to reveal new models, or showcase its wackiest one-off concept cars. However, in 2007, with only two months to go before the festival opened, VW had no centerpiece.

VW's engineers filled the gap with the W12-650 concept car. It had the rear axle and brakes from a Lamborghini Gallardo, the front brakes from an Audi RS4, and the twelve-cylinder biturbo powerplant from the Bentley Continental GT. The 366-cubic-inch (5,998-cc) engine was mid-mounted in an aluminum subframe from the Audi R8, and mated to an automatic DSG gearbox from VW's Phaeton. While the W12-650 had a body shape similar to the Mark VI Golf GTI, it was actually much wider and lower than the original. The only parts it actually shared were the hood (bonnet), doors, and light assemblies; all other body panels were made of lightweight plastic and carbon fiber.

VW's Über-Golf certainly wowed the crowds. While the W12-650 will never be put into full production, it showed what enormous potential the car's platform has, and was testimony to the technical skill, energy, and vision of its German designers. **DS**

Reventón | Lamborghini

I

2007 • 396 cu in/6,496 cc, V12 • 640 bhp/477 kW • 0–60 mph/97 kph in 3.3 seconds • 221 mph/335 kph

When launched at the 2007 Frankfurt Motor Show, the Lamborghini Reventón was the most expensive road car the Italian maker had ever produced. Priced at a cool $1.5 million (£950,000) in the United States, the limited run of twenty were all earmarked for "Lamborghini friends and collectors."

According to Lamborghini tradition, the Reventón is named after a famous fighting bull, although in the Spanish vernacular it can also mean "explosion." That is an appropriate name for a brutally powerful, lightweight hypercar capable of 221 mph (335 kph).

The official Lamborghini press release explains how the Reventón's matte gray paint scheme and angular carbon-fiber bodywork was inspired by modern combat aircraft. Soon after its launch, a Lamborghini test driver raced the Reventón against an Italian Air Force fighter along a 1.9-mile (3-km) runway; only when the jet became airborne did it overtake the Lambo in the last moments of the race.

Beneath its futuristically styled exterior, the Reventón shares its mechanics with the Lamborghini Murciélago LP640-4. The four-wheel-drive system gives the car superb grip that helps to launch the car to 60 mph (97 kph) in just 3.3 seconds. The aerospace-inspired air scoops help cool its enormous brake callipers and carbon discs, while driver information is given via two liquid-crystal displays, similar to those found in the cockpits of modern aircraft.

In 2009 a further fifteen Reventón Roadsters were produced, based on the LP 670-4 Super Veloce; they cost an estimated $1.6 million (£1 mllion). Ralph Lauren has one of these in his automobile collection. **DS**

R8 | Audi

(D)

2007 • 256 cu in/4,200 cc, V8 • 414 bhp/309 kW • 0–62 mph/100 kph in 4.6 seconds • 188 mph/302 kph

The Audi R8 supercar, unveiled at the Paris Motor Show of 2006, appeared as from nowhere but actually had a long evolution. The company that had built the A3 hatchback and A4 family car had looked at a world-beating supercar for two reasons. First, Audi's motorsport division had progressed from its Quattro-based rally successes of the 1980s to building GT track cars to tackle the 24 Hours of Le Mans Race. Second, Audi had taken Lamborghini in 1998.

Audi had created one of the most successful race cars of all time, also called the Audi R8. This had won Le Mans five times and the U.S. Le Mans Series seven times. That R8 was a mid-engined, rear-drive race car built of carbon fiber with a 220-cubic-inch (3,600-cc) twin-turbo V8 producing about 670 bhp (500 kW). The R8 was superseded by the diesel-powered R10.

The R8 unveiled in Paris was a very different-looking machine. The platform underneath was shared with the 202-mph (325-kph), V10-powered Lamborghini Gallardo. But instead of the Lamborghini's exotic Italian look, the new R8 had a more purposeful, Germanic, two-door-coupe body made of aluminum. It also had a Quattro permanent four-wheel-drive system and a mid-mounted V8 engine.

By 2009 the engine was replaced by a 317-cubic-inch (5,200-cc) V10 similar to the Gallardo's powerplant. There was a convertible Spyder R8 version, too, which was featured in the 2010 movie *Iron Man 2*. A GT version in 2010 boosted performance to 199 mph (320 kph) with a 0–62 mph (100 kph) time of 3.6 seconds. The car is still evolving; the 2014 R8 is expected to use Audi's 244-cubic-inch (4,000-cc) twin-turbo V8. **JI**

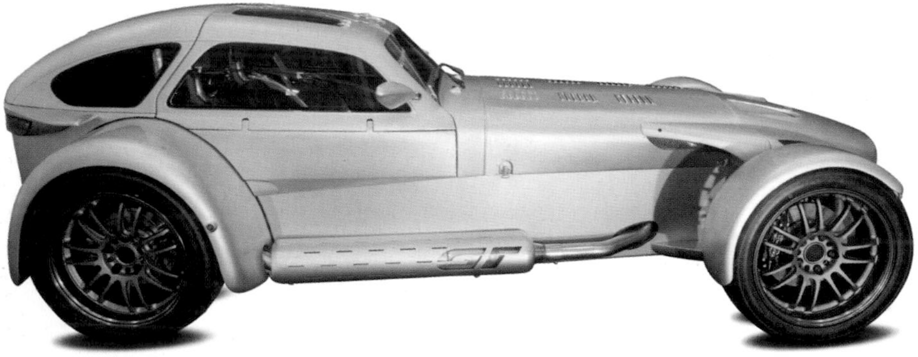

D8 GT | Donkervoort

NL

2007 • 110 cu in/1,800 cc, S4 • 270 bhp/200 kW • 0–60 mph/97 kph in 3.6 seconds • 155 mph/250 kph

The Donkervoort D8 GT may look like a Caterham that has taken too many steroids, but it is a proper high-performance car in its own right. Like the Caterham, it evolved from the classis Lotus Seven, but this car has grown into something very different.

The D8 GT was the Dutch company's first car to have a roof. Built on the basis of thirty years of European track experience, it was a purebred, high-tech racer combined with the personality of a stylish long-distance grand tourer. The distinctive body was hand-built in Donkervoort's new factory in Lelystad, the Netherlands. Thanks to the body's carbon-fiber construction, the D8 GT weighs just 1,433 pounds (650 kg). The semi-gull-wing doors provide easy access to the interior, although luggage is put in through the hinged rear window instead.

Under the hood (bonnet) is a choice of Audi turbocharged engines—180 bhp (132 kW), 210 bhp (154 kW), or 270 bhp (199 kW). The most powerful engine is extremely fast in such a light body. At the time of writing, the roofless version, the Donkervoort D8 270, is one of the ten fastest production cars ever to lap Nürburgring. Recently, a D8 GT won the Dubai 24 Hour Race.

Donkervoort Automobielen may not be a household name, but it has been building sports cars since 1978. Joop Donkervoort originally started in a shed, making versions of the Lotus Seven with a 122-cubic-inch (2,000 cc) Ford engine. His cars always lack electronic aids such as electronic stability programs, but enthusiasts love his back-to-basics approach. More than 1,100 Donkervoorts have been sold. **SH**

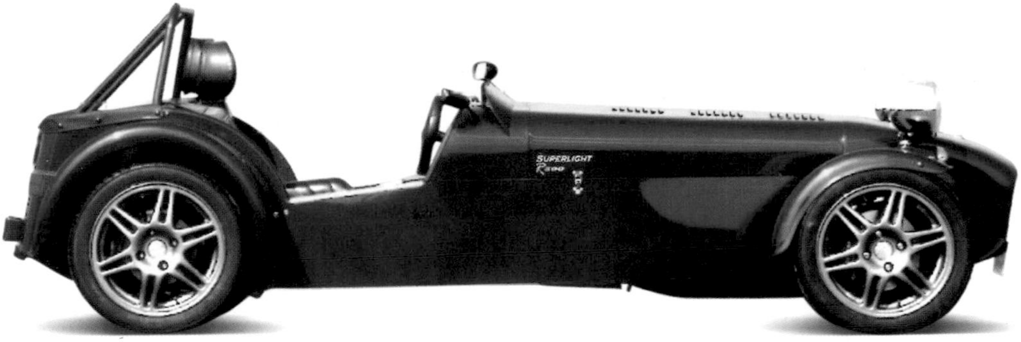

Superlight R300 | Caterham

GB

2007 • 122 cu in/2,000 cc, S4 • 175 bhp/129 kW • 0–60 mph/97 kph in 4.5 seconds • 140 mph/225 kph

Sports-car builders often talk about their products' power-to-weight ratio—the amount of grunt the engine can produce in relation to the weight of the car it has to propel. A big, heavy car may have a big, powerful engine, but can still be slow if the power-to-weight ratio is not in its favor.

The opposite is true, too. Caterham owners often mention the power-to-weight ratio because their cars are so ridiculously light that any engine can make them fast. That is why this entry-level Caterham has one of the smallest and least powerful engines found in any supercar. A mere 175 bhp (129 kW)? In a supercar?

Drivers only have to spend a few minutes in the R300 to realize that 175 bhp is plenty. If the road is wet and they are not expert at handling rear-wheel drive, the small engine can even feel like too much.

The Superlight R300's engine is a slightly tuned Ford Duretec 122-cubic-inch (2,000-cc) version, such as might be found under the hood (bonnet) of a mild-mannered family hatchback. Yet in this Caterham it translates to a power-to-weight ratio exceeding that of any BMW M3 or Porsche 911.

The R300 formula is much the same as any other Caterham—so spartan that it barely qualifies as a car in any normal sense. The R300 feels like an old single-seat track-going race car, but with another seat squeezed in alongside the driver. There are no luxuries or gadgets at all. A windshield, doors, or roof are optional extras.

Yet the handling and performance are so good that most buyers treat their R300 as a weekend toy to be driven purely for the fun of driving. Rock singer and car enthusiast Chris Rea is a big fan. **SH**

caparo

Few road-legal supercars resemble track models quite so closely as the 2007 ultra-aerodynamic Caparo T1.

T1 | Caparo (GB)

2007 • 213 cu in/3,496 cc, V8 • 575 bhp/422 kW • 0–62 mph/100 kph in 2.5 seconds • 200 mph/322 kph

An orange Caparo T1 was officially unveiled by Prince Albert II of Monaco and TV motorsport commentator Murray Walker at the exclusive Top Marques car show in Monte Carlo in 2006. The first question everyone asked was "Can it be driven on the road?" It certainly looked like a track car and was clearly inspired by Formula 1 technology, but, yes, the T1 was road-legal. *Evo* magazine went one step further; it was "as close as you'll get to an F1 car for the road."

Cutting-edge technology and materials were employed in all areas of the T1's construction. The body was a carbon-fiber-and-aluminum honeycomb unit, and even the steering rack was made from magnesium. The seats had six-point harnesses for both the driver and passenger (slightly behind the driver), and the car was fitted with a fire-extinguishing system.

The engine was a 214-cubic-inch (3,500-cc), thirty-two-valve, naturally aspirated V8 from U.S. engine builder Menard. Exceptionally light at 260 pounds (116 kg), it revved to an incredible 10,500 rpm. The car was mid-engined with rear-wheel drive. It could hit 100 mph (161 kph) in five seconds, and, thanks to the huge downforce generated by its Formula 1-inspired aerodynamics, it was theoretically possible to drive the car upside down in a tunnel at 150 mph (241 kph).

The price for all this technology was $333,000 (£210,000) before options. Fifteen cars had been sold up to the time of writing. Perhaps there might have been more sales had one not caught fire on the U.K. TV show *Fifth Gear* while being driven by Jason Plato at 160 mph (257 kph). Formula 1 performance, certainly, but with Formula 1 risks, too. **RD**

GTM Supercar | Factory Five (USA)

2007 • 427 cu in/7,000 cc, V8 • 515 bhp/379 kW • 0–60 mph/97 kph in 3 seconds • 160 mph/257 kph

Factory Five Racing's idea for the GTM was to produce a head-turning supercar at the price of $20,000 (£12,750), that of an ordinary family hatchback. However, buyers had to build the car themselves, not to mention provide their own chassis and engine. What they ended up with was an American rear-wheel-drive two-seater supercar with a mid-mounted aluminum V8, along with a shapely, aerodynamic, composite body and a lightweight steel tube frame chassis and roll cage.

Buyers can opt for a 348-cubic-inch (5,700 cc) or 427-cubic-inch (7,000 cc) Chevrolet Corvette C5 engine, with sports suspension, huge brakes, and a Porsche 911 transaxle. Parts can be bought off the shelf or from a donor vehicle. Factory Five Racing estimates that the total cost will be about double the price of its original package, which is still very low for a high-performance supercar. The estimated time required to build the car is around 250 hours.

After years of computer design, clinics, and prototypes, the New England–based company came up with a sophisticated design, with excellent weight distribution and precise handling. The GTM Supercar clearly is not limited to track work. It has a large and fairly quiet cockpit, good visibility, modern temperature control, air-conditioning, and power windows. It may not compete with the luxury brands, but it has plenty of leather and simple, clear instrumentation.

Factory Five Racing was set up in 1995. Since then it has produced a very successful roadster kit car based on a Ford Mustang donor car. More than 5,000 of those have been sold, making it one of the most popular kit cars ever produced. **SH**

500 | Fiat

(I)

2007 • 53 cu in/875 cc, S2 • 85 bhp/63 kW • 0–60 mph/97 kph in 11 seconds • 108 mph/174 kph

Fiat was the third major carmaker to jump on the bandwagon of retro-styled versions of favorite classic cars. First came Volkswagen's New Beetle; then the MINI; in 2007, fifty years after the introduction of the original, Fiat reinvented the iconic Cinquecento.

Marketed largely at female, fashion-conscious motorists, the car can be customized from a dazzling array of body colors, interior trims, wheel choices, and body decals. At the time of writing, 549,396 different combinations of Fiat 500 were on offer. Special editions have ranged from a metallic-pink Barbie version to the 180-bhp (134-kW) Abarth 695 Tributo Ferrari.

Under the curvaceous bodywork, the 500 shares its mechanical underpinnings with two frumpy cousins, the Fiat Panda and the Ford KA. For those wanting a stylish, superfrugal city car, Fiat's revolutionary TwinAir turbocharged two-cylinder engine has tiny CO_2 emissions. Also, the perky 85-bhp (63-kW) engine can run at 76.3 mpg (32.4 km per liter).

The Fiat 500 launch party on July 4, 2007, was one of the largest in automotive history. Across Italy, thirty of the most beautiful and historic town squares were cordoned off to showcase the new baby Fiat. Amid street parties, food stalls, car displays, and live entertainment, the only vehicles seen were Fiat 500s, both new and old. Fiat's first production run of nearly 60,000 cars was sold in the three weeks that followed.

Since its launch, the new Fiat 500 has received numerous accolades for its design, innovation, and ecological credentials. In 2008 it became the twelfth member of the Fiat family to win the coveted European Car of the Year award. **DS**

Clubman | MINI

GB

2007 • 95 cu in/1,560 cc, S4 • 110 bhp/81 kW • 0–60 mph/97 kph in 10.4 seconds • 120 mph/193 kph

In August 2011 Prime Minister David Cameron drove the two millionth BMW-made MINI off the U.K. production line. It was a landmark occasion; in just ten years the revived MINI brand had become the world's favorite retro-styled runabout.

In 2007 the second generation of the new MINI was launched, and for the first time a slightly longer station-wagon (estate) version, called the Clubman, was in the lineup. The new model took several design cues from the original Mini station wagon, including its rear "barn doors." In 2010 the MINI Clubman was voted *What Car?* magazine's Estate Car of the Year.

Technically, the MINI Clubman is a shooting-brake, meaning a cross between a station wagon and a two-door coupe. Interestingly, the Clubman features a small rear door (officially called the "Clubdoor") on its right-hand side; this allows easier access to the rear bench seat, which can now comfortably accommodate three passengers. While this might seem desirable, it irked British and Japanese customers who, it seemed, were expected to debark their families into oncoming traffic.

With a longer wheelbase and a 143-pound (65-kg) weight gain over the standard MINI, performance was slightly dented. However, buyers who opt for the Clubman are mainly looking for a degree of practicality; figures for the Cooper Diesel are given above.

BMW's MINI Clubman is a fun, fine-handling, and well-equipped package, but one thing irritates many car buffs, and that is the name itself. Original station wagons were branded the Morris Mini Traveller or Austin Mini Countryman; the "Clubman" moniker applied only to 1969's slab-fronted, face-lifted Minis. **DS**

CCXR | Koenigsegg

S

2007 • 287 cu in/4,700 cc, V8 • 1,064 bhp/793 kW • 0–62 mph/100 kph in 2.8 seconds • 250 mph/400 kph

An environmentally friendly supercar seems almost a contradiction, yet the monstrously powerful engine of the CCXR from Swedish high-performance specialist Koenigsegg runs on ethanol, which can be made from potatoes. Surprisingly, the special cooling properties of ethanol mean that the CCXR is even faster than its almost identical gas-powered sister. This custom-built rocket is hardly the "green" supercar, though, as its fuel consumption is extreme. At its best it drinks ethanol (or gas) at around 12 mpg (22 liters per 100 km).

It has a standard supercar layout, with two doors, two seats, and the engine in the middle driving the rear wheels. But the rest of the specification has more in common with race cars than standard family machines: huge ceramic brakes with eight-piston calipers, carbon-fiber wheels, six-speed paddle-shift gearshift, and a system that sprays cooled oil onto the pistons in the engine.

For buyers unimpressed by all that, Koenigsegg developed an even more special version, the CCXR Trevita. A new technique was used to coat the fibers of the composite body shell with diamonds during construction to give a unique shimmering look to the car. The price: $4,850,000 (£3,115,000).

In 2010 the new owner of Harrods department store in London caused a stir by parking his CCXR right outside. A traffic warden promptly gave the bright blue supercar a parking ticket. The multibillionaire Arab owner ignored the ticket so the CCXR was then clamped. The car was eventually released after a representative of the owner paid Kensington Council the $109 (£70) parking fine. **SH**

Fetish | Venturi

F

2007 • electric motor • 300 bhp/220 kW • 0–62 mph/100 kph in 4 seconds • 124 mph/200 kph

Venturi builds by hand the sexy-looking open-top Fetish, one of the world's first production electric sports cars, in its workshop in the tiny municipality of Monaco in the south of France.

On the surface it is a classic two-door, two-seater, rear-wheel-drive roadster. The engine even sits behind the seats in a typical mid-engined layout. Under the skin, the advanced electric engine can attain 12,500 rpm. Its power has been tuned to provide acceleration to match the best sports cars, but its top speed is limited to the level of an ordinary family car.

On one battery charge, the Fetish can run for 211 miles (340 km) at a steady 56 mph (90 kph) with no emissions. Recharging of the alternative-fueled car can be done in just one hour at a fast-charge socket, or three hours at a normal mains socket.

It is no spartan eco-car. Instead, the Fetish is a luxury vehicle, with a leather and carbon-fiber hand-trimmed cockpit. Buyers can receive regular checkups on their car by plugging it into a Wi-Fi Internet connection to the Venturi technicians in Monaco during the two-year warranty period.

Millionaire businessman Gildo Pastor, who took over Venturi in 2001, has pushed the brand toward producing pioneering electric vehicles. As part of this aim, Venturi built a one-off vehicle called Jamais Contente ("Never Happy") that claimed the electric-powered land-speed record at Bonneville in the United States in 2010, with a speed of 307 mph (495 kph).

Venturi limits production of the Fetish to ten cars a year. The price ensures it will remain an exclusive choice: it costs around $475,000 (£300,000). **SH**

DBS | Aston Martin

GB

2007 • 366 cu in/6,000 cc, V12 • 510 bhp/380 kW • 0–60 mph/97 kph in4.3 seconds • 191 mph/307 kph

Incredible as it seems to most of us, some car owners find the Aston Martin DB9 a bit too, well, mundane and sluggish—they need an even sportier machine. That is why Aston Martin launched the thunderous DBS.

Of course, this Aston line is forever linked with James Bond. An earlier version of the DBS featured as 007's car in *On Her Majesty's Secret Service* (1969), while the current car was driven by Daniel Craig's Bond in *Casino Royale* (2006) and *Quantum of Solace* (2008).

This new DBS was based on the DB9R race car, which means that it is lower, wider, and more aggressive-looking than a standard DB9. Cooling ducts dominate the nose, which houses the uprated, hand-built V12 engine. The purposeful lines are still discreet in a British way, with merely a small carbon-fiber lip spoiler at the rear. With a fabulous, deep, inspiring engine note, brutal performance, and an overwhelming sense of Britishness, the DBS has proven a worthy flagship for the Aston Martin brand.

Ultralight carbon-fiber body panels on an aluminum structure keep down the weight. The engine features an extra air intake, which opens at high revs, flooding the engine with more fuel-air mixture for a surge in performance. With adaptive damping, traction and stability control, and carbon-ceramic brakes, the DBS has the technology to handle all that power.

The DBS costs around $286,000 (£180,000) and—from insurance to tires, fuel to servicing—it costs a fortune to run. However, experts suspect that buyers who hold onto it for long enough will make a profit. A 1960s Aston Martin can be worth up to $397,000 (£250,000) at auction today. **SH**

LS 600h | Lexus

J

2007 • 305 cu in/5,000 cc, V8 with electric motor • 439 bhp/327 kW • 0–62 mph/100 kph in 6.3 seconds • unknown

The LS 400 had kicked the doors in, now its hybrid grandson is booting the occupants out into the street. The luxury sedan (saloon) from Toyota's premium brand had swamped the established premium brands with its blend of technology and quality. The LS 600h has carried on that tradition by offering environmentally conscious buyers the first V8/electric hybrid. It is the world's most powerful hybrid car.

At lower speeds, the big car's progress is often free of emissions because it runs on its electric motor alone. As the speed increases, the V8 takes over. At full throttle, both electric and gas power combine for enormous performance. The allocation of power between the two systems is seamlessly controlled by a computer, which also ensures constant recharging of the electric motor's batteries. However, fuel economy is only slightly better than a normal version. A diesel-engined model would do better. Meanwhile, the price tag made it the most expensive Japanese luxury car ever, with a starting price around $100,000 (£80,000).

At least the LS 600h has a spacious, ultraluxury cabin to match the price: it is full of fine leather, of course, and buyers can specify four or five seats, long or short wheelbase. Rear seats recline and even massage their occupants. Other technological marvels include a self-parking system, adaptive pneumatic suspension, intelligent cruise control, an 8-inch (20-cm) touch-screen infotainment system, and doors that close themselves. Ultimately it is the refined, smooth, swift, and almost silent progress that impresses most, though. The Lexus LS 400 started the dynasty, and the LS 600h takes it one step further. **SH**

GT-R | Nissan

J

2007 • 232 cu in/3,799 cc, V6 • 540 bhp/400 kW • 0–60 mph/97 kph in 3.5 seconds • 193 mph/311 kph

The GT-R badge (meaning "Grand Turismo Racing") first appeared on Nissan's boxy five-door Skyline back in 1969; this staid-looking giant-killer was soon showing European sports-car manufacturers that the Japanese could mix it with the best of them. Generations of Skyline GT-Rs have carried on this tradition, culminating in this car, unveiled at the 2007 Tokyo Motor Show.

Nissan's chief creative officer is quoted as saying, "The GT-R is unique because it is not simply a copy of a European-designed supercar; it had to really reflect Japanese culture." Retaining its forefather's nickname, this new generation "Godzilla" looks monstrously fast even when parked. Inside its carbon-fiber-trimmed cockpit is a digital multifunction dashboard display, developed by the same video-game designers who produced *Gran Turismo 5* for the PlayStation.

On release, this 2+2 twin-turbocharged supercar appeared to have the Porsche 911 Turbo as its

key performance target. The two models have similar acceleration times, top speeds, and levels of practicality. However, the Porsche price tag is 50 percent more than the Nissan. The GT-R actually costs about the same as a Range Rover, but it can lap the Nürburgring faster than a Bugatti Veyron.

Before Nissan could even get its official imports into North American and European dealerships, the motoring press had started to dole out awards; between 2007 and 2009 the GT-R had been given Car of the Year awards by the TV show *Motor Trend*, and *Evo*, *Autocar*, and *Automobile* magazines. After it took BBC TV *Top Gear*'s Supercar of the Year award, Jeremy Clarkson suggested that the GT-R had been "designed to go faster than you ever thought possible, possess more grip than is physically allowed, change gear more quickly than you can blink, and stop with such ferocity that you can actually feel your face coming off." **DS**

S5 Coupe | Audi (D)

2007 • 256 cu in/4,200 cc, V8 • 354 bhp/264 kW • 0–60 mph/97 kph in 5.1 seconds • 155 mph/250 kph

Audi's formula for the S5 is a story of gradual evolution. First there was the A4 executive sedan (saloon) range. Then there was a two-door coupe version: the A5. The S5 was the high-performance version of this line, and it came as either a Coupe, Cabriolet, or Sportback. With Audi's Quattro four-wheel-drive system giving it excellent grip, the Coupe is the modern equivalent of Audi's trendsetting Coupe Quattro of the 1980s. It matches that car's performance, and in many ways it is a more practical and comfortable car, although the old Quattro had the edge in driver involvement. Audi calls it "a modern grand tourer."

At its launch the Coupe was powered by a 256-cubic-inch (4,200 cc) V8 (its figures are given above). The Cabriolet and Sportback came along with a supercharged 183-cubic-inch (3,000-cc) V6 engine, and in 2012 the Coupe was given this more modern and slightly faster engine too, along with a seven-speed semiautomatic gearbox and a "stop-start" system for better fuel economy. The S5's body was tweaked to look slightly more aggressive, with LED running lights and a new grille, 19-inch (48-cm) alloy wheels with ultra low-profile tires, and a discreet rear spoiler. The S5 had bigger brakes to cope with the huge increase in power, and stiffer suspension for more agile handling. **SH**

8C | Alfa Romeo (I)

2007 • 287 cu in/4,700 cc, V8 • 444 bhp/331 kW • 0–60 mph/97 kph in 4.2 seconds • 181 mph/292 kph

When Alfa Romeo pulled the wraps off its 8C model at the 2006 Paris Motor Show, more than 1,200 people immediately placed an order for one. That was awkward because they had decided to build only 500. The 8C was a spectacular-looking creation. Few cars have been quite so acclaimed for their styling, from the shiny quad exhaust pipes to the gaping front air intakes.

The gorgeous retro-styled carbon-fiber body was matched to a wonderful 287-cubic-inch (4,700-cc) V8 with an exhaust tone described as "epic" by one reviewer. The engine and suspension were tuned versions of Maserati units. The Ferrari-built engine was just behind the front axles. The computerized six-speed semiautomatic gearbox was just in front of the back axle that it drives. So the two units balanced the car's weight and kept everything neatly within the wheelbase.

The modern Alfa supercar was named after the brand's historic race cars and was clearly designed for enthusiasts. The luggage space was minimal, it was built only in left-hand drive, and it cost an enormous $267,000 (£174,000). BBC TV *Top Gear* host Jeremy Clarkson called it "quite simply the best-looking car ever made," but on the show's test track its wayward handling was exposed; it recorded one of the slowest laps ever. **SH**

CL600 | Mercedes-Benz (D)

2007 • 336 cu in/5,500 cc, V12 • 510 bhp/377 kW • 0–60 mph/97 kph in 4.3 seconds • 155 mph/250 kph

It was like a coupe except that it was not cramped and awkward to get into, and it had plenty of luggage space. And it was like a big luxury car except that it had sumptuous acceleration, loads of grip and agility, and revved up to 8,500 rpm. The Mercedes CL600 was simply one of the best all-around cars in the world when it appeared in 2007.

It was also a showcase of all the latest automotive technologies. With a fast-changing seven-speed semiautomatic gearbox with an adaptive shift pattern, an electronic trunk (boot) lid closer, adaptive brake lights that flashed during emergency stops, and ventilated seats that massaged on demand, this was a car that catered to every whim. Other assets included an infrared night-vision system for seeing pedestrians after dark, radar-based intelligent cruise control for keeping a safe distance from cars in front, and a park-assist system with front and rear radar sensors for spotting a suitable parking space.

The best component of all was housed under the hood (bonnet): a state-of-the-art twin-turbo twelve-cylinder engine with huge pulling power, right up to its 155-mph (250-kph) limited top speed. As the reviewer from insideline.com reported, "Its luxury-to-performance ratio is perfect." **SH**

Mondeo | Ford (GB)

2007 • 134 cu in/2,200 cc, S4 • 173 bhp/127 kW • 0–60 mph/97 kph in 8.1 seconds • 139 mph/224 kph

The successor to the Ford Sierra family car was the more modern, front-wheel-drive Mondeo (called the Contour, Mystique, and Fusion in North America). What Ford came up with in 1992 was a curvily styled, well-equipped, spacious medium hatchback and sedan (saloon) that was better to drive than any rival.

In North America and Australia, it was less well received, so Ford abandoned its world-car pretentions in favor of locally tailored vehicles. But in Europe, and especially in the United Kingdom, the Mondeo became part of popular culture. "Mondeo Man" became a stereotype of a middle-class white-collar worker. Even so, the Mondeo confounded critics with its excellent driving characteristics and choice of fine engines. Figures for the 134-cubic-inch (2,200 cc) diesel are above.

By the time of its fourth generation, in 2007, the Mondeo was based on a shared platform with Volvo. Some say it was the best Mondeo yet. It was built in Belgium, Russia, China, Taiwan, and Thailand, but this fourth Mondeo was no world car—North America and much of South America got Ford Fusion versions. During its life, the Mondeo's fortunes have mirrored economic conditions and the changing car market. So the Mark V, planned for 2013, will again be a world car, simply badged as a Fusion in North America. **SH**

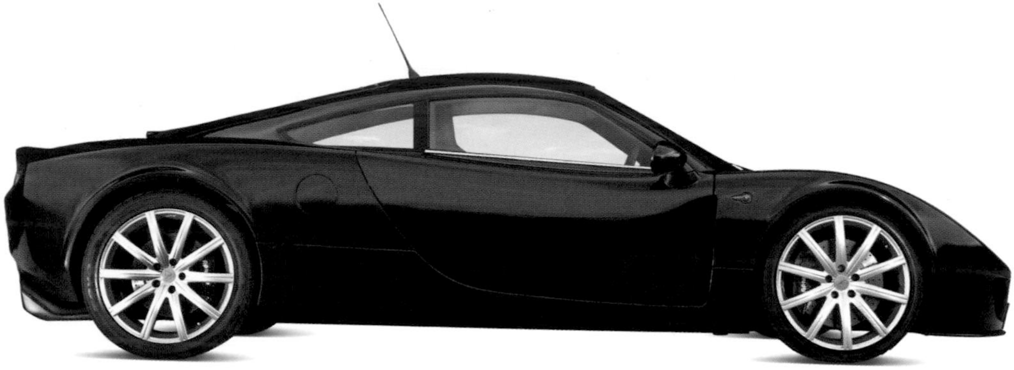

F400 | Ginetta

GB

2008 • 183 cu in/3,000 cc, V6 • 384 bhp/286 kW • 0–60 mph/97 kph in 3.7 seconds • 175 mph/282 kph

This is one sexy-looking supercar. Powered by a supercharged Ford V6, the F400 is an exclusive mid-engined two-door, two-seater coupe with performance to rival the world's best supercars. Its history is not straightforward, though. It's a tale that shows how hard life is for small independent sports-car makers, struggling to produce a supercar in difficult economic conditions. The car's name has changed several times in recent years as its ownership has switched hands and the car evolved.

A small niche carmaker called Farboud originally came up with the car, calling it the GTS. Farboud was bought out by another maker called Farbio, based in southwest England and run by former race driver Chris Marsh. Farbio was expert at carbon-fiber production and had a factory at Bath in Somerset, England.

Then Ginetta took over Farbio and rebadged the GTS project as its own F400; it was launched with a ceremony at Silverstone racetrack. Ginetta, an English sports-car maker founded in 1958, has itself changed hands and location more than once. In recent years it has become a much bigger name in motorsport than in road-car sales. It is now based in northern England and guided by businessman Lawrence Tomlinson.

Ginetta used its track expertise to redevelop the Farbio car. The F400 was renamed the G60 in 2011. Prices have varied along with the name, but the latest tag is around £100,000 ($150,000).

Whatever its history, the end result is this lightweight carbon-bodied two-door coupe sitting on a space-frame chassis. Performance is impressive, and the top speed is over 175mph (202kph). **SH**

FX50 | Infiniti

J

2008 • 305 cu in/5,000 cc, V8 • 390 bhp/291 kW • 0–60 mph/97 kph in 5.8 seconds • 155 mph/250 kph

The FX first appeared in 2003, aimed directly at upmarket crossover pioneers such as the Volvo XC90, BMW X5, and Porsche Cayenne. The Japanese sport utility vehicle (SUV) shared a platform with the Nissan 370Z sports coupe and was designed to combine a coupe's curves with an off-roader's imposing stance.

Somehow Infiniti—Nissan's luxury arm—got the styling slightly wrong. After the FX's looks were criticized as being like "a giant beetle," this redesigned version appeared in 2008. The second-generation model was the first to be sold in the United Kingdom.

Even with its improved styling, the SUV's looks divided opinions. The FX50 had the height of an off-roader with the sweeping lines of a sports car. But it seemed wide for European roads and its 21-inch (53-cm) alloy wheels looked overlarge. Nevertheless, buyers discovered a luxurious cabin inside, on a par with the quality of Lexus, Toyota's rival brand.

Under the controversial body there was sophisticated technology at work. This included a "rear-active steering system" that used an electric motor to turn the back wheels slightly to preserve stability during high-speed lane changes. In normal driving all power went to the rear wheels, but it was apportioned to the front when more grip was required. The gadget list was long, too, including active cruise control, lane-departure warning, and 360-degree cameras.

The range-topping engine, a 305-cubic-inch (5,000-cc) V8, certainly delivered sporting performance, but at the cost of high fuel consumption. Some reviewers reported that they had achieved only 14 mpg (17 liters per 100 km). **SH**

F16 Sport | Secma

F

2008 • 98 cu in/1,598 cc, S4 • 105 bhp/77 kW • 0–60 mph/97 kph in 5.5 seconds • 110 mph/180 kph

The Secma F16 is a factory-built super buggy with sports-car performance and handling but the price tag of a small hatchback, around $23,500 (£15,000).

The French two-seater, built in Aniche in northern France, is named after a U.S. fighter jet—mainly because it is rather swift. It is also rather small, measuring just 9 feet (275 cm) long and 5 feet 8 inches (176 cm) wide. That tiny body is made from molded polyethylene set on a strong steel-beam frame. The whole car weighs just 1,235 pounds (560 kg). The fuel-injected 98-cubic-inch (1,600-cc) sixteen-valve Renault Mégane powerplant sends drive to the rear wheels via a five-speed Renault manual gearbox.

The F16 Sport's modest mass means that the humble Renault family-car engine provides impressive performance while keeping fuel consumption down to ordinary family-car levels, at an average of 43.5 mpg (6.5 liters per 100 km).

Secma also builds tiny beach and track buggies, and the little F16 Sport is actually the company's biggest and most powerful vehicle. But enthusiastic drivers got everything they needed: disk brakes all around, sports suspension, alloy wheels, a stainless-steel exhaust, and peerless, go-kart-style handling.

In this car, gadgets and comfortable extras are few. Optional extras include a cockpit cover, retractable top, luggage rack, colored leather seats, and a leather-covered steering wheel. The two black leather sports seats are not adjustable, but the pedals are. There are no floormats, and no trunk (boot) or glove box for storing valuables. Buyers even have to pay extra for doors—but then they are gull-wing doors. **SH**

MiTo | Alfa Romeo

F

2008 • 107 cu in/1,750-cc, S4 • 237 bhp/177 kW • 0–62 mph/100 kph in 5 seconds • 155 mph/250 kph

Taking ingredients of the Alfa Romeo 8C supercar and the common small hatchback platform used for the Fiat Punto and Opel/Vauxhall Corsa, Alfa designers mixed them with typical brio to create a sporty mini hatchback. The MiTo took many design cues from the 8C—the bulbous nose, teardrop-shaped windows, and round taillights—to make an exciting supermini. The name MiTo is an abbreviation of Milan, where the car was designed, and Turin (Torino), where it was built.

Drivers could choose from three settings in a new Alfa DNA (Dynamic, Normal, and All-Weather) system. The settings controlled the behavior of the engine, brakes, steering, suspension, and gearbox. The DNA system also oversaw the sophisticated electronic differential on the front axle that varied the level of the car's traction to match conditions.

The sporty little coupe's shape rekindled memories of the popular Alfa Bertone Coupes of the 1960s and '70s. The sportiest version was given a 107-cubic-inch (1,750-cc) engine—as used in the acclaimed sporty Bertone GTV of 1967. The figures given above are for this high-performance GTA prototype model. Sadly, due to economic conditions the MiTo GTA may never go into full production. Humbler MiTos gave lesser performance, although most gas models make the 0–60-mph (97-kph) sprint in around eight seconds.

Alfa included a Windows-motif button on the steering wheel for connection to an information and entertainment system. This allows voice control of music playback and Bluetooth cell (mobile) phones.

In Italian *mito* means "myth" or "legend," and Alfa is still hoping that the car will become one. **SH**

SL | Mercedes-Benz

(D)

2008 • 336 cu in/5,500 cc, V12 • 510 bhp/380 kW • unknown • unknown

The Mercedes SL (Sports Light) was first produced in 1954 and has been a range of luxury grand tourers ever since. More than 630,000 SLs have been sold. Sales were helped by Apple founder Steve Jobs, who swapped his SL every six months. All have been two-door roadsters with an engine at the front driving the rear wheels, but details have constantly evolved.

The suave and sophisticated 2008 model was the last, and best, incarnation of the fifth-generation SL (it was superseded in 2012 by the sixth generation, the first all-aluminum line). It arrived with Mercedes' new, fast, seven-speed semiautomatic gearbox; engines ranged from a 214-cubic-inch (3,500-cc) version to the 366-cubic-inch (6,000-cc) V12 used in the AMG special high-performance models. Figures for the 336-cubic-inch (5,500-cc) SL600 are given above.

All of the 2008 models had an elegant powered folding roof made of metal, rather than canvas. A rollover bar automatically popped up if the car detected a risk of turning over while the roof was down.

Mercedes tweaked the 2008 design to achieve the youthful, sporty look combined with traditional cues that SL buyers favor. Wraparound headlights replaced old-fashioned double-light units, the grille and the three-pointed star were simplified, and power bulges appeared in the hood (bonnet).

The SL continued to showcase interesting technology: the 2008 model had bixenon headlights with an intelligent light system offering different modes for various driving conditions—country, motorway, fog, cornering, and "active," which pivots the beam in the direction of the wheels. **SL**

Phantom Drophead Coupe | Rolls-Royce

GB

2008 • 412 cu in/6,749 cc, V12 • 453 bhp/338 kW • 0–60 mph/97 kph in 5.7 seconds • 149 mph/240 kph

At the launch of the Phantom Drophead Coupe, Rolls-Royce chief designer Ian Cameron said, "Simply removing the roof would have made a great convertible . . . but it wouldn't have made a perfect one." So every exterior panel on the Drophead was new, echoing the style of the sedan (saloon), but with proportions better suited to its shorter body.

Cameron explained that the team decided to use natural surfaces wherever possible, so the enormous hood (bonnet) and A-pillars were brushed steel; the rakish grille was also finished in steel.

The rear deck comprised thirty individual pieces of solid teak, and special techniques were developed to preserve the wood without relying on a thick layer of varnish. The team checked out Americas Cup J-class yachts of the 1930s for inspiration, but the boat deck also evokes 1930s coachbuilt cars, 1950s Riva speedboats, and the automotive star of the 1968 children's movie *Chitty Chitty Bang Bang*.

The fabric roof was made like a bespoke suit. It was chosen over a retractable metal lid because it took up less storage space and seemed more appropriate. The poetic Cameron also said that "There is nothing more romantic than driving a convertible at night and hearing the drops hit the roof."

Naturally the Drophead delivered a sumptuous drive, with the exceptionally strong and light aluminum space frame banishing the slightest convertible shiver.

Even the "Spirit of Ecstasy" figure on the nose had been remodeled in the year of the Drophead's launch to make her more lifelike. Standing on the prow of this exquisite machine, she had good reason to smile. **LT**

Despite holding numerous records, the Ariel Atom was too slow for some buyers—and so the Atom 500 was born. ⊳

X6 Falcon | AC Schnitzer (D)

2008 • 269 cu in/4,400 cc, V8 • 655 bhp/482 kW
0–60 mph/97 kph in 4.4 seconds • 186 mph/300 kph

AC Schnitzer is a tuning company based in Aachen (hence the "AC"), Germany. It works exclusively on improving BMW cars and motorcycles. As well as selling replacement parts, such as custom sports exhaust systems and fancy alloy wheels, the firm tunes customers' engines for more performance and creates whole Schnitzer versions of BMWs for sale. The AC Schnitzer X6 Falcon, for example, is the big BMW X6 sports crossover with extra style and muscle.

Schnitzer boosts performance by up to 100 bhp (75 kW) using a new engine-control unit and a sportier exhaust system. A reworked suspension allows the Falcon to handle that extra performance, even in the case of the uprated BMW X6 M, whose figures are given above. At the same time, Schnitzer converts the interior, with new carbon trim everywhere and a neat new Schnitzer steering wheel. The pedals and cover for the BMW iDrive system controller are made of aluminum. The dashboard now contains Schnitzer instruments—the dials now have a white background and red pointers, and their lighting is red.

The biggest changes occur to the exterior. The full Schnitzer Falcon carbon body includes front and rear spoilers, 1.5-inch-wide (40-cm) wheel arches, hood (bonnet) vents, and a trunk (boot) wing. The ride is lowered and there is a new, sportier exhaust system with quad chrome tailpipes. There are bigger and wider alloy wheels with low-profile tires. One optional extra is a plexiglass hood that shows off the engine.

For those who consider the original all-wheel-drive X6 overweight and pretentious, the Falcon transforms it into a Porsche-beating monster with attitude. **SH**

Atom 500 | Ariel (GB)

2008 • 183 cu in/3,000 cc, V8 • 500 bhp/368 kW •
0–60 mph/97 kph in 2.3 seconds • 170 mph/274 kph

"I have never driven *anything* that accelerates so fast," shouted BBC TV *Top Gear* host Jeremy Clarkson above the engine noise, his face distorted by G-forces. His review on the international motoring show plunged the strange little Atom, built by enthusiasts in England's rural Somerset, into the supercar big league.

Yet compared to any other supercar, it is a ridiculous, tiny two-seater, with no doors, roof, screen, or even body. It is like a race car with the panels taken off. Somehow it is road-legal, which means that the Atom is a uniquely exciting driving experience.

The Aerial Atom holds records all over the place, including the fastest-ever indoor car—70 mph (110 kph) on a 220-yard (200-m) track in Birmingham, England—and *Autocar* magazine's fastest car—0–100 mph (161 kph) in 6.86 seconds.

Some buyers, amazingly, judged the "normal" Atom to be too slow, so in 2008 the limited-edition Atom 500 V8 version was launched. It had a distinctive gold painted chassis. The standard Honda VTEC engine was replaced by a U.S. Hartley V8 engine built from two Suzuki motorcycle engines combined. Speed was also increased by the lightweight build—it weighs only 1,213 pounds (550 kg)—and the superfast sequential gearbox—paddle gearshifts take less than forty milliseconds. The race-car suspension ensures that the Aerial is agile and nimble, with plenty of adjustability for enthusiasts who want to use it on the track.

Only twenty-five Atom 500 V8s were built. The price was high, around $240,000 (£150,000), but twenty were sold before the version was even launched, and the rest were sold soon after. **SH**

Q1 | Rossion (ZA)

2008 • 183 cu in/3,000 cc, V6 • 450 bhp/340 kW • 0–60 mph/97 kph in 3.2 seconds • 189 mph/304 kph

South African supercar enthusiasts Ian Grunes and Dean Rosen used to import supercars such as the Noble M400 into the United States. They liked the British track-focused car so much, they purchased manufacturing rights and decided to convert the rather spartan car into a more luxurious, refined, and practical supercar of their own.

The Q1 is the result, a completely new lightweight two-seater supercoupe. The name stands for "quick one," and the badge appropriately features a peregrine falcon, the fastest creature on earth. The car is built in a modern factory in Port Elizabeth, South Africa, although the Rossion firm (combining "Ros" and "Ian") is based in Pompano Beach, Florida.

The Q1's body is fiberglass, the powerful twin-turbo Ford V6 is mid-mounted and drives the rear wheels, and it all sits on a steel space-frame chassis. The power-to-weight ratio means that the Q1 is very fast, especially from a standstill, but the chassis design and sophisticated suspension make the ride less bone-crashing than more track-focused sports cars.

The Rossion's interior is surprisingly smart and comfortable for a supercar. The leather-coated Momo steering wheel and aluminum pedals are all adjustable to fit the driver's size. **SH**

X-Bow | KTM (A)

2008 • 121 cu in/1,984 cc, S4 • 237 bhp/177 kW • 0–62 mph/100 kph in 3.9 seconds • 134 mph/217 kph

In 1954 Kraftfahrzeuge Trunkenpolz Mattighofen started to manufacture motorcycles, mopeds, and bicycles in Graz, Austria. In 2006 KTM, as it is now known, instigated a project to build a lightweight sports car for track use only, with input from Italian Grand Prix car chassis experts Dallara. The resultant car featured a carbon-fiber tub clad in plastic panels. Inspired by KTM's motorcycles, and powered by Volkswagen's popular four-cylinder turbocharged engine, it weighed just 1,738 pounds (790 kg).

After launch, three models were offered: the Clubsport and Street retained the original 237-bhp (177-kW) output, and a tweaked R version gave 300 bhp (223 kW). In its street-legal specifications the car, named the X-Bow (pronounced "crossbow"), features a weatherproof interior, which is handy, given the lack of doors, roof, or windshield. The X-Bow has no traction control, no brake servo, and no power steering. Four-point harnesses are standard, as are a limited-slip differential and individually adjustable pedals.

In 2008, *Top Gear* magazine awarded the X-Bow the title Sports Car of the Year. The car comes only in KTM's classic orange-and-black paint scheme. The list price is a hefty $77,000 (£50,000) before extras such as fire extinguishers are added on the options list. **RD**

FCX Clarity | Honda

J

2008 • hydrogen fuel-cell electric • 134 bhp/100 kW • 0–60 mph/97 kph in 10 seconds • 99 mph/160 kph

BBC *Top Gear* called it "the most important car since the car was invented." Honda's FCX Clarity is an electric-powered car that generates the electricity itself using a hydrogen "fuel cell." The technology is this: the car's fuel tank is filled with compressed hydrogen. That combines with oxygen in the car's fuel cell to create electricity, which operates the electric motor at the front of the car. The motor drives the front wheels. The only emission produced is pure water. There is no recharging, no consumption of mains electricity (and the energy that requires), and no pollution.

At present the Clarity costs so much to build that Honda is only planning to produce around 200. They are available only to lease, mostly in California, with a few in Japan and Europe. Their use is limited to areas that have hydrodgen pumps at service stations. The car travels around 240 miles (386 km) between fill-ups. An onboard battery is used to store electricity generated by the braking and deceleration process.

Honda—and most other car manufacturers—is watching closely to see how this new technology performs. Most experts believe that fuel-cell cars, much more than hybrids or electric cars, are the future of motoring. The best news? Hydrogen will never run out. It is the most abundant element in the universe. **SH**

M3 | BMW

D

2008 • 244 cu in/3,999 cc, V8 • 414 bhp/309 kW • 0–62 mph/100 kph in 4.7 seconds • 155 mph/249 kph

Unveiled at the 2007 Geneva Motor Show, the BMW M3 type E90/92/93 was built on the success of the outgoing six-cylinder E46 M3. The new BMW M3 was the first in the series to use a V8. Along with the bigger engine came a larger base-level price of $78,000 (£50,000), with a list of expensive options.

The new M3 was soon making an impression in motorsport circles. It won the American LeMans Series of 2009, the 24 Hours at Nürburgring, and the GT2 category of the Intercontinental Le Mans Cup 1,000 km (621 miles) at Zhuhai in China. In addition to the huge horsepower and firm ride, the M3 was equipped with plenty of luxuries as standard. There was technology aplenty, too: an optional Electronic Damping Control system provided Sport, Comfort, and Normal modes, which were selectable through the M3's i-Drive system.

The V8 engine was relatively light at 444 pounds (202 kg) and was coupled to a six-speed manual gearbox. A later option was a double-clutch gearbox from Getrag with seven gears and rapid gearshifts. Three body types were available: two-door sedan (saloon), cabriolet (with powered retractable hardtop roof), and four-door sedan. *Car and Driver* magazine was full of praise: "Based on our experience, the current M3 is the world's all-around best car for the money." **RD**

Q5 | Audi

D

2008 • 120 cu in/1,968 cc, S4 • 168 bhp/125 kW • 0–60 mph/97 kph in 9.5 seconds • 126 mph/203 kph

In the late 1970s there was a children's craze for putting empty potato-chip bags in the oven, where they would shrink down to form miniature versions of themselves. The Q5 is a bit like that. From a distance it looks remarkably like its big brother, the rather brutish Audi Q7, but smaller, as if it has been parked farther away.

When it was launched in 2008, the Q5 was aimed at the slot in the marketplace occupied by the BMW X3, Land Rover Freelander, and Volvo XC60. These were all premium-brand soft-roaders that were slightly smaller than their siblings (the X5, Discovery, and XC90, respectively). Though they may never go farther off road than mounting the curb outside school at pickup time, they all have some all-terrain credibility.

Audi, knowing the Q5 had to be good, built it on a new medium-large platform it shared with the A5 coupe. This would make it bigger than the Volkswagen (VW) Tiguan and Skoda Yeti, both part of the Audi-VW-Skoda-Seat family but in the lower price range.

There was a choice of engines at launch, including the 120-cubic-inch (1,968-cc) gas turbo used in the Golf GTI and Audi A3. Many drivers opted for the diesel turbo version of this engine, which offered good power and efficiency; its figures are given above.

On the road (which is where 90 percent of Q5s are found) the car handled more like a modern hatchback than an off-roader, helped by the permanent four-wheel-drive and excellent chassis. Then again so did its many of rivals. The Q5 had great build quality, plenty of passenger room, and a lot of equipment. For many it brought an affordable slice of luxury, prestige, and quality to the mid-sport utility vehicle market. **JI**

X6 | BMW

(D)

2008 • 268 cu in/4,395 cc, V8 • 555 bhp/408 kW • 0–62 mph/100 kph in 4.7 seconds • 155 mph/250 kph

This bastard child of BMW's M6 and X5 models was the first ever car to be marketed as a sports activity coupe (SAC). It was followed by the MINI Paceman, showcased at the 2011 Detroit Motor Show. According to BMW press releases at the time, the SAC was a new breed of vehicle that combined the high ground clearance and off-road abilities of an sport utility vehicle (SUV) with "the athletic and elegant lines of a coupe."

The X6 was BMW's attempt to tap into the lucrative luxury crossover market, dominated by the Range Rover Sport and the Porsche Cayenne. However, unlike its key rivals, the maker of the X6 made few pretentions that it was any sort of off-road "mud-plugger"; its natural environment was firmly on the highway.

Road testers from the U.K. TV show *Fifth Gear* were seriously impressed with the X6's road manners: "Taking into account the size and weight of the X6, the way it goes around corners is quite astonishing. Thanks to advanced all-wheel drive with torque vectoring, power can be sent from the front to rear wheels and side to side too . . . It's so good, you wouldn't complain if you had a hatchback that handled this well."

However, while some drivers considered the X6 to be quite stylish, and it definitely had road presence, the SAC remained an expensive mass of contradictions. It was the size of a multipurpose vehicle (MPV) but only seated four; it had a high ride height but was hopeless off-road; and, weirdest of all, the ActiveHybrid X6 was less economical than the base model.

If people really wanted to buy an X6, then the 555-bhp (414 kW) M-Sport was the one to go for. It was still pointless, but it went like a rocket. **RD**

Chairman | SsangYong

ROK

2008 • 305 cu in/5,000 cc, V8 • 302 bhp/225 kW • 0–60 mph/97 kph in 6.6 seconds • 155 mph/250 kph

The fact that South Korea's big, comfortable Chairman sedan (saloon) looks like an East Asian Mercedes-Benz is no coincidence—SsangYong has been working with the luxury German carmaker since the 1990s.

SsangYong —which means "twin dragons"—went into business in 1954, making jeeps for the U.S. Army. By the 1960s the company was building buses, too, followed in the 1970s by sport utility vehicles. Then came the partnership with Mercedes, which gave the Koreans access not only to new design ideas but also mechanical components. The first generation of the Chairman was based on an old Mercedes E-Class platform. It even looked a lot like the by-then obsolete German executive car.

The second-generation model of 2008 was known in Korea as the "Chairman W." This time it had moved up a notch to target the range-topping Mercedes S-Class. It was an entirely new car, but still made with lots of help and components from Mercedes. There was a Mercedes seven-speed automatic transmission, suspension, four-wheel drive, and radar cruise control. Even the range of engines was Mercedes-derived. The Chairman W looked more like a generalized mix of BMW, Mercedes, and Lexus than the previous model, but there was still little originality on show.

Even so, the Chairman W was South Korea's most expensive car at launch, costing around $105,000 (£67,000). It has electronically controlled air suspension and four-wheel drive, vibrating backseats, surround-sound hi-fi, ten air bags, powered doors and trunk (boot) lid, and voice recognition. Both the seats and the drinks holders are heated and cooled. **SH**

Challenger SRT8 | Dodge

(USA)

2008 • 370 cu in/6,100 cc, V8 • 428 bhp/315 kW • 0–60 mph/97 kph in 4.7 seconds • 170 mph/274 kph

Launched in 1970, the original Dodge Challenger crashed into the fuel crisis that killed off the muscle car. The car is also famous for crashing into immortality at the end of the iconic 1971 road movie *Vanishing Point*.

The 2008 model was a latecomer to the muscle-car revival, appearing just in time to collide with financial meltdown and soaring gas prices. It was a welcome arrival, nonetheless, more overtly retro than the Dodge Charger, retaining its predecessor's classic short deck, long hood (bonnet), and four-headlight "bandit" grille.

Under its skin was a short-wheelbase version of the platform used for the Chrysler 300C and the Charger, with suspension from the Mercedes S-class upfront and from the E-class at the rear. The growl was provided by another classic revival—the Hemi, or at least a modern, 370-cubic-inch (6,100-cc) reinterpretation of it.

The price was reasonable, starting at $40,495 (£25,800); the car achieved 13 mpg (22 liters per 100 km) in the city and 18 mpg (16 liters per 100 km) on the highway. A less expensive, more frugal 214-cubic-inch (3,500-cc) V6 was offered from 2009.

The Challenger proved popular with hip-hop, rap, and soccer stars, and was frequently seen with even bigger wheels and wide-body kits. The enthusiastic team at Dodge, led by ultracool Haitian-born Ralph Gilles, who progressed from designer to president of Dodge Brand, revived original colors such as Sub Lime and Plum Crazy, offering limited-edition paint and trim options. Gilles took the role of the blind DJ Super Soul in *Vanishing Point* and drove a white Challenger on the One Lap of America; the attempt ended in a minor crash that was a fitting tribute to the movie's ending. **LT**

500 Abarth 500 Assetto Corse | Fiat

I

2008 • 83 cu in/1,368 cc, S4 • 190 bhp/142 kW • 0–60 mph/97 kph in 7.4 seconds • 130 mph/210 kph

Fiat's race version of the cheeky Cinquecento was revealed at the 2008 Paris Auto Show. Modified by Fiat's in-house tuning company Abarth, the Assetto Corse (or "Racing Trim") featured 17-inch (43-cm) ultralight race wheels, adjustable suspension, a winged rear spoiler, and twin tailpipes. Painted pastel gray, the car bore Abarth's scorpion logo and red race stripes; the four white roof checkers pay tribute to the all-conquering Abarth 850 Turismo Competizione car of the 1960s.

Replaced by carbon fiber where necessary, 3,971 pounds (180 kg) of surplus interior trim were removed. The single race seat, complete with six-point safety harness, was shifted slightly nearer to the car's center to help with weight distribution. With a turbocharged 83-cubic-inch (1,368-cc) engine pushing out 190 bhp (142 kW), and a curb weight of only 2,050 pounds (930 kg), the Assetto Corse had a better power-to-weight ratio than the Porsche Cayman.

Only forty-nine examples of the Fiat 500-based track cars were built in 2008; almost all were snapped up by race drivers looking to enter the Abarth 500 Trophy race series held at circuits across Europe. Before taxes, the Assetto Corse costs a whopping €32,800 ($43,150/£26,970), while the championship's entry fee is another €12,000 ($15,800/£9,875). But Abarth threw in branded race overalls, helmet, gloves, and shoes.

In 2011 an even hotter, track-focused Cinquecento entered the one-make race series. The Abarth 695 Assetto Corse wrung another 15 bhp (11 kW) from the same 83-cubic-inch engine and featured a sequential gearbox, welded roll cage, and lightweight Lexan windows. Who said the Fiat 500 was a woman's car? **DS**

iQ | Toyota

J

2008 • 61 cu in/996 cc, S3 • 67 bhp/50 kW • 0–60 mph/97 kph in 14.1 seconds • 93 mph/150 kph

The iQ is the world's smallest production four-seater at 10 feet (3 m) long, but it is a premium-economy ride. Its name comes from the intelligence quotient test, but Toyota elaborates that the "I" stands for individuality, innovation, and intelligence, and "Q" for quality.

The iQ's quirky look came from Toyota's European design studio. Its comfortable interior and nippy handling won praise worldwide, but its performance was lackluster. Appearing in Japan in 2008, it had a 61-cubic-inch (996-cc) three-cylinder engine; an 81-cubic-inch (1,329-cc) followed, plus an 83-cubic-inch (1,364-cc) diesel for European markets. An electric version was launched in 2012. In the United States the iQ slotted perfectly into the lineup of Toyota's youth brand, Scion. It went on sale in 2009 with the 81-cubic-inch engine for the price of a larger Ford Fiesta. Strangely, considering its lack of oomph, the press launch was on the steep streets of San Francisco.

The iQ was well received by the motoring press, but no one expected to see it wearing an Aston Martin badge. The Aston Martin Cygnet arrived in the United Kingdom in 2011. Its cabin required as many hides as a DB9 for its leather trim, and it cost $49,000 (£31,000). The tiny luxury car helped Aston Martin to comply with new European Union average fleet emissions regulations because its 60.7-cubic-inch (1,000-cc) engine achieved 54 mpg (5.2 liters per 100 km).

The iQ and Cygnet are helping to answer the question asked by Mercedes when launching the Smart: are there really buyers out there who want a premium-brand car they can park anywhere, with excellent green credentials? The jury is still out. **LT**

Nagari | Bolwell

AUS

2009 • 214 cu in/3,500 cc, V6 • 268 bhp/200 kW • 0–60 mph/97 kph in 4 seconds • 180 mph/290 kph

Starting in the 1960s, sports-car enthusiast Campbell Bolwell built a small business making cars from fiberglass and parts from used cars. The 1970 Nagari was the best of the bunch, having an attractive coupe design, a brand-new Ford V8 and suspension, and Austin 1800 steering. Performance was strong, with a top speed of 130 mph (209 kph). Much of the design was inspired by a visit to Lotus in the United Kingdom by Bolwell's younger brother, Graeme.

In total, around 800 Bolwells were sold before stricter type-approval regulations and the fuel crisis forced Australia's most successful independent sports-car maker to switch to making ocean-going yachts.

In the 2000s Campbell Bolwell again began to build prototypes in his factory in Melbourne, and in 2009 he launched a completely new Nagari. The new car had a few styling links to the old coupe but was a much more serious proposition. It was a mid-engined, rear-wheel-drive, two-seat super coupe with the classic arrangement of a light composite and carbon-fiber body on a steel frame. The whole car weighed only 1,874 pounds (850 kg).

The Bolwell brothers continued their tradition of raiding the surplus shelves of other manufacturers. Power came from the 214-cubic-inch (3,500-cc), twenty-four-valve alloy V6 from Toyota's luxury Aurion sedan (saloon). The light clusters were from the Honda Integra. There was a six-speed semiautomatic gearbox with sequential paddle shifters on the steering column. And this time the specification was up to supercar standards, with antilock brakes, adjustable double-wishbone suspension, and Recaro seats. **SH**

GT MF5 | Wiesmann

(D)

2009 • 305 cu in/4,999 cc, V10 • 507 bhp/373 kW • 0–62 mph/100 kph in 3.9 seconds • 193 mph/310 kph

The Wiesmann GT MF5 is a powerful sports car with a classic retro look, characterized by a long, curvaceous hood (bonnet) and a low profile.

Yet there is nothing old-fashioned about the materials and technologies used in its construction. Each car is handmade, taking 350 hours, in Wiesmann's factory at Duelmen, Germany. Wiesmann's company logo features a gecko, and some say the excellent road handling of the cars emulates the gecko's ability to stick to challenging surfaces.

Even before the distinctive V10 engine starts to sing, this car's high-quality feel justifies its $275,000 (£169,000) price. Buyers can specify right- or left-hand drive, as well as the leather and color of the interior.

The body is constructed using reinforced fiberglass. The aluminum chassis is also lightweight, helping to ensure that the BMW engine and gearbox technology used in the carefully crafted Wiesmann GT MF5 do not have superfluous weight to propel.

The Wiesmann GT MF5 has a closed, aerodynamic body with a small, smart tailfin that improves road handling at high speeds. A limited-edition version of the car, the open-topped Roadster MF5, was also manufactured, but the production run of this convertible was capped at just fifty-five vehicles.

With a seven-speed manual gearbox, the Wiesmann GT MF5 is a car that drivers can enjoy taking out onto curving, rolling roads and open stretches. The sports car has rear-wheel drive and nippy acceleration. That it was chosen as the safety car for the 2009 FIA GT racing season speaks volumes about this well-crafted, desirable product from a niche carmaker. **SF**

In the Mojave Desert, California, the British Steam Car broke the steam-powered land-speed record on August 25, 2009.

G50 EV | Ginetta (GB)

2009 • electric motor • 121 bhp/90 kW • unknown • 120 mph/193 kph

The small British specialist company of Ginetta had been building and racing sports cars since 1958, but the G50 EV was surely its most exciting vehicle. It was planned to be the first all-electric supercar. A prototype was tested by journalists from *Autocar* magazine, who said it had "race-car levels of feel and response." The car was very closely based on the gas-powered Ginetta G50, which was undefeated in the British GT Championship; in 2009 it took the European title, too.

Like that gas-powered, 300-bhp (220-kW) track car, the EV was a rear-wheel-drive, two-door, two-seat coupe. But instead of a mid-mounted Ford Duratec 214-cubic-inch (3,500-cc) V6, the EV had a state-of-the-art 121-bhp (90-kW) electric motor mounted in front of the rear axle. Three sodium nickel-chloride batteries, placed in the car's nose, could be recharged from a standard household electricity socket in around six hours. Ginetta guaranteed the car's range would be at least 150 miles (240 km), even if used for track racing.

The car was the pet project of Ginetta's Leeds-based chairman, Lawrence Tomlinson. He appealed to the British government for £1.7 million ($2.7 million) to help develop the electric car but was told that the project was "too niche" for government support.

Nevertheless, the Ginetta G50 EV was the first car to be actually driven through the Channel Tunnel linking England and France, in 2009. At the wheel was veteran race driver John Surtees, the only winner of both two- and four-wheeled world championships. Surtees took the EV through the Eurotunnel's 31-mile (50-km) service tunnel to mark its fifteenth anniversary, raise money for charity . . . and help promote the car. **SH**

Steam Car | British (GB)

2009 • 12-boiler turbine • 360 bhp/268 kph • unknown • 148 mph/238 kph

The car racing across Edwards Air Force Base in the Mojave Desert, California, looked like another jet-powered land-speed record bidder. Yet this sticker-covered, rocket-shaped vehicle was powered by steam.

The British Steam Car (BSC) was the result of ten years of development by a team working in farm buildings in the New Forest. Their sophisticated steam engine used a 3-megawatt liquid gas burner to heat water for a turbine engine capable of 13,000 rpm. The steam was superheated to 752°F (400°C) and driven into the turbine at more than twice the speed of sound.

This was the equivalent of boiling 1,500 kettles at once, or twenty-three cups of tea a second. The twelve boilers had more than 2 miles (3 km) of piping and used more than 440 gallons (2,000 liters) of distilled water per hour. One officially verified test session by the "flying kettle," as the car was dubbed in the media, beat the previous long-standing record of 127 mph (204 kph) set by the U.S. Stanley Rocket steam car in 1906. A Florida-based team has since announced that they will build a high-speed steam-powered vehicle to attempt to return the world record to the United States.

At one point, test driver Don Wales, the grandson of British high-speed Bluebird ace Sir Malcolm Campbell, piloted the BSC to a world record speed of 148 mph (238 kph) averaged over 2 miles (3.2 km), although at some stages Wales claimed to have achieved more than 150 mph (241 kph).

The 25-foot-long (7.7-m) car has a lightweight steel space-frame chassis, sleek aerodynamic carbon-composite and aluminum body panels, and powerful SiC (silicone carbide) brakes. **SH**

CALOR
RS

V12 Vantage | Aston Martin

GB

2009 • 366 cu in/6,000 cc, V12 • 510 bhp/380 kW • 0–62 mph/100 kph in 4.2 seconds • 190 mph/305 kph

The release of the V12 Vantage, Aston Martin's most powerful production sports vehicle, created a stir of excitement. It is everything an aficionado would expect from the British manufacturer with a long tradition of producing exclusive, high-performance cars. It is refined and sharp—both in looks and capabilities.

At a time when credit was increasingly hard to come by, and environmentalists were telling anyone willing to listen that reducing the size of our carbon footprint was essential for the survival of the world, it might have seemed improbable that a car costing £135,000 ($180,000) and pumping out exhaust fumes from a 366-cubic-inch (6,000-cc) engine would have people clamoring to buy it. Yet reviews for Aston Martin's V12 Vantage were so enthusiastic, and demand for the vehicle so strong, that a specially adapted version, featuring Carbon Black metallic body paint, was created for release in North America in 2010.

Wheels magazine, based in the Middle East, named it as its Supercar of the Year. The car's power enabled Aston Martin employees to drive it to victory in the SP8 class over twenty-four hours of racing at the Nürburgring. This was a car for serious drivers, built using components and technology based upon the V8 Vantage and developed for racing.

Comfort, though, is by no means lacking. The seats are lightweight but cozy, and the fittings are finished to the very high standard expected of the Aston Martin name. But under normal road conditions, it is unlikely that either the acceleration of this high-quality and dynamic car or its 700-watt audio system can ever be given a full workout. **SH**

Ghost | Rolls-Royce

(GB)

2009 • 398 cu in/6,529 cc, V12 • 563 bhp/420 kW • 0–60 mph/97 kph in 4.7 seconds • 155 mph/249 kph

Many Rolls-Royce buyers hunted out this Ghost because it offered all the quality and prestige of its bigger sister, the Phantom, without bellowing their wealthy presence quite so loudly in the street. And it came cheaper: at £192,000 ($250,000), it was about two-thirds of the price of the Phantom.

When it was launched in 2009, the Ghost was the most powerful and driver-focused car the venerable brand had ever produced. Unusually for Rolls, its design was deliberately modern. Speaking of the distinctive prow, design director Ian Cameron said, "We wanted this to be less reminiscent of the traditional Parthenon style and more like a jet intake."

While many Phantom owners preferred to travel behind a chauffeur, those choosing a Ghost wanted to get behind the wheel themselves. The baby Rolls was quiet and well behaved at low speeds; pushed harder, it rewarded a driver with sheer power, balance, and dynamic ability. It was never intended to be as sporty as some rivals, however, and the eight-speed shift-by-wire gearbox was not offered with paddle or sports modes. The Ghost's intelligent air suspension also preserved a touch of traditional Rolls-Royce waft.

The car was loaded with luxury features, including cooling and massage functions through the perforated leather seats. There were even wood-veneer picnic tables for the rear. Cameras allowed the driver to view the rear, front side, and overhead, and the car had night vision (where allowed by law).

In 2010 tuning specialists Mansory produced the White Ghost version, with 630 bhp (470 kW) and a rather undignified top speed of 180 mph (290 kph). **LT**

Scirocco BlueMotion | Volkswagen

D

2009 • 120 cu in/1,968 cc, S4 • 142 bhp/103 kW • 0–62 mph/100 kph in 9.3 seconds • 138 mph/222 kph

This 2009 diesel coupe is a significantly redesigned incarnation of the popular Scirocco. That sports car was originally launched by Volkswagen in 1974 and was so successful that it went on to sell 795,650 units by the time production was ended in 1992.

The BlueMotion is the diesel sister of the powerful gas-engined R Coupe. It shares the same low profile, sporty side skirting, and subtle, liplike rear spoiler. Perhaps belying its aerodynamic design, the car is built on an adapted version of the chassis used for the Golf Mark V, which has prompted some observers to joke that this is a "Golf GTI in disguise."

The timing of the release of the R series, in the depths of the most serious global economic crisis since the Great Depression, was unfortunate, yet may have persuaded some drivers to take this diesel version of the six-gear sports car. This model utilizes Volkswagen's BlueMotion technology to achieve the impressive fuel efficiency of 55.4 mpg (51.4 liters per 100 km), while still being perky enough to accelerate from 0 to 60 mph (97 kph) in under ten seconds.

On sale in an era when environmental concerns affect image and tax, the BlueMotion's carbon emissions of 214 g/mile (134 g/km) are a further selling point. Piezo injectors help maximize efficiency.

Like the other models in the Scirocco R series, this car was developed in Germany but is produced at Volkswagen's AutoEuropa plant in Palmela, Portugal. The production site is located far enough south for the workers to feel, from time to time, the effects of the warm Scirocco wind, after which the car is named, that blows over the Sahara toward Europe. **SF**

G37 Convertible | Infiniti

J

2009 • 226 cu in/3,700 cc, V6 • 325 bhp/242 kW • 0–60 mph/97 kph in 6.4 seconds • 155 mph/250 kph

The G37 is a classy, fast sports coupe and convertible range built by Infiniti, Nissan's luxury wing, to tackle prestige brands such as Mercedes-Benz and BMW.

The G37 tries hard to be a premium product. The convertible features a three-piece, twenty-five-second powered retractable hardtop roof, a Bose "Open-Air" hi-fi sound system, heated and cooled leather seats, and a sophisticated adaptive climate-control system that reacts to the roof position.

As a sign of its times, the G37 was the subject of a major online marketing campaign in the United States; visitors were invited to enjoy interactive experiences and "own the sky" on popular Web sites, social media pages, and even on cell (mobile) phones.

Both the coupe and convertible are designated as 2+2 cars, although the backseats are cramped for adults. The G37's biggest downfall in Europe is its thirsty engine and the lack of a diesel alternative.

In true Japanese style, the car is packed with modern features such as a reversing camera, touch-screen navigation system, and seven-speed paddle-shift automatic gearbox (or six-speed close-ratio manual). While some of the underpinnings are shared with the Nissan 350Z and the engine comes from the 370Z sports coupes, the body is that of a distinctively luxurious grand tourer, fitting the Infiniti brand image.

Inside, details such as a traditional oval analog clock and instrument dials that glow purple in the dark create a premium aura, even if it is a little cheesy. It is hard for a global company like Nissan to pretend to be an upscale specialist manufacturer. Some of the G37's switchgear is sourced from the Navara pickup. **SH**

Evora | Lotus

GB

2009 • 211 cu in/3,456 cc, V6 • 345 bhp/257 kW • 0–60 mph/97 kph in 4.6 seconds • 172 mph/277 kph

The Lotus Evora is a rarity: a mid-engined 2+2. It is also the first all-new model produced by the British sports carmaker since the first Elise was launched in 1995.

Lotus invented the name "Evora" by combining the words "evolution, vogue, and aura." This was to be the flagship model that signaled Lotus's ambitions to develop the brand, and take on the likes of Porsche (and ultimately Ferrari), with a new lineup of fine-handling luxury grand tourers and hardcore sports cars.

The Evora's lightweight modular aluminum chassis is wrapped in a svelte fiberglass shell. Luggage space is quite generous for a supercar, and can accommodate a set of golf clubs at a pinch; however, the optional rear seats are really only usable by children. Up front, Recaro bucket-seats, brushed aluminum switchgear, and a sumptuous leather interior show that Lotus is serious about moving upmarket. Despite that, engineers claimed that, during handling tests at the famous Nürburgring in Germany, the prototype Evora was actually quicker, and more stable at speed, than its track-focused little brothers, the Elise and Exige.

In 2010 the Evora S was launched as a rival to the Porsche 911. With a 345-bhp (257-kW) supercharged version of Toyota's 214-cubic-inch (3,500-cc) engine, it featured a sport button that sharpened throttle responses, raising the rev limit and opening a valve to give the V6 a "race-inspired" exhaust note.

Since its launch, the car has won numerous awards. In 2011 *GQ* magazine made the Evora S its Best Car Under £60k ($100k), stating that "when it comes to blending ride, handling, and serious performance, no one can touch Lotus as it stands right now." **DS**

S1 | Invicta

GB

2009 • 305 cu in/5,000 cc, V8 • 600 bhp/447 kW • 0–60 mph/97 kph in 3.8 seconds • 200 mph/322 kph

The Invicta S1 is the world's first road car, with a one-piece carbon-fiber body and the strongest chassis ever tested in the United Kingdom. Adding a big Ford Mustang V8, tuned to give 600 bhp (447 kW), was to furnish the ingredients for a very potent supercar.

The car is new, but the Invicta badge dates back to 1900, when it sat on a series of sports cars that rivaled Rolls-Royce for quality and Bentley for speed. The company reappeared in the 1940s when it built a rare sports sedan (saloon) called the Black Prince.

The current incarnation of the Invicta company is based in the country town of Chippenham in the west of England, near the historic Castle Combe racetrack. Invicta is a small, independent company producing hand-built, high-performance, rear-wheel-drive S1s at a planned rate of one per month.

The S1 is a big car for a two-seater—particularly in its width of 8 feet, 2 inches (250 cm). With its big trunk (boot) and practical cabin, it is more suited to grand touring on highways than day-to-day pottering in towns or on minor roads. Launch prices in 2009 were around £150,000 ($237,000). Cheaper versions with smaller, less powerful engines than the 305-cubic-inch (5,000-cc) V8 are available.

The specification includes huge, ventilated, race-quality disc brakes, adjustable finely tuned sports suspension, limited-slip differential, and tubular steel chassis and roll cage. The floor is completely flat to aid aerodynamics but soundproofed to create a relaxed cabin. It is spacious, with heated and powered Recaro seats, and satellite navigation, climate control, and hi-fi present in the brushed aluminum and leather. **SH**

XFR | Jaguar

GB

2009 • 305 cu in/5,000 cc, V8 • 503 bhp/375 kW • 0–60 mph/97 kph in 4.7 seconds • 155 mph/250 kph

Jaguar's fastest-ever four-door sedan (saloon) has the big, muscular supercharged engine from the Range Rover Sport to achieve supercar speeds. How fast is it? Well, a slightly modified XFR with the usual engine limiter removed reached 226 mph (363 kph) during a speed trial on Bonneville Salt Flats in the United States.

With such performance, plus a heavy dose of Jaguar luxury inside and state-of-the-art technology under the skin, the car admirably lives up to its maker's slogan from the 1960s: "Grace, space, and pace."

Swift and agile, the XFR manages to be smooth, quiet, and comfortable, too. Acceleration is refined and linear, automatic gearshifts are imperceptible, the seats are big and luxurious, and the ambience retains the XF's standard mix of modern style and British elegance. The equipment list is long and sophisticated, ranging from adaptive cruise control with emergency brake assistance to touch-screen satellite navigation.

In fact, the XFR could be seen as an upgraded version of the standard rear-wheel-drive XF. The changes are discreet: a more purposeful stance, lower and wider, with bigger wheels and more aerodynamic trimmings and cooling ducts. The six-speed paddle-shift semiautomatic gearbox has been tweaked, the suspension stiffened, and the brakes beefed up. Under the hood (bonnet), the engine has immense torque that gives it an edge over its German rivals. In particular, mid-range acceleration is effortlessly brutal.

The XFR is "possibly the best fast large saloon in the world," said BBC *Top Gear*. *Autocar* magazine's verdict was "Jaguar has produced a real world beater." The *Daily Telegraph* simply trumpeted "Rule Britannia." **SH**

TT RS Quattro | Audi

(D)

2009 • 153 cu in/2,500 cc, S5 • 335 bhp/250 kW • 0–62 mph/100 kph in 4.5 seconds • 155 mph/250 kph

The RS Quattro was Audi's ultimate TT model. At first it was not available in the United States, but an Internet petition was started. After Audi received more than 11,000 signatures, the car started shipping stateside.

Audi's curvy, stylish, two-door coupe had almost been turned into a supercar, the spiritual successor of Audi's all-conquering Quattro Coupe rally cars of the 1980s. Like those original Quattros, the TT RS had permanent four-wheel drive for fabulous roadholding and traction on difficult surfaces. It also had blistering performance, thanks to an all-new turbocharged engine with Audi's FSI direct fuel-injection system.

The TT Quattro was Audi's first coupe to wear the high-performance "RS" badge. Unlike the original Quattro, it was available as a hardtop or a roadster. And it was the first RS vehicle to be built at Audi's regular TT factory in Gyor, Hungary, where build quality had proved to be high, rather than at the Audi Quattro headquarters in Neckarsulm, Germany.

Of course, creating the RS Quattro was never just a question of simply adding more power to the TT. The TT's Quattro system was upgraded to deal with the RS's extra power, and its suspension was made stiffer and lower, too. The brakes were uprated and enlarged. Visible through the distinctive 18-, 19-, or 20-inch (46-, 48-, or 51-cm) alloy wheels, the gloss-black calipers clearly show the RS logo.

The TT RS soon fell into the hands of extreme tuners. By 2010 German VAG specialist MTM offered a 466-bhp (343-kW) upgrade. This even hotter TT RS did 0–62 mph (100 kph) in 3.9 seconds and reached a top speed of 194 mph (312 kph). **SH**

XJ | Jaguar (GB)

2009 • 305 cu in/5,000 cc, V8 • 503 bhp/375 kW • 0–62 mph/100 kph in 4.9 seconds • 155 mph/250 kph

The current XJ luxury car is the latest in a long line of big Jaguar sedans (saloons) from the 1960s. But this XJ was different. It did away with Jaguar's lingering retro obsession and tackled its German rivals head-on.

The XJ was unveiled in 2009 at a smart London art gallery by American comedian and auto enthusiast Jay Leno and supermodel Elle McPherson. The launch was shown live on Jaguar's Web site. The new XJ was bigger and more modern than predicted, but all the major Jaguar qualities were there: smoothness, comfort, sporty but graceful handling, and an opulent cabin.

The XJ's muscular exterior has class-leading aerodynamics—it is Jaguar's least air-resistant car ever. The all-aluminum chassis and body keep weight low, making it fast, agile, and frugal.

The interior is as well-trimmed as ever, but also spacious. There is an enormous glass sunroof. An 8-inch (20-cm) infotainment touch-screen, 1,200-watt hi-fi, and virtual instrumentation keep gadget lovers happy. Luxury addicts can specify a leather-lined roof.

To loosen the stability control and stiffen suspension for a sportier handling experience, drivers press a small button bearing a checkered flag motif. How perfectly Jaguar. No wonder this big cat quickly became the top-selling U.K. luxury car. **SH**

Scirocco 2.0 TSI R Coupe | VW (D)

2009 • 120 cu in/1,968 cc, S4 • 268 bhp /195 kW • 0–60 mph/97 kph in 8.9 seconds • 155 mph/250 kph

The 2.0 TSI R Coupe stands out as being the most powerful production Scirocco ever produced.

Klaus Bischoff, Volkswagen's chief designer, led the company's special-projects team in restyling and reengineering the Scirocco ahead of its public unveiling in 2009 at the Nürburgring, where a GT24 race version of the car participated in the challenging twenty-four-hour race (finishing eleventh overall of 200 starters, and securing two class wins).

The 2.0 TSI R Coupe is a smartly packaged two-door vehicle. Its sleek, low profile offers drivers speed yet a reassuring sense of being in control. The Adaptive Chassis Control (ACC) system contributes to the smoothness of the drive, allowing drivers to select between comfort, normal, and sport settings. The ACC sensors constantly measure the car's behavior as it corners, accelerates, and brakes, adjusting the shock absorbers for an enjoyable and safe driving experience.

The front-wheel-drive R Coupe has six gears as standard, either manual and automatic. Bucket front seats, five-spoke wheels, and low front air intakes contribute to the model's sporty look and feel. The TSI R Coupe can seat four adults; the trunk (boot) has an 11-cubic-foot (312-liter) capacity. Consequently, the car is seen as a practical but very sexy hatchback. **SF**

GT | Artega

(D)

2009 • 220 cu in/3,600 cc, V6 • 300 bhp/220 kW • 0–62 mph/100 kph in 4.8 seconds • 168 mph/270 kph

The Artega GT is a sleek and sexy new German supercar created by Aston Martin designer Henrik Fisker, Porsche technical designer Hardy Essig, and former CEO of Rolls and Maserati Karl-Heinz Kalbfell. Its twenty-four-valve V6 engine, from the high performance Volkswagen Passat R36, is slung low in the middle, driving the back wheels, and it has an alloy chassis and composite body.

Drivers enjoy light, ultradirect steering and responsive, precise handling. The standard specification includes a six-speed semiautomatic DSG gearbox with steering-wheel shift paddles and a state-of-the-art switchable electronic stability system.

The simple leather-and-Alcantara-clad cabin is surprisingly spacious for a two-seater, with pride of place going to a touch-screen infotainment computer system and satellite navigation. There are sports bucket seats, and plenty of luggage space for this class of car.

The Artega is built by hand at a new factory in Delbrück in Westphalia, Germany, and at the time of writing costs around $113,000 (£74,000). An impressive electric version, the Artega SE, was unveiled at the 2011 Geneva Motor Show. It has 380 bhp (280 kW). Artega claims it can accelerate from 0 to 62 mph (100 kph) in just 4.3 seconds, with a 155-mph (250-kph) top speed. The SE has a range of around 125 miles (200 km). **SH**

E63 AMG | Mercedes-Benz

(D)

2009 • 378 cu in/6,200 cc, V8 • 518 bhp/386 kW • 0–60 mph/97 kph in 4.3 seconds • 200 mph/320 kph

Ask Mercedes racing arm AMG to build by hand a sedan (saloon), and this is what happens—a supercar disguised as an executive car. The E63 AMG was loosely based on the Mercedes E-Class but was given a huge power boost. Once AMG had done its work, the refined E-Class sedan could do 200 mph (320 kph).

From the outside, the aerodynamic body adds aggression to the looks and channels air more effectively at speed. The side skirts, rear apron, and big front air intakes cool the naturally aspirated V8 under the hood. The front wheel arches are flared for a wider, lower, and more stable stance. Stiffer suspension (with three driving settings), unique lightweight alloy wheels, a sports exhaust, uprated braking system, and even AMG lights are added to the car's specification.

AMG started life as a race-engine builder in 1967. By 1990 the firm was Mercedes's high-performance specialist. Bought outright by Mercedes in 2005, it now operates as a sports subsidiary. The E63, AMG's first entirely hand-built car for Mercedes, adds a heavy price premium to the standard car but is a very different sort of vehicle. It retains the build quality, smoothness, and refinement of the E-Class, but adds almost over-the-top sporting ability. BBC *Top Gear* called it a "street-race Q-car that can crush continents." **SH**

GranTurismo S | Maserati

Ⓘ

2009 • 286 cu in/4,691 cc, V8 • 433 bhp/323 kW • 0–62mph/100 kph in 4.5 seconds • 183 mph/294 kph

In 2007 Maserati returned to profit after a long time in the red. The same year also saw the launch of the GranTurismo, a 2+2 coupe that was derived from the Quattroporte V sedan (saloon). Unfortunately, the GranTurismo did not quite manage to deliver the superperformance that buyers expected. Buyers of that GranTurismo possibly made their expensive choice based on the Pininfarina styling alone, but in 2009 the GranTurismo S was released, with major changes. This time the performance did not disappoint.

The S had the same engine-block casting as the Ferrari F430 and Alfa Romeo 8C, but bored to 286 cubic inches (4,691 cc). It shared its six-speed semiautomatic design with Ferrari, and offered clever "Skyhook" adaptive suspension. Power was up to 433 bhp (323 kW) and the car was transformed. It became the fastest production GT that Maserati had ever made, capable of 183 mph (294 kph). The S model added larger, 20-inch (51-cm) wheels with an elegant trident pattern that suggested the Maserati logo.

Maserati cars had previously struggled to match Ferraris and Porsches for handling. That story changed with the GranTurismo S because the revisions gave the car grip, balance, and feedback that had previously been lacking. These factors took the appeal of the GranTurismo S beyond the boulevard and made it a viable performer on the circuit, too, with less leather and more carbon fiber in the "MC racecar" specification.

Autocar magazine called it "a handsome, rare, and desirable GT with as much pace and handling panache in its locker as cruising refinement." At last Maserati had made a car as good to drive as it was to look at. **RD**

Panamera Turbo | Porsche

D

2009 • 293 cu in/4,800 cc, V8 • 493 bhp/368 kW • 0–60 mph/97 kph in 3.3 seconds • 188 mph/303 kph

Porsche's legion of loyal sports fans begrudges any deviation from the original raw driving experience of the early rear-engined cars. But Porsche's top-seller of recent times is not among their sports cars—it is the Cayenne sport utility vehicle (SUV). So who can blame Porsche for trying to widen its appeal by launching a four-door luxury sports sedan (saloon)?

The Panamera's elongated Porsche 911 appearance was greeted with predictable dismay from the brand's enthusiasts, but it received rave reviews and continues to sell well. The Turbo, in particular, is an ultimate modern crossover vehicle. It offers supercar speed and four-wheel drive. The load space is huge; normally 15.7 cubic feet (440 liters), it grows with the rear seats folded down to an impressive 44 cubic feet (1,250 liters), accessed via a large tailgate.

The Panamera features an adaptive air-suspension that combines a constantly smooth ride with accurate handling. The leather and walnut-covered cabin features more than a hundred buttons for gadgets that include a touch-screen infotainment system and a 585-watt hi-fi rated as one of the best factory-fitted audio systems in any vehicle. There is also climate control, traction control, ride height control, optional wireless rear-seat entertainment package, fourteen-direction power-adjusted heated seats with memory, and an optional voice control system.

Since the Panamera's launch, a 542-bhp (405-kW) Turbo S version has been added with even more performance potential. Porsche has also horrified its traditional enthusiasts by introducing an economical version of the Panamera powered by diesel. **SH**

The 2009 Tesla Roadster offers guilt-free motoring by combining supercar performance with zero emissions.

Roadster | Tesla (USA)

2009 • AC induction motor • 299 bhp/223 kW • 0–60 mph/97 kph in 3.7 seconds • 125 mph/201 kph

The Tesla Roadster was the brainchild of American entrepreneurs Martin Eberhard and Marc Tarpenning. These committed environmentalists saw a gap in the market for an all-electric supercar that would allow enthusiastic drivers like themselves to enjoy the California hills without causing pollution. PayPal founder Elon Musk joined the team in 2004 and became the company's CEO.

In 2005 Tesla and Lotus began to work closely together, with the British sports-car maker providing technical input and part-assembling the Roadster on its Norfolk-based production lines. However, less than 7 percent of the Elise's parts went into the Tesla.

In the first four years of production, 2,100 Roadsters were delivered to customers in thirty-one countries. With a base price of $109,000 (£87,945), the up-front costs are around three times those of its Lotus-badged cousin. But the Tesla can achieve the electric equivalent of 135 mpg (57 km per liter), with zero emissions and an estimated running cost of only two cents per mile.

In 2010 journalists from *Evo* magazine praised Tesla's upgraded Roadster Sport: "With so much torque, from literally no revs, the acceleration punch is wholly alien. Away from traffic lights you'd murder anything . . . all you have to do is floor the throttle and wave goodbye." Its performance figures are given above.

As a pollution-free U.S. product, with awesome performance and stunning looks, the Tesla is fast becoming the default choice of Hollywood's A-list celebrities. Leonardo DiCaprio, Matt Damon, and Brad Pitt have all hung up their Prius keys in favor of the electric supercar—and who can blame them? **DS**

Nano | Tata (IND)

2009 • 38 cu in/623 cc, S2 • 33 bhp/24 kW • unknown • 68 mph/109 kph

The Tata Nano is a cute four-door city car. It has a rear engine and rear-wheel drive, but, most important, it is the world's cheapest car. The Tata Nano was expressly designed to be the people's car of India, and was intended to be affordable by as many people as possible. The Nano was launched with a price tag of just 100,000 rupees ($2,100/£1,350).

It does not take long to begin to understand where the money savings have come from: the engine is a tiny, 38-cubic-inch (623-cc), two-stroke unit. There is only one wing mirror, one wiper, no power steering, no air bags, no air-conditioning, manual windows, and manual door locking. The radio is an optional extra. Tata saved more by having no tailgate access to the luggage space—users have to get to it by lowering the back seats inside the car instead.

Everything has been trimmed back: the gearbox only has four speeds instead of five, there are drum brakes not discs, and there are only three nuts holding on each wheel instead of the normal four.

Yet the design is quite eye-catching. The Nano is about the size of the original Mini, but the body is much taller and rounder. The tiny 12-inch (30-cm) wheels are at each corner. It is like a giant mobile egg.

The Nano drives better than an egg, though. The supple ride is capable of soaking up the worst of India's potholes, the turning circle is good, and the car is very economical on gas (65 mpg/4.3 liters per 100 km).

The interior is roomy, with lots of head height and legroom because the engine is under the trunk (boot) floor, not squeezed in front of the driver. It is strangely reminiscent of another "people's car"—the Beetle. **SH**

Yukon Denali | GMC

USA

2009 • 378 cu in/6,200 cc, V8 • 403 bhp/301 kW • 0–60 mph/97 kph in 8.7 seconds • 97 mph/156 kph

The 2009 Denali sits at the top end of the GMC Yukon range of powerful sport utility vehicles. One of its chief selling points is its high safety rating; the U.S. National Highway Traffic Safety Administration gave it five stars for performances in front and side crash testing.

This is a big vehicle. The four-wheel-drive version is able to tow up to 8,100 pounds (3,674 kg). The standard model is 202 inches (513 cm) long. The XL version is even bigger, a prodigious 222 inches (565 cm), and able to seat eight rather than seven people across three rows of seats. The Yukon Denali has much to offer big families; British soccer star David Beckham reportedly bought a version to drive in the United States.

Despite GMC's research into hybrid fuel technology and its commitment to the environment, this is not a vehicle that will appeal to drivers who put a premium on low fuel bills. The more efficient two-wheel-drive version of the six-speed automatic Denali returns just 12 mpg (19.6 liters per 100 km) in urban areas and 19 mpg (12.38 liters per 100 km) on the highway. The engine is built to run on unleaded gas, E85 ethanol, or even a combination of the two.

The Denali can be distinguished from other Yukons by its distinctive upper and lower honeycomb grilles, and its sporty 20-inch (51-cm) chrome-finished wheels, which are fitted as standard. The interior is smart and comfortable, characterized by the use of soft leather and chrome dashboard highlights.

This powerful vehicle offers owners the option of a blind-zone alert, especially useful when towing, that is displayed in the driver's side mirror when radar detects vehicles entering the Denali's blind spots. **SF**

Golf GTI | Volkswagen

D

2009 • 121 cu in/1,984 cc, S4 • 213 bhp/155 kW • 0–60 mph/97 kph in 6.9 seconds • 148 mph/240 kph

This model is the sixth generation of Volkswagen's punchy yet affordable turbo-charged version of the Golf, a car that has had broad appeal for more than a generation. Around 1.7 million Golf GTIs have sold since 1975. This Mark VI model, revealed at the 2008 Paris Auto Show, offered a host of subtle enhancements of the Mark V. Volkswagen did not break with its winning formula of providing practical yet stylish cars that consistently meet drivers' expectations.

This model offered a smoother, more powerful drive than its predecessor. Improvements to the soundproofing made it all the more enjoyable to drive. The backlit dashboard dials were changed to white, part of a makeover of the interior that raised the quality of the fittings and met the Zeitgeist for sleek cars. The soft plastic dashboard was given chrome and aluminum highlights and the three-spoke steering wheel helped to enhance the car's sporty feel.

All drivers are told that lowering carbon emissions is imperative to help arrest global warming and save humanity. The Golf GTI allows drivers to release a guilt-free lungful of carbon dioxide into the atmosphere as they car share with up to four other adults in a vehicle whose emissions fell to 170 g/km (274 grams per mile)—19 g/km (31 grams per mile) less than the Mark V—while offering a thrifty 39 mpg (6 liters per 100 km).

And in a safety-conscious world, Volkswagen has introduced a range of technical enhancements, including seven air bags as standard. The redesigned front fender (bumper), sporting a honeycomb grille, helps to create an impression of greater width in this new version of the Golf GTI. **SF**

R | Tramontana

E

2009 • 336 cu in/5,500 cc, V12 • 720 bhp (530 kW) • 0–60 mph/97 kph in 3.6 seconds • 200 mph/325 kph

In the Tramontana R, the driver sits in the center of the cockpit; it is like being in an Formula 1 car or a modern fighter jet. The pedals and driving position are factory-built to the driver's dimensions. Press the accelerator, and the 336-cubic-inch (5,500-cc) engine pumps out 720 bhp (530 kW) in a car that weighs about the same as a plate of rice. Acceleration from 0 to 60 mph (97 kph) takes just 3.6 seconds and the top speed is 200 mph (325 kph).

Named after a wind that sweeps over the mountains of Spain, that country's first supercar was designed by Josep Rubau, an automotive designer trained at the Royal College of Art in London. Rubau turned down a job designing machines for the *Star Wars* movie franchise in Hollywood to concentrate on car design. At first he worked for Volkswagen in Germany, but he left to create a space-age vehicle of his own.

Incredibly, his futuristic-looking idea made it into production. No more than a dozen of his idiosyncratic, rear-wheel-drive machines are built each year at a small factory on the Costa Brava.

Driver and passenger sit in line under an aircraft-style canopy, with the passenger slightly higher than driver. The hood (bonnet) badge is made of solid white gold, and the entire carbon-fiber body is fine-tuned to the physical dimensions of the buyer. Even door handles and pedals are adjusted to the driver's dimensions. And instead of a chassis number, each Tramontana R is inscribed with a line of specially composed poetry.

Power comes from a twin-turbo Mercedes V12. If the standard 550 bhp (405 kW) is not enough, a button boosts output to 720 bhp (530 kW). In a perhaps futile gesture, buyers are told not to do this in countries that restrict emissions levels. **SH**

Camaro 2SS | Chevrolet

(USA)

2009 • 378 cu in/6,200 cc, V8 • 426 bhp/318 kW • 0–60 mph/97 kph in 4.9 seconds • 155 mph/250 kph

Chevrolet's fifth-generation Camaro appeared with a stunning macho body, as though the long-standing pony car had been working out after the last generation finished. And in addition to hairy-chested retro looks, this was a muscle car that could hang on in corners as well as sprint in a straight line.

The Camaro series was first launched in 1966 to tackle the original Ford Mustang. Production of its fourth distinct version ended in 2002. General Motors then spent the next seven years creating a new car good enough to tackle the contemporary Mustang. With an engine borrowed from the Corvette, the fifth-generation Camaro had supercar performance.

The top-of-the-line 2SS model came with different engines to match the choice of gearbox. Figures for the more powerful six-speed manual transmission version are shown above. Onboard technology included launch control, adaptive stability and traction control systems, and park assist.

The car had a full leather interior but some cheap plastic, too. Traditionally it was the low quality of the cabin and the vague cornering that had put some European buyers off U.S. pony cars, and the new Camaro was only a slight improvement in their eyes. And the heavy Camaro was clearly more of a classic muscle car than its sportier Corvette stablemate.

A popular special edition in yellow with black stripes recognized the Camaro's link with the 2007 *Transformers* movie, which features Bumblebee, a device that transforms from a Camaro into a formidable fighting robot. That was just about the right image for a machine that aimed to restart the pony car wars. **SH**

Continental Supersports | Bentley

GB

2009 • 366 cu in/6,000 cc twin turbo, W12 • 621 bhp/463 kW • 0–62 mph/100 kph in 3.7 seconds • 204 mph/329 kph

Bentley makes refined grand tourers, not crazy high-performance two-door coupes . . . or does it? In 2009 Bentley unveiled the Supersports version of its Continental. The gentleman's express had become a track-day hooligan. It was the fastest, most powerful Bentley to date, with supercar levels of performance.

Bentley's new flagship was launched by American comedian and car fan Jay Leno at the Geneva Motor Show. Its specification was tantalizing: the 366-cubic-inch (6,000-cc) twin-turbo W12 had been tweaked to produce 621 bhp (463 kW). In each corner were the largest brakes ever fitted to a production car—17-inch (420-mm) carbon ceramic discs that "can tear your face off" according to BBC TV's *Top Gear* host Jeremy Clarkson.

The Supersports uses a Continental body as a base, but plenty of luxury has been ripped out in the name of saving weight. For example, there's no rear seat at all, carbon-fibre trim replaces slabs of walnut and the front "sofas" are replaced by lean carbon sports buckets.

The four-wheel-drive system has been adjusted so that most power goes to the rear, there's an upgraded active shock-absorbing system, new anti-roll bars and suspension bushes, and new 20-inch (cm) alloy wheels with high-performance Pirelli tires. All this has made the Supersports the best-handling Bentley, ever.

A Continental Supersports broke the world ice-driving speed record on the frozen sea off Finland in 2011. World Rally Champion Juha Kankkunen drove a convertible model to 206 mph (331 kph). The car had slight safety modifications, but the engine was standard. Sadly for Bentley, however, three weeks later an Audi RS6 beat the record by 0.5mph (0.8 kph). **SH**

A 2010 advertisement from Aston Martin draws attention to the sculptural aesthetics of the One-77. ⊡

Type 5 Sports Car | Harper (ZA)

2010 • 98 cu in/1,600 cc, S4 • 175 bhp/130 kW • 0–62 mph/100 kph in 6.8 seconds • 115 mph/185 kph

African track and rally driver Craig Harper was forced to cut short his race career due to the cost of the sport. Instead, he decided to create a fast, comfortable, fun, low-maintenance sports car for both road and racetrack. He came up with an acclaimed mid-engined kit car that costs no more than a small hatchback.

To check his creation, Craig drove it from Botswana to Zimbabwe to take part in an endurance track race against serious track cars, including Porsches. After coming seventh, he and his girlfriend drove 1,800 miles (3,000 km) back to Cape Town in the same car.

Now the Harper Type 5 Sports Car is being produced and sold from a workshop near Cape Town. The engine, gearbox, steering, brakes, and cooling system are standard road-going units from the Toyota Corolla, so parts and servicing costs are kept low. Buyers can build their own car or have it built for them.

Harper's body design includes huge air scoops on either side of the body that drive cooling air into the radiator, which is mounted behind the seats. The fiberglass body sits on a light, tubular steel spaceframe to give a total weight of just 1,433 pounds (650 kg). Harper claims that the Type 5 Sports Car, with tuning, is easily capable of 143 mph (230 kph). Crash protection, spaciousness, and ample luggage storage have not been forgotten, and the only thing limiting the Sports Car's practicality is the complete absence of a roof.

Owners can choose higher-performance engines, including a Honda VTEC and a Volkswagen/Audi twenty-valve turbo. At the time of writing, Harper is building a 244-cubic-inch (4,000-cc) V6-powered Type 6 version that promises astonishing performance. **SH**

One-77 | Aston Martin (GB)

2010 • 446 cu in/7,312 cc, V12 • 750 bhp/559 kW • 0–60 mph/97 kph in 3.5 seconds • 220 mph/355 kph

Every aspect of this luxury sports car indicates its exclusivity, even its name. The Aston Martin brand is widely recognized for engineering excellence, yet the "seventy-seven" in the car's name has special significance: only that total of the car will ever be made.

Some people think of the One-77 as automotive art. In 2009 the Chicago Athenaeum Museum of Architecture and Design gave Aston Martin its prestigious Good Design Award in recognition of the One-77's technical inventiveness, concept, and originality. But it is not just the appearance of the One-77's sweeping aerodynamic curves that has won plaudits; it is also the technology and engineering that went into this supercar.

The components within the svelte aluminum body paneling are hand-crafted on top of the carbon-fiber chassis at Gaydon in Warwickshire, England. The result is a highly desirable object that also happens to house the world's most powerful normally aspirated road-car engine. The blistering acceleration of the One-77 draws upon Aston Martin's racing technology and was honed following rigorous testing at the Nürburgring.

The dynamic-looking car has a low, sporty profile. Weighing 3,594 pounds (1,630 kg), it is able to produce a thrilling 553 pound-feet (750 Nm) of torque, making the One-77 a dream drive for enthusiasts. But for most people, driving the Aston Martin One-77 will remain just a dream. The basic price of this masterpiece of craftsmanship was initially reported to be $1.5 million (£1.05 million), a price that is later said to have risen to $1.75 million (£1.2 million). The first customers took delivery of their new cars in the spring of 2011. **SF**

Mulsanne | Bentley

GB

2010 • 412 cu in/6,750 cc, V8 • 505 bhp/377 kW • 0–60 mph/97 kph in 5.1 seconds • 184 mph/298 kph

Traveling in a car, have you ever thought to yourself, "This is nice, but my living room at home is nicer"? Or maybe even, "Okay, so I'm travelling at high speed, but what I really need is to feel like I'm in the drawing room of a country house"? In the unlikely chance that you have, maybe you should consider taking a ride in a Bentley Mulsanne.

This car is big and weighs 2.5 tons. It is powerful, with a 412-cubic-inch (6,750-cc) twin-turbo V8 running through an eight-speed automatic gearbox to the rear wheels, and it is quick: 184 mph (298 kph). But it is also ridiculously comfortable, with masses of space in the back for two passengers. There is a third seat in the middle, but most have this folded down to access the air-conditioning controls, entertainment system, and überupmarket cup holders.

At its launch in 2010, the Mulsanne was Bentley's flagship vehicle. Named for the fastest straight on the Le Mans circuit (the scene of many a Bentley triumph in the past), it was also the first Bentley to be entirely designed and built at the company's Crewe plant since 1930. As an indication of who the car's key customers were, the Mulsanne was unveiled in California, at the prestigious Pebble Beach Concours d'Elegance classic car event. California is Bentley's biggest market in the United States, and the country is the company's biggest global market.

What drives millionaire Americans to buy a car built in Crewe? It is not just its power, style, or comfort, but its Britishness. One American reviewer said, "In most cars you comment on the quality of the plastics. In the Bentley we couldn't find any." **JI**

Ampera | Vauxhall

USA

2010 • 85 cu in/1,400 cc, S4, and electric • 80 bhp/59 kW (gas) • 0–60 mph/97 kph in 9 seconds • 100 mph/161 kph

General Motors (GM) has produced a new version of the hybrid concept. Called the Volt in the United States and Australia and the Ampera in Europe, the car has a 149-bhp (111-kW) electric motor but switches to a gasoline engine when it runs out of charge. The gasoline engine helps out by powering the electric motor, recharging the batteries at the same time to extend the car's range.

The system is a truly innovative solution to the problem plaguing all electric cars to date: the limited range of a single battery charge. The Volt/Ampera's batteries can only guarantee a 40-mile (64-km) range, but with the help of the gasoline engine this is extended to around 310 miles (500 km).

The interaction between gasoline and electric power is complicated. For climbing long, steep hills, for example, the car uses both powerplants at the same time to maintain full performance. The batteries can be recharged in the normal way from a mains socket in about six hours.

The car is expensive for a small, five-door family hatchback, but costs far less to run than a gasoline-only equivalent. It is difficult to work out the mileage of such a complex powertrain, but GM claims up to 175 mpg (1.6 liters per 100 km) is possible. CO_2 figures are very low, about a quarter of a purely gasoline-powered car. Tax and additional charges are low or nonexistent, depending on the country. And the maker reckons that on about 80 percent of trips, drivers will not use the gasoline engine at all—meaning that for most of its life the Volt/Ampera will be completely emission-free. **SH**

Focus RS500 | Ford

D

2010 • 154 cu in/2,521 cc, S5 • 345 bhp/257 kW • 0–60 mph/97 kph in 5.4 seconds • 165 mph/265 kph

Do the engineers at Ford Europe never know when to stop? First they made the Focus, probably the best-handling family hatchback there is. Then they made the excellent turbocharged ST, which took peak power to 223 bhp (166 kW). They then went on to produce the Focus RS, with power up to 301 bhp (224 kW) and a top speed of 164 mph (264 kph).

Now, most people might think that was enough: they had effectively raised the bar to an all-time high in terms of hot-hatch performance. But the Ford team just couldn't let it lie and came up with the limited-edition Focus RS500 (the "500" referring to the total that they would build) This made even more power: 345 bhp (257 kW) at 6,000 rpm.

The RS500 underwent a range of engine modifications, including a new engine control unit (ECU), new exhaust downpipe, larger intercooler for the turbo, and bigger air filter. The six-speed manual transmission system also got an upgrade. A sophisticated limited-slip differential helped feed all that power through the front wheels without too much torque steer.

Inside the cabin, there were subtle touches such as a metal plaque with each car's production number. But the most obvious difference was on the outside: every RS500 was "wrapped" in a matte back body covering by a specialist German firm close to the Ford factory. The wrap made it look like a stealth machine which, given the throatiness of the new exhaust, it certainly was not.

It is a sign of how much the British love their hot hatches (and the Focus) that, of the 500 RSs made, 101 were earmarked for the United Kingdom. **JI**

Range Rover Evoque | Land Rover

GB

2010 • 122 cu in/1,999 cc, S4 • 237 bhp/177 kW • 0–60 mph/97 kph in 7.1 seconds • 135 mph/217 kph

The Range Rover Evoque is summed up by the decision to use soccer wife and fashion queen Victoria Beckham as a consultant before its launch—it is all about style. The Evoque was launched in 2010 at a glittering party in London to celebrate forty years of the Range Rover—the vehicle that shocked the world by adding luxury to the previously utilitarian Land Rover.

As the Range Rover had grown more opulent and city-bound, a smaller, urban fashion statement was a natural progression. The small Evoque is sleek and mean, and its body shape is closer to a coupe than a sport utility vehicle, especially as a three-door.

The production Evoque stuck close to Land Rover's wedgy LRX concept, which made a splash at the 2007 Detroit Auto Show. Land Rover took 18,000 orders before production began. Each Evoque took twenty-nine hours to build, and in the first year, one was rolling off the line every seventy seconds. The vehicle shared the same D-class platform as the Land Rover Freelander, Ford Mondeo, and Volvo S60, among others. It felt lighter and more nimble than previous Range Rovers and extremely carlike on the road.

The 122-cubic-inch (1,999-cc) four-cylinder turbo gasoline engine was the smoothest and most powerful engine option, but Europe's favorite was the gruff 134-cubic-inch (2,200-cc) TD4 diesel. Two- or four-wheel drive were offered and, to keep the brand DNA intact, the four-wheel-drive version offered proper off-road and wading capability for those who wanted it. In real life, however, you're more likely to see Victoria's stilettos churning up the mud than an Evoque's big, shiny wheels. **LT**

GTX | Devon

USA

2010 • 513 cu in/8,400 cc, V10 • 650 bhp/478 kW • unknown • unknown

The Devon GTX supercar was the result of Los Angeles–based American entrepreneur Scott Devon asking Swedish designer Daniel Paulin to draw a spectacular body for a high-priced, high-performance two-seater. Race driver Justin Bell was employed to help fine-tune it.

Paulin's design was a blend of classic sports car and futuristic science fiction. Front and rear overhangs were minimal, the doors opened in an up-and-over style, and the front and rear wheel surrounds were made a different color from the rest of the body.

The interior design was minimalist. Swathes of black and white leather led to a clean electronic dashboard. The six-speed manual gearbox was operated by a retro 1970s muscle-car gearshift sprouting from the central transmission tunnel, topped by a white knob. Seats were lightweight carbon fiber.

An aircraft-quality carbon-fiber body was mounted on a steel frame, with a V10 engine sourced from the Dodge Viper driving the rear wheels. The independent suspension had a damping system; the brakes, tires, and wheels were all high-performance components.

With this setup the performance was staggering, as was the price, about $500,000 (£300,000). An even lighter and faster track-going version was also available for an extra $24,000 (£15,000). Devon claimed the engine was the most powerful naturally aspirated production powertrain on the market. It set production car lap records at Willow Springs and Laguna Seca.

After the excitement of its launch at the 2009 Pebble Beach Concours, however, the GTX seemed to stall on the startline for business reasons. At the time of writing, only two cars had been produced. **SH**

458 Italia | Ferrari

(I)

2010 • 275 cu in/4,500 cc, V8 • 652 bhp/413 kW • 0–62 mph/100 kph in 3.4 seconds • 202 mph/325 kph

Ferrari claimed that its new supercar had the highest power-per-liter output of any nonturbo car. With its maximum power coming at a screaming 9,000 rpm, the Italia was the highest-revving Ferrari of all time.

But then things started to go wrong. A spate of 458s were destroyed by fire erupting in their rear wheel arches. After five of the $270,000 (£170,000) supercars were wrecked, Ferrari engineers discovered that one of their glues melted at high temperature, dripped onto the hot exhaust pipe, and ignited. The lightweight aluminum body simply melted in the ensuing blaze.

Ferrari had to write to all 1,200 buyers of the 458 so far, asking them to bring back their $336-million (£212-million) worth of cars to be adapted with old-fashioned rivets instead of glue. Owners included rock star Eric Clapton and U.K. media personality Chris Evans.

As if that was not bad enough publicity, Ferrari was also hit by news that another brand-new 458 with a special $104,000 (£65,000) Dolce & Gabbana interior was completely destroyed by an unrelated fire at a London airport. Mischievous Web sites carried a spate of photographs of 458s involved in serious crashes.

Whether this was a jinx or just jealousy, the negative press overshadowed the fact that the 458 was an extraordinary car, with an ultra-aerodynamic body, superlight, record-breaking engine, and classic mid-engine layout. It had active aerodynamics and a superfast seven-speed semiautomatic gearbox. With extensive testing assistance from race champion Michael Schumacher, Ferrari used Formula 1 technology for the brakes, transmission, and handling to create a sensational race car for the road. **SH**

⟨ A bird's-eye view of the 2010 Aston Martin Rapide sports car reveals the unusually spacious seating for four people.

Rapide | Aston Martin (GB)

2010 • 362 cu in/5,935 cc, V12 • 470 bhp/350 kW • 0–62 mph/100 kph in 5.3 seconds • 188 mph/296 kph

Describing a vehicle as a sports car with four seats might sound a little bit like wishful thinking; some people might suspect a compromise. The Rapide, though, really is a sports car and, despite the sleek exterior of this Aston Martin, it is easily large enough to transport four adults.

That might come as a surprise, given the low, sweeping form of this supercar. The curves of the Rapide, reminiscent of an elongated coupe, have been compared to the "muscular haunches of a race horse." Given the kick that this rear-wheel-drive car offers its pilot, it might seem strange that passengers could ever be anything other than thrilled by the ride. Yet, should the attention of those in the rear seats wane, they can watch movies on the LCD screens of the entertainment system located in the backs of the seats ahead of them. A Bang & Olufsen system can provide the sound, unless the passenger chooses to use headphones.

The concept of this car was shown at the 2006 Detroit Auto Show and plans for production started a year later, after Aston Martin had been sold by Ford. Built in Graz, Austria, the powerful yet elegant Rapide, priced at £139,950 ($190,000), allowed the carmaker to broaden its ability to compete with other luxury automotive brands.

The Rapide's 20-inch (50.8-cm) diameter ten-spoke wheels and swept back bixenon headlights look sporty and contemporary, and this car has a performance to match its looks. The damping system aids handling, and Aston Martin's Hydraulic Brake Assist system enables safer braking within short distances. This is a vehicle either to drive or be driven in. **SF**

Spirra | Oullin (ROK)

2010 • 165 cu in/2,700 cc, V6 • 493 bhp/363 kW • 0–60 mph/97 kph in 3.5 seconds • 186 mph/300 kph

The Oullin Spirra of South Korea has the rare automotive distinction of being produced by a husband-and-wife team.

In the early 1990s, Han-chul Kim and his wife, Ji-sun Choi, both automotive experts, quit their jobs in leading Korean car companies to work as consultants for other carmakers. They wanted to make their own supercar, and what began as a dream developed into a full-blown development project. In 2001 their "PS-II" prototype was presented to the press.

Despite being the world's fifth-largest auto-manufacturing country, Korea had never produced high-performance cars. Establishing a small-scale, hand-built production line for such an exotic car was problematic. A decade and four generations of complete reengineering proved necessary.

But the result is impressive. The Oullin is powered by a Hyundai V6 that is available with four different outputs. The most powerful version uses twin-turbos to create up to 493 bhp (363 kW). With a six-speed manual gearbox, this version has true supercar performance.

The car is built to the modern race-bred formula of lightweight carbon-fiber body, stiff tubular space-frame chassis, and lightweight high-power engine mounted in the middle for balance. The look, while definitely in supercar territory, is deliberately less overtly aggressive than that of many rivals.

How good is it? The couple raced a Spirra with a tuned 600-bhp (450-kW) version of the V6 in the Korean GT Masters Championship, taking two consecutive wins against fully race-prepared Porsche 911 GT3 RSRs, BMW M3s, and Nissan 350Zs. **SH**

Plethore | HTT

CND

2010 • 378 cu in/6,200 cc, V8 • 750 bhp/552 kW • 0–62 mph/100 kph in 2.8 seconds • 241 mph/388 kph

Canada's first homemade supercar was made to the same formula as many rookie supercars. Its Corvette ZR1 supercharged V8 engine is mounted in the middle of a rigid lightweight carbon-fiber chassis and an outrageous, head-turning body.

In this Montreal-built street race car, the driver sits centrally for perfect balance, as in the McLaren F1. Two passengers can sit on either side. The engine is mounted low to reduce the center of gravity and the aluminum sports suspension and drivetrain help to keep weight down to just 2,750 pounds (1,250 kg).

HTT claimed the Plethore was the "best balanced car that's ever been built." The engineering team had also managed to squeeze 750 bhp (552 kW) from the Corvette V8 engine. The figures above are estimates as none had been released at the time of writing.

Rather playfully, the "HTT" of the company name stood for "High-Tech Toy." Buyers found plenty of state-of-the-art technology and gadgets to justify the name, including suspension that is electronically adjustable, two rear cameras with internal dash-mounted LCD screen, a hands-free phone system, and sophisticated automatic climate control. The Plethore's scissor doors open by remote control to reveal a leather-clad cabin, seven-speaker hi-fi, and a six-speed sequential gearbox.

In 2011 HTT founders Sébastien Forest and Carl Descoteaux presented their supercar on Canadian TV's version of *Shark Tank* (*Dragon's Den*). Two of the judges were so impressed that they immediately invested $1,500,000 (£1,000,000) for a 20 percent stake in the company. They also ordered a car each for themselves. **SH**

Superlight | Rapier

USA

2010 • 378 cu in/6,200 cc, V8 • 638 bhp/469 kW • 0–60 mph/97 kph in 3.2 seconds • 222 mph/357 kph

Knowing that even supercar buyers feel the recession, Rapier came up with a payment plan: pay 50 percent of the Superlight's price tag, then sit back for nine months while the Boston-based team build by hand the super coupe. In the meantime, buyers can access an online photo diary of their car being built. At the end of the wait they get one of the world's fastest supercars . . . and the bill for the rest of the $179,000 (£113,000) car.

The nine months are well spent. The Rapier team build each car around the buyer's physical dimensions and personal preferences. For example, there are fourteen different colors (including pink and purple), three engines (the Corvette ZR1 unit is most powerful—its figures are given above), various interior trims, and a long list of gadgets buyers may want fitted. There are nine types of wheels to choose from.

Rapier claims the Superlight to be "the most exotic custom-built supercar on the planet." It certainly looks the part with its aircraft-style cockpit canopy, scissor doors, and huge rear wing. The Superlight lives up to its name, too; the chassis is aluminum, the body is composite. Rapier claims a weight of 2,375 pounds (1,077 kg)—1,000 pounds (454 kg) less than the Corvette that features the same engine. The engine sits behind the passengers, powering the rear wheels through a six-speed manual gearbox.

With its 222-mph (357-kph) top speed, it is no surprise that the Superlight is considered a semitrack car, so a roll cage and quick-release steering wheel are incorporated. The suspension is race standard, too. And to slow them down to legal speeds, drivers will appreciate the enormous race-specification brakes. **SH**

Vantage N420 | Aston Martin (GB)

2010 • 289 cu in/4,735 cc, V8 • 420 bhp/313 kW • 0–62 mph/100 kph in 4.9 seconds • 180 mph/240 kph

The V8 Vantage N420 was a sportier, special-edition version—produced both as a roadster and coupe—of Aston Martin's V8 Vantage. The look is essentially that of a classic sports model rather than an overtly aggressive racer. The wheels, though, with a glossy black finish and ten spokes, could be made to work hard.

The N420 is 60 pounds (27 kg) lighter than the standard car, mainly due to the use of carbon fiber, including in the seats. The interior has a smart contemporary feel and includes graphite instruments. The basic price of this vehicle, £96,995 ($137,000), included a classic leather or stylish black Alcantara steering wheel.

One of the chief differences between this and the V8 Vantage is that the Sports Pack suspension came as standard on the N420. Lessons learned by Aston Martin at Nürburgring also inspired enhancements to the shock absorbers, springs, and anti-roll bars, making for a more responsive driving experience.

For fans of motorsport, the distinctive, powerful sound of the N420's exhaust system was a thrill. Pushing a car through its six gears, either in manual or using the Sportshift option to maximize the engine's performance during changes, had never sounded so good, according to Aston fans. **SF**

New Stratos | Lancia (I)

2010 • 263 cu in/4,308 cc, V8 • 540 bhp/397 kW • 0–62 mph/100 kph in 3.3 seconds • 170 mph/274 kph

When the Bertone-styled Lancia Stratos prototype was unveiled at the 1971 Turin Auto Show, it completely reshaped the way people thought about automotive design. The "Plastic Dart," with its wraparound windows and aggressive stance, made such an impact on German businessman and Stratos aficionado Michael Stoschek that, for more than a decade, he pursued his dream to resurrect the iconic rally car in a modern form.

Stoschek first backed the Fenomenon Stratos concept car, which was one of the stars of the 2005 Geneva Motor Show. When that project started to stall, Stoschek commissioned Bertone to build him a one-off Stratos for his own use, based on the shortened chassis of a Ferrari 430 Scuderia. The New Stratos's body structure paid homage to the 1970s rally-honed supercar but was made entirely of carbon fiber. Powered by a V8, it had more than twice the power-to-weight ratio of the original roadgoing Stratos.

In 2010 a short production run of fifty cars was announced. However, the same internal politics that killed off the original Lancia Stratos would also cause Stoschek's New Stratos to remain a one-off. In 2011 Ferrari, perhaps fearing that the New Stratos would be a strong competitor to its own 458 Italia, forbade its suppliers from continuing to support the project. **DS**

DS3 Racing | Citroën (F)

2010 • 98 cu in/1,598 cc, S4 • 205 bhp/157 kW • 0–60 mph/97 kph in 6.9 seconds • 146 mph/235 kph

As far as car buyers are concerned, Citroën has never really capitalized on its successes in the World Rally Championship (WRC). There was a special-edition C4, named after driving genius Sebastién Loeb, but that was just an exercise in sticker placement and white wheels. Only with the DS3 Racing's arrival has Citroën's motorsport success been shouted from the rooftops.

The recipe was simple: take one DS3 (Citroën's current weapon of choice in WRC competition). Throw in a turbocharged 98-cubic-inch (1,598-cc) engine as used in the BMW Mini Cooper S John Cooper Works. Have the racing division work on the suspension, to make the car lower and wider than the standard DS3, and beef up the braking so the car can stop on a dime. And tune the steering to enable the car to handle 205 bhp (157 kW) coming through the front wheels.

The result is a car with astonishing power for its size, coupled to incredible roadholding and the ride of a much bigger car. Would-be WRC heroes can switch off the DS3 Racing's clever handling electronics.

Oh, and one more part of the recipe: throw in some mystique by telling the world that only 1,000 will be built (well, maybe 2,000 is closer to the truth) and watch orders flood in, even at an asking price of $35,400 (£23,000). **JI**

Ibiza Cupra Bocanegra | Seat (E)

2010 • 85 cu in/1,390 cc, S4 • 178 bhp/133 kW • 0–60 mph/97 kph in 7.2 seconds • 140 mph/255 kph

As part of the Volkswagen (VW) group, the Seat Ibiza is part of the same family as the Skoda Fabia and VW Polo. All three come in various hot versions, so Seat, marketed as "sporty with a bit of character," had to find a niche to call its own. With the Ibiza Cupra Bocanegra it went for lots of power and a front end painted black (Bocanegra means "black nose"). The engine and mechanics were the same as the slightly cheaper Cupra model so the changes for the Bocanegra were cosmetic, with splashes of black around the car, different wheels, and a central exhaust.

The engine was supercharged and turbocharged to give a broad spread of power plus good economy. VW's clever seven-speed DSG electronic transmission could operate in manual or automatic mode. The latter made driving much easier in traffic, while the paddle changes were quick to respond out on the open road. The Bocanegra had an electronic system that mimicked a mechanical limited-slip differential, braking individual wheels to aid grip when cornering.

The problem was that the Skoda Fabia vRS was equipped with the same engine and gearbox and gave the same performance. It also offered more room inside. Worst of all for the Seat, the Skoda cost a lot less—but then it did not have a black nose. **JI**

With its distinctive gull-wing doors, the 2010 Mercedes SLS AMG is a sleek update of Mercedes's 300SL, a 1950s classic. ▷

SC7 | Orca (FL)

2010 • 256 cu in/4,200 cc, V8 • 850 bhp/634 kW • 0–62 mph/100 kph in 2.6 seconds • 248 mph/400 kph

After around twenty years of experimenting with prototypes, trying to build a rival to the world's quickest road cars in his tiny workshop in Vaduz, Liechtenstein, Swiss engineer and designer René Beck came up with the amazing Orca SC7.

This exotic car had the lightweight aluminum twin-turbo V8 from the Audi A6 in the middle of an ultralightweight hyperaerodynamic carbon-fiber body. It weighed just 1,874 pounds (850 kg) and had the classic mid-engine, rear-wheel-drive configuration. German specialists MTM tuned the engine to produce 850 bhp (634 kW), and a seven-speed sequential gearbox was installed to handle all that power.

The chassis was very sophisticated. It comprised three large carbon-fiber, aluminum, and nomex pieces with ten composite panels screwed in place to form the body. An active suspension system raised or lowered the ride height, while electronically controlled damping optimized roadholding at speed.

The body's styling cues seemed to come from the Stealth bomber rather than from any other current cars. It incorporated gull-wing doors, two rear spoilers, and plenty of vents and cooling ducts, including two just above the cockpit roof.

With 1,874 pounds (850 kg) propelled by 850 bhp (634 kW), the Orca was one of the few cars ever to achieve the engineer's holy grail of a power-to-weight ratio of just one—hence its extraordinary performance.

Beck made only seven of the "Street Competition" cars, a fact reflected in the SC7 name. They are believed to have been sold to very wealthy buyers. After that, Beck move on to other supercar projects. **SH**

SLS AMG | Mercedes-Benz (D)

2010 • 379 cu in/6,208 cc, V8 • 563 bhp/419 kW • 0–62 mph/100 kph in 3.8 seconds • 197 mph/317 kph

The Mercedes-Benz SLS was created by AMG's Gorden Wagener, who needed a replacement for the McLaren-developed SLR. The sensational replacement was unveiled at the 2009 Frankfurt Motor Show. The SLS was deliberately evocative of the Mercedes 300SL, one of the company's most graceful designs.

The first things to gasp at were the gull-wing doors, which opened on gas struts. But the rest of the car was pretty awesome, too. The aluminum space-frame chassis was made by hand. Under the hood (bonnet), AMG installed a mighty V8, with a seven-speed, dual-clutch, semiautomatic gearbox controlled by metal paddles behind the steering wheel. Various chassis settings were available to ensure the SLS performed as well on the boulevards as it did on the back straight of racetracks. Other advanced technical quirks included lightweight carbon-fiber mechanical components and explosive bolts that freed the gull-wing doors in the event of their being forced shut by an accident. Race-style carbon-ceramic brakes were an option.

The SLS AMG had nearly perfect 50:50 weight distribution and a reputation for being easy to drive despite the huge power available. Nevertheless, eight air bags and a plethora of electronic safety aids were in place should the driver struggle to cope with a top speed of almost 200 mph (321 kph).

Hollywood actor Eddie Murphy owned one in black, and the SLS gained considerable exposure as the safety car in the 2010 Formula 1 series.

At the time of writing, Mercedes is working on a new SLS with improved performance . . . powered by an electric motor at each wheel. **RD**

197 MBC

RCZ | Peugeot

F

2010 • 98 cu in/1,600 cc, S4 • 197 bhp/147 kW • 0–62 mph/100 kph in 7.6 seconds • 147 mph/237 kph

Peugeot had made a crazy concept car in 2007. It was a futuristic sports coupe that bore no relation to the French company's rather bland current offerings. Peugeot had no plans to build such a mad contraption, but the outcry from press and public was so positive, it began to have second thoughts. Maybe, thought Peugeot, it could recapture some of the kudos it had lost since the 205GTi, the Mi16, and the 406 Coupe.

So the concept car went into production and the RCZ was the result. The striking, sporty coupe was an instant success and Peugeot sold 30,000 within a year.

This car is all about its looks. Underneath is a small, front-mounted turbo engine, shared with the MINI, that drives the front wheels. The car has the mechanical trimmings of a mildly hot hatchback, and its handling and performance are similar, too.

The body is a truly innovative design, with a "double-bubble" cockpit roof curving down into the rear window. Aluminum-effect pillars, chunky wheel arches, knife-slash headlights, and a self-raising rear spoiler, all combine to give the RCZ real road presence.

Buyers can opt for an alternative 122-cubic-inch (2,000-cc) diesel version and choose luxuries such as heated leather seats, JBL hi-fi, bigger alloy wheels, and directional xenon headlights. But inside the car, apart from a chunky sports steering wheel, this could be a Peugeot 308 family hatchback—except that there is less space in the back of this coupe.

A hybrid RCZ concept car using an all-wheel-drive system and a diesel–electric power mix has been built by Peugeot. At the time of writing it is only a project—but then again, so was the RCZ at one time. **SH**

CTS-V | Cadillac

USA

2010 • 376 cu in/6,162 cc, V8 • 550 bhp/410 kW • 0–60 mph/97 kph in 3.9 seconds • 191 mph/308 kph

The Cadillac CTS-V is a car that has pulled off a pretty amazing feat. It is an all-U.S. sedan (saloon) that has successfully managed to challenge the very best offerings from the United Kingdom and the Continent.

This car began life as the fairly humdrum CTS rear-wheel-drive family sedan, part of Cadillac's U.S.-market lineup. But the CTS-V's engine is a supercharged V8, based on a motor from the C6 Corvette. It produces 550 bhp (410 kW), through either a six-speed manual transmission or an automatic box with paddle shifters.

But all this power would be nothing without great handling—something that few U.S. cars are famous for. That is where the CTS-V excels. It has fully independent suspension (with not a live axle or leaf-spring in sight) and a multilink setup at the rear. The car has MagneRide technology, where fluid-filled shock absorbers are automatically adjusted as the car moves, on the basis of sensor readings taken every one-thousandth of a second. The steering is also speed-sensitive.

Inside the CTS-V are plenty of details and gadgets, including a gauge that measures lateral g-forces and a flashing LED alert to tell forgetful or inexperienced drivers when to change gear upward.

The most important question, of course, is how well does the car handle on the road or track? Or to be more precise, how well does it handle compared to rivals such as a BMW M5 or Jaguar XFR? The answer is absolutely brilliantly. One of the CTS-V's claims to fame is that it broke the record for the fastest lap at the Nürburgring for a production sedan car.

Without question, this was a car that the motoring world beyond U.S. shores had to take seriously. **JI**

B2 | Marussia

(RUS)

2010 • 171 cu in/2,800 cc, V6 • 450 bhp/310 kW • 0–62 mph/100 kph in 3.8 seconds • 160 mph/250 kph

Having created Russia's first supercar, the sexy, curvy B1, the Moscow-based Marussia operation took the same chassis to build its second supercar, the more aggressive B2. The pair have the same Cosworth engine choices, lightweight chassis, high-powered brakes, and luxury features. They even have the same price: about 4 million rubles ($133,000/£85,000).

The new ultrarich Russian elite can customize either of the body styles, and custom-design the interior, too. Marussia is even considering offering a race version, a sport utility vehicle version, and one with electric power—all of them sitting on the same space-frame chassis with carbon-fiber panels.

The exciting B2 is a lightweight, mid-engined two-seater of Italian-influenced design. The V6 engine sits transversely on the rear axle and operates through a six-speed automatic gearbox. Various engine sizes and outputs are available, with the top of the range being a 450 bhp (310kW) unit (performance figures above). The interior is a mix of high-tech LCD information screens (using 4G communications and a 320-GB hard drive) and traditional, finely stitched, soft-touch leather coverings on everything from seats to gear lever.

The man behind the project is Russian singer, TV personality, and race driver Nikolai Fomenko. He claims that around a third of the car parts are sourced from Russia, and the rest from established makers elsewhere.

Marussia does not lack financial backing. Its first showroom opened in Moscow in 2010, and in that year Marussia also acquired a significant stake in the Virgin Racing Formula 1 team. New showrooms in London and Monaco are also planned. **SH**

ST-1 | Zenvo

(DK)

2010 • 427 cu in/7,000 cc, V8 • 1,104 bhp/812 kW • 0–60 mph/97 kph in 2.9 seconds • 233 mph/375 kph

Denmark's first car ever is built by hand in a small workshop on the island of Zealand. The country is not known for having an automotive tradition, so people might expect something rather amateur and experimental from such a rural spot.

But they would be wrong. Zenvo makes a world-class sports machine for which customers gladly pay more than $1.8 million (£1.2 million). Zenvo plans to build only fifteen cars to maintain the ST-1's exclusivity, which is a shame because the ST-1 has one of the most striking bodies of any modern supercar, and some of the hottest performance figures around.

The ST-1 is designed to the modern supercar norm—rear-wheel drive for handling, mid-engine for balance, and an aerodynamic carbon-fiber body for lightness and rigidity. Its body has huge air intakes to cool the engine and brakes, and arch contours to manage the high-speed airflow, but Zenvo seems to have incorporated the elements into an attractive whole. Zenvo says the design was inspired by stormtroopers' uniforms in the *Star Wars* movies.

The huge Zenvo-made engine has a monstrous power output thanks to both supercharging and turbocharging. The top speed is limited to 233 mph (375 kph), mainly to protect the tires.

Incredibly, an even hotter version has been produced for the United States, with a power hike to 1,233 bhp (907 kW). Only three examples of this ST-1 50S will be built, and its performance will be even more eye-watering. And if that is not enough to swing the sale, buyers also get a "free" exclusive Swiss watch with the car, worth around $50,000 (£30,000). **SH**

Leaf | Nissan

J

2010 • electric motor • 107 bhp/80 kW • 0–60 mph/97 kph in 9.9 seconds • 93 mph/150 kph

The Nissan Leaf was the world's first mass-produced zero-emission electric car. Built in Japan, the United States, and the United Kingdom, it is a five-seater, five-door hatchback with an electric motor driving the front wheels. Its conventional layout and good performance gave the Leaf mainstream appeal; Nissan bosses expected to churn out 250,000 vehicles a year when its three car plants were working at full capacity.

While the Leaf has cutting-edge aerodynamics, designed to improve performance and extend range, it is not universally praised for its looks. Nor is the Leaf a cheap car to buy, although the retail price varies across the world; in 2012 it cost $27,700 (£25,990) after considerable government subsidies.

What really did appeal to early adopters were its frugal running costs. *Consumer Reports* magazine found, during one extended road test, that the Leaf had an average running cost of 3.5 cents per mile; by comparison, the best-selling Toyota Corolla cost around 12 cents per mile. It could achieve the electric equivalent of 106 mpg (45 km per liter).

Nissan claims that the Leaf has a typical range of 73 miles (117 km) under normal driving conditions, and 95 percent of the world's population commute fewer than 62 miles (100 km) per day. Fully recharging the Leaf typically takes eight hours using a 240-volt power supply, while Nissan's DC fast-charger recharges the battery to 80-percent capacity in just thirty minutes.

In 2010 the Leaf won the World Car of the Year award. Later that year, *Wired* magazine declared, "Nissan hasn't built a remarkable electric car. It's built a remarkable car that happens to be electric." **DS**

New Beetle | Volkswagen

D

2011 • 122 cu in/2,000 cc, S4 • 197 bhp/145 kW • 0–62 mph/100 kph in 7.3 seconds • 139 mph/224 kph

The first version was a pioneering showpiece of Hitler's Third Reich. The second was a cartoonlike, retro-kitsch machine. This third version is, at last, the desirable car the Volkswagen (VW) Beetle always wanted to be. The New Beetle is still a reinvented icon, but now it looks better than ever, with a lower, wider stance and a curving coupe rear that conjures up the long-lost link between Porsche and the original Beetle.

Under the three-door-hatch skin, the car is mostly a retro-bodied version of the VW Golf and Jetta, built in the same factory in Mexico that made some of the first- and second-generation cars. This time it is more macho, and VW hopes it will attract more male buyers.

The 2.0 TSI model is based on the VW Golf GTI with an optional seven-speed DSG double-clutch gearbox. The TSI figures are given above. VW has not confirmed whether a superhot Beetle R concept, shown at the Frankfurt Motor Show in 2011, will ever join the line.

The New Beetle is good, but, like the 1998 remake, it is mostly aimed at those who value style above substance. It is slower and less agile than the equivalent Golf, but appears to have more character and style. To cement this appeal, the Beetle Mark III comes with a range of premium features and options. These include a Fender-branded 400-watt hi-fi, Bluetooth system, keyless entry, push-button start, and tilt-slide sunroof.

The New Beetle's launch in 2011 was another sign of the times. It is hard to imagine what the makers of the original model would have thought of the global musical launch events that VW arranged for the car in conjunction with MTV. They were held simultaneously in Berlin, New York, and Shanghai. **SH**

1-Series M Coupe | BMW

D

2011 • 182 cu in/2,979 cc, S6 • 335 bhp/246 kW • 0–62 mph/100 kph in 4.9 seconds • 155 mph/250 kph

The BMW 1-Series was on sale for eight years before the German carmaker finally launched its M version. It was worth the wait. The 1-Series M Coupe was less a range-topper for the baby BMW range and more a mini-supercar. It was still a compact rear-wheel-drive car, but its lightweight chassis, stiffened sports suspension, and high-performance compound disk brakes came from the M3, the race-bred flagship of the bigger 3-Series.

Further, the big turbocharged 182-cubic-inch (2,979-cc) engine came from the BMW 335, which gave the small two-door a hefty 155-mph (250-kph) electronically limited top speed.

On the road, there was no mistaking the lines of the new 1M Coupe. Its body was a widened pastiche of a BMW 1-Series with bulging wheel arches accommodating a wider track and bigger wheels for better handling. Four exhaust pipes poked out from under the chunky rear end, where a spoiler ensured reduced body lift at high speeds. At the front end, an aerodynamic air dam forced cooling air into the engine through big ducts. The car was only available in white, black, or bright orange.

Inside, the 1M Coupe was dominated by black leather with contrasting stitching. A short, stubby lever operated a lightweight six-speed manual gearbox, and an "M" button on the multifunction steering wheel gave drivers the chance to immediately sharpen all the car's responses for extrasporty driving.

The cramped rear seats really only suit children or very short journeys. But at least they fold down for extra trunk (boot) space—although that was probably the last thing on most buyers' minds. **SH**

C30 Electric | Volvo

S

2011 • electric motor • 110 bhp/81 kW • 0–62 mph/100 kph in 10.5 seconds • 81 mph/130 kph

The Volvo C30 Electric looks like a normal Volvo C30 hatchback and has all the style, safety, and comfort of the standard car. The difference is that it is powered solely by electricity, entirely without exhaust emissions, and has a range of up to 93 miles (150 km) on a single charge. When it first appeared in 2010, the C30 Electric was one of the first genuinely attractive and usable mainstream electric cars. It was even a little faster and better-handling than the diesel version.

The C30's electric motor is housed under the hood (bonnet) and is powered by U.S.-made lithium-ion batteries sited where the fuel tank and transmission tunnel would normally be. Trunk (boot) space is unchanged. The batteries add 617 pounds (280 kg) to the weight. The lower center of gravity enables the car to hold the road better than the regular version.

The battery is charged from the mains via a socket under a flap in the front grille. A depleted battery takes about eight hours to recharge, but a 150-minute charge will add 25 miles (40 km) to the car's range.

There is no exhaust pipe. Inside the car the rev counter is replaced by a power-flow meter that shows whether the battery is being depleted or regenerated by the braking system. A small display shows the range remaining to the driver. The gear lever is now a stubby chrome lever that pushes forward to engage reverse, or backward to activate drive.

The C30 Electric has a DRIVe heating system that uses bio-ethanol fuel to warm the car without depleting battery power. As in all electric cars, progress is generally silent, and initial performance is impressive because all the power is delivered instantly. **SH**

M600 | Noble

GB

2011 • 271 cu in/4,439 cc, V8 • 650 bhp (484 kW) • 0–60 mph/97 kph in 3.5 seconds • 225 mph (362 kph)

The M600 is a sports car from British low-volume manufacturer Noble Automotive. Company founder Lee Noble learned his trade in Formula 1, and although he left Noble to form Fenix Automotive before the M600 was launched, the car is clearly inspired by the low weight and high power of Formula 1 cars. Unlike the Ford V6-engined M12 and M400 that preceded it, the M600 has a mid-mounted Yamaha-built V8 boosted by twin turbochargers. The only gearbox on offer is a six-speed manual. The chassis is stainless steel and the panels are carbon fiber.

Noble trims the interior to the buyer's taste, but there are few luxuries—this is a sports car above all else. In uncertain financial times, a delayed launch, an expensive model, and an obscure brand spell that the car is seldom encountered on the road, but anyone who does will remember its sound for life.

Autocar magazine called it "one of the most exciting British sports cars in history." With the same power-to-weight ratio as a Bugatti Veyron, things are made even more "exciting" on wet roads thanks to a complete lack of safety aids. The car does have traction control, activated from under a red toggle-switch cover lifted from an RAF fighter-bomber. In this analogue supercar, it is probably best not to touch it. **RD**

SV12 R Biturbo | Brabus

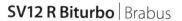

D

2011 • 384 cu in/6,300 cc, V12 • 800 bhp/588 kW • 0–62 mph/100 kph in 3.9 seconds • 217 mph/350 kph

The SV12 R Biturbo—the Brabus version of a Mercedes S-Class—is the world's fastest limousine, and an extreme example of what today's tuning specialists can do. Brabus starts by increasing the standard engine size from 336 cubic inches (5,500 cc) to 384 cubic inches (6,300 cc). The powerplant is then tuned and tweaked with high-performance components. A stainless-steel sports exhaust is added, as is a limited-slip differential for better traction, and a five-speed automatic gearbox that is reinforced to take the extra power.

The businessman's executive express has never looked so macho. Brabus adapts the exterior with a new aerodynamic body kit, including spoilers and side skirts. Then big 21-inch (53-cm) alloy wheels are fitted. Under the skin are high-performance brakes with twelve-piston calipers; an uprated, lowered, and stiffened suspension; and special speed-resistant tires.

Inside the cabin, which is swathed in leather, Alcantara, or wood depending on the buyer's preference, customers can specify a state-of-the-art Apple multimedia system that is integrated into the Mercedes electronics—all controlled by an iPad. Rear-seat passengers each get a leather-covered table designed to hold an iPad, with an integrated docking station to recharge its batteries. **SH**

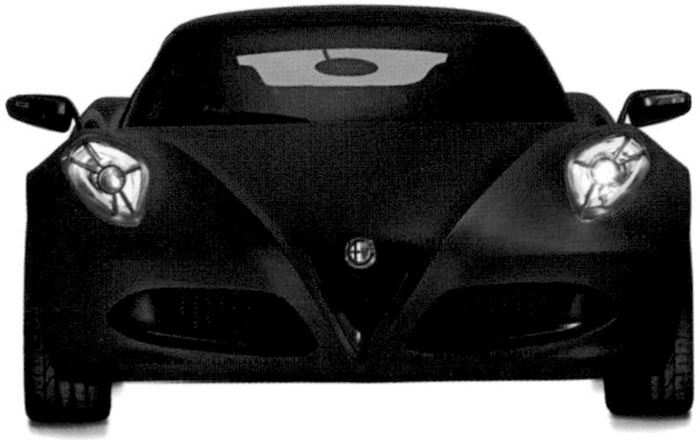

4C | Alfa Romeo (I)

2011 • 107 cu in/1,750 cc, S4 • 230 bhp/169 kW • 0–60 mph/97 kph in 5 seconds • 155 mph/250 kph

The 4C was an off-the-wall concept first revealed at the Geneva Motor Show in 2011. The tiny red supercoupe was an instant hit. Reaction was so good that Alfa engineers were initially told to get the mid-engined car into production as quickly as possible. That surprised most people inside and outside Fiat because it is a fairly extreme model, even for Alfa. It is a chunky little mid-engined high-performance car, smaller than the MiTo, but as powerful as a Porsche.

With a blunt short tail and minimal overhangs, it combines cues from the bigger 8C and some of its ancestors, too. However, at the time of writing the plans to build the two-seater appear to be delayed. The 4C may even spearhead Alfa's relaunch as a brand in the United States, starting with 2014's Detroit Motor Show.

The compact 4C's carbon-fiber central tub and aluminum subframe evolved from the innovative underpinnings of the KTM X-Bow, which was also conceived in Italy by specialists Dallara. The outer skin is a fiberglass composite. The driver will have paddle-shift controls on the steering wheel to flick through the dual-clutch semiautomatic sequential gearbox. There will be no manual option. Alongside will be a "DNA" switch to change all the car's dynamic settings for different driving styles. **SH**

911 GTS | Porsche (D)

2011 • 232 cu in/3,800 cc, F6 • 408 bhp/300 kW • 0–62 mph/100 kph in 4.2 seconds • 190 mph/306 kph

The GTS is the final version of the 997 generation of the classic rear-engined Porsche 911 sports car. A new 998 range was introduced in 2012, but the GTS deserves to linger in car buyers' attention because it is one of the best-ever 911s—and that's saying something.

The GTS is a well-sorted combination of the best bits of all the various 911s on offer, with simple rear-wheel drive housed in the wider body of a four-wheel-drive model, a tuned engine for higher output, and a few tweaks to the body kit to make it look lower, meaner, and more purposeful.

The GTS is also fast. Its engine features a special new free-flowing exhaust and a few plumbing tweaks to boost mid-range power—something that does not show in the performance figures above but makes a big difference to everyday driving.

Buyers who tick the Sports Suspension option get a limited-slip differential for better traction, and a lower ride height for even better roadholding. Yet the GTS is no roll-cage racer—it is comfortable and practical enough to drive to work every day.

BBC *Top Gear* reported it to be "the best all-around balance of price, performance, and comfort in the whole of the 911 Carrera range." *Auto Express* magazine was unequivocal: "It's Porsche's best car yet." **SH**

M5 | BMW

D

2011 • 268 cu in/4,395 cc, V8 • 560 bhp/418 kW • 0–62 mph/100 kph in 4.4 seconds • 155 mph/250 kph

In the early 1970s, BMW motorsport engineers took a standard sedan (saloon) and, with a tune-up here and a bolt-on there, turned it into a sports car by hand. This started a kind of arms race with both Mercedes-Benz's AMG tuning arm and tuning firms associated with other carmakers. Thirty years later, BMW's 5-Series-based M5 arrived to prove that BMW's M-men had come a long way since tweaking carburetors—this new M5 had an almost nuclear 560 bhp (418 kW).

The outgoing model relied on a naturally aspirated V10 engine, but regulations concerning emissions and fuel consumption meant that the new M5 had to do things differently. The M5 had a 268-cubic-inch (4,395-cc) V8 with twin-scroll turbocharged power; the engine also found in the X5 M and X6 M. Transmission was BMW's own seven-speed dual-clutch system. As with all fast BMW cars, the top speed was limited to 155 mph (250 kph), but buyers specifying the "M drivers package" could raise this to 190 mph (205 kph) . . . and still have room for the family. Utilizing "Efficient Dynamics" technology, including a brake-energy regeneration system comparable to the "KERS" system found in Formula 1 cars, the M5 had a frugal fuel consumption of 28.5 mpg (9.9 liters per 100 km), despite its weighing 4,288 pounds (1,945 kg).

Further weaponry was to be found in the cabin, with an active head-up display and night vision. Only geeks could spot the external differences between a standard 5-Series and the M5, though. Blue brake calipers and a subtle diffuser were the main differences. The M5 might pack atomic power . . . but it was delivered in a Stealth bomber package. **RD**

Geneva | Bufori

(MAL)

2011 • 372 cu in/6,100 cc, V8 • 430 bhp/316 kW • 0–62 mph/100 kph in 5.4 seconds • 166 mph/267 kph

At the 2011 launch, Bufori's marketing boss explained, "The Geneva is targeted at individuals who are . . . unable to identify themselves with a bland mass-produced luxury car." So, buyers who find a Rolls-Royce or a Cadillac unpalatably commonplace might find this ultraluxury retro sedan (saloon) to be the answer.

The Geneva is aimed at a money-is-no-object market where features such as mood lighting, champagne minibar (with flutes), and locking safe for valuables can win over super-rich customers. And few rivals can offer a leather and wood-swathed interior with a built-in china tea set, an instant boiling water tap and sink, an espresso coffee maker, and a cigar humidor.

The underlying rear-wheel-drive car is not bad either. Classic design elements such as long running boards and rear-hinged doors mix rather well with modern styling cues such as integrated bixenon headlights and LED taillights. The tuned Chrysler V8 supplies plentiful power but can be optionally supercharged to provide 600 bhp (441 kW) and a correspondingly jaw-dropping performance.

There is plenty of new technology in the recipe. A state-of-the-art carbon fiber/kevlar mix is infused with "vinylester resin" to create an extremely strong, light, and rigid body. Bufori claims that it is the world's first sedan with such technology. Every modern device is included: traction control, head-up display, a thermal-imaging night-vision camera, lane departure warning, and active cruise control.

Particularly security-conscious buyers can specify a Geneva with bulletproof armor, although the Bufori brochure describes it as "ballistic resistance." **SH**

Hot Rod Jakob | Caresto

S

2011 • 154 cu in/2,521 cc, S5 • 265 bhp/385 kW • unknown • unknown

To celebrate Volvo's eightieth anniversary, Swedish designer and coachbuilder Leif Tufvesson and his company, Caresto, created an extraordinary hot rod. It was based on the first mass-produced Volvo, the 1927 OV4—standing for "Open Car Four Cylinders"—which the Swedes had nicknamed the "Jakob." The one-off car toured Europe and the United States and soon won awards such as Hot Rod of the Year and Most Innovative Car. Volvo was delighted and displayed the Hot Rod Jakob in its museum in Gothenburg.

The new car mimicked many of the OV4's features. It had the same characteristic radiator grille pattern, and, as in the original, the chrome pillar holding up the flat windshield extends down the side of the body. Many dimensions and materials match. Caresto even used the same number of screws as the OV4. The hot rod's body was made by hand by bending aluminum panels into shape using a hammer and an English wheel—the method that was used back in the 1920s.

The Hot Rod Jakob is a rear-wheel-drive two-seater with typically hot-rodding big, uncovered, aluminum-spoked wheels. The wheels—19-inch (48-cm) at the front, 22-inch (56-cm) at the back—are modern versions of the original's wooden wheels.

Massive, specially made Pirelli Scorpion tires with a milled tread, along with huge brake discs, add street credibility to the cartoonlike OV4 copy.

Volvo engineers of eighty years ago could not have dreamed of using the Hot Rod Jakob's carbon-fiber chassis, which includes a steel subframe to support the engine (from a modern Volvo T5) with a flexi-fuel conversion to run on both gas and ethanol. **SH**

Z-One | Perana

ZA

2011 • 378 cu in/6,200 cc, V8 • 434 bhp/330 kW • 0–62 mph/100 kph in 3.9 seconds • unknown

Mix famous Milanese coachbuilder Zagato and ambitious South African carmaker Hi Tech Automotive and what happens? The answer is the stunning Perana Z-One. They borrowed the name Perana from a series of high-performance cars produced in South Africa in the 1960s and 1970s, but this time sophisticated virtual-reality development techniques allowed the first car to be built from scratch in just four months. The car is already in full production in Port Elizabeth, South Africa.

The lightweight two-seater supercoupe has the classic configuration of front engine and rear-wheel drive to achieve the perfect 50/50 weight distribution essential for predictable handling. The styling is impressive. The fiberglass body on a tubular-steel chassis has an aggressive muscle-car front end with muscular flanks that rise up over the rear wheel arches.

All that V8 power in such a lightweight car means shocking acceleration: 0–100 mph (160 kph) in less than ten seconds. And yet the limited-edition Perana costs less than some executive sedans (saloons). That is due to Hi Tech's back-to-basics approach. There are no gadgetty driver's aids and only modest luxuries.

Nevertheless, Hi Tech has used the best components, including hefty Brembo brakes, Bilstein shock absorbers, and Recaro seats. The all-aluminum V8 comes from the Corvette and Camaro, and the six-speed high-performance manual transmission from the Cadillac CTS-V. For any buyers insane enough to want even more power and performance, Hi Tech will be offering the option of a bigger engine, the 505-bhp (371 kW), 427-cubic-inch (7,000-cc) powerplant from the Corvette Z06. Performance will be awesome. **SH**

Fabia vRS S2000 | Skoda

CZ

2011 • 85 cu in/1,400 cc, S4 • 180 bhp/132 kW • 0–62 mph/100 kph in 7.3 seconds • 139 mph/224 kph

The Fabia vRS S2000 is a limited-edition rally-style hot hatch built to celebrate Skoda's victory in the Intercontinental Rally Challenge.

Just a generation ago, that opening sentence would have seemed like fantasy. Skodas were the butt of everyone's jokes—they were the car you could double in value by filling with fuel, and had heated rear windows to warm your hands while pushing them, and could be overtaken if you just ran a bit faster. The marketing power of the Volkswagen Group, which now owns Skoda, has helped, but really it is the quality of today's cars that has reversed people's perception of the historic brand. Now, the existence of a desirable, rally-bred Skoda does not seem extraordinary at all.

This latest version of the Fabia vRS comes in the works team's color scheme of bright green with a white roof, with striking white alloy wheels and all the graphics and logos expected of race cars. It is produced in a limited edition of just 200 cars. The S2000 also marks Skoda's centenary in motorsport.

The car misses out on the extreme modifications that allowed Skoda to win the IRC Constructors' Title, namely a 270-bhp (199-kW), sixteen-valve, 122-cubic-inch (2,000-cc) engine, four-wheel drive, and an extensive body kit. But it is one of the sportiest Skodas ever to go on sale. The vRS engine produces a huge dose of power from such a small unit. Drivers also get to enjoy the sophisticated race-style DSG gearbox, with paddle-shift sequential changes mounted on the leather-trimmed steering wheel. And, beyond all that, it is an economical, well-built, practical, small family hatchback, and that is no joke. **SH**

VXR8 | Vauxhall

GB

2011 • 378 cu in/6,200 cc, V8 • 425 bhp/317 kW • 0–60 mph/97 kph in 4.9 seconds • 155 mph/250 kph

This brutal BMW M5-eater derives from Holden, Vauxhall's Australian General Motors stablemate. It is a muscle-car version of Holden's big, award-winning sedan (saloon), the Commodore.

Putting a big V8 upfront got tire-squealing performance from the big four-door sedan. Its stately body shape is now disfigured with LED strips, air ducts, cooling vents, and aerodynamic bolt-ons. It looks like something cooked up by a couple of backstreet Aussie hoodlums. Almost. The VRX8 was the brainchild of Holden Special Vehicles, the equivalent of M-Sport or AMG for the Australian manufacturer.

The engine may be a tuned-up leftover from the old Monaro, but the rest of the specification is serious: the monstrous disc brakes can stop the VXR8 from 60 mph (97 kph) in just 118 feet (36 m), and giant alloy wheels hide multilink independent rear suspension controlled by electronic active safety chassis control. There are antilock brakes, traction control, and a "launch control" system for optimum acceleration from a standstill. The Enhanced Driver Interface touch-screen computer system dominates the dashboard, feeding the driver with real-time performance data: g-forces, lap times, power, and torque. The word "Oversteer" flashes up if the driver misses the mark while cornering.

Yet the big Vauxhall is also a practical vehicle with plenty of room in the leather-swathed interior for four adults. There is a big trunk (boot), and a rear parking camera and tire-pressure monitor are standard, too.

Vauxhall is also marketing a station wagon (estate) and, unusually for the British market, a fire-breathing pickup truck version. **SH**

LFA | Lexus

J

2011 • 293 cu in/4,800 cc, V10 • 553 bhp/407 kW • 0–60 mph/97 kph in 3.6 seconds • 202 mph/325 kph

Lexus makes luxury limousines for business people, but for a long time the company has been trying to raise its high-performance credentials, too.

The LFA is immodestly described by its maker as "the supreme supercar." It certainly has classic supercar ingredients: a slippery two-door coupe body with a powerful V10 engine . . . and an enormously long development period. In fact, an LFA prototype was tested at the Nürburgring in 2004, and Lexus engineers have been fiddling with the design ever since.

The LFA's high-revving nonturbo engine sits behind the front axle and powers the rear wheels through a six-speed sequential gearbox that can change in the blink of an eye (200 milliseconds). That is the kind of shift a driver needs in a car that can rev from idle to 9,000 rpm in 0.6 seconds.

The body is carbon-reinforced polymer and many components are carbon fiber or aluminum to keep the weight down. The suspension is aluminum, and the big wheels are aluminum with wide thin tires to keep the LFA on the road. At speed a rear spoiler adjusts automatically to increase aerodynamic downforce.

Inside, the LFA's cabin is purely for two but still relatively spacious. The sports steering wheel is carbon fiber. Some overfiddly complexities perhaps show that developers spent too long dithering with technology. For example, selecting neutral requires two paddles to be pulled simultaneously, and choosing reverse involves pressing two buttons in the correct order.

None of this will bother the lucky 500 able to buy a limited-edition Lexus LFA, although they will have to find $375,000 (£236,000) for each car. **SH**

MXT | Mastretta

MEX

2011 • 122 cu in/1,999 cc, S4 • 240 bhp/180 kW • 0–62 mph/100 kph in 4.9 seconds • 162 mph/260 kph

The MXT is the first whole production car made by brothers Daniel and Carlos Mastretta, who had previously built buses and Volkswagen-based kit cars in a factory near Mexico City for twenty years.

The low-slung high-performance two-seater is an impressive debut. The budget mid-engined sports car spurns most high-tech drivers' aids for the classic formula of lightweight body, sporty suspension, and a hot engine driving the rear wheels. The MXT's looks are distinctive, chunky, and purposeful, with magnesium wheels and a carbon-fiber-reinforced plastic body. Headlight units swoop down to become air intakes, and the wheels sit in muscular arches.

The car, weighing just 2,050 pounds (930 kg), has a Cosworth-tuned turbocharged sixteen-valve aluminum Ford engine, an innovative high-performance aluminum chassis with carbon-fiber floor, and double-wishbone suspension all around, with powerful four-piston brakes. The no-frills cockpit comes complete with a built-in roll cage; carbon-fiber, leather-covered racing bucket seats; and safety harness. There is a small suede-covered, flat-bottomed steering wheel, five-speed manual gearstick, and closely placed aluminum pedals for fast heel-and-toe footwork.

For use on the road, the MXT has antilock brakes, xenon lights, two air bags, air-conditioning, and an in-car media center featuring GPS navigation, Bluetooth hands-free phone system, DVD player, and iPod dock.

The exterior styling hints at a flamboyant Italian influence. In the 1930s, the Mastretta brothers' father was a student in Milan, Italy, where he was taught by a young engineering professor called Enzo Ferrari. **SH**

Agera R | Koenigsegg

S

2011 • 305 cu in/5,000 cc, V8 • 1,115 bhp/820 kW • 0–62 mph/100 kph in 2.9 seconds • 275 mph/443 kph

Late in 2011, at the Koenigsegg test track in Angelholm, Sweden, the Agera R supercar broke several world speed and braking records for production cars. At one point it accelerated from 0 to 186 mph (300 kph) in just 14.5 seconds, then braked back to zero in just seven seconds. The Agera R's top speed has yet to be verified, but this Swedish two-seater is clearly one of the fastest production cars ever built.

Yet the R is just a special edition of the standard Agera two-seater, built with an in-house engine adapted to run on biofuel. Amazingly, biofuel makes it faster than the regular gas model. The Agera R can also run on gas, but not as efficiently.

Like any Agera, the R has all the ingredients of a world-beating supercar: an enormously powerful mid-mounted V8 driving the rear wheels, a very light body made of carbon fiber and Kevlar, and a very stiff and light carbon-fiber chassis. Intelligent design and high-tech efficiency combine all over the car. The adaptive aerodynamic rear wing, for example, is not powered. Instead it uses the pressure of the wind created at high speeds to change its angle, creating downforce on the car, while at the same time drawing hot air from the engine bay. The system is lighter, simpler, and more responsive than any powered hydraulic spoiler.

The car has sophisticated features such as a seven-speed paddle-shift transmission, forged aluminum wheels, fiberoptic interior lighting, a removable targa roof panel that stows under the front hood (bonnet), and beautifully engineered scissor-opening doors.

Not surprisingly, the Agera R's price tag is astronomical—around $1.7 million (£1.1 million). **SH**

T5 Clubman | Elfin

AUS

2011 • 346 cu in/5,665 cc, V8 • 329 bhp/245 kW • 0–60 mph/97 kph in 3.7 seconds • 175 mph/281 kph

Australia has never been a big player in the world of mass-produced motor vehicles, so learning that Elfin is the world's second-largest producer of race cars comes as a surprise. Garrie Cooper founded the South Australia–based company in 1957 and produced 250 race and sports cars up until his death in 1982. His father sold the company, but production never ceased and continues to this day. That is a pretty good survival story in a country littered with evidence of the work of failed automotive visionaries.

Manufactured from premium-grade aluminum sheeting painstakingly hand-riveted then sealed for maximum strength, the chassis of the T5 Clubman is built to exacting race-standard specifications. All fixing points are welded for rigidity and longevity. The completed chassis is prepared for sandblasting, and then painted to a mirrorlike depth of 50 microns. The T5 is another Elfin doorless design (although a cloth roof and "doors" are options) and the cockpit is easy to climb into and out of. Drivers with neck trouble or loose fillings should avoid taking it over rough or corrugated roads, however, as every bump is keenly felt.

A modern incarnation of Elfin's original 1961 Clubman, the rear-wheel-drive T5 is a mix of Formula 1 and pure hot rod. The British press had criticized Elfin's MS8 Streamliner for being too heavy, possessing too much brute force, and being difficult to handle. In response, the Clubman was given a lighter frame and an upgraded suspension that was more "user friendly." But do not think for a moment that performance was sacrificed. The T5 Clubman still has a better power-to-weight ratio than a Porsche 911 Turbo. **BS**

Karma | Fisker

(USA)

2011 • 122 cu in/2,000 cc, S4, two electric • 400 bhp/298 kW • 0–60 mph/97 kph in 6.3 seconds • 125 mph/201 kph

In 2007, after spells at BMW, Ford, and Aston Martin, Dane Henrik Fisker joined forces with Bernhard Koehler to form Fisker Automotive in California. After a legal spat with Tesla, and a $529-million (£337-million) loan from the U.S. government, the company unveiled the Fisker Karma, claiming it to be the first true electric luxury vehicle with extended range. Fiska's marketing spin doctors described the Karma as "a bold expression of uncompromised responsible luxury."

The Karma runs for up to 50 miles (80 km) on its two battery-powered 201-bhp (150-kW) motors alone, or up to 300 miles (480 km) when using the gasoline engine. The gasoline engine does not actually power the wheels, but a 3.3 kilowatt-hour battery charger for the Lithium Ion batteries. Drivers traveling more than 300 miles have to find somewhere to connect the built-in 120-volt "convenience cord." The upside of the electric power is the huge torque available—959 foot

pounds (1,300 Nm)—although the relatively modest performance figures tell the true story of a 2,404-pound (5,300-kg) luxury car with green ambitions.

The Karma has some unusual technical features: a roof-mounted solar panel to assist the air-conditioning, reclaimed-wood trim, and 22-inch (56-cm) alloy wheels. Despite the hefty U.S. loan, only half of each Karma comes from the United States; it is assembled in Finland at a factory more familiar with Saabs.

The car was named *Automobile* magazine's Design of the Year and *Top Gear* magazine's Luxury Car of the Year as well as being listed by *Time Magazine* as one of the "The 50 Best Inventions" of 2011. Actors Ashton Kutcher and Leonardo DiCaprio were among the first customers for the Karma. If Fisker's ambitious plans are to be met, it will have to find another 14,998 people who have $100,000 (£62,000) to spend on the ultimate green fashion statement. **RD**

MP4-12C

⊲ A 2010 McLaren MP4-12C shows off its "butterfly" doors; its orange paint finish is a tribute to early McLaren race cars.

MP4-12C | McLaren (GB)

2011 • 232 cu in/3,799 cc, V8 • 592 bhp/441 kW • 0–62 mph/100 kph in 3.1 seconds • 205 mph/330 kph

The MP4-12C is the first all-new McLaren to be built at the company's production center in Woking, England, since the awesome F1 was launched in 1993. By applying the same attention to detail to the MP4-12C as it does to its Formula 1 race cars, McLaren has developed a road-going engineering masterpiece.

By its own admission, McLaren turned weight saving into an obsession. Toward the end of the MP4-12C's development, when every superlight component had been designed, engineers were sent away to reduce weight by another 5 percent. This final push shaved 154 pounds (70 kg) off the production version. Central to the car's construction is its carbon-fiber Monocell chassis, weighing just 176 pounds (80 kg). Intelligent design features, such as side-mounted radiators, reduce the need for extra plumbing and coolant; similarly, exhaust pipes exit straight from the back, allowing them to be shorter and lighter.

McLaren ransacked its treasure trove of outlawed Formula 1 technology for this car. The car features "Launch Control" and active Brake Steer, a system that helps it to corner at high speeds by slowing the inside wheels (banned in 1997 after McLaren claimed easy victories at the European Grand Prix). Costing £168,500 ($229,000) when launched, this British-built supercar is capable of lapping the Nürburgring circuit more quickly than its price-matched Italian rivals, the Ferrari 458 Italia and Lamborghini's Gallardo.

Adding to the McLaren's sense of drama, the MP4-12C has "butterfly" doors that open upward and out to allow access, via wide carbon-fiber sills, to the dark cabin. A convertible version is also available. **DS**

Roadster | Chinkara (IND)

2011 • 110 cu in/1,800 cc, S4 • 114 bhp/85 kW • 0–62 mph/100 kph in 6.7 seconds • 116 mph/187 kph

The Chinkara Roadster, one of India's first genuine sports cars, is a neat little Lotus Seven derivative built from locally made components to keep costs and repair bills down. The doorless two-seater is powered by an Isuzu engine used in the Hindustan Ambassador, and its suspension, steering, and brakes come from the Maruti Suzuki Alto, India's best-selling hatchback.

Chinkara is run by Guido and Shama Bothe, a husband-and-wife team based near Mumbai. He is German; she is Indian. Their company is named after the smallest Asian gazelle and their main business is building boats, so their expertise is in the use of fiberglass. They also make the Jeepster (a retro sport utility vehicle), and plan to make an AC Cobra clone.

The Roadster has all the traditional Lotus Seven features: a featherlight fiberglass body on a tubular chassis, fat tires under suspended mudguards, stand-up headlights, a rudimentary soft-top, and rear-wheel drive. Chinkara adds red and black leather bucket seats, a wooden steering wheel, a shiny side-silencer pipe, and red three-point safety belts.

Customers can choose a manual or auto gearbox, and a hardtop with gull-wing doors. The Roadster's overspecified chassis is more rigid and stronger than a Lotus Seven's to cope with India's wayward road surfaces. The car is designed to appeal as a pure driving toy for the subcontinent's wealthy new business class.

The Roadster does not have modern technology such as traction control, antilock brakes, or even power steering. Instead, it is a pure driving experience, just as Colin Chapman of Lotus originally conceived it. The Roadster is a sports car unplugged. **SH**

CLS63 AMG | Mercedes-Benz

(D)

2011 • 336 cu in/5,500 cc, V8 • 518 bhp/381 kW • 0–62 mph/100 kph in 4.4 seconds • 155 mph/250 kph

While good performance and handling are possible in a big, heavy luxury car, it is a difficult job to create such a machine. That is why executives are happy to pay more than $127,000 (£80,000) for this coupe.

The performance of the Mercedes CLS63 AMG is not just good, it is phenomenal. It weighs 4,210 pounds (1,910 kg) and is a spacious and luxurious four-door, four-seater, but it can out-accelerate a Porsche Carrera all the way up to its 155-mph (250-kph) limited top speed. The AMG version of the CLS executive coupe range has slight changes in its aerodynamic body, but they are all appropriately understated in the Mercedes way. Essentially, the AMG's long, sleek, sweeping body looks much like that of the standard CLS. It is only under the hood (bonnet) that the refined E-Class cruiser has been turned into a bestial rebel.

The all-aluminum V8 puts out 518 bhp (381 kW). That is already fairly extreme, but for buyers who opt for the "Performance Pack" costing $10,000 (£6,495), the output edges up to 549 bhp (404 kW). That is debatable value: the package works out at around $317 (£200) per 1 bhp and yet knocks only 0.1 second off the 0–62 mph (100-kph) acceleration time.

The "basic" AMG is a sophisticated machine without any extras. A slick seven-speed auto gearbox, active damping and air suspension, and a precise speed-sensitive steering system are included to help the driver. There is an option of race-style carbon-ceramic brakes and limited-slip differential for extra traction.

With so much grip, agility, and responsiveness, this big Mercedes is very engaging to drive. It adds up to being one of the best AMGs ever seen on the road. **SH**

Mégane 2.0T Renaultsport 250 | Renault

F

2011 • 122 cu in/1,998 cc, S4 • 247 bhp/184 kW • 0–62 mph/100 kph in 6.1 seconds • 155 mph/181 kph

A hot hatch with some clever technology, the Mégane 2.0T Renaultsport 250 was built at Renaultsport's factory in Dieppe, France, where a selection of Renault's mainstream models are turned into sports variants.

The Mégane yielded its sports performance thanks to a 122-cubic-inch (1,998-cc) turbocharged engine giving 247 bhp (184 kW). But in addition to packing more power than its nearest rivals, the Golf GTi and the Ford Focus ST, the Mégane had a trick up its sleeve. For a front-wheel-drive car it had incredible cornering ability due to steering and suspension technology called Perfohub. Unlike other hot hatches, the Mégane didn't lose speed by understeering in corners, and consequently it set the standard for handling. *Evo* magazine said, "It never bites or snaps. It just serenely takes everything in its stride, utterly unruffled by quick progress." The twin-scroll turbocharged power was delivered in a predictable and consistent manner, without taking the driver off the road. *What Car?* magazine named the Mégane 250 as its Hot Hatch of the Year three years running.

Renault styled and marketed the 250 as a Coupe, further distancing it from its three- and five-door hatchback rivals. The gadget-laden cabin offered technology such as "keyless go" and a panoramic roof, along with interesting extras such as yellow-faced instruments, switchable engine maps at the driver's fingertips, and even a g-force meter for recording the fun enjoyed while cornering. The price was competitive, too, at just $38,000 (£24,145). More was charged for the upgraded 265 model, which achieved 261 bhp (192 kW) and had further chassis tweaks. **RD**

In line with Lamborghini tradition, its new 2012 supercar was named after a bull—Aventador was known for his courage.

MS8 Streamliner | Elfin (AUS)

2011 • 346 cu in/5,665 cc, V8 • 328 bhp/245 kW • 0–62 mph/100 kph in 4.5 seconds • 171 mph/275 kph

Anyone who ever wanted to be a Formula 1 driver and gets excited by high-tech specifications is likely to fall head-over-heels for the Elfin MS8 Streamliner. This car has everything to make the would-be Formula 1 driver feel like a winner: suspension springs by Eibach, Koni 8211 shock absorbers, ventilated disc brakes with alloy mounting hats, aircraft-quality braided brake hoses and suspension arms, to say nothing of its 0.001 mm-tolerance nuts, bolts, and threads.

The Elfin Sports Car Company, founded in 1957, is the oldest continually operating manufacturer of sports cars in Australia. It has given the world some of the most desirable and competitive open-wheel and sports racers of its era.

The rear-wheel-drive Streamliner, designed by Elfin and styled by the team at Holden Design, is a hand-built supercar with gull-wing doors that open forward rather than out, making it easier to park in tight spaces. The interior is beautifully crafted with sunken leather seats bringing the wide door sills to shoulder-height, giving drivers a snug sense of being cocooned as they attempt to come to grips with its 328 bhp (245 kW).

Oil and water gauges are flanked by aircraftlike heater vents, and the tachometer has no red line. There are no side windows, and the roof is a removable hardtop. Low-backed racing seats come equipped with four-point racing harnesses, and there are individual driver and passenger roll bars. Body panels are made from glass-reinforced plastic (GRP), and the chassis is rose-jointed to prevent flexing. The list goes on.

The Streamliner can outrace a Porsche GT3, costs less than half the price, and is built to win. **BS**

Aventador | Lamborghini (I)

2012 • 397 cu in/6,500 cc, V12 • 691 bhp/515 kW • 0–62 mph/100 kph in 2.9 seconds • 217 mph/349 kph

Forty years ago, only Ferrari and Lamborghini built serious supercars, but new supercars are now being hatched all over the world by specialist companies. So can this latest offering from Audi-owned classic sports-car constructor Lamborghini compete against the scores of rival mid-engined carbon-fiber machines?

Lamborghini is clearly going full tilt at this. The Aventador, named after a famous brave bull in Spanish bull fighting, is a completely new car. The lightweight body is baked as one carbon-fiber and plastic monocoque shell. The shape is low, sleek, and dramatic.

Huge air scoops cool the engine, which is displayed at the back of the car under a window of its own. The naturally aspirated alloy V12 makes its excitingly loud and rude screaming noise while driving all four wheels—the smooth, superquick engine is the unique selling point of this Lamborghini. Inside the cockpit are two electrically adjustable bucket seats and a seven-speed manual gearshift. There is no storage space, although there is room for some luggage under the hood (bonnet). But of course, no one buys a supercar just for its practicality.

The completely digital dashboard is not entirely satisfactory. It gives digital representations of a speedometer and rev counter at the touch of a stalk, but not both at the same time, so drivers find themselves constantly flicking between the two.

The Aventador has three driving modes that govern the responses of the engine, gearbox, steering, and dynamic controls. "Road" is the most easygoing, "Sport" gets rather hairy-chested, and as for "Track," take a deep breath and hold on tight. **SH**

Golf R | Volkswagen (D)

2012 • 122 cu in/2,000 cc, S4 • 266 bhp/196 kW • 0–62 mph/100 kph in 5.5 seconds • 155 mph/250 kph

Is this the ultimate Golf? The R, a four-wheel-drive turbocharged evolution of the familiar German hatchback, is being launched gradually across the world at the time of writing. The fastest Golf ever produced, it has a limited top speed of 155 mph (250 kph); its acceleration makes it not only the fastest Golf ever but also the fastest ever Volkswagen.

The Golf R is distinguished from more humble members of its hatchback family by discreet styling cues: new front fenders (bumpers) that include LED running lights and a trio of deep airdams, gloss-black wing mirrors, sill extensions, and 18-inch (46-cm) five-spoke alloy wheels, although 19-inch (48-cm) gloss-black wheels can be specified. There is a tiny roof-mounted spoiler at the back, and twin exhausts. The lowered ride height signifies a sportier suspension.

The Golf R uses a revised version of Volkswagen's "4motion" four-wheel-drive system, which reacts quickly to maximize traction and minimize wheelspin. A six-speed manual gearbox is standard, but a six-speed DSG gearbox, available as an option, shaves two-tenths of a second from the acceleration figures.

The high-performing Golf R keeps up other Golf traditions, too. It returns 33 mpg (8.6 liters per 100 km), and has low CO_2 emissions:195 g/km. **SH**

335d | BMW (D)

2012 • 183 cu in/3,000 cc, S6 • 265 bhp/195 kW • 0–60 mph/97 kph in 6 seconds • 155 mph/250 kph

Around thirty years ago it took some brave French makers to change our perception of diesel cars. Now carmaking has reached a point where this German diesel-powered executive car is more desirable, faster, and more economical than many gas-driven rivals.

The first models of the wider, longer, and sleeker "F30" incarnation of the BMW 3-Series were launched in 2012. The range-topping diesel is expected to be the 335d. At the time of writing, before that model arrived, it was expected to produce sports-car performance while cutting fuel consumption by around a third.

Diesel engines produce more torque, or pulling power, than gas equivalents and this translates to impressive mid-range grunt—the sort of performance that makes most impact in real driving. The hot new 3-Series diesel is expected to have around 425 pound-feet (576 Nm) of torque, which is more than that achieved by the gas-powered V8 of the BMW M3.

Figures given above are only industry estimates, but it is likely that the 155-mph (250-kph) 335d diesel sedan (saloon) will also be among the most fuel-economic nonhybrid luxury cars. The previous generation's top diesel was the 330d, which also set a high standard for stunning performance allied with more fuel-efficient motoring. **SH**

Lancer Evo XI | Mitsubishi (J)

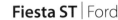

2012 • 98 cu in/1,600 cc, S4/electric motor • unknown • 0–60 mph/97 kph in 5 seconds • unknown

The aim of the Mitsubishi team currently working on the concept of the next-generation Evo (Evolution) is to produce the first hybrid supercar. Fans of performance cars were shocked to hear that the latest Evo would be powered by a mix of diesel and electricity, but most were delighted that the series had not ended.

Its predecessor was the tenth-generation Lancer Evo of 2007, a high-tech car which could accelerate from 0 to 60 mph (97 kph) in 4.8 seconds. But emission controls and economic conditions threatened the Evo project. In the marketplace, fuel economy and low emissions were becoming just as important as high performance in attracting car buyers.

Mitsubishi announced that a team was working to develop an eleventh-generation Lancer Evo using a combination of electric power—to reduce emissions—and turbodiesel power—to maintain the famous mid-range acceleration of the Evo range.

The Evo XI is expected to feature an uprated version of the tenth generation's sophisticated S-AWC four-wheel-drive technology, which combines traction control, braking, and steering in one system. Performance may well exceed that of the Evo X. With few technical details available at the time of writing, the figures above are industry estimates. **SH**

Fiesta ST | Ford (GB)

2012 • 98 cu in/1,600 cc, S4 • 180 bhp/130 kW • 0–60 mph/97 kph in 7 seconds • 137 mph/220 kph

At the time of writing the Fiesta ST is still a concept car, but it is the high-performance version of the newest Fiesta generation. The Fiesta front-wheel-drive hatchback series has been Ford's supermini since 1976.

The Fiesta Mark VII features Ford's new family front end, with a gaping black grille and slanted headlights. Inspired by the Fiesta RS World Rally Championship car, the ST version of the new generation has been given more aggressive looks to match its performance. The muscular exterior features a deeper front fender (bumper), rear spoiler, rear diffuser, a set of twin exhausts, and bold 17-inch (43-cm) alloy wheels. The suspension is lowered and stiffened, and the track is wider, all to help make the handling sharper.

Power comes from Ford's new Ecoboost engine. This has variable valve timing, direct injection, and turbocharging to boost performance while reducing emissions and improving fuel economy. The six-speed manual transmission is more sporty than before.

The production car will feature many of the gadgets of the new Mondeo Ecoboost and the Focus ST, including electronic stability control. Drivers will enjoy the cockpit, which includes Recaro bucket seats, chrome gauges, a Sony CD player rather than the standard Ford unit, and colored courtesy lights. **SH**

Camaro ZL1 | Chevrolet

USA

2012 • 376 cu in/6,162 cc, V8 • 580 bhp/433 kW • 0–60 mph/97 kph in 3.9 seconds • 184 mph/296 kph

Even the threat of global warming and rising oil prices could not kill off the the all-American muscle car. The Chevrolet Camaro ZL1 boasted the "most powerful supercharged engine in the world"—a 376-cubic-inch (6,162-cc) V8, borrowed from the Cadillac CTS-V.

Chevrolet wanted to build a car with the same reputation as its original 1969 ZL1, a fairly ordinary-looking Camaro, except for the air scoop in its hood (bonnet) that had been the drag-strip king.

The 2012 car was a lot more sophisticated, of course, with a highly tuned suspension system depending on magnetic fluid. Constantly monitoring conditions, the suspension system was capable of adjusting itself up to 1,000 times a second.

Putting all that V8 power down required either a six-speed manual gearbox or an electronic automatic. The latter was tuned to hang onto the lower gears in order to make the most of the power. But it had a manual mode, too, with quick-shifting paddles around the steering wheel.

The bodywork was understated, yet still managed to project an air of menace. Even the exhaust was tuned to create an aggressive sound when the car was just ticking over. In this respect the Camaro's appeal was boosted by appearing as "Bumblebee" in the *Transformers* movies. In fact, the car was a movie star before production models were even available.

With the Camaro ZL1, the updated Ford Mustang at last had a credible rival in the muscle stakes. It reached 60 mph (97 kph) in under four seconds and achieved a top speed of 184 mph (296 kph). As the Camaro's own publicity put it: "Barely street legal." **JI**

Corvette ZR1 | Chevrolet

USA

2012 • 376 cu in/6,162 cc, V8 • 638 bhp/476 kW • 0–60 mph/97 kph in 3.4 seconds • 205 mph/330 kph

No account of the 2012 Corvette ZR1 should omit some very impressive facts. It is the most powerful production car General Motors has ever built, thanks to a supercharged V8 that can push the car beyond 65 mph (105 kph) in first gear alone—which means using the gearstick in city traffic is largely unnecessary. In tests at the Nürburgring track in Germany, the ZR1 improved on the previous ZR1 model's lap time by more than six seconds, and bettered the Dodge Viper by three seconds. The car is aided in cornering by a performance-control system, and new, lightweight aluminum wheels with extrawidth Michelin "Zero Pressure" tires—designed specifically for the ZR1—provide all the grip drivers will ever need.

Enhancements in 2012 include a traction-control program that adjusts engine torque up to a hundred times a second, increasing safety in icy or treacherous conditions, and much-needed lateral and shoulder bolsters in the seats to keep drivers from sliding side-to-side, from door to center console, as they corner.

To pacify the U.S. Environmental Protection Agency, the ZR1 has an electronically controlled exhaust flap that plugs the rear silencer and keeps the "noise" down. Rebellious drivers have noted that it takes less than a minute to remove its 10-amp fuse. Muzzling the gorgeous notes of the ZR1 might stop birds from fleeing their nests as the ZR1 flies past, but, as any motorsport enthusiast or opera aficionado will contend, it is the high notes that can separate the good from the sublime. Whether it be Placido Domingo or the ZR1, high notes are an indicator of perfection, and something is lost when they are tampered with. **BS**

SLS AMG E-Cell | Mercedes-Benz

D

2012 • four electric motors • 535 bhp/399 kW • 0–62 mph/100 kph in 4 seconds • 155 mph/250 kph

At the time of writing, the Mercedes-Benz SLS AMG E-Cell is only a concept car. Mercedes celebrated the 125th anniversary of Carl Benz's patent for a "vehicle with gas engine" by suggesting that this amazing, forward-looking project could start production in 2013.

The brilliant, high-performance coupe with gullwing doors is almost as quick off the mark as its gas-powered production sister, which has a thirsty, polluting, 378-cubic-inch (6,200 cc) V8. The E-Cell's performance comes from the innovative layout of an electric motor for each wheel. This creates an electric version of permanent four-wheel-drive, with all its benefits of optimized traction in cornering and on slippery surfaces. Each motor can rev to 12,000 rpm and supply maximum power immediately from a standstill. Formula 1 driver David Coulthard was filmed testing a bright-yellow E-Cell prototype. He was visibly shocked by the acceleration. "Awesome," he grinned. "You will not believe the performance. It's more responsive than the V8!"

The electric energy is stored in liquid-cooled, high-voltage, lithium-ion batteries dotted around the car to balance the weight and improve the center of gravity. They can be recharged from a normal domestic power socket and allow a range of about 81 miles (130 km).

Inside, the cockpit is similar to the sexy SLS, except for a battery-power dial that shows remaining power and whether the battery is being depleted or recharged in the course of the journey.

The E-Cell is a hint that the future of motoring will not only concern stop-start technology and hybrid power. Whatever happens, cars will still be fun. **SH**

Focus ST | Ford

GB

2012 • 122 cu in/2,000 cc, S4 • 247 bhp/184 kW • 0–62 mph/100 kph in 6.5 seconds • 154 mph/248 kph

The new front-wheel-drive Focus hatchback is Ford's first truly global car, and the ST is its first performance car to be sold almost identically in the United States, Europe, and most of the rest of the world.

With its big alloy wheels, roof spoiler, and menacing front nose job, the new Focus ST was developed by Ford's hot-hatch experts, the RS Team in Europe, with input from the Special Vehicles Team in the United States. The car comes in orange, red, white, or blue. The wheels are black, the brake calipers red.

The five-door ST is powered by the new all-aluminum Ford Ecoboost engine working the front wheels through a six-speed close-ratio semiautomatic sequential gearbox. The engine features three sophisticated technologies: low-inertia turbocharging, high-pressure direct injection, and double overhead variable cam timing. These help boost performance while reducing emissions and fuel consumption. Ford describes the appeal of the vehicle as "refined engineering and undiluted adrenaline."

Inside, the ST is no stripped-out racer. The predominantly black cabin has top-of-the-line features available, such as Recaro sports seats, keyless starting, dual-zone climate control, and automatic lights and rearview mirror dimming. There is also a Windows-based infotainment system with an 8-inch (20-cm) touch screen that provides satellite navigation, audio, and Wi-Fi Internet access throughout the car.

Ford has also launched a station-wagon (estate) version of the ST in Europe only—surely one of the fastest ways to carry an old cupboard or a baby stroller. Ford describes the car as a "unique niche model." **SH**

SR8 RX | Radical

GB

2012 • 165 cu in/2,700 cc, V8 • 460 bhp/343 kW • 0–60 mph/97 kph in 2.7 seconds • 178 mph/286 kph

At the time of writing, the Radical SR8 holds the lap record for road-going cars on the famous Nürburgring circuit in Germany. The lightweight British sports car was almost half a minute quicker than anything before.

Some questioned the Radical's eligibility. Is that ridiculously low-slung two-seater really a road-legal car? Radical's race driver Michael Vergers had the perfect reply: he had driven the SR8 from the United Kingdom to Germany the day before the test.

Nevertheless, the SR8 is not much like many road cars. From the foam-filled fuel tank to the paddle-shift gears, track compenents and styling dominate. The potent engine, built from two Suzuki four-cylinder motorcycle engines, produces incredible acceleration. The car weighs just 1,496 pounds (680 kg). Take into account a long list of sophisticated race features, such as the fuel-induction system, aerodynamic rear wing, and fully adjustable suspension, and it is easy to see why this is one of the fastest point-to-point road-legal cars in the world.

Founded by enthusiasts Mick Hyde and Phil Abbott in 1997, Radical is a small British company that uses superbike technology to build lightweight, superfast sports cars. It has built more than a thousand cars in its workshop in Peterborough, England.

A team of students from Imperial College London converted an SR8 into an electric car and drove it the full length of the Pan-American highway in 2010 to demonstrate the performance and range of electric vehicles. With a top speed of 124 mph (200 kph) and a range of more than 250 miles (400 km), it completed the 16,500 miles (26,500 km) in seventy days. **SH**

F1 | Hulme

(NZ)

2012 • 427 cu in/7,000 cc, V8 • 600 bhp/447 kW • 0–60 mph/97 kph in 2.8 seconds • 200 mph/322 kph

Named in honor of Denny Hulme, New Zealand's only Formula 1 (F1) World Champion, this supercar is a high-performance, mid-engined road car that aims to provide an experience akin to driving an F1 race car on the road. The striking two-seater is the brainchild of former Rolls-Royce engineer Jock Freemantle and his design team; they are based in New Zealand.

The muscular, hand-built alloy V8 engine is supercharged and comes from General Motors' Corvette C6. The Hulme's body is very light—just 2,183 pounds (990 kg). Performance is likely to be sensational, but the figures given above are industry estimates.

The weight savings start with its state-of-the-art carbon, Kevlar, and titanium chassis and composite body panels. The uncompromising open-top body creates the sort of aerodynamic downforce usually found in F1 cars, with hefty spoilers both front and rear. Early test drives suggest roadholding and performance will be among the best available among road cars.

The car has a sophisticated double-wishbone and pull-rod suspension, huge Pirelli tires, and AP Racing brakes. Gearbox options are a six-speed manual, six-speed sequential, or six-speed paddle-shift. The rear-wheel drive operates through a limited-slip differential.

The car has been designed and built, and a prototype widely tested. Now the team are trying to finalize investment to put the car into production. It is expected to be launched with a modest sales target of just nine cars a year, with a total run of just twenty cars.

Jock Freemantle hopes to sell the first F1 in 2012, commemorating the twentieth anniversary of the death of New Zealand racing hero Denny Hulme. **SH**

◁ The 2012 Renault Twizy accommodates just two people. The optional doors are recommended for driving in the wet.

Twizy | Renault (F)

2012 • electric motor • 20 bhp/15 kW • unknown • 47 mph/76 kph

Is the Twizy really a car? Should Renault's strange city vehicle even be included here? Yes, of course, because this innovative form of electric transport marks another significant step forward in motoring.

With an electric motor at the back powering the rear wheels, the Twizy is designed for short, quick urban journeys. Its range is between 34 and 72 miles (55 to 116 km), after which a recharge from a standard electricity point takes about three-and-a-half hours.

The Twizy has four wheels and a steering wheel, but not much else in common with other cars. It has no gears, no doors (although doors are an option), and no fuel bills. There are two seats, with the passenger sitting behind the driver as on a motorcycle, but no helmet is required because legally the Twizy is a car.

The cockpit is an open-sided plastic pod that sits on a tubular-steel chassis. The optional doors have a scissor action. The whole thing weighs just 992 pounds (450 kg) and is less than 4 feet (1.2 m) wide, making it easy to park and highly maneuverable. With its low center of gravity and agile suspension, it is great fun to drive, more like a tiny electric go-kart than a car.

Other features of the Twizy include a luggage box behind the rear seat, an iPod link to its audio speakers in the roof, and an optional "apron" that protects the driver's lower body from spray.

The Twizy has no emissions and is cheap to run, but not cheap to buy—around $11,000 (£7,000), plus another $70 (£45) per month to lease the battery. The Twizy is safer and more comfortable and practical than a scooter, and cheaper and smaller than most electric cars. But is it the urban runabout of the future? **SH**

Mondeo Ecoboost 240 | Ford (GB)

2012 • 122 cu in/2,000 cc, S4 • 237 bhp/174 kW • 0–62 mph/100 kph in 7.5 seconds • 153 mph/246 kph

At the time of writing, this car, going by the full name of the Mondeo 2.0 Titanium X Sport Ecoboost 240, is Ford's fastest car in Europe and the quickest version of the long-standing Mondeo line of large family cars.

Environmental and economic concerns have moderated the top end of many manufacturers' ranges. That is because fuel economy is a bigger seller than performance for most buyers. This big, heavy Ford Europe flagship's stop-start system can reduce fuel consumption by up to 5 percent and can return an impressive 37 mpg (6.4 liters per 100 km).

The X Sport Ecoboost 240's interior has a sporty feel, with Alcantara seats and contrasting red stitching. And under the hood (bonnet), the X Sport features what used to be regarded as high-performance technology: an aluminum engine with variable valve timing and direct injection, and a six-speed twin-clutch semiautomatic sequential gearbox. Adaptive shock absorbers adjust the suspension so the five-door Ford can cruise smoothly on the motorway or zoom into sporty action on bendier roads. As usual, the Mondeo's agile chassis provides very rewarding handling.

The Mondeo line took a step upmarket when the 2007 generation arrived. Its latest upgrades take it even further into premium territory. Sophisticated technological driver aids include lane-departure warning, automatic headlight dipping, driver weariness alert, reversing cameras, and blind-spot notification.

Today's buyers may opt for the diesel TDCi version, which offers more miles per gallon. But most true driving enthusiasts are likely to prefer the sound, response, and performance of the Ecoboost. **SH**

Mustang Super Cobra Jet | Ford

USA

2012 • 330 cu in/5,400 cc, V8 • 430 bhp/316 kW • unknown • unknown

Ford built only fifty of these Super Cobra Jet Mustangs for 2012. The few lucky owners got what is basically a factory-built, stripped-out, track-specification car. The Cobra Jet is not a street-legal road car. Instead, the specialists at Ford Racing produced a drag-strip competitor with optimized suspension and adjustable shock absorbers, race-prepared automatic or manual transmission, a full roll cage, and five-point racing harnesses. There is even a push-button starter on the dashboard, and a battery cut-off switch on the rear end for safety in the event of an accident.

The heart of the car is the supercharged Ford V8, which tackles the quarter-mile (0.4-km) sprint in less than ten seconds. New drag-style wheels and tires add to the aggressive looks of the Cobra Jet trim, which includes "Powered by Ford" badges and Cobra graphics. Everything is fine-tuned to make an impact at the track. For example, the Goodyear tires developed for this car have minimal tread, designed for low rolling resistance, which is great for straight-line speed but hopeless for roadholding on wet corners.

The factory-built Cobra Jet costs around $104,000 (£66,000) and comes only in blue, white, or red (the silver launch model is shown above). It can also be assembled using a regular Mustang as a donor car along with components from the Ford Performance Parts Catalog.

Fans of the Mustang who want high-performance cars that legally can be used on the road can turn to the Boss versions and the Shelby GT500. The latter produces a claimed 650 bhp (478 kW) and reaches over 200 mph (322 kph), with a 0–60 mph (97 kph) time of less than four seconds. **SH**

GT 86 | Toyota

J

2012 • 122 cu in/2,000 cc, F4 • 197 bhp/145 kW • 0–62 mph/100 kph in 7 seconds • 149 mph/240 kph

When Toyota first wanted to make an impact on the world's motoring marketplace, it created great sports cars like the Celica, MR2, and Supra. These helped to make Toyota one of the world's top-selling motor brands, but then the company relaxed, stopped the sports cars, and its big sellers became bland. Toyota soon realized it had work to do. Under the slogan "Fun to drive, again," it has surprised the car world once more.

Rivals had opted for bigger and bigger engines, turbos, four-wheel drive, and multiple driver aids. But the cars cost too much and were often boring to drive. Toyota wanted to return drivers to the simple pleasures of rear-wheel drive and a nonturbocharged engine.

So it launched the Toyota GT 86 (also called the Subaru BRZ and Scion FR-S, depending on the market). A chunky, retro 2+2 coupe, the car looks like an updated version of an early Japanese sports coupe. It has decidedly average performance but the kind of handling that, at any speed, is likely to raise a smile.

Inside, the car is designed around the driver. The cosseting cockpit has two front sports bucket seats and two almost unusable backseats. The 14-inch (36-cm) buckskin-trimmed steering wheel is the smallest ever fitted into a Toyota. The dashboard is dominated by the Toyota Touch system's 6-inch (15-cm) touch-screen interface for satellite-navigation, music, rear view camera, and hands-free Bluetooth.

The GT 86 is just short of 14 feet (424 cm) long, which makes it the most compact four-seater sports car currently available. Toyota and Subaru collaborated to create this new sports coupe, and some are already calling it the "Toybaru." **SH**

Grand Cherokee SRT8 | Jeep

USA

2012 • 391 cu in/6,400 cc, V8 • 465 bhp/347 kW • 0–60 mph/97 kph in 4.8 seconds • 155 mph/250 kph

Jeep's marketing team are not underselling their new sport utility vehicle, calling it "the ultimate performance SUV." At least this Grand Cherokee looks the part, having one of the most aggressively sporty body kits ever to grace an SUV, dominated by a huge front air scoop.

And the SRT8 certainly has the muscle to meet the hype; the 391-cubic-inch (6,400 cc) V8 powers the chunky SUV to supercar speeds. Top speed is limited to the most unlikely off-roader pace of 155 mph (250 kph). The new hot Jeep can even stop from 60 mph (97 kph) in just 116 feet (35.4 m), thanks to high-performance six-piston Brembo antilock brakes.

Jeep has clearly thrown technology at its familiar old Grand Cherokee to create this innovative SUV/performance crossover. Handling has been transformed with an electronic limited-slip differential that gives more control on the road by eliminating rear-wheel slip. A new adaptive damping suspension interacts with the rest of the car's dynamics, including the stability control, transmission, differential, and throttle. This means the ride is generally smooth and cornering stays composed, even at high speeds.

Inside the four-door shell, the cabin seems more like a performance car, with black leather and suede sports seats, carbon-fiber panels, a small leather-trimmed and heated steering wheel, and even drilled aluminum pedals. Onboard toys include a nineteen-speaker Harmon Kardon surround-sound hi-fi, adaptive cruise control, and blind-spot monitoring.

Chrysler has been making Cherokee SUVs since 1984, but they were never like the SRT8. "This," say the marketeers, "is the most powerful Jeep ever built." **SH**

Overfinch | Land Rover

GB

2012 • 305 cu in/5,000 cc, V8 • 510 bhp/375 kW • 0–62 mph/100 kph in 5.9 seconds • unknown

If it looks like a very naughty Range Rover indeed, and passes at a very high speed, take a look at the name on the hood (bonnet). Chances are it will say "Overfinch." This small tuning and styling company has become a favorite among British celebrities. The Leeds-based specialist only works on Range Rovers, but the vehicles it produces are often spectacular.

For example, the Overfinch Holland & Holland edition appears in two-tone paint and is trimmed throughout in luxurious leather. It has a wood veneer gun and drinks cabinet, and a fridge that is regularly restocked with champagne and spirits during the first year of ownership. The latest Overfinch Sport GTS has an aggressive new body kit including LED running lights and new wheels. The Range Rover interior has a complete makeover, including Overfinch instruments and multifunction steering wheel. The vehicle can be resprayed in one of Overfinch's bright custom colors.

But Overfinch began life as a tuning company, and it reworks Range Rover mechanicals, too. Generally this involves replacing standard engines with either a Corvette engine or a Jaguar V6 or V8 (figures given above). Overfinch once fitted a special new gearbox to a Range Rover entering the Paris–Dakar rally. It won.

Overfinch cars have become popular with British soccer players. England and Liverpool captain Steven Gerrard has owned several. His latest was said to have had £30,000 ($47,000) worth of extras fitted. Manchester United and England striker Wayne Rooney has one. His wife, Coleen, who has her own TV show, bought a diesel-powered Overfinch that her husband once accidentally filled with gasoline. **SH**

Polo R | Volkswagen

(D)

2012 • 98 cu in/1,600 cc, S4 • 210 bhp/157 kW • 0–62 mph/100 kph in 6 seconds • 150 mph/241 kph

There is still life in the hot-hatch concept. Almost forty years after Volkswagen (VW) launched the first trendsetting Golf GTI, it is planning a high-performance version of a small, apparently sedate little car.

This time it is the Polo that is getting the go-faster treatment, and it looks to be a classic in the making. Like so many of its hot predecessors, the Polo R will be a front-wheel-drive small hatchback with a powerful rally-bred engine. The new hot Polo is scheduled to launch soon after the time of writing, and may even be on sale by the time this book is published.

The latest R is certainly going to be a looker—early photographs show a distinctive paint job and wheel arches filled by sexy big alloy wheels clad in ultra-low-profile tires. VW's R Division has made no announcement about the exact specification of the latest member of their "R club," but industry experts believe the Polo version will definitely outperform the existing 85-cubic-inch (1,400 cc) Polo GTI. It may actually give its big brother, the current Golf GTI, a scare, although figures above are only estimates.

The new car comes as VW makes a return to the World Rally Championship after a long absence. Its rally car—the Polo R WRC—has already been launched. This 300-bhp (224-kW) turbocharged four-wheel-drive superhatch is designed to compete against the Citroën DS3, Ford Fiesta, and MINI Countryman.

The road-going Polo R is expected to share many of the rally car's high-performance components. So the seven-speed DSG semiautomatic dual clutch gearbox is very likely, and perhaps even the same four-wheel-drive system as the WRC car. **SH**

Paceman | MINI

GB

2012 • 98 cu in/1,598 cc, S4 • 211 bhp/157 kW • unknown • unknown

The MINI Paceman concept was unveiled at the 2011 Detroit Auto Show. It is set to become the seventh member of the MINI family to enter the 2012 model lineup. Based on the Countryman sport utility vehicle, this upmarket three-door "sports activity coupe," as MINI likes to call it, is likely to become a cut-price rival to Land Rover's three-door Evoque and the BMW X6.

In John Cooper Works (JCW) specification, the gas-powered 98-cubic-inch (1,598-cc) twin-turbocharged engine delivers a sporty 211 bhp (157 kW). It can be specified with MINI's "ALL4" permanent four-wheel-drive system. Typical Paceman customers want access to usable grunt, and a healthy 192 pound-feet (260 Nm) of torque makes the Paceman an easy machine to pilot on the school run, while an overboost function takes that up to 207 pound-feet (281 Nm) for swift overtaking.

Built at the BMW plant in Graz, Austria, the Paceman shares the same floor and inner structure as the Countryman. However the Paceman's wider track and sloping roofline give it a squat, purposeful stance. While the JCW version also features twin tailpipes and a rear diffuser, all models receive MINI's trademark central speedometer and retro-styled switchgear. According to BMW, the MINI Paceman "meets the needs of modern, lifestyle-oriented customers, but it also remains true to the character of the MINI brand."

In 2011 MINI returned to World Rally Championship (WRC) after a forty-two-year absence. From just six selected WRC events, the 300-bhp (224-kW) Prodrive-prepared MINI Countryman took two podiums, and seven stage wins. The Paceman is set to become MINI's WRC weapon of choice in 2013. **DS**

FF | Ferrari

(I)

2012 • 382 cu in/6,262 cc, V12 • 651 bhp/485 kW • 0–60 mph/97 kph in 3.5 seconds • 208 mph/335 kph

"The fastest four-seater car in the world" is a pretty bold claim for any manufacturer to make about one of its products. But if the carmaker in question is Ferrari, that claim is very likely to be true. Further, the FF (Ferrari Four) is also the Italian company's first four-wheel-drive car. Hard to believe—a four-wheel-drive Ferrari.

Unveiled at the Geneva Motor Show, Ferrari claims the FF to be a whole new car concept, although others use the term "shooting brake," a phrase more commonly heard in the 1960s, which meant a kind of funky three-door station wagon (estate). From the front profile, the FF is clearly a Ferrari, with styling cues from the 458 Italia, but as soon as you see the side view it's clear that this is something different. This is a full four-seater, not a miserly 2+2, even though it is not as long as the 612 Scaglietti it replaces.

Under the hood (bonnet) is the biggest engine Ferrari has ever used: a 382-cubic-inch (6,262-cc)

normally aspirated V12 producing 651 bhp (485 kW). This runs through a transmission system called 4RM, designed and patented in-house at Ferrari. When a dial on the steering wheel is set to "comfort" or "snow," it switches into intelligent four-wheel-drive mode, sending power to each wheel as it is needed. The system is highly complex, with a second gearbox used to control the distribution of the car's immense torque. The system can be switched off altogether with a turn of the dial to leave the FF in standard rear-wheel-drive mode. Moreover, it boasts a 20 percent power increase with a 25 percent reduction in fuel consumption.

The world's reaction to the FF is best described as shock and awe—shock that the car delivers everything that Ferrari boasted it would, and awe at the supernatural way it goes around corners at any speed and in almost any conditions. And, of course, it is a four-wheel-drive Ferrari. Just deal with it. **JI**

Index of Cars by Model

Glossary

Antilock brakes (or ABS)
A modern braking system that prevents wheels from locking up and skidding during severe braking, allowing drivers to steer out of danger.

Bhp/kW
Brake horsepower (or kilowatts) measure the overall pulling power of an engine. It is related to, but not the same as, torque (see opposite).

Camshaft
A spinning rod in the engine that operates the inlet and exhaust valves—the vital ways in and out of the combustion chambers. The performance of the camshaft is crucial to the performance of the engine. Double or twin camshafts are more efficient as they operate the inlet and exhaust valves separately.

Carburetor
A device that mixes air and fuel to optimize combustion in the cylinders. Carburetors were largely replaced by less temperamental and more accurate fuel injection systems during the 1980s.

CC
Cubic centimeters (cc) are the standard measure for the volume of an engine—technically, the total swept area of the cylinders. In the United States cubic inches are used instead, although cc are now becoming the global standard.

Column gearchange/shift/lever
The gear stick is mounted on the steering column instead of the floor.

Coupe
From the French word "to cut," a coupe has a tapered rear end that usually comes with extra sportiness, either real or apparent.

Crossover
Marketing people like to label the various categories of vehicles. Crossovers bridge at least two categories. The most recent crossovers are a mix of off-roader and sports car.

Differential
The outer wheel rotates faster while cornering than the inside wheel because it travels farther. A differential gearing system under the car allows that to happen. A limited-slip differential is a more sophisticated version designed to counter wheelspin.

Disc brakes
These replaced the old fashioned drum brakes with a more efficient stopping system based on a wheel disc that is gripped by brake pads to slow the vehicle.

Flat engine
An engine configuratiuon where the cylinders are arranged in two horizontal opposing banks. The movement of the pistons looks like they are punching each other—hence the nickname "Boxer" engines.

Front-wheel drive
The power of the engine is transmitted to the front wheels and the rear wheels just roll along. In rear-wheel drive the power goes to the back wheels instead, leaving the front wheels to concentrate on steering. In four-wheel drive all the wheels get some power to increase traction on slippery surfaces.

Gull-wing doors
A flamboyant design where the car doors are hinged at the top and open upward and outward like wings. A modern supercar variant is the "scissor" door, which articulates upward, outward, and forward.

Homologation
To compete in motor sport, manufacturers often have to show they have produced a minimum number of road-going models that are the same as the competition car. This can mean the road cars are very, very sporty.

Hot hatch
Europe, 1970–1990. Sports versions of mundane compact hatchback

cars were the coolest cars to own. Some were extremely fast.

Hybrid
Any car that uses more than one propulsion system. It could be electric and petrol/gasoline or it could involve diesel, liquid gas, or biofuel. The general goal is to produce a more environmentally sound vehicle.

Hydraulic
A car's shock absorbers, or dampers, absorb violent suspension movements in oil-filled hydraulic cylinders.

Hydrolastic
Unusual hydrolastic rubber units filled with fluid were used in British cars to operate the primary suspension system.

Hydropneumatic
Hydropneumatic suspension systems were Citroën's own complicated way of keeping a car level whatever the terrain. It used hydraulic pumps to maintain a constant ride height at each wheel.

Independent suspension
Better handling and comfort come from this suspension arrangement that allows each wheel to move up and down independently.

Intercooler
Air from a turbocharger is cooled in a special radiator before it is forced into the engine for more efficiency.

Kei car
A Japanese taxation category that restricts overall size and engine volume in return for financial benefits. The Kei class has spawned some of the most unusual and creative car designs ever made.

Pony car
Compact, sporty cars arrived in the United States with the Ford Mustang. This led to a wave of similar hot coupes—all dubbed pony cars.

Roadster
A car with a removable or collapsible roof—also called a cabriolet, convertible, rag-top, spider or open-topped car.

Paddle gearshift
Semiautomatic gear system that allows drivers to change gear using "up" and "down" paddles attached to the steering wheel.

Straight (or inline) engine
An engine where all the cylinders are simply arranged in one line (as opposed to a V shape or flat arrangement).

Supercharger
A compressor driven by the engine, that pumps more air into the engine, increasing the power.

SUV
Sport utility vehicle—a marketing term for a leisure off-roader such as a Toyota RAV4.

Torque
A measure of the potency of an engine that specifically means the maximum twisting force it produces. It's subtly different from bhp/kW, which measures the overall pulling power. More torque usually means more low rev "grunt," more bhp/kW usually means a higher top speed.

Transverse engine
The car's engine is mounted sideways across the car (as opposed to longitudinal, where it is in line with the car).

Turbocharger
A device that uses the power of the exhaust gases to drive a turbine that forces more air into the engine for increased power.

V engine
A "V" engine has the cylinders arranged in a V formation. The number of cylinders is usually mentioned when a V engine is specified (eg: V12).

Contributors

Sue Baker (SB) has been a full-time specialist motoring writer for British national newspapers and magazines for over thirty years, and has tested cars on every continent. She is a former host of BBC TV *Top Gear* and is a past chairman of the U.K.-based international Guild of Motoring Writers. Sue is a U.K. judge for the Women's World Car of the Year.

Jeroen Booij (JB) is based in Amsterdam and has been a motoring journalist since 1998. He prefers describing the weird and wonderful of the automotive industry, specializing in classic, specialist, or simply unusual cars. His articles are published in eighteen countries.

Rich Duisberg (RD) has lived and worked in England, Germany, and Scandinavia. He was once personal fitness advisor to F1 driver Luca Badoer. He has written for magazines such as *Practical Performance Car* and *Evo*, and blogs at www.s2b2.net.

Stuart Forster (SF) is a British writer who has driven on five continents. He has contributed to several books, including *Driving Holidays Across India*, which won India's 2010 National Tourism Award for best travel publication in English.

Mike Gerrard (MG)'s first car was an Austin A40, which did nothing to prepare him for a career as an award-winning travel writer. He divides his time between England and his home in Arizona, where he and his wife drive a 1984 Pontiac Sunbird station wagon and publish a Web site devoted to the Pacific Coast Highway: www.Pacific-Coast-Highway-Travel.com.

Simon Heptinstall (SH), the main writer and general editor of this book, is a former taxi driver and garage manager who became an award-winning writer. His credits include helping to launch *BBC Top Gear* magazine and working on Jeremy Clarkson's *Big Boys' Toys* TV series.

Jerry Ibbotson (JI) has been a BBC radio journalist, a freelance writer, and has even worked in the video games industry as a sound designer. When he's not writing about cars he's likely to be sticking a microphone up their exhaust pipe to record the sound. He's also an author of urban fantasy novels. The car he drives is sadly not among the 1,001 in this book.

Bob Kocher (BK) is an award-winning automotive writer who has been writing reviews on new and old cars, motorsports articles, automotive aftermarket product reviews, and automotive lifestyle stories for the past twenty-five years. His articles have appeared in numerous newspapers and magazines. His professional affiliations include serving as president of the Midwest Automotive Media Association, and he has also been a judge at the Greenwich Concours d'Elegance in Greenwich, Connecticut.

George Lewis (GL) has been in all of the cars that he writes about here, except, to his disappointment, the ZiL. He has consumer-tested almost every supermini produced for the U.K. market since 1987 and has reported on them for both the manufacturers and consumer magazines.

Darryl Sleath (DS) is a writer, photographer, and classic car restorer who lives in South Wales with his family and assorted British jalopies. His work has been published in several motoring magazines and he is currently writing a book on sports car family trees.

Barry Stone (BS) is an internationally published author of numerous general history titles on topics ranging from religious hermits to contemporary architecture, who, in his alter ego as a travel writer, spends far too much time daydreaming about future destinations. He lives in Picton, a quiet rural hamlet an hour's drive south of Sydney, Australia.

Liz Turner (LT) has enjoyed driving and writing about cars for twenty years. She spent five years on staff at *What Car?* and four years at *Autocar*. As a freelancer she has written regularly for many national magazines and newspapers, including the *New York Post*, *The Independent*, *Car*, and *Classic & Sports Car*.

Richard Yarrow (RY) is a respected freelance journalist based in the United Kingdom. He has written about the auto industry full-time since 1998, and his clients include national newspapers, consumer publications, and the auto business press. He's a former associate editor of *Auto Express*, the U.K.'s top-selling weekly car news magazine.

Picture Credits

Every effort has been made to credit the copyright holders of the images used in this book. We apologize for any unintentional omissions or errors and will insert the appropriate acknowledgment to any companies or individuals in subsequent editions of the work.

2 Tom Wood/Alamy **20** Kimball Stock **22** Bettmann/Corbis **23** Bettmann/Corbis **24** Megashorts/Flickr **25** Car Culture/Corbis **26** Bettmann/Corbis **28** Getty Images **29** Daimler AG **30** James Mann **31** Kimball Stock **32** Motoring Picture Library **33** Giles Chapman **34** AF archive/Alamy **36l** Rover Group/Heritage Motor Centre **36r** FIAT S.p.A **37l** The Lanchester Legacy by C.S. Clark **37r** James Mann **38** FIAT S.p.A **39** Kimball Stock **41** Getty Images **42** GM Company **43** Louwman Museum **44** Motor Snaps **45** FIAT S.p.A **46** Vauxhall **48** Kimball Stock **50l** Motoring Picture Library **50r** Michael Whitesel **51l** Louwman Museum **51r** Car Culture/Getty Images **52** Giles Chapman **54** Newspress **55** John Cook **56** Martin Prokop **57** magiccarpics.com **59** Getty Images **60** Motoring Picture Library **61** Renault **62** Getty Images **64l** Car Culture/Getty Images **64r** magiccarpics.com **65l** James Mann **65r** Giles Chapman **66** James Mann **69** Ei Katsumata/Alamy **70** James Mann **71** James Mann **72** James Mann **73** magiccarpics.com **74l** British Car Auctions **74r** AFP/Getty Images **75l** Giles Chapman **75r** magiccarpics.com **76** Louwman Museum **77** Car Culture/Getty Images **78l** Motoring Picture Library **78r** Motor Snaps **79l** Kimball Stock **79r** James Mann **81** Motoring Picture Library **82** Car Culture/Getty Images **85** Car Culture/Getty Images **86** magiccarpics.com **87** Giles Chapman **88** FIAT S.p.A **89** Kimball Stock **92** Car Culture/Getty Images **93** James Mann **94** Detectandpreserve/Wikimedia Commons **95** Motoring Picture Library **96** The Kobal Collection **97** Getty Images **98** Getty Images **100** Motoring Picture Library **101** Getty Images **102** Kimball Stock **104l** Leo Mason/Corbis **104r** Wouter Melissen **105l** magiccarpics.com **105r** Swiss Museum of Transport/Stefan Waefler **106** James Mann **107** Giles Chapman **108** Motoring Picture Library **109** David Wall/Alamy **110** Kimball Stock **112** Car Culture/Corbis **113** Newspress **115** Mary Evans Picture Library/Onslow Auctions Limited **116l** Mark Scheuern/Alamy **116r** Paul Debois/Alamy **117l** Wouter Melissen **117r** Lane Motor Museum **118** BMW Group **119** James Mann **120** Motoring Picture Library **121** Kimball Stock **122** Daimler AG **123** Jaguar Land Rover **125** Time & Life Pictures/Getty Images **126** James Mann **127** Audi **129** Kimball Stock **130** FIAT S.p.A **131** Kimball Stock **132l** Newspress **132r** GM Company **133l** Kimball Stock **133r** Motoring Picture Library **135** Spaarnestad Photo/Mary Evans **136** Motoring Picture Library **137** The Kobal Collection **138** 20th Century Fox/The Kobal Collection **139** Chrysler **140** Kimball Stock **142** Universal/The Kobal Collection **143** Rolls-Royce Motor Cars Ltd. **144** Renault **147** Time Life Pictures/Getty Images **148l** magiccarpics.com **148r** Giles Chapman **149l** Giles Chapman **149r** David Askham/Alamy **150** Motoring Picture Library **151** magiccarpics.com **153** magiccarpics.com **154** Giles Chapman **155** Giles Chapman **157** Time & Life Pictures/Getty Images **158** Lucasfilm Ltd/Paramount/The Kobal Collection **159** The Kobal Collection **160** PA/PA Archive/Press Association Images **162** Giles Chapman **163** Motoring Picture Library **164** magiccarpics.com **166** Design Pics Inc. - RM Content/Alamy **167** Tampa Bay Automobile Museum **168** James Mann **170l** Ford Motor Company and Wieck Media Services, Inc. **170r** LAT Photographic **171l** Wouter Melissen **171r** Giles Chapman **172l** Wouter Melissen **172r** Tom Wood/Alamy **173l** Giles Chapman **173r** Kimball Stock **175** The Advertising Archives **176** magiccarpics.com **177** Toyota **179** Getty Images **180** The Kobal Collection **181** Kimball Stock **183** Getty Images **184** culture-images GmbH/Alamy **185** Car Culture/Corbis **186l** Bentley Motors Limited **186r** Time & Life Pictures/Getty Images **187l** magiccarpics.com **187r** Motoring Picture Library **188** Getty Images **190** Kimball Stock **191** GM Company **192** Giles Chapman **193** magiccarpics.com **195** Getty Images **197** Bettmann/CORBIS **198l** FIAT S.p.A **198r** Kimball Stock **199l** magiccarpics.com **199r** magiccarpics.com **200** FIAT S.p.A **201** James Mann **203** Car Culture/Getty Images **204** Kimball Stock **205** Kimball Stock **206** The Kobal Collection **207** Getty Images **208** Kimball Stock **209** magiccarpics.com **210** James Mann **211** James Mann **212** PSA Peugeot Citroën **213** Popperfoto/Getty Images **214l** BMW Group **214r** Kimball Stock **215l** Kimball Stock **215r** Chrysler **216** BMW Group **218** Kimball Stock **219** James Mann **220** Kimball Stock **222** Kimball Stock **223** Transtock/Corbis **224l** magiccarpics.com **224r** James Mann **225l** James Mann **225r** Kimball Stock **227** Gamma-Keystone via Getty Images **228** James Mann **229** magiccarpics.com **230** Kimball Stock **231** Kimball Stock **232** magiccarpics.com **234l** Giles Chapman **234r** James Mann **235l** Kimball Stock **235r** Boyd Jaynes/TRANSTOCK/Transtock/Corbis **237** magiccarpics.com **238** Kimball Stock **239** Kimball Stock **241** Columbia/The Kobal Collection **243** Volvo Car Corporation **245** FIAT S.p.A **246** James Mann **247** Kimball Stock **248** Giles Chapman **250** Jaguar Land Rover **251** Daimler AG **253** Berliner Verlag Jochen Moll/DPA/Press Association Images **254** magiccarpics.com **255** magiccarpics.com **256** Mary Evans/Toscani Archive/Alinari Archives Management **258** Giles Chapman **259** magiccarpics.com **261** Getty Images **262** Kimball Stock **264** Kimball Stock **265** James Mann **266** Volvo Car Corporation **267** Fuji Heavy Industries Ltd. **269** magiccarpics.com **270** magiccarpics.com **271** Giles Chapman **272** James Mann **273** Kimball Stock **274** Getty Images **276** magiccarpics.com **277** Kimball Stock **278** Kimball Stock **279** James Mann **281** Columbia/The Kobal Collection **282** Giles Chapman **283** Giles Chapman **284** Kimball Stock **285** magiccarpics.com **286** Kimball Stock **289** Giles Chapman **290** Gamma-Keystone via Getty Images **292** Kimball Stock **293** Kimball Stock **294** PSA Peugeot Citroën **296** James Mann **297** magiccarpics.com **298** magiccarpics.com **299** James Mann **301** MARKA/Alamy **302** magiccarpics.com **303** Ford Motor Company and Wieck Media Services, Inc. **304** magiccarpics.com **307** magiccarpics.com **308l** magiccarpics.com **308r** magiccarpics.com **309l** Kimball Stock **309r** Nissan Motor Co.,Ltd. **310** Don Heiny/Corbis **311** James Mann **312l** Giles Chapman **312r** Giles Chapman **313l** Magic Car Pics **313r** magiccarpics.com **314** James Mann **316** James Mann **317** James Mann **318** Kimball Stock **320l** Giles Chapman **320r** Jeep **321l** magiccarpics.com **321r** James Mann **323** DANJAQ/EON/UA/The Kobal Collection **324** magiccarpics.com **325** magiccarpics.com **326** Giles Chapman **327** Giles Chapman **328** Motoring Picture Library **330** magiccarpics.com **333** magiccarpics.com **335** Central Press/Getty Images **336** magiccarpics.com **337** Kimball Stock **339** Getty Images **340** SSPL via Getty Images **341** James Mann **342** Warner Bros. Pictures/The Kobal Collection/Bennett Tracy **344** Kimball Stock **345** magiccarpics.com **347** The Kobal Collection **348** Kimball Stock **349** Kimball Stock **351** Car Culture/Getty Images **352** Car Culture/Getty Images **353** Getty Images **354** The Advertising Archives **356** Aston Martin **357** Phil Talbot/Alamy **358** Phil Talbot/Alamy **359** James Mann **361** Mike Long **362l** magiccarpics.com **362r** Nissan Motor Co.,Ltd. **363l** Nissan Motor Co.,Ltd. **363r** FIAT S.p.A **364** Andy Crawford /Getty Images **365** magiccarpics.com **367** Kimball Stock **368** Kimball Stock **369** Dodge **370** AF archive/Alamy **372** Phil Talbot/Alamy **373** Kimball Stock **375** Photos 12/Alamy **376** James Mann **377** magiccarpics.com **378** magiccarpics.com **379** magiccarpics.com **381** magiccarpics.com **382l** Toyota **382r** magiccarpics.com **383l** Group Lotus PLC **383r** Giles Chapman **384** magiccarpics.com **386** James Mann **387** Audi **388** Kimball Stock **390** Toyota **391** FIAT S.p.A **393** magiccarpics.com **394l** magiccarpics.com **394r** Performance Image/Alamy **395l** Car Culture/Corbis **395r** Roy Zukerman/www.vignale-gamine.com **396** Ford Motor Company and Wieck Media Services, Inc. **397** Maserati **399** Warfield/United Artists/The Kobal Collection **400** Giles Chapman **402** magiccarpics.com **403** martin berry/Alamy **404** James Mann **405** James Mann **406** Jaguar Land Rover **407** James Mann **408** ZUMA Wire Service/Alamy **409** Oleksiy Maksymenko/Alamy **410** magiccarpics.com **411** Daimler AG **412** magiccarpics.com **413** Courtesy of Toyota USA Archives **414** CBS-TV/The Kobal Collection **416** Tom Wood/Alamy **418** Ford Motor Company and Wieck Media Services, Inc. **419** Datsun **421** Getty Images **422** Porsche **423** Nissan Motor Co.,Ltd. **424** James Mann **425** magiccarpics.com **426** Getty Images **428** Phil Talbot/Alamy **430** Giles Chapman **431** Phil Talbot/Alamy **432** magiccarpics.com **433** magiccarpics.com **434l** Giles Chapman **434r** Kimball Stock **435l** Giles Chapman **435r** Surdin Photography/Alamy **437** Bettmann/CORBIS **438** CW Motorsport Images/Alamy **439** Giles Chapman **440** Kimball Stock **441** Kimball Stock **442** magiccarpics.com **444** Ford Motor Company and Wieck Media Services, Inc. **445** magiccarpics.com **446** James Mann **447** Kimball Stock **449** Jaguar Land Rover **450** Robert Genat/TRANSTOCK/Transtock/Corbis **451** James Mann **452l** Motoring Picture Library **452r** Courtesy of Ford Motor Company of Australia Limited **453l** Performance Image/Alamy **453r** Giles Chapman **454** James Mann **455** Tom Wood/Alamy **457** DANJAQ/EON/UA/The Kobal Collection **458** Kimball Stock **459** Kimball Stock **460** Kimball Stock **462** magiccarpics.com **463** magiccarpics.com **464** magiccarpics.com **466l** Motoring Picture Library/Alamy **466r** magiccarpics.com **467l** Dariusz Majgier/Alamy **467r** magiccarpics.com **469** AIP-Filmways/The Kobal Collection **470** LAT Photographic **471** magiccarpics.com **471** Kimball Stock **473** magiccarpics.com **474** Giles Chapman **475** Kimball Stock **476** magiccarpics.com **477** Giles Chapman **478** magiccarpics.com **479** Kimball Stock **481** Universal/The Kobal Collection **482** James Mann **483** Giles Chapman **484** Kimball Stock **485** Kimball Stock **486** Giles Chapman **489** magiccarpics.com **490** Giles Chapman **491** Giles Chapman **492** magiccarpics.com **493** PSA Peugeot Citroën **495** Car Culture/Corbis **496** magiccarpics.com **497** Giles Chapman **499** magiccarpics.com **500** magiccarpics.com **501** FIAT

S.p.A **503** Giles Chapman **504l** Daimler AG **504r** Giles Chapman **505l** magiccarpics.com **505r** Group Lotus PLC **506** magiccarpics.com **507** Volkswagen **508l** Terry Borton/www.panthercarclub.com **508r** magiccarpics.com **509l** Richard McHowat **509r** Maserati **510** DIOMEDIA/Alamy **511** Suzuki Motor Corporation **512** Giles Chapman **513** magiccarpics.com **514l** magiccarpics.com **514r** magiccarpics.com **515l** Dikiiy/Shutterstock.com **515r** magiccarpics.com **516** Car Culture/Corbis **517** Peter Harholdt/CORBIS **518** Performance Image/Alamy **519** Mazda Motor Corporation **520** N/A **521** Anthony Fosh **522** magiccarpics.com **523** Ford Motor Company and Wieck Media Services, Inc. **525** Giles Chapman **526** magiccarpics.com **527** magiccarpics.com **528** Kimball Stock **530** Giles Chapman **531** magiccarpics.com **532** magiccarpics.com **534** Giles Chapman **536l** Giles Chapman **536r** Octane Magazine **537l** GM Company **537r** Matt Garrett/www.GM-Classics.com **539** Kimball Stock **540l** Richard McDowell/Alamy **540r** Giles Chapman **541l** magiccarpics.com **541r** magiccarpics.com **543** NBC via Getty Images **544** magiccarpics.com **545** Kimball Stock **547** magiccarpics.com **548** magiccarpics.com **549** Giles Chapman **550** Fabiano Guma **551** Kimball Stock **552** magiccarpics.com **553** magiccarpics.com **554l** Motoring Picture Library/Alamy **554r** magiccarpics.com **555l** Renault **555r** Kimball Stock **556** Kimball Stock **557** magiccarpics.com **558** Kimball Stock **560** James Mann **561** magiccarpics.com **562** Giles Chapman **563** Giles Chapman **564** magiccarpics.com **565** magiccarpics.com **566** magiccarpics.com **567** Kimball Stock **568l** magiccarpics.com **568r** Giles Chapman **569l** Giles Chapman **569r** FIAT S.p.A **570** magiccarpics.com **572** Paul Fievez/Associated Newspapers /Rex Features **574l** magiccarpics.com **574r** Giles Chapman **575l** Neill Bruce **575r** magiccarpics.com **577** magiccarpics.com **578** magiccarpics.com **579** magiccarpics.com **581** magiccarpics.com **582** Kimball Stock **585** magiccarpics.com **586l** magiccarpics.com **586r** magiccarpics.com **587l** magiccarpics.com **587r** Giles Chapman **589** magiccarpics.com **590** Kimball Stock **592l** Giles Chapman **592r** GM Company **593l** Giles Chapman **593r** FIAT S.p.A **594** Audi AG. **595** Giles Chapman **596** Kimball Stock **598** Giles Chapman **599** magiccarpics.com **600** Giles Chapman **601** magiccarpics.com **603** Jaguar Land Rover **604** Giles Chapman **605** Nissan Motor Co.,Ltd. **606l** Richard Spiegelman **606r** magiccarpics.com **607l** Giles Chapman **607r** Citroen **608** Giles Chapman **609** Giles Chapman **611** Getty Images **612** Group Lotus PLC **613** magiccarpics.com **614** Kimball Stock **617** Kimball Stock **618** Transtock Inc./Alamy **619** Les Barrett/www.**454**ss.com **620l** Giles Chapman **620r** Courtesy of Toyota USA Archives **621l** Giles Chapman **621r** Giles Chapman **622** Nissan Motor Co.,Ltd. **623** James Mann **624** magiccarpics.com **625** Motoring Picture Library/Alamy **626** magiccarpics.com **627** magiccarpics.com **629** James Mann **630l** Motoring Picture Library/Alamy **630r** Giles Chapman **631l** Volvo **631r** Mazda Motor Corporation **633** Transtock/Corbis **634** magiccarpics.com **636** Suzuki Motor Corporation **637** FIAT S.p.A **638** Phil Talbot/Alamy **639** Transtock Inc./Alamy **640** Phil Talbot/Alamy **641** Kimball Stock **642** BMW Group **645** Giles Chapman **646** Kimball Stock **647** Kimball Stock **649** John Decker/Sacramento Bee/ZUMA/Corbis **650** Phil Talbot/Alamy **651** Kimball Stock **652** Patrick Sautelet/Renault **654** Morgan Motor Company Limited **655** GM Company **656** Kimball Stock **657** Giles Chapman **658** magiccarpics.com **660l** Toyota **660r** GM Company **661l** Richard Warburton/Alamy **661r** Subaru **662** Giles Chapman **663** Transtock Inc./Alamy **665** Kimball Stock **666** The Colt Car Company Ltd **667** Kimball Stock **668l** Ford Motor Company and Wieck Media Services, Inc. **668r** Dodge **669l** Audi AG. **669r** Audi AG. **670** FIAT S.p.A **671** Phil Talbot/Alamy **672** Honda **673** FIAT S.p.A **674** magiccarpics.com **675** Kimball Stock **676** Drive Images/Alamy **677** Transtock Inc./Alamy **678** magiccarpics.com **679** Jaguar Land Rover **680** magiccarpics.com **681** James Mann **682** Group Lotus PLC **683** magiccarpics.com **684l** PSA Peugeot Citroën **684r** magiccarpics.com **685l** Phil Talbot/Alamy **685r** Trinity Mirror/Mirrorpix/Alamy **686** Getty Images **688** Kimball Stock **690** Giles Chapman **691** Kimball Stock **693** Kimball Stock **694l** Toyota **694r** FUJI HEAVY INDUSTRIES Ltd. **695l** PSA Peugeot Citroën **695r** Nissan **696** magiccarpics.com **698** Maserati **699** Kimball Stock **701** The Advertising Archives **702** FIAT S.p.A **703** magiccarpics.com **704** The Advertising Archives **706l** magiccarpics.com **706r** Car Culture/Corbis **707l** Phil Talbot/Alamy **707r** Kimball Stock **708** magiccarpics.com **709** Giles Chapman **711** James Mann **712** Audi **713** Kimball Stock **714** The Advertising Archives **716** Car Culture/Getty Images **719** Mark Jenkinson/CORBIS **720l** BMW Group **720r** FUJI HEAVY INDUSTRIES Ltd. **721l** magiccarpics.com **721r** Giles Chapman **722** Guy Spangenberg/Transtock/Corbis **724** TVR GmbH **725** Group Lotus PLC **726** Kimball Stock **727** magiccarpics.com **728** MGM/EON/The Kobal Collection/Maidment, Jay **730** Motoring Picture Library/Alamy **731** Trinity Mirror/Mirrorpix/Alamy **733** Transtock Inc./Alamy **734** Morgan Motor Company Limited **735** Ford Motor Company and Wieck Media Services, Inc. **736** Kimball Stock **737** James Mann **738l** Audi AG. **738r** Volvo Car Corporation **739l** Seat **739r** Suzuki Motor Corporation **740** Kimball Stock **741** BMW Group **743** Kimball Stock **744** Daimler AG **745** Dodge **747** Kimball Stock **748** BMW Group **750** Toyota **751** Ford Motor Company and Wieck Media Services, Inc. **753** Kimball Stock **754** Kimball Stock **755** magiccarpics.com **756** Daihatsu Motor Co., Ltd **757** Daimler AG **758** Kimball Stock **760l** BMW Group **760r** Vauxhall **761l** Lamborghini **761r** Guy Spangenberg/Transtock/Corbis **762** Rolls-Royce Motor Cars Ltd. **763** Daimler AG **765** magiccarpics.com **766** Kimball Stock **767** Maserati **768** Caresto **769** Donizetti Castilho **770** Aston Martin **771** Kimball Stock **772** Audi AG. **773** Bufori Motor Car Company **774** Kimball Stock **775** Kimball Stock **776l** John Early/TRANSTOCK/Transtock/Corbis **776r** magiccarpics.com **777l** Robert Kerian/Transtock/Corbis **777r** Giles Chapman **778** The Colt Car Company Ltd **779** Rick Chou/TRANSTOCK/Transtock/Corbis **780** magiccarpics.com **782** Kimball Stock **783** Morgan Motor Company Limited **784** Kimball Stock **785** Kimball Stock **787** James Mann **788** Ford Motor Company and Wieck Media Services, Inc. **789** Daimler AG **790l** BMW Group **790r** The Colt Car Company Ltd **791l** Kimball Stock **791r** GM Company **792** Jaguar Land Rover **793** Kimball Stock **795** James Mann **796** TVR GmbH **797** Chrysler **798** Kimball Stock **799** FIAT S.p.A **800l** GM Company **800r** BMW Group **801l** BMW Group **801r** Spyker Cars N.V. **802** Audi AG. **803** Motoring Picture Library/Alamy **805** Kimball Stock **806** Kimball Stock **807** Caresto **808** magiccarpics.com **809** magiccarpics.com **810** Kimball Stock **811** Kimball Stock **812** Ford Motor Company and Wieck Media Services, Inc. **814** Kimball Stock **815** Kimball Stock **816** ALEXANDRA BEIER/X01172/Reuters/Corbis **818** Vauxhall **819** Drive Images/Alamy **820l** magiccarpics.com **820r** Kimball Stock **821l** Daimler AG **821r** Kia Motors Corp. **823** Kimball Stock **824** Ascari **825** Seat **826l** Hyundai **826r** Audi AG. **827l** Bristol **827r** Volkswagen **828** Lamborghini **829** Audi AG. **830** Car Culture/Corbis **831** Caterham Cars **832** T1 Cars Limited **834** magiccarpics.com **835** Kimball Stock **836** Koenigsegg **837** Venturi Automobiles **838** Aston Martin **839** Toyota **840** Kimball Stock **842l** Audi AG. **842r** FIAT S.p.A **843l** Daimler AG **843r** magiccarpics.com **844** Goddard Automotive/Alamy **845** Drive Images/Alamy **846** Secma Automobile **847** FIAT S.p.A **848** Daimler AG **849** Rolls-Royce Motor Cars Ltd. **851** James Mann **852l** Rossion **852r** KTM **853l** Honda Motor Europe Limited **853r** Drive Images/Alamy **854** Audi AG. **855** BMW Group **856** SsangYong Motor Company **857** Kimball Stock **858** FIAT S.p.A **859** Toyota **860** Bolwell **861** Kimball Stock **863** Getty Images **864** Aston Martin **865** Rolls-Royce Motor Cars Ltd. **866** Volkswagen **867** Infiniti **868** Kimball Stock **869** Invicta Car Company **870** Kimball Stock **871** Audi AG. **872l** Jaguar Land Rover **872r** Volkswagen **873l** Artega Automobil GmbH & Co. KG **873r** Daimler AG **874** Kimball Stock **875** Kimball Stock **876** Kimball Stock **878** GM Company **879** Volkswagen **880** Kimball Stock **882** H. Lorren Au Jr/ZUMA Press/Corbis **883** Bentley **885** Aston Martin **886** Bentley Motors Limited **887** Vauxhall **888** Ford Motor Company and Wieck Media Services, Inc. **889** Jaguar Land Rover **890** Kimball Stock **891** Kimball Stock **892** Aston Martin **894** HTT Automobile **895** magiccarpics.com **896l** Aston Martin **896r** Martyn Goddard/Corbis **897l** PSA Peugeot Citroën **897r** Seat **899** Daimler AG **900** PSA Peugeot Citroën **901** WireImage /Getty Images **902** Car Culture/Corbis **903** magiccarpics.com **904** Nissan Motor Co.,Ltd. **905** Volkswagen **906** Mark Scheuern/Alamy **907** Volvo Car Corporation **908l** Noble Automotive **908r** Brabus **909l** FIAT S.p.A **909r** Kimball Stock **910** BMW Group **911** Bufori Motor Car Company **912** Caresto **913** H. Lorren Au Jr/ZUMA Press/Corbis **914** magiccarpics.com **915** Vauxhall **916** Toyota **917** Kimball Stock **918** Bloomberg via Getty Images **919** Elfin Heritage Centre **920** Kimball Stock **922** McLaren Automotive Limited **924** Daimler AG **925** Renault **926** Bloomberg via Getty Images **928l** Volkswagen **928r** BMW Group **929l** The Colt Car Company Ltd **929r** Ford Motor Company and Wieck Media Services, Inc. **930** GM Company **931** Kimball Stock **932** Daimler AG **933** Ford Motor Company and Wieck Media Services, Inc. **934** Radical Sportcars Ltd **935** Hulme Supercars Ltd **936** Renault **938** Ford Motor Company **939** Toyota **940** Wes Allison/Transtock/Corbis **941** Jaguar Land Rover **942** Volkswagen **943** BMW Group **944** Bloomberg via Getty Images

Acknowledgments

Quintessence Editions would like to thank the following individuals and organizations for their assistance in the creation of this book:
Richard and Vicky Dredge at Magic Car Pics, Jon Day at Motoring Picture Library, Will Taylor-Medhurst at LAT Photographic, Chris Taylor, Mark Johnson Davies, and OMNiON PreMedia Private Limited.

OIL-TEMP
TANK
2/4
4/4
30
20
10